NATURE and CULTURE
Ethical Thought
in the French Enlightenment

NATURE and CULTURE
Ethical Thought
in the
French Enlightenment

by Lester G. Crocker

BALTIMORE: THE JOHNS HOPKINS PRESS

BJ
702
C7

Printed in the United States of America by Vail-Ballou Press, Inc.
Distributed in Great Britain by The Oxford University Press, London

Library of Congress catalog card number 63-10813

This book has been brought to publication with the assistance
of a grant from The Ford Foundation

TO

Roger and Leslie

operibus meis prae omnibus dilectis

EDITORIAL NOTE:

As in the preceding volume of this study, all quotations, except poetry, are translated, and the place of publication, when it is Paris, is omitted. The end bibliography includes only titles which are not listed in the bibliography of *An Age of Crisis. Man and World in Eighteenth Century French Thought.* Fuller bibliographical data for titles listed in the earlier volume are supplied in the footnotes, at the first mention only.

CONTENTS

NATURE and CULTURE
Ethical Thought
in the French Enlightenment

INTRODUCTION

To a certain extent, the problem of morality is changeless. "The moral state of men," wrote Christian Wolff, "is that which is determined by their rights and by their obligations. Moral man is man considered as the subject of these rights and obligations." [1] But if the problem remains the same, the answers have differed widely. There was perhaps more homogeneity, a greater *consensus gentium,* during the Christian Middle Ages than there has been at any other time. The break up of the Christian metaphysical hegemony led to new views of man and of morals.

Although, strictly speaking, no positions were discovered that had not been anticipated by the Greek philosophers, we may nonetheless speak of a renewal of ethical thought in the seventeenth and eighteenth centuries. The rationalistic emphasis of Descartes, and later of the Cambridge Platonists and others, brought about the powerful reaction first of Hobbes and then of Mandeville. Hobbes sees no real moral difference inhering in actions, since he derives obligation from power and justice from the social compact. Mandeville uncovers the path to utilitarianism, while apparently conserving the rigoristic distinction between virtue (nonegoism) and vice (egoism). In France, Bayle's corrosive skepticism questioned all accepted notions and abetted the upsurge of a "morale laïque" which social and psychological changes in the cultural

[1] *Principes du droit de la nature et des gens,* I, p. 13.

complex of his time were fostering. The rise of rational scientific materialism threw a new light on man's place in the world, on his nature and motivation. He was seen as moved by appetite, fear, and pride; his reason was often derogated as an instrument of self-interest, his moral conscience reduced to habituation or fear of sanctions.[2] To many it now seemed doubtful that a divine influence was immanent and operative in the conscience, or at least that it produced a firm, valid, and (in the Kantian sense) practical awareness of obligation—a doubt which had already been announced by the Augustinian and Reformation conceptions of Christianity. Even deists, men of moderate tendencies, although hoping that somewhere in the universe there is a power which is on the side of right, thought they had better seek out a more concrete foundation in man's nature as a social being, a naturalistic foundation independent of metaphysics.

Such solutions at least left the hope of either inducing or compelling men to conform to moral principles in their conduct. Where Christianity broke down, something had to be put in its place, lest the human moral world succumb before the onslaught of those who insinuated that there was no right but only might, no valid law but only tyranny, and no hope for changing what had to be. Somehow, the light would be kept burning in the human habitation, even if it were true that outside was nothing but the dark night of an indifferent universe.

The history of eighteenth-century ethical speculation is, then, one of challenge and response. The first challenge came from the emptiness which ensued in the minds of many thinking men from the collapse of the Christian cosmos. It seemed at first not too difficult to replace what had been lost, and even to set the new structure on firmer ground.[3] But then the second challenge came

[2] I have already pointed out that confidence in reason—at least in a kind of practical reason—was reintroduced by some of the same writers in the doctrine of enlightened self-interest, and in the belief that "enlightenment" can be increased among men. (L. G. Crocker, *An Age of Crisis. Man and World in Eighteenth Century French Thought*, p. 253.) Rationalism increased in the second half of the century, even as its antithesis, sentimentalism, also did.

[3] "Eighteenth century philosophers," writes J. L. Talmon, "faced a mighty challenge." The Church accused secular philosophy of destroying the two essential conditions of morality—an absolute point of reference, and the unity of human existence—thereby undermining society. "The *philosophes* felt the challenge so keenly that, as Diderot put it, they regarded it their sacred duty to show not only that their morality was just as good as religious ethics, but much better." [Cf. *An Age of Crisis*, chap. 13.] "A great deal of eighteenth century thought would assume a different complexion, if it was constantly remembered that though a philosophy of

from those who tore down whatever such humanists tried to build. These challengers declared that mankind had to live permanently in the ruins and rubble of the collapsed moral world, perhaps with armed guards to keep looters and snipers in check, perhaps with none. This group of radicals, although they were few, could not be ignored. They reintegrated man within the all-embracing fold of nature to a degree which denied him any transcendence or exceptional status. Diderot, for instance, warns us that "it's every man for himself in this world," and that "the world is the house of the strong." This was the second challenge. It grew out of the critical rationalism of the eighteenth century, its psychology, its theories of determinism and materialism. Robespierre, speaking to the Convention on the eighteenth Floréal of year II, summarized with understanding this aspect of the century which lay behind him. "In a large part we owe them [the *philosophes*] that kind of practical philosophy which, reducing egoism to a system, considers human society as a war of ruse, success as the rule of justice and injustice, probity as an affair of taste and convention, and the world as the patrimony of clever crooks." How accurate this diagnosis was we shall have ample occasion to observe in this volume. But any student of the eighteenth century will realize to what extent it is confirmed, even outside of the philosophic writings, in the theatre from *Turcaret* to *Le Mariage de Figaro* and in the development of the novel.

Robespierre's diagnosis, however, is only a partial truth. The vast majority of writers were concerned, quite to the contrary, with a positive response to the challenge, with avoiding that position which he sets forth as the heritage of the *philosophes*. The facts of nature, they recognized, may include those which the immoralists cited as their justification. There is, however, another fact: the moral world in man. It is here that the problem of the genesis of moral experience becomes important, and we can understand why so many writers were concerned with it. If we knew the origin, it was thought, we would know the status of the moral life: whether it was natural or artificial (to use the vocabulary of the time); whether it was primary—that is, coequal with the egoistic

---

protest, revolt and spontaneity, [it] was intensely aware of the challenge to redefine the guarantees of social cohesion and morality. The *philosophes* were anxious to show that not they, but their opponents, were the anarchists from the point of view of the natural order." (*The Rise of Totalitarian Democracy*, pp. 21–22.)

impulses, even though at variance with them—or secondary, the product of culture; and whether it was instinctual, emotional, or rational. The two principal traditional approaches to ethics, the intuitional and the utilitarian, reveal their shape in this inquiry and foreshadow their responses to the major substantive problem of ethical value.

Certainly, the epistemological inquiry would not in itself solve the moral problem. No matter what the truth happened to be concerning the origin and status of "moral knowledge," it could never do away with the ineradicable reality of moral dilemmas and decisions. It would not tell us, in any troubled situation of life, what *is* the right thing to do, or determine us to do that right thing even if we knew it. Indeed, in some cases it may have had a contrary effect and discredited moral conventions by uncovering irrational or scandalous origins. At the least, it seemed evident that the development of the moral notions in any culture does not, in itself, confer absolute authority on our traditional and instinctive moral feelings.[4]

On one thing the defenders of morality, religious or humanistic, were agreed, although they would not have expressed it in the same phrases or concurred on the ultimate motivating goal. The essence of the moral problem, it was clear to all, was that of the socialization of the egoistic individual. This was the basic reason why ethics and politics became inseparable. The nihilists were precisely those who denied any status to this problem or solved it in favor of the natural egoistic propensities. On the one hand, there is the moral conscience, whatever its origin, commanding us to think in terms of others, or more exactly, of standards and acts which underlie and safeguard the existence of society.[5] On the other hand, there are the instinctual, egoistic drives of the individual toward pleasure, power, and pride. Since men are free, as many observed, from the compelling fixity of instinctual animal behavior, they are free to violate conscience and prefer self to collectivity. The measure must be balanced, or social life and the survival of the species become impossible. And yet there were some who asserted, and innumerably more who acted as if they, too, asserted that such limitations on the individual egoistic

[4] Cresson: *Le Problème moral et les philosophes,* p. 182.
[5] This is clearly and precisely stated by Raynal, *Histoire des Deux Indes,* Livre XIX, chap. XIV.

vitalities violated the universal natural law which makes the weak the victims of the strong. For them moral law was an artifice of the weak to frustrate nature, and as such can command no status in the eyes of the strong.

Eighteenth-century ethics, consequently, does not separate theory from the practical need to make men virtuous. A twentieth-century ethical philosopher writes: "The author does not undertake to teach the duties of the gentleman, nor to show that virtue is preferable to vice and that he who submits to its rules is not the dupe of his prejudices."[6] Such a statement would have been deemed most strange in eighteenth-century France. The basis of values, the nature of virtue, the reasons why we should be virtuous, and the methods of making men virtuous were all considered as the phases of a single problem, and the last two phases tormented philosophers not the least. Mandeville, for instance, contrasts the state of nature in which the self only is considered with the social state. In the latter, the problem is to make men believe "it was more beneficial for every Body to conquer than indulge his interest, and much better to mind the Publick than what seemed his private interest."[7]

Furthermore, this problem supplied the link between ethical and political speculation which were so closely allied at that time. "All men," states Hume, "are sensible of the necessity to maintain peace and order, and all men are sensible of the necessity of peace and order for the maintenance of society. Yet, not withstanding this strong and obvious necessity, such is the frailty or perverseness of our nature! it is impossible to keep men faithfully and unerringly in the paths of justice. Some extraordinary circumstances may happen in which a man finds his interests to be more promoted by fraud or rapine than hurt by the breach which his injustice makes in the social union. But much more frequently he is seduced from his great and important, but distant interests, by the allurement of present, though often very frivolous, temptations. This great weakness is incurable in human nature. Men must, therefore, endeavour to palliate what they cannot cure."[8]

This problem, in France at least, was further conditioned by

---

[6] Dupréel, *Traité de morale*, p. v.

[7] Kaye, *The Fable of the Bees*, I, p. 28 (original pagination).

[8] "Of the Origin of Government," in *Hume's Moral and Political Philosophy*, ed. H. D. Aiken, New York, 1948, p. 311.

the prevailing theory that the quest for happiness or pleasure and the avoidance of pain or displeasure were the motives of all action. Such a supposition slants the problem in a definite direction and leads to d'Holbach's concise formulation: *"To make men happy through virtue:* that is the great problem which ethics must undertake to resolve." [9] This direction of thought was, in fact, apparent much before d'Holbach. Butler had already written, "I suppose it may be spoken of as very much the distinction of the present to profess a contracted spirit and greater regards to self-interest than appears to have been done formerly." [10] This turn toward naturalism projects another aspect of d'Holbach's problem. If self-love is the center of the psychic life and its unique motivation (a debated question which we analyzed in the first volume of this study), how could one explain the fact that man is inevitably a moral being? Nor could one escape this fact by denying, as some sought to do, the existence of God and valid imperatives. The moral facts, such as self-sacrifice, and the ethical judgments were irremovable.

There were, then, two principle general questions (each having many facets) in eighteenth-century ethical speculation. The first concerns the origin of our moral judgments. Does "right" refer to inherent characteristics of actions, or does it only indicate approval? By what principle of our constitution are we led to form such distinctions? Is it, for instance, by our reason, which also perceives the distinction between truth and falsehood, or perhaps by some other peculiar power of perception or of intuition? Why do we approve of some acts as right and disapprove of others as wrong? Is the root to be found in the emotion of pity or in self-interest? Are these distinctions necessary or local and conditioned? This entire problem which was not of interest to the ancients now becomes important, in part because it is related to the wider problem of knowledge.

The second question relates to the object of moral approbation. Is there a common quality of rightness in the different modes of virtue (benevolence, rational self-love, proper action in a given situation)? If this quality is the unegoistic, that which tends toward the common good, what is its relation to the egoistic? Again we inquire, first, how it made its appearance beside the egoistic, and

[9] *Le Système social,* III, p. 164.
[10] *Five Sermons,* Sermon IV, p. 1.

then, wherefrom it derives a superior validity in choice, and after that, why men should be guided by its sway (the practical problem of inducing them to be so guided).

On the question of origin, it might be held that both egoistic and altruistic impulses are among the original endowment of human nature, or that the egoistic becomes altruistic as a result of rational meditation, or again, that the altruistic grew out of the facts and needs of society.[11] In the first case, man is held to be naturally a moral being. This does not necessarily mean that he would be a moral being without society, but that he brings to social experience innate moral attitudes, predispositions, and even, perhaps, criteria. The Natural Law and moral sense theories fit in here. The other two theories implied that the moral life is an artificial accretion, resulting in different ways from society. These theories did not, in turn, deny innate potentialities, but they emphasized the implantation and inculcation of moral experience. They also held such experience to be a valuable and necessary supplement imposed upon the natural.[12] This attitude contrasted with the view of the immoralists, who also considered the ethical as an artificial adjunct, but concluded that it was invalid and to be abandoned, if not by all of society at least by the superior and the strong.

Other questions followed from these, inevitably, but they were mainly rephrasings or special aspects of the main question. Is justice prior to law or does it derive from law? This is really to ask again whether the feeling of right and wrong is prior to society, or whether it stems from it, or is at least validated by it. Either of these views involved the assumption that society—in the sense of stable relations and codes—came into being. Still another way of approaching the problem hinged on a decision as to whether moral notions depend on an immutable, absolute order, such as God's will, universal reason, or human nature, or whether they grew up as an empirical reaction to the particular experience of various cultures. Followers of the traditional Natural Law theories adhered to the idea of an immutable order. Moral sense theorists found another absolute basis in human nature. Utilitarians and naturalists might prefer the solution of experiential development; but often,

---

[11] See A. Schweitzer, *Civilization and Ethics,* London, 1946, p. 71.

[12] "Natural" is taken here in the sense of "original," "spontaneous." For definitions of these and other terms, see *An Age of Crisis,* Prefatory Note.

like Voltaire and Diderot, they mingled two or more theories. The force of the belief in a universal human nature was too great to be ignored entirely by most writers, but the content of this universal was subject to a variety of interpretations.[13] Rivarol, near the close of the period, summarizes this thinking. "Morals, like the political body itself, is founded on homogeneity: for there is none between man and beast, nor between man and God. Among animals, they would be founded on animality; among angels on spirituality; among men, they would be founded on humanity, mother of all virtues, for it leads first to justice and then to beneficence." [14] A *natural* morality, then, would be one based on universals in the human psyche, which might, in turn, depend on universals in our physical and social life. "The *philosophes*," writes R. R. Palmer, "obtained the advantages of theology by appealing to an absolute humanity . . . they invoked the judgment of man in general. Diderot in particular took this course. He deplored the fact that Helvétius should call ideas of right and wrong mere local and variable conventions." [15] Morality might be "artificial," in the sense that it developed from social living, but it was nonetheless a natural development. With this even Rousseau would have agreed. On the other hand, it was also possible to conceive of nature not as a fixed order, but as a living process devoid of finalities, as a history pregnant with the unforeseeable. Either attitude permitted the belief that mankind could be organized for the achievement of definite objects, and in ways so opposite as to foreshadow the cleavage between a totalitarian or a liberal society.

Reason in the Age of Enlightenment, as in any other age, demanded a conceptual morality objectifying and projecting its own existence. Whether such concepts formed a body of knowledge or truth was another question which vexed inquiring minds. It was also assumed by most that the will has the capacity to direct action in accordance with such universals and the demands of a particular situation. Here, however, great complexities arose for those who argued that actions are necessarily determined, and for those who maintained that reason is only the servant of the passions.

[13] See *An Age of Crisis,* chap. 7.
[14] *Maximes et Pensées,* in *Oeuvres,* 1950, I, p. 248.
[15] *Catholics and Unbelievers,* Princeton, 1939, p. 191.

We shall encounter many other problems which grew out of the effort of exploration and reconstruction. We shall see that the French writers of the eighteenth century—both *philosophes* and others—were deeply and constantly concerned with abstract questions relating to the moral life (even as they were with abstract questions relating to human nature, the political and economic organization of society, the origins of religion, societies, myth, etc.). They could not easily forget their preoccupation with the basic, multifaceted problem of our moral and social coexistence.[16]

History is a succession of evolving cultural complexes, each of which is a tension of conflicting polarities, themselves ever-evolving, creating moments of unstable stability like the points in the flight of Zeno's arrow, leading to a new cultural complex. The "unity" or "character" of a period lies in the unique dynamic equilibrium it achieves; that is to say, in the peculiar forms and emphases given to the polarities, resulting in the unique form of the relatively stabilized tension of evolving contraries which prevails; a uniqueness which includes, among the factors, the peculiar shape of the questions that are asked and the "preconceptions" and other tools which are brought to bear in the quest for their solution. Independence and dependence (the individual and the whole), the universal and the particular, the absolute and the relative; authority (conformity) versus criticism (originality), reliance on pure intellect versus trust in feeling (in its physical and emotional forms), nature versus art—these are among the unending polarities whose metamorphoses and recombinations, impelled by the changing facts of culture and the natural restlessness or dissatisfaction which characterizes the species, lead us, insensibly or by brusque revolution, from one cultural complex to its equally self-liquidating successor.

It is the aim of this study to supply a view of many of the conflicting elements of the cultural complex of eighteenth-century France, a view of their peculiar nature (reflecting the facts of that cultural moment), and of the peculiar balance of their opposing

---

[16] Cf. J. L. Talmon: "But Carcassonne himself had to admit that the nearer we get to the French Revolution, the more prevalent, not to say universal, becomes abstract and dogmatic thinking, and that in the more strictly political field." (*Op. cit.*, p. 261.) The statement is even truer in regard to ethical thinking and the two are, as we shall see, indissolubly linked.

force which created a dynamic tension with sufficient stability to warrant the appelation, "Age of Enlightenment." [17]

[17] A word of caution. The reader will, it is hoped, discriminate between the objective analysis of eighteenth-century ideas and the author's critical perspective upon them. It is nowhere suggested that materialism and amoralism are interchangeable words; or that there is any logical connection between moral idealism (or lack of it) and a given metaphysical position. Where a logical connection is asserted, in this volume or in *An Age of Crisis,* between ideas and events, reference is usually to a particular historical framework, outlook or intellectual climate, that of the period under study, rather than to abstract logic. Finally, it is worth repeating that the word "nihilism" is always to be taken in the ethical sense, as the denial of the validity of all distinctions of moral value.

*The Nature and Genesis
of Moral Experience*

One

NATURAL LAW

I. A Brief Historical View

BROADLY SPEAKING, THERE ARE only three possible sources of our moral judgments. We may hold them from a direct revelation of God's will, communicated to a silent humanity by his prophets or vicars. In this case they are above all experience and are commands from a superior which may conceivably contradict our reason and our notions of utility. Contrariwise, they may be held to derive from experience and to be subsequently formulated by arbitrary custom, by affective reactions, or by rational reflection, in other words, by a purely human moral process. Somewhere between these two stands the doctrine of Natural Law. It holds moral truths to be prior to experience and yet involved in experience, to be above expediency and yet fundamentally more useful than expediency, to be set forth by the will of God and yet directly discoverable by each human being through that intuitive aspect of his rationality commonly denominated "right reason."

Natural Law may be properly considered as a doctrine, when we contemplate it as a part of the mainstream of Western philosophy and jurisprudence. In reality, it is something much more important and profound, for the doctrine only formulates an intuitive belief, rationally conceived or not, which always reasserts itself within a given tradition; namely, that there is an objective right and wrong in the very nature of things and their relationships, divorced from general utility, self-interest, or emotional

3

preference.[1] Such a belief has perforce been modified into typical forms corresponding to the peculiar outlook of a given moment or milieu. Its validity and even its existence have been denied by various philosophical sects, such as the Sophists, the utilitarians and positivists, and the Hegelian idealists, all of whom, through the exercise of discursive reason, have evolved systems to which such a notion would be inimical. Yet, like the intuition of our self or of our freedom, the belief in Natural Law persists, and even as a doctrine of jurisprudence has enjoyed a powerful revival in recent years. The historian can obviously follow it only through its written formulations.[2] He will find it in systems of law, from Justinian's Code to the American Constitution; in literature and philosophy from Sophocles and Aristotle to Maritain and Proust.

The content of Natural Law has always been somewhat vague and imprecise. It changes somewhat according to the formulations of its various exponents and is consequently not quite the same for Cicero, Voltaire, or Burke. Some recent apologists of Natural Law, Catholics or political conservatives, have gone too far in an attempt to unify a "Natural Law tradition," from Plato up till Hobbes and Grotius—generally deriving a theory which happens to be that of Aquinas. This is a patent distortion, for the history as well as the philosophy of Natural Law is extremely complex, with significant differences not only between pagans and medieval Christians, but also among the writers of each of these groups. Nonetheless, we find throughout a consistent basic attitude toward the relation of positive law to justice and right, and a common core of prescriptions and of rights. The prescriptions involve an intuitive grasp of justice in human relations: the fulfillment of contractual obligations, gratitude, or the return of good for good, the accomplishment of other undeniable obligations in the family, in the cultural group, and even among nations. Obligations imply rights, and it is on this subject that we find the widest differences of opinion among the proponents of Natural Law, though the right to life, and to what is necessary to maintain life, would be granted by all.

Occidental thought has conceived of two rather different kinds of Natural Law. From the time of the Greeks until the middle of

---

[1] An intuitive notion may be true or false. No judgment is intended here.

[2] Thus he will find no direct evidence of it among the ancient Hebrews, who did not work it out as a formulation, but who tacitly conceived of such a truth.

the seventeenth century, there was a major tradition, growing in magnificence throughout that long period despite variations and contradictions. Then, as a result of the collapse of the inherited value system during the late Renaissance and the concomitant rise of empirical science, a different kind of law of nature was gradually evolved by Hobbes and his successors, one that had new and often unexpected ramifications.[3]

In the major tradition, nature, and not abstract reason, is supposedly the norm. The laws of ethics thus endeavor to escape the vagaries of individual human reason and will which are so often fallacious or corrupted by the egoistic propensities. And yet the "nature" that is involved in the Natural Law concept is not at all that nature of which we conceive in the broad and universal sense of the word: the laws which make the planets revolve in their courses and the plants to grow; nor yet the impulses which govern the affective and instinctual existence, or the animal souls in men and in beasts. It is that nature, or that part of nature, which is perceptible alone to beings who enjoy a rational mode of existence, and its laws are applicable to such beings alone. Natural Law is considered inseparable from the law of reason, for reason is the natural structure, or at least the obligation of men. It is not a law for angels, since its function is to confine, to direct, and to regulate the impulses of the animal soul. It is, then, a law made by God for man, independent of his will and dependent on his reason (that is, his "right reason," not his logical powers) only for its perception and not for its existence. Reason then is a guide or discoverer, but not a creator.

As a law of nature, the Natural Law is universal and immutable. It is nonconventional and transcends culture itself. "It was conceived as an ultimate law inherent in the nature of things and centered in man himself. Clearly, belief in Natural Law assumes a noble idea of man, of his unique value both as a free and rational individual and as a social being." [4] The Natural Law in sum was immutable because it emanated from God; universal because of the common nature of man and because its foundation was rational. We must, however, go beyond this. Natural Law is "natural" only because of a certain concept of nature, one which holds

[3] See L. G. Crocker, *An Age of Crisis*, chap. 1. Cf. A. P. d'Entrèves, *Natural Law*, p. 12. The theories of Hobbes and later radicals actually had antecedents among the early Greeks.

[4] P. J. Stanlis, *Edmund Burke and the Natural Law*, p. 8.

it to be definable in terms of proper ends, and which takes certain regularities to be indicative of those ends. "Unnatural acts" occur in nature but violate the ends conceived of as natural.

The seventeenth-century shift in viewpoint on man and the universe brought about a corresponding revision in the concept of Natural Law. The world was no longer seen, by advanced thinkers, as an ordered cosmos. The State was the highest expression of power, not of morality. And man, far from being an essentially rational being, was selfish and cruel, moved by his egoistic impulses and passions. A new idea of "natural law" dawns, reminding us of Ulpian's "regrettable" intrusion into the more comforting classical doctrine: the only universal law is "the law of nature" (as we shall call it, to distinguish it from Natural Law theories), one which does not distinguish man from beast, but embraces them both, and perhaps all living things, in the pursuit of the elemental needs of life, therefore of power. For Ulpian, however, and for others who adhered to his view, the problem was to "moralize" nature, transposing to it moral categories of social origin. And now it is the categories of natural science that will be applied to the social state to give it stability.

Hobbes rejected the notion that man is a political and social animal as an error of political idealism. Man is an animal mechanistically determined, living in a godless and amoral world. In such a philosophy there was obviously no place for the traditional Natural Law. "Where there is no common power there is no law; where no law, no injustice" (*Leviathan,* Ch. XII, 1651). Although Hobbes continues to use the traditional terminology, he revolutionizes the concept, for he starts not from natural order, but from natural chaos as the human condition. Power, will, and need now become the naturalistic components of a law which operates entirely within the human experience, and has no existence outside of it. Law, for Hobbes, "is the world of him, that by right hath command over others." [5] "Traditional natural law," writes Leo Strauss, "is primarily and mainly an objective 'rule and measure,' a binding order prior to, and independent of the human will, while modern natural law is, or tends to be, primarily and mainly a series of 'rights,' of subjective claims, originating in the human will." [6]

[5] *Leviathan,* chap. XV. Cf. *De Cive,* chap. XIV, art. 1 and R. Polin, *Philosophie et politique chez Hobbes,* p. 179.
[6] *Natural Right and History,* p 183.

This law, existing in the state of nature, has no ethical content, no normative function. It is based on a fundamental "nature" which results in necessary tendencies; this nature is the fear of violent death and the desire for security. The law of nature is a factual experience of man's power and faculties which lead him to seek what is good. It asserts the individual's right to life and to what he needs for life: the right to the end includes the right to the means.[7] Since man possesses reason, he is sole judge of what is his good and of the best means to secure it. He has a "right to anything which he so pursues and gets."

When men voluntarily enter into the social compact, the state of nature gives way to positive law. Hobbes, then, separates clearly the two ideas in the word *"droit,"* law and right. A law is a command with the power to enforce it. A right is the free and legitimate use of power.[8] And "right reason" is only the most efficient calculation. But positive law is not limited by a prior and superior moral law by which it is to be judged for its worth and moral rightness. It is the only source of justice and there is no appeal as long as power can prudentially maintain itself. Law founds right and maintains it. The State and primarily its head, the monarch, may be absolute and arbitrary (although he is in practice limited by what the sensible sovereign will do and by what the people can do against him). Hobbes, by his concepts of man and the state of nature, makes absolutism, within the realistic bounds of power, and unlimited sovereignty both necessary and morally justifiable.

Once the social contract is entered upon, relationships and, consequently, laws change. We may properly apply to Hobbes Rousseau's warning, that we must not confuse what is natural in the state of nature with what is natural in the social state. The social compact has certain essential or "natural" implications which derive from its essence and from right reason. These are obligations, "artificial" calculations which are not, however, anti-natural. They constitute a "Natural Law" which the ruler of a society may not disregard with impunity. In society, then, we have a Natural Law, but rights are dependent on positive laws. The situation of the state of nature is thus reversed. Obligation now comes into being because mutuality is expressible in society, and Hobbes, the realist, recognizes no obligation which is not an effective, external

---

[7] *De corpore politico,* in *The Moral and Political Works of Thomas Hobbes,* London, 1750, p. 36.

[8] Polin, *op. cit.,* p. 181.

constraint.[9] What characterizes Hobbes's derivation of Natural Law in the social state is the fixity of his prescriptions, resulting from his effort to achieve certainty and stability by conceiving moral rules very much as one would mathematical axioms.[10]

For Hobbes, then, there are really two forms of Natural Law. In the state of nature, his doctrine is purely one of "rights of nature," and not one of limits upon rights, or obligations. Moral Natural Law arises only in society, out of a transformation of the conditions of egoistic self-realization. On the one hand, civil law may not contradict Natural Law (except at its own risk). On the other hand, Natural Law becomes obligation only in the form of civil laws (enforceable commands), and Natural Law itself commands obedience to all the laws of a State; so that no civil law can be charged with violating the Natural Law—it is the only interpreter of Natural Law—nor is there any prior definition of justice to limit positive laws.

The influence of Hobbes was complex. On the one hand, a strong and persistent adverse reaction denounced his concept of man in the state of nature, its lack of rational and moral law, and the absolutism which it justified. On the other hand, his imprint on Natural Law theory, with its shift to empirical realities of the human will, was indelible.[11]

Although Locke denied Hobbes's view of man and refuted his political theories, he was nonetheless influenced by him to the point of absorbing some essential aspects of the new doctrine of Natural Law. Locke, it is true, desired to reaffirm the traditional Natural Law and to put it on a sounder basis. The essential difference is that for Locke the world is a moral order in which man participates; for Hobbes it is merely a natural order, in which man is called upon to build a moral order. Because of the many natural obstacles, declares Hobbes, force is necessary to moral obligation. Locke, on the other hand, insists that even in the state of nature man was bound by a natural moral law, inasmuch as he is a ra-

---

[9] In the view of the traditional doctrine, Hobbes confuses the moral order with the juridical. Natural Law concerns knowing, not legislating, man as man, not a political community. Each man has within himself the judiciary authority of humanity. (J. Maritain, "Natural Law and Moral Law," pp. 69–70.)

[10] The laws are listed both in *De Cive,* chap. III, and in *Leviathan,* chap. XIV, XV. For an excellent summary, see R. Polin, *op. cit.,* pp. 191–93, and the table on pp. 200–1.

[11] Many of his basic views were followed and reinforced by Spinoza; see *Tractatus theologico-politicus,* chap. XVI.

tional creature, a part of the divinely established order of the world, an order operating through laws. "Natural Law" includes the free power of the rational individual, but this freedom, as a condition of its own existence, calls forth obligation.[12]

On several major points, however, Locke departs from the traditional Natural Law doctrines, for instance, in his emphasis on rights. Also, man, not having innate ideas, lacks an immediate perception of Natural Law—although it is "natural" to him in the sense that it is a natural result of the use of his natural rational faculties. But it is not immediately discoverable to his conscience, not readable in the "heart," not ascertainable by a *consensus gentium*. Conscience and therefore the laws and customs of peoples are relative and diverse. The discovery of moral truths depends, then, on correct reasoning, and moral truths are considered to be fixed rules, as provable and ultimately as self-evident as a mathematical theorem. Furthermore, Locke's account of motivation stresses the pleasure-pain principle, leading thereby to the utilitarian criterion of the greatest happiness—which also confirms the utilitarian emphasis on rights as the means to attain this goal. (Here we must remember that for Hobbes—as for Rousseau, but under quite different conditions—society puts an end to natural rights, or at least transforms them; while for Locke, the whole purpose and justification of a society lay in the protection and enhancement of these rights.) Although Natural Law is not "justified" by its utility, the motive for conforming to it is one of self-interest.[13] Finally, Locke swerved from the main stream of Natural Law theory by rooting his theories in a presocial "state of nature." The consequences are manifold. The natural equality of this state becomes the source of natural rights. It follows also that although society is in conformity with human nature, men are not at once compelled by a social instinct to live in political communities. From this, the social contract doctrine ensues inevitably. The contract theory severs the State from nature. It assumes an individual will to establish "a relationship of mutual obligation which would not otherwise exist by the law of nature."[14]

We come now to the second source which feeds into the new stream. As Hobbes is the fountainhead of the first, so Grotius is

[12] See R. Polin, *La Politique morale de John Locke*, p. 100.

[13] *Ibid.*, II, chap. 28, art. iv, ii.

[14] D'Entrèves, *op. cit.*, p. 57. See G. H. Sabine, *A History of Political Theory*, New York, 1950, p. 529.

of the second.[15] It is the unfortunate tendency on the part of some recent writers to confound Hobbes, Locke, and Grotius into a single monstrous faction of secularists. No one, however, would have been more horrified than Grotius by Hobbes's philosophy of naturalism. He belonged to an entirely alien school of thought.

Grotius, an Arminian Protestant, was concerned with countering the doctrine of Luther and Calvin (one which had its precedent in William of Occam and the Nominalists), that law depended on the arbitrary will of God and, *mutatis mutandis,* on the arbitrary will of the State, as affirmed by Machiavelli and Bodin.[16] This doctrine, ultimately, was not unlike that of Hobbes who also placed will above reason or an eternal moral order. Law, Grotius felt, must be independent of arbitrary will and of particular facts or historical experience. Natural Law is the source of obligation which in turn is the mother of civil law.[17] It must be based on pure reason, not on power. In establishing this abstract or independent validity, he gave Natural Law a renewed vitality and restored its importance. But he did it at the price of a concession that was fraught with unexpected consequences. Like the Stoics, and unlike the Roman jurists and Aquinas, he considered law as possessing a logical or mathematical certainty which even God could not change; so that, even though it is the will of God, it is, in a sense, independent of his will. It was in this framework that Grotius wrote these famous lines:

> What we have been saying would have a degree of validity even if we should concede that which cannot be conceded without the utmost wickedness, that there is no God, or that the affairs of men are of no concern to him. . . . Just as even God cannot cause that two times two should not make four, so he cannot cause that that which is intrinsically evil be not evil.[18]

The consequences of this statement went beyond Grotius' intention and turned out to be the support of a humanistic ethics and a secular Natural Law. "He proved that it was possible to build

---

[15] In point of time, Grotius precedes Hobbes. His *De Iure pacis et belli* dates from 1625; Hobbes's *De Cive* was published in 1642, the *Leviathan* in 1651.

[16] Luther and Calvin could not accept Natural Law as the sign of the dignity of human nature and as the mediator between man and God.

[17] *Le Droit de la guerre et de la paix,* ed. Pradier-Fodéré, 1867, I, p. 21.

[18] *Prolegomena,* par. 11; I, i, x. Actually this idea had already been expounded by Suárez and the group of Spanish jurists. See W. A. Dunning, *A History of Political Theories,* I, pp. 134, 138.

up a theory of laws independent of theological presuppositions." [19]
From the traditional viewpoint, this began a schism in which
Natural Law ceased to be a participation in Eternal Law and God
became merely its guarantor. In Pufendorf (1672), Burlamaqui
(1747), and de Vattel (1758), Natural Law becomes a purely
rational construction. "What Grotius had set forth as a hypothesis
has become a thesis. The self-evidence of natural law has made
the existence of God perfectly superfluous." [20] Although this
statement is essentially true, all these writers do express their belief
that Natural Law has its source in God. Moreover, the individualism characteristic of the modern natural rights or Natural
Law theory is rooted in the doctrine of the social contract, which
is *not* accepted by Grotius (and which is, at best, only implied by
Burlamaqui). Grotius intended Natural Law to be an abstract
theory, not a revolutionary doctrine; he was, we recall, an upholder
of slavery and the divine right of kings. It is true, on the other
hand, that Grotius did reinterpret the idea of natural rights, giving
them a greater importance than previously. Rights, he thought,
depend not merely on eternal principles, but on qualities inherent in persons, on "that quality in a person which makes it just
or right for him either to possess certain things or to do certain
actions." Therefore, the end of positive law was, in part, to protect
these rights.[21]

In the eighteenth century, there will gradually be, after de Vattel
especially, an adamant demand for specific and rigidly conceived
rights, compared to the vague, pliable, and prudential rights of
the earlier theory—"rights" which could be modified to suit almost any regime. The modern theory "was not, properly speaking,
a theory of law at all. It was a theory of rights." [22] This momentous

[19] D'Entrèves, *op. cit.*, p. 52. Hans J. Morgenthau comments: "Thus he took the
decisive step from the concept of a theological world, whose divine government is
above human understanding as well as action, to the concept of an inherently rational world of which man is a part and which he can understand and act upon."
(*Scientific Man vs. Power Politics*, Chicago, 1940, p. 13.) For J. Maritain, Grotius'
error was to concentrate on the order of nature as deciphered by human reason,
rather than on the relation between the order of nature and eternal reason (*op.
cit.*, p. 67).

[20] D'Entrèves, *op. cit.*, p. 53.

[21] For Pufendorf's attempt to "save the phenomena," see *Le Droit de la nature
et des gens*, Amsterdam, 1734, Bk. VII, chap. 1, 2, etc.

[22] D'Entrèves, *op. cit.*, p. 59. But we must recognize the fact that totally different
political systems are developed: absolutist (Hobbes, Grotius, Spinoza, Pufendorf), or
liberal (Locke and some eighteenth-century French writers).

change and the ensuing ambiguity of "Natural Law" rested partly
on an ambiguity of vocabulary, the words *ius* and *droit* referring
both to a system of law and to rights. On the other hand, it should
also be noted that the eighteenth-century proponents of natural
rights did not deny, as is charged, normative limits on rights and
make of them a pure experience of will and power. There was an
ethical norm inherent in their theory of natural rights, in its basic
principle of equality or reciprocity. It is therefore equally inaccurate to assert that this theory held natural rights to be absolute.
Rather it declared them to be unalienable to other individuals or
to the State.

Now we must note a curious historical phenomenon which is
usually overlooked by historians of Natural Law. Even as the new
natural rights version of Natural Law was growing in strength,
with its valuation of individual prerogatives and satisfactions,
there was an increasing tendency, which we shall later observe in
some detail, toward theories of utilitarianism and social control
for the good of all. While with some writers (notably in England),
this concept was designed to include the *rights* of the individuals
within the purlieu of general welfare, with many others (especially
in France), the locus of these rights is displaced from the individual to the community. In this process as we see it, for instance
in the works of Morelly, Helvétius, Mably, and Rousseau, the
"natural rights of the individual" vanish.[23] It is the good of the
community which it is the absolute right of the community to
realize, even, or more exactly, necessarily at the cost of individual
rights, since private natural rights and social utility are often, in
view of the egoistic nature of man, incompatible. This new demand for natural rights, combining then the social or communal
with private rights, but emphasizing the former, became that
doctrine of natural rights, absolutist in character, which Burke correctly denounced as contrary to the moral prescriptions of traditional Natural Law and as being equivalent to power, and not to
right at all.

Let us summarize the two divergent doctrines, remembering
that this résumé is schematic and that there are many important

[23] "Morelly and Mably completely rejected the current individualism and declared
that happiness is to be found only in an organized society where the individual
satisfaction is deliberately subordinated to the public good." (K. Martin, *French Liberal Thought in the Eighteenth Century*, Boston, 1929, p. 242.) Mably, however, also
asserts the rights of individuals, and even the right to revolt.

variations in each. The classical-Christian theory maintains a God-given moral law which is prior and superior to the individual and his claims. It is "known by human reason, but human reason has no part in its establishment." It includes certain general rights of the individual inasmuch as he is a moral being. Although these rights inhere in nature and will (subjective motivation), their ultimate source and justification is God's moral law. Willed personal interests are irrelevant, unless they are reconciled with objective reason which does not derive from self-interest and is the corrective of self-interest, the latter being an atomizing and not a societal force. However, there is no antithesis between nature and society, and therefore no "natural rights" claim against society. Society is given equally with the person. Social institutions are part of the natural order and must respond to the Natural Law which is superior to them, but not antecedent or separate from them. They must, then, take into account man's natural rights as a moral being under Natural Law. However, these rights do not exist independently of the social context or against it, but rather achieve their reality and their realization within a specific cultural context, and their concrete forms are modified thereby. No rights can be asserted, on an individual, natural, or communal basis, against the moral law or the social institutions which properly reflect it; for those rights, like man himself, do not exist prior to them or independently of them. Natural Law, social institutions (properly conceived), and human rights are one complex, inseparable and indivisible. The individual is not independent of history or of institutions, and to think of him in this way is invalid. We must therefore separate civil rights from natural rights: the former derive from civil society, not from nature or God.

The "modern Natural Law doctrine" emphasizes the individual and the empirical reality of his actual experience, needs, and claims. It is really an exaltation of human will for human ends, without a contemplative participation in divine reason. Yet it is not, as conservatives charge, a pure doctrine of will and power. It is a theory of right, one which involves the use of power for its realization; but power is not made equivalent to right. The right is *to* the means or power. The whole sense of the doctrine is precisely a revolt against force or power, as embodied in existing institutions. It leads to a demand for abstract, that is, for rigid and specific rights which are held to be natural and God-given. Although natural rights are admittedly only a corollary of Natural Law, in some writers, notably Locke and numerous partisans of the French Revolution, they acquire the primary importance; they are ultimately, in the nineteenth century, severed from Natural Law which is abandoned by positivist sociology and jurisprudence as a metaphysical doctrine. The "modern theory" assumes a state of nature as a historical or a hypothetical reality. The state of nature concept inevitably throws emphasis on natural freedom and equality. It makes rights (and with some writers, obligations) both prior to and independent of any given society. The natural rights theory emphasizes the break between nature and culture or convention (between nature and art, as it is sometimes phrased). The traditional Natural Law theory had distinguished the two without making them antithetical—in fact it had usually emphasized that the realization of Natural Law came about *naturally* through conventional institutions. For the theorists of the later view, individual rights inhere in each individual as a human being and are limited or conditioned only by the same rights of all other individuals, according to the principles of equity and equality. Their source is human nature and will alone, that is, the natural desire for satisfaction and self-fulfillment, although these may be held ultimately to derive from God. Our rights remain valid and unmodified (though limited) in society, which is a voluntary association whose only justification is their furtherance. Therefore they are superior to any particular established form of government, which must adhere to them, failing which, revolution becomes legitimate. The mere existence of institutions is, then, no argument for their validity or for their conformity with Natural Law. One might well say the contrary, for history is the history of irrationality and error. But reason is capable of creating a rational and just society, *de novo*. It has the right and the duty to do so. The historical outcome of this theory was the severance of juridical law and moral law (already evident in Montaigne, Descartes, and Pascal)—a process which has begun to be reversed only in recent years.

There remains an important point, one that has also been usually overlooked. What we have called the secondary source of modern Natural Law theory, stemming from Grotius, was essentially not a theory of rights or of voluntarism, but a theory of moral knowledge and of the origin of moral experience. In England, this factor was relatively unimportant, because of the influence of Hobbes and Locke, and also, perhaps, because of the empirical shape of mind. As a result, many English defenders of innate objective moral truth turned away from Natural Law to what seemed like more empirical solutions, such as the moral sense theory, moral intuition, or natural sympathy. In France, however, where Hobbes was also universally condemned, there was no Locke to transform appealingly and to perpetuate certain elements of his doctrine, for in that country Locke was known and admired for his metaphysical more than for his political thought. Rousseau, who absorbed much of Hobbes, wrote after the middle of the century and, moreover, went in an opposite direction from Locke. Consequently, Natural Law could still flourish in France, even if with some secularization, as a true ethical theory, and there was no need to resort to the moral sense hypothesis which, as we shall see, had little appeal to the French. And yet when the French Revolution broke out, the Natural Law doctrine was no longer the chief support of moral certitude. Just as in England, it terminates in the natural rights doctrine, in the *Déclaration des Droits de l'homme.* French and Anglo-Saxons fuse in Thomas Paine's ardent support of the Revolution, and in his unforgettable rebuttal of Burke. How extensive, then, and how deep did the Natural Law current remain in eighteenth-century French ethical speculation? This is the question we must principally examine. Why and when did it cease to be an ethical theory and become one of voluntarism and natural rights? This question, too, although outside the scope of pure ethical inquiry, demands at least a brief reply.

II. Natural Law in Eighteenth-Century France

What thief will abide a thief?—Saint Augustine

The Christian apologists had found themselves ever since the rise of the seventeenth-century *libertin* movement in an ambivalent position. On the one hand, they desired to confirm the status of Natural Law as a part of the Christian tradition and structure, and a needed defense against amoralism and immoralism. On the other hand, in response to the new foe, it became equally urgent to limit the role of Natural Law, or at least, to decry its supposed sufficiency and self-sufficiency; for freethinkers and deists were now asserting that Natural Law made revealed and institutionalized religions superfluous, and some went so far as to find it independent of divine establishment.

The apologists' defense of Natural Law combines a basic unity with significant divergences of approach and argumentation.[1] We have already noted the existence of such disparities among Christians before the eighteenth century, despite the superficial appearance of a unified traditional Natural Law doctrine. Now they will become more marked, and are characterized by their reflection of and response to certain current notions and problems. Among the most important of these are the pervasive belief in a unique self-interest motivation and the state of nature theories deriving from Hobbes.

One of the main threats to Christian Natural Law was the development of a naturalistic Natural Law which asserted the same moral principles but divorced them from God and a moral universe, predicating them solely on the kind of utilitarianism which was later to be embodied in the theory of natural selection. Another danger came from a small group of thinkers who admitted only a "law of nature" which amounted to a denial of any moral Natural Law. Against both of these groups the apologists had to maintain the existence of a moral order in the world duplicated by a moral realm in man, which, in effect, became the explanation of the genesis of moral judgments and obligations.

The problem in relation to the first group was clearly set forth by the apologist Postel, from the vantage point of the year 1769. "There is almost none of our *philosophes* who does not admit a Natural Law. But several of them make it consist of that innate human tendency to seek in everything our welfare and what is useful to us; others, with a more refined and spiritual feeling, make it consist of that inspiration of reason which prescribes certain principles to every reasonable creature. . . ."[2]

As for the second group, it is most interesting to see Crousaz, in his refutation of Pope (1737) written before radical materialism had received much expression outside of clandestine manuscripts, attacking its basic position as he found it expressed in the writings

---

[1] The exception to the unity was the Jansenists. "They were the only group who consistently refused to see in Natural Law a standard of right and wrong . . ." (Palmer, *Catholics and Unbelievers*, p. 28).

[2] *L'Incrédule conduit à la religion catholique*, Tournay, 1769, pp. 135–38.

of the Leibnizian optimists. Pope had argued that if such natural disasters as earthquakes do not upset the natural order, why should the existence of a Borgia or a Cataline? The implication is that everything is natural and necessary in a necessary world, the best world possible. And Crousaz correctly points out that such words confuse the moral with the physical and make pleasures, virtues, and vices the inevitable results of an eternal chain.[3]

As early as 1692, Abbadie assumed a connection between Natural Law and self-interest. By this time, the self-interest reduction of motivation was already a widespread theory, as a result of the writings of Pascal, La Rochefoucauld, the *libertins,* and certain theologians.[4] The full implications and "dangers" of this position were not yet evident. Abbadie, attempting to establish the origin and validity of obligation, is concerned rather in showing that it does not come from education. He finds two innate forces in man. The first is sensitivity to pleasure and pain which is attached to self-preservation; the second is reason. The error, he argues, is to dissociate the two; whereas the natural use of reason is the proper direction of self-love. From this it is clear that duties and moral laws have a natural derivation as mechanisms of self-preservation, and such virtues as temperance, justice, moderation, beneficence are the result.[5] Abbadie in this fashion resolves the dilemma of nature and reason. Yet he seems acutely aware that the moral problem is not solved thereby; that, as Hobbes and Pascal had made plain, law exists only insofar as it is realized and enforced. For he adds at once that the validity of his concept is conditioned by our immortality. The tendency to lasciviousness, injustice, and greed are *also* so natural that the law deriving from "reasonable nature" is ineffective by itself. "Thus the Natural Law is in man, but the perfection and extent of that law is in man immortal." [6] Abbadie thus reaches an accord with Christian doctrine and simultaneously rejects the *libertin* appeal to the sufficiency of Natural Law.

Two or three later apologists also bowed to the pressure of the current psychology. Nicolas Bergier, one of the most able Catholic writers and one who for a while frequented the d'Holbach clan,

---

[3] *Examen de l'Essay de Monsieur Pope sur l'homme,* Lausanne, 1737, p. 82.
[4] See *An Age of Crisis,* chap. 10, and especially p. 258.
[5] Compare the argument of the materialist, d'Holbach, in chap. 3, *infra.*
[6] *L'Art de se connoître soi-mesme, ou La Recherche des sources de la morale,* La Haye, 1692, pp. 60–64.

inquired into the nature of obligation, which he properly saw as
the nucleus of the moral problem.[7] Man therefore has two orders
of judgment, moral and selfish. Why, he asks, should the moral
win out over the selfish? Why should I sacrifice my happiness?
"The reason will be the foundation of moral obligation." And it is
this: I am happy when I have made the sacrifice. Bergier's answer
is not only a *petitio principii,* but is (as Kant was to show) unmoral. He thinks only in terms of interest. And yet he fails to ask
the main question: suppose that in making the sacrifice my happiness and self-interest come out less well than in *not* making it, then
where is my obligation? But Bergier makes matters even worse by
the assumption which enables him to avoid this question. The
sacrifice is a reasonable pleasure, he avers, not madness, because of
God's future rewards and punishments; and if this is not true,
then "man has no other laws or duties than those of animal packs
in the forest." After this, his statement that Natural Law—pity,
beneficence, justice—is written in our conscience loses the force
of a moral imperative.[8]

In this utilitarian confirmation of Natural Law by means of a
supposed virtue-happiness (and vice-unhappiness) equivalence, we
have one of the key ideas of the century, and we shall later find it
interesting to follow its fortunes among the opponents of Christianity. Other apologists, however, took a different tack and either
denounced the utilitarian trap or shied away from it. The littéra-
teur and apologist, Denesle, for one, tried to separate moral experience and pleasure by considering as quite distinct the pleasure
felt in doing good.[9] This brings us to a moral dilemma which
could not be solved in eighteenth-century terms of the "unique
pleasure motive," which would have required action to be un-
pleasurable in order to be moral. Eighteenth-century thinkers
were unable to distinguish between the pleasure, immediate or
consequent, we take *in* an act, and the pleasure (or satisfaction)
we experience in contemplating ourselves as the subject of that
act (which may itself be unpleasant), according to a projected ego-

[7] *Examen de la religion,* 1771, II, pp. 314–25. On Bergier, see the authoritative
article by Alfred J. Bingham, "The Abbé Bergier: An Eighteenth-Century Catholic
Apologist."
[8] Similar concessions were made by Ph.-Louis Gérard in his *Comte de Valmont*
(I, pp. 454–67), a work that went through fifteen editions.
[9] *Examen du matérialisme,* 1754, I, pp. 81–84.

image.[10] Such an image may be of ourself as a moral being, who selects higher values and performs obligations inherent in the relations of things.[11]

In their defense of Natural Law as the origin of our moral experience, most apologists took care to emphasize the necessity of Revelation as a completion and corrective to the intuitively perceived moral law which characterizes man as a rational animal. Reason, says the abbé Sigorgne (who was also a professor of philosophy and a physicist), adds something to animality, imposes requirements of its own. Man has his own destiny.[12] Yet, he adds, reason is obviously insufficient as a principle of conduct.

The more astute apologists also denied a state of nature. The motive is evident in the refutation of Helvétius' *De l'Homme* by the theologian Pichon.[13] Helvétius had demonstrated that there could have been no virtue before society, since virtue is only respect of mutual obligation. Therefore the larger number of the

---

[10] See Arthur O. Lovejoy, "Terminal and Adjectival Values," *Journal of Philosophy*, 46:593–608, 1950.

[11] This statement is not intended to exclude the possibility of loving the right for its own sake.

Let us note briefly the most widely read of the other writers in this group. The popular abbé Pluche sought to divorce ethics from a social origin, and obligation from interest; he denied the state of nature with its resulting unmoral independence. His traditionalism is contaminated by introduction of the "fear of injustice" motivation and by this interesting idea: "if [man] had a sixth sense, he would experience new duties which would govern the use and condemn the abuse of that sense. It is therefore relatively to his needs that man feels turned toward the immutable principles of a morality which rules his condition." (*Le Spectacle de la nature*, 1746, VI, pp. 6–17; V, pp. 188–90.) The good abbé would have been shocked to know that he was anticipating the evolutionary materialism implicit in Diderot's *Lettre sur les aveugles* (1749).

In the second half of the century, Hayer, in his sprawling twenty-one volume refutation of the *philosophes* devotes many pages to the support of Natural Law. His criticisms of Voltaire and Diderot are of particular interest. (*La Religion vengée*, 1752–60, VIII, p. 3 ff.; X, pp. 168–93.) Hayer's error—a not uncommon one, in the Natural Law group, was to make reason the "essence" of man, instead of a distinguishing characteristic. In his chapter on d'Alembert, Hayer bases Natural Law on well-regulated self-love, the desire to have others do good to us. This again approaches the "naturalistic Natural Law" of certain *philosophes!*

The abbé Guidi naïvely places Natural Law above Revelation (*Entretiens philosophiques sur la religion*, 1772, I, pp. 156–57; his work, incidentally, contains a very good statement of the materialistic philosophy and some of the most interesting arguments against it).

[12] *Le Philosophe chrétien*, Avignon, 1765, pp. 9–10, 37. His view is fundamentally not dissimilar from that of a contemporary biologist, George Gaylord Simpson, *The Meaning of Evolution*, New Haven, 1950.

[13] *Les Arguments de la raison, ou Examen de l'Homme, de M. Helvétius* (Londres, 1776, pp. 81–84).

defenders of Natural Law insisted that men have always been social. Even this hedge was insufficient in the eyes of most apologists,
since it only made Natural Law coextensive with men. Consequently they insisted further on the imposition of Natural Law
by God; and a few, placing the existence of Natural Law above the
danger of its self-sufficiency, even asserted its independence from
God.

Defense of Natural Law continued, then, throughout the century. It acquired renewed force in the writings of Bernardin de
Saint-Pierre, who was concerned about the danger of nihilism.
For this reason he condemns Locke. "He did not suspect that by
denying man innate ideas, he was supplying arguments to anarchism and materialism" by making moral judgments conventional.[14]
But we have been provided with Natural Law which identifies
personal interest and the general interest. These reflections lead
Bernardin to a practical law, analogous to Kant's: "Do you desire
to know whether a maxim is just in relation to others? apply it to
yourself. In relation to yourself? apply it to others, extend it to all
men: if it cannot be applied to all, it can be applied to none." [15]

Bernardin's most significant and best-reasoned piece on ethics is
one that has generally been overlooked. Entitled "De la Nature de
la morale" (1798), it is really a report on a prize contest of the
Institut National in which he was a judge.[16] He is critical of papers
which placed the basis of morals in education, laws, or "our so
fickle heart." [17] He will not allow morals to be derived from self-
love, which is tied to our passions; nor from the social order,
which is often oppressive, unjust, and conducive to unhappiness;
nor from the general interest, which is frequently contrary to
private interest (a notable admission, for the time!); nor from
Adam Smith's sympathy, since it omits duties toward ourselves.
The fact is that we are subject to two kinds of morality, explains
Bernardin. There is a human kind, deriving from passions and
varying with customs; and a divine morality springing from reason,

[14] *Harmonies de la nature,* in *Oeuvres posthumes,* 1833, pp. 259–60.

[15] *Ibid.,* p. 295. The posthumous *Harmonies* were left-overs from the *Etudes de la
nature* (1784), therefore contemporaneous with Kant. Note also the use of the word
"maxim." The treatment in the published *Etudes* is less interesting, declamatory,
poorly reasoned. (*Oeuvres complètes,* 1818, V, p. 4 ff.)

[16] *Oeuvres,* VIII, pp. 423–41.

[17] Compare with his attack on reason in the *Etudes, loc. cit.*

"an intuition of the laws which God has established between men
. . . a conscience given by nature." The first, the morality of
passion, Bernardin declares, embracing in anticipation both Freud
and Adler, has two parts, love and ambition. It separates men;
whereas the morality of reason unites them in harmony and shows
them that the reward of virtues is in heaven. The rational law does
not vary with special interests but is immutable. Thus Bernardin,
like Kant, reacts against the winds of eighteenth-century doctrine
by reaching for a rigoristic moral absolutism.[18]

Samuel Formey, the prolific Protestant apologist who flourished
in the middle of the century at the Academy of Berlin, offers the
rather curious case of a defender of traditional Natural Law who
has fallen under the influence of Christian Wolff's new interpretations. As early as 1745, Formey seems to have been swayed by
Wolff, whose monumental *Ius naturae methodo scientifica per-
tractatum* had appeared in 1741. In a paper read before the
Académie de Berlin ("Sur la Loi naturelle"), Formey asserts that
the denial of God has nothing to do with the validity of moral
law: "the foundation of rectitude is in the nature of man. . . . It
is not enough to deny God, you must also deny and strip humanity." [19]

By making Natural Law purely "natural" and also by his emphasis on rights, Formey takes an important step toward the newer
conceptions of natural right doctrine. He advances still further in
that direction in a later work, *Le Bonheur* (1754), by defining the
propriety of acts as a relation with our happiness, this relation
forming Natural Law or moral law. It is obvious that the accent is
now completely displaced. "Since man can be motivated (*déter-
miné*) only by his appetite for good and his aversion for ill,[20] and
since nonindifferent actions have a fixed and determinate relation
with man's happiness [an assertion not substantiated by Formey],

[18] We must note Marmontel's statement: "Man's duties, if we take away the law
imposed by God, are only conventions, calculations of a free intercourse, in which
each would have the right to protect his own interests and to break agreements
whenever he felt himself hurt." If God were eliminated, then Marmontel would
find himself in accord with the most rebellious of atheists, and he virtually admits
this. (*Leçons d'un père à ses enfants sur la morale*, in *Oeuvres complètes*, 1819,
XVII, pp. 232–34, 276.)

[19] *Histoire de l'Académie de Berlin*, 1745, Berlin, 1746, pp. 102–3. Cf. Diderot, in
"Droit naturel."

[20] Formey uses the words "le bien" and "le mal," terms which have a utilitarian as
well as moral denotation.

it follows that our actions have immutable relations with our happiness. . . . Consequently, natural laws are immutable laws." [21] If all men are moved by the same motives, and if this relationship is fixed, it is obvious that "given the same circumstances, what obliges one obliges all." Formey thus attempts to prove the universality and immutability of Natural Law in a way which, though still a priori in its reasoning, rests on utilitarian and naturalistic premises more than on divine.[22]

Among the deists, too, and among those nominal Christians who cannot be classified as apologists or theologians, we easily observe the persistence of traditional Natural Law throughout the century, though with a definite falling off in the last decades, and with the same traces of infiltration by the new doctrines.

Bayle, as might be expected, both confirms and weakens Natural Law. In chapter CLXXII of the *Pensées diverses sur la comète,* he assures us that "there are ideas of honor in the human species, which are the work of nature, that is, of general Providence." But in the *Continuation des Pensées diverses,* he declares that "nothing is more confused" than Natural Law, for every moral law is contradicted by opposite usages. On a later page, however, he adds, "Even scoundrels have the idea of justice." [23] Bayle's principal statement in support of Natural Law is found in the *Réponse aux questions d'un provincial.* "We must be virtuous" is a proposition, he says, which is "as eternally true, necessary and immutable as this other one, *man is a reasonable animal.*" Natural Law is thus grounded on rationality; but Bayle turns away from the usual concomitant support, its origin in God's will. God cannot change the essence of things—of a sphere, of arithmetic, or of

---

[21] In Formey's Preface to his abridged translation of Wolff, the statement is even more radical. Morality is not a matter of self-sacrifice or altruism. All a man does for his neighbor makes himself better and happier; or else, "we must strike [such acts] out from the category of duties." (*Principes du droit de la nature et des gens,* Amsterdam, 1758.)

[22] In another piece published the same year, Formey lays greater weight on the voice of conscience. "It is, then, a divine voice, it is the eternal voice of truth which is speaking within me." This voice coincides with Natural Law. ("Du vrai bonheur," in *Mélanges philosophiques,* Leyde, 1754, II, p. 74 ff.) The little known Bernard Lambert, whose writings appeared under the name of Frère Thomas Jacob, pointed out the "dangerous" implications of Formey's theorizing. Jacob's work is valuable as a criticism of all the important Natural Law doctrines of the seventeenth and eighteenth centuries. See *Essai sur la jurisprudence universelle,* 1779, pp. 15-91.

[23] *Oeuvres diverses,* La Haye, 1737, III, p. 221. On pp. 405-8 he gives us a closely reasoned argument supporting the traditional Natural Law doctrine which is too long to reproduce here.

virtue. "Virtue was therefore morally good before God knew it to be such, but God has known it to be such because it was such." Otherwise, before God willed virtue and vice in acts, it must be admitted that he saw them indifferently, that he might have willed the vicious to be virtuous, and that he may, some day, change his mind and abrogate existing moral laws. In such a view, $3 + 3 = 6$ only so long as it pleases God and may be false elsewhere in the universe.[24] Bayle thus carries forward Grotius' "paradox," and in this regard, at least, helps prepare the way for new ideas of Natural Law.

Bayle's comparison of Natural Law with mathematical laws overlays his basic skepticism. Unlike physical laws, mathematical laws do not necessarily correspond to reality. Bayle never doubts the truth of moral precepts, any more than he does the properties of an ideal geometrical figure, but their existence is in an ideal world, one without passions. "I mean that, without exception, all moral laws must be submitted to that natural idea of equity which . . . illuminates every man as he comes into the world." [25] But then he goes on to hint that, unfortunately, this "illumination" fades before the brighter light of passions, self-interest, custom, and education. We must always bear in mind both domains, abstract right and the world as it is, for each has its own reality. "Natural Law differs from all other laws in that what it commands is good in itself, and what it forbids is bad in itself, whereas other laws make something illicit by forbidding it, or good by commanding it." [26] Clearly, then, Bayle realistically recognizes the need for both concepts of law, that of essential right, that of pragmatic command.

A group of writers in the middle years of the century support, in one way or another, the traditional approach to Natural Law.[27]

[24] *Ibid.*, III, pp. 987, 675.

[25] *Ibid.*, II, p. 369. See also the strong statement, *ibid.*, III, pp. 964–65, which is almost identical with Voltaire's defense of Natural Law. Also, IV, pp. 258–60.

[26] *Ibid.*, IV, p. 262.

[27] Among lesser writers, we should note Père André's formalist absolutism, which is in many ways close to Shaftesbury. (*Essai sur le beau* [1741], Amsterdam, 1749, pp. 38–74.) Richer d'Aube's stout defense of Natural Law against Carneades, Grotius and Hobbes anticipates Diderot's "Droit naturel." He attributes to the "social body" the right of decision in moral matters; unless, indeed, "stripping himself of the prejudices which self-interest might have given him, he [the individual] puts himself in a position to decide as the social body would, if it were assembled." (*Essai sur les principes du droit et de la morale*, 1743, pp. i–xix.)

Morelly, the deistic totalitarian communist, assumes the Natural Law in his *Code de la nature* (1755), but treats it more fully in his earlier work, *Essai sur le coeur*

Strube de Piermont's *Ebauche des loix naturelles et du droit primitif* accepts pleasure and chagrin as related to the experience of obligation.[28] However, they are not necessarily related to the utility of an act, according to Strube, but rather to its propriety for a man. The interesting fact about Strube is that while, on the one hand, he reaffirms traditional Natural Law, stating, for instance, that the union of men in society supposes a pre-existing order, and that men have a deep desire to be useful to their fellows even at their own cost; on the other hand, he takes a step forward toward a naturalistic view. He does this when he declares that the unity of the *genre humain* is only an intellectual, not a real, notion; [29] the only real union is that which derives from common needs and the need for mutual help, the latter being a variable.[30] From this he concludes that Natural Law must be looked for not in the intellect, but in the passions of love (leading to acts of self-preservation) and hate (prevention of destructive acts). Strube carries this interesting analysis one step further when he notes, "We must however admit that there are some cruel men who, insensitive to the keenest sufferings of their fellows, seem even to take joy in inflicting suffering on them." [31] Thus men are instinctively propelled to proper acts of self-preservation, and, in "perverted" cases, to improper destructive acts. But there can be no natural principle authorizing us to treat others any way we wish, or else "there would be no more injustice or wrong in anything we do, whatever hurts and sorrows we may cause others. The rule, or rather the privilege, which would result from such a principle, would make us the judge of all our acts, and we would no

---

humain (1745). Man "brings at birth if not the first idea of morals, at least the facility of grasping them when they are presented to him"—that is, the relation of acts to the public interest, and of the latter to his own. (Pp. 172, 193–96.) The law of equity has its root in the equality involved in the relation of reciprocity. A formalist and a rigorist, Morelly insists that an act, to be virtuous, must be performed with no thought of reward, and only for the sake of virtue. Ten years later, Morelly's ideas have evolved. Natural Law is now a principle of self-interest, instilled in us by God. The moral truths it leads to have a rigorous mathematical certainty. (*Code de la nature*, ed. Chinard, pp. 157, 244.)

Toussaint offers a classic model of Natural Law doctrine. Unlike Voltaire, he denies that virtue is conformity with positive laws. "Sovereigns can proclaim and abrogate laws; but they cannot create, or annihilate virtues." *Les Moeurs* (1748), Amsterdam, 1777, pp. xxv–xxvi.

[28] "Nouvelle edition" (?), Amsterdam, 1744, p. 59.

[29] Compare a similar denial by Rousseau, in the second chapter of the first version of the *Contrat social*.

[30] P. 29.

[31] P. 35–48.

longer be accountable to anyone."[32] Strube, in this remarkably clairvoyant statement, poses the problem of nihilism, especially in its sadistic form.

Burlamaqui, writing in 1747, exercised considerable influence through his *Principes du droit naturel.* A comparison with Montesquieu's *De l'Esprit des lois* would illuminate some of the dichotomies and disparities of that complex of ideas which is embraced under the phrase, "Eighteenth-century political thought." In regard to Natural Law, Burlamaqui holds it to consist of rules which are imposed by God through human reason.[33] But *droit* is an idea relative to human nature and must be deduced from it. From reason and its judgments, inasmuch as they indicate the way to perfection and happiness, arises obligation, "for to approve is to recognize that one should do something; and to condemn is to recognize that one should not do it."[34] Obligation may be defined, then, as "a restriction on natural freedom, produced by reason. . . ."

Right is defined as "the power which man has to use his freedom and natural forces in a certain way . . . insofar as this exercise of his powers is approved by reason."[35] Reason, then, is one link to the normative character of *droit.* It distinguishes our "right" from our power; and Hobbes's definition, or Spinoza's, is avoided by the inference of the moral character of this reason. And so, "anything which man can reasonably do becomes for him a right." A second link to *norma agendi* is the essential indivisibility of right and obligation. If reason approves an act, that is, grants it to be a right, it simultaneously imposes the idea of obligation on others. Obligation, now, is derived only indirectly or ultimately from reason, but immediately from rights. We have an obligation *because* men have rights. Burlamaqui does not say, like the traditional theorists, that because men are obliged to certain duties, rights (usually in some vague and uncertain way) are involved in these moral commands.

As soon as we go outside man's essential nature and consider his various states and relations of dependency, we see him subject to the will of a superior. "This is the right we call law." Law must be in accord with reason, however, to be obligatory,

---

[32] P. 50.
[33] *Principes du droit naturel,* Amsterdam, 1748, II, p. 2.
[34] *Ibid.,* I, p. 92.
[35] *Ibid.,* I, p. 101.

that is, in accord "with the nature and constitution of man, and [must] be ultimately related to his happiness, which reason requires him to pursue." [36] Law, when it conforms to the conditions of legitimacy, is the highest source of obligation.[37] The morality of an act is its conformity to the law which should rule it. Nevertheless the sole supposition that a creature is reasonable, and that it is reasonable to do or not to do certain things, constitutes obligation and suffices to establish a system of moral duties. A father must care for his children, since their welfare depends on it; the approval of his reason makes the act morally good. Therefore, the common arguments that the person who obliges and who is obliged cannot be one and the same, and that a superior is necessary so that one may not release himself from obligation, are untenable.

In this way Burlamaqui unfolds a theory of obligation and of Natural Law which is in many respects classical, but which also contains some new ideas. The emphasis on rights and the right to happiness and on the self-sufficiency of reason are among these. He also brings to the fore the vexed question of the relation of "right" to "good" or "useful." Although he is obviously not a utilitarian, there is no doubt in his mind that the word "right" is indissolubly related to a functional end, human happiness and welfare. It consists, however, of general and immutable rules. The coincidence of the right and the good is the working of Providence.

Montesquieu is closer than Burlamaqui, in some regards, to the classical doctrine of Natural Law, and yet, in a more important sense, he is further away from it.[38]

In the *Lettres persanes* (1721), he asserts his belief in the universality of physical laws and in the existence of natural economic laws.[39] There are also moral natural laws, whose principle is summarized in his defense of justice. "Justice is a relationship of propriety, which really exists between two things; this relation is always the same, regardless of the being who contemplates it,

[36] *Ibid.*, I, pp. 115–16.

[37] *Ibid.*, I, p. 141.

[38] The *Essai touchant les lois naturelles* (*Oeuvres*, III, pp. 175–99) is probably not by Montesquieu. See R. Shackleton, *Montesquieu*, p. 249n. This essay, perhaps by a disciple, emphasizes the involvement of self-interest in moral judgments, alongside the objective distinction between right and wrong. It also separates virtue (right action) from obligation, which derives from laws (of God or men) that effectively oblige.

[39] Lettre XCVII, and note 2 in Antoine Adam's edition.

be it God, angel, or man." [40] Justice is eternal and independent of human conventions—if it were dependent on them, "this would be a terrible truth, which we should hide from ourselves." Our experience of justice involves an inner feeling, but also requires rational intuition. It is inhibited by self-interest and the passions. It does not depend on this other important truth: "justice to others is charity to ourselves." [41] Thus moral value, while not separated from self-interest, is made independent of it, prior and superior to it.

As Montesquieu's thought matures and evolves, his interest in Natural Law recedes.[42] In the *Esprit des lois* (1748), he is preoccupied almost exclusively by the dynamic power forces of statecraft, and by the nonmoral physical and historical factors. The art of government is seen as a pragmatic art. Basically, Montesquieu believes as firmly as ever in Natural Law, and his conception of it is close to that of Aquinas—or to that of Burke; in other words, it is the traditional view. It is still a matter of basic laws to be discovered in objective relationships stemming from human nature and needs, and linked with a rational universe ordained by God.[43] The moral and political spheres, as well as the physical, are considered subject to natural laws, and there too the order of nature is constant. The moral laws are normative; the physical and political laws, though descriptive, may become normative, judging from Montesquieu's subsequent treatment of them. These relations, abstractly considered, are absolute, prior to intelligent beings and their positive laws.[44] Such laws may therefore be unjust.

Here Montesquieu's analysis and his interest in the subject come to an end. He seems almost to wish to point out the place of this inherited, rationalistic basis of politics and to be rid of it.[45] He draws no precise political precepts nor does he attempt to

[40] Lettre LXXXIII. Also in 1721, in the *Traité des Devoirs* (Pensée 1226).

[41] Lettre XII.

[42] As Shackleton remarks, "he is not interested in speculation on the presocial condition of mankind or the mode of its emergence from that condition into the State" (*op. cit.*, p. 249). This, however, is in accord with the traditional doctrine.

[43] Livre Premier, chaps. 1, 2.

[44] "To say that there is nothing just or unjust except what positive laws command or forbid is to say that before a circle had been drawn, all the radii were not equal." (*De l'Esprit des Loix*, ed. Jean Brethe de La Gressaye, 1950, I, chap. 1.) The formulation is, of course, old. Cf. Samuel Clarke, *A Demonstration of the Being and Attributes of God*, Part II.

[45] L. Stapleton points out that the comparative and historical method tended to discard the idea of universal law applicable to "men of different habits and customs, living in different stages of development." (*Justice and World Society*, p. 82.)

apply Natural Law to any of the real problems of government. He is aware that the concrete, effective forms of law vary, and these conditions are the ones that seem to him really significant.[46] The basis of any morality, for Montesquieu, is a metaphysical assumption about the world and man which overrides individual and cultural differences; but his practical morality is founded on human psychology. Inasmuch as this is so, the natural laws relating to human behavior and needs are always present in his mind. But the positive form which they take and the concrete conditions in which they are given form and in which they operate are his immediate concern. Natural Law thus recedes to a background, even to a nominal position as Montesquieu advances toward the positivist, utilitarian view which, paradoxically, was to arouse the hostility of other utilitarian political theorists who followed him.

G. H. Sabine, consequently, errs in claiming that Montesquieu "had never considered Natural Law with any care." [47] On the other hand, he is correct in stating that this was "a conventional way of getting started," and that "what interested him was the idea that this fundamental natural law in society, which he identified in the usual way with reason, must operate in different environments and so must produce different institutions in different places."

Sabine also accuses Montesquieu of including in his concept of Natural Law "disparate features," moral, social, physiological. Sabine is here involved in a serious confusion which occurs again in Sergio Cotta's treatment—a confusion of the laws in the second chapter of the first book with those of the first chapter.[48] As a result of this confusion, Cotta himself accuses of confusion critics who have found a Natural Law concept in these opening pages. In the first chapter Montesquieu does sketch a theory of Natural Law, including its metaphysic, its juridical logic, and its specific content (in the ninth paragraph). None of the latter is physiological; it is explicitly referred to as "the intelligent world," in open contrast with the physical world. It is clearly a matter of equity; of the "ought," not of descriptive law.[49] In this chapter

[46] "The effort of reason should therefore bear less on abstract, general, uniform, immutable law, flowing directly from human nature, than on positive law which a given society has made for itself under the influence of certain factors." (I, chap. 18.)

[47] *Op. cit.,* p. 554.

[48] *Montesquieu e la scienza della società,* p. 356 ff.

[49] "We must therefore admit relationships of equity prior to the positive law which establishes them: such as, for example, supposing there were a society of men, it would be *just* to obey their laws; if they were intelligent beings who had

Montesquieu uses the phrase, *"loi naturelle."* The second chapter, however, headed by a significantly different phrase, *"Des Loix de la nature,"* no longer treats this subject, as Sabine and Cotta have erroneously assumed. It refers rather to the laws which "derive solely from the constitution of our being," or as he has put it in the preceding paragraph, from man "as a physical being." [50] The laws in the first chapter, however, constituting Natural Law, are outside of these factors—in their origin and import. They are rational, not empirical-naturalistic. It is for this reason that Montesquieu is obliged in the second chapter to postulate a hypothetical state of nature in which he does not believe, in order, like Rousseau later, to conceive for a moment of a presocial, premoral, physical man-animal. Cotta's amazing "discovery" that Montesquieu's natural laws, as sketched in chapter II, are physiological and not moral rests, then, on two misconceptions: first, that there can be no Natural Law theory without a belief in a state of nature; second, that Montesquieu is writing about the same kind of law in chapters I and II, when, in fact, he is opposing to positive laws (which he goes on to treat in the third chapter) *two kinds* of prior law, moral Natural Law (chapter I) and the laws of (physical) nature (chapter II). It is much more accurate to say, with Brunschvicg, that the conflict in Montesquieu is between a Natural Law deriving from man's reason and moral nature (a law superior to positive laws) and his continuing demonstration that laws are only the result of conditions of fact. It is therefore important to recall once again the distinction between the doctrine or theory of Natural Law and the fact that there are "laws of nature." In the latter sense, Montesquieu's whole object is to discover natural laws which are pure descriptions of what is indispensable as a result of the nature of the State in question; such laws are normative only in the quite different sense that they are necessary if the State is to survive.

---

received some benefit from another being, they *ought* to have gratitude for it; if an intelligent being had created another intelligent being, the created being *ought* to remain in the dependency which he had from his origin; an intelligent being, who has done harm to an intelligent being, *deserves* to receive the same hurt, and so on with the others." (Italics added.)

[50] Shackleton's list of Montesquieu's natural laws (*op. cit.,* p. 250) refers to these laws, and to their development in Book XXVI. So do his astute comments on the character of these laws as descriptive rather than normative, characterizing in simple principles "the activities of man in relation to nature." Montesquieu then proceeds to "treat them as normative principles."

The second of the century's great figures in whose thought Natural Law theory is interwoven was Voltaire. His writings are especially fascinating in regard to this subject, for they are the clearest testimonial to the difficulties traditional Natural Law was experiencing in the intellectual medium of the Enlightenment. Voltaire desired most earnestly, even desperately, to maintain the truth of Natural Law and also the existence of God and freedom of the will, in order to provide a secure foundation for ethics. A reading of *Candide* or several of his other tales or poems reveals how well he appreciated the menace of moral nihilism. His intellectual life was a struggle within himself. He had to give up freedom; he clung to God as a drowning man to a timber; and he defiantly asserted Natural Law, time and again, with a varying admixture of alien emphases.

The difficulty was that such a doctrine involved him in conflict with other aspects of his ideology. As a "purist" believer in sensationism, he assumes the *tabula rasa,* which was precisely (and more logically) the fount of antithetical theories, such as Helvétius', that men are susceptible to conditioning without any limitation from Natural Law. Voltaire was quite aware of the difficulty. In the second part of the *Poème sur la loi naturelle* (1756), he attempts to refute four objections to a universal morality. Two of the four are variations of the problem inevitably raised by sensationism: that remorse and conscience may be only a habit.[51] That Voltaire's own philosophy might well have been pointed in the same direction is evidenced by his later article, "Imagination," in which he maintains that all our abstract ideas are based on concrete representations and concrete experiential images.[52] In the *Poème,* he poses the problem frankly.

> On insiste, on me dit: "L'enfant dans son berceau
> N'est point illuminé par ce divin flambeau;
> C'est l'éducation qui forme ses pensées;
> Par l'exemple d'autrui ses moeurs lui sont tracées;
> Il n'a rien dans l'esprit, il n'a rien dans le coeur;
> De ce qui l'environne il n'est qu'imitateur.[53]

[51] The other two are the variability of laws and customs, and the prevalence of crimes.

[52] *Oeuvres,* ed. Moland, Vol. 19, p. 428 (published in 1765, written perhaps in 1757).

[53] Compare the verses in *Zaïre* (1732, I, p. i):

> Je le vois trop: les soucis qu'on prend de notre enfance,
> Forment nos sentiments, nos moeurs, notre croyance. . . .
> L'instruction fait tout, et la main de nos pères
> Grave en nos faibles coeurs ces premiers caractères. . . .

In his reply, Voltaire does not belittle the power of environment, but insists on the real existence of an unchangeable basis for the reception or interpretation of experience.

> Mais les premiers ressorts sont faits d'une autre main;
> Leur pouvoir est constant, leur principe est divin.

These "springs" are the instincts, which in man include a "moral instinct," or the necessity of reacting morally to experience, that is, of making moral judgments. Such judgments are, although a result of experience, generated necessarily.

> Il faut que l'enfant croisse, afin qu'il les exerce;
> Il ne les connaît pas sous la main qui le berce.

Comparisons with animals follow to sustain the argument. "Tout mûrit par le temps, et s'accroît par l'usage." Voltaire thus rejects what he conceived to be Descartes' innate ideas, already present at birth; [54] but since certain universal ideas are necessarily generated, although as a product of experience, the terminal result is substantially the same with a difference only in the process. As he puts it in the *Eléments de Newton* (1738), all ideas come from the senses, but identity of senses produces the same needs and feelings which give rise to roughly the same notions.[55] To express the matter differently, it is obvious that an action cannot appear just or unjust, cannot evoke a moral reaction, unless we are equipped to bring such a category of judgment to bear on the data of experience. Consequently, moral experience may be spoken of as natural, as well as derived from culture; it is not secondary, but imposed on culture by the same human nature which makes culture.

A second difficulty for Voltaire was the unity of human nature. Both in the *Traité de métaphysique* (1734) and in the *Essai sur les moeurs* (1753–56), he emphatically denies the unity and common descent of mankind, qualifying the differences between whites, Negroes, and Indians or other races as greater than, or as great as, that which separates families or species of animals. "Moreover," remarks one commentator, "he not only assigns to what he

---

[54] This is a misinterpretation of Descartes, who held innate ideas to arise, not at birth, but with the developing mind; they are self-generating, however, and not contingent on experience.

[55] *Oeuvres*, Vol. 22, p. 419. He is astonished that "the wise Locke" concluded that because there are no innate ideas, there are no universal notions of good and evil. He correctly and astutely remarks that savages may eat their parents as a way (which he calls "perverted") of demonstrating their love, that is, to deliver them from old age or enemies. (He might have added, to give them immortality.)

calls the various human species 'a character different from ours,' but he also attributes to them different outlooks. For instance, he explicitly says about the natives of India that 'since their physical nature differs from ours, their morality must also necessarily be different from ours.' " [56] This statement, however, gives a rather inaccurate account of Voltaire's thinking. The morality which is "different" is customary, or related to what we should now call instrumental values. Apparently Voltaire does not think physical differences so great as to exclude unity of terminal values. For he also writes, concerning the Indians: "All these people resemble us only by their passions, and by the universal reason which counterbalances the passions, and which imprints this law in all hearts: 'Do not do unto others what you would not want them to do unto you.' Those are the two characteristics which nature impresses in the many different races of man, and the two eternal links by which she unites them, despite all which divides them." [57] We must remember that Voltaire's opposition to the unity of the races was largely motivated by his polemical attitude toward Christianity, here involving the myth of the Creation in Genesis, and perhaps also, to a lesser degree, by his opposition to the newly-rising theories of evolution.

Be that as it may, the essential fact is that Voltaire does unflaggingly maintain the immutability and universality of the basic moral judgments and terminal values which constitute Natural Law —the supremacy of the group interest, the parent-child relation, the "silver rule," the right to the fruit of one's labor, the sanctity of the pledged word, the prohibition of unjustified murder, the return of good, not evil, to one who has done us good. In the *Epître à Uranie* (1722), the *Remarques sur les Pensées de Pascal* (1734), the *Traité de métaphysique* (1734), the *Poème sur la Loi naturelle* (1756), these ideas are well known. We must emphasize that they are proclaimed in many other writings and at all periods of Voltaire's life. In the *Eléments de Newton* (1738), he writes, "I understand by natural religion the principles of morality which are common to the human kind . . . for, all having the same reason, the fruits of that tree must sooner or later resemble others." [58] In *Le Philosophe ignorant* (1766), he still marvels that

[56] Jerome Rosenthal, "Voltaire's Philosophy of History," *Journal of the History of Ideas*, XVI, 153, 1955.
[57] *Essai sur les moeurs et l'esprit des nations*, Oeuvres, XII, p. 370.
[58] *Oeuvres*, Vol. 22, p. 419.

despite all the differences between men, they all have the same fundamental ethics (*"le même fond de morale"*), a rough notion of justice; and all, he says, have acquired it "at the age when reason unfolds, as they acquire naturally the art of lifting loads with sticks. . . . It seemed to me then that this idea of just and unjust was necessary in them. . . ." If the Egyptian and Scythian have the same basic ideas about justice, it is because God has given to both "that reason which, as it develops, makes them perceive the same necessary principles, just as he has given them organs which, when they have reached the degree of their energy, perpetuate necessarily and in the same way the races of the Scythian and the Egyptian." [59]

Voltaire's opinion has not changed in forty years. To be sure, some of his statements now betray the influence of materialism: body and mind both undergo analogous and necessary development, and there is an ultimate identity. The moral law is comparable to the law of gravitation. This materialism does not diminish one whit his belief in a good God as the creator of matter, of its laws of development, and particularly of Natural Law—although there is another area of shadow in this notion, too, of God's goodness. [60] The coexistence of materialism and belief in God is perhaps Voltaire's deepest dilemma, and we have already referred to this uneasy partnership. [61] But as he needed Natural Law to establish the primacy and objectivity of moral experience, so he needed God to establish the certainty of Natural Law. Its precepts are always, for Voltaire, from beginning to end, "engraved in our hearts by God," who "speaks to us" in this way. [62] In the *Philosophe ignorant,* it is "the supreme intelligence which . . . has therefore willed that there be justice on earth, so that we could live there a certain time." He mocks Pufendorf's idea that men

---

[59] *Oeuvres*, Vol. 26, pp. 77–79. Cf. *L'Orphelin de la Chine, Oeuvres*, Vol. 5, p. 318. Compare the verses that end the first part of the *Poème sur la loi naturelle:*

> Le Ciel fit la vertu; l'homme en fit l'apparence.
> Il peut la revêtir d'imposture et d'erreur;
> Il ne peut la changer: son Juge est dans son coeur.

[60] See the discussion of Voltaire and the problem of evil, in *An Age of Crisis,* pp. 63–67.

[61] *Ibid.,* p. 65. In *Le Philosophe ignorant,* he declares that even if there is only matter, "whoever thinks must be just, because the atom to whom God gave thought can have merit or demerit, be punished or rewarded. . . ." (Vol. 26, p. 77.)

[62] The same phrase is used in the *Epître à Uranie* (1722, Vol. 9, p. 361) and in *La Henriade* (1723, Vol. 8, p. 172).

can create moral values ("moral entities"), or "certain modes which intelligent beings attach to natural things or physical movements, in order to direct or restrict the freedom of man's voluntary acts, so as to put some order, propriety and beauty into human life." [63] All of Voltaire's ideas are renewed in the article "Loi naturelle," in the *Questions sur l'Encyclopédie* (1771). Differences in moral ideas? "Laws of convention, arbitrary usages, fashions which pass: the essential remains forever." [64] Man, it is unhappily certain—for Voltaire has not forgotten the lessons of life and of history which he expounded in *Candide* and the *Essai sur les moeurs*—can be diabolical. But he can also be noble. "Well," asks Voltaire, "do storms prevent us from enjoying a fine sun?" It is natural to be one-eyed, lame, misshapen—or vicious; but we prefer well-shaped people. Yet there is a logical defeat in this conclusion. Is it not to admit what the materialists had been saying, that if a supposed Natural Law is natural, so is its opposite? [65]

Voltaire, we have noted, was aware of the arguments for an amoral universe and an immoral mankind, aware, that is to say, of what seemed to him the menace of moral nihilism. Another indication of this unavowed apprehension is clear, if disguised, in the verses near the close of the first part of the *Poème sur la loi naturelle*.

> Jamais un parricide, un calomniateur,
> N'a dit tranquillement dans le fond de son coeur:
> "Qu'il est beau, qu'il est doux d'accabler l'innocence,
> De déchirer le sein qui nous donna naissance!
> Dieu juste, Dieu parfait! que le crime a d'appas!" [66]

These lines seem to be almost a protest aimed at the writings of a Duclos or a La Mettrie. But his reassurance that no one would give either theoretical or personal approval to such deeds is contingent on the existence of Natural Law. Without this law, men might indeed say and do such horrible things.

> Voilà ce qu'on dirait, mortels, n'en doutez pas,
> S'il n'était une Loi terrible, universelle,
> Que respecte le crime en s'élevant contre elle.

[63] "Droit" (1771), *Oeuvres*, Vol. 18, p. 426.

[64] *Oeuvres*, Vol. 19, pp. 604-6. See also article, "Lois," Vol. 19, pp. 623-24, and *L'A, B, C*, Vol. 27, pp. 338, 351.

[65] This was pointed out in refutations of the *Poème sur la loi naturelle*. See Crowley's edition, pp. 225-26.

[66] Verses 69-74.

Voltaire's struggles and dilemmas are again visible in his dialogues, *L'A, B, C* (1768). At this time, utilitarianism and naturalism
are strong in his outlook, but he still feels the need of saving Natural Law. In a long note to the first dialogue he refutes Horace's
line, *"Nec natura potest iusto secernere iniquum"* ("Nature cannot
discern the just from the unjust"), by citing another verse of
Horace: *"Iura inventa metu iniusti fateare necesse est"* ("It must
be admitted that laws were invented because of fear of injustice").
Justice, then, was conceived of before convention and is natural.
Actually, there is no contradiction in Horace, as Voltaire asserts.
It only seems one to him, because he confuses (as was typical both
of eighteenth-century naturalism and of Natural Law thinking)
cosmic nature with human nature. This confusion accounts for
the ensuing statement: "If nature made no distinction between
right and wrong (*"le juste et l'injuste"*), there would be no moral
distinction in our actions; the Stoics would apparently be right
in contending that all crimes against society are alike." [67] While
the nihilist made the error of considering cosmic nature as all
nature, and thus, accepting the truth of the condition in Voltaire's
first phrase, asserted the truth of the conclusion; Voltaire apparently makes the contrary error of extending what is true of human
nature to cosmic nature.[68] In reality, however, all he intends to
assert is that such distinctions are necessary and natural to any
reasonable being. In the third dialogue, however, Voltaire himself
takes the contrary position. He now asserts—in contrast to the
traditional Natural Law doctrine which he usually upholds—the
radical opposition between nature and art. Hobbes was right:
"everything is convention or force." [69] Is there, then, no Natural
Law? "There is one to be sure, self-interest and reason." This
definition puts Voltaire in the naturalistic camp, but he avoids
Hobbesian radicalism by denying evil in man and by the implicit
emphasis on reason. He does not, however, solve the contradiction

---

[67] *L'A, B, C*, in *Dialogues philosophiques*, ed. R. Naves, p. 254-55n.

[68] The source of the confusion is rather obvious. The nihilist observes the non-
teleological character of natural events (of the motion of planets, for instance); recognizing that human nature is also natural, he concludes that human nature refuses
a teleological analysis, which is a non-sequitur. Voltaire, observing the necessity of
a teleological analysis of human behavior, remarks that man is natural and that the
rest of the universe is, too. He concludes that moral purposes must have a basis
which extends beyond the sphere of human experience—which is also a non-
sequitur.

[69] P. 272.

between a natural moral law which is prior to convention and a moral law which arises (however "naturally") from convention. Furthermore, his own utilitarian definition of virtue as obedience to law makes all crimes offenses against society or convention, and only indirectly, if at all, against nature.

Natural Law is, then, for Voltaire, the source and the guarantor of our ethical life, a criterion of judgment for other moral and legal notions, and also a substitute for religious ethics. It is the universal essence of justice from which we derive our ideas concerning justice. Voltaire's strategy, in the hope of erecting an unassailable foundation for moral values, is to unify reason and nature, and at the same time, the natural and the transcendental, in the truth of the traditional doctrine of Natural Law. For Voltaire's Natural Law theory, as he expresses it, is the traditional doctrine, relatively free of contagion. The moral law is posited directly on right and only indirectly on the right to happiness; there is no stress at all on a natural rights theory; and there is no claim for rigid specificity in all situations or for mathematical certitude.[70] And yet, the greatest problem for our understanding of this aspect of Voltaire's thought is his growing emphasis on utility. No act, for Voltaire, has an intrinsic or formal value, its effect on men alone confers value on it.[71] It cannot be judged outside of its results in a specific situation. The theory of Natural Law, as I have made clear, and indeed any theory of moral right or justice, is ultimately related to the welfare of human beings— even a theory which justifies evil on earth as a test of merit for future reward. Utilitarianism, however, makes a specific good the immediate and pragmatic test of right—which is a quite different matter. Elements of utilitarianism are visible in Voltaire's thinking relatively early, as when in 1738, he cites as a proof of Natural Law the fact that in any society "one gives the name of virtue to what is believed useful to society." [72] And it can be said, in a more general way, that Voltaire's espousal of Natural Law is to some degree at variance with his constant belief in limited pragmatic solutions, with his refusal to pretend that we can attain to abstract truths, to metaphysical or cosmic certainties.

[70] In the article "Souverain Bien," of the *Dictionnaire philosophique*, Voltaire rejected the current belief that virtue was in itself a source of happiness.

[71] He explicitly states this in the *Traité de métaphysique*, ed. H. Temple Patterson, Manchester, 1937, p. 60.

[72] *Eléments de Newton*, Vol. 22, p. 421.

However, while utilitarianism will assume a dominant position in Voltaire's outlook, I do not think it correct to say that Natural Law gives way before it or is supplanted by it. On the contrary, he never ceases to reassert his belief in Natural Law, even as late as 1775 in the *Histoire de Jenni*. Nor, it must be further stressed, is it a case of Natural Law terminology masking a new meaning given to old words. The fact is rather that the two theories accompany each other without overtly coalescing. Is this a contradiction of which Voltaire is unaware? It is rather, I believe, that Voltaire, rightly or wrongly, conceives of them as complementary and not contradictory. It is partly that for him the universality and immutability of basic moral judgments are the evidence of their usefulness. But even more, the very indefiniteness of traditional Natural Law precepts allows him to conceive of modifications relative to the needs of a specific circumstance. The laws which God has put into our hearts are only tendencies and forms, with variable content. "Do unto others" is an immutable law, but its implications may differ somewhat. Laws change; but virtue, everywhere, is obedience to law. General tendencies, equated with what is universally useful to human society, may preserve the consonance of formal and utilitarian value. Value judgments, for Voltaire, cannot escape an objective human reality which is largely immutable. This reality may be conceived of as "laws" (ethical judgments), now concrete, now only tendentious. In obeying them we carry out God's wisdom which makes our notion of right coincide with our good. This ground of reality may also be viewed as the welfare of society, which has some basic, immutable elements, and others that are variable. We are bound in all that regards the former. Seeking what is useful, we will encounter invariant Natural Law. If we look into our hearts, we will find that the same law, though we may not realize it, represents what is most useful.[73] If Voltaire goes beyond Natural Law, it is because he is not satisfied that it is a sufficient or effective solution to the moral problem. How he goes beyond it we shall see later.

Returning now for a rapid glance at other writers of the second half of the century, we shall once more note the persistence of Natural Law theory.

In the *Encyclopédie*, according to René Hubert, the main ques-

---

[73] The latter sentences are taken from my article, "Voltaire's Struggle for Humanism" in *Studies on Voltaire in the Eighteenth Century*, Geneva, 1957, IV, p. 157.

tion is whether there is a natural morality "prior to the social institution and to laws, or whether all moral notions, virtues and vices, appear only with the State." [74] Jaucourt ("Loi naturelle," "Devoir") contends that the prescriptions of Natural Law "derive solely from the constitution of our being before the establishment of societies"; they are religion, self-love, sociability, and beneficence. He, too, quotes Cicero's definition. Boucher d'Argis offers no significant variation in the article, "Droit naturel." He defines the prescriptions as the duty to hurt no one and to give to each what belongs to him. While Jaucourt is closer to Grotius, Boucher holds to the orthodox theories without deviation.

The abbé Yvon's articles are in some respects similar to Voltaire's thinking. In "Bon," he contends that our organs are "in proportion to the rank which we occupy in the universe." This is more than a figurative expression. It assumes the hierarchy of a scale of beings, a finalism and Providentialism that sees to it that a man gets what he needs in order to be a man, and a dog what he needs to be a dog. "We are obliged to recognize the goodness and wisdom of Providence equally in what it gives and what it refuses." It follows that God has provided us with moral rules and an awareness of them, making social life possible.

Yvon's article, "Athée," is largely a refutation of Bayle in which he actually weakens the structure of Natural Law by diminishing the role of right reason and objective relations, and by making God not merely its origin and support, but the effective agent in each moral act. He is forced to admit that his system is formally similar to Hobbes's.[75]

---

[74] *Les Sciences sociales dans l'Encyclopédie*, 1923, p. 270.

[75] Rousseau's fellow Genevan, E. Beaumont, attributes obligation to relationships and reason; the will must prefer the good, that is, "anything which can contribute to the self-preservation, protection and pleasure of man." The dangerous implications are avoided by the arbitrary assertion of "true" and "false" values—a notion Sade will shake. Interestingly, Beaumont, a year before Rousseau's *Discours sur l'inégalité*, contrasts natural with instituted relations; the latter are derived from new needs developed by society, which produces new passions—some to be satisfied, some to be repressed. (*Principes de philosophie morale*, Genève, 1754, pp. 17, 26.)

Condillac's theory reminds us of Voltaire's in its combination of experience, utility, and divinity. Mutual needs give rise to moral conventions, but as a result of God's planning. "There is therefore a Natural Law, that is, a law founded on God's will and which we discover by the sole use of our faculties." (*Traité des animaux* [1755], *Oeuvres*, 1798, III, p. 587.)

In the same year Sulzer read a paper on Natural Law at the Academy of Berlin (reprinted by Robinet in his *Dictionnaire universel*). It is a strange paper, in which he affirms that Natural Law differs from morality in that its prescriptions, being more specific, are obligatory. It tells us, for instance, to return what we have bor-

The year 1758 brings us to the publication of another landmark in Natural Law theory, the *Droit des gens* of the Swiss jurist, de Vattel. The emphasis on happiness as the function or goal of Natural Law instead of on moral duty (although happiness was never totally separated from the latter concept), an emphasis which we have noted from time to time in this chapter, is expressed even more strongly by de Vattel. The laws which man, as man, must naturally obey arise from the basic axiom, as he terms it, that "the chief end of any being endowed with intelligence and feeling is happiness." Even more, obligation itself depends on this axiom. "It is solely by the desire for this happiness that a thinking being can be bound, that we can form the knots of obligation which are to submit him to some rule." Natural Law is nought but "the rules which man must follow to reach his goal, to obtain the most perfect happiness of which he is capable." The rules are fixed and obligatory and derive from his nature, regardless of God's existence. Of course God does exist and has willed these rules for our happiness. God and nature coincide in us. Together they oblige us, that is, oblige us to be happy.[76] Inasmuch as de Vattel draws a continual analogy between Natural Law and international law (*droit des gens*), the following declaration is particularly significant for the rise of the "modern" or "revolutionary" doctrine of Natural Law.

But duties towards oneself being incontestably prior to duties to others, a Nation's first and overriding duty is to do all it can for its own happiness and development [*perfection*]. . . . So that when it cannot contribute to another's welfare without essentially hurting itself, its obligation in that particular occasion ceases. . . . Nations being free and independent of each other, since men are naturally free and independent, the second general law of their society is that each nation should be allowed the peaceful enjoyment of that freedom which it has from nature. The natural society of nations cannot subsist, if the rights which each has from nature are not respected. From

---

rowed, whereas the moral rule, "Give to each what is due him," fails to tell us what is due. Sulzer's conclusion is one which announces an autocratic society. The legislator must demand all the duties he can; "he must leave to the citizens' pleasure only what, by its very nature, cannot be required by force. For the more that is left to the will of the members of society, the more one risks seeing duties badly fulfilled, and the more widely one misses the ultimate goal of civil society" [happiness]. It is interesting to compare this formula with Rousseau's in the *Contrat social.* (*Histoire de l'Académie de Berlin*, XII, pp. 450–58, 1756.)

[76] *Droit des gens*, 1835 edition, I, pp. 87–89.

this freedom and independence, it follows that it is for each nation to judge what its conscience requires of it . . . what is proper or improper for it to do. . . . The right of constraint against a free person belongs to us only when he is obligated towards us in a specific thing, which does not depend on his judgment. . . .[77]

Now de Vattel would undoubtedly have admitted that the social contract creates what he terms "external obligation" (i.e., not dependent on conscience) toward others, and he might have been willing to admit—had he been pushed to it by the abbé de Saint-Pierre—that a "social contract" between nations would be desirable; but the development of his theory obviously represents a marked shift in emphasis, by justifying morality only in terms of happiness. There is an equally important (and logically connected) departure in his stress on natural rights. Men "are naturally equal, and their rights and obligations are the same, as coming equally from nature. . . ."[78] And again, he states that a nation has a right to whatever it needs for its self-preservation. "For Natural Law gives us a right to all things without which we cannot satisfy our obligation [and we recall how he has defined that word]; else it would obligate us to do the impossible, or rather would contradict itself. . . ."[79] De Vattel would probably not have denied that positive law and custom produce distinctions—even as Burke was to insist—but it is difficult to guess how he would have resolved the problem of the correspondence of Natural Law, as he conceived of it, to positive law.

Mably, as might be expected, is interested in the political applications of Natural Law as well as in moral theory. In the *Entretiens de Phocion* (1763), he praises Lycurgus for ending unrestricted exploitation and oppression—an accepted but false idea of happiness. Instead, he consulted nature, "descended into the depths of the human heart, and penetrated the secrets of Providence." In those dark chambers Lycurgus found the need to repress passions and to be guided by reason.[80] In his *Doutes sur l'ordre naturel des sociétés politiques* (1768), a work written in refutation of the Physiocrat Le Mercier de la Rivière, Mably agrees with

---

[77] *Ibid.*, pp. 93–94.

[78] *Ibid.*, p. 95.

[79] *Ibid.*, p. 109. The argument, of course, was by now old. He does make the reservation that the means must not themselves gainsay Natural Law, which is to argue in a circle.

[80] *Oeuvres*, Londres, 1789, X, pp. 42–43.

the latter that Natural Law is the basis and criterion of positive laws, but denies its sufficiency: "it is not enough to urge us to make just laws; never has a precept been both more widely known and more neglected." This is nowhere more obvious, claims Mably, than in Le Mercier's own treatise, which establishes property and inequality of wealth as basic natural laws, thereby making just political laws impossible.[81] Mably is more positive in his later work, *Droits et devoirs du citoyen* (1783). There he tells us that natural laws, being only the precepts of reason, are simple, clear, and luminous, and command assent when we are not blinded by the enemy of reason, passion. The most stupid peasant finds the "silver rule" self-evident.[82]

In his longest development on the subject, Mably has one interlocutor in the same dialogue assert, following Hobbes and Rousseau, that in the state of nature the egoistic search for happiness was the only law and guilt did not exist. Obligation, and the human moral life, began only with the social contract. "By obliging himself to respect in others the rights he wanted respected in himself, the citizen undoubtedly set narrow limits to the unlimited power he had as a man." But Mably's clear intention is to refute the modern versions of Natural Law. Having set up this argument, he proceeds to demolish it. If there ever was such a time in mankind's infancy, it was only a brief moment of physical development, and such creatures were not really men at all. "What can this situation matter to us? It is not ours and perhaps never existed." As soon as pleasure and pain produced ideas, and reflection grasped relationships, then distinctions of good, propriety, and justice and the limits of rights became self-evident, and even more, became operative by virtue of the authority of reason. "Before any civil conventions, good faith was distinguished from perfidy, cruelty from beneficence; since man was made in such a way that he had to feel pleasure or pain from the beneficent or cruel actions of his fellows, and thereby has to develop that moral instinct which honors our nature." If this were not true, men would never have thought of making laws. How would they have known what should be forbidden or commanded?[83]

[81] *Ibid.*, XI, pp. 53–54. A similar view had been expressed in Morelly's *Code de la nature* (1755), éd. Chinard, 1950, p. 211, but this work was little read in the eighteenth century.
[82] *Oeuvres*, XI, pp. 334–35.
[83] *Ibid.*, pp. 253–58.

Although Mably reaffirms the traditional doctrine, or intends to, there are significant differences. To begin with, he makes no mention of God, or of a rational or moral universe. Natural Law seems confined entirely within the human experience.[84] It is, moreover, a result of sense experience; it does not exist as a priori judgments, but as logical conclusions. Most telling of all, Mably's emphasis, as he proceeds to apply his exposition, is on what "the citizen has a right to require" from society. He must obey laws and rules, but only "so long as he knows nothing wiser." He is not condemned to sacrifice himself to error. "If citizens have made absurd conventions; . . . if in seeking the road to happiness they have taken the opposite road; if unfortunately they have let themselves be led astray by perfidious and ignorant leaders; will you condemn them inhumanly to be the eternal victims of error or wandering? Shall the quality of 'citizen' destroy the dignity of 'man'? Shall the laws made to aid reason and support freedom degrade and enslave us?" The flow of eloquence runs on, foreshadowing already the orators in the Revolutionary tribunes.

Mably's position may be contrasted with that of the youthful Sabatier de Castres, who, in 1769, insists that Natural Law is of divine, not human, institution.[85] The traditional theory is also reasserted by Barbeu du Bourg, in 1774, and by Du Pont de Nemours, in 1792.[86] The same may be said of Delisle de Sales, who in 1796 bitterly assailed the French Revolution for having crushed Natural Law, which provided "a morality independent of social laws." [87]

We may close our investigation of this phase of eighteenth-century Natural Law theories with the widely read deist Volney. In 1793 Volney published his *La Loi naturelle, ou Principes physiques de la morale*. This little essay, coming at the end of the period, is an excellent indication of an average state of mind among liberal thinkers.

According to Volney, Natural Law depends on general and

---

[84] In another work, *Principes de morale*, Mably sketches a completely empirical or experiential explanation of the genesis of obligations (*Oeuvres*, X, pp. 280–81).

[85] *Dictionnaire des passions*, II, pp. 24–26, 31–32.

[86] Barbeu du Bourg, *Petit Code de la raison humaine*, 1789 ed., pp. 19, 105–6; Du Pont de Nemours, *Philosophie de l'univers*, pp. 99–100.

[87] *De la Philosophie du bonheur*, II, p. 78; see also his earlier work, *De la Philosophie de la nature*, Amsterdam, 1770, I, pp. 1–83. On the other hand, J. N. Moreau, the arch-conservative author of the notorious diatribe, *Mémoire pour servir à l'histoire des Cacouacs* (1757), expounds a Natural Law theory which is infused with naturalistic viewpoints. See his *Variétés morales et philosophiques* (1785), pp. 142–57.

constant rules of conduct which inhere in the order of things. It comes from God, is "presented" by him to each man, through his reason, and is the criterion of all positive laws, in all times and places. Thus far, then, Volney gives us the classical doctrine. He then declares that Natural Law, by itself, suffices to make men happier and better. Furthermore, he adds, it is not obvious, except "in its bases," but forms "in its developments and consequences, a complex ensemble, which requires the knowledge of many facts and all the sagacity of reasoning." When these are understood, it forms "a science as precise and as exact as geometry and mathematics." The basic principle of Natural Law is self-preservation, and not happiness, which is "un objet de luxe." Pleasure and pain are the mechanisms by which it works: pleasure is "an encouragement to live," as pain is "a warding off of death." Men can have no awareness of these principles when they live alone, but only in society which is, however, man's true natural state, since it is necessary for his self-preservation, while in the state of nature he was only a miserable brute. The purpose of Natural Law and of all our moral ideas is, then, the development of our faculties toward the sole natural end of self-preservation.[88] Thus Volney's theorizing reveals clearly the infiltration of naturalistic viewpoints into Natural Law theory. The new doctrine is grafted on to the old and effectively "corrupts" it. The whole moral dimension of human life is squeezed down into a basic animal law, and all of morality becomes a narrowly utilitarian self-seeking.[89]

[88] Compare Volney's *Les Ruines:* man in the state of nature "did not see at his side beings descended from the heavens to inform him of his needs which he owes only to his senses, to instruct him of duties which are born solely of his needs." (*Oeuvres complètes,* 1821, I, p. 29.)

[89] The development of Natural Law theories in eighteenth-century England is far less interesting than in France. When adopted as a reaction to Hobbes, Mandeville or later utilitarianism, the traditional theory is expressed. See the following: S. Clarke, *A Demonstration of the Being and Attributes of God* (6th ed., London, 1725, p. 116; Pt. 2, Prop. 1); Shaftesbury, *Characteristicks* . . . (6th ed., n.p. 1737 [1711], I, p. 109, etc.); William Wollaston, *The Religion of Nature Delineated* (London, 1727, p. 26); Joseph Butler, *A Dissertation upon the Nature of Virtue* (Appendix to I, chap. 3 of the *Analogy,* 1736); Kames, *Essays on the Principles of Morality and Natural Religion* (Edinburgh, 1751, pp. 122–126); William Blackstone, *Commentaries* (referred to in D. J. Boorstin, *The Mysterious Science of the Law,* Boston, 1958, p. 47 *et passim*). Kames, however, really belongs to the moral sense group. Nor does Butler proclaim a Natural Law, and we can properly speak only of a kinship. For Burke's theories of Natural Law, understanding of which has recently been clarified, see Charles Parkin, *The Moral Basis of Burke's Political Thought,* Cambridge, 1956, pp. 10–28, and P. J. Stanlis, *Edmund Burke and the Natural Law,* Ann Arbor, 1958.

III. Variations and Vicissitudes of
Natural Law Theory

The influence of Hobbes and the inferences that could be drawn from a similar naturalism are attested to by a defender of traditional Natural Law, the Swiss Protestant, Claude-Marie Guyon. In his *L'Oracle des nouveaux philosophes,*[1] he refers to those who claim that primitive rights still subsist, "and that it is permissible to enjoy them whenever we can without danger." These errors, he continues, were introduced into France about twenty years ago, and since then we have been "assailed by books which teach them." It is absurd, according to Guyon, to suppose centuries of a state of nature during which men "knew no internal law which taught them to distinguish order and disorder, humaneness and ferocity." It is equally absurd to say (with Rousseau, of course) that people had no idea of property, or that only pity and not obligation, marked the limit of egoistic aggressiveness.

Guyon seems acutely aware of the menace of nihilism. He attacks the view that love of domination, being natural, is therefore legitimate, or that right and wrong are no more than ways of thinking. It is unnatural, precisely, to say that respect and gratitude to parents (or other prescriptions of Natural Law) are only conventional obligations. Before Burke, he affirms that the state of nature concept is the chief weapon against Natural Law, since it dehumanizes man, and turns ideas of rightness into conventions devised for general utility, and dependent on education. He comes finally to the point of his charge. The *philosophes* have nihilistic intentions. They wish to destroy "the innate idea of general principles of moral truths," destroy the moral order, "by putting all the vices in the place of, and on the throne of virtue." Guyon's paroxysm carries him so far that, although he believes in the most traditional Natural Law, he ends up by denouncing it and crying out against the "blind and interested partisans of Natural Law." Natural Law is not enough; men cannot or will not contemplate it. It is evident that he must have been thinking of another kind of Natural Law, propounded by the secularists.

Inevitably, many writers in the second half of the century were

[1] Berne, 1759, pp. 30–61.

more or less under the influence of a naturalistic view of the universe and man. Those who were thoroughgoing naturalists were not, with few exceptions, immoralists, but were trying to reconstruct a more human ethics, a more valid and efficacious ethics—more valid and efficacious because of its adherence to natural laws. While some of these writers scoffed at any idea of a moral Natural Law having a place in a purely physical Nature, others concluded that human nature, in its distinctive moral development, did possess a natural moral law. This being so, the phrase "Natural Law" is appropriate and meaningful in describing their theories.

The points of difference with the traditional doctrine, and also with its "modernizers," are marked but not fatal. First, the notion of a moral universe outside of man himself is excluded. Second, the moral law is not necessarily a law of God, nor is it necessarily apprehended by conscience; it is, rather, a derivation of experience and reflection. It is these suppositions, more fundamentally than an emphasis on rights or subjective will (as it is often argued), which distinguish the empirical rationalists. Cassirer summarizes the problem in this form: "Do our logical and ethical concepts express definite objective content existing by itself; or are these concepts merely verbal symbols which we arbitrarily attach to contents?" [2] It would be more exact to say that there are two separate positive ideas involved, and not to reduce the choice to the Platonic or Sophist. The traditional Natural Law doctrine is indeed Platonic, since the just is absolute, independent of and prior to human experience. Furthermore, as Cassirer has aptly indicated, the "newer" doctrine of Grotius and Pufendorf is even more Platonic in its transposal of the concept of law from the realm of empirical reality or application to that of arithmetical ideality or logical definition, in which demonstration is possible.[3] The naturalistic viewpoint, on the other hand, limits the moral reality of right and just to human experience, but attempts to seat their reality on natural (therefore objectively ascertainable) facts of

[2] *The Philosophy of the Enlightenment*, Princeton, 1951, p. 235.
[3] "Just as the mind is capable of constructing the realm of quantity and number entirely from within itself by virtue of its 'innate ideas,' so it has the same constructive ability in the field of law. Here too the intellect can and should begin with fundamental norms, which it creates from within itself, and then find its way to the formulation of the particular." (*Ibid.*, p. 238.) Cassirer errs in considering the Natural Law as "created" by the mind, which only "discovers" it. The pure reason involved in Natural Law is common to God and man, and might be spoken of as a manifestation of the *Logos*, therefore not dependent on God's arbitrary will.

human nature, needs, relationships. In other words, the two earlier groups held moral distinctions to be absolute, or the same for every possible rational being, while the eighteenth-century naturalists who perceive the necessity of a Natural Law consider it to be a derivative of the particularities of human nature and experience, rather than a body of abstract truths. It is only the few, but historically important, nihilists who will renew the Sophist position, and this is precisely their role. They are the ones who do not fall into Cassirer's formulation: "The philosophy of the Enlightenment at first holds fast to this apriority of law, to this demand for absolute universally valid and unalterable legal norms. Even the pure empiricists and the philosophical empiricists are no exception in this respect." [4]

D'Alembert believed in an empirical genesis of moral judgments. Inasmuch as he also believed in Natural Law, he furnishes a clear example of the possible confluence of the two approaches. There is no doubt that for d'Alembert a moral law exists. "That which belongs essentially and uniquely to reason and which consequently is uniform among all peoples, is our duty toward our fellow men. Consciousness of this duty is what is called morality." The principles involved are therefore objective and discoverable to reason. Their function is "to procure for us the surest means of being happy by showing us the intimate connection between our true interest and the performance of our duty." [5] In this work d'Alembert gives us no clear statement as to the genesis of obligation, though he doubtless means that the pursuit of happiness is not merely its function but its origin. He does clarify this matter in his *Discours préliminaire* to the *Encyclopédie,* which we shall examine in greater detail in another context. There he shows that moral judgments arise from experience, from the egocentric sensation of injustice perpetrated by a stronger individual. No independent moral sphere, conceived of as coexisting with the physical, is allowed. But once men enter into the realm of moral experience, universal notions deriving from human needs, relations, and sensual experience become a self-evident Natural Law.[6]

---

[4] *Ibid.,* p. 243.

[5] *Eléments de philosophie,* in *Oeuvres,* 1821, I, Sec. VII.

[6] Sylvain Maréchal is an example of a notorious atheist who supported a natural moral law, related to the calculation of happiness (*Examen des critiques du livre intitulé "De l'Esprit,"* Londres, 1760, pp. 103–5, 117 ff., 152 ff.)

The mystical philosopher-scientist, Charles Bonnet, derives moral experience from

While Count Honoré de Mirabeau does allow that everything in the chain of beings has its particular law which comes from God, the source of Natural Law, as he describes it, is purely physical.[7] Duty is the fulfillment of law; law is order, and order is founded on physical sensations and needs. Natural Law, consequently, does not have its source in our reason, but is beyond it. It hinges on our necessary dependency. Now, the work of culture, for Mirabeau (contrary to Rousseau), is not to supersede or abolish nature, but to protect it. Society must therefore "give the greatest possible liberty to the individuals who compose it," and extend their *jouissances* (pleasures, enjoyment of rights). The formation of society is no more than "the extension of primitive relations, not their abolition." It so happens that the first relations are those of mutual assistance, rooted in utility, whence the dependency from which Natural Law results. There is some logical confusion in Mirabeau's writings. If natural and human institutions, as he also claims, contradict each other, it is difficult to see how his main premise is tenable. And if nature is not reason, is it the passions? There is no other choice; and yet Natural Law tells us to dominate our passions.

With d'Holbach, we have an excellent example of a radical naturalist who formulates a notion of Natural Law, derived a posteriori from the facts of experience. He assumes that "experience and reason" lead to general truths and judgments. These, he assures us, are "not founded on conventions among men, and still less on the chimerical will of a supernatural being, but on the eternal and invariable relations which subsist among beings of the human species living in society. . . ."[8] For d'Holbach these laws are based exclusively on utility. His fellow atheist, Naigeon,

---

the fact that our rationality and freedom give us a different way of *being* in nature, one which inevitably puts all our mutual relations, necessary or voluntary, in a unique light of right and ought, the moral plane of existence. "From this there arises a new order of actions; among these are the ones called *moral*, because they are subject to a law. This law is Natural Law, which is in general the result of the relations man has with the beings around him." (*Essai sur l'âme*, Sec. 272, *Oeuvres*, Neuchâtel, 1781, 1782.)

For the association of Natural Law with anarchism, see Dom Deschamps, *Le Vrai Système*, p. 169. For a version with egalitarian socio-political overtones (equality is the foundation of duties), see the article "Etat de nature," in Robinet's *Dictionnaire universel*.

[7] *Essai sur le despotisme* (1772), in *Oeuvres*, 1835, VIII, pp. 29–32, 40.

[8] *Système de la nature*, Londres, 1771, I, p. 145. Also, *La Morale universelle*, Paris, 1820, I, p. xxx.

uses the interesting phrase, "revealed by nature to every reasonable being"—an obvious transposition of the traditional phrasing.[9]
Indeed, for Naigeon and for d'Holbach, the end result is no different. "This voice of nature and of reason," continues Naigeon,
"speaks in the same tone to all inhabitants of the earth. It teaches
love between husband and wife, between father and son, friendship, humaneness, justice." He then adds, "if they desire to obtain
for themselves the attitudes [on the part of others] which they
need to make themselves happy here below." There is, of course,
much more to be said about the theories of these naturalists, but
we must leave this for our third chapter.

The Physiocrats were a solidary group representing the most
important segment of economic thought, a nascent laissez-faire
capitalism in a broad philosophical setting. While their doctrine
may be considered as a link between the two concepts of Natural
Law, naturalism and utilitarianism predominate in it. Thus the
Marquis de Mirabeau writes: "Moral principles are linked to
physical principles, as the soul is to the body. . . . It is not from
the civil or public order that I derive my principles; it is in the
very nature of things, in the physical compatibility, or incom-
patibility, of human conditions, and not, I say, in the moral and
positive constitution of society, always subject to interpretations
and debate." [10] Laissez-faire flows from a belief in the natural
harmony of nature's workings: "It is clear that each of your subjects fills your [i.e., the King's] coffers in looking after his own
interests." [11]

If you believe in a natural order, writes Mirabeau, if you believe in a law governing the growth of plants from a seed, then
you must also believe that happiness depends on constant laws of
movement, imprinted in matter. The individual, as a part of "the
universal concert," cannot escape from it without hurting himself
and his kind, without producing chaos.[12] It is therefore useless
to study Natural Law, as has usually been done, divorced from its
base, the physical order, as if we were purely intellectual beings.
Like Helvétius, d'Holbach, and the other materialists, Mirabeau
and all the Physiocrats insist on the close connection of physical

[9] *Le Militaire philosophe*, Londres, 1768, pp. 181–82. (This work was edited by
Naigeon from an earlier anonymous ms.)
[10] *Théorie de l'impôt*, n.p., 1761, pp. 14, 339, 360.
[11] *Ibid.*, p. 339. Compare Mandeville.
[12] *Ibid.*, I, pp. xxxiv–xxxvii.

and moral laws, and the derivation of the second from the first.[13] This natural order does, it is true, dictate that the strong shall grab what belongs to all; but it also creates dependence, commerce, and competition, and therefore a limit to cupidity. Thus each, working for himself, works for all by the linkage of reciprocal needs.[14] (This thesis is typical of the failure of laissez-faire theorists, including Adam Smith, to foresee the capacities for monopoly in capital and labor.)

Mirabeau also attempts to combat nihilism, or what he terms "moral pyrrhonism." The metaphysical reality of Natural Law, he contends, cannot be denied without a simultaneous rejection of a physical order.[15]

Although Mirabeau, like the other Physiocrats, refers to God as the creator of all natural laws, his concept clearly relegates the deity to a shadowy and figurative position.[16] His emphasis on scientific exactness and discursive reason is not traditional doctrine; and, though he predicates a universal human reason and nature, they exist only as forms or functions of the physical world, not as a self-existent moral world. In no place does he substantiate the rise of the moral from the physical. His argument is the naturalistic or "evolutionary" view, that self-interest produces a reciprocity of interests; right and wrong, rights and obligations, are no more than these.[17]

Unlike the proponents of what some have called "the revolutionary natural rights theory," the Physiocrats did not put much stock in a state of nature. Le Trosne, for instance, argues that once we realize that man is *naturally* social, *la conclusion s'impose:* there are *natural* laws to govern him in society.[18] The whole function of society is "to protect all the rights by the observation of all

---

[13] Any moral order is subject to "the primitive, essential and fundamental law of physical necessity." (Baudeau, quoted by Weulersse, *Le Mouvement physiocratique en France*, II, p. 111.)

[14] *Ibid.*, II, pp. 98–101.

[15] *Ibid.*, III, pp. 6–9.

[16] The Divinity is fused and confused with the natural order, as is Providence; its legislation is only "the code of nature." (Weulersse, *op. cit.*, II, pp. 115–16.)

[17] Similar concepts are found in Quesnay's article, "Droit naturel," and in the second chapter of Lemercier de la Rivière's *L'Ordre naturel et essentiel des sociétés*, which Diderot so admired and which Mably caustically criticized. For Du Pont de Nemours, writing in the *Ephémérides du citoyen*, immutable physical laws "constitute exactly the *droit naturel* of all men." (In Quesnay, *Oeuvres*, 1888, p. 645.)

For Mably's important criticism of the Physiocrats, see *Doutes sur l'ordre naturel des sociétés politiques, Oeuvres*, XI, pp. 25–28.

[18] *De l'Ordre social*, 1771, p. 13 ff.

the duties." All this is inscribed in the great book of nature. "Indeed, all is physical in this matter, and everything works by physical means." The laws of social order are only deductions from the same laws that make plants grow. Le Trosne does say, however, that there are also "moral affections," natural ideas of justice, duty, and rights. All that is needed is to grasp the connection between the physical laws of reproduction and moral truths, and to deduce "an exact and calculated science." Were Le Trosne able to substantiate such a mechanical connection, the moral problem would be solved, and, indeed, "moral" would become a merely figurative word, since nothing "physical" or "natural" would have to be contravened. But he can "prove" this linkage only by a dubious appeal to self-interest—properly conceived, of course.[19]

Le Trosne's emphasis on rights is typical of the newer theories. The first right, and the source of all others, is the right to life. It involves the use of the natural physical means to enjoy it, property and mobility. These rights are absolute (i.e., unalienable), and universal.[20] Being such, they imply the obligation of each to respect the same rights in others. It is impossible, Le Trosne avers, to separate rights and duties. We may conclude, then, that for Le Trosne, moral obligation has its source in the possession of rights, rather than the reverse. "Men cannot therefore reflect on themselves without discovering what they owe to others. They cannot demand their rights without recognizing the extent of their duties, without admitting they are prescribed by their own interest. . . ."[21]

---

[19] *Ibid.*, pp. 73–75.

[20] "Personal freedom and personal property are then two social laws, primitive, indispensable, and self-evidently deduced from the right to life" (p. 29). The right to real property is deduced from agriculture. Cf. M. Albaum, "The Moral Defenses of the Physiocrats' Laissez-faire," *Journal of the History of Ideas*, 16:179–97, 1955, p. 182: "Whatever made for the greatest pleasure in a world governed by natural law was justified by natural rights."

[21] Le Mercier de la Rivière also emphasizes the principle of the priority of rights to society (which serves to protect them), and to justice and injustice. "There are no duties without rights," adds Le Mercier, "the latter are the fount and measure of the former . . . duties, in short can be established in society only on the fact that they are needed for the preservation of the rights which result." Le Trosne criticizes collectivistic or anarchistic theorists who, because self-interest is a cause of disorder, think that men can be stripped of it by abolishing property. He seems to realize to what extremes conditioning would have to be carried, and how disastrous would be its consequences—even if it could succeed. "To deprive man of this passion is to denature him, and reduce him to the state of a purely passive and inert being." (P. 35.) Rousseau, precisely, will demand that we denature man. (*Op. cit.*, p. 8.)

This maintenance of self-interest is, in effect, another illustration of the Physiocrats' fundamental naturalism, of their negation of transcendence over nature.[22] As long as the natural order is not disturbed by man, it will tend toward his happiness. They therefore deny that nature's law leads to oppression or exploitation, to the happiness of one at the expense of another, but see it rather as a process of conciliation. *Ex natura, ius.* "Where will justice be found," inquires Roubaud, "if it is not in the natural course of things?" [23] Man, then, must submit to the natural order. The result, following Malebranche, is to make love of order "the unique virtue." The ultimate aim and effect of the Physiocratic philosophy is to reconcile, if not to fuse, nature and culture. It does so only by making morality secondary and derivative. As Baudeau writes, "Virtue, modesty, justice, beneficence are of course worthy of the deepest respect; but subsistence, freedom, property are names which awaken more attractive ideas, those of the real values (*biens*) with which men are concerned. . . . Net product, such is the infallible touchstone of justice and injustice."[24] As with d'Holbach, there is only one natural law—pursuit of our own advantage, which is automatically countered by another: fear of reprisals. Injustice carries the seeds of its own destruction and cannot perpetuate itself—as even Sade was to show, despite himself.

Leaving the theories of Rousseau until a later point in our inquiry where we shall be able to examine them to better advantage, there remains for us to analyze Diderot's attitude toward Natural Law. With Diderot, we must always remember that we are dealing with a man whose real convictions are not always readily ascertainable. He was an experimenter in ideas, and his thinking follows along several different lines, which not only evolve across the years, but which, at any given time, may be both extremely radical and conservative or conventional. That he would oppose the traditional foundations of Natural Law is obvious from his atheism. Richard Hooker had written, "The being

[22] In theory they accepted the transcendence and adhered to "a modified Cartesian dualism largely derived from Malebranche" (Albaum, p. 184). The realm of spirit, however, is not scientifically knowable; and apparently, it does not really signify in actual existence, since it is assumed to be in perfect agreement, or even identity, with the physical, which we can know.

[23] Weulersse, *op. cit.*, II, p. 113.

[24] Quoted by Weulersse, *op. cit.*, II, p. 108.

of God is a kind of law to his working; for that perfection which
God is, giveth perfection to that he doth." [25] Diderot makes it
quite clear in the *Lettre sur les aveugles* (1749) that the world, if
we look at it as it is, cannot, for this very reason, be the work of
God. Earlier, it is true, in his translation of Shaftesbury's *Essai
sur le mérite et la vertu* (1746), he had apparently espoused a
rationalist, innatist Natural Law, rooted in the universal wisdom
which governs the universe, and linked to the happiness of each
person.[26] In the following year the same theory is maintained in
De la Suffisance de la religion naturelle, but it is more directly
pointed in the direction implied by the title.[27] It is after this initial
period that Diderot's atheism asserts itself.[28] He does not, however,
cast off his belief in Natural Law along with that in some kind of
God. As a pure naturalist, he will continue to assert that law (as
well as to deny it), but finds it embedded in nature itself.

There are two articles in the *Encyclopédie* in which Diderot
treated this subject; and there is ample evidence from other aspects
of his ethical thought that they represent his sincere opinions. In
"Droit naturel," he declares that almost every man has a subjective intuition of the self-evidence of Natural Law. The average
person, however, can only refer to his conscience when challenged,
while the philosopher, in his attempts to define *droit,* is frustrated
by finding himself engaged in a vicious circle. Here Diderot postulates a premoral state of nature ("in which perhaps a distinct
idea of obligation would not yet exist").[29] The philosopher's
sequence of ideas would be: right (in the sense of "rights") is the
foundation of justice; justice is the obligation to give to each what
belongs to him—but what, if anything, belongs to any one? "It is
at this point that the philosopher begins to feel that of all notions
of ethics, that of *natural right* is one of the most important and
one of the most difficult to determine." This Diderot now attempts
to do. It is necessary to break out of the circle. First, unless man
is a free and responsible agent (and not merely a voluntary one),
there is no justice or injustice, no virtue or vice, no obligation
or right, but only "animal goodness or malice." Second, man is

[25] Quoted by L. I. Bredvold, "The Meaning of the Concept of Right Reason in
the Natural Law Tradition," p. 121.
[26] R. Legros, "Diderot and Shaftesbury," p. 188 ff.
[27] *Oeuvres,* ed. Assézat et Tourneux, 1875-77, I, pp. 261, 269.
[28] See Aram Vartanian, "From Deist to Atheist," in *Diderot Studies,* pp. 46-63.
[29] *Oeuvres,* XIV, p. 297.

wicked, since he is impelled to find happiness at the expense of others; he must, moreover, either recognize his wickedness, or grant to others the same privilege toward himself.[30] Third, on what basis could we reproach a man who freely accepts this reciprocity of evil and who, "to acquire the right to dispose of others' lives, offers up his own?" What shall we reply if he has the honesty and courage to say:

> I realize that I am bringing terror and chaos to mankind; but I must either be unhappy or make others unhappy; and nobody is more precious to me than I am to myself. Do not reproach me for this abominable predilection; it is not free. It is the voice of nature which is never clearer and louder in me than when it speaks in my own favor. . . . Who is there among you who, on the point of death, would not buy back his life at the price of most of the human species, if he were sure of impunity and secrecy? But . . . I am equitable and sincere. If my happiness requires me to destroy all lives which are an obstacle to me, then any other individual should be able to destroy mine if it hinders him. . . . I am not so unjust as to require of another a sacrifice that I am unwilling to make to him.

This is a very important statement. It draws a clear consequence from materialistic determinism—which even the moralistic d'Holbach was to accept as a basic postulate and problem. It indicates Diderot's awareness of the challenge of moral nihilism and sets forth that challenge in terms that are not only clear, but entirely representative of the formulation given to it by others in this period, from La Mettrie and d'Argens to Sade, and in several of the novels of the time. Foreshadowing Sade, especially, is the frank willingness to incur the risk of similar treatment, if in the game of war which is life another should assert superior strength. In this passage, the rights of nature or the laws of nature (as contrasted with Natural Law) are given full statement and undisputed sway. The prerogatives and constrictions of culture are denied any validity.

The question of the origin of moral value, and of its validity, is now dramatically at stake. Diderot has assumed the role of defender and will attempt to assert moral "right" over the "right" of nature, the latter phrase, it must be noted, being construed in

---

[30] Diderot is in a sense begging the question here, since the "must" and the reciprocity, as well as the notion of wickedness already contain the essence of Natural Law.

its egoistic or biological sense. He approaches his defense indirectly, in his fourth step. The nihilist's speech reveals that man is "a reasoning animal," one who must reason. (Diderot is careful not to say, "essentially" or "exclusively"; and he means that man cannot escape the activity and judgments of reason.) The nihilist is therefore *obliged,* like any other man, to seek the truth, under the penalty of giving up his human status—which would justify others in treating him like a wild beast and exterminating him.[31] In his fifth point, Diderot reaches the core of the problem. "What shall we reply then to our violent reasoner, before strangling him?" Diderot now adroitly points out the implicit admission of a moral law in the very concept of reciprocity, even in evil-doing.[32] "His entire speech comes down to discovering whether he acquires a right over others' lives by abandoning his to them." This argument for reciprocity, this self-justification, reveals a desire to be not only happy, but also to be equitable, and not to be termed wicked.[33] But Diderot only makes this point in passing. He is more interested in another thrust: the nihilist "has no legitimate authority" to make others accept the deal; and he is offering only one life in exchange for many. This argument is valid only on Diderot's assumption that the nihilist, by wishing to justify himself, wishes to be just. The assumption is indeed contained in the hypothesis as stated; and the nihilist who does not wish to justify himself is taken care of by the assumption that he would lose his human status and could be destroyed like a wild beast.[34]

[31] But suppose, after discovering the truth, he will still refuse to conform to it? Diderot realizes this crucial difficulty; "whoever refuses to conform to it is mad or wicked with moral wickedness." (P. 298.) That is, once right is established (and known), its existence and our awareness of it carry their own power of obligation. The nihilist would probably reply that the part of his nature which urges him to selfish happiness is necessarily more powerful, and more precious to him, than the other part. And so we are brought back to the question of freedom, to that of happiness, etc. Rousseau, we shall later see, understood this weakness in Diderot's position and proposed a radically different solution.

[32] In a subsequent chapter we shall see in more detail how nihilism is ultimately self-contradictory and self-defeating.

[33] Sade's heroes rejoice in being wicked but display the same need for self-justification. But Diderot again begs the question: if the nihilist did not desire to be equitable, "we should have to strangle him without a reply." Diderot has logically indicated that such a recourse would be justified if the nihilist refused to use reason, but he has not proven that the nihilist would lose his human status by refusing to be morally *good,* since this is the whole point at issue. Such "strangling" could, then, be only an arbitrary (though self-protective) use of force against force and would in itself confirm the nihilist's contention.

[34] The idea was inspired by Cicero; see chap. 1, *supra.* See Kant's argument supporting constraint of those who do not treat others justly. It is summarized by

With perspicacity, Diderot realizes the further consequence of what he has established. It is simply this: the individual has been deprived of the right of subjective determination of right and wrong. Where, then, will this determination lie? This is Diderot's sixth point. In reply, he proposes his notion of a "general will." The general will alone is right, and always right, and so it automatically overrides the individual will. And this general will *is* Natural Law, "an order of knowledge and ideas peculiar to the human species, which come from and create its dignity." It encloses both the obligation and the privilege implied by the phrase *droit naturel.* It sets the limits of duties and gives to each person "the most sacred *natural right* to whatever is not denied by the entire species." But how can we know this general will? The answer, this time, is more vague; it demands both rational inquiry and emotional introspection. The general will is partly a consensus, consisting of "universal principles of right" of civilized nations, social actions of primitive peoples and tacit conventions of moral anarchists and partly, subjective feelings of resentment. All of this is, of course, abstract, vague, and scarcely usable. The consensus supposes a unity which many, in the eighteenth century and since, have denied, but which probably does exist at a basic level, such as Voltaire conceived of in his Natural Law theory.[35] Perhaps because he realizes the abstractness of his solution, Diderot also offers a more convenient *modus operandi:* our *subjective* decision that an act is "in the common and general interest," that is, "whatever you require for your happiness and theirs"; a decision which is "a pure act of the understanding which reasons in the silence of passions on what man may require of his fellow, and on what his fellow has a right to require of him." [36]

In this fashion, then, Diderot explains the basis of obligation in Natural Law, and the obligation to fulfill it. Its rule obtains in all societies, as the very condition of their being, "not excepting those which are of a criminal nature"—a truth which Sade's "societies for crime" were to confirm. This Natural Law inheres,

---

E. F. Carritt: "This infringement is justified, because either they recognize the obligation to justice and know they are doing wrong, and therefore approve, while disliking, the constraint, or they do not recognize it; and on neither alternative have they any right to be 'treated as ends.' . . . We are justified, then, in compelling rational beings to behave justly." (*Morals and Politics*, p. 94.)

[35] For modern confirmations, see *An Age of Crisis,* chap. 7.

[36] This criterion is also Rousseau's, but the means of discovering the general will and other implications are radically different from Diderot's.

then, in the species and would change if it did. Unfortunately, Diderot's Natural Law has no prescriptive content. It is an effort to base the rights of culture, or moral law, in nature, and thereby to counteract the nihilism which the analysis of human nature and motivation, the submersion of man in nature, and the supremacy of a "natural" criterion encouraged. Whether or not it be regarded as a satisfactory logical reply to the nihilist's argument, as set forth by Diderot himself, here and elsewhere, it is nonetheless of very limited value. In its abstractness—which was the very character and weakness of most eighteenth-century thinking—it fails to come to grips with the *existential* claims, experiences, and realities of both individual and social life.[37]

Diderot's later article, "Loi naturelle," also carries the stamp of his personal thinking, as is obvious especially in the image drawn from painting.[38] To be sure, the definitions are much closer this time to the traditional doctrine. But they do tally with the ethical formalism which consistently marks one aspect of his moral theorizing. "Natural Law is the eternal and immutable order which should serve as a rule for our actions. It is founded on the essential difference between good and evil." Diderot admits a diversity of opinion and difficult boundary cases, but this fact does not "prevent there being, really and essentially, a very great difference between right and wrong." The proof is in our conscience, which always tells us when we are doing wrong, and approves when we do the right. Diderot repeats approvingly Cicero's dictum, that Natural Law is not an arbitrary, human invention, but "the impression of the universal reason which governs the universe." We may take this as a conventional phrase, or as a figurative expression of Diderot's belief in rational natural laws and immutable truths of reason.

That Natural Law and formalist moral concepts form one essential current in Diderot's ethical speculations is confirmed by their recurrence in one of his last and most significant works, the

[37] "Droit Naturel" was probably written (and Rousseau took it to be written) in reply to the individualistic rebelliousness of the *Discours sur l'origine de l'inégalité* against social sanctions and limits. We must remember that Diderot's defense of Natural Law—like much of his speculation—is a hypothesis, and that he is not necessarily committed to it. But, contrary to Vaughan's hostile criticism, there is no reason to doubt his sincerity, either in the development of his reasoning or in his opposition to Rousseau's.

[38] *Oeuvres*, XVI, p. 1.

Réfutation d'Helvétius (1773–76).[39] Even in the earlier and also unpublished *Réflexions sur le livre de l'Esprit* (1758), Diderot had objected to Helvétius' reduction of justice to the mere dictates of self-interest. Helvétius has been deluded by *facts* and their apparent relativism. His paradox is false:

> false because it is possible to find in our natural needs, in our life, in our existence, in our organization and our sensitivity which expose us to pain, an eternal basis for right and wrong, whose notion general and personal interest then vary in a hundred thousand different ways . . . but its essence is independent of them.[40]

The proof is another fact: there are universals; giving water to a thirsty man is approved in all times and places. In the *Réfutation* Diderot develops his argument in more concrete form. There is a knowledge of moral right and wrong built into the human animal—this is the sum of Diderot's refutation of Helvétius' moral doctrine. If a primitive man steals the fruits of another's labor, he will run away. What does his flight denote, if not consciousness that his action is bound to evoke resentment, in other words, his awareness of an injustice, subject to punishment? The robbed man, on his side, will feel indignation, and be conscious of a wrong done to him. It is not a mere contest of force, unaccompanied by emotions or ideas pertinent to moral distinctions. "It seems to me that between these two savages there is a primitive law which characterizes actions, and of which the written law is only the interpretation, the expression, and the sanction. The savage possesses no words to designate right and wrong; he cries out, but is his cry empty of meaning? Is it no more than the cry of an animal? The thing would take place, as [Helvétius] paints it, between two wild beasts; but man is not a beast [and] we must not overlook this difference in the judgments we make of his actions." [41]

The greatness and depth of Diderot's humanism glow in these

---

[39] One should also refer to his statement in the *Plan d'une Université* (1775), III, p. 493.

[40] *Oeuvres*, II, p. 270. A similar idea is expressed in the *Entretien d'un philosophe avec la Maréchale* (1776), *ibid.*, p. 517, and in the *Fragments échappés* (1772), VI, pp. 444–45.

[41] *Oeuvres*, II, pp. 387–88. Helvétius' position is stated in the opening paragraph of chapter VIII of Section IV of *De l'Homme*. The savage knows only force and has no glimmer of an idea of justice or injustice, since there are no positive laws.

lines. It is a conviction rooted in the distinctiveness of the human,
and that distinctiveness lies, more than anywhere else, in man's
moral life. To sacrifice that would indeed be to do what he had
threatened the nihilist with, in "Droit naturel"—to retrogress
from the human to the animal status. This is precisely the threat
of moral anarchism, of a narrowly conceived naturalism, such as
Helvétius had developed to a logical fullness, and no feat of logic
can overcome Diderot's resistance to it. "I should very much like,"
he concludes, "not to authorize the wicked man to appeal from
artificial, conventional law to the eternal law of nature; [42] I should
much like that he not be enabled to say to others, and to himself,
'After all, what am I doing? I am returning to my first rights.' "
From this it is clear that Diderot is not asserting the supremacy
of culture over nature. He is seeking rather to establish their
underlying identity, by discovering the moral law of right and
wrong inscribed in nature itself, in that Natural Law which for
him is the human appanage. This law is not created by societal
organs or structures; it is what Montesquieu described as "the
necessary relations which derive from the nature of things"—as
things are experienced by men. For Diderot, the humanist, we are
obliged to behave like human beings because we are human beings;
unless, indeed, like the theorists of nihilism, such as Sade and
Stirner, or its practitioners, such as the Nazis, we wish to cease to
hold that title.[43]

As it may be expected, Natural Law theories, even in their most
secular dress, had their opponents. These were to be found among
the more radical materialists. The ambiguity of the words "law"
(descriptive, normative) and "nature" (universal, human, physical,
moral) made it possible to interpret them in opposing senses. We

[42] I have inverted the original order of these phrases in order to express the exact
meaning of the French.

[43] This discussion should make clear the erroneous syncopation of Diderot's
thought which is expounded by Cassirer (*The Age of Enlightenment*, pp. 246–47).
Cassirer turns into an evolution what is a persistent dualism. The abstract command
of reason does not simply give way to a solely biological uniformity of inclinations,
instincts, and appetites. (The Cartesianism of the *philosophes* has been recognized
by Talmon in *The Rise of Totalitarian Democracy*, Boston, 1952, pp. 28–29, and by
others.) Cassirer does not seem to realize that the "natural law" of the *Rêve de
d'Alembert* is not a moral law. We shall return to this. It is correct to say that for
Diderot "no mere obligation can presume to annul or to alter fundamentally the
empirical nature of man." But Diderot's whole purpose, in this aspect of his
thought, is to prove the existence of obligation, by making it an essential part of
his empirical nature. Cassirer therefore fails to understand the real sense and character of Diderot's moral philosophy.

can observe this clearly in the work of two consistent mid-century materialists, d'Argens and La Mettrie.

In his *Songes philosophiques*,[44] d'Argens asserts that men should live "according to the laws of nature . . . the only ones that can make creatures fortunate and that can deprive them of nothing which belongs to their happiness." The language is guarded, but the implication clear. "All those [laws] made by certain men, who have pretended to rise above their sphere, are only unbearable bonds; but those of nature give only what is needed and forbid only what should be forbidden." One can scarcely doubt the import of these words. Men are denied the power or the right to rise above their physical or instinctual demands, except as those same demands may themselves dictate. Human laws are good, or valid, only insofar as they support those demands, invalid and onerous whenever they contradict them. A precise application of this principle is to be found, in more outspoken terms, in d'Argens' anonymous novel, *Thérèse philosophe*.[45] In this story—a most immoral testimonial to amoralism—Thérèse's confessor advises her to practice onanism to assuage her desires: "those are sexual needs (*"des besoins de tempérament"*) as natural as those of hunger and thirst. . . . Now, as we know that natural law is of divine provenance, how would we dare to fear to offend God by relieving our needs by means which he has given us . . . ?" There is no offense in any act, as long as the social order is not disturbed.

La Mettrie, with his usual logical consistency and unwillingness to halt halfway, came to see an effective discrepancy between determinism and a natural law of "ought." That is why in 1751 he added to his *Histoire naturelle de l'âme* (1745) this comment on Spinoza: "In Spinoza's system . . . good-bye to Natural Law, our natural principles are only customary principles! . . . According to Spinoza again, man is a true automaton, a machine subject to the most constant necessity. . . . The author of *L'Homme machine* seems to have written his book purposely to defend this sad truth." [46]

In 1747 in *L'Homme machine*, La Mettrie had emphasized his contention that there is no special natural law or way of being which puts man into a different category from beast. Both are

[44] Berlin, 1746, pp. 45–46.
[45] La Haye, s.d. [1748], pp. 70–71, 86.
[46] Quoted by A. Vartanian, *La Mettrie's L'Homme machine*, p. 48.

entirely subject to the determinism of natural laws, and these are
identical for all animals. To establish this contention, it was necessary to face the objection of a natural moral law perceptible only
to human rationality. As a positivist, La Mettrie's appeal is to experience. "There is, it is said, a Natural Law in man, a knowledge
of good and evil, which has not been engraved in the hearts of
animals. But is this objection, or rather, this assertion, founded
on experience, without which a philosopher may reject anything?" [47] Our only experience is a subjective one of remorse.
From outer signs we assume an identical experience in other
men. Since the behavior of gods and other animals give us similar
signs, we must again assume an identity of experience or feeling.
By this logical but simplistic reasoning, La Mettrie thus tries to
extend a natural law of "moral" reactions to animals.[48] He is on
firmer ground when he points out that men are capable of being
fiercer and more inhuman "than all the lions, tigers and bears."
This fact, moreover, would give weight to the opposite assumption: animals do not have a Natural Law, but neither do men.
"Man is not fashioned from a more precious clay; Nature has used
a single and same dough, in which she has varied only the leaven."

La Mettrie, however, prefers the first conclusion. Evidence
abounds that normal men must make distinctions between virtue
and vice, and approve or blame others. The distinction, it seems
to La Mettrie, is an easy one, being merely a matter of pleasure or
repugnance, which are the "natural effects" of virtue and vice.
And such a reaction belongs to animals as well as men, for it is
one of the "prerogatives of animality"! More even than a prerogative, it is indestructible like any law of nature. Even tigers have
their moments of remorse. La Mettrie has, of course, performed
a simple but fallacious reversal of what is, to begin with, a dubious
formula. The judgment of virtue is assumed to be one of pleasure,
that of vice, one of displeasure. By reversal, an experience of
pleasure or displeasure is assumed to contain a judgment of virtue
or vice. Nor does he stop to inquire whether the objects of pleasure
and of displeasure are identical or belong to entirely different
categories.

La Mettrie has degraded moral experience to the level of a

[47] *L'Homme machine,* ed. Solovine, p. 95 ff.
[48] We might also point out that he forgets what he himself has said about differences resulting from greater complexity of brain structure.

mechanical pleasure-pain reflex, like that of hunger or sex. This is essential to an understanding of his naturalistic, nonmoral definition of Natural Law—one which actually annuls any of the usual meanings of the phrase. "It is a feeling which teaches us what we should not do, because we would not want others to do it to us. Shall I dare add to this conventional idea that it seems to me that this feeling is only a kind of fear or fright, as salutary to the species as to the individual." By this process of reduction, La Mettrie takes what is doubtless one genetic factor of moral experience —the self-protective reaction—and makes of it the totality of that experience. Natural Law is therefore "only an intimate feeling which again belongs to the imagination. . . . Consequently, it evidently presupposes neither education, nor revelation, nor legislation. . . ." There is nothing *moral* in La Mettrie's definition of Natural Law. It is not an innate idea nor an acquired idea, but an innate affective reaction. We shall shortly see that for d'Alembert the idea of right originates in oppression by power, as an innate reaction. For d'Alembert, however, there is a leap from power to the ought; an idea of right is immediately implied. In La Mettrie there is only a doctrine of prudence—fear of retaliation, fear of remorse.[49] Ultimately, the Natural Law concept is an impossible contradiction for La Mettrie. It unites two different and opposing realms of being: nature and moral-social conduct. Nature refers to the physical, and in this realm we can indeed speak of truths. Culture, however, is the domain of human action, and here we can speak only of the useful. Morality is an invention of man, of culture.

In England, meanwhile, Hume (*Treatise of Human Nature*, 1739–40) was subverting the whole edifice of Natural Law "by questioning the epistemological validity of rational self-evidence in this field," in an analysis which was to provide the basis for nineteenth-century positivistic thought.[50] By analyzing the opera-

[49] In his *Anti-Sénèque, ou Discours sur le bonheur* (1748), La Mettrie reduces Natural Law to ideas received in childhood (*Oeuvres philosophiques*, Amsterdam, 1774, II, p. 177). "People think they do great honor to nature by trying to ornament it with a supposed law, born with it, as with so many other acquired ideas. It is not the dupe of that honor . . . a well organized soul disdains everything attributed to it over and above what really belongs to it. . . ." In his *Discours préliminaire* (1751), he affirms that the principle stated in his definition of Natural Law "is rarely natural"; it comes from fear or self-love (*Oeuvres*, Berlin, 1764, I, p. 36).

[50] Sampson, *Progress in the Age of Reason*, pp. 149–50. The ensuing discussion follows in part Sampson's excellent analysis.

tions of reason in the formulation of ethical beliefs, Hume sought
to destroy the possibility of universal moral truths intuited by
right reason. Causal relationships and value statements are not
provable by the operations of reason, nor do they result therefrom.
They are only "conventions," or convictions of "common sense,"
which are inescapable, useful, and customary, and so seem rationally valid. They imply more regularity than is certain. They are
not necessary since "the contrary could always be assumed." [51]
While common sense makes us think that acts are in themselves
right or wrong, Hume, like Spinoza and other naturalists, considers all such qualifications to be the expression of subjective approval and disapproval which are unverifiable expressions of
taste.[52] Consequently ethical terms are deemed by Hume to have
no abstract or universal validity. They must be defined as psychological and emotional phenomena, as responses to their assumed
consequences in terms of our desires and aversions (which may
include benevolence, as well as egoistic pleasure and pain).[53] Right
and wrong, however, are not merely individual subjective prefer-
ences. They can be distinguished, but only empirically, by inves-
tigating the reactions of the majority of men to establish which
actions do in fact evoke approval or disapproval. In this way
Hume intends to introduce the experimental method into morals.

The result of Hume's analysis is to confer a "divine right" upon
the majority. It is also to eliminate any meaningful distinction
of "ought" and "is." Might may become right, the degradation of
men in such institutions as slavery may become legitimate, and
mankind is condemned to be the prisoner of its given cultural
moment. Such thinking leads to a nihilism of social arbitrariness
or tyranny. Since the whole problem in morals is to determine
what actions give "to a spectator the pleasing sentiment of approbation," [54] Hume does not so much "overcome the conflict between
the *is* and the *ought*," as Sampson says, as he eliminates any true

[51] Sabine, *op. cit.*, p. 601. This statement is not certain, nor empirically verifiable!
Can one imagine a society based on a law of returning evil for good, or a law of
deliberate deception and breaking of contracts, on doing hurt to other persons?

[52] See *An Enquiry Concerning Human Understanding*, in *The English Philosophers
from Bacon to Mill*, ed. E. A. Burtt, New York, 1939, p. 689.

[53] Sampson points out that Hume's hedonism is benevolent rather than egoistic.
It is true that he does not fall into the simplified view of human nature characteristic of French hedonism. On the other hand, the French went beyond him in their
analysis of evil in human nature. "Absolute, unprovoked, disinterested malice,"
writes Hume, "has never, perhaps, place in any human breast. . . ." (p. 150).

[54] *Treatise on Human Nature*, quoted by Sampson, *op. cit.*, p. 152.

significance of the latter term, since it can indicate only conformity to what *is*, reason being powerless to generate or to justify values.[55]

Hume effectively unseats reason as "the arbiter and authority for our ethical knowledge." [56] Reason, by calculating results, can adjust means and ends, but it cannot determine the ends we should follow, and only our emotional constitution may (or may not) determine us to follow ends that are benevolent rather than malevolent. Here, as elsewhere, one of the weaknesses of Hume's analysis is its restrictive definition of reason, one which narrowly confines its operative function to the determination of fact rather than of value, and to analytical deduction of a mathematical type. The result is to exclude judgment from the sphere of norms, leaving moral beliefs "at the mercy of caprice, impulse, prejudice or habit." [57]

"The periods of greatest concern with questions of natural law," writes Georges Gurvitch, "have coincided with critical epochs in which the established order has been beset by new currents of thought and new social aspirations." [58] The importance of the controversy over theories of Natural Law was recognized by contemporaries. Hume warns his readers that he will not enter a

[55] *Ibid.* "Where a passion is neither founded on false suppositions, nor chooses means insufficient for the end, the understanding can neither justify nor condemn it. It is not contrary to reason to prefer the destruction of the whole world to the scratching of my finger."

[56] *Ibid.*

[57] *Ibid.*, p. 154. Moreover, Hume's argument that in moral enquiry you must ultimately reach a final end-in-itself, desirable on its own account with no possibility of rational justification outside of human sentiments evades the real moral issues of choice which confront us. Is it certain that reason is impotent to bring wants and sentiments under rational control, through judgment on conflicting wants in terms of causes and effects? This process is the transformation of wants into values, which Hume mistakenly identifies with satisfaction or enjoyment. Reason goes beyond desirability (already given in the term "desire") and enables us to judge whether a desire, or a propensity, is worthy of becoming a value, or the determining motive of our behavior. Hume has underestimated both the cognitive and the empirical functions of reason. In the broadened view of empiricism in our own day, experience and reason are not held to be necessarily separate. "Reason is itself empirical when it observes and respects experience and weaves it into some coherent meaning." (V. Ferm, "Varieties of Naturalism," p. 439.) We should also note Adam Ferguson's criticism of Hume. A moral judgment, he contends, is an act of a peculiar nature. Not a mere desire or aversion, it is rather "a censorial act in the mind of man, having cognizance of a *right* or a *wrong* in the measure or tendency of his own desires or aversions even when they have most entirely determined his will." (*Principles of Moral and Political Science*, Edinburgh, 1792, II, p. 116.) Ferguson, like Kant, notes the transcendent character of reason. He also places the locus of moral approbation in good will, not in utility or sympathy (pp. 119–26).

[58] "Natural Law," p. 285.

polemic, "which of late years has so much excited the curiosity of the publick, whether these moral distinctions be founded on natural and original principles, or arise from interest and education." [59] Natural Law, in one of its forms or another, was one of the principal recourses of those who felt the need to reaffirm and to secure the validity of moral distinctions by methods outside the arbitrariness of Revelation. For this reason it was accepted on both sides, by orthodox and by freethinkers. The former, as we have seen, were somewhat worried by the latter's claim for the sufficiency of Natural Law. Deists, on the other hand, embraced the doctrine in order to ward off both Christians and amoralists. The extremists, on both sides again, rejected Natural Law (in any of its shapes); these included Jansenists, convinced of the total corruption of nature, and atheistic nihilists, who shared a similar conviction.

Doubtless one of the reasons why many deists, like Voltaire, did not drift into atheism was the support for moral values provided by God's existence. The traditional Natural Law doctrine was built on that belief. It implied a universe which included the "ought" as a phenomenon natural to any rational being. It was far more secure—provided the original premise was accepted—than the modern versions, grounded solely in nature. The function of traditional Natural Law "was no less than to provide the original and fundamental premise from which the central tradition of European values was derived." [60] With the scientific revolution and its mechanistic explanation of the world, God was no longer needed to explain natural phenomena, and no longer was he narrated to all eyes by the glories of the heavens; but he was still needed as the source and protector of ethical values. Natural Law kept the command and the certainty of God, yet removed him from the universe and its day-to-day functioning; it made of him a remote Creator and law-giver rather than an immanent force. The moral command of the Natural Law was contained in the nature of things, as created by God's will and reason, before the birth of human will or law. It placed the origin of moral obligation outside of an autonomous experience, in which the creativity of the individual or the species would be controlling. It was conducive to the dependence of the individual, and thus to harmony. The

---

[59] *Treatise of Human Nature*, Bk. II, Sect. VII.
[60] Sampson, *op. cit.*, p. 143.

universal took precedence over the particular, and reason over nature, but *in the name of* nature. An act of discovery, by reason in its intuitive aspect, revealed certain relationships in which a proper course of action inheres objectively. The advantage of Natural Law was thus to take morals outside of human will and constructive reason, to give them a cosmic status, a certainty, indisputable, eternal, readily known. This advantage the naturalistic versions weakened or destroyed, by placing law within man, like will itself, though objectivity was still sought.

Natural Law required, then, an assumption of a universal human nature and rationality. If there were only particulars of individual experience, there could be no laws governing human phenomena, especially conduct. To the partisan of this view, it seemed clear enough that to say there is only positive law is to make the latter entirely arbitrary and devoid of a necessary validity from a universal viewpoint. One might even go further and challenge its validity in a given local situation, argue that since it is arbitrary, it cannot compel respect and thus drift into nihilism.

The doctrine of Natural Law is one of man's great attempts to unite reason and nature by making moral judgments natural. This is clearly expressed in Raynal's summary of Confucianism: "His code is only Natural Law. . . . Reason, says Confucius, is an emanation of Divinity; the supreme law is only the accord of nature and reason. . . ."[61] But while Natural Law reconciles nature with reason, in the sense of intuitive moral judgments (and thus, indirectly, reconciles nature with the requirements of culture), it definitely separates the moral and the physical world by its selective definition of nature. It corresponds to the rest of nature only in the sense that the principles of both, originating in God's mind, are rational. For human beings, to be "natural" is to be moral. On the other hand, Natural Law did not pretend to make angels out of men. It did not refuse properly controlled physical satisfactions. It recognized legitimate (nonharmful) egoistic needs, such as the acquisitive impulse. Its legitimation of property was a defense of natural instinct as opposed to rationally conceived anti-property-right ideas. We again see that Natural Law serves to unite nature with reason, though on a selective basis for both terms, one which its opponents could denounce as arbitrary.

On the other hand, Natural Law had various weaknesses and

[61] Quoted by H. Wolpe, *Raynal et sa machine de guerre*, Stanford, 1957, pp. 121–22.

shortcomings, as a support for the moral life. Some of these took on importance for men of the eighteenth century especially, others had always been obvious. The sanctions and penalties for infraction were vague and remote—reputation or reciprocal treatment; they acquired somewhat more force, if no more immediacy, for the Christian. At all events, few were so optimistic as to believe that the added support of religion or of institutions of the State was not necessary. We may say, in other words, that Hobbes's and Pascal's analysis of law was a realistic appraisal. Natural Law did not contain sufficient motivating or coercive force. Bayle, Montesquieu, Rousseau, and others recognized the difference between goodness and virtue. Many who believed that men were moral beings, in the sense of having natural knowledge of moral distinctions, admitted that passions and self-interest are the more powerful and more usual motivating forces.

The word "natural," in traditional Natural Law and in other applications, was often corrupted. It was likely to signify, in actuality, the civilized rather than the original or primitive.[62] It could, on one interpretation, become conducive to conservatism and resistance to change. Rousseau was aware of both these characteristics when he attacked Natural Law and the usual concept of the state of nature. These transformations of meaning resulted from another characteristic trait. One might venture to say that the strength (as well as the weakness) of Natural Law lay in its vagueness. The result of this vagueness was precisely what we have indicated—to tend to make Natural Law the simple equivalent of the moral conscience or level of a given cultural complex—despite its supposed absoluteness. What, indeed, was the content of Natural Law? Sanctity of word and contract, and of life, the law of reciprocity, the preference of justice and beneficence over excessive egoism (or the right to pursue one's own good provided there was no trespass of the right of others), the right to property or the fruits of one's labor. Clearly, several of these are variables. While Natural Law sets up an ostensibly objective "ought" besides the objective "is," it tended, in practice, to merge the prescriptive with the descriptive, and to define the "ought" in terms of the "is." An outstanding example of this was the doctrine of Blackstone and Burke, who tried to arrive at Natural Law through a study of history and of present institutions.[63] A principal ground for the

[62] See B. Willey, *The Eighteenth Century Background*, London, 1953, p. 20.
[63] See D. J. Boorstin, *op. cit.*, pp. 59–61.

opposition of many *philosophes* to Montesquieu was that he found his "laws" of what ought to be and what had to be in what "was." This is one reason why a new absolute version of "natural rights" arose, and why conservative writers attacked the latter and preferred the former. Traditional Natural Law was a conservatism, and modern Natural Law a reform movement in which law "ceases to be mainly a regulating principle, and becomes mainly a liberating principle." [64]

Our reference to criticism of Montesquieu involves a related cause for hostility to traditional Natural Law. While cosmic status was a support for moral values, in the minds of some men, like Rousseau, it was a limit as well. It also ran counter to the most advanced trends of scientific thought. It postulated a finalism and Providentialism which see to it that a man gets what he needs to be a man. It assumes that what we are was given to us from the outside, not developed by the dynamism of the organism itself seeking a *modus vivendi* with its natural context.[65] In both senses, natural and willful, man's power to construct his own world was limited. The modern Natural Law theories, as we can already observe in Locke's "revolutionary" version, have confidence in man's creative capacity and consider it a sign of human nobility. They do not merely accept nature, but consciously seek to modify it. They insist on the antithesis of nature and art, or culture.[66]

The human dynamism which thus forms one aspect of opposition has a wider bearing. The naturalistic, or biological view of life is directly connected with the ultimate ambivalence of the word "natural," which we have already touched on, and which is the core of weakness in Natural Law. By particularizing among all the meanings of that word, and only by so doing, Natural Law makes it possible to apply the attribute "unnatural" to acts, with both descriptive and prescriptive connotations. By its selection of a rational-moral sphere of human experience, it delegates that sphere to be the defining, therefore the prescriptive or law-making meaning of "natural" for man. The naturalist was aware, even in the eighteenth century, that there are other laws of nature, that

[64] Willey, *op. cit.*, p. 16.

[65] Eighteenth century transformism replaced externally imposed finalities with inherent, organic, natural finalities. Natural Law theory conflicts as well with Darwinian forms of evolutionism, which replace organic finalism with "chance" or "random variations" whose effects are perhaps equally mysterious and magic.

[66] See Strauss, *op. cit.*, p. 248; L. I. Bredvold, "The Meaning of the Concept of Right Reason . . ."; H. V. S. Ogden, "The Antithesis of Nature and Art. . . ."

the most perfect point of impartiality and disinterestedness in human reason "remains in organic relation to a particular center of life, individual or collective, seeking to maintain its precarious existence against competing forms of life and vitality." [67] Man's nature and reason, or natural reason, cannot escape this situation, if they are to function. They are ambivalent: reason is more than an instrument of self-interest, but it can never be entirely dissociated from it; it can be an instrument of justice, but not a pure instrument of justice. It is a deceptive short cut to conclude that because man is endowed by nature with reason, life in accord with reason is life in accord with nature—just as it is to reverse the proposition, as the nihilist does.[68] On the other hand, if nature is to be our criterion, and if we are immersed in nature, why do we need rules to prevent deviations from nature when it is impossible for action to deviate from nature? Is slavery, for instance, natural? It is opposed to moral Natural Law, but Aristotle thought it was natural, and so it is.[69] To critics of the *philosophes,* the confusion was obvious. Sabatier de Castres taxed them with being ridiculous when they qualified as *"loi naturelle,* as *religion naturelle,* what is most opposed to nature and its demands." [70]

The idea that rational will must transcend given nature becomes more important as the great countercurrent to Natural Law first takes shape and then swells almost unchecked in the second half of the century. This counterforce was utilitarianism. In regard to theoretical ethics, the utilitarians urged, "be good so that you will be happy," whereas Natural Law said, "if you are good, as you should, you will also be happy." In practice, there was inextricable confusion between the two viewpoints and the distinction tended to fade into the utilitarian perspective, especially in the "modern" or "naturalist" theories of Natural Law. But there were other points of opposition. As Natural Law involves the transcendence of an intuitive rational nature over irrational nature

---

[67] R. Niebuhr, *Children of Light and Children of Darkness,* New York, 1949, p. 71.

[68] According to Franz Neumann, Natural Law theories "destroy the unity of the whole of human relationships; they arbitrarily elevate one aspect of human nature, one impulse, one drive, to the rank of the absolute, and deduce from it a whole set of postulates for the ordering of human society." (*Op. cit.,* p. 71.) On the other hand, we must not forget Kant's view that this aspect is the ordering function in human nature, the aspect which is naturally able to give a law to the whole; however it is not the only kind of "natural law" we find operative in man.

[69] Freedom and equality were made parts of Natural Law by canon lawyers, but *ius gentium* and positive law legitimized slavery.

[70] *Lettres critiques, morales et politiques,* F~furt, 1802, pp. 88–89.

(the superego over the id), so does utilitarianism assert the supremacy of analytic reason over intuitive reason. Nevertheless, the basis of utilitarianism, before it reaches the stage of social judgment and social planning, is a natural instinct, one associated precisely with that aspect of irrational nature which Natural Law is supposed to check and to confine within the limits of its disciplinary rule. "I shall prove," declares Helvétius, "that in all times, in all places, in regard both to morals and to intellect, it is personal interest which dictates the judgment of individuals, and general interest that of nations." [71] To utilitarians, it seemed that the compass of a Natural Law or a natural government was too circumscribed and would produce a static society, when nature itself was process and change, which human will could channel into what was called progress. They did not mean, however, that nature was to be ignored or disregarded, but rather that it was to be known and used, that the social machine was to be reduced "to a few easily controllable forces." [72] Paradoxically, in the systems of certain utopian writers like Morelly and Rousseau, the goal was a relatively static pattern of social institutions.

Natural Law was thus opposed to the idealistic hopes of many in the second half of the eighteenth century. It was also opposed to the growing positivistic spirit. In those later years it was not only the other meanings of "nature" which came increasingly to be noted, but also the relativism of facts. Both history and travellers' accounts brought home that variability of conscience which Montaigne, Locke, and Bayle, as well as countless travel books, had already asserted, but which now acquired renewed force. What was right and wrong for modern European civilization had not always been so for ancient peoples, nor was it presently for the primitives of the island of Bougainville. Facts did not seem to tally with the idea of Natural Law, or the voice of God speaking through the conscience. In the third section of *Le Rêve de d'Alembert,* for instance, Diderot challenges the idea that there is such a thing as normal or natural human sexual behavior. Natural Law was particularly alien to the rising spirit of historicism which remained, however, in a subordinate position. The historical outlook on the march of human affairs is either cyclical or dialectical. There is no absolute pattern of social organization which corre-

[71] *De l'Esprit,* p. 47.
[72] G. Chinard, introduction to Morelly, *Code de la nature,* p. 97.

sponds to an absolute nature or right. From the absolutist viewpoint of Natural Law, the past has been a series of errors and crimes. Pessimists might conclude that this would always be so, and traditional Natural Law did not encourage reform. Paradoxically, however, optimistic political thinkers were often opposed to historicism, though not to the idea of progress in history. Optimists of a certain kind hoped to utilize natural laws in willful rational patterns to reach a new and sometimes static state. History would have to be disregarded and by-passed, and a rational pattern imposed. Partisans of modern Natural Law theories, with their emphasis on natural rights, political conservatives like the Physiocrats, or pure utilitarians like Helvétius, all were impervious to historicism, all believed, in contrast with their avowed empiricism, in a natural or rational order that was the basis of a perfect society. Montesquieu, Voltaire, Turgot, and Condorcet, on the other hand, did possess the historical viewpoint. Since their attitudes to Natural Law were not identical, we must conclude that although Natural Law is in essence superhistorical and anti-relativistic, the question of historicism is a broader one which involved other political and intellectual attitudes. Moreover, to be paradoxical again, traditional Natural Law was in a sense more historical than the modern, since it held that natural rights (however weakly and vaguely it conceived of them) can be conceptualized and realized only in a given historical context and are relative to particular situations. It led to that historicism, to which Burke came perilously close and into which Blackstone fell, according to which "things are right either simply because they already exist, or because they occupy a certain place in the process of historical development." [73] Thus Natural Law could be either anti-historical or excessively historical, according as one chose to interpret it.

What is spoken of as modern (or by some, revolutionary) Natural Law is a loose conglomeration of theories which were a partial response to the shifting tide from a priori thinking to empiricism and experience. We must take special care to distinguish those theories which stem from Grotius, Pufendorf, and Locke, and which are, after all, a "heretical" offshoot or variation of the traditional doctrine from the naturalistic theories discussed in this chapter. To be sure, they have much in common. But the

[73] H. D. Aiken, introduction to *Hume's Moral and Political Philosophy*, New York, 1948, p. xlii.

naturalistic views have Hobbes as their true ancestor. They considered men to be ruled not "by an abstract command of reason but by the uniformity of their inclinations, instincts and appetites. It is here that we must look for the true organic unity of man. . . ." [74] As the empiricists viewed it, the same faculties and tendencies everywhere develop according to the same laws, and reason progresses toward the same level. Different ways of thinking and feeling are only accidents due to external factors. The general laws of life apply to man as to other species; he too is essentially the faculty of feeling and desiring.[75]

Such naturalistic theories made happiness the motivating force of duty, rather than its result. There was no question, however, of giving free rein to nature. Moral law, it seemed indubitable, inheres in the objective natural and social relations of rational beings. As Spinoza had written, "a law which depends on natural necessity is one which necessarily follows from the natural, or from the definition of the thing in question." [76] If man is endowed with a fundamental nature which determines necessary tendencies, moral distinctions and laws are among these tendencies and, as a regulatory agency, are related to their fulfillment. That is to say, the natural tendencies toward the welfare of society and of the individual require and clearly indicate the necessary restrictions and sacrifices. Natural Law, then, is man's natural law which can supersede "the law of nature." In other words, while utility might be held to be the basis of moral law, it was also accepted that there are universal and unvarying factors in utility. The two notions were not deemed to be basically exclusive. The moral judgment, it seemed, though developed by education and culture, is not—despite sensationist psychology—enslaved to them. No Leviathan

---

[74] Cassirer, *op. cit.*, p. 246.

[75] We can do no better than repeat R. R. Palmer's formulation:
"The *philosophes* could not feel law as an obligation imposed from on high. They were deferential, indeed, to nature and the natural law, but they included themselves in nature, and thought that the natural law legitimized the empirical facts of their existence, their needs, wishes, impulses, and capacities for enjoyment. Law, natural or divine, was not for them a rule to which men must force themselves; it was a cosmic authorization for them to do what gave them happiness in the world. It was a charter of liberty, under which men as individuals need observe only the rights of each other, and men as a whole, free from obligations not fixed by themselves, had the right to master the world and do with it as they pleased, and to make such changes in their government and society as they might suppose would be useful to these ends." (*Op. cit.*, pp. 204-5.)

[76] *Tractatus theologico-politicus*, in *The Chief Works of Benedict de Spinoza*, London, 1909, I, p. 57.

or totalitarian state can define justice in such a way as to extirpate it. That is why these utilitarian theorists were believers in unalienable natural rights. Moreover, whereas traditional Natural Law, lacking a rigorous determinism, was unable to satisfy a scientific concept of law, the newer theories contained more objective (and, some pretended, quantitatively formulable) elements. One major difficulty, however, is that these natural rights were rooted in the presocial state of nature, whereas the "ought" involved in Natural Law pertained, in good part, to the relations of society. Nevertheless, for the adherent of this type of theory, any attack on Natural Law "resulting in a weakening of belief in the self-evidence of rights grounded on Natural Law would necessarily leave a wide hiatus concerning the fundamental status of moral and political values." [77]

Christian apologists were aware of the dangerous connotations of the newer theories; yet, as so often happened, they absorbed some of the novelties in the very effort to blunt their force. The ideas of Hobbes and Grotius were not utterly without impact. An objective right is conceived of, independent of God's will. Self-interest and utility infiltrate into all corners. And a desperate note is sounded in the oft-repeated claim that we must accept God and Natural Law or remain with nothing—nothing, that is, but might and success.

In the wider view of Natural Law, there still remained an unresolved problem of attributes. Is Natural Law natural, considering its denial of powerful instincts and drives? Is it rational when it denies constructive reason in favor of intuitive reason? Is it teleological when it asserts a formalism opposed to the utilitarian, while claiming to be designed for human good and human needs? The intuitionist, moreover, goes beyond subjective feeling, despite his insistence on the immediate nature of the moral experience. He asserts that this experience provides knowledge, and so removes the arbitrary from the subjective immediate experience. To justify this viewpoint, however, a supporting metaphysic becomes necessary, one that can establish values as self-existent essences. Only supernaturalism could provide one, and supernaturalism, precisely, was waging a losing battle in the course of Western cultural history. The eighteenth century was moving in various directions that were bound eventually to weaken Natural Law. It moved

[77] Sampson, *op. cit.*, p. 144.

toward the emotional, toward systematic rationalism, radical naturalism, dogmatic utilitarianism. Scientific positivism, the development of relativism and historicism, the all-pervasiveness of the happiness criterion, all undermined traditional Natural Law. The influence of political reconstructionists, culminating in Rousseau, with their inquiries into the requirements of society, the demand for political and civil rights, fostered most of all by the American Revolution and the spirit of 1776, were powerful forces working in the same direction. Very deeply, there was a cleavage between the belief in culture's struggle for enlightenment and the belief in a natural moral rationality or in conscience the voice of God, which did not stem from culture and perhaps made its efforts supererogatory. Traditional Natural Law was too intimately associated with the crumbling metaphysical and social structure of the Old Regime not to be involved in its downfall.

Natural Law theories of one type or another were nevertheless one of the two great efforts of the moderate group to protect moral values, to ground them in objective truth, to unite nature and reason in the service of culture. This they did by accepting as "natural" the impulses and emotions that are harmonious with culture. By selecting as ultimate criterion that aspect of nature which is involved in reason, they were able to assert the validity of the moral and social imperatives by which culture denies the claims of other natural instincts that are inimical to its survival. Duty, they maintained, was not merely a general obligation to use discretion in the pursuit of personal good. There are rules, fixed in our nature, that give structure to our conduct and qualify some ways of reaching our ends as definitely right or wrong. This statement applies to all but the most radical of the empiricists. The empiricists ridiculed innatism; but the belief, to which most clung, in a human nature and in some universal moral laws and judgments was really another way of eating the same cake.[78] The "experimental" (experiential) was for them, in the final analysis, only an efficient cause of a predetermined end. Their supposed inductions from experience were most often rational constructs. The result was in many ways substantially the same, if formally different. They knew that pure ethical relativism would neces-

---

[78] For modern confirmation of universals, by an empiricist, see E. Westermarck, *The Origin and Development of the Moral Ideas*, London, 1917, II, pp. 742–44, and *An Age of Crisis*, pp. 196–98.

sarily result from a moral life entirely formed and determined by local experience, and that experience itself belies such a complete relativism.[79] Thus Maupertuis, for instance, criticizes Montesquieu for asserting that equity is the ultimate basis of law, instead of the principle of greatest happiness; but he admits that the two principles produce the same basic legislation.[80]

The strength of Natural Law was in its correspondence to common sense. The restrictive power of culture and its laws—it is generally felt—would be arbitrary were it not informed by a general principle of justice definitive of the right order of life in a human community. All societies, it is felt, have some notions of justice beyond their laws, which laws must embody under penalty of condemnation by the conscience of the just. Basically, Natural Law asserted that moral obligation must arise from the freedom and responsibility of a moral being to act in accord with his own nature.[81]

[79] "The *philosophes* obtained the advantages of theology by appealing to an absolute humanity." A primary virtue was benevolence. "The *philosophes* somewhat altered the idea, making it not a commandment but an inclination, and teaching . . . that men in particular *should* be humane because men in general *were* humane, thus keeping up the appearance of deducing values from facts, and duties from actual behavior" [more exactly, from what we actually approved]. (R. R. Palmer, *op. cit.*, pp. 191–92.)

[80] *Eloge de Montesquieu, Oeuvres*, III, pp. 404–8.

[81] The powerful revival of Natural Law theories, especially since World War I, is a phenomenon of more than passing interest to the student of intellecual history. While on the one hand, traditional theories are reasserted in the course of the so-called "Catholic Renascence," naturalistic theories have been revised in the light of recent psychological, anthropological and juridical thought. One noteworthy example of the latter (among others) is the theory of F. S. C. Northrop, as expounded in his article, "Ethical Relativism in the Light of Recent Legal Science" (*Journal of Philosophy* 52:649–62, 1955).

Two

MORAL SENSE THEORIES

THERE WAS ONE RIVAL to Natural Law theories for the allegiance of those who believed that moral experience was the immediate result of innate endowment rather than the mediated lesson of culture. The distinctive characteristic of moral sense theory was its removal of moral judgment from the province of intellect, and its attribution to an inner sentiment or feeling which is primary and therefore not subject to analysis or logical disproof. The advantages and disadvantages of such a theory are obvious. By attempting an epistemology which gave to moral judgments the same empirical origin as other sensual perceptions, its proponents sought to establish their status as knowledge, on the same basis as Locke's simple ideas, and in defiance of Locke's own explanation of those judgments. As post-Lockeans, the moral sense school abjures innate ideas, but substitutes an innate source of ideas. The adjectives "immediate" and "natural" and the noun "perceptions" become effective guarantees, more universal and secure than the whims and convolutions of intellectual judgment. On the other hand, the physical existence of such a sense and its proper organ were points of weakness easily seized upon by its enemies, who could also allege the varieties of moral judgments as the very empirical confirmation of the intellectualism and relativism which it denied. One might also justifiably inquire how an instinct becomes a voluntary activity influenced by principle, and whether, if this cannot be established, instinct by itself merits the qualification of "ethical."

Although in some writers moral sense forms a crystalline theory, at times it becomes obscured by tinctures of other doctrines. Its

75

pure form postulates only the perception of the moral quality inhering in particular acts, arousing the innate moral feelings. Yet
sometimes we see it shading off into the intuition of principles
and axioms, which are really judgments self-evident to reason. On
the other hand, while the theory was nonrational rather than
positively anti-rational since it concluded that there are a priori
eternal truths, with some French writers it became transformed
into the romantic attitude that feeling or "heart" can alone perceive moral truth. Elsewhere it became clouded by fusion with an
aesthetic theory of beauty. Thus we have Shaftesbury's and Hutcheson's identification of the good, the true, and the beautiful,
which enjoyed considerable vogue in France. A good act, or life,
and a beautiful one were interchangeable expressions. Virtue is
a proportion of internal affections and a relation of these to the
rest of the universe. This synthesis is found in Crousaz's *Traité
du beau* (1725), the abbé Batteux's *Les Beaux Arts réduits à un
seul principe* (1746), and Duclos' *Considérations sur le goût* (date
uncertain).

Still another apparent deviation—a far more heretical one—
was due to John Gay's notion of association, later developed systematically by David Hartley. It is necessary, writes Gay, "in order
to solve the principal Actions of human life, to suppose a *Moral
Sense* . . . and also public Affections; but I deny that this Moral
Sense, or these public Affections, are innate, or implanted in us:
they are acquired either from our own *Observation* or the *Imita-
tion of* others." [1] And Hartley will declare the moral sense to be
"factitious," acquired through the association of pleasurable sensations with certain objects.[2] Here, however, the "deviation" is
only apparent. What we are really witnessing is an entirely alien
theory which has appropriated or misappropriated the title and
attributed a different meaning to it. Gay and Hartley belong in
our next chapter.

The moral sense theory rose and flourished in England, where
it owed a particular debt, despite its rejection of rationalism, to
the school of Cambridge Platonists. It was not indigenous to
France. Toward the end of the seventeenth century, a French
writer who lived in England, Saint-Evremond, asserted that real

---

[1] *Dissertation Concerning the Fundamental Principles of Virtue or Morality*,
quoted by B. Willey, *The Eighteenth Century Background*, London, 1953, p. 140.
[2] *Ibid.*, p. 143.

honnêtes gens do not need moral lessons. "They know the right by the sole finesse of their taste, and are spontaneously carried to it." [3] But this, like others, is a passing reference and is qualified by limitation to "honnêtes gens" and to situations not having great complexity. The first of these limitations is, indeed, a crucial one, since it leads as easily to the materialistic theory of being "fortunately born" or "unfortunately born."

The formulation of the moral sense theory and its influence in France are due largely to Shaftesbury. The metaphysical basis of his doctrine is the Platonic postulate that goodness is immutable and eternal, a necessary factor of the order of things, which neither divine nor human legislation can alter. But the English moral sense school breaks completely with the Cambridge school in an essential respect: In the atmosphere of British empiricism the metaphysical essence becomes an actual part of nature, an empirical, affective experience rather than an a priori revelation. What is then needed is a sure mechanism to perceive it. With this we are endowed, since we possess a "natural and just sense of right and wrong"—although this sense can be corrupted by custom and superstition. [4] We have a kind of instinct which belongs to the mind itself. [5]

While the moral sense does not depend on the processes of reasoning, it is found only in rational beings. In these, it exists necessarily, and in absolute form. The recognition is "an immediate feeling and finer internal sense." [6] Shaftesbury's theory actually involves a sublimation of reason itself, to make it *natural*, absolute, part of the universal, divine harmony. Ethics is cemented to nature, and nature to the universal harmony—which man is meant to experience in himself, just as God expresses himself in the spiritual being of man.

Not long after Shaftesbury, Hutcheson also linked the good and the beautiful in *An Inquiry into the Original of our Ideas of Beauty and Virtue* (1725). He announces his desire to prove that by a moral sense some actions are immediately found to be good; that we approve of them, in ourselves or in others, without any

---

[3] *Oeuvres mêlées,* Amsterdam, 1706, III, p. 113.
[4] *Characteristiks,* II, pp. 40, 46 (*An Inquiry Concerning Virtue*).
[5] *Ibid.,* II, pp. 28–30.
[6] B. Willey, *op. cit.,* p. 58. "Babbitt has signalized him as the precursor of the 'Rousseauist' moralists who transform the conscience from an inner check into an expansive emotion."

view of advantage from them; and that it is not an intuition of pleasure which gains approbation, nor "any other natural good, which may be the consequence of virtuous action; but an entirely different principle of action from self-love, or desire of private good." [7] Benevolence, he argues further, excites our approbation, and we feel differently toward a person who benefits us out of his own self-interest than toward one who does it for love of us. Therefore we have other perceptions of moral actions than those of advantage. "And that power of receiving these perceptions may be called a moral sense. . . ." [8] Contrary to Hume, Hutcheson maintains that the sensation of pleasure could never produce the desire for public good, or approval of an action, in life or in literature, which promotes the happiness of others. Is it because we project ourselves? Perhaps; but if we had no sense of the moral good in virtues, our sense of natural good (self-love) would "engage us always to the victorious side, and make us admire and love the successful tyrant, or traitor." An heir would admire the parsimony of a miser rather than his generosity to a friend. God has given us the moral sense "so that while we are only intending the good of others, we undesignedly promote our own greatest private good." [9] Hutcheson thus reaches a conclusion which is opposite to that of Mandeville (whom he is particularly desirous of refuting), of Hume, and of the later French materialists.

Hume's moral philosophy is far more complex and involves a number of disparate elements. In some ways he belongs with this group. His theory is predicated on an instinctual feeling in all men of benevolence or humanity, which he terms sympathy. This is an other-regarding, nonegoistic sentiment, whose origin and strength, however, come out of the association of observed behavior with our own experience.[10] For Hume man is "preeminently a social being," comments H. D. Aiken, "not in the

[7] Third edition, London, 1729, p. 109.

[8] *Ibid.*, p. 112.

[9] *Ibid.*, p. 128. Unlike Hume, Hutcheson claims that another's pleasure is indifferent to us. But our apprehension of another's virtuous acts "raises sentiments of Approbation, Esteem, or Admiration, and the affection of good-will towards him." (According to the analysis of the pessimists, cynics and nihilists, observing another's joy would give rise to jealousy and ill-will.) Hutcheson seems to fall into some confusion later, when he posits benevolence as the foundation of moral sense, defines it as "usefulness to the public," and adds that it is for reason to determine what is really useful to the public (pp. 199–207).

[10] *Treatise of Human Nature* (1739), in *Hume's Moral and Political Philosophy.* Edited with an Introduction by H. D. Aiken, New York, 1948, p. 132 ff.

sense of being altruistic or in the sense that the fulfillment of his wants requires the aid of others, but in the more important sense that whatever others do, their joys and sorrows, loves and hates, have an immediate and continuous impact upon our own sentiments. It is this capacity for reciprocity of feeling which renders possible a common moral life." [11] Hume also relates the "sense of beauty" with our "sentiments of morals." [12] In these regards, then, we may speak of a kinship with the moral sense school. Yet Hume distinctly disassociates himself from that group on the major premise. The feeling of moral approbation is not the perception of a moral truth, since only reason can conceive of truth. Moral judgments are not the same thing for him as the instinctive emotion of moral approval or disapproval, but this feeling, which is one of pleasure or displeasure, makes them possible. Before Rousseau, Hume sketches the idea of "the other" as spectator, determining our reactions (and our opinions); though he doubles it with a reverse projection.[13] But he never holds moral values to be grounded objectively in reality, in a "natural order of things," or in "eternal rules of reason." He demands, instead, a naturalistic theory, related to experience and to the passions (by which he means appetites, desires, emotions).

Hume's theory, moreover, reserves a large sphere of moral experience for what we may call culture, as opposed to nature. If "natural" be interpreted as opposed to supernatural, he explains, both vice and virtue are natural. If it be taken to mean what is usual, then great virtue is as little natural as great brutality. If it be what is opposed to the artificial, then "both vice and virtue are equally artificial and out of nature," at least in regard to acts.[14] The feelings of approbation and disapprobation, rooted in sympathy and involving pleasure or displeasure, are natural. We may

[11] *Ibid.*, p. xxiii. The sentiments of approval, esteem, pleasure, are evoked by whatever promotes the happiness or welfare of mankind or of other individuals. Hume's analysis is precisely the counterpart of that of Sade and his predecessors. (See p. 143, etc.)

[12] *Ibid.*, pp. 133–34.

[13] "A violent cough in another gives us uneasiness, though in itself it does not in the least affect us. A man will be mortified if you tell him he has a stinking breath, though it is evidently no annoyance to himself. Our fancy easily changes its situation; and, either surveying ourselves as we appear to others or considering others as they feel themselves, we enter by that means into sentiments which no way belong to us, and in which nothing but sympathy is able to interest us." (P. 143. See also, pp. 146–47. Here Hume, like Rousseau, extends the process to its counterpart, comparison, leading to rivalry and malice.)

[14] *Ibid.*, pp. 47–48.

feel sympathy (pain, disapprobation) for a distressed person, but may or may not be generous, the latter trait involving a reflective or "artificial" virtue.[15] The former responds to the "seeming tendencies" of objects, the latter distinguishes their "real consequences." [16] Either, or both together, arouse our moral "sentiments." Since Hume does not admit natural, intuitive, or affective perceptions of relations of justice or equity, he belongs in larger measure within the compass of our next chapter.[17]

When we turn to France and the continent, we find the echoes of the moral sense theory to be weak and lusterless. It attracted not a single first-rate mind, not even one capable of a sustained, systematic development. We have really only a series of passing references, or brief outlines which are undoubtedly faint echoes of their English inspiration. We must glance at these, however rapidly, to determine the extent, character, and durability of the moral sense hypothesis in France.

The first fact one encounters is one of chronology. There seem to be almost no references to such a theory before the middle years of the century. This is not surprising in view of the expected lag in intercultural influence, and the fact that Diderot's translation of Shaftesbury's *Inquiry Concerning Virtue* (*Essai sur le mérite et la vertu*) appeared in 1745. (Paillet's little-known translation appeared in 1744.) Obviously Shaftesbury had been read by some in English, although the vogue of that language was yet to reach its crest.

The earliest reference I have found is in a *Recueil de divers écrits*, published in 1736 by Thémiseul de Saint-Hyacinthe. It contains an anonymous piece, "Réflexions de M. le Marquis de xx sur l'esprit et le coeur." One suspects that the author was one of the *libertin* group, such as the Marquis de Lassay, and that the piece dates from the early years of the century. He sketches an anti-rational but nonemotive theory. The "heart," he claims, operates as "a kind of instinct." This instinct is actually "a kind of judgment," capable of discerning "the good, the true, the delicate."

---

[15] *Ibid.*, p. 141. Hume generally distinguishes "immediate pleasure or uneasiness" from sympathy, but sometimes, as here, unites them. They are, in any case, related, and distinguished from self-interest. For Helvétius and others they are of course the same.

[16] *Ibid.*, pp. 141, 144.

[17] Kames, who appears to have been little known in France, also accepts the moral sense theory, but not without criticism of his predecessors (*Essays on the Principles of Morality and Natural Religion*, Edinburgh, 1751, pp. 54–118).

This instantaneous operation, "this instinct which moves our heart, is an infinitely surer guide than the *lumières* which enlighten our minds."[18] As is usual, we find this type of theory associated with an expressed optimism about human character and motives, which the marquis justifies by our instinctive reaction of pain at the sight of innocence oppressed or of crime rewarded.

We can again detect the presence of moral sense theory in an original work by Saint-Hyacinthe, published in 1743.[19] But that adventurous writer had eloped to England in 1722, at the age of thirty-eight, and had settled there. Since he knew English even before and had read widely, we may assume his acquaintance with the leading English writers on the subjects that interested him. His argument, then, is that man is born with instincts of mind as well as of body; and particularly with an instinct for knowledge of moral actions on which depend his satisfaction and well-being and the happiness of others. Since moral knowledge is involved, it must also be concluded that we possess "an instinct for truth" which forestalls the dilatoriness of reason and the sophistry of passion.[20]

Saint-Hyacinthe goes further, however, than most other French writers. He inquires into the substance and forms of this instinct. His theory may be described as a mélange of idealistic self-perfectionism and eudaemonism. All seek happiness—there is no other motivation—and happiness consists of the perfecting of our present state. "Well-being must be the goal of being."[21] Moral values—as Hume had maintained—justice and injustice, and rights and duties must be the expression of a furtherance of human welfare and perfection. In this sense rights and duties are natural; and the reason which formulates them (Hume would say, "invents" them), being a tendency to happiness and perfection, is properly called "law of nature," by which is meant "the properties necessary to the existence [of things]." So far, so good, despite the egocentric focus. But Saint-Hyacinthe now falls into the trap which others in his time also did not avoid. Anything, he continues, which makes me happy is virtue, whatever people may say. Even a so-called "criminal" act is virtuous if it makes me happier. Does this

---

[18] *Ibid.*, pp. 287–91.
[19] *Recherches philosophiques, sur la nécessité de s'assurer par soi-même de la vérité*, etc., Londres, 1743.
[20] *Ibid.*, pp. 15–17.
[21] *Ibid.*, p. 249 ff.

make of Saint-Hyacinthe a nihilist, a predecessor of Rameau's nephew? Not so, because his purpose is to refute and avoid this conclusion. The nihilistic argument, he counters, would indeed be valid if there were no after-life, in which all wrong will be set right and justice meted out. Since there is an after-life, the greater happiness (or misery) makes such egoistic acts vices. Otherwise, he repeats, there would be no obligation except suitability, and it would be reasonable and proper to commit crimes when the danger is small and the gain great; for well-being is the goal of being, and virtue, vice, just, unjust, without God, are only terms representing variable matters of opinion. In fact, "man is a moral being only insofar as he is an immortal one." Has Saint-Hyacinthe accomplished his intention to rescue morality? Or has he rather most seriously undermined it?

Probably the most important author who defended the moral sense idea was the Swiss jurist, Burlamaqui. Referring to "Hutchinson" (*sic*), he defines the notion, and then proceeds to defend it.[22] The moral instinct, or sense, comes to us, like our others, from God. Its function is to forestall reason, and to compensate for its inequalities. Countering several objections, he insists that all men possess it, and that, if there are a few "moral monsters," their disposition is the result of corruption rather than of nature. Burlamaqui, however, wants something stronger than the moral sense theory. He goes on to describe the second origin of moral discernment—reason—and to expatiate on its many advantages over the first. His commitment is only half-hearted.

In the *Encyclopédie,* Jaucourt's article, "Sens moral," gives us little beyond a definition. We are told that moral sense, also called moral instinct, involves the immediate recognition of good and evil "by a sort of sensation and by taste, independently of reasoning and reflection." The definition is accredited to Hutcheson. Jaucourt, whom we cannot consider seriously as a thinker, approves the notion. God has given us this instinct so that we can make up our minds when reason is too slow.

For our next adherence to this theory, we must travel to the Academy of Berlin, before which body the Swiss philosopher and philologist, J. B. Merian, expounded his version of it.[23] After a eulogy of Shaftesbury, Merian defends the idea of a moral sense as

---

[22] *Principes du droit naturel,* II, chap. 3.
[23] *Histoire de l'Académie de Berlin,* 14:390–413, 1758.

a philosophical principle. It is not reason, he contends, but sentiment which distinguishes moral good and evil. Like physics,
morals are a generalization from experience, and moral experience
is like that of hot or cold—an immediate sensation. Approbation
is caused by pleasure or pain, as indeed it is with other perceptions,
including those of beauty. "To judge an action good or bad is to
be agreeably or disagreeably affected by it." This reads like a
simplified version of Hume. The difficulty with Merian's contention—one which Hume had to overcome—is that it does not
bring in the *moral*—virtue, or the "ought"—since pleasure-pain
reactions are in themselves not susceptible of such qualifications,
except on the theory of egoistic hedonism, or if virtue is postulated
as the sole cause of pleasure. Merian concedes that in the absolute
sense disinterestedness is impossible and cannot even be conceived
in the mind. (We must assume, then, that the moral sense does not
approve of disinterestedness.) On the other hand, he argues, his
hypothesis separates moral judgment from (calculated) self-interest,
since we are not the masters of the impressions which objects make
on us. They precede reflection and so are independent of personal
considerations. Virtue is therefore really meaningful, in the light
of a moral sense, whereas reflective virtue is mere calculation. And
yet, self-love for Merian is not opposed to moral sense; the former
tends to individual good, the latter to the good of the species which
is the sum of individual goods. So that we reach a conclusion not
dissimilar from that of the Physiocrats: "Let each individual seek
his true good; the species will be happy." Merian gives evidence
of a thorough knowledge of the British moralists. Like others of
this school, he confuses what we now recognize as conditioned
reflexes with immediate reactions of instinct.

The title of Part III of Robinet's *De la Nature* (published in
1766) is "De l'Instinct moral." He begins by retracting his earlier
opinions. Formerly he had believed, like Malebranche, Clarke,
Wollaston, and Montesquieu, in "the system of moral relations,"
but now he knows better. "Everywhere I was sure I saw constant
relationships, necessary and immutable, but I couldn't discover
their supposed morality. . . ." [24] No longer can he accept the
notion of an abstract conformity with universal order and reason.
"But it does often happen to me, I said to myself, to approve or to
blame by an involuntary impulse, before I have formed any dis-

---

[24] I, pp. 227–52. For Robinet's earlier view, see I, p. 64, and note pp. 64–65.

tinct notions of order"—before having examined or compared an action with such a rule. At this point his reason, "its back to the wall," tried to convince him that he had an innate idea of order, or one that developed with his understanding, or again, that we all have a kind of universal logic of moral values. But all this was so little in conformity with experience, "so far above human imbecility, that I concluded it was not the role of reason to establish the morality of our actions; and I made up my mind to turn to the decisions of feeling." He now concludes we have an instinct which approves or disapproves actions, "an internal feeling which can best be compared to the taste of sweet and bitter," regulated by the Creator in accordance with the essential and immutable relations among beings. This might also be called "a feeling of moral beauty." Because "we feel justice and injustice by a natural impulse," by "an involuntary instinct," even children and the ignorant are aware of them. Because the rule of our actions is within us and is not hinged on reasoning, because it is universal and immutable, it is independent of all laws of men or churches. Moral differences, concludes Robinet, are immediately known to us by an organic disposition; "they must be the fruit of a sixth sense entirely similar to the others . . . the beauty and difformity of actions become perceptible to us like the beauty and ugliness of faces." Consequently, we must possess "a moral organ." Unfortunately, "what leaves some obscurity in this operation, is that we are not in a position to identify precisely this organ."

Robinet's subsequent summary of Hutcheson and of Hume reveals to us the sources of his ideas and gives them a content. We naturally approve any useful or agreeable action or quality, as we distinguish pleasant from unpleasant odors. Realizing, however, that such an instinct is not equivalent to one for discerning right and wrong, he adds that the reaction is not moral unless accompanied by a desire to do good. Intention, or good will, thus becomes an essential ingredient in moral judgment, but Robinet fails to integrate it with the reactions of the moral sense, and we have the impression that it is dragged in as an afterthought, to "save the phenomena."

Several brief references, in other writers, now call for passing note. The puzzling abbé Dulaurens whom we saw in our earlier study taking both moralistic and nihilistic stances, at one point approves the moral sense doctrine. Even if there is no God (and this may be a significant conditional clause), the just and unjust exist. We know them through a sixth sense, the moral sense which makes a person "perceive the essential and necessary propriety of certain acts, which flows from certain equally necessary relations he has with surrounding beings." [25] The Protestant, Holland, attempts to refute d'Holbach's assertion that the moral sense involves innate ideas. The sense of sight, he argues, surely does not imply innateness of the ideas of colors. We approve of moral good, wish evil punished, just as we find sugar sweet and absinthe bitter. "They are natural dispositions of our soul . . . of attraction and repulsion." Holland thus also endeavors to make moral values certain by reducing them to a physical basis. He not only places them beyond the uncertainties of reason, but beyond those of experience; for, he says, experience can exercise a sense (a power which is part of our nature), but not create it.[26] He, too, calls on Shaftesbury, Hume, and also on Robinet for support of his contentions. Still another writer worthy of mention is the Netherlander, Hemsterhuis. He believes that the organ which Robinet was unable to specify is the heart. Through the heart, we perceive not only relations among other objects, but our relations to them, and this in turn gives rise to the "sensation of duty." [27] There can, then, be no moral experience without social relations, as there can be no seeing without light, no hearing without sound.[28]

Only a few French writers, in the latter part of the century, were attracted by the moral sense theory. Delisle de Sales, writing in 1770, also summons the authority of Hume, Hutcheson, and Robinet, "the first who have assigned to the moral instinct the foundation of the laws of nature," to support his concept of this instinct, as a "sixth sense more excellent than the others, since . . . it preserves the human species, while the other five preserve only individuals." If moral decisions had to depend on reasoning, our drowning friend would die while we calculated. Although this instinct is not incompatible with reason, reasoning alone would

---

[25] *Le Porte-feuille d'un philosophe*, Cologne, 1770, IV, pp. 152–53.
[26] *Réflexions philosophiques sur le Système de la Nature*, Neuchâtel, 1773, I, pp. 161–63. See also Béguelin's paper read to the Academy of Berlin, in *Nouveaux Memoires de l'Académie de Berlin*, 1774, p. 418 ff.
[27] "Lettre sur l'homme et ses rapports," in *Oeuvres philosophiques*, 1792, I, pp. 177–82.
[28] *Ibid.*, pp. 190–91.

make a man less than a man. Delisle confesses that the mechanism of the moral instinct is mysterious and that it sounds like an occult quality—but then, so is gravitation, and the value of both theories lies in their power to account for phenomena.[29]

The moral sense theory was ignored by most in France, but denounced by some. In an early article in the *Encyclopédie*, Diderot cast doubt upon the aesthetic facet of the theory, as developed by Hutcheson.[30] Later, in one of the moralizing episodes of the *Salon de 1767*, he raises the question which was used so often as an argument by moral sense doctrinaires: "Why does the recital of those [i.e., virtuous] actions seize the soul suddenly, in the strongest and most unreflective way; why do we let others see the full impression we receive for them? To believe with Hutcheson, Smith, and others that we have a moral sense made to discern the good and the beautiful is a vision which may be pleasing to poetry but which philosophy rejects."[31] Diderot's own reply to this question we shall examine in the next chapter. But it is noteworthy that, at about the same period, he included Hutcheson in the list of moralists admitted to his *Plan d'une université pour le gouvernement de Russie*.[32]

Saint-Lambert notes in passing, "It is astonishing that in the land of Locke and Bacon, philosophers speak to you about a moral sense in the light of which we divine all our duties."[33] In his posthumous work, *De l'Homme*, Helvétius reduces the so-called moral sense to an attitude of *bienveillance*, which is always reciprocal to the usefulness of others to ourselves.[34] This is no sense, he declares; unless we are to speak of a "mathematical sense," or a "chemical sense."[35] A moral sense would make morality a natural phenomenon, whereas it is the product of culture. Ethics is "the science of the means invented by men to live among themselves

---

[29] *De la Philosophie de la nature*, Amsterdam, 1770, I, pp. 6, 281, 75–80. See also, Sabatier de Castres, *Dictionnaire*, 1779, II, p. 391 and the apologist, Chiniac, *Essai de philosophie morale*, 1801, I, p. 102.

[30] "Du Beau," in *Oeuvres*, X, pp. 23–24.

[31] *Ibid.*, XI, p. 25.

[32] "I recall a little work on ethics written in Latin by the Englishman Hutcheson; it seemed a classic to me. The author establishes the general principles of the science of morals . . ." (III, p. 492).

[33] *Analyse de l'Homme*, "Discours préliminaire," in *Oeuvres philosophiques*, 1801, I, p. 27.

[34] Londres, 1776, IX, pp. 138–39.

[35] Curiously, Sabatier does make and accept the analogy with the perception of truth in geometry. (*Op. cit.*, II, p. 391.)

in the happiest way possible." Shaftesbury's system, explains Helvétius, is really one of innate ideas, a notion Locke had already done away with. According to the British philosophers, man, when indifferent, desires the good of others—but he is never indifferent! In order to feel compassion we must first know that another is suffering, and to know it we must suffer first ourselves. Compassion is only the remembrance of our own suffering and fear, and the ensuing discomfort. We are sorry for ourselves, and relieve ourselves.

D'Holbach twice vents his distaste for the moral sense theory in his last major work, *La Morale universelle* (1776). This supposed instinct, he declares (in a fashion reminding us of Hartley), is nothing but habit, based on associations, a habit which allows us to make quick decisions. He does admit our "esteem, admiration and love for virtuous deeds, and our horror of criminal deeds. . . ." But our reactions are like taste in the fine arts, a faculty acquired by experience, and weak or inexistent in some men. There are men who admire crimes and violence; only reflection and habit can develop the proper taste.[36]

Although the apologist, Father Richard, would completely disagree with the materialists' arguments, he, too, rejects the moral sense theory.[37] Writing in 1773 in refutation of Robinet's exposition, he characterizes instinct as "a natural, blind, unreflective movement." To assert that an instinct has all the necessary qualities of a moral rule and that it suffices for the discernment and practice of the right is to reverse everything. How can a blind, natural impulse be an ethical law? We must rather look for that rule in Natural Law which even little children and ignorant people "carry written like an open book in the depths of their soul." No "intimate feeling" can make moral distinctions unless it is so enlightened, and then its voice is that of conscience which is also an "inner, immediate rule." We may conclude from Richard's observation that conscience and moral sense function alike, and that both are inner feelings and natural impulses. Their difference, it appears, is that the one involves "pure intellection . . .

[36] *La Morale universelle*, 1820, I, pp. 52–53; III, p. 205. D'Holbach's idea, in regard to judgments of taste, had already been developed by Diderot, in his *Lettre sur les sourds et les muets*.

[37] *La Nature en contraste avec la religion et la raison . . .* , 1773, pp. 111–22. Richard returned to the assault in 1785 (*Exposition de la doctrine des philosophes modernes*, Malines, 1785, pp. 43–44).

[of] spiritual objects" (Richard), the other a physical or "organic disposition" (Robinet). Moral sense would, then, deprive man of *evidence,* the immediate intuition of clear truth.

Richard also attacked the moral sense theory on two other grounds. Its identification of the just and the pleasurable places moral quality in pleasure. Its dependence on organic dispositions (tastes) makes ethics impossible. Now these were precisely the grounds on which Kant was to base his criticism in 1785. The principle of moral feeling, Kant contends, must be classed under that of happiness, since agreeableness is a matter of our well-being. He excludes all empirical principles, such as happiness, or "moral feeling, this supposed special sense," on a number of counts, including their inability to lead to general and necessary laws. "Feelings which naturally differ infinitely in degree cannot furnish a uniform standard of good and evil, nor has anyone a right to form judgments for others by his own feelings. . . ." [38]

Other criticisms may be added to those expressed by contemporaries. While, as Shaftesbury makes it clear, "there is no virtue or goodness in acting from hope or fear," and the moral sense doctrinaires were possessed of high ideals, they succeeded in separating moral judgment from *calculated* self-interest only. As Schweitzer has shown, they do not establish a higher principle of ethics, in contrast to utilitarianism, in such a way that "a higher and more comprehensive content of ethics can be derived from it." [39] They do not show an inner connection between the tendency to self-perfection and obligation. One wonders, too, on what grounds it can be claimed, as Delisle de Sales does, that certain customs of various peoples contradicted their moral sense; surely a higher and rational source of moral discrimination, such as Natural Law, is implied by the possibility of such a criticism. There are other latent dangers in the moral sense theory. As is evident in Saint-Evremond and again in Hemsterhuis, it could lend itself to the materialistic view that individuals are not morally respon-

---

[38] *Fundamental Principles of the Metaphysic of Morals,* in *Kants' Critique of Practical Reason and Other Works,* translated by T. K. Abbott, London [1954], p. 61. See also p. 80. It would be interesting at this point to turn to Adam Ferguson's espousal of moral sense theory, late in the century, but our exploration must end here. The curious reader should consult his *Principles of Moral and Political Science,* Edinburgh, 1792, II, pp. 127–34. For his criticism of other predecessors, see *ibid.,* p. 166 ff.

[39] *Civilization and Ethics,* London, 1946, pp. 84–89.

sible, since they are not responsible for their endowment.[40] The moral guide, furthermore, becomes entirely the individual who is deemed innately good and inclined to virtue. Such a view led, it has been pointed out, to romantic self-indulgence.[41] It is, in fact, difficult to distinguish these theories in some important respects from the sentimental intuitionism of conscience, as we encounter it in Rousseau.

The persistence of moral sense theory can only be accounted for by certain advantages which made an appeal to some minds or hearts. In the psychological emptiness of Lockean psychology it was, in a way, a savior, for it supplied a natural mechanism for swiftly and surely filling the void left by the abolition of innate ideas. Doubtless this explains its presence and function in *Pamela* and novels of that sentimental school. Such a natural tendency to virtue, moreover, made an appeal to our selfish instincts unnecessary (as their opponents had to do), although ultimate utility was always implied. There was, too, a primal certainty in this "natural, blind, unreflective movement." The diversity of intellectual capacity among individuals, the vagaries of reflection and ratiocination, all became unimportant. (No one before Kant conceived of a special kind or power of reason with which man is endowed, whose function it is to give the moral law to his will and intellect.) The moral sense theory, moreover, made it possible to ascribe our moral sentiments and reactions to nature, not to culture, even though society is required to develop them. The moral laws are primary in man, not secondary; part of his nature, not of habit, his "other nature." The universe is moral, and the moral realm of being, though uniquely experienced by man, is not created and added to the world by him.

The frequent references to the British moral sense theorists confirm the fact that this doctrine was not of native French origin. To a great extent this explains its limited penetration. It grew and

[40] Duties, affirms Hemsterhuis, are proportionate to the perfection of the moral organ, "and that is the true reason for the constitution of those unfortunate men who have become famous by atrocious cruelties." *Op. cit.*, p. 199.

[41] W. E. Alderman, "Shaftesbury and the Doctrine of Benevolence in the Eighteenth Century," *Transactions Wisconsin Academy of Science*, XXVI, p. 142 ff. Alderman quotes Chatterton: "Then, friend, let inclination be thy guide." The theory led also to lachrymosity, as seen in the novel. "By way of escape from the nightmare of Mandeville, even many of the orthodox and humanists join hands with the sentimentalists."

thrived in the soil of British empiricism, with its anti-rationalistic trend, and with its persistent optimism, countering Hobbes and Mandeville. In France, the predominance of rationalistic Natural Law theory, or of a contrary rationalistic materialism, as well as a deep pessimism and cynicism about human nature, provided an ungrateful soil for this foreign seed.

Three

EXPERIENTIAL ORIGINS OF MORAL VALUES

THE "NATURE" WITH WHICH THE *philosophes* were concerned, remarks René Hubert, "is only the sensitive constitution of man,
the ensemble of his perceptions and his affective tendencies. At no
time . . . do they admit in man an ideal nature, summoned to
ends which would go beyond the coordination of his perceptions
and the satisfaction of his tendencies." [1] While this statement calls
for some modification, it is essentially true. It is difficult to conceive of Natural Law and natural rights without having an ideal
man in mind, in contrast to existing moral and political realities;
but for the *philosophes* the goal is always the realization of a certain constitution and certain impulses, which we have received
from nature. According to Mornet, the *philosophes* held this to be
the necessary goal, lest man "engage in an eternal, hopeless struggle
with himself." [2] Again the generalization is somewhat sweeping.
But Mornet has touched upon the heart of the ethical problem,
the relation of moral values to nature and to culture, and the struggle between the two, one which some, like Voltaire, accepted as
man's fate, and which others, like Diderot and Rousseau, dreamed
of abolishing—though in polar directions.

The traditional Natural Law theory and moral sense theory as
well postulated an objective world of moral value which was not
man's creation, though he alone on earth could discover and experience it. Although it grew and flourished in society, it was not

[1] R. Hubert, *Les Sciences sociales dans l'Encyclopédie*, 1923, pp. 272–73.
[2] D. Mornet, *Diderot, l'homme et l'oeuvre*, p. 95.

91

the creation of society either, since it obtained with equal validity in the isolation or the fleeting contacts of the state of nature. According to these theories, we have intuitive or instinctual knowledge of moral truths, a knowledge inspired by God or by some force operating in a way unlike the forces of nature which are subject to formulation in terms of scientific laws. Society has only an instrumental function, that of efficient cause, and is not the real source or basis, not the final authority.

Some writers, we have seen, sought to preserve the objectivity, or even the absoluteness of Natural Law, while discarding its supernatural origin and refusing it an a priori basis. Were it not for their adherence to an ideal law, such theories might be classified with those we are about to investigate—theories which rely entirely on the creative force of human experience, involuntary and voluntary, and which tend (though not always successfully or consistently) to avoid universals and absolutes, in view of a strong feeling for human complexity and diversity. Custom, some of these writers might say, makes anything right. The supernatural is a myth. Every force governing man must be explained in terms of nature's laws. But in such a view as this, we see at once two difficulties. The first is which idea of nature is to be adopted—that of a general "Nature," or that of a differentiated human nature, one, moreover, which contains not merely ethical potentialities but ethical actualities. Is the moral (in the latter case) already implanted in us, as a real and self-subsistent normative function of the rational faculties? Or does it arise from constituents which are themselves a nonmoral nature? The second difficulty is contained in our very statement of an experiential theory. What is the relative importance of custom (habituation, education) and of physical nature (self-preservation, passion) in the genesis of moral experience? This subject, notes Hume, has been much discussed in recent years.[3] While he inclines to giving greater weight to the former, he sees little practical difference, since pain and pleasure are the basic elements in either case.

Society, furthermore, becomes the prime generative factor. Whereas Natural Law is law prior to and independent of the existence of society and is innate or inevitably developed, experiential theories hold moral laws and judgments to be generated by conditions of fact, not self-deduced from the moral nature of man.

[3] *Treatise of Human Nature*, Vol. II, Pt. I, Sec. VII.

Right and duty are invented norms which derive from, or inhere in the forms and functioning of the social group, not from prior natural laws embodied in the individual's self-contained natural reactions or perceptions. On this view, moral judgments which have common elements in different cultures may be said to have a natural foundation, while variants are customary—but all must be learned. The emphasis is, then, not on innate predispositions or criteria, but on implantation and inculcation of moral habits, with criteria arising from social or physical facts. Consequently, some writers will emphasize man's physical nature as the chief generative factor, while others will stress the acculturative factors of social groups, and still others will concentrate on a factor implied in both of the preceding: self-interest and its sublimation. In any case, it is not an innate moral faculty which each individual automatically develops, but rather a way of coping with innate nature, of disciplining the egoistic vitalities, one which is created by a separate order of facts, social facts, as distinct from natural or individual facts.

We see this clearly in Montesquieu. That great jurist, as we have seen, believed in Natural Law—even as he admired democracy. But these were ideal choices, and Montesquieu operates essentially in the realm of concrete possibilities.[4] When he analyzes the role of virtue in a democracy, we can observe his effective thinking on the subject. The advantage of monarchy is that it does not count on virtue, but on self-interest. Virtue is "a renunciation of oneself, which is always a very painful thing." Since everything in a democracy depends on this, "it is to inspire it that education [up-bringing] must devote itself." [5] Clearly, then, the ethical life is for Montesquieu largely an artificial product of acculturation, designed and instilled in order to suppress or control nature.

Many eighteenth-century moderates, like Montesquieu, hoped that somewhere in the universe there is a power which is on the side of right. But as a basis for their philosophy, they sought a

---

[4] There is a particular affinity between Montesquieu and Burke; both belong, despite salient differences in political philosophy, in the same group with Machiavelli, Guicciardini and Hobbes, as opposed to those (Morelly, Mably, Rousseau, Paine) who theorize about the functioning of the State abstractly or *de novo* rather than on the basis of existing tradition and law, or to those who attempt to idealize the existing norms (Grotius, Hooker).

[5] *De l'Esprit des lois*, Livre IV, chap. V. Montesquieu, it is true, pretends to speak only of "political virtue," but analysis of his concepts shows them to be fundamentally identical with "moral virtue."

foundation more concrete and secure than this hope, one based on man's nature as a social being, which they envisaged either realistically like Montesquieu, or pessimistically like Rousseau, or optimistically like Chastellux. In any case, their ethical thought, while it was usually not in conflict with the traditional religion, was entirely independent of it. The a priorists posited an all-or-nothing justification of moral imperatives on an eternal order, instituted by God or self-existent. Empiricists also sought out the laws of a natural order. But their "nature" was independent of metaphysics and theology. It was a dynamic, living nature, empty of finalism, historical and evolving; it worked out a new order of relationships, utterly unknown in nature, through the ingenuity of a species whipped on to creativity by the necessity of reconciling the conflicting demands of ego and community. Such an ethics assumed that mankind can be organized, and that it had to be, in a way which would secure definite objectives; these were, indeed, entirely natural demands, but could be obtained for men only in a special "unnatural" way. This is creation as opposed to discovery; a creation continuing through all the past time of the species (a necessary product of the new order of facts, social facts), and yet having constantly to be re-created, at each cultural moment and in each individual atom of the cultural complex, through the formative processes of will and custom.

In the eighteenth-century cultural complex, two of the important conflicting polarities were Cartesian rationalism and the sensationism developed by Locke and his successors. While the former remained a live and powerful force, a force, moreover, which infiltrated and shaped the thought even of those who opposed it, there is no doubt that the new and more potent formative influence was that of the revived, modernized sensationist psychology and epistemology. The forms of ethical theory we are discussing in this chapter are in harmony with, and to a great extent derive from, sensationism and are in open opposition to its adversary. They are also in harmony with the general scientific empiricism whose rise accompanied that of sensationism. Moral laws may be described as generalizations from data rather than as derived by the mind, by virtue of an intellectual necessity, from its own operations.

We may summarize the trend, in Hume's words, as an "attempt

to introduce the experimental method of reasoning into moral subjects." [6] Following the persistent Newtonian model of analysis and synthesis of observed phenomena, the laws of moral behavior should be discoverable. The actual methodology was far from empirical. But the contrast with the rationalists, who often claimed that moral laws were of a nature to be expressed as mathematical certainties, is striking.[7] The mathematical analogy is a priori and is associated with innateness which, in turn, implies that truths exist before they are conceived, that is, independently of our conceiving them. Innatism, it seemed to many, tried to explain existent knowledge by an unverifiable hypothesis, whereas sensation was itself a real phenomenon, and so more satisfactory.[8] It is not difficult to find ridicule of innatism in the writings of Voltaire, Condillac, and d'Alembert. Perhaps no criticism is more germane to our subject than that of Diderot in his very brief entry in the *Encyclopédie* under the title "Inné."

> There is nothing innate except the faculty of feeling and thinking; all the rest is acquired. Suppress the eye and you suppress at the same time all ideas which belong to seeing. . . . Now with all these ideas and all these senses suppressed, no abstract notions remain. But after having proceeded by means of suppression, let us follow the contrary method. Let us suppose a shapeless but sensitive mass; it will have all the ideas which can be obtained from touch. Let us complete its organisation; let us develop this mass, and at the same time we will open the door to sensations and to knowledge. By both of these methods a man can be reduced to the condition of oyster and an oyster raised to the condition of man.

These ideas and their formulation are typical of Diderot and immediately bring to mind passages in *Le Rêve de d'Alembert*. It is all the more surprising, then, to find the statement in the final sentence, since it omits completely the function of the *sensorium commune*, or brain, to which he elsewhere assigns a crucial role.

[6] *Treatise*, Introduction.
[7] This method takes empirical science as its model. Thus Helvétius: "I have thought that morals should be treated like all other sciences, and ethics constructed like experimental physics." (*De l'Esprit*, pp. i–ii.) It may also terminate in arithmetical formulation, but on the basis of phenomenological analysis. For Newtonianism and morals, see G. Chinard's edition of Morelly's *Le Code de la nature*, pp. 142–43, and Cassirer, *op. cit.*, p. 7 ff.
[8] The sensationist explains identity of knowledge by an innateness of structure, but this allows for a relativism due to variability of stimuli.

Diderot, indeed, belonged more characteristically to the man-machine group than to the sensationist school.[9]

It was typical of the French sensationists to slight the contribution of faculties and structures.[10] They did not attribute to structure an active importance in determining the meaning, content, and utilization of experience, and underplayed the basic phenomenon, the transformation of sensation into psychic experience, which required pre-existing faculties, and which sensation does not explain. Innate categories of judgment, if not types of reaction, are excluded. Kant, therefore, was to insist that forms of sensibility and reason are prior to experience, perhaps basing his criticism on Leibniz's *nisi intellectus ipse*—nothing except what is already present as part of the innate nature of the intellect. At the very least, it must be admitted that no moral need as such is included by sensationists in their theory of human nature. They are consequently faced with the problem of genesis in an acute form which the apriorists escape. Their theories involve a scission between moral judgments or values and an assumed primary human nature. This is seen, actually, even outside the sensationist school, in the wider perspective of the genetic method. As early as 1701 the *libertin* Baudot de Juilly wrote: "For we must draw near the cradle in order to know what nature wants, because it is in children that it acts with greatest freedom . . . so that one may say they are the mirrors of nature." [11] Indeed, when one separates the child from the adult in this way, one discriminates between nature and culture. The separation of morality, which is not found in the child, from nature is bound to ensue.

There are other instances of the new tendencies among writers

[9] This is obvious in his opposition to Helvétius. For the significant differences between the two viewpoints, see A. Vartanian's critical edition of La Mettrie's *L'Homme machine*, pp. 116–23. The sensationist postulates the identity of moral and physical laws, no hereditary predisposition other than conformation of physical organs, unlimited malleability, and (for some) Providence. (See G. Chinard, *op. cit.*, p. 141.) Proponents of the man-machine hypothesis, and many others as well, protested against this false scientism, the simplification of man and society implied by the analogy with the physical world.

[10] For Locke, see Gibson's *Locke's Theory of Knowledge*, Cambridge, 1917, pp. 155–57, and Locke's *Essay*, ed. A. C. Fraser, Oxford, 1894, Book I, chap. 2. As Fraser interprets him, "our mind is not originally like white paper, in the sense of being equally disposed to accept any proposition regarding conduct," thus implying there is good and bad antecedent to human institution (p. 66). For Locke, moreover, God has "joined virtue and public happiness together" (p. 70) while for the French philosophers virtue is simply definable as public happiness (except when it is made equivalent to private happiness).

[11] *Dialogues entre Messieurs Patru et D'Ablancourt sur les plaisirs*, 1701, I, p. 182.

of the transition period. "Justice," writes Saint-Evremond, "is simply a virtue established in order to maintain human society; it is the work of men. . . ." [12] Maubec, a member of the Faculty of Medicine at Montpellier, already attempts a physical approach in 1709. In an interesting but little known work, *Principes phisiques de la raison et des passions des hommes,* published in Paris, he assumes the *tabula rasa* and the development of ideas from sensations—probably under the influence of the Gassendist philosophy. All ideas leave traces in the brain, forming paths through which spirits flow again, reawakening the traces "by a mechanical necessity." [13] Prejudices—and other customary ideas—are such traces deposited by education and example.[14] In the following year Simon Tyssot de Patot published his utopian novel, *Les Aventures de Jacques Massé,* in which he denies any intrinsic moral value to acts. If they "are capable of *becoming* good or evil, it can only be in relation to certain institutions." Doubtless Spinoza's statement, "wrong is conceivable only in an organized community," if not Hobbes, is at the source of such ideas.

In the hearts of men, asserts Fréret, "it is true that I see a law engraved from the first instant of one's existence, the law of love of pleasure and aversion to pain." [15] But pleasure and pain are not only physical; and, in any society, moral judgments and the establishment of moral values are inevitable, though they "vary according to the diversity of the customs, needs and opinions which have prevailed in each of these societies." [16] Fréret emphasizes the rational elaboration of moral values, based on physical and social needs. Like many other rationalistic naturalists, he holds up the goal of universal law: that of a "natural morality"—supplied by the human intellect.

The main difficulty for the experientialists should already be obvious. It is to explain the leap from the natural to the ethical. The ethical is without meaning in their nature philosophy. Moral values are artificial (invented or established by men), but it is natural for men to set them up. However, the step from mere sensation (pleasure-pain) or desire to the "ought" of right and

[12] "Sur l'Amitié," in *Oeuvres,* III, p. 359, quoted by Vyverberg, p. 33.

[13] P. 47.

[14] P. 100.

[15] *Lettre de Thrasibule à Leucippe,* in *Oeuvres complettes,* Londres, 1775, III, p. 107 ff. The attribution of particular works to Fréret is uncertain, but he was taken to be their author.

[16] *Ibid.,* p. 115.

wrong is a gap which demands to be filled. There is another but similar challenge in the analysis of human nature. The will to live and the will to power, it was often recognized, impel our nature to hurt others, to dominate or exploit them. Having thrown aside transcendence of self and of nature, we are left with the epigrams of Diderot: "everybody thinks of himself in this world" (*La Religieuse*), and "the world is the house of the strong" (*Le Rêve de d'Alembert*).[17] This result of eighteenth-century psychology, determinism, and materialism is the challenge which had to be met—unless, indeed, it were accepted (as nihilism) and declared to be the touchstone of value. With man replaced among other natural beings, with innateness and free will denied him, with original goodness and original wickedness either combined or both denied, what was left was "an animal capable only of receiving sensations, of feeling needs, and of combining ideas derived from those sensations."[18] Somehow, one had to build a bridge to the ethical world: from self-interest to virtue, from egoism to sacrifice for the equal right of others to the will to live, and to their equal share in self-realization in society. The experientialists could not, like the apriorists, assume the independent origin and coexistence of man's ethical world nor, consequently, its justification. They had to show a path which leads from the natural value to moral and cultural value.

An experiential morality may emphasize the artificial, the natural, or combine both origins. Ultimately, the natural basis could never be excluded. Often—especially in the first part of the century—it was taken to lie in universal constituents of the human psyche. In an early eighteenth-century manuscript we can observe the hesitations of transition.[19] On the one hand, there is a universal recognition of the basic moral law of reciprocity, universal reactions to certain acts. On the other hand, our moral approbation and disapprobation extend to a new order of facts, arbitrary convention. Men can decide that acts are to be considered good or evil, "and then their agreement constitutes right." Adultery was right in Sparta, "because right and justice are not such and such a thing, but in general not to do wrong to any one and to conform

[17] Or with the revolt of the nihilist in his article, "Droit naturel."

[18] Hubert, *op. cit.*, pp. 270–71.

[19] *Difficultés sur la religion, proposées au Père Mallebranche* (called *Le Militaire philosophe*), Maz. 1163, Pt. IV, fol. 33–39. J. S. Spink dates the manuscript between 1706 and 1710 (*French Free Thought from Gassendi to Voltaire*, pp. 293–95).

to convention." In Sparta, adultery was a mutual right, agreed upon by the social group; and virtue and vice consist in obedience or disobedience to such conventions. In this writer, then, the natural (in the shape of an a priori) is diluted by cultural creativity to a serious extent.

With the rise of the new sciences, especially of mechanistic biology in the 1740's, the universal natural basis of ethics is occasionally transferred to the human physical constitution.[20] Materialists from La Mettrie on, who reduced the psychic to the physical, generally emphasized the contrast between moral convention and physical nature, considering the former to be natural only in the sense that man naturally creates artifices.

Hartley, who was well-known in France, was the first important writer to stress the physical basis of moral reactions, as the result of a mechanical process of association in the brain, similar to what we call the conditioned reflex, by which we associate pleasurable sensations with certain objects, acts, or ideas. No moral judgments "arise in us independently of prior associations determining thereto." [21] Such a process leads from love and hatred of persons, "by farther associations to the love and hatred of the virtues and vices considered abstractly and without any regard to our own interest." [22] Some associations are so early and so strong, so close to the "common nature of man," that they appear to be instincts. Hartley also assumes a Providence which usually prevents us from associating pleasure with the "wrong" objects. But the admitted role of education belies his own statement, and materialists from La Mettrie to Sade were to assert the equal naturalness of "wrong" associations.

Condillac, though his work is seminal in the history of French naturalism, is another borderline figure. In the *Traité des sensations* (1754), carrying forward his extreme sensationism, he admits no moral notions generated by the mind itself. "Good" is a quality referring to the contributions of things to our pleasures. Its attribution is consequent to our organism and our experience. It follows that "the good and the beautiful are not absolute: they

---

[20] The fountainhead is Descartes, then the school of iatrophysicists. On this subject, see A. Vartanian, *Diderot and Descartes*, p. 17 ff. and chap. IV; E. Guyénot, *Les Sciences de la vie aux XVII* et XVIII* siècles*, p. 154 ff.; and J. S. Spink, *op. cit.*, p. 215 ff.

[21] *Observations on Man* [1749], London, 1801, I, p. 498.

[22] *Ibid.*, p. 496.

are relative to the character of the person judging, and to the manner in which he is organized." [23] Value judgments, it is clear, are for Condillac the result of a physical determinism which is an entirely natural process. But it is also clear, if only implicit, that stimuli may be supplied by society—and this is what Helvétius and others will develop. Condillac, like them, bases the physical re-action on utility, among other qualities (novelty, rareness) which his successors will subsume under self-interest (prestige, etc.). All value judgments, one must conclude, are made (at least initially) as a function of the sentient ego.

Condillac, in fact, answers practically all questions concerning knowledge from the standpoint of physical organism. Life is built around needs and the necessity of satisfying them. From these grow habit, emotion, value judgment. The mind and the personality are "created" out of sensations, and all higher faculties depend on associations.[24] However, Condillac, a conservative, also seeks a return to God and Providence. In *La Logique* (1780), he uses the nigh-universal definition of morality as "the conformity of our actions with the laws," which are "conventions made by man." [25] Are these conventions, then, and the ensuing moral standards, purely arbitrary? Many—too many—are; nevertheless

> those which determine whether our actions are good or bad are not, and cannot be. They are our work, because they are conven-tions which we have made; yet we have not made them by our-selves; nature made them with us, dictated them to us, and it was not in our power to make others. Given the needs and the faculties of men, the laws themselves are given; and although we make them, God, who created us with such needs and such faculties is, in truth, our only legislator.

Now, while the materialists would not have accepted Condillac's escape to supernaturalism and final causes, they did embrace the explanation of a natural substructure for convention and will. Condillac's own substructure is entirely physical, and, though he will not admit it, it creates a complete natural (physical) determin-ism. His "divine Providence" is no more than its justification. His combination of universals ensuing from structure and will operat-

[23] *Traité des sensations*, IV, p. 3. In a footnote Condillac warns the reader, "Every-thing he judges good will not be morally good."
[24] See also Condillac's *La Logique*, I, chap. IV.
[25] Chap. VI.

ing through convention is precisely an epitome of the new naturalistic moral theories.[26]

The idea of the physical basis of moral experience becomes absorbed in the broader outlines of the materialistic ethical philosophy. We shall shortly encounter it again as an integral part of the doctrines of Diderot, Helvétius, La Mettrie, and d'Holbach. We must note, however, that the idea of the physical origin of moral experience attained its widest acceptance in the closing decades of the century, even among writers who cannot be classified as strict materialists. This fact bespeaks the increasing penetration of the new "scientific philosophy," and also the gradual focusing of ideas in a direction which leads to the work of the *idéologues*.[27]

The reduction of human behavior to physical terms was a solution which could also be cheerfully embraced by the nihilist. As early as 1787, in *Les Infortunes de la vertu*, Sade, with his remarkable lucidity and courage, notes an inverse relation between moral feelings and the sexual instinct. "It is unfortunately [*sic!*] only too common to see debauchery of the senses completely extinguish pity in man; its ordinary effect is to harden; whether it is because most of its delinquencies require a kind of apathy in the soul, or because the violent shock it imprints on the nervous system diminishes the sensitivity of their action, the fact remains that a professional libertine is rarely a compassionate man." [28] In his more

[26] For a divergent interpretation, see Charles Frankel, *The Faith of Reason*, New York, 1948, p. 50.

[27] Naigeon founds ethics on man's unchanging physical needs and pleasures. (*Discours préliminaire pour servir d'introduction à la morale de Sénèque*, 1782, p. 129.) J. H. Meister, who succeeded Grimm as editor of the *Correspondance littéraire* reduced moral reactions (and all else) to electrical phenomena. (*Mélanges de philosophie, de morale et de littérature*, Genève, 1822, I, pp. 69–72.) Again this amounts to physical sensations of pleasure and pain, which involve universals modified by habits acquired to form "an order which suits the economy of my being." One basic component is compassion (the feeling of identification), and reflection in relation to the tendency to order. (*De la Morale naturelle*, Londres, 1788, pp. lx–xll, 1–18.) Delisle de Sales and Du Pont de Nemours also make physical needs the basis of Natural Law, which they consider to be a metaphysical reality. Dupont assures us that morality must eventually be put on the basis of physics: "everything is physical, metaphysics and morality, too; moral affections are themselves physical effects," and moral laws are therefore as provable as those of chemistry. (*Opuscules morales et politiques*, an XIII, pp. 349–63.) Sabatier de Castres clearly shows a drift analogous to the views of the *idéologues*, explaining human behavior on the organic, or physical level. (*Pensées et observations morales et politiques*, Vienne, 1794, pp. 377, 403n.)

[28] *Les Infortunes de la vertu*, 1930, p. 42.

important novel, *Histoire de Juliette* (1791), Sade devotes one of his philosophical interludes to this proposition, and to the consequences he wishes to draw from it. "All moral effects," sermonizes one of his chief corrupters, Mme Delbène, "are due to physical causes to which they are irresistibly chained. . . . Certain tendencies of our organs, the nerve fluid more or less irritated by the nature of the atoms which we breathe, by the kind or quantity of nitrous particles contained in the food we take, by the course of the secretions [*humeurs*] and by a thousand other external causes, determine a man to crime or to virtue." [29] Later, another teacher of Juliette, Lady Clairwil, repeats the lesson, but adds a section on the influence of education and habituation in modifying our original nature. Virtue results from the conditioned resistance of organs to the nervous fluid. [30]

Other writers went beyond the physical organism and concentrated on the most important psychic factor it generated; the various forms and expressions of self-interest. The typical phenomenon of the transition from the seventeenth- to the eighteenth-century cultural complex was the revaluation of self-interest and the satisfactions it demands. Defense of the passions was a particular phase of this movement. Joseph Butler notes in one of his sermons, "I suppose it may be spoken of as very much the distinction of the present to profess a contracted spirit and greater regard to self-interest than appears to have been done formerly." [31] Some defenders of self-love did not attempt to solve the riddle of its transformation into other-regarding affections. Others, from Shaftesbury to Rousseau, posited two original and conflicting impulses in *homo duplex,* the selfish and the compassionate. But the materialistic sensationist followed (in a more "scientific way") the current initiated by La Rochefoucauld which reduced compassion and altruism to forms of self-love. A mode of transition had therefore to be indicated.

Abbadie, in his apology of self-love, fails to do this. He declares that virtue is only a more noble way of loving oneself, but stops short of an explanation. [32] An anonymous manuscript, *Examen de*

[29] *Histoire de Juliette,* ed. Pauvert, 1954, I, p. 22.

[30] *Ibid.,* II, pp. 93–94.

[31] J. Butler, *A Dissertation upon the Nature of Virtue,* p. 50. See *An Age of Crisis,* chap. 10.

[32] *L'Art de se connaître soi-même,* La Haye, 1711 [1692], II, pp. 161–62. The same may be said of La Placette (*Essais de morale,* Amsterdam, 1716, II, pp. 2–3).

la religion, does better: it is the social, pleasurable reward of praise, and its contrary, the pain caused by scorn, that impel us to overcome selfish instinct.[33] For writers such as these, altruism has its source in egoism, of which it is a refined manifestation, imposed by society and developed by education. The desire for superiority, writes Mandeville, is always greater than the love of virtue, but it is often overcome for the sake of appearances.[34] Natural impulse, he continues, is purely egoistic. However it does not exclude compassion, which may lead to altruistic deeds in order to relieve the unpleasant feeling it provokes. Other good deeds result from love of praise and fear of blame—the mechanisms created by society for its self-preservation against the disintegrating effects of natural egoism. Virtue is, then, a conversion of evil, effectuated by the mechanism of pride, and imposed by the need to compensate for vices in human nature. In general, the naturalness and strength of a desire can be inferred from the fact of a general prohibition against it.[35]

For Fréret, moral imperatives result, inevitably, from the act of reflection on our self-interest and the quest for happiness—inevitably, because of our own weakness and dependence.[36] Here we can see the optimism of an early radical. Morelly, who was a totalitarian collectivist, takes an ambiguous attitude. On the one hand, self-interest is the mother of property and evil. In his "heroic poem," the *Basiliade,* Fahdilah describes self-interest as a god worshiped by the people, a giant "whose feet stand on an immense pile of skeletons. . . ."[37] On the other hand, Morelly paints self-interest as the origin of social virtues through mutual needs. "Would you believe it, oh happy Zainzemin! almost nowhere do men help each other because they love each other, but because otherwise they would be condemned to perish: those are the sad links of any society among us; that is the horrid principle of our virtues and our vices. Hope or fear lead us to self-control or to excesses." Morelly's thoroughly naturalistic explanation, like Hobbes's, envisions men as evil and, after passing through a state

[33] Written between 1710 and 1720; see Wade, *op. cit.,* p. 151. Published, "Londres, 1761," pp. 99–100.

[34] *Fable of the Bees* [1714–1729], ed. by F. B. Kaye, Oxford, 1924, II, pp. 254–57.

[35] *Ibid.,* I, pp. 41–43, 51; II, pp. 134–37, 196; I, pp. lxiv, n. 1. For Butler's reply, see Sermons 1 and 11.

[36] *Oeuvres,* III, pp. 84–96.

[37] *Naufrage des Isles flottantes, ou Basiliade du célèbre Pilpaï,* Messine, 1753, II, pp. 35–47.

of war, as discovering that the best way of helping themselves is honesty and reciprocity. There is also some analogy with Nicole and with Montesquieu's Troglodytes, especially in the implications of the word "sad." There is perhaps some confusion here (as was frequent among adherents of the genetic methodology) between two senses of the word "origin": origin as cause, or how a thing arises, and origin as what constitutes, defines, or justifies. Of course, continues Morelly, if there were no private property, men would love each other and this subterfuge would not be necessary; we should have a true morality instead of an inefficacious one based on pride, shame, idealistic speculation, and fear of punishment. We have only to eliminate property, and men will be free in their passions, and yet good, because united "in a single will," straining toward a single goal, the common happiness.[38]

Similar viewpoints are found in the *Encyclopédie*.[39] For Edmund Burke, too, natural forms of self-interest contain or imply the acceptance of obligation and do not necessarily produce "that appetite for domination which springs from illegitimate desire and mere willful self-interest." [40] Charles Leroy places moral experience after social experience. "Then the interest of each establishes in his mind an idea of proportion between the pleasure he seeks and the hurt he would suffer if he alienated others. From this arises the mutual respect which, by nature, is as superficial as interests, but to which habit and the feeling of compassion . . . impart much strength." [41] Even apologists, like Bergier and Gérard, were swept away by the tide. Bergier accepts self-interest as the origin and contents himself with reminding his readers that there is an eternal self-interest in the other world.[42] Gérard, in his apologetic novel, goes so far as to exclaim, "Oh worthy self-love! . . . which so exalts man, makes him so great a being, in his ideas, his penchants and his views, and distinguishes him from the stupid animal who ruminates and is content." [43] What has happened to original sin?

---

[38] *Ibid.*, and also pp. 227–28, 291–92. Similar ideas will be found throughout *Le Code de la nature.*

[39] E.g. Yvon's "Vérité, Bonté, Beauté," and Séguiran's "Vérité, Bonté, Beauté" [out of place, in XVII, p. 184].

[40] C. Parkin, *The Moral Basis of Burke's Political Thought*, p. 34.

[41] *Lettres philosophiques* [1768], an X, pp. 166–67; but cf. pp. 268–70, where compassion is emphasized.

[42] *Apologie de la religion chrétienne*, 1769, I, p. 43.

[43] *Le Comte de Valmont, ou les égaremens de la raison*, 1774, I, pp. 500–13.

There is little to be gained from following this current in its many repetitions throughout the years. We may, however, tarry briefly on those writers, or groups of writers, who gave the self-interest theory a significant form.

First among these were the Physiocrats. In contrast to the radical groups on the left, of socialists, collectivists, or primitivists, they stood on the far right. Property, laissez faire and a strong monarch were the keynotes of their program. We have already seen, in our first chapter, how their economic theory was part of a general philosophy of Natural Law—not traditional Natural Law, but one based on physical laws and self-interest. In the hands of the Physiocrats, these concepts led to a startling number of ethical absolutes, including rights, and duties derived from rights.[44] It follows that moral judgments and values are not the conscious work of man, but are generated by physical facts operating in the elementary conditions of human culture.[45] Right and duty become "claims and obligations which men must recognize among themselves to insure their own well-being."[46] It also follows, from the physical and necessary nature of moral facts that self-interest promotes the general interest and is, in fact, identical with it; for the self-interest of each man is identical with that of others, and in advancing one's own cause one contributes to that of all. In other words, there is no abstract "general interest," set up in opposition to an anti-social self-interest.[47] Private interest commands us to use our faculties, provided we do not hinder others from using theirs, since such a hindrance would take away our assurance, as Quesnay puts it in his "Droit naturel," that we could keep the use of ours. We cannot become aware of our rights without at the same moment becoming aware of our duties, and the two are not psychologically dissociable.

Essentially, then, though the formulation and general theory are different, we have the pervasive naturalistic view that self-protection and mutual interdependence in a social structure

[44] "Absolute justice," states Le Mercier de la Rivière, "can be defined as an order of duties and rights which are physically necessary, and consequently absolute." (*L'Ordre naturel et essentiel des sociétés politiques* [1767], 1910, p. 8. See M. Albaum, "The Moral Defenses of the Physiocrats," *Journal of the History of Ideas*, 1955, p. 184.

[45] For an interesting account of the economic basis of ethics, see Mirabeau, *Philosophie rurale*, Amsterdam, 1764, I, pp. 134-36.

[46] Albaum, *op. cit.*, p. 185.

[47] "The magic of a well ordered society makes each one work for others while he thinks he is working for himself." (Mirabeau, quoted by Weulersse, *op. cit.*, II, p. 95.) It may be noted that this theory is antithetical to Rousseau's.

necessarily generate norms of conduct. We also have a typical note of eighteenth-century optimism (one denied by pessimists and nihilists), that we automatically recognize the reciprocity of rights and an advantage to ourselves in respecting those of others. Morality, asserts Mirabeau, "is everywhere and in everything our most real self-interest." [48] This naturalistic optimism makes minimal the requirement for the intervention of culture and its rational organs. At the same time, nothing is more rationalistic, and nothing more false, than this optimistic naturalism, which is based ultimately on Providentialism. And yet nothing is more typical of a certain kind of thinking generated by the social and intellectual complex which was the Enlightenment than this peculiar combination. Here we do not have a theory according to which one natural law (egoism) is countered by another (altruism, sympathy, compassion). We have two equilibrated impulses of self-interest, the one dynamic or aggressive, the other disciplinary and repressive. An individual, declares Quesnay, "cannot refuse to play his part in the universal concert without dragging himself and his species, as far as his sphere extends, into revolt, ruin (*la misère*), death and chaos." [49] The Marquis de Sade, who was to deny the truth of suppositions such as those of the Physiocrats, nevertheless was to prove in his very denial the consequences alleged by Quesnay.

Turgot, though not officially a Physiocrat, was in some ways sympathetic to their philosophy. Morals, he writes, depends "on self-love regulated by justice, which itself is only an enlightened self-love." [50] With his deep realism, he denied that property or society makes men evil. Evil is in human nature.[51] There is no use in telling a child to be virtuous—the word has no meaning to him (for *ideas* of justice are not in our original nature); make him rather experience the pleasure (and the utility) of being just. In order for charity to flourish, he writes elsewhere, "the passion for public weal must give men the same benefits as the vanity of founding charitable institutions . . . in this regard the general interest must be the result of the efforts of each individual to further his private interest." Any time you wish to increase the people's ardor for any good, "increase their self-interest" in it.[52]

---

[48] *L'Ami des hommes,* quoted by Weulersse, II, p. 97.
[49] *Philosophie morale,* quoted by Weulersse, II, p. 111.
[50] *Oeuvres,* ed. Schelle, 1913, I, p. 311.
[51] Lettre à Mme de Graffigny (1751), *Oeuvres,* I, pp. 243–46.
[52] "Fondations," *Ibid.,* I, 587 ff. (From the *Encyclopédie.*)

Although the Physiocrats may have borrowed from Helvétius, he differs from them in his radical elimination of all elements other than the physical. Self-interest, by which he means pleasure and pain, is held to be the sole motive of action. By elaborate and at times absurd gyrations of reasoning, he reduces all motives to pleasure, and all pleasure to purely physical sensation.[53] In the *nature* of man, then, there is no such element as a moral faculty, intuition, need or impulse, for morality is the denial of *natural* impulse. Morality is purely the work of culture, partly involuntary and partly voluntary, and nature merely supplies the raw elements out of which it is built. "Born without ideas, without vices and without virtue, everything, even his humanity, is an acquisition in man; it is to his education that he owes this feeling." [54] Helvétius denies compassion and altruism as natural facts.[55] We help others, or sympathize, only to relieve ourselves, to make others or ourselves think highly of ourselves, to obtain gratitude or reward of some kind, to demonstrate our power or to enjoy its exercise. Outside of man, the universe is utterly empty of moral value or meaning; there are no "absolutes."

Nevertheless, moral experience is a reality and is essential to society. We must realize that Helvétius fancies himself the defender of morality, not its foe. His purpose is to exclude idealistic and theological claptrap, and to rebuild the structure of ethics on the basis of natural phenomena as experience demonstrates them really to be. He does not deny that compassion is developed in men, but wishes to indicate its true place in the affective economy. It is thus necessary to understand the actual genesis of self-disciplinary and other-regarding feelings. His concept of the origin of moral experience is conditioned by his concept of the ethical, and the latter is clearly visible in the former.

Once at this truth, I easily discover the source of human virtues: I see that without sensitivity to physical pain and pleasure, men, without desires, without passions, equally indifferent to

[53] See, among innumerable examples, *De l'Homme* [1772], Londres, 1776, pp. 206-9.

[54] *Ibid.* For Helvétius' denial of Natural Law, see *De l'Esprit*, 1758, pp. 278, 323-24, 344, and *De l'Homme*, p. 82n. The idea of "good" derives meaningfulness from the child's association of something good to eat with a pleasant sensation, and is later widened by application to anything which is pleasing by its physical sensation. (*De l'Homme*, VIII, pp. 55-56.)

[55] "Men, sensitive to themselves alone, indifferent to others. . . ." *De l'Esprit*, p. 238. Primitive man has no idea of justice, no word to express it. (*De l'Homme*, p. 202.)

everything, would never have known self-interest; that, without self-interest, they would not have gathered together in society, would not have made conventions amongst themselves, that there would not have been a general interest, consequently no just or unjust actions; and so physical sensitivity and self-interest are the sources of all justice.[56]

For Helvétius, in sum, right and wrong are voluntary conventions referring to the community interest (which is ultimately requisite to private interest). We have, then, a natural fact—men are governed uniquely by self-interest—and a social fact: private interest must be subordinated to the general interest. This constitutes the moral-political problem. Since morality arises from experience, we must give children experiences which will be conducive to it, creating the desired habits.[57] Omitting criticisms of detail, it is obvious, from the preceding analysis, that Helvétius confuses the moral order with the physical order. Animals, too, are sensitive to pleasure and pain, but have no moral life. Helvétius has cavalierly thrown out the peculiar human endowment, the human need to make moral evaluations—a need which is as natural and compulsive as physical demands, as natural as society, in abstraction from which it is absurd to consider mankind. Diderot wrote the most thoroughgoing critique of his fellow materialist. He pointed out, among many other things, that sensitivity is a condition of all animal experience, not a cause of human moral experience. The jump is too great, even with the intervening steps, to account for the psychic life by sensitivity alone.

Many other writers who saw moral experience as the creation of social living accepted the importance of the organic and of self-interest, but broadened their view of the social to include other elements, such as sympathy, pleasure of association for its own sake, and the emergence of an autonomous rationality. There was, in fact, a wide spectrum of interpretations.

As early as 1721, we find a quite Christian writer, Ladvocat, attributing moral value to conscious social creativity. It is evident, he declares, that things are good or evil "only in relation to pleasure and pain." From this premise he concludes that these qualifi-

---

[56] *De l'Esprit*, p. 276. In a note, Helvétius adds, "This proposition cannot be denied without admitting innate ideas." See also p. 230; *De l'Homme*, Sect. X, chap. VII.

[57] See, *inter alia, ibid.*, p. 547n. The similarity to Freud's theories will be noted later.

cations are nothing more than the conformity of our actions with a certain law, representing "the will and power of the legislator." [58] In this we can already see Voltaire's definition of virtue in the *Traité de métaphysique* (1734).

As we have already noted, Montesquieu's account, despite his theoretical acceptance of Natural Law, actually depends on an experiential basis. This is particularly striking in his parable of the Troglodytes, who "were so evil and ferocious, that there was no principle of equity or justice among them." [59] It is only through the bitter experience of the effects of natural egoism that the Troglodytes learn to create, with conscious will, the concrete forms of justice and law, together with the social limitations which they impose on the individual's independence. This is the answer to Mirza's question, whether justice is a quality "which is as intrinsic [to men] as existence." [60] The reply is ambiguous: justice is necessary to their existence, but its realization must be developed from experience. Painfully we have learned (and perhaps keep learning) that there is such an entity as the common interest, that our own is not divorced from it, that virtue and justice are "charity for ourselves." [61] Moral experience is, then, only a sublimation of selfishness, and repression of egoism is only a higher form of egoism.

To be sure, Montesquieu still believes in the reality and objectivity of moral values, inhering in relationships which constitute Natural Law. Following Malebranche and Shaftesbury, he recognizes an objective order of the world, an order which *ipso facto* creates value. Justice is eternal. But the perception of these values is the work of cultural experience, and adherence to them is voluntary. It is not the values that are created by the will of men, but their formulation in effective social law which expresses their agreement to recognize and respect them. In contrast to theories such as those of Helvétius, Montesquieu's is ultimately rationalistic and banks on the rationality of men (though not on their virtue). He specifically denies that sensual experience can in itself

---

[58] *Entretiens sur un nouveau système de morale et de physique*, 1721, pp. 41–43.
[59] *Lettres persanes* (1721), Lettre XI.
[60] Lettre X. In an illuminating note, Antoine Adam points out the importance of the question of the unnaturalness of virtue, as posed by Hobbes, La Rochefoucauld and the Augustinian tradition, and as contrasted with Shaftesbury. (*Lettres persanes*, éd. critique, Genève, 1954, p. 31.)
[61] Lettre XII.

be the basis of moral value, since the whims of subjectivity cannot create recognizable value.[62] On the other hand, one of his unpublished *Pensées* places him in the vanguard of his time in its emphasis on the physical mechanisms of habituation. "We all have machines which submit us eternally to the laws of habit. Our machine accustoms our soul to thinking in a certain way. It accustoms it to thinking in a different way. It is here that physics could find a place in ethics, by making us see how inclination towards human vices and virtues depends on the mechanism." [63]

Much thought in England was devoted to similar problems, and some of it had considerable penetration and influence in France. Hobbes was universally seen as the fountainhead of the idea that virtue and justice are arbitrary conventions. (Spinoza, too, was interpreted in the same way.) Locke's empiricism had led him to distinctions which resemble those of Bayle and were not distant from Montesquieu's. Virtue and vice, he notes, are supposed to stand for actions "in their own nature right or wrong." In reality, they are everywhere given "to such actions as in each country or society are in reputation or discredit." Thus men "establish among themselves what they will call virtue and vice," by this "approbation and dislike." [64] But Locke acknowledges, as we saw in relation to his theory of Natural Law, that many of these ideas are the same everywhere, since they express what men find to their advantage; and this corresponds to "the unchangeable rule of right and wrong, which the law of God has established."

Mandeville, in *The Fable of the Bees* (1714–1728), continued this empirical tradition. It was David Hume, however, who gave it greatest amplitude and most significant form. Hume achieves a synthesis of the natural-sympathetic and the artificial-utilitarian theories of the genesis of moral judgment. His principal targets were the rationalists, especially Clarke, who conceived moral relationships to be abstract truths like mathematics, directly perceptible to the mind. Reason, Hume argues, can tell us whether an action is in conformity with a rule or end, but no more; only feeling can win our adherence to it. There is a basic universality

---

[62] Lettre XVII.

[63] *Pensées*, in *Oeuvres complètes*, ed. André Masson, 1950–55, II, pp. 93–94. In contrast, we note the traditional statement in *Lettres persanes*, that we are born with an innate predisposition to specific virtues. (Lettre XXVI, Adam, p. 73.)

[64] *An Essay Concerning Human Understanding*, Bk. 2, chap. 28, Sec. 10–12. "There is not one of ten thousand, who is stiff and insensible enough to bear up under the constant dislike and condemnations of his own club."

in moral judgments (despite the apparent relativity of instrumental values induced by varying cultural structures). But this universality derives from the approval or disapproval which our acts encounter in those around us. Virtue, consequently, is any action or quality of soul which provokes a feeling of pleasure and approbation in those who witness it.

Thus far, all this might seem like a development of Locke's theory. But Hume's analysis cuts much deeper. And one important difference is already apparent. Reason, according to Hume's thesis, cannot motivate will or control passion.[65] It is, in fact "the slave of the passions," for all determinations of the will come from desire and aversion, pleasure and pain. By this Hume means only that objective reason has a practical function, the satisfaction of human desires. No passion can be deemed unreasonable in itself, but only if it is founded on objects which do not exist or if it chooses insufficient means for its end. Otherwise, "it is not contrary to reason to prefer the destruction of the whole world to the scratching of my finger." [66] Hume means that there is no sense in talking of passions in terms of rationality, for they are two different kinds of things. He does not mean that a rational knowledge of consequences will not affect behavior; the passions will be repelled or attracted by what they see as their objects. Hume, in a word, is attacking pure reason in ethics (as in Aristotle, Plato, or Descartes), and not reasonableness. There is, further, no "abstract, rational difference betwixt moral good and evil." [67] Moral values are not immutable, universal, inherent in things or discernable to human reason. Even if they were, no obligation would be involved unless we could also prove a necessary and universal connection between such objective relations and the will, which alone controls action. But there is no such causal connection.

While at first blush Hume may seem to give food to the nihilist, his effort is only to escape from the bonds of a false rationalistic structure which makes morality a matter of truths, that is, objective relationships independent of the sentient human being and his needs. Incest in animals, for instance, is—formally—the same as in men, and we cannot argue that it is because of our superior reason that it is for us a vice. "For before reason can perceive this turpi-

---

[65] We must keep in mind Hume's abstract and rather narrow concept of reason. Compare also Bayle, in *Pensées sur la comète.*
[66] Aiken, *Treatise of Human Nature,* p. 25.
[67] *Ibid.,* p. 39.

tude, the turpitude must exist, and consequently is independent of
the decisions of our reason. . . ." [68] The question then becomes,
what makes it a turpitude? It is not the act itself, considered as a
purely objective relation.[69] Vice comes into being only when "you
turn your reflection into your own breast and find a sentiment of
disapprobation which arises in you towards this action." The
disapprobation is a matter of fact, discernable to reason;

> but it is the object of feeling, not of reason. It lies in yourself,
> not in the object. So that when you pronounce any action or
> character to be vicious, you mean nothing, but that from the
> constitution of your nature you have a feeling or sentiment of
> blame from the contemplation of it. Vice and virtue, therefore,
> may be compared to sounds, colours, heat, and cold, which, ac-
> cording to modern philosophy, are not qualities in objects but
> perceptions in the mind.

But why do we experience a sentiment of approval or of blame?
Only, according to Hume, because an act or character "causes
a pleasure or uneasiness of a particular kind. . . . The very *feeling* constitutes our praise or admiration." [70]

We must remember that Hume's account is a genetic one. It
does not commit him to the confusion which we have previously
noted in others, between origin and validity. They are not identical for Hume. Benevolence is a criterion in a way which does not
make the morality of actions equivalent to pleasure. To confuse
the origin of judgment with its basis is not to talk of morals. It is
true that I would not make a particular moral judgment if I did
not like it; but the basis of judgment, and its validity, is its usefulness to mankind. There are, moreover, different kinds of pleasure, corresponding to quite different sensations. "It is only when
a character is considered in general, without reference to our
particular interest, that it causes such a feeling or sentiment as
denominates it morally good or evil."

But why do we have this particular kind of pleasure, which
causes us to take a wider view than our particular interest? The
answer is sympathy. Sympathy is an emotion aroused by the per-

---

[68] *Ibid.*, p. 41. Reason, then, does not create value.

[69] Hume would not admit that the objects (animals, man) being different, the
nature and meaning of the relationships involved in an act are also essentially
different.

[70] *Ibid.*, p. 44.

ception or imagination of similar feelings in others; it is the cause
of common attitudes and of benevolence; furthermore it is instinctual and not a form of egoism, as Hobbes, Mandeville, and
others had held.[71] Our pleasure in the utility of any quality comes
from our sympathy with the happiness of those affected. Sympathy
works by association of ideas to produce an identification with
our own experience, but the direction of the emotion is toward
others, toward beings who feel and behave like ourselves.[72] For
Hume, moral sentiment "is an outgrowth of natural human fellow-
feeling, extended by sympathy, and 'corrected' and 'stabilized' by
convention and habit." [73] Thus Hume avoids the reduction of
ethical judgments to egoistic or sentimental relativism. In judging,
we unconsciously assume the position of a "benevolent impartial
spectator." Since others do the same, basic moral judgments are
universal, although there is variation due to passing individual
factors. In the same way, we can see that moral distinctions are
real, and it could not be claimed that a villain is entitled to our
regard.

The question now remains, what are the objects of sympathy?
Sympathy is aroused by what is "useful or agreeable to ourselves
or others." Our approbation or blame is consequent to this reaction. But Hume goes beyond this empirical datum. The origin
of sympathy and benevolence excludes an instinctive love of mankind as such. In addition to the "natural" instincts of sympathy
which account for the "natural" virtues, we need the "artificial"
virtues (such as justice) which result from conventions. It is obvious that "artificial" is taken by Hume to mean what man adds to
natural impulse through custom or rational will. We develop a
sense of interest which binds us to these conventions as desirable
and useful, or ultimately, as right. The utility of many acts of
judgment is not apparent, but lies in "the maintenance of the
whole fabric of rules and customs whereby the stability and order
of society is assured." [74] This fabric is a necessary supplement to
nature and our interest lies in its universal observance. This in-

---

[71] See the second Appendix to the *Enquiry* for a refutation of egoistic theories.
For sympathy, see pp. 132–34, 142–43, *et passim.*
[72] See *An Inquiry Concerning the Principles of Morals*, Section V, "Why Utility
Pleases."
[73] Aiken, *op. cit.,* p. xxxv.
[74] Aiken, *op. cit.,* p. xxlx.

terest leads, by way of moral sentiment, to "a *new* obligation upon mankind." [75]

Justice or equity, for Hume, is a conventional or "artificial" virtue, arising "from education and human conventions." [76] It is not an immediate reaction of sympathy, pleasure, or utility. Justice is artificial in the sense that its rules are an invention of culture, necessitated by the fact that men act from self-interest (since if men acted naturally out of a regard for public interest, the rules of justice "would never have been dreamed of").[77] It is not a "natural law." In a situation of selfish interest, there is no natural principle of justice in us, for natural feeling makes us prefer self or family to others. The remedy derives from artifice; that is, from the *natural* faculty of reason which produces conventions, the latter being a reasoned decision about our best interest.[78] Hume may then state that justice is also the most natural virtue—in the sense that, although invented, it is universal and necessary to the species.[79]

Hume's distinction lies, then, in his separation of affective reactions as natural, and of the products of the understanding as invented and artificial: a distinction which he himself effectively abolishes and which, at best, can be reduced to a contrast between the spontaneous and reflective. The importance of culture and its accompaniments in the furtherance of the reflective process are not gainsaid. We may say that justice (and virtue) are natural developments of the self in relation to experience in society.

Hume does not rest at the reduction to the utilitarian "greatest happiness" principle. He recognizes that moral judgments of conduct concern intention or good will, and that moral responsibility is based thereon. The values, to be sure, which are or should be

[75] As Aiken phrases it, first common self-interest expresses itself in conventions, then their utility evokes moral approbation, thus giving rise to moral obligation, and finally our interest is transferred to the maintenance of the rules for their own sake (formalistic sense of duty). (P. xl.) See p. 134–36.

[76] P. 54.

[77] P. 64.

[78] Pp. 58–60.

[79] Pp. 54–55. There is no natural principle of justice in us (pp. 58–60), and no "eternal, immutable and universally obligatory" principles of reason or relations of ideas, but only what experience teaches us to be useful to our interest (pp. 64–65). Hume's opponents, and most French writers, would have answered: it is true that men are naturally selfish; but it is equally natural that reason necessarily perceive a relation between my desire to keep what is mine and another person's desire, with the necessary rational intuition of the moral law of reciprocity which constitutes justice and virtue

the objects of motives are expressions of what is useful and agreeable to mankind, that is, of human interest. But moral goodness refers to character and not to consequences; it refers to the sympathy and benevolence which motivate preference or approbation of the useful. Hume, moreover, recognizes a sense of duty which is different from moral sentiment, sympathy, or benevolence. It springs from "a regard for virtue," which is really a regard for the approval of a virtuous person or for the maxims he would approve.[80] Nevertheless, in the last analysis there would be no obligation to follow our sense of duty, or what an "impartial spectator" would approve, if we did not also approve, that is, if our pleasurable reactions and awareness of utility did not impel us to do so. It is useful or pleasurable to us to promote others' welfare and to pursue objects of disinterested approval.

Fundamentally, then, moral experience remains empirical and utilitarian.[81] But these characteristics assume forms which correspond to reactions or judgments which are universal and objective values and become subject to the approval of intention and good will. Hume does not really escape the identification of moral goodness with the utilitarian "greatest happiness principle," but rather circumvents it by defining moral goodness as the benevolent will to conform to the utilitarian principle. But disinterested approval which constitutes this moral quality is a value only because it is, in itself, useful and pleasing, and the same must be said of actions. Nonetheless, disinterestedness functions as the *principle* of moral action.

Hume's empirical account may indeed explain why some people prefer duty to self-interest. It does not explain our obligation to do so, especially if we feel no concern with the end to which the obligatory act is addressed. In other words, why should we do what is approved, or what secures approbation, if we conceive it to be in our self-interest not to do so? Ultimately, for Hume, we do the

---

[80] Aiken, *op. cit.*, p. xxxv. We see an analogy here with Rousseau's "spectator" and similar theories. What is involved are "adjectival values," the desire to consider ourselves as a certain kind of person, and to be so considered, in fact or in imagination. Hume's explanation, however, assumes a transfer of value from an end to an act which is the means to it, or similarly, from motive to the act which expresses it. For Hume this is not a moral motive—the only moral motives are those of moral sentiment. In fact, however, the desire for approbation of others is not distinguishable from the desire for self-approbation, and it is difficult to understand why the desire to think of ourselves as moral is not a moral motive.

[81] For a contrary view, see C. W. Hendel's edition of the *Inquiry*, p. xxxvi.

right because it is agreeable to us so to do, not because it is right.[82] But doing wrong may be more agreeable—the empirical proof being that many (or all) people do it. This is so because—as empirical evidence shows—we are not always bound by sympathy, by the (rational) regard for an impartial spectator, or by the desire to consider ourselves (or to be considered) as a moral person.[83]

It may be argued, to be sure, that this objection refers only to the genetic level of moral judgment, and not to the level of validity. For Hume, we have seen, morals have nothing to do with self-interest, though their genesis lies in pleasure and pain. Obligation exists in virtue of the principle of benevolence. What Hume really admits is that we cannot offer any reason to convince a man that he ought to be moral, if he does not experience benevolence. No one can demonstrate the obligation to prefer duty to self-interest, regardless of the kind of human being who is involved. On the one hand, Hume recognizes the dominance of self-interest; on the other, he asserts that the moral decision is one of benevolence, not of self-interest. If you then ask, "Ought I prefer duty to self-interest?" Of course the moral answer is "Yes." But if you prefer self-interest to the moral, there is no answer. In other words, the question "Why should I be good?" when "should" refers to a moral ought is simply tautological.[84] An analysis of this kind, however, was not likely to satisfy the imperious demand of eighteenth-century minds for an answer of what was considered the basic ethical problem.[85]

Hume gives us the impression that he is less interested in the substance of the moral life than in its origin and psychology. In his analysis along these lines, sometimes utility seems the dominant factor,[86] and at other times it is sympathy.[87] This is equivalent to his "artificial-natural" distinction. Actually, the significant thing is that he ultimately unites them as forms of pleasure-pain reactions,

---

[82] In fact, Hume admits that we often do the right from self-interest, habit or other nonmoral motives (among which he classes the sense of duty). But he argues that such acts would still be approved by the impartial spectator and involve no discredit to human nature. (Aiken, *op. cit.*, p. xxxix.) This is quite inconsistent with Hume's distinction between value and intention.

[83] Pp. 144–45. We may also inquire what it means to say that the virtue of what is useful lies in its utility (p. 168).

[84] For a similar view, see C. W. Hendel, *op. cit.*, p. liii.

[85] Compare Diderot's reply in "Droit naturel."

[86] E.g., p. 145.

[87] E.g., p. 156.

the reaction to what is useful being sometimes immediate, sometimes rational. Similarly, one may perhaps say that he sees value on a dual basis, first as self-interest, pleasure, and pain, and then in its objective, rational extrapolation.[88] Hume's method is far more empirical than that of any French writer of the eighteenth century. It consists of a close analysis of experience, which is always supreme.[89] His most significant accomplishment is perhaps to have united the natural (organic) and the cultural as inseparable parts of moral experiences.[90]

Many minor French writers upheld the social genesis of moral experience to the exclusion of innate faculties and abstract intellectual perception of absolute moral truths. Since it would be of little value to analyze all of these writers, we shall tarry instead on several of the major thinkers.[91]

[88] E.g., pp. 144, 155.

[89] E.g., pp. 166–67, 179.

[90] The reader interested in Hume's ethical thought is urged to consult Thomas Reid's refutation, in *Essays on the Active Powers of the Human Mind* (*Works*, ed. by Dugald Stewart, New York, 1822, III, pp. 255–315). Reid foreshadows the Kantian position and insists that moral approbation is a real act of judgment, as well as a feeling. He denies the objective equivalence of acts performed by men and by other living things; the "ought" establishes a new relation, between me and a certain action in my power. He maintains that there is moral value in actions as well as in persons, in actions which ought to be done by those able to perceive their obligation to do them.

Adam Smith, on the other hand, develops the theory of sympathy. He holds that the initial perception of right and wrong comes from "immediate sense and feeling," but admits that by reason we discover general rules as inductions from experience. We may apply to Hume Smith's criticism of Hutcheson: we approve and disapprove of approbation itself (as proper or improper). Smith's chief criticism of Hume is that utility is not the first or principal source of approbation, or else there would be no difference between moral approbation and approbation of a well-contrived machine or building. The first ground is rather "a sense of propriety" which is quite distinct from usefulness, and which may lead us to approve of what is not obviously useful. Utility has no reference to the sentiments of others, since it would be felt by persons brought up alone, whereas shame or self-esteem would not: these suppose the idea of another who judges us. (*The Theory of Moral Sentiments*, London, 1892 [1759], pp. 270–77, 461–81.)

[91] See Vauvenargues, *Introduction à la connaissance de l'esprit humain*, 1746, *Oeuvres*, I, pp. 76–77, and Lesage de la Colombière: "Nature provides no moral law." (*Principes naturels des actions des hommes*, Genève, 1749, pp. 8–10.) Another Swiss writer, E. Beaumont, sees the importance of mental association and training; he insists that morality belongs to the intelligence, though it begins with the physical sensation of compassion. In some ways he foreshadows Rousseau's pedagogical methods in *Emile*. However, we have, he claims, natural penchants to vice, but none to virtue, which must be learned. He denies any foundation to obligation other than that of self-interest, "since one's own interest is the highest reason." To make men moral, then, you must make it their interest to be so. (*Principes de philosophie morale*, Genève, 1754, p. 37 ff.) For the anarchist, Dom Deschamps, moral categories and content are due to society, but, paradoxically, true moral

La Mettrie's empiricism is in some ways close to Hume's, closer, probably, than that of the other *philosophes,* but his conclusions and general attitude are quite different. As the great proponent of the man-machine hypothesis, he excludes any purely psychic endowment. Moral experience must be understood as a derivative of physical (organic) mechanisms. "If we assume the least principle of motion, then animated bodies will have all they require in order to move, to feel, to think, to repent, and in short to conduct themselves physically and, which is dependent on this, morally." [92] This limitation to the physical excludes (as Hume does) innate moral feelings or perceptions, such as Natural Law, but also (contrary to Hume) immediate moral reactions to experience such as those of benevolence. Innateness he terms a vain attempt to make virtue and vice seem real. But if moral discernment were born within us, he adds with some sophistry, we could not be deserving.[93] It is inculcated in us only by education, especially by example, rewards, and punishment, and its maintenance depends on its association with *amour-propre.* Hence it is secondary, and frequently our real, original nature breaks out, and education is forgotten. In other words, man has no natural moral endowment or inclination to virtue, no moral drives or needs; sacrifice for the good of all is not natural.[94]

This is the role of social pressure. Since moral judgments stem from artificially inculcated reactions, we cannot treat ethics as a part of philosophy or science. "Such is morals; the arbitrary fruit

principles cannot exist until the social state is terminated (*Le Vrai Système,* 1939, pp. 83–84). Also worthy of mention: Mably, *Principes de morale, Oeuvres,* X, p. 280 ff.; Duclos, *Considérations,* 1751, p. 10; Charles Levesque, *L'Homme morale,* Amsterdam, 1775, pp. 12–26. Hemsterhuis (*op. cit.,* II, p. 58 ff.) defines moral experience as the capacity "to contemplate oneself, so to speak, from the center of another individual" and signals this objectifying power as the distinguishing human trait. Raynal (*Histoire des Deux Indes,* Livre XIX, chap. XIV) makes society both the condition of moral experience and the source of its corruption through rivalry. Saint-Lambert counts economic factors as the determinants of history, politics and progress, but also gives credit to love ("the sixth sense") as a prime source of needs; moral notions come from rational reflection on our relationships, based on generalizations from sensual experience. The need for sacrifice of egoism and will (obligation) and for authority is born in the family experience; later, it is supplemented by the rational concept of happiness. (*Oeuvres philosophiques,* I, pp. 44, 293–94; II, pp. 1–10; III, pp. 30–31; for a critique, see Barni, *Les Moralistes français au XVIIIe siècle,* III, p. 176 ff.)

[92] *L'Homme machine,* ed. Solovine, p. 134. Man differs from other animals only by having a slightly higher intelligence. ("Discours préliminaire.")

[93] *Discours sur le bonheur,* in *Oeuvres philosophiques,* Amsterdam, 1774, II, pp. 133–37.

[94] *Ibid.,* and p. 183.

of politics," but not of nature, reason, or philosophy, which are synonymous terms. Philosophy deals with things, laws, truth; ethics, with manners, feeling, arbitrary convention. Convention was necessary, to be sure: "Men having formed the project of living together, it was necessary to devise a system of political morals, for the safety of this intercourse." [95] It was necessary because men —far from feeling sympathy and benevolence—are vicious.[96] By our according esteem to forbearance from hurting others for egoistic profit, "many animals with a human face have become heroes." Gallows and torture are necessary to protect the weak from the depredations of the strong. In this way education "can give us feelings and a happiness contrary to what we would have without it," and modify our instincts. But not only do organs and instincts often reassert their natural ways; "we are not even the master to profit from our education as much as one might wish for the good of society." [97] La Mettrie, who ridicules religion and the supernatural, strongly urges their use as a powerful weapon to make men conform to the desired order. This sharp contrast with the efforts of other *philosophes* to free men from religious fears and imperatives is highly significant. It may, in several cases, indicate a belief on their part in a natural moral experience, or in the power of other social factors, or both. But most strikingly, it illustrates the uncompromising consistency of La Mettrie's materialism. He recognizes only the two empirical facts, man's selfish and cruel nature and society's needs. Morals are a product of these two, and the use of "false" repressive means cannot be distinguished in any way from other utilitarian mechanisms to a desired end. Moral restraints are a social tyranny, necessary and useful, but they have no other status whatsoever, in nature, human nature, or reason.

Beneath the moral conventions of man lies a law of nature, but it is not our moral law: "so much does nature's morality (for it has its own) differ from that which an admirable art has wisely invented." [98] Nature's "morality" consists of tastes, pleasures, and voluptuousness. This is indeed the proper subject of "philosophy," which is concerned with truth, regardless of consequence. The legislator, on the other hand, either is indifferent to truth or fears

[95] "Discours préliminaire."
[96] *Discours sur le bonheur*, p. 139.
[97] La Mettrie here points out the flaw in the deterministic theory of moral responsibility. See *An Age of Crisis*, chap. 6.
[98] "Discours préliminaire."

it and is concerned only with right and wrong, justice and injustice, which are his inventions to control men. Obviously, then,
La Mettrie is telling us that truth and morality are in contradiction, and that the philosopher, in his private world at least, will
follow the former. Philosophical morality is opposed to religious
and political morality, "as nature is to art." We cannot expect
either that nature and reason will deny themselves, or that society
will conform to nature. The last statement again sets La Mettrie
in sharp conflict with the moralizing materialists and explains
their hatred of him, which we find expressed in Diderot's writings.
Despite La Mettrie's reassurances that all his ideas were only
abstract theory, not to be applied to daily life, they saw his basic
nihilism. When he asserts that the "truth" can only strengthen
the social bonds, what else can he mean except that an arbitrary
social tyranny must be imposed? [99] His own praise of individual
revolt in pleasure belies his self-defense, and his separation of life
and thought is the enthronement of Machiavellian immoralism in
the shape of a "social morality." Morality, in a word, is morally
unjustifiable, but necessary.

D'Alembert's analysis is of interest because of its preciseness
and its attempt to conciliate the new experiential approach with
the traditional rationalistic doctrine. Moral notions, he explains
in the *Discours préliminaire* to the *Encyclopédie,* are "reflective
ideas" and not original sensations. They are not like mathematical
truths or abstract knowledge of general properties of bodies, but
are arrived at inductively from "the idea of ourselves." [100] D'Alembert amplifies his theory in the *Eléments de philosophie.* The
initial fact from which moral experience derives is mutual needs,
which automatically imply mutual duties. All moral rules flow out
of this reciprocity "by a necessary linkage" which is immediately
cognized as a form of self-interest, "the principle of all moral
obligations." [101] Since the creation of man as a social animal is
a divine act, "moral principles belong with eternal decrees." [102]
Apparently, however, this fact is of no pragmatic significance.

[99] "We know as well as you [the magistrates] this hydra [the people] with a hundred and a hundred thousand mad, ridiculous, imbecilic heads; we know how difficult it is to lead an animal who does not let himself be led, we applaud your
laws, your morals, even your religion, almost as much as your gallows and scaffolds."
[100] *Discours préliminaire,* ed. Picavet, pp. 22–29.
[101] *Eléments de philosophie,* p. 137.
[102] *Ibid.,* p. 208.

Societies preceded knowledge of God and grew out of human motives. And our knowledge of our mutual relations and needs was learned from sensual experience. The basis is, then, physical. Our sensations suffice, "without any operation of our minds, to give us the idea of physical hurt," which is the usual result of moral hurt. It is evident that in the order of knowledge, the idea of physical hurt "leads us to that of moral wrong, although they are of different natures." If man were impassive, he would never have the notion of wrong, whence derives that of right.

Returning to the *Discours préliminaire,* we find the last idea explained more fully by d'Alembert.[103] Pleasure and usefulness are the cement of social bonds. But since men are egoists, each wants a greater part of these advantages for himself. The ensuing rivalry prevents equality of usufruct, although all have an equal right. D'Alembert now expresses an idea which approaches that of La Mettrie, and which bears comparison with Rousseau's discussion of the "right of the strongest." There is, unfortunately, he says, another kind of right, prior to social and moral right, a barbarous right, to be sure, but inscribed in the law of nature, "called the law of the strongest, whose use seems to merge us with the animals, and of which it is nevertheless so difficult not to take advantage." The result is abuse and oppression. Men do not accept this oppression

> because they feel that nothing ought to have submitted them to it. This is the origin of the notion of injustice, consequently of moral good and evil, whose source so many philosophers have sought, and which the cry of nature, resounding in all men, evokes even in the most primitive peoples. . . . Thus what we experience through the vices of our fellows produces in us the reflective knowledge of the virtues opposite to those vices.[104]

We have, then, two natures, corresponding to the two notions of right. One is animal and primary, the other, though no less natural, is social and secondary, "the fruit of the first reflective ideas which our senses occasion." It constitutes Natural Law. D'Alembert's assumption that the second right is "right" is, as he presents it, arbi-

---

[103] Pp. 19–21.

[104] The abbé Hayer criticized the idea that protest gave rise to the idea of just and unjust. To have such a feeling of protest, he maintains, implies that the idea of just and unjust already exists. "One cannot say that oppression is unjust except on the basis of a notion of injustice." (*Op. cit.,* p. 153.)

trary and without justification. "Thus force," he says, "given by nature to certain men, and which they without doubt ought to use only for the support and protection of the weak, is on the contrary the origin of their oppression." But this is precisely the nub of the problem, and precisely what the nihilist was to challenge.

Disentangling the elements of d'Alembert's thought, we see that rights are prior to moral judgments; first, the basic, but immoral right of the strong and second, the subsequent, but also natural right to an equal participation in the benefits of society. The second, however, is purely theoretical. The interplay of the two leads to the natural but hitherto latent judgment of moral wrong, which, in turn, produces conscious formulation of moral right.

Voltaire's reflections are entirely devoid of originality. Their only importance lies in the diffusion they enjoyed and their representative value. Their only interest is the internal conflict to which they testify. Voltaire, as we have seen, held to the Natural Law theory: there exist God-created laws of right and wrong which are immediately intuited by conscience. But he was also a leading proponent of sensationism and an opponent of innatism. In this regard, however, he did not go so far as Condillac or his followers; remaining close to his admired Locke, he did not deny the innateness of faculties which would, for instance, be able to intuit truths of moral relationships. Despite this recourse, to which he long held, Voltaire later had doubts (at least occasional doubts, for his thought fluctuates) [105] about an instinctual conscience. Moving closer—in this regard as in several others—to the materialists, he asserts that we have no other conscience except "that which is inculcated by the times, by example, by our temperament, by our reflections." [106] A savage will readily treat others as he would not want to be treated by them—unless he has learned otherwise. Implicit in this declaration are several ideas: our primary, original nature is purely egoistic and nonmoral; moral notions are dependent on our organic endowment and the formative pressures of our upbringing. In both these ideas, Voltaire is remarkably close to a man whose philosophy he detested, La Mettrie. Again, partly out of his desire to attack Rousseau—another detested man —he asserts that virtue is not natural (Rousseau never claimed

---

[105] Cf. *Histoire de Jenni.*
[106] "Conscience," 1771, *Oeuvres,* ed. Moland, XVIII, pp. 234–36.

that it was!), that it does not exist in savages, but is developed gradually with the increasing cultivation of reason.[107]

From these statements, we are entitled to conclude that it is men who, making a choice from natural data, construct a value system that is not necessarily given, one subject only to their own judgments, individual and collective. If Voltaire goes a long way toward such a teleological value concept, it is doubtless because of its consistency with the social orientation of his definitions of right and virtue. The universality of certain moral principles may still be maintained; but it depends only on the empirical usefulness or harmfulness of certain acts to all societies. This is purely a matter of self-interest. No act has an intrinsic or formal value, its effect on men alone confers value on it. Voltaire even came to reject the current belief that virtue is in itself a sure source of happiness.[108] He is thus divided between the traditional account, with its security and rational neatness, and the pull of the new science and philosophy. As one scholar has aptly put it, his ethics are aprioristic only on the surface; more deeply, he exemplifies the drift to pragmatic, utilitarian, anti-metaphysical values.[109] As we have seen in the discussion of Natural Law, it is quite likely that he conceived his utilitarian and formalistic theories as perfectly complementary. Yet the contradictions are ineffaceable. They apply not only to the genesis of moral judgments, but to the substance. The "obedience to law" definition rests upon benefit to social order. Such a notion contains two debatable assumptions: first, that a particular law is not itself destructive to social order and welfare; second, that the prevailing social order is a just and moral order. And Voltaire has told us that justice is immutable, and precedes law. It is clear that these several values may lead to an inextricable dilemma.

In d'Holbach, on the other hand, we do not find conscious conflict, but a superficiality which allowed acceptance of incompatible premises and principles. D'Holbach was one of the most radical and proselytizing materialists of the eighteenth century, endlessly repeating a limited number of ideas in dull tomes heavy with ponderous rhetoric. His major work is called—in harmony with the dominant note of his time—*Le Système de la Nature* (1770);

---

[107] *Ibid.*, XXVI, p. 21.
[108] Article "Souverain bien," in *Dictionnaire philosophique*.
[109] H. Dieckmann, "An Interpretation of the Eighteenth Century," pp. 306–7.

a title which expresses his cardinal tenet, that if man is to be happy, he must learn—and follow—the chain of natural causes and effects. Only in this way can he know and remain in harmony with his own nature. The basic natural fact is that thought and feeling are only qualities of matter, organized in a certain way. Love, hate, desire, and aversion are only modifications of the specialized matter which is nervous tissue. Moral man is only physical man considered from a special point of view: that of the effects of his actions on other men. And physical man has only one motive, to be happy.

Given these facts, d'Holbach desires only one thing: to substantiate the indisputable bases of a universal, immutable natural morality of virtue, and to outline its content. He "saw no contradiction between determinism and a doctrine of moral imperatives. The combination of outright atheism and of a neo-Christian ethics was one of the most striking features of [d']Holbach's thought." [110]

His starting point is the denial of an innate conscience, of any inherent or essential moral qualities, judgments, or tendencies.[111] From nature we receive only sensitivity; all judgments are habits formed from pleasant or unpleasant feelings—just like taste. In nature there is neither good nor evil, but a sentient being feels good or evil in relation to his self-interest and self-preservation. Human nature and the conditions of life make association in societies necessary for these two ends.[112] Obligation is the simple product of "the need which men living in society have of each other." Duty is the means man is forced to take to obtain the well-being he longs for. Duty is only a means to get others "to work for his own happiness or to unite interests with him. . . . Moral obligation is the necessity of being useful to those whom we find necessary to our own happiness and to avoid what may alienate them." [113]

By this reasoning, d'Holbach reaches the conclusion that a virtuous life is necessarily happy, and a vicious one unhappy. This calculation is designed to provide the motivating stimulus and solve the problem of *why* we should be virtuous. A *reasonable*

---

[110] Vyverberg, *Historical Pessimism in the French Enlightenment,* p. 213.

[111] *La Morale universelle* (1776), 1820, I, pp. 3–4 ff. Also, p. 52, and III, p. 205.

[112] *Système social,* Londres, 1773, I, pp. 70–75. See also, *Morale universelle,* XIX–XX; *Système de la Nature,* I, pp. 131, 144–46.

[113] Adam Smith's theory of the genesis of justice and remorse is similar to this view of d'Holbach's. However, Smith enlarges it to include Hume's idea of the impartial spectator (*op. cit.,* pp. 119–24).

man will give up passing pleasures and advantages in favor of doing what is useful to others, and so to himself. "To speak to us of
a disinterested obligation is therefore to show complete ignorance
of human nature." [114] The more necessary and useful others are to
us, the stronger and more sacred our obligations to them, as in
the relationship between father and son. Since we must do good
to others, "that is what virtue consists of." When we say virtue is
desirable for itself, or justice is its own reward, we are really referring to the advantages and happiness they bring us. We love virtue
because we love ourselves. When we admire virtues that can do us
no personal good, it is because of a psychological substitution and
pride in the species.

The fact of selfishness does not, however, exclude compassion
and benevolence. Only we must not attribute those attitudes "to
a certain sympathy, an occult, chemical cause." [115] D'Holbach's
explanation is the usual materialistic one, of vicarious suffering
and egoistic relief, productive of a variety of pleasures. But compassion varies with one's physical constitution and experience,
and many men do not experience it. "What do I say! Men, for the
most part, believe themselves authorized, by the weakness or misfortune of others, to outrage them impudently, and take a barbarous pleasure in afflicting them, in making them feel their
superiority, in treating them cruelly, in covering them with
ridicule." Compassion, then, cannot be the origin of moral virtue.
But self-love, in the man who thinks, is always accompanied by
affection for others. In brief, then, experience and reason teach
men desirous of self-preservation and happiness that they need
other men to contribute to these goals; that certain actions which
they approve will produce this effect. The resultant ideas constitute judgments of virtue and vice, of just and unjust. [116]

D'Holbach realizes that relativism and subjectivity are the
dangers implicit in his theories. To avoid them, he insists on the
identity of human nature—of feelings, reactions, needs, and relations in society. This is the foundation of a "universal morality,"
and of values which are as objective and immutable, for d'Holbach,
as for any believer in Natural Law. [117] It is for the same reason that
he establishes ethics as a "system of nature." Unlike most of his

[114] *Système social*, I, p. 71.
[115] *Morale universelle*, I, pp. 100–4.
[116] *Système de la Nature*, I, p. 144.
[117] *Morale universelle, I*, xix–xx.

fellow materialists, he denies that moral values and judgments have their source in more or less arbitrary conventions. "It is on the necessary diversity of these effects that the distinction between good and evil, vice and virtue, is founded; a distinction which is not founded, as some thinkers have held, on conventions among men, and still less on the chimerical commands of a supernatural being, but on the eternal and invariable relationships which subsist among beings of the human species living together in society, and which will subsist as long as men and society do." [118]

D'Holbach's moral theory purports to rest exclusively on empirical data. Even if this were so, it must be said to be based on certain selected aspects of human nature, and on certain phases of experience. While he insists on the experiential origin, he excludes the relativism induced by "false customs." However, if experience alone were consulted, this relativism could not be excluded. Indeed, d'Holbach admits the great variety and contradictoriness of the moral rules by which men actually do live. Relativism is avoided only by the rationalistic assumption that these customs are based on "error," and do not in fact lead to self-preservation and happiness.[119] Despite its pretense of being a naturalistic theory, based on the physical organism and self-interest, d'Holbach's ethics is essentially a rationalistic system, in which a preconceived theory of virtue and a moralistic spirit seek justification in a naturalistic genesis. He selects his data so as to exclude two classes of facts: facts about man's moral experience which do not fit into his scheme of genesis, and facts about man's immoralism which belie his virtue-happiness equivalence and the universals he assumes to be necessary. As d'Holbach develops his theory, we see time and again that real experience and moral truth are implicitly or explicitly dissociated, and that the latter is made a function of reason, which alone (in his framework) can avoid relativism and egoism. Conscience is of little avail. "Only profound and persistent reflection on the immutable relationships and the duties of morality can enlighten the conscience, and show us what we should avoid or do, independently of the false notions which we find established." [120] When we read some of d'Holbach's pages on the rational basis of natural morality,[121] we cannot help doubting that it is "natural"

[118] *Système de la Nature*, I, p. 145; *Système social*, I, pp. 121–23.
[119] *Morale universelle*, I, pp. 44–47.
[120] *Ibid.*, pp. 57–59.
[121] E.g., *Système de la Nature*, II, pp. 254–55.

for most men to reason in this fashion, or that he has held to his proclamation: "the morality of nature, founded in the essence of man living in society." [122] This "experiential morality" assumes an absolute which human experience has nowhere attained, and the deduction of a certain happiness from the formula for behavior is a non-sequitur.

"The true system of our duties," writes d'Holbach—and there is only one—"must be the one which results from our own nature, properly modified." [123] Such a statement does not answer the essential question which it conceals. What makes one modification more "suitable" or "proper" than another? Why should I prefer someone else's judgment? If happiness is the only criterion, may we not suppose that different "modifications" lead to this result, especially since d'Holbach emphasizes the different natural constitutions and inclinations of all individuals? Are they not, then, all "proper"? On what grounds, moreover, can we make an ethical value-judgment among differing individuals or cultures? D'Holbach is doubtless aware of this aspect of the problem, for he proposes an answer to it. He tells us that we can evaluate competing moral judgments and value systems by comparing their usefulness for the race and their effect on its happiness.[124] This is at least consistent in its standard. But what has authorized him to change the locus of value from the sentient individual to the race? Again he says, "it is not the usefulness of an individual, of a body, of a nation which give it [virtue] its worth: it is the general utility of men, it is its conformity with the permanent interest of the human race"—with what reason shows us to be useful in all times and places.[125] The individual's happiness may be lost; what is useful here and now may be ignored. We are handed that great abstraction, "the human race," in the name of which men, guided by "abstract reason," have committed the greatest inhumanities. Nowhere has d'Holbach (any more than Helvétius or the other materialists) explained why we have the feeling that we *ought* to suppress an instinctive desire. But the sentient individual, amoral

---

[122] *Ibid.,* II, p. 268.
[123] *Morale universelle,* I, p. xi.
[124] *Système social,* I, pp. 93–94.
[125] *Ibid.,* I, p. 82. This inevitably leads him to ethical formalism. "Now there are actions and tendencies which by their nature or essence are useful and pleasant to men." Virtue and vice are not mere experimental conventions. Actions and things have an "intrinsic value." (*Ibid.,* I, pp. 116–19.)

and self-seeking, whom d'Holbach posits, will not cheerfully sacrifice his happiness to an abstraction. He will remember the *natural* laws d'Holbach has proclaimed, and the *natural* goals he is
entitled and required to seek by virtue of his constitution. For him,
d'Holbach's ethics will either become the dead letter which it is;
or if, like Sade, he is an outspoken rebel, he will call d'Holbach his
spiritual father.

It is well known that Diderot had anticipated several of Condillac's ideas by his publication of *La Lettre sur les aveugles* in 1749,
an event he was to regret because of his incarceration which followed. Although this brilliant work is far from being a complete
or systematic statement of Diderot's evolving materialism, it does
already contain its essential organismic basis. And there are no
reservations or escapes. Supernaturalism and final causes are refuted. Our entire moral and mental life is only the physical
activity of complex, highly integrated material structures, our
organs.

"I have never doubted," declared Diderot (with some exagger-
ation), "that the state of our organs and of our senses has great
influence on our metaphysics and on our morals, and that our
most purely intellectual ideas, if I may express myself that way,
follow closely the conformation of our bodies. . . ." [126] Thus a
blind man will not make a vice of immodesty in dress, but will
hold disorderliness and theft (against which he cannot easily protect himself) to be capital vices. The sympathy and pity assumed to
be a part of our inherent make-up will at least be modified (even
as they are by distance and size for us who see). "Ah, madame!"
exclaims Diderot, entranced with his illumination, "how different
is the morality of the blind from ours! How different again would
be a deaf man's, and how imperfect, or worse, a man who had an
additional sense would find our morality!" [127]

In the combination of internal, organic compulsions and external sensual stimuli, Diderot will increasingly emphasize the
former, thus leading to his eventual refutation of Helvétius. Contrary to Helvétius and to Condillac, he will underline the importance of the brain (the mind) as a kind of universal sense, the

[126] *Lettre sur les aveugles,* in *Oeuvres philosophiques,* ed. Paul Vernière, p. 92.
[127] Cf. *Eléments de physiologie:* "Our vices and our virtues depend very closely on
our organs" (IX, p. 334).

creative interpreter of sensations rather than their mere depository. The moral experience is in this sense rational, belonging only to men.

That sensationism led him to the same conclusions as his belief in the man-machine hypothesis is made obvious in his *Apologie de l'abbé de Prades* (1752), in which he asserts the complete dependence of moral judgments on sensations and on "the exercise of our corporal faculties." [128] They are really *judgments,* however, and not merely instinctual or affective reactions. They are cognitive intuitions, "an immediate induction from physical good and evil." Through this derivation, Diderot is able to rejoin his naturalistic concept of Natural Law, which we examined in an earlier chapter.

> Man cannot be susceptible of pleasant or disagreeable sensations, and consort at length with beings similar to him, thinking beings, free to procure him the one or the other, without having experienced them, without having reflected on the *circumstances* of his experiences, and without passing quite rapidly from the examination of these circumstances to the abstract notion of injury and benefaction; a notion which may be considered as the elements of Natural Law, whose first traces are impressed on the soul very early, become stronger daily, become ineffaceable, torment the wicked man within himself, console the virtuous man, and serve as an example for legislators.[129]

Moral judgment is not natural in the sense of "original," but only in the sense of necessarily generated habits of thought and feeling.[130]

This explanation persists throughout Diderot's writings. Even in the *Réfutation d'Helvétius* (1773–75), in which he poses the limits of materialism, he declares that "the diaphragm [makes] compassionate and moral men," and that a moralist should be a natural philosopher, a physiologist and a doctor.[131] In the very radical *Supplément au Voyage de Bougainville* (1772), he denies any native endowment other than similarity of physical organization, and in consequence, common needs and sensations of pleasure and pain; this "constitutes man as he is and should be the

[128] *Oeuvres,* I, pp. 450, 470–72.
[129] *Ibid.,* p. 471.
[130] *Salon de 1767,* XI, p. 25.
[131] *Oeuvres,* II, pp. 332, 338.

foundation of the morality which is proper for him." [132] In this
dialogue, as in *Le Rêve de d'Alembert* and *Le Neveu de Rameau*,
Diderot draws out the implications of his theory, and as we shall
see later, they hold anarchistic and nihilistic potentialities. It is especially significant that in these works he denies the creative role or
legitimacy of convention, in other words denies that social conventions are the source (rather than the mere formulation) of moral experience. In this he differs from many of the writers we have been
examining. His aversion to this common naturalistic explanation
may be accounted for on two opposing grounds. When speculating
in the vein of radical materialism, his locus of value is the individual, and he denies the "right" of societal organisms to override
the natural "right" to satisfy one's needs and proclivities. When
he is acting, contrariwise, as defender of moral values, his effort
is to reach a naturalistic version of Natural Law, to which the
relativism and arbitrariness of conventions would be inimical.
The latter tendency is again obvious in a piece doubtless written
for Raynal in 1772.[133] There is a universal morality, he there
affirms, eternal and immutable. The idea of justice, goodness, compassion, friendship, faithfulness, gratitude, of all vices and virtues
is not subject to change. The constancy and unanimity which persist through all apparent diversity have their roots in a constant,
eternal cause—a physical cause. "And where is this cause? It is in
man himself." And again, he tells us that similarity of organization,
needs, pleasures, etc., lead to the common enterprise which is
society.[134]

How different is the note Diderot strikes from d'Holbach's!
While the dour host of the philosophers constantly insists on a
calculus of self-interest as the result of the given conditions, his
friend, less system-bound, stresses the experience of right and
wrong, and the cognition of moral truths. Such truths derive from
utility, to be sure, and from self-interest. But the very notion of

[132] *Oeuvres philosophiques*, ed. Vernière, p. 505. The same idea will be once more
repeated in the *Réfutation d'Helvétius*: "Morals are founded on identity of organization, source of the same needs, the same pains, the same pleasures, the same
aversions, the same desires, the same passions." (*Oeuvres*, II, p. 356.)

[133] *Fragments, Oeuvres*, VI, pp. 444–45.

[134] A more spirited defense of this viewpoint is to be found in his earlier "Réflexions sur le livre de l'esprit." (II, p. 270.) On the other hand, Diderot was
always alive to individual differences. He does not deny that each culture has its
own moral character and interpretations, and in moments of paradox, will go so
far as to propose a separate moral code for the artist or for the superior person.
(See VI, p. 444, XI, p. 124 and *L'Entretien d'un père avec ses enfants*, V, p. 279 ff.)

self-interest is incomparably broader and more humane. Reporting to Sophie Volland on a conversation with d'Holbach, Diderot tells of upholding opinions such as these:

> . . . that the reasons for our being moved by the recital of fine deeds are innumerable; that we revealed [thereby] an infinitely estimable quality; that we promised others our esteem if they ever merited it by some rare and fine act; that we thus encouraged them to it; that fine deeds made us conceive the hope of finding among those around us someone capable of doing them; that, by the extreme admiration we gave them, we imparted to others the idea that we would ourselves be capable of them if the occasion arose; that, independently of all these views of self-interest, we had a notion of order, and a taste for it, which we could not resist . . . ; that no fine deed was ever without some sacrifice, and that it was impossible for us not to pay hommage to the person who sacrificed himself; that, although in sacrificing we were only doing what pleased us most, we were rightly impelled to honor those who gave up the most precious advantages for the one of doing good and having a better opinion of ourselves. . . .[135]

In an outburst such as this, we can see the full dimension of the humanism and spirit which Diderot adds to the narrow, dogmatic materialism of his time, and which on occasion breaks into open conflict with it. To a mind unusually aware of the complexities of all things, of life and of human beings, it was bound to become evident that the socio-physical story of moral genesis was inadequate, though not false, because of its exclusion from what man brought to experience of anything but a raw physical capacity for sensation. While it was not possible for him to conceive of such aspects of our inheritance as the "racial unconscious," nor even of such aspects of mental structure as the Kantian categories of thought, he did increasingly realize that man is possessed of unique psychic demands which, however dependent in the long reach on physical structure, are not to be entirely explained by phenomena so primitive and so universal to all forms of life as sensitivity and goal-seeking. This apprehension would again tend to reinforce his innermost tendency toward a revised doctrine of Natural Law—innermost, I believe, because it responded to the demands of his "heart," of his moralizing sentimentality, without being repugnant to the corrosive logic of his intellect. Over and against his reflective

[135] *Lettres à Sophie Volland*, éd. Babelon, 1938, II, p. 167 (septembre 1767).

theory of moral judgments, moreover, he at times insists on the spontaneous nature of virtue, rising out of our natural sympathy with others. This sympathy, which is taken to be innate in the *Essai sur le mérite et la vertu* and becomes biological in the later writings, overcomes the self-directed impulses.[136] Philosophically, this is important; for it testifies to his separation of the love of right from knowledge of it, contrary to sentimentalists or moral sense theorists.[137] Even in one of his radical pieces, the *Introduction aux grands principes,* where he adheres to d'Holbach's view and summarizes it in two lines;[138] even here, he admires forgiveness for offenses as "belonging to a great soul."[139] In this latter phrase he gives us the secret of his attitude toward life. Throughout his essays, fiction, and art criticism, we see a fervent admiration for "great souls"—great in evil, it is true, as well as in virtue—but one that bucks hard against any mechanistic reduction.

Diderot's insistence on the uniqueness of man grows as he advances in years and in wisdom. To understand morals, he tells us, we must know the nature of man, for otherwise there can be no definition of good and evil. This is what La Mettrie, Helvétius, and d'Holbach had proclaimed. But then Diderot drives his point home—perhaps against these same men: "What is a man? An animal? Of course; but the dog is an animal, too; the wolf is an animal, too. But man is neither a wolf nor a dog. . . . How many philosophers, failing to make these simple observations, have given to man the morality of wolves, as stupidly as if they had prescribed for wolves the morality of men!"[140] Diderot does not here define the nature of man. Doubtless it is still basically as he had stated it elsewhere: tendency, sensation, pleasure or pain, desire—leading, by reflection, to moral judgment. Doubtless he would still adhere to his definition of virtue (in the article "Juste"), as "an action which is or is not appropriate to the nature of the being who produces it." But these definitions do not exhaust the human situation.

The break becomes clearest in the *Réfutation d'Helvétius.* In

---

[136] R. Hubert, *op. cit.,* p. 185. Elsewhere Diderot derives sympathy from self-projection; when we hear about a fine action, we become all at once "the author or the object" of the deed. (*Correspondence,* ed. G. Roth, V, p. 76.)

[137] See *Oeuvres,* II, p. 397.

[138] [Man's duties are] "To make oneself happy. Whence the necessity of contributing to others' happiness, or in other words, of being virtuous." (*Oeuvres,* II, p. 85.)

[139] *Ibid.,* II, p. 87.

[140] *Salon de 1767,* XL, p. 124.

his withering demolition of Helvétius' system, one of Diderot's major points is the real distinction between "physical man" and "moral man." [141] He does not claim the moral to be independent and autonomous; but he does make it devastatingly clear that it is another mode of existence, neither comparable to nor congruent with the physical. He realizes with utmost clarity the weakness of the naturalistic genesis: even if true, neither the original genesis of the specifically human moral phenomenon, nor the elementary physical conditions that make it possible can explain what it *is* and *means* now. "I am a man, and I must have causes belonging specifically to man." [142] And for a man, moral experience is different from, and as real as, physical. Once more this brings us back to moral intuition and Natural Law.[143] Behind the shadow of Helvétius, it is the nihilist, the real foe, that Diderot is combatting. His defense, most curiously, returns the locus of moral judgment to the individual; whereas years earlier, in writing "Droit naturel," he had based his defense on a shift from the individual to the human race.[144]

Diderot differs, then, at least in his mature thinking, from both d'Holbach and from Rousseau in giving to presocial man a positive sense of justice.[145] Nature is amoral. Man's nature includes Nature's amoral forces and goals, but it has emerged to a new level or status of being. The process has involved different elements which Diderot never brings together in a systematic presentation. We can, without doing him injustice, bring together and interpret his major ideas. The problem is to overcome nature, which cares only for self-preservation and procreation, and supplies the power-

---

[141] II, p. 304.

[142] See *ibid.*, pp. 300–4.

[143] See the passage quoted earlier, pp. 57, 129.

[144] Diderot had written, "I am a man, and I have no other truly unalienable natural rights except those of mankind." Only the general will has the authority to pronounce in moral values. See above, chap. 1.

[145] For Rousseau there was injury but no offense. However in his *Apologie de l'abbé de Prades* (1752), Diderot had said that presocial man knew only resentment, which was "the only brake on injustice," and that men had no duties since there were no social conventions. (I, p. 455.) Antoine Adam summarizes Diderot's theory in this book: Primitive man had only one will and duty, to live. Similarity of interests and need led to herd life. But the conflict of egoisms, according to "barbarous natural right" [the phrase, we recall, is d'Alembert's] contradicts the right to life. Humanity would have destroyed itself. This led to the formation of legal or civil societies, the juridical state, founded on conventions. ("Rousseau et Diderot," in *Revue des Sciences humaines*, 53:23 ff., 1949. See especially *Oeuvres*, I, pp. 466–67.) Much of this development seems to be closely based on Montesquieu's Troglodytes. We shall discuss this point further in the next chapter.

ful egoistic, anti-social instincts. But in man egoism has learned to become altruism, in its own self-expression, sublimating itself through his higher rationality even to the paradox of denying its original impulses. Similarity of organization and needs, sympathy and community living, interdependence, all these lead to a natural taste for order, to a new need for the esteem of our contemporaries and even of future generations. There is no doubt that rational thought plays a large part in this journey of mankind, especially in the moments of struggle between nature and culture. Then we may have a rational vision of an ultimate good and an abstract ideal which often involve partial or complete sacrifice of the original good. Sentiment may or may not accompany such decisions, or motivate them.[146] In this way, then, men may hope to create a human world in place of the natural world of the struggle for existence. In this way, too, Diderot answers the challenge of nihilism, which he understood only too well: when happiness is my natural desire, why should I want to be unhappy? But this is not his only answer.

To understand Rousseau's theories, we should keep in mind Diderot's, to which they are, in part, in conscious or unconscious opposition. For this reason, we are obliged to begin with the matter of Natural Law, which produced one of their first major ideological differences.

The place of Natural Law in Rousseau's thought is, in fact, a vexed question. One primary datum for understanding this problem is his severance of the two components of *droit:* moral obligation, and rights. The question of rights, as the century advanced, became almost uniquely, in the atmosphere of the time, a political one, a matter of the civil rights of the individual vis-à-vis the power of sovereignty. While it has been tempting to accuse Rousseau of having accentuated this growing scission within Natural Law, the fact is that his political ideas had little influence until well into the 1780's or later.[147] The separation must rather be attributed to the general drift of political writings and to events of the times in France and in America. Rousseau rejects the doctrine of natural rights in society, and we shall later return to this issue. His attitude toward Natural Law, in the sense of natural

---

[146] *Essai sur la peinture,* X, pp. 519–20.
[147] See (but with caution) D. Williams, "The Influence of Rousseau on Political Opinion, 1760–95."

moral obligations, is complex and, on the surface, ambivalent. There is, however, a fundamental structural unity in his thought, despite the fact that not everything he wrote fits neatly into it.[148]

The basic structure of Rousseau's thought undermines the possibility of Natural Law as it is generally understood. The picture of man in the *Discours sur l'origine de l'inégalité* (1755) is incompatible with the idea of Natural Law as an innate experience. In that work, as in all his other works of socio-political theory, nature and culture are deliberately and completely divorced. This is perhaps the essential distinctiveness of Rousseau's philosophy and explains, as much as anything else, his battles with the encyclopedists, his former friends and associates. We need not enter into a refutation of the common notion, now disproven, that he preferred nature to culture.[149] In summary, we may say that he held social man to be in some ways worse off than "natural man," and that he felt romantic longings for the independence, immediacy, and guiltlessness of the original state; but that he considered the moral and even the rational development in the social state to be inherently of greater worth. It allows men, miserable and at war with each other because of the mixture of the two states in which they are now living, to conceive of ways of moving on to a purely social state, in which equality and happiness will be regained through the complete sublimation of natural independence.[150]

This conclusion is entirely consonant with Rousseau's highly original description of man in the state of nature. The chief element of that picture which concerns us here is the total absence

[148] There is no problem of a chronological development here. Rousseau's system was conceived in 1754–55, when he wrote the *Discours sur l'origine de l'inégalité* and the first version of *Du Contrat social,* and it remained whole despite some modifications. These two works, the article "Economie politique" (1755), and the published *Contrat social* (1762) form a generally coherent theoretical structure. While "Economie politique" already shows significant differences with Diderot's thought in "Droit naturel," it is in the second chapter of the unpublished version of *Du Contrat social* that he undertakes a thorough refutation of Diderot's position.

[149] See the excellent article by H. V. S. Ogden, "The Antithesis of Nature and Art . . ." pp. 645–49.

[150] For Rousseau's definitive statements in the second chapter of the first version of the *Contrat social,* see Vaughan, *The Political Writings of Jean Jacques Rousseau,* Cambridge, 1915, I, pp. 448, 449, 454; these passages are supplemented by the hortatory appeal in a fragment: "Make man one, and you will make him as happy as he can be. Give him all to the State, or leave him all to himself, etc." (I, p. 326). See also L. G. Crocker, "The Relation of Rousseau's Second *Discours* and the *Contrat social,*" pp. 42–44.

of a moral or conceptual life.[151] To transpose Rousseau's terminology (but not his ideas), we may say that his natural man is devoid
of any superego and possesses only a rudimentary ego. His life
unfolds at the biological level of the id. His fleeting relations with
others of his species are governed by an instinctual sympathy and
an instinctual self-protectiveness. These may be spoken of as a
"droit naturel," but not as a moral Natural Law of obligation. The
advantage of this state lies in the absence of the aggressive impulses
asserted by Hobbes, and denied by Rousseau who explains how
they are the product of social life. (There is no need for us to
discuss the fact that Rousseau's concept of what we call the id is
erroneous, and Hobbes's correct.) On the one hand, then, moral
experience (and consequently, Natural Law) does not exist prior
to society; on the other hand, while society in its present form has
made man a moral being, it has created a state of war and developed
vice more than virtue. It is clear why Rousseau conceives of a
state beyond these two. If social institutions have deformed men,
they can *reform* him.[152]

Rousseau, then, more than any other eighteenth-century writer,
is dominated by the idea of cultural evolution, as distinct from
mere historical progression.[153] Through acculturation, man creates
himself. Moral obligation is implicit in man's perfectibility—the
main characteristic which separates him from other animals—but
it is not functional in his original nature. The moral conscience,
operating in the conceptual realm of right and wrong, must be
awakened and developed in him by social living. "These words,
virtues, vices, are collective notions which are born only from con-
sorting with men." [154] Originally, then, there was no virtue or
vice.[155] One cannot therefore speak of a Natural Law as the

---

[151] He criticizes philosophers who, like Locke and Pufendorf, "have not hesitated
to suppose in man, in that state, the notion of right and wrong, without bothering
to show that he must have had this notion, or even that it was useful to him."
(Vaughan, *op. cit.*, I, pp. 140–41.)

[152] In the first version of the *Contrat social*, he writes: "And so the sweet voice of
nature is no longer an infallible guide for us, nor the independence which we received from her, a desirable state. . . ." (Vaughan, I, p. 448.) By comparing Rousseau's projected state beyond the present social state, with that of Dom Deschamps
or other primitivists and anarchists, we can see how his thought evolves in an
antithetical direction.

[153] It is noteworthy that Diderot never applied to societies his poetic vision of
cosmic evolution in *La Lettre sur les aveugles.*

[154] *Préface à Néron* (1752), *Oeuvres*, V, p. 108, n. 1.

[155] This is explicitly described in the second *Discours* and restated in the first
Contrat social, Vaughan, *op. cit.*, I, p. 448. See also *ibid.*, I, p. 335. When Rousseau,

original source of obligation. In fact, insofar as culture must be conceived (as Rousseau does conceive it) as the negation of nature, we may even say that morality, exactly like reflection, is *unnatural,* "a state against nature," as Rousseau puts it, the sign of *"un animal dépravé."* The "law of nature" is the law of the strong: "Nature deals with them ["natural men"] precisely as the law of Sparta did with the children of citizens; it makes strong and robust those with a good constitution, and eliminates all the others." [156] Although it is true that Rousseau here refers to this process with a nuance of approval, the essential point is that he realizes the danger (or the impossibility) of equating moral value and natural value. Nihilists, precisely, were to use for their own purposes the idea of the supreme or unique validity of nature. Rousseau understands that moral value depends on our perfecting transcendence of nature (understood as the qualities he attributes to natural man, or to animal nature in general). He consequently rejects the state of nature as a normative state, or as one in which norms exist.[157]

Rousseau has established the thesis that the moral dimension of human life is a product of cultural evolution rather than an original function or a direct result of biological evolution.[158] He has brought out a truth which Montesquieu had glimpsed and which Kant was to emphasize, that innocence cannot maintain itself. In other words, morality involves a loss as well as a gain for

in the first chapter of the *Contrat social,* writes that "the social order is a sacred right which is the basis of all others," he means that rights, like obligations, are moral notions which do not exist in the natural state of force. Voltaire and Diderot also believed that man has naturally compassionate and selfish impulses and that the latter are exacerbated in society; but for them (though on different grounds for each) man was naturally and inevitably a being who made moral judgments.

[156] *Discours sur l'inégalité,* in Vaughan, *op. cit.,* I, p. 143. Men also have their specific natural law of compassion. Rousseau deliberately rejects current notions of Natural Law on the ground that they require intellectual development, and as being a mere assemblage of useful rules fictitiously denominated "law." (*Ibid.,* I, pp. 136–38.)

[157] On the 18th of November, 1762, Rousseau proclaimed the unity of his philosophy and confirmed his earlier analysis in a letter to Christophe de Beaumont, archbishop of Paris (Rousseau: *Oeuvres,* Hachette, III, pp. 62, 64–65). "Conscience is developed and acts only with enlightenment. It is only by his *lumières* that he [man] gets to know order, and it is only when he knows it that his conscience brings him to love it. Conscience is therefore inexistent in a man who has not compared and who has not seen his relationships. In that state, man knows only himself; he does not see his own good as opposed to or in conformity with that of anyone else; he neither hates nor loves anything; limited to mere physical instinct, he is nothing, he is stupid: that is what I proved in my *Discours sur l'inégalité."*

[158] Man, he repeats in the same letter, is originally only an animal with physical instincts, knowing no good or evil (*loc. cit.*).

mankind, in its acquisition of guilt. But we must not let this thesis conceal the fact that for Rousseau moral experience does develop naturally, *with the natural coming into being of cultures.* The willful creation of moral value on which, to a considerable extent, he comes to rely is not exclusive of natural moral evaluation understood in this way. Although culture is artificial, its creation is inevitable for man in the course of events. This is Rousseau's constant opinion. As soon as transactions between men become settled, regular, formalized, language comes into being and the intellectual realm along with its accompanying moral realm, hitherto dormant, spring to life. Moral experience may thus be spoken of as the result of culture, but its coming into being is, like that of culture itself, entirely "natural," that is, unreflective, an unwilled and spontaneous process.

How does this process take place? Rousseau offers us various explanations. They are not mutually exclusive. At one point, in the second *Discours,* he merely says that established relations between men "required different qualities in them from the ones they had from their original constitution," and that morality was "beginning to be introduced into human actions." [159] Although he follows this with the statement that natural pity was attenuated and makes no affirmation here about the genesis of morality, it is difficult to conceive that the feeling of compassion, which he had described so eloquently a few pages previously, was not involved in the process. This interpretation is substantiated by a passage in the Preface in which Rousseau speaks from an abstract analytic viewpoint, before he actually undertakes his genetic account of culture.[160] After mentioning the necessity of going back to the beginnings in order to determine the real meaning of *droit naturel,* he rejects two well-known versions: that of certain Roman jurists for whom it was a purely descriptive "law of nature" applied to all living beings, and the rationalist modern version, that of a prescriptive rule for men alone, which is not only vague and contradictory, but assumes a level of intellectual development that cannot be attributed to primitive man. A "Natural Law" must compel self-conscious obedience, and it must also "speak immediately through the voice of nature." The only two such principles that Rousseau can find are self-preservation and compassion. The

[159] Vaughan, *op. cit.,* I, p. 175.
[160] *Ibid.,* pp. 136–38.

latter feeling checks the former and tells man "His duties towards others." [161] Yet this is not really virtue, nor a conscious knowledge of moral right and wrong; and that is why the attainment of the moral level in culture makes it necessary to re-establish these rules "on other bases." This would not be possible, he tells us, without pity, from which "quality flow all the social virtues." [162]

The brief but important "Note O" furnishes us with clues to other possibilities.[163] We recall how Rousseau accepts Abbadie's separation of *amour de soi* and *amour propre*.[164] The former is natural and good; "directed in man by reason and modified by pity, [it] produces humaneness and virtue." This would indicate an origin in combined self-interest and pity. *Amour de soi* is operative both in the state of nature and in society. In the latter state, however, *amour propre* begins to function. A man is no longer the sole spectator of himself and in consequence his own and only judge. He can no longer look upon other men merely as "animals of another species," and injuries are therefore no longer without moral connotations. In this way there takes place the major psychological development, involving merit and demerit, pride and shame, esteem and self-esteem, all involved in the comparative process in which we see and judge ourself through the eyes of the spectator, of the "other." [165] It is logical to suppose (and Rousseau may well have had in mind) a process in which this consciousness of the "other" as spectator becomes an internalized self-consciousness, a process in which the phrase "spectator of oneself" is transformed from a subjective to an objective mirroring. This would indeed be a plausible explanation of the genesis of the moral conscience, a more subtle version, perhaps, than the internalization of the superego expounded by Freud and, in cruder form, by La Mettrie and other eighteenth-century materialists.[166] Shame and pride, rooted in our need for approval and self-approval, would then be the origin of our moral judgments—a natural product of social relations (which Rousseau considers to result from the natural growth of artificiality).

---

[161] The word "duties" is unhappy and misleading, since Rousseau makes it abundantly clear that there is no idea of obligation or virtue.

[162] *Ibid.*, p. 161.

[163] *Ibid.*, p. 217. It is completed by the important passage on pp. 195–96.

[164] See *An Age of Crisis*, pp. 279–80.

[165] Vaughan, *op. cit.*, I, p. 174. Only Rousseau points out that identity of nature is a cause of dissension as much as of union (*ibid.*, I, p. 447).

[166] There is no question of Hume's "impartial benevolent spectator."

Yet such an explanation, while sufficient for certain naturalists, may have been considered inadequate by others who, like Rousseau, believed in the creative power of the self and of reason. It is certain that we feel shame (objective and subjective), the disesteem of others and of ourselves ("adjectival values"), the projection of the ego-image and its violation—an image which to a large degree has been formed by the internalization of accepted values, mores, standards. But if man can transcend nature through culture, and culture through his own self, then that ego-image and our value judgments are not entirely ingested. We are capable of independent or creative judgments of the rightness or wrongness of an act or situation.

Thus Rousseau maintains that when the natural feeling of humaneness is stifled by the competitive drives, a so-called "Natural Law" develops in us, "which should better be called the law of reason." [167] In this way, the natural feeling, or its effect, comes into being again, because "the more we become enemies of our fellow men, the less we can get along without them . . . such are the foundations of that universal benevolence, the feeling of which is stifled even as we recognize its necessity." [168] In an important fragment, "L'Etat de guerre" (1753–55?), Rousseau again recognizes Natural Law. In a brief statement, he reveals his ambivalent feelings toward it, an admission of its existence and a distrust of its efficacy. "As for what is commonly termed international law (*droit des gens*), it is certain that, for lack of sanctions, its laws are only chimeras weaker even than Natural Law. The latter at least speaks in the heart of individuals. . . ." [169] It is also significant that in the same piece he goes beyond the attribution of Natural Law to reason. "If Natural Law were written only in human reason, it would be scarcely capable of directing most of our actions. But it is also engraved in man's heart in ineffaceable letters; and it is there that it speaks to him more strongly than all the precepts of philosophies; it is there that it cries out to him that he is not allowed to sacrifice the life of his fellow man except to preserve his own. . . ." [170] We might attribute this dissonant remark to the polemical purpose of refuting Hobbes. But the

[167] *Ibid.,* p. 449.
[168] *Ibid.,* p. 447.
[169] *Ibid.,* p. 304.
[170] *Ibid.,* p. 294.

idea occurs too frequently in Rousseau's writings. The idea and the tone leads us inevitably to a work which lies outside the basic structural group of writings in which Rousseau oulines his theory of the individual and society, one which seems to have little intellectual relation to them, the *Profession de foi d'un vicaire savoyard* (1762).

As we have seen, the belief in an innate or intuitive judgment of right and wrong is not contradictory to the affirmation that "natural man" has no moral experience until he is no longer "natural" but social.[171] From one end of his career to the other, Rousseau consistently proclaims the intuitive knowledge of right and wrong, which is associated with the conscience and is akin to Natural Law. "We have an internal guide," he writes in rejoinder to the King of Poland's refutation of his *Discours sur les sciences et les arts* (1749), "far more infallible than all books, and which never abandons us in time of need. It would suffice to guide us guiltlessly, if we were always willing to listen to it." [172] This principle leads to an extreme subjectivism, which doubtless is one reason for Rousseau's lack of reliance on this resource in his social theories, a point which is often overlooked. The Savoyard Vicar also finds rules of conduct "written by nature in ineffaceable letters at the bottom of my heart." He draws a logical conclusion from this belief. "I have only to consult myself on what I want to do: everything that I feel to be right is right, everything that I feel to be wrong is wrong. The best of all casuists is my conscience." [173] Rousseau does realize the duplicity of nature's laws, nonmoral and moral, in man, but gives priority—arbitrarily, it may be said—to the moral law.[174] "We think we are following nature's impulse, and we are resisting it; in listening to what it tells our senses, we scorn what it says to our hearts." Here we have a common assumption of many eighteenth-century writers who sought to ground moral law in natural law.

This spontaneous judgment also emphasizes the link to compassion which has been suggested. "Iniquity is pleasing only insofar as

---

[171] Also in the *Lettre à d'Alembert*: "Man only has to establish the first relations of society to give to his feelings a morality always unknown to animals." (Ed. Fuchs, p. 116.) The universality and immediacy to reason of the clauses of the social contract (chap. VI) are another instance.

[172] *Oeuvres*, I, p. 35.

[173] *Emile*, ed. Richard, Garnier [1951], p. 348.

[174] See also Vaughan, *op. cit.*, I, pp. 322–23.

we profit from it; in all else, we want the innocent to be protected. If we see in a street or road some act of violence and injustice, at once a surge of wrath and indignation wells up at the bottom of our hearts and impels us to defend the victim." [175] The passage continues, citing, as moralists from the beginning of the century had done, our reaction to crimes and virtuous deeds in the remote past, concluding that we hate the wicked because we hate wickedness, and for no egoistic reason. All this is in harsh contrast to the second *Discours,* in which we are told that such sentiments are stifled in society, overcome by a sadistic pleasure in hurting others. "There exists, then," concludes the Vicar, "in the bottom of our souls an innate principle of justice and virtue," which we call conscience.

This analysis must be completed by a statement earlier in *Emile,* which indicates the actual mechanism of the genesis of moral reactions. We are conscious, first, not of right, but of wrong.[176] "Our first duties are to ourselves; . . . all our natural impulses relate first to our self-preservation and welfare. Thus the first feeling of justice does not come to us from what we owe, but from what is owed to us; and it is still another *contre-sens* of usual upbringing that, speaking first to children of their duties, never of their rights, we begin by telling them the opposite of what we should. . . ." [177]

This last statement is extremely curious. It is in accord with Note O of the *Discours,* but goes beyond it. It largely negates the Vicar's theory that the genesis of moral feelings is connected with natural compassion and attaches it instead to natural self-interest— a derivation which was that of the naturalists and materialists. Its emphasis on the primacy of rights is also similar to the "revolutionary" theory of Natural Law. The importance of this passage is heightened when we recall that it is by virtue of an innate sense of the right of property, and its violation, that Emile's tutor actually awakens in him the idea of justice.[178]

Rousseau's belief in the inevitable evil of human nature in society does not, then, exclude Natural Law of a kind. On the other hand, he considers the individual rationality and conscience

---

[175] *Emile,* p. 350.
[176] Cf. d'Alembert and Diderot.
[177] *Ibid.,* p. 88.
[178] *Ibid.,* p. 91.

as pragmatically inadequate or untrustworthy, despite their theoretical or subjective self-sufficiency.[179] These are the two positions in Rousseau's thought which are difficult to reconcile, the one taken from the viewpoint of the sentient individual, the other from that of the collective organism. The reason for the inadequacy of conscience and Natural Law is the very reason for his rejection of the solution to the moral problem proposed by most of his former comrades, enlightened self-interest. Both in the *Discours* and in the first *Contrat social* (and again in the fourth *Rêverie*), he denies the hypothesis that the general good and the good of the individual are ever the same. (It is only the general will as incarnated in the individual that is the same as the general good; therefore they may become identical in the projected good society.) [180] In the former work he asserts that the individual has always more to gain by preferring his own interest.[181] In the *Contrat*, refuting Diderot's "Droit naturel," he tells us that the private and general interest are "mutually exclusive in the natural order of things; and social laws are a yoke that each is willing to impose on others, but not to burden himself with." Even if a person were willing to make this sacrifice, he would have no certainty that he would not merely be exposing himself to the exploitations of the strong, "without daring to make it up on the weak."

In other words, there is a natural law of egoism which counters and tends to nullify the natural moral law. Culture transforms both elements of the original *droit naturel*—self-interest and compassion—in a way which is not favorable to moral life in society. The progress of society, reasons Rousseau, only stifles any such Natural Law and strengthens personal interest, because such a Natural Law could only be known after an intellectual development had taken place, and by that time passions would also have developed and made all its precepts impotent. "Indeed," he concludes in a moment of extreme negation, "if the notions of the

---

[179] Rousseau's dubious attitude toward the efficacy of subjective moral experience is illustrated by his statement ("Lettre sur la Providence") that a belief in immortality, in the reparation of injustices in the next world, is a necessary moral motive, and also by his introduction of a civil religion in the *Contrat social*.

[180] See Vaughan, *op. cit.*, I, pp. 323–24.

[181] Vaughan, *op. cit.*, I, p. 203. He expressed the same opinion in "Economie politique": "But unfortunately personal interest is always in inverse proportion to duty" (*Ibid.*, I, p. 243). This will be one of Sade's basic tenets.

Deity and of Natural Law were innate in all hearts, it was an unnecessary task to teach them both." [182]

When Rousseau, in the first chapter of the published version of the *Contrat social,* declares that *droit*—by which he surely means a code of rules and values, as distinguished from spontaneous moral reactions—derives from the social order, that it is artificial and not natural, he is planting a signpost to the interpretation of all his thought. Rousseau understood that it is man's nature to transcend nature, to create himself and to elaborate his own historical existence. The fixity of Natural Law was not suitable for his revolutionary thinking. When we think of remaking society, of the good society, it is not nature we must think of, but human will and reason; not those of the individual, to be sure, subjective and corrupted. We need not go into details, but the evidence is ample in support of one critic's formulation of Rousseau's thinking: "The laws of society must be laws against human nature, a yoke curbing human selfishness, not a code imposed by the reason of the individual." [183] Independence must be transformed into interdependence, the atomism of individuals transmuted into the unity of an organic whole. In short, any fixed prior limit, such as Natural Law or unalienable natural rights, would prevent the individual and social transformation Rousseau has in mind by confining the sovereignty of the new *moi commun* (the collective or corporate self).

In reply to Diderot's hypothetical nihilist of the article "Droit naturel," Rousseau would not propose a mythical general will existing naturally among all mankind. Such a will can only be the artifact of a cultural group. "Let us show him, in art perfected, the remedy for the evils that art begun did to nature. . . . Let him see in a better constitution of things the reward for good actions, the punishment of bad ones and the sweet accord of justice and happiness." [184] Man is brutish and unmoral in the state of nature, "unhappy and wicked when he becomes sociable." Living in a hybrid state in which nature and culture are in perpetual contradiction and at war, "at once in the freedom of the state of nature and submitted to the needs of the social state," he cannot know

---

[182] *Ibid.,* I, pp. 449–51. See also the quotation from a letter to Mirabeau, in Vaughan, *op. cit.,* I, p. 49n.

[183] Ogden, *op. cit.,* p. 649. See also L. G. Crocker, "The Relation between Rousseau's second *Discours* and the *Contrat social.*"

[184] Vaughan, *op. cit.,* I, p. 454. (*Contrat social,* first version.)

justice, equality, happiness. Can he leave this state by dissolving culture? Rousseau always proclaimed this to be impossible and undesirable. The other alternative is the one he chose. Diderot, in "Droit naturel," had found no way to overcome the natural order of egoism except to postulate an equally natural moral order of Natural Law. Rousseau denies the latter, in the state of nature, and makes it inefficacious in society. Far more naturalistic than proclaimed naturalists like Diderot (and later, d'Holbach), he sees nature for what it is, but (unlike Sade, for instance) rejects it and calls on men to correct, overcome, and surpass it through culture. This is what he calls "virtue." This is his answer to the problem of the nihilist posed by Diderot, "the man who brings terror and chaos into the human kind."

To Rousseau, Diderot's reply seems futile. Even if we were to suppose a natural moral law and knowledge of it, the vital question, why I should sacrifice my egoistic interest to it, remains unanswered according to Rousseau. More accurately, Diderot's proposed answer, that the recalcitrant egoist excludes himself from the human kind and joins the ranks of wild beasts, is not merely ineffective, but irrelevant. The very analysis of human nature practiced by Diderot and all the naturalists has shown that we must act on pleasure-pain (or self-interest) motivation. "It is a matter," then, "of showing me what interest I have in being just." [185] This, as we have seen, cannot be demonstrated.[186] But even beyond this, even if we accept—as Rousseau here does— Diderot's definition of general will as "an act of pure understanding which reasons in the silence of the passions on what man can expect of his fellow and on what his fellow can expect of him," this definition is again irrelevant and without value. "But where is the man who can separate himself from himself?" Certainly *nature* does not support this possibility, for nature orders us to consider ourselves before the generality. And how many men are capable of attaining to such a speculative level? Or capable, with the best of good will, of reasoning correctly, without mistaking inclination for reason?

This point is of maximum interest; for Rousseau is here denying the validity and prerogatives of the individual conscience,

---

[185] Vaughan, *op. cit.*, I, p. 452.
[186] In society, it is advantageous and even necessary to hurt others (Vaughan, *op. cit.*, I, pp. 179, 202–3).

which he was to exalt in the *Profession de foi*—and I can see no way of reconciling the two opposites. Here he not only reduces the moral problem to naturalistic terms of self-interest motivation, but treats conscience in the same terms. Here conscience is not the voice of God, but exactly what it was for La Mettrie, Helvétius, or Sade: "This voice, it is said, is only formed by the habit of judging and feeling in the midst of society, and according to its laws; it cannot therefore establish them." [187] Thus Rousseau accepts Diderot's definition of general will as an act of pure intellect, but demonstrates its inadequacy. Diderot has ignored the emotional and instinctive forces in man in their exacerbated social form. The society which gives man intellect also develops passions which destroy reason's harmony. In similar fashion he adds a bit farther on:

> All justice comes from God, he alone is its source; but if we were able to receive it from up-high, we should not need government or laws. Certainly there is for man a universal justice, emanating from reason alone and founded on the simple right of humanity. But this justice, to be operative, must be reciprocal; to look at matters in a human way, the laws of justice are impotent among men; they only profit the wicked and burden the good. . . . It is a beautiful and sublime precept to do unto others as we would want them to do unto us. But is it not evident that far from serving as a foundation for justice, it needs a foundation for itself? For what clear or solid reason is there why I, being I, should act according to a will which I might have if I were someone else? [This is the nihilist's question.] It is also clear that this precept has a thousand exceptions which have only been given sophistical explanations.[188]

"We must therefore have conventions and laws in order to unite rights with duties," Rousseau concludes. But what is Natural Law, except this reciprocity of rights and obligations? Rousseau, quite plainly, holds it to have no effective existence by itself, either *before* society or *in* society, because of human nature.

Rousseau uses his naturalistic analysis to show that if we would speak of moral value, we must rise above nature, and above the motivation, the experience and the self of the individual. For

---

[187] Rousseau will later be trapped in the same vicious circle, in his concept of the Legislator.

[188] Vaughan, *op. cit.*, I, pp. 491, 494. (Also in final edition, II, chap. 6.)

even if we look for the general will, as Diderot suggests, outside
of conscience, in written law, in the social actions of all people, in
the tacit conventions of the very enemies of mankind, we shall
find that any ideal order we can imagine is projected from
the social order we know. "We really begin to become
men only after we have become citizens." Rousseau's appeal, it
follows, is not to an abstract sense of justice, manifest to right
reason everywhere.[189] His appeal is to a new cultural entity, the
"general will," a metaphysical conception based on the cultural
creation of "a collective self" (*"le moi commun"*). This "general
will," which theoretically at least, is "susceptible of empirical examination in terms of existing beliefs and aspirations,"[190] is his
substitute for Natural Law, or more precisely, his supplement to
it, that which gives it effective existence. While for Diderot general
will was a synonym for Natural Law, for Rousseau it is a supervening collective conscience, whose validity lies in the "collective self"
which is created out of the fusion of atomistic individuals into a
true organism.

This is why, in "Economie politique" (and also in the *Discours*),
Rousseau takes care to sever completely the authority of the State
from the model of the natural authority of the *pater familias*. The
family relationship is natural; for the father "the voice of nature
is the best guide," and he "has only to consult his heart." The
magistrate, however, functions in a cultural situation. Natural impulse is "a false guide" for him, and must, in fact, be overcome by
"the most sublime virtue." The sole rule for him is "public reason,
which is the law."[191] Law is the expression of the general will (we
may take this to be a normative rather than an empirical definition); and Rousseau pays significant attention to the means of
determining that will. The essential matter is that the general will
becomes the standard of justice for individual and for State. This
is possible because "the political body is thus also a moral being
which has a will"; and this general will "tends always to the preservation and welfare of the whole and of each part."[192] Consequently, it is "for all the members of the State, in regard to them
and to it, the rule of right and wrong"; for "everything that the

---

[189] R. V. Sampson, *Progress in the Age of Reason*, London, 1956, p. 149.
[190] *Ibid.*
[191] *Ibid.*, I, pp. 239–40.
[192] "Economie politique," Vaughan, *op. cit.*, I, pp. 241–42.

Law orders" is legitimate.[193] Right and wrong thus become not only what has been a *natural* creation of culture (conscience, Natural Law), but a rational, willful, teleological creation, one which surpasses nature, although its purpose is to realize the profound natural aspiration of men—happiness.[194]

The essential principle of Rousseau's social ethics is the same as Diderot's: "that each prefer in all things the greatest good of all." [195] For Diderot this is an absolute dictate of rational Natural Law.[196] For Rousseau it flows, directly and specifically, from the social contract, an act of will: it substitutes a *droit juridique* for *droit naturel,* legality for morality. Although in this passage he

[193] This should not be taken as a Hobbesian phrase, but in relation to the previous definition of law. The opposition between Natural Law and general will may be illustrated by the fact that as early as 1789 Isnard, the future Girondist, rejected the theory that law was the expression of general will; Natural Law, he declared, existed apart from the will of the people. Robespierre and the Jacobins were to follow Rousseau's doctrine.

[194] D'Entrèves points out that the voluntarist notion of law as pure will is associated with Calvinism (*Natural Law,* p. 67). He also shows that the doctrine of absolute sovereignty (which Rousseau is logically obliged to proclaim in order to *create* right through the general will) excludes the possibility of Natural Law. "Natural Law is not properly law if sovereignty is the essential condition of legal experience." Rousseau's conception of the political body leads directly to Hegel's "ethical State," which holds that the State is the highest manifestation of ethical life and that "absolute ethical totality is nothing but a people or a nation." The "right" of the State stands above any other—"the power of reason actualizing itself as will." This doctrine is a complete substitute for Natural Law, holding that the welfare of the community has claims to recognition "totally different from those of the welfare of the individual." Will is the supreme arbiter of all human values. It should be noted that in Rousseau's mind there is no contradiction between such a theory and the denial that might is right. The power exercised by the general will is power used to realize ethical right.

Vaughan speculates (*op. cit.* I, pp. 440–41) that Rousseau suppressed Chapter II of the unpublished *Contrat social* because he realized that in refuting Natural Law, "he had unwittingly made a deadly breach in the binding force of the Contract," since the assertion that there is no obligation in the state of nature discredits the contract in advance. This explanation is plausible, all the more because Rousseau had studied Hobbes and Locke. Nevertheless this defect within the framework of Rousseau's own argumentation was not fatal, since obligation is assumed to be added to nature as a rational and willful creation of culture.

Vaughan is also unfair to Diderot in his assessment of his theory as compared to Rousseau's (*op. cit.,* I, pp. 426–28). It is not certain that Rousseau's theory is in all respects the better one, or even the more valid. For him, general will is the source of rights (which are therefore civil) and of obligation—the limits to rights. For Diderot, rights are natural ("droit naturel") and so are the limits to them ("general will"). Rousseau's chief concern is one of efficacy. As we shall see in our last chapter, their views of the relation of the individual and the State, flowing from these basic considerations, are antithetical

[195] Vaughan, *op. cit.,* I, pp. 493–94.

[196] That is, in "Droit naturel." In other writings, it may be a formulation of enlightened self-interest, or is even denied.

still uses the conventional phrase, *droit naturel,* Rousseau knows that his principle is not natural in a descriptive sense, and he has made it plain that it cannot be normative in present societies (in which, however, the usual Natural Law has come into being), since it would contradict the *droit naturel* of self-interest and self-preservation. In a word, there can be no answer to Diderot's nihilist in present societies, but only in the creation of a true organic collectivity. In such a community, with its reformed constituents, the menace to self-preservation will be removed, and men will no longer hesitate to do what is right and virtuous for fear of being taken advantage of by others. Then, instead of saying, like Diderot, that the anarchist reads himself out of the human family, we can, without positing such a fictitious entity, read him out of the State, declare him to be *an enemy of the State.*[197] In such a community, the basic principle may, in Rousseau's words, be spoken of as *"droit naturel raisonné,* different from Natural Law properly speaking, which is founded only on a true but vague feeling and often stifled by self-love."[198] This *droit naturel raisonné* stifles egoism, instead of being stifled by it. It implies an organized society which can bring it into functional being, a collectivity whose will, relative and not universal, is monistic. For the moral precept itself, though it is *droit naturel* in the sense of a spontaneous perception of right, is only a form; its substance must be created by the general will. Moral right and legal right are thus completely fused, as the conscience or introspected Natural Law of the individual is in part absorbed into the new moral person or collective self and its rational will. This will is always right "because it is against nature to want to hurt oneself."[199] Therefore no collective or general will can want to hurt itself. This fact serves to unite the natural and the rational on a new level of culture, in which juridical monism absorbs all partial wills and sublimates them into a general will, so that the independent self of natural man is transmuted into a social self and can be "forced to be free," forced to attain the happiness he "really" wants.

There are, as Robert Derathé has pointed out, two passages in

---

[197] *Contrat social,* II, chap. 5; also IV, chap. 8.
[198] Vaughan, *op. cit.,* I, p. 494.
[199] *Ibid.* And not, Rousseau states, because it is based on justice, since it creates justice; we shall return to the question of the priority of justice and law in the following chapter.

which Rousseau declares the Natural Law to be incontrovertible by the laws of the general will.[200] Aside from the fact that almost any idea of Rousseau's is contradicted by something else he wrote, his uncertainty in this matter is largely due to the need to legitimize the social contract by the prior idea of the obligation to respect mutual engagements, and perhaps also by the wish to defend himself. But this is not the essential point. We cannot discard Rousseau's statements, or assume that he did not mean them. However, we must interpret them properly. When, in the fourth chapter of the second book of the *Contrat social* he writes that the sovereign power is limited by "the natural right which they [men] must enjoy inasmuch as they are men," he means only and exactly that he is unable to conceive of the *possibility* that the higher moral self (the *moi commun,* higher because it transcends the natural self with its egoistic flaws) should ever *wish* to violate the humanity of man, just as he cannot conceive of its "hurting itself," or its being "unjust to itself"—but decision is left entirely in the hands of the general will itself. This is precisely what Rousseau states again in the sixth *Lettre de la montagne,* and only five lines below the passage quoted by Derathé: "I say that this engagement is of a special kind, in that, being absolute, without conditions, without reserve, it cannot, despite that, be unjust or open to abuse; since it is not possible that the body should want to hurt itself. . . ." [201] In "Economie politique" Rousseau had, in unmistakable terms, set forth his belief in the moral superiority of the general will to the individual's conscience.[202] The brief mention of natural right in the *Contrat,* moreover, is, then, an idea of pure logic, having no meaning in the realm of political reality—Rousseau frequently passes all too conveniently from the metaphysical to the empirical level, and confuses them—a realm in which we are dealing with majorities and minorities, power, conflicting wills, and individuals who suffer and protest. The real significance of his thinking is to be found in his earlier statement

[200] The only really pertinent passage cited by Derathé is this one, from the sixth of the *Lettres de la montagne:* "For it is no more permissible to break the natural laws by the social contract than to break positive laws by private contract." (*Rousseau et la science politique de son temps,* pp. 157–58.) Of course the natural laws *are* broken by the social contract, since that is its purpose!

[201] Vaughan, *op. cit.,* II, pp. 200–1. Also p. 219: "Now, it is of the essence of sovereign power that it cannot be limited . . . it can recognize no other rights but its own and those it may grant." On p. 235, n. 1, Vaughan notes the "discrepancy."

[202] Vaughan, *op. cit.,* I, pp. 241–42, 243, 245.

that the Sovereign has no need to give any guarantees to the citizens, in his failure to state any effective principle of rights or to stipulate any positive rights (though he does stipulate denials of rights, such as censorship, and says that even life is "a conditional gift of the State"), and in his failure to provide or to permit any mechanism for protecting whatever those "rights" might be.

We may summarize by emphasizing the three major elements in Rousseau's thinking on this subject. Before society ("naturally"), men have no moral experience. Social relations produce ("naturally") the development of our faculties, including the conscience, the idea of right and wrong, Natural Law. Finally, the social contract, properly understood and implemented, creates a moral being which supervenes and becomes the ("artificial") source and standard of right and wrong, one which cannot ["cannot" is here more accurate than "ought not"] violate the individual intuition of Natural Law, but which perfects it, illuminates it, applies it, and makes it efficacious.

The key to Rousseau's thought is, I believe, the tension between two polarities. These may be diversely envisaged as nature and culture, independence and dependence, the existentially concrete and the abstract. Now one pole achieves ascendancy, now the other (with the dominant intellectual direction toward the second, the dominant emotional direction toward the first). At times there is an effort to compromise and conciliate. In *La Nouvelle Héloïse*, Julie is deeply engaged in precisely this struggle, and harmony is her longing. This is the profound meaning of her prayer: "I wish everything that is related to the order of nature which Thou hast established and to the rules of reason which I hold from Thee." [203] Indeed, such a conciliation might be possible, when we consider Rousseau's belief in an intuitive knowledge of right and wrong; a knowledge which is both the product of reason (transcending the egoistic vitalities and foreseeing ultimate self-interest), and a spontaneous outgrowth of compassion and aggrieved *amour de soi*. But because society—itself an artificial product of nature—creates a war within man and between men and exacerbates the egoistic vitalities, Julie's subjective desire is unreliable and insufficient. We must "mutilate [human] nature" and accede to the superior moral person, the State—expression of the communal Whole—which is impersonal and rational.

[203] *La Nouvelle Héloïse*, ed. D. Mornet, 1925, III, p. 66.

It is little wonder that many have been baffled by the rich complexity of Rousseau's thought or shrugged off his apparent contradictions and paradoxes. This was as true in his time as in later times. We need only think of the charges of contradiction which Helvétius leveled at him.[204] There are some contradictions in Rousseau; more often these are complementary facets of a many-sided human truth. Consistently, he fights for his principles: that there is more than nature; that there is a moral or spiritual realm in man to be realized; and that the invariable goal is "the lovable harmony of justice [ethical value] and happiness." [205]

To gauge the mean state of opinion among advanced thinkers at the close of the period, we can do no better than to turn to that most representative of *philosophes*, Condorcet. For Condorcet, the moral derives from experience or habituation, not directly from natural endowment. While men have natural feelings of compassion, this does not constitute moral judgment, and besides, he points out, men will hurt each other when their interests are opposed.

> Man could neither perpetuate nor form a family society without the painful sensation which is born from the view of the pain of suffering beings becoming transformed into a feeling of *malaise* . . . ; a feeling from which the desire of solacing these needs must soon have been born, and, when he helped to provide for them, an impulse of pleasure, the natural recompense for this almost mechanical benevolence. A keener attachment to those for whom he daily felt such sentiments was an infallible consequence, and they became his first moral habits.[206]

These "habits" involved feelings of indignation for harm needlessly and willfully done and of remorse for one's own injustice, which later evolved into a generalized horror of injustice. A feeling of equality of rights is also generated from one's own suffering and from aversion to making others suffer.

> . . . carried thus towards justice, now by their own interest, now by that of beings whom feelings of benevolence caused to be confused with themselves, [men were] able to begin thenceforth to regard the practice of justice as the common

[204] *De l'Homme,* Sec. V, chap. 1.
[205] Vaughan, *op. cit.,* I, pp. 323, 454.
[206] *Esquisse d'un tableau historique du progrès de l'esprit humain* (1793–94), Deuxième Partie, Première Epoque.

interest of all, as a kind of obligation, since they could not violate it without exposing themselves to suffering either from the injustice of others or from the reproaches of their conscience.

Thus we have "a coarse morality, born of self-interest and of natural sensitivity." And it may be said that our ideas of justice and duty, of good and evil are determined by our very nature and are neither arbitrary nor vague. "Truths that bear upon these ideas have then the same certainty, the same precision as those of all the speculative sciences. If, further, we examine our own heart, we shall find that the attraction of a good action or the aversion towards doing a bad one, the remorse that follows it, are necessary consequences of our moral constitution."

The social experience, then, is first, according to Condorcet. Only subsequently does sensitivity in its form of self-interest, aroused by personal injury, and also in its peculiarly human form of sympathy, fostered by association and interdependence, develop into habits which become the norms of proper behavior. Conceptualization follows still later, at which point men reach an awareness of what we may properly call moral truths and universals. However, Condorcet does not really define the notion of duty or obligation, nor does he succeed in telling us why it is a duty to be just.

In this fashion, Condorcet and other *philosophes* saw nature and culture working in unison, generating a novel moral experience, a new level of being in the universe. Its purpose and effect is to repress or control some of the most vital and basic aspects of man's nature in order to foster other natural aspirations, whose realization in culture also acquires novel, artificial forms. Obligation to others is shown to rise out of pleasure and self-interest, out of our claim that others have obligations to us, and out of fellow-feeling, in a mélange of processes consisting of spontaneity and reflection, conventions, laws, and sensitivity to the opinions of others. In all of this, most of the experientialists claimed there were certain universals, rooted in similarity of body, mind, and social structure. The basic laws of behavior are not moral; they remain consistent with the analysis of human motivation and behavior. They are self-interest, in its many guises and disguises, and the opinions or pressures of the social group. But they eventuate in moral laws.

Albert Schweitzer has classified the answers of this period to the problem of the passage from egoism to altruism in three groups, which attribute the evolution to individual reason, to society, or to the original coexistence of egoism and altruism.[207] Since, in the last solution, altruism is weaker than egoism, the first two are also brought in as reinforcements. All agree that nothing is ethical in itself, but only in its effects on the general welfare and happiness. Little weight is given to a self-perfecting dynamic within the individual. There is a blurring of the two distinct components of natural judgment: the perception of conduct as right or wrong (according to certain desirable effects), and the perception of the merit or demerit of the agent. The latter is inevitably sacrificed, largely because of the sway of mechanistic determinism and the associationist theory of knowledge, but partly also because of the social locus of value and the empirical theory of knowledge. It should be noted, too, that when reason is brought in, its function is not, as for Cudworth, Clarke, and the Natural Law theorists, the perception of abstract moral distinctions. From Hutcheson on, it is accepted that right and wrong express agreeable and disagreeable qualities in actions, experienced by feeling. The function of reason is rather that of a practical operation on the basis of psychological or social facts. Similarly, sympathy is seen as the need to see happiness around oneself in order to be happy. Convention and opinion derive their weight from our desire for approval, prestige, admiration, fame, and ultimately, for self-approval. We have the deep need of considering ourselves in the light in which we wish to appear to others. Here Hume and Adam Smith bring in the notion of the "impartial spectator," but this concept never appears in French thought.

There is universal agreement that the ethical consists in a willing sacrifice of immediate egoistic satisfaction out of consideration for the equal rights of others to seek self-realization in society, a right which is expressible in terms of "general interest." The impulse to this sacrifice is not natural. It may develop from natural sympathy or from the transmutations of self-interest into convention, ingested by reflection or by conditioned reflexes. The second process involves the controlled utilization, or the suppression (as in La Mettrie and Rousseau), of the aggressive tendencies inhering in the "pride complex" of motivation, by means of the stated mechanism. Its *terminus,* but not its *origin,* is the intuition

[207] *Civilization and Ethics,* London, 1955, pp. 71–84.

of right and wrong as objective and self-existing truths. This, primarily, is what distinguishes the experientialist from the Natural Law theorist. Both agree that the existence of right (obligation) is a limit on will.

The experientialists were certain that they had found the real source of ethical experience, and thereby a conclusive justification of the validity of moral judgments against the rebellion of any Thrasymachus of the past or present. The reality of egoism was not diminished or denied, but eagerly accepted. By inextricably linking the welfare of the self-loving self with its attitudes and behavior to others, the empiricists showed how nature and culture have evolved moral values as the most refined mechanisms of ego-protection and satisfaction. To the enemy who asserted that if self-interest is the criterion, acts are equal in other respects provided they suit our interest, so that the word "right" adds nothing and has no meaning, the inevitable shift from the self-centered self to the other-oriented (but still self-regarding) self supplied a persuasive reply. To the scoffer who put forward the endless variations of personal and historical experience as an argument against universal rational norms derived from experience, the answer was the basic uniformity of experience and of the endowment with which men react to it; history, moreover, is only a process of superficial distortion, deviation, or perversion. To those who persisted in the notion that man cannot be a responsible moral agent if he is not free, it was made clear that the perception of the difference between right and wrong through conditioned reflexes and reflection on the requirements of approval and self-approval furnished adequate motivation for proper determination.[208] Good will, it is true, is swallowed up by calculation and social pressure, but it remains, for some, at least, as an original element of sympathy. In these ways, then, a human moral order is evolved and created out of a nonhuman, nonmoral physiological order, without appealing to the intervention of a cosmic moral source or to the fiction of a native, autonomous moral realm in human nature.

The triumph of these eighteenth-century views in the nineteenth century is incontestable. Lamarck brings the integration of man in nature to its fruition by means of a comprehensive evolutionary theory in which the ethical is held to develop from feeling

[208] On the problem of free will, see *An Age of Crisis*, chap. 4, 5, 6.

and needs, through environment, education, and hereditary modification.[209] According to the evolutionary theories of Darwin and
Spencer, altruism was not originally coexistent with egoism, but is
rather a derivative of it. Experience and natural selection promoted the principle that the individual welfare is best secured in
working co-operatively for the common good. In fact, Darwin tells
us, any social animal, "if its intellectual faculties were to become
as active and as highly developed as in man . . . would gain . . .
some feeling of right and wrong, or a conscience." [210]

In the twentieth century, anthropology and psychology have
added to the findings of biology and philosophy. According to one
anthropologist, Robert Briffault, morality arises out of no altruism,
but is "a heavy weight of necessity laid upon man's development
by the unbending conditions that govern it." Man by the law of
his development seeks power over his fellows. However, the exploited competitor is a fellow man, so that the condition of the
exploited reacts upon the exploiter himself. The will to power at
the expense of others hurts the whole; power must be of the group
over nature. Anger at abuse of power thus becomes righteous indignation, reinforced by the dread of the community's disapproval
and wrath. The experience of indignation, in the company of
others, leads in turn to the sense of shame, self-respect, the desire
for approval, and the point of honor. (The last is older than any
feeling of sympathy and humanity, and it may coexist with callous

[209] See H. Hastings, *Man and Beast in French Thought of the Eighteenth Century,*
Baltimore, 1936, pp. 171–72.

[210] *The Descent of Man,* chap. IV. Moral experience is, apparently, rational and
reflective, for Darwin; but in truth, he could in no other way account for its absence
among other social animals. Nevertheless he goes on to place the origin of moral
distinctions in the social instincts. The latter, in his view, are dissociated from the
pleasure or selfishness principle (whether as immediate reaction or as calculation),
and are somewhat analogous to the instinct of ants and bees, seeking the good of
the community. These autonomous instincts have their demands and frustrations,
their habits which become hereditary and produce certain moral intuitions that
have no basis in individual experiences of utility. Here, indeed, is a very important
difference from the eighteenth-century theories. But in many respects Darwin's
theory seems like a perfected version of eighteenth-century explanations. The origin
of the moral conscience lies, then, in the social instincts, and especially in their
unique human derivative, sympathy, which makes us responsive to the needs, suffering, and most of all, the approbation and blame of our fellows. As proof of his
analysis, Darwin offers the fact that primitive people are indifferent to, or even
delight in the sufferings of strangers. He also holds that human nature and experience lead to moral universals. It is not in Darwin that we find an extreme relativism,
or a refusal to evaluate cultures in terms of higher and lower. For this we must
await Sumner's *Folkways* and the so-called "scientific" school of sociology and
anthropology.

ferocity.) Justice is not merely a demand of self-interest or a cry of the weak. It is "the condition of human adaptation to the facts of human life. . . . It is the call of the paramount interests of the race." [211] Moral sentiment is not the outcome of natural sympathy and commiseration. "The moral *feeling* is posterior to the fact of moral practice. It is after a course of conduct has been set as right . . . that corresponding feelings of pity, sympathy, become developed." [212] The Spaniards accepted the Inquisition with no feelings of pity or horror. However Briffault's view is not entirely convincing. Did pity arise because the Inquisition was abolished? Or was it rather the reverse?

John Dewey represents a modern humanistic naturalism. "Moral conceptions and processes grow out of the very conditions of human life," he writes. "The fundamental conceptions of morals are therefore neither arbitrary nor artificial. . . . Particular aspects of morals are transient; they are often, in their actual manifestation, defective and perverted. But the framework of moral conceptions is as permanent as human life itself." However, Dewey also reduces right to fact, to "the concrete demands" of social pressures, in contrast with a preconceived standard of what ought to be. This is more typical of his thinking.[213]

Some psychologists have also denied any native moral component in human nature. A. A. Brill declares that the child "above all feels no sense of sympathy, morality, or disgust. In fine, he acts and feels like any other animal." [214] Morality, according to Brill, is entirely ingested by social conditioning. The psychological aptitude for this experience, its origination in society, and the relation between these two phenomena are not explained by this psychologist. Sigmund Freud, in his fashion, has attempted this task. Both individual development and the cultural processes, according to Freud, are life-processes. They must partake of the basic condition of "organic life in general"—the struggle between Eros and the death instinct (we might say, between creativity and aggressive destructiveness). The cultural process "is the particular modification undergone by the life-process under the influence of

[211] *The Making of Humanity*, pp. 298–300.
[212] *Ibid.*, pp. 261–64, 276–86.
[213] *Human Nature and Conduct*, p. 320, comment by M. C. Swabey, *The Judgment of History*, pp. 140–41.
[214] "Sexuality and its Rôle in the Neuroses," in S. Lorand, *Psychoanalysis Today*, p. 177.

the task set before it by Eros and stimulated by Ananke, eternal
necessity; and this task is that of uniting single human beings into
a larger unity with libidinal attachments between them." [215] The
process is essentially the same, whether applied to individual
development or to cultural units: the incorporation of an individual as a member of a group, the creation of a single group.

> The development of the individual is ordered according to the
> programme laid down by the pleasure-principle, namely, the
> attainment of happiness, and to this main objective it holds
> firmly; the incorporation of the individual as a member of the
> community, or his adaptation to it, seems like an almost un-
> avoidable condition which has to be fulfilled before he can
> attain this objective of happiness. . . . To express it differ-
> ently, we may say: individual development seems to us a
> product of the interplay of two trends, the striving for happi-
> ness, generally called "egoistic" and the impulse towards merg-
> ing with others in the community, which we call "altruistic."

In individual development, the accent is on egoism, while the
cultural tendency amounts to the institution of restrictions. But
in culture, the objective of happiness is only incidental, the important aim being the creation of a single unity.

In Freud's analysis, as it has proceeded thus far, we must first
note the basic similarity to that of the eighteenth century. It may
be interpreted, as it was by Morelly, Helvétius, Rousseau, and
others, in a way that justifies what we should call a totalitarian
socio-political system. "It almost seems as if humanity could be
most successfully united into one great whole if there were no need
to trouble about the happiness of individuals." [216] Freud does not
make it entirely clear whether the "altruistic impulse towards
merging" is a separate and original instinct, or whether it results
from the egoistic, as many eighteenth-century writers would have
claimed. He describes it as a discrete force and declares that the
eternal struggle between love and aggression is an innate ambivalence.[217] However, since it must have arisen in individuals, we
may perhaps assume its genesis from the pleasure principle, which
is called the unique motive of behavior. Where Freud departs entirely from the eighteenth-century frame of reference is in the role
he gives to guilt feelings as the source of conscience. These origi-

[215] *Civilization and its Discontents,* pp. 132–33. Compare Rousseau.
[216] *Ibid.,* p. 135.
[217] Pp. 121–22.

nate in the Oedipus complex and are intensified in society by the extension of the same conflict, that is, between love and aggression. Culture can achieve its unifying aim only by fomenting an ever-increasing sense of guilt.

Despite the weight of evidence and the weight of authority, this type of naturalistic explanation of the ethical life was challenged in the eighteenth century and has been denied or modified in more recent times. Joseph Duhamel, in 1753, turned the barbs of his logic against Alexander Pope who, foreshadowing d'Holbach, had praised self-interest as the source of moral judgment, which he attributed to a renunciation out of fear of reprisal. Glimpsing the confusion between "origin" in the sense of cause and in the sense of justification or validity, Duhamel inquires whether it would be legitimate to steal if there were no vengeance or punishment to fear. Is it a question of avoiding making enemies, or of being unjust? [218] Natural Law theorists and others held to an innate conscience which intuited formal truths and qualities of acts, or as some would have put it, "relations." Father Richard, a professor of theology, took it upon himself to refute d'Holbach's *Système social*. He denies that a system based on selfish interest can be an ethical system. "To love others only because they are useful or necessary to us is not to love them at all; it is only to love our-selves." He thinks its ultimate logic leads to the sacrifice of others wherever it benefits the self—the typical nihilistic position. D'Holbach makes the "moi" far more hateful than Pascal, he charges. But we do forgive enemies, help strangers, and love virtue for itself.[219] In another work, Richard directs his fire at d'Alembert. If our duties and rights depend on reciprocal needs, then "it is clear from this text that the measure of my duties to society is the extent of my needs which it can and must satisfy. I then owe it nothing if I can or do wish to be self-sufficient, or if it does not wish to satisfy my needs as I please." [220]

---

[218] *Lettres flamandes*, Lille, 1753, pp. 112–13.

[219] *La Défense de la religion . . .* , 1775, pp. 83–96. Moral obligation, declares Richard, does not consist in being useful to those who are useful to us, but rather in the requirement for a free and intelligent being to conform to moral law. The former is to recognize only "the mechanical instinct of blind nature. . . . The man who is activated by the impulse of sensitive self-interest is not moral man, but animal man." (P. 128.) Another long refutation of d'Holbach was offered by the abbé Bergier, in his *Examen du matérialisme* (1771, II, p. 317 ff.).

[220] *Exposition de la doctrine des philosophes modernes*, Malines, 1785, pp. 31–33. Where d'Alembert writes that all of morality is founded "on a single factual truth . . . on men's mutual need for each other and on the reciprocal duties imposed by

Immanuel Kant provides us with a more searching criticism. Compassion, for Kant, is not a moral principle, since "inclination is blind and slavish whether it be of a good sort or not," and does not come from deliberate maxims.[221] Taking a wider view, he assails experiential theories in general, on the ground that "they do not distinguish the motives which are prescribed as such by reason alone altogether a priori, and which are properly moral, from the empirical motives which the understanding raises to general conceptions merely by comparison of experiences."[222] For Kant, moral principles "are not based on properties of human nature, but must subsist a priori of themselves, while from such principles practical rules must be capable of being deduced for every rational nature, and accordingly for that of man." Contrary to Hume, he believes that the moral reason is practical, that is, can influence the maxims of action. He sets practical reason (the moral) against nature. Whatever is deduced from the peculiar natural characteristics of humanity, from feelings and propensions, may only supply us with a maxim, but not with a law; with a subjective principle, "but not with an objective principle on which we should be *enjoined* to act, even though all our propensions, inclinations and natural dispositions were opposed to it. In fact, the sublimity and intrinsic dignity of the command in duty are so much the more evident, the less the subjective impulses favor it and the more they oppose it, without being able in the slightest degree to weaken the obligation of the law or to diminish its validity."[223] Kant's ethics is nonetheless a human one, made by and for men: "the laws to which he is subject are *only those of his own giving,* though at the same time they are universal," and "he is only bound to act in conformity with his own will; a will, however, which is designed by nature to give universal laws."[224]

Jean Piaget has explored with great depth and acumen the

need," Richard notes, "Thus the recluse has no moral duty—and he will watch one of his fellows die of hunger at the door of his grotto. I do not need anybody, and so I have no moral duty." (This is in fact conceded by Raynal [*op. cit.,* Livre XIX, chap. XIV] who equates morality with social utility and ascribes its origin to social convention.) But Bergier claims for Christianity the original formulation of enlightened self-interest! (*Examen du matérialisme,* 1771, I, pp. 216 ff.)

[221] *Critique of Practical Reason,* ed. cit., p. 214.

[222] *Fundamental Principles of the Metaphysic of Morals, ibid.,* p. 6, see also pp. 27–28, 44, and especially p. 59–61, where Kant argues that empirical morality involves an infinite regression which must ultimately rest on an unconditioned good will.

[223] *Ibid.,* p. 43. This is similar to Rousseau's concept of virtue-sacrifice.

[224] *Ibid.,* p. 51.

development of the child's moral world. His investigations show that it contains two levels, that of moral experience, and one which is theoretical, verbal, reflective. It is of particular interest to us that the utilitarian and the formalistic approaches, which consider value as referring to acts (or their consequences) rather than intentions, correspond to the primitive level, when duties are imposed upon the small child and conformity is required. (What do intentions matter? If we trip, we fall to the ground by the law of gravity; so it seems to the child, a lie brings punishment.) The problem of responsibility is simply to know whether a law has been respected or violated. Subsequently, in his first associations with other children, the child applies the same attitude toward them and judges by the outward shape of acts and by the objective criterion of rules. It is a fundamental fact of human society, as compared with the instinctive social animals, that rules cannot be constituted or transmitted by means of an internal biological heredity, but only through the external pressures exercised by individuals upon each other. (In theory, however, moral rules once arose, and would arise again, without seniors imposing their authority—which is equivalent to Natural Law.) Moreover, states Piaget, this "does not prevent some rules from containing more than others an element of rationality, thus corresponding to the deepest functional constants of human nature."

It is co-operation, according to Piaget, which "leads to the primacy of intentionality, by forcing the individual to be constantly occupied with the point of view of other people so as to compare it with his own." Thus the child attains the stage of autonomy of moral judgment. He discovers that truthfulness is necessary to relations of sympathy and mutual respect.

> Reciprocity seems . . . to be the determining factor of autonomy. For moral autonomy appears when the mind regards as necessary an ideal that is independent of all external pressure. Now, apart from our relations to other people, there can be no moral necessity. . . . Conversely, any relation with other persons, in which unilateral respect takes place, leads to heteronomy. Autonomy therefore appears only with reciprocity, when mutual respect is strong enough to make the individual feel from within the desire to treat others as he himself would wish to be treated.

The autonomous conscience is, then, a new construction superimposed on constructions already formed by action, and arises

later than action proper.[225] Piaget's analysis, it would seem, confirms in a modern, scientific way the essential notion of Natural
Law, interpreted as an experiential unfolding of the psyche.

Some general limits to the validity of eighteenth-century experiential theories may now be formulated. These theories, as
they were developed, tend to diminish the function of ethics as a
relation between individuals, and to replace the latter by a relation
of an individual to an organized society taken as an abstract entity.
Social conditions become the limit of the ethical, so that there is
no need to go beyond the standard given in the situation; indeed,
one may argue that it becomes morally wrong, or else even impossible, to transcend the cultural complex. There is a constant
tendency to confuse altruistic action with virtue, although in
certain situations altruism may be opposed to justice, which is
often proclaimed to be the cardinal virtue. A more rigorous view
would be that moral virtue assumes the *capacity* of altruism, since
it implies rising above self to an impersonal and objective viewpoint. Among the materialists, we encounter a further difficulty.
They were monists, and denied a mind-body dualism. But dualism
persists in disguised forms: man is egoistic and other-directed,
social and antisocial.

The empiricists' account of our anguish at the suffering of
others is not convincing. Of course we feel sorrow and pity because
the suffering hurts us; this is tautology—to feel sorrow *is* to suffer.
The question is why a man experiences suffering when, for instance, he sees a woman weeping forlornly and desperately. The
misfortune and suffering of a fellow being, especially when helpless or wronged, evokes in him a fellow-feeling, a protest, and a
desire to help. This is not because he places himself specifically in
the place of the woman, as it was asserted, but because he *imagines*
the suffering, whether or not he actually experiences it; and there
is a natural aversion to suffering. The ability to imagine the
suffering of others derives from the unique objectifying power of
the human mind, which enables us to conceive of other beings as
other selves, and not just in relation to our own subjectivity. Without this power, there would be no possibility of treating other

[225] J. Piaget, "The Child and Moral Realism," in R. N. Anshen, *Moral Principles
of Action*, New York, 1952, p. 417–35. For an interesting eighteenth-century view
somewhat analogous to Piaget's, but with greater emphasis on the ideas of approbation and self-approbation, see Dugald Stewart's introduction to Adam Smith, p.
161–94.

human beings as ends rather than as means, and so no obligation to do so.

All these criticisms add up perhaps to one major point. Ethics may have originated in biological and psychological needs for happiness, security, unguiltiness, rewards, or utility. Our moral intuitions and judgments may originally have evolved, in the dark night of human time, as survival mechanisms. Such a formula, however, does not satisfactorily account for our moral judgments. Once the moral life exists, it is not confined by its genetic factors. It makes demands of its own which are no longer within the frame of its origin. Right and wrong are distinctions demanded by the species and by the individual, and it is impossible to conceive of a group of men who, thrown together from infancy on an isolated island, would not develop such distinctions with the unfolding of their faculties. It is a biologist of our own time who has written that the "basic mechanism" of morality is innate, a part of our biological inheritance.[226]

A further confusion ensues from the thesis that an individual has no natural moral endowment, but receives his moral conscience from the conditioning processes of his upbringing. Such a statement confuses the mere mechanism by which conscience is developed with an explanation of the existence of moral conscience. It also conflicts with the evolutionary hypothesis. The latter implies that the moral mechanisms, developed as survival needs, eventuated in a biological selection, therefore in a biological inheritance. Otherwise the social process would involve an infinite regression with no explanation of the original impulse. We have already noted that the inadequacy of the socialization explanation, even when combined with that of self-interest, is attested to by individual rebellion in favor of "higher" standards. We should ask, too, how it explains the phenomenon of our greater esteem for a defeated Cato than for a triumphant Caesar. Cato miscalculated his personal interest and did not have opinion on his side. Cato, the *philosophes* would have replied, was happier in his conscience despite his ruin. However our moral judgments are not arrived at by such calculations. It would require a most sophistical logic to show that pity, self-interest, or conventions motivate our judgment in such a case, rather than an intuition that an act or attitude is right or wrong, and an involuntary approbation of what is conceived of

[226] G. G. Simpson, *The Meaning of Evolution*, p. 294.

as right. The simplistic notion that our moral life results entirely from education and conditioning falsely denies the autonomous power of what Kant termed "the moral reason," which enables individuals to arrive at their own conception of moral value and to love the right because the conception of right attracts allegiance from those who conceive of it.[227] Such a theory minimizes the faculties which, as Durkheim said, make it possible quickly to educate a child morally, but not a chimpanzee or an elephant.[228]

The empiricists frequently spoke of their desire to achieve a "natural" ethics. By this they meant a contrast in origin with the supernatural, and simultaneously an ethics that satisfied human needs and desires. In regard to the first point, we should note that most (excepting a few extremists who were relativists) believed in universal moral laws grounded on empirical identities of human nature; however, such identities do not, by themselves, denote or reveal a universal natural morality and standard of ethical values. In regard to the second point, it would be futile to overlook the fact that human needs and desires are complex and contradictory. From one viewpoint, the psychology of Diderot's Rameau's nephew or of Laclos' hero represents the natural laws and forces of the universe in their human form. From another viewpoint, our nature revolts against these and makes opposite demands. But if we are to set up moral value as a natural phenomenon, can we make it compete with the egoistic vitalities? In what way is it more valid, or more compelling, than other natural urges? The *philosophes* were well-aware of this problem, and their "natural" morality is (save for the nihilists) never anything but the application of reason to experience.[229] It is, however, natural for men to do this, and some will go so far as to agree with Kant, that it is natural to arrive at certain universal principles. Still, moral valuation cannot be termed "natural" in quite the same way as our animal impulses. It is natural only insofar as it is a terminal result of our natural impulse to social living. But social living is on a conscious and cultural level; its forms are not naturally outlined beyond the family relationship. Both culture and its consequences are, in a

[227] This is admitted by Darwin (*op. cit.*, p. 110).

[228] Cresson, *Le Problème moral et les philosophes*, p. 185.

[229] Raynal (*loc. cit.*) furnishes an excellent example. Neither the *natural* feelings of compassion, benevolence and honor, nor the equally natural feelings of hatred, vengeance, jealousy, pride, lust for domination, can be the source of morality, he argues; it arises only from the idea of a common good. (The escape to the abstract social entity is obvious.)

real sense, anti-natural, though they spring from our nature. Here Rousseau was right in opposing moral man and natural man. His error was to sever his "natural man" from social impulse and to give him a real status in being.

The naturalistic, experiential account of moral genesis contains many basic and essential truths, without which it is impossible to understand the human ethical world. Nevertheless, by its adherence to the genetic method as a complete explanation of the end product, by its self-limitation to physiological sensitivity and social conditioning, it does not do full justice to the mind's distinctive expressions and to the unique demands of human nature.

Four

COROLLARIES

I. Conscience

THE QUESTION OF THE MORAL CONSCIENCE has been implied or discussed throughout the preceding chapters. If one believes the knowledge of right and wrong to be intuitive, as did the Natural Law theorists, one also believes conscience to be intuitive, since conscience is that awareness. For the same reason, there is no substantial difference between Shaftesbury's moral sense and conscience, although in this case it is conceived of as experience which is concerned with a special kind of object. On the other hand, if one holds moral judgment to be the product of experience and conditioning, then, as we have seen, we can conceive its object to be either the truths of objective relations or mere habituation and conformity to given standards. We have, then, either an a priori conscience or a generalization from subjective experience.

A reaction to Church absolutism, especially after the Council of Trent (1545–63), encouraged the rise of deism, Pyrrhonism, and even atheism. The conscience was not challenged, by these rebellious movements, as operative in the terrestrial realm (with or without metaphysical implications). Many used it, on the contrary, to support the idea that man and nature are not intrinsically evil or meaningless, and that improvement is possible. But the dominant seventeenth-century attitude was distrust of conscience, as subjective and as subservient to our powers of self-delusion.[1] The

[1] P. Bénichou, *Morales du grand siècle*, 1948, p. 105.

Jesuits emphasized a formalistic morality in which conscience was no longer a light but a dupe. Bossuet's pronouncement was that the Roman Catholic Church is the ultimate guide to morality, and the revocation of the Edict of Nantes was made in this spirit. The Jansenists, with their insistence on depravity redeemable only by grace, were even more hostile to the sufficiency of conscience. Nevertheless, Catholics admitted that evil, though it gives pleasure, also brings remorse.

An important part of eighteenth-century ethical thought consists in the re-evaluation of conscience. There is at first a movement —which continues unabated throughout the period—toward re-establishing the authority of conscience. One part of this movement derives from the Enlightenment's refusal to accept the doctrines of original sin and innate depravity. A typical example is Mme de Lambert, about whom Sainte-Beuve writes:

> She is also one of the first moralists who, as the seventeenth century closes, came back to the very un-Jansenist idea that the human heart is essentially good, and that conscience, if one knows how to consult it, is the best witness and the best judge: "By the word conscience, I understand that internal feeling of a delicate honor which assures you that you have nothing with which to reproach yourself." She gives, in her way, the signal that Vauvenargues will take up in his turn, and which, in the hands of Jean-Jacques, will become an instrument of universal revolution.[2]

With some important qualifications, Voltaire may be put in this group. A second part of the movement derives from the more balanced and impartial investigation of moral experience which was the necessary accompaniment of the whole movement of ideas, the growth of naturalism and rationalism, the desire to build a secular ethics. Locke and Bayle may be considered as among the chief sources. The utilitarians, in particular, found it necessary to cope with the reality of the moral conscience, and to enlist it in their program. The few but significant writers who were attracted by nihilism were obliged to diminish conscience, and especially to get rid of its manifestation as remorse.

Bayle considers conscience to be the intuition of Natural Law. In his famous "impious paradox," he makes it the touchstone of conduct, regardless of the consequences of an act, provided it operates free of prejudice. Real morality is the result of personal

[2] *Causeries du lundi*, IV, p. 231.

experience rather than of external authority.[3] He maintains "that any action done against the lights of conscience is essentially bad." Those who assert the contrary argue that a good action sometimes results from acting against the dictates of conscience. "Monstrous doctrine," he exclaims, "which upsets all morality." [4] Intention (good will) alone is the object of moral judgment. Conscience is adviser, consoler, witness, judge, executioner, and rewarder. Bayle's emphasis is not on remorse; and it is especially curious that he does not mention remorse as a factor in his defense of the possibility of an atheistic society. He makes another interesting and highly valid point: although the child has no moral feelings and knows only pleasure and pain (which is the reason why punishment and enforced good habits are necessary), conscience itself is not the *result* of education, either in function or content.[5] The function of conscience, moreover, is not to intuit absolute qualities, or "what objects are in themselves," but their "putative truth," or probabilities for action in relation to our needs. This also helps to explain why, in his "impious paradox," Bayle maintains that the erring conscience is not subject to blame.[6] On the other hand, despite these speculative theories, he does not believe that in real life the conscience often operates freely, untainted by passion or prejudice. "We always judge things in relation to ourselves. What is useful to us seems just to us; but if the same thing is contrary to us, we find it unjust." We think we are sincere and see a difference in the act, but it is "only an illusion of our heart." [7] Bayle is too much the realist to *trust* in conscience. He despaired of men's ability to follow its dictates to any broad regeneration of morality. Caught in his own web, he cannot get back to the Christian God and is left with the materialist's view that though man may know good from evil, he is incapable of governing his choices. God is as much a principle of evil as of good, and original sin is a mechanical principle forcing men to evil: "for all act criminally because of a certain corruption which comes to us from the body." [8]

[3] Cf. the modern theories of Jean Piaget and Erich Fromm.

[4] *Dictionnaire*, I, p. 172.

[5] *Oeuvres diverses*, II, p. 468; I, p. 671. See also *ibid.*, I, p. 441; II, pp. 224–25, 263, 422–30, 510–16; III, p. 986.

[6] Montesquieu satirizes this famous paradox as the delight of casuists. (*Lettres persanes*, LXII.) For Bayle, it is one of the foundations of his defense of tolerance.

[7] *Ibid.*, II, pp. 176–77.

[8] He also believes that some acts are intrinsically good or bad, according to Nat-

Pufendorf, juridically inclined, had emphasized conscience as cognition of truth, as well as its function as judge (evoking tranquillity or remorse). Only insofar as it partakes of the law, which alone obliges, is it valid. A view such as Bayle's, according to Pufendorf, would lead straight to anarchy. We must therefore distinguish three cases: right conscience, probable conscience (in cases outside the law or where there is conflict between law and equity), and doubtful conscience, which permits of no licit action.[9]

The attitude of Catholic and Protestant apologists swerved notably in the eighteenth century toward the enhancement of conscience. It was impossible not to feel the imprint of the intellectual milieu and the prevailing tides of thought. Conscience is made the instrument of Natural Law, "a sure mark," the rule of our actions, and is at times clearly set up in opposition to the opinions of others—a view which at first blush might make us think of the subjectivity of Rousseau or other romanticists, but which, in the minds of the apologists, refers to an objective standard (in Natural Law or Revelation) that can be opposed to existing norms. Again the opposition is clear between this type of thinking and the experientialist approach. Conscience, writes the abbé Sigorgne, is not "the effect of prejudice or of education."[10] The widely read abbé Gauchat, however, remains closer to Pufendorf. For him conscience, unless it interprets higher law, has no value and is only "a prejudice of childhood." Wishing to provide a firmer anchor than subjective experience, he thus plays into the hands of the radical materialists, by leaving anarchism and nihilism as the only alternative to supernaturalism.[11]

---

ural Law. Reason tells us it is unjust to rob a weak man in the desert, even though there is no risk and much gain. He rejects utility as "a gross error."

[9] *Op. cit.*, I, pp. 44–49. In a note, Barbeyrac disagrees with the remark about anarchy.

[10] *Le Philosophe chrétien*, Avignon, 1765, pp. 23–27. See also Père André "Sur les Merveilles de la Conscience," *Oeuvres philosophiques*, 1843, pp. 289–302; Bergier, *Examen du matérialisme*, 1771, II, p. 330; Chaudon, *Anti-Dictionnaire philosophique*, 1775, 4th ed., II, pp. 14–17; Para du Phanjas, *Principes de la saine philosophie*, 1774, p. 117.

[11] "For after all, why should we feel a repugnance towards certain actions, remorse after having done them, secret esteem for certain deeds? Because these impressions have been instilled in us since childhood. . . . As soon as they do not express a law, they are only a sterile, deceitful image." He presses home his point, arguing that no moral link can come from men, nor from arbitrary convention or civil law. "All men, united together, would not form a degree of authority over a single one, *by nature*." Laws are only customs which we may violate without moral guilt. (*Lettres critiques*, 1755–63, XVI, pp. 216–22.) Jaucourt, in the *Encyclopédie*, also warns us

Chief among the Protestant defenders of a priori conscience was Samuel Formey, of the Academy of Berlin. For him conscience is a necessary consequence of the use of our faculties and is not dependent on education for its functioning. Formey, unlike Gauchat, does not deny the existence or validity of moral law without God, but only its effectiveness. What is more, defining conscience as an internal judgment of actions in relation to conceived obligations, he denies what Rousseau was later to claim, that conscience is "a sort of voice of God, different from natural lights and the exercise of reason." It is the voice of man, he asserts, not of God. Judging and willing are a single act. There is, in fact, no separate tribunal, called conscience, nor any way of distinguishing it from the total self. Nor is it an original imprint on our soul. Conscience is simply "the development of reason, relative and proportional to the knowledge of duties." Its judgments are not intuitive, but discursive, embodying the knowledge and application of our duties and of principles, of the circumstances of any particular act, and of the right of the agent to do it. Since conscience is proportional to reason and intelligence, "there are not two consciences exactly alike." Which conscience, then, is best? "That which responds to the widest extent and the most exact notions of duties which man has been able to acquire." And the standard of judgment is man; "because man is man," he must approve or disapprove of certain acts, in view of their moral sequel. To deny the moral difference between acts is not to abjure God, but humanity.[12] Here, certainly, is a humanistic moral outlook, although it is not clearly and consistently thought out.

While Voltaire's ideas on the conscience present no originality, they do bear a personal stamp. Conscience comes from God and is man's universal law.[13] In the *Poème sur la loi naturelle* (1752), he, too, denies that it is formed entirely by education and example; it develops rather as an instinct, or as "the first fruit of reason," without having an instinct's compulsiveness, however. Voltaire's emphasis, in contrast to Bayle's, is on remorse, as "the defender" of Natural Law, and he is at particular pains to refute the argu-

---

not to follow our conscience, unless we have the necessary enlightenment with which to judge it. ("Conscience.")

[12] See *Le Philosophe chrétien*, Leide, 1752, II, pp. 272–84; *Mélanges philosophiques*, Leide, 1754, II, pp. 180–82; *Système du vrai bonheur*, Utrecht, 1771, pp. 40–44; *Mélanges philosophiques*, II, pp. 151–96.

[13] "*Catéchisme de l'honnête homme*," *Oeuvres*, Vol. 24, p. 539.

ments of those who dismiss remorse as mere habit developed from experience.[14] "The first springs come from a different hand." The moral experience, then, is primary, not secondary. As with all adherents of Natural Law, the a priori conscience, for Voltaire, is its inseparable adjunct. We have already noted the gradual displacement of the center of gravity, in Voltaire's thinking, toward utilitarianism. This is one of the innermost characteristics of the evolution of eighteenth-century thought. Consequently it is not surprising that in later years his idea of the conscience was modified in an empirical direction. In 1771, he wrote in *Questions sur l'Encyclopédie:*

> It results from all this that we have no other conscience but the one which is infused into us by the age, by example, our temperament, our reflections. Man is not born with any priniciple, but with the faculty of receiving them all. His temperament will make him more inclined to cruelty or to gentleness; his understanding will make him understand one day that the square of 12 is 144, that he must not do to others what he would not want to be done to him. . . .[15]

That Voltaire's thinking in this passage is somewhat confused is all too evident. He begins with an empirical development and ends with the self-generating perception of an a priori moral truth, not of one deduced from experience. He goes on to say that a savage will readily treat others as he would not want to be treated, unless he has learned otherwise, and to balance this statement by the admission of two innate forces: pity and the power of understanding truth. We cannot therefore speak, in relation to Voltaire, of a clear and consistent concept of conscience.

While Rousseau's concepts of the conscience also seem to lack unity, there can be no doubt about the great influence exercised by his romantic proclamations of the validity of the subjective moral judgment. In the *Discours sur l'origine de l'inégalité*, as we have seen, Rousseau seems to derive virtue, and so the conscience, from sensibility, or the feeling of pity. Reason is denounced as the source of *amour-propre*. But in the *Lettre à d'Alembert* we are told that "Nature and reason give man the love of goodness." In *La Nouvelle Héloïse* (1761), Julie defends reason as the revealer

[14] *Poème sur la loi naturelle*, ed. by F. J. Crowley, pp. 240–41, 248 (1. 49–50), 251 (1. 1–8), 253 (1. 49–54), 254–55.
[15] "Conscience," *Oeuvres*, Vol. 18, pp. 234–36.

of right, and her own moral debates are a model for the theory of conscience as reason—not merely intuitive, but discursive.[16] The Savoyard Vicar, in the *Profession de foi* (1762) makes conscience the sole judge of good and evil, a judge whose task is to control the instincts and the passions. Conscience is innate, therefore a natural instinct; its function, then, is to control other natural instincts.

> Following my usual method, I do not take these rules from the principles of a lofty philosophy, but I find them inscribed by nature, at the bottom of my heart, in ineffaceable characters. I have only to consult myself about what I want to do: whatever I feel to be right is right, whatever I feel to be wrong is wrong. The best of all casuists is conscience; it is only when one haggles with it that one has recourse to the subtleties of reasoning. The first of all cares is for oneself; yet how many times does the inner voice tell us that in furthering our own good at the expense of others, we are doing wrong! We think we are following nature's impulse, and we are resisting it; in listening to what it tells our senses, we are despising what it tells our hearts; the active being is obeying, the passive being is commanding. Conscience is the voice of the soul, passions are the voice of the body. . . . Too often reason deceives us, we have earned only too well the right to reject it; but conscience never deceives; it is man's true guide; it is to the soul what instinct is to the body; who follows it obeys nature, and need not fear going astray. . . . The sole morality of actions is in the judgment we make of them ourselves.[17]

In this statement we must first note that conscience or moral judgment is made to be entirely natural or instinctual. It is in no way the product of culture (although, as we saw in our earlier discussion, it is not awakened until social experience arouses all the higher faculties). Conscience has two enemies. The first is physical nature, or ego-satisfaction (which Rousseau assumes incorrectly to be identical). The second is reason, which is the child of culture and the slave of the passions.

[16] *La Nouvelle Héloïse*, III, pp. 85, 65 ff.

[17] *Emile*, ed. P. Richard, pp. 348–49. Cf. the famous exclamation, admired by Kant: "Conscience! Conscience! divine instinct, immortal and celestial voice; sure guide of an ignorant and limited, but intelligent and free creature; infallible judge of right and wrong, which makes man like unto God, it is you that makes the excellence of his nature and the morality of his actions; without you I feel nothing in me which raises me above the beasts except the sad privilege of straying from error to error with the help of an understanding without rule and a reason without principle" (pp. 354–55). Rousseau's implied distinction between the understanding and reason is also worthy of note.

Many readers, in Rousseau's time and later, understood him to have defined conscience as feeling, and to have preached a morality of feeling. (It is also possible to interpret his conscience as a moral sense.) Although there is no doubt about his attachment to the principle of subjectivity, in this phase of his writings, the essential thing is to understand the nature of that subjective experience. And there is ample ground, in the *Profession de foi,* for the sentimentalist reading. Denouncing the empirical explanation of conscience, Rousseau admits that all our ideas are acquired; but he claims that "the acts of conscience are not judgments, but feelings." To exist is to feel, and feelings precede ideas. Feelings do not come from outside ourselves. It is by feelings alone that we know "the propriety or impropriety which exists between ourselves and the things we should respect or avoid." [18] Feelings include the ego-protective and the social or moral.[19] Clearly, then, it is in part the desire to preserve the innate and natural character of conscience, in view of the sensationist theory of knowledge, that has impelled Rousseau to sever it entirely from the rational or intellective aspects of the self.

But Rousseau does give a role to reason. Feeling cannot "know." Man "does not have the innate knowledge" of right and wrong; "but as soon as his reason gives him that knowledge, his conscience impels him to love it. It is this feeling which is innate." God has given us "reason to know the good, conscience to love it, and freedom to do it." [20]

However there is a second fatal weakness in rationalistic moral theories which has led Rousseau to the severance of reason and conscience. Reason, he holds, cannot refute the nihilist—as Diderot had tried to do in "Droit naturel." [21] Reason cannot successfully establish the essential of morality:

[18] *Ibid.,* p. 352–53.
[19] "It is from the moral system formed by this double relationship to oneself and to one's fellows that the impulse of conscience is born." (P. 354.)
[20] This phrase also appears in *La Nouvelle Héloïse,* Part 6, Letter 7. In his defense of *Emile,* in the *Lettre à M. de Beaumont* (1762), Rousseau equates conscience with love of order and again declares that it is developed and functions only with "*lumières,*" which enable it to know order. Once it is known, conscience makes us love it.
[21] As Charles Frankel has put it, "reason could never argue anyone into having a feeling of obligation." (*The Faith of Reason,* New York, 1948, p. 78.) Rousseau's preoccupation with the challenge of nihilism is frequently apparent. In *La Nouvelle Héloïse,* for example, Julie searches her soul, admits the beauty and usefulness of

There is no use trying to establish virtue by reason alone; what solid basis can we give it? Virtue, they say, is the love of order. But can this love, and should it, win out in me over love of my own good? Let them give me a clear and sufficient reason for preferring it. At bottom their supposed principle is a mere play on words; for I say also that vice is the love of order, taken in a different sense. There is some moral order wherever there is feeling and intelligence. The difference is that the good man orders himself in relation to the whole, and the wicked man orders the whole in relation to himself. The latter makes himself the center of all things; the former measures his radius and limits himself to the circumference.[22]

This thought, concerned now with God as the center of concentric circles, continues to this conclusion: "If God does not exist, only the wicked man reasons, the good man is just crazy."

The whole point for Rousseau is, then, precisely this: reason does not supply us with the reason (or motive) for being virtuous, for adhering to a principle of limit (the "circumference"). It only lets us know what virtue is. The instinctive principle of conscience urges or compels our adherence, so that there is no need to refute the nihilist by reasons; nature itself refutes him, aided by faith in God.

Nevertheless there is a lack of consistency in Rousseau's presentation. At the outset, he made conscience more than a motivating force toward the right. It seems rather to be concrete perception of what *is* right or wrong, either an intuitive judgment or a moral sense, and not merely an admonition telling us, "Do this which reason says is right," or "You are doing what reason says is wrong, therefore I disapprove and you are doing wrong." Rousseau's frequent declarations, in his own defense, to the effect that he *feels* he is right, indicate a conscience which discriminates. But that is not his theory as he outlines it in the *Profession de foi*. Nor is it the theory of an "enlightened conscience," according to which reason would transform conscience from a sentimental impulse to something that can be reasoned about. By separating conscience from reason and giving to the latter sole power to discern what is right and wrong, and to conscience the power to move the affective

virtue, then asks: "but what does all that count in comparison to my personal interest, and which, at bottom, matters most to me, my happiness at the expense of all other men, or the happiness of others at the expense of mine?" (III, p. 67.)
[22] P. 356.

allegiance of the self, he transforms conscience from a cognitive or a judicial faculty to a sentimental impulse.

Rousseau here seems to believe in the intuitive value of reason in discerning right and wrong—the process being apparently immediate, for the more one reasons, the more one falls into error. But frequently, too, he denies any value to reason, and *opposes* it to conscience and feeling. "In all difficult moral questions . . . , I have always found it well to solve them by the dictate of my conscience rather than by the lights of my reason: the moral instinct has never deceived me." [23] And so we are brought back to the immediate judicial power of conscience, or to its cognitive function as a moral sense.[24] However he also writes of himself (speaking in the third person) that he was not virtuous, that is, not able to overcome his self-interest in favor of his duty. "How could he be, always having for his guide only his own heart, never his duty nor his reason?" [25] This leads into still another confusion. He has told us that conscience is our real nature, or again, that part of our nature whose function it is to control our animal nature. But in this same passage he says that nature can only make people good (that is, disposed to taking pleasure in doing good), but not inclined to the sacrifice which is virtue. "The law of nature, its voice at least, does not go that far. Another must then command, and let nature be silent." Virtue requires reason. Does this oppose conscience to nature? Or does it indicate that nature (including the individual conscience) must be superseded by culture?

It would perhaps be a kind of rough summary to say that reason (rationality) awakens the moral conscience, and then prepares its own abdication to the conscience; it also assists the conscience and justifies it. "Thus my rule to abandon myself to feeling more than to reason is confirmed by reason itself." Conscience is an immediate perception of a special kind of truth.

By and large, Rousseau's subjective ethics is one of sensibility and not of reason, but there are strange confusions which result

[23] *Rêveries, Oeuvres,* IX, p. 350, also p. 357.
[24] We find the same uncertainties in *Emile.* First he writes: "Reason alone teaches us to know good and evil. Conscience, which teaches us to love one and hate the other, although independent of reason, cannot then develop without it." (P. 48.) And later: "I know only that truth . . . is not in my mind which judges [things] . . . and so my rule, to give myself up to feeling rather than to reason, is confirmed by reason itself." (P. 327.)
[25] *Dialogues,* IX, p. 209.

from the lack of rigorous thinking.[26] Moreover, he is aware of the uncertainty of the power of one natural instinct (conscience) to control another. Consequently, it is not surprising that the same uncertainties persist in his other writings. In the *Contrat social,* though the focus is social, distrust of the individual conscience is implied in his theory of the "guide." In *La Nouvelle Héloïse,* we have both the contrast between natural goodness and social morality, and the symbolic alliance between Julie and Wolmar. Convention, the opinion and esteem of others, as well as reason (as in the problems of dueling and suicide, among others) time and again prove Saint-Preux to be wrong in following his conscience. If Rousseau's purpose is to change man into an artificial social being, then natural instincts like conscience are not sufficient to the task. Nevertheless, he will at the same time maintain the absolute validity of conscience.[27]

Doubtless Rousseau feels that in an ideal social order, the unity of presocial man would be restored, with the significant difference that it would be established on a moral level. Virtue would then unite reason and feeling, each strengthening and guiding the other, feeling animating reason, and reason illuminating feeling. In the present social state, which is itself a contradictory dualism of nature and culture, this unity is impossible.

Typical of the attacks on Rousseau's ethical conceptions were those of Charles Bordes and of Bouchaud, a professor of theology. The former, in a biting satire, writes: "The wicked have passed the word around: this man delivers us from the yoke of laws and religion; he reduces everything to conscience, which tells us nothing." [28] Bouchaud points to the inconstancy and uncertainty of conscience. To act against conscience is to violate Natural Law; "but it does not follow that someone who followed all the impulses of conscience would always be doing just actions." [29]

---

[26] Jean Starobinski's solution is that "reason appears dangerous to him only insofar as it claims to grasp the truth in a non-immediate way." Reason and feeling are not contradictory insofar as they are immediate. (*Op. cit.,* p. 50.) This explanation is correct and most helpful, but it does not resolve fully the multiple facets of the problem.

[27] In one and the same letter, it is both categorically denied and affirmed. Cf. *La Nouvelle Héloïse,* ed. D. Mornet, III, pp. 67, 77. There are similar uncertainties about reason; e.g., II, pp. 110n., 263, 297, 300; IV, p. 245 n. 3.

[28] *Profession de foi philosophique.*

[29] Bergier and Bouchaud, *Principes de métaphysique et de morale,* 1780, p. 18–19. The theory of conscience as subjective sentiment was developed further by Bernardin de Saint-Pierre. See "De la Nature de la morale," *Oeuvres,* 1818, Vol. 7. Some

The empiricists, taking a diametrically opposing position, considered conscience as nothing more than the internalization of outside standards and pressures. (How conscience originated is a matter we have examined in the preceding chapter.) Face to face with this fact, it was still possible to accept the validity of conscience. But there were some who chose to view moral judgment as a question of experience, with conscience as variable and as flexible as any other human reaction. They did not deny the existence of conscience, but rather its validity.

Citing many examples of enormities practiced in good conscience, either in other cultures, or in any culture when the threat of punishment and censure is removed, Locke had supported both the empirical formation of conscience and its cognitive and moral unreliability.[30] For Hume, conscience was more a matter of the approbation of others than of self-approval.[31] Unlike Rousseau, he does not confuse the role of conscience (or that of reason) in its function in motivation with its function of cognition, denying only the latter in moral matters. Collins argued that conscience went well with determinism, but he reduced it to remorse, that is, fear of or regret for the consequences of what a person necessarily did.[32]

This emphasis on remorse dominates the materialistic approach. The key is given in some of the early manuscripts. In one we find remorse dismissed as the result of instilled prejudices and "a particular disposition of our organs," a view which the author attempts to substantiate by citing varying reactions to the same deed. If we could get rid of these prejudices, we should be free from remorse.[33] Boulainvilliers, an important writer and circulator of skeptical manuscripts, thought that shame indicates weakness. It befits souls which lack greatness and the courage to be evil. Remorse applies only to the past and is useless for the future. He calls it "an importune and painful sensation, which is the first

---

further proponents of the a priori conscience: Meister, *De la Morale naturelle,* Londres, 1781, pp. 73–79; Mme Necker, *Nouveaux Mélanges,* 1801, II, p. 98; Du Pont de Nemours, *op. cit.,* pp. 99–101; Delisle de Sales, *op. cit.,* I, pp. 21–22. In England, Butler and Reid, but they were little known in France. For Kant's concept of conscience as the judiciary faculty, related to God, see *op. cit.,* pp. 173, 182 and especially 321–22.

[30] *Essay,* Bk. I, chap. II.
[31] B. Willey, *op. cit.,* p. 122.
[32] *A Philosophic Inquiry concerning Human Liberty,* London, 1717, pp. 105–6.
[33] *Examen de la religion,* Londres, 1761, pp. 121–22. The manuscript dates from about 1711.

punishment of the guilty." [34] This tendency is continued in Vauvenargues, but with a peculiar admixture of elements. Vauvenargues makes light of conscience as a changing and uncertain rule
of conduct. He also belittles reason. "The mind is the eye of the
soul, not its force. Its force is in the heart. . . . I rarely take the
cause of feeling before the tribunal of reason." But he uses this
attitude as a weapon against remorse, which, he thinks, derives
from reflection. Remorse makes us unjust toward ourselves.[35]

All of these writings may be considered as preparations for the
principal theorist of materialism in the first half of the century,
Julian Offray de La Mettrie. Fundamentally a nihilist in his moral
theory—although admitting the necessity for society to impose
arbitrary standards—La Mettrie considers remorse the principal
obstacle to the emancipated individual. He poses this problem as
the starting point for his reflections: if moral principles are
arbitrary and human, why are men tortured by remorse? [36] There
is no Natural Law. Remorse is instilled during childhood and in
adults is a retrogression to childhood. "At first it was only a simple
feeling, received without examination and without choice, and
which engraved itself as deeply into the brain as a seal into soft
wax." Passion stifles it temporarily; but then it returns, "for then
the first principles which form the conscience, those with which
it has been imbued, come back, and that is what we call remorse.
. . . It is, if you will, a brain-path which is renewed, and consequently an old prejudice which voluptuousness and passions do
not put to sleep well enough for it not to reawaken sooner or
later. Thus man carries his greatest enemy within himself. . . .
Fortunately this cruel enemy is not always the winner. Any other
habit, either more permanent or stronger, must necessarily conquer it. The best trod path becomes effaced." A new mechanism
abolishes earlier structure.

In this way La Mettrie, the medical scientist, dispassionately
analyzes the origins and power of remorse (we should say "guilt"),
to which he reduces conscience. Then the moralist steps in. The

---

[34] *Réfutation des erreurs de Spinoza*, Bruxelles, 1731, pp. 208–9. The manuscript
predates 1722. See Wade, *op. cit.*, p. 116 ff. and the revealing article by N. L. Torrey,
"Boulainvilliers, the Man and the Mask."
[35] *Oeuvres morales*, 1874, pp. 28, 32 (*Réflexions*, pp. 133, 134, 135, 149), I, pp. 142–
143.
[36] *Anti-Sénèque, ou Discours sur le bonheur*, pp. 127–33, 100.

moralist condemns remorse as the "executioner" of happiness. If we want to be virtuous, moreover, it should be by reason, not by habit. The irony, for La Mettrie, is that it is the good who are tormented by remorse, while the wicked have learned to stifle it. Besides, he asserts, remorse does not prevent crime, but only puts in an appearance *post facto*. The best thing for us to do, he urges, is to throw off this yoke. "Since remorse is a vain remedy for our ills, since they trouble even the clearest waters, without clearing even the least troubled, let us then destroy it; let there be no more chaff, mingled with the good grain of life, and let this cruel poison be expunged forever. . . . We have, then, every right to conclude that if the joys drawn from nature and reason are crimes, the happiness of men lies in their being criminals." To be sure, happiness can come from not doing what will provoke remorse. But we are necessarily determined, not only in our actions, but in our way of finding happiness. The result of a moralistic course, for many men, would be to give up pleasure, and to repent of pleasure is a mere puerility. From another viewpoint, since virtue is a simple matter of arbitrary social institution and is enforced by policemen, remorse is unnecessary to society.

In these statements, La Mettrie has not yet revealed the full power of his speculative nihilism, as we shall see in a later chapter. However his nihilism was obvious to his contemporaries. Voltaire wrote his *Poème sur la loi naturelle* at least partly to refute him. Diderot mentioned him only with an angry detestation exacerbated by the fact that he was himself unable to write the refutation he would have liked to write. Gauchat, who could speak from a different viewpoint, did undertake a refutation. He concludes that La Mettrie is himself one of those "mad dogs" which he gives society the duty to destroy.[37]

---

[37] *Op. cit.*, I, pp. 190–201. In *L'Homme machine*, La Mettrie's analysis of the nature and power of remorse is substantially the same, though briefer and attenuated in its nihilistic tendency (pp. 100–3, 133–34). See also *Discours préliminaire*. To attribute La Mettrie's tendency to "irony" or "paradox" is to deny the essential meaning of his thought and to fall into the trap which he set out in self-defense. It is true that many of his observations may be taken as positivistic descriptions of fact rather than as value statements, but he often crosses the line.

We should note in passing an opinion expressed by Turgot, in a letter to Du Pont de Nemours, that there is no remorse for injustice when that injustice is not condemned by prevailing opinion. (Cf. Locke.) Where slavery is established, there is no remorse. "Do you think that Philip felt any for crushing Greece, and Alexander for conquering the kingdom of Darius?" This statement is of interest, for it implies

In Diderot's references to the question we encounter the bi-
furcation of his thought, according to whether he is donning the
bonnet of the defender of morality or of the radical with speculative nihilistic tendencies. In "Loi naturelle," he proclaims the
universality of conscience, although he does not inquire into its
origin. In "Droit naturel," his appeal to the general will comes
dangerously close to nullifying the personal responsibility he is
trying to establish. But the general will is reached through the
conscience of individuals, and in his thinking he approaches a
form of categorical imperative. "There is no quality essential to
your species except the one you require from all your fellows for
your happiness and for theirs." Without this universal, conscience
will become confused. Here, as elsewhere, Diderot is aware of the
precarious balance of a morality which has only the human as its
foundation; yet, this is our lot. His formalistic view of conscience
is most evident in his repeated insistence on the virtue-happiness
equivalence, a belief which implies that actions are good in themselves.[38] In *Jacques le Fataliste,* a work in which Diderot puts his
divergent theories to the test of experiment, the characters, "without taking into account the very deterministic wherefore which
would have to be known for complete explanation . . . instinctively *know* that such an act is desirable, another to be discouraged
and punished." [39]

Elsewhere Diderot pursues a different line of thought. The abbé
Hayer warned his readers that although the article "Conscience"
in the *Encyclopédie* (by Jaucourt) was acceptable, they should
beware of "Fragilité" (by Diderot). Indeed, some of the remarks

a permanent, universal right which has been violated—Turgot, we recall, supported Natural Law; and yet the conscience is not always aware of, or affected by
the wrongs one does. We have, then, the unusual combination of an a priori moral
law and an empirical conscience (*Oeuvres,* III, p. 378).

Condillac's statement is equivocal. He follows Locke in making all knowledge, and
so moral knowledge, the result of experience. "One consequence is that good and
evil are not absolute: they are relative to the character of the person who is judging, and to the manner in which he is organized." (*Traité des sensations,* Part IV,
chap. 3, par. 3.) In a note, however, Condillac protests that he is contemplating only
a state of isolation. But since he does not allow even innate mental faculties or
structures, no other conclusion is possible. His views could not help but lead others
toward determinism and exclusive self-interest. We recall other statements: "The
statue can love only itself." "Sensations force it to flee pain and to seek the pleasurable." The social and moral are therefore superimpositions. In the earlier *Traité
des systèmes,* Condillac opposed conscience as a criterion of certitude, inasmuch as
that would imply innatism. (*Oeuvres,* II, pp. 98–99.)

[38] See the next chapter and L. G. Crocker, *Two Diderot Studies,* pp. 15–17.
[39] J. R. Loy, *Diderot's Determined Fatalist,* p. 179.

in the latter article are not unlike the views of La Mettrie. In *Le Neveu de Rameau,* Diderot's protagonist finds no place for conscience in his nihilistic view of man and the world. In the *Entretien d'un père avec ses enfants,* remorse is characteristically reduced to fear.[40] Diderot rarely speaks of the conscience, but if we follow his materialism, it seems evident that we are no more responsible for the feeling of shame after wrong-doing than for the desire to do what society has chosen to call wrong.

It scarcely need be said that for Helvétius conscience is entirely introjected and is a result of conditioning; this fact he considers a most useful mechanism for society. Like the other materialists, he makes a strong attack on the notion of an innate conscience and is most concerned with remorse. Remorse, he assures us, "is only the foresight of the physical punishment to which crime exposes us."[41] If a man is without fear or above the law, he will indulge in bad actions without remorse, provided he has not contracted the habit of virtue. Remorse (conscience) depends on custom and education and varies widely. This proves that it is nothing more than fear of punishment or shame—which, in turn, is always reducible to physical pain.

D'Holbach, like Diderot, believes in the universality and the efficacy of conscience and in the reduction of remorse to fear. There are only two elements in behavior according to his analysis. Our passions are a natural part of our temperament; the use we make of them depends on our habits and ideas, which come from education and society. "These are the things which necessarily decide our conduct." [42] Remorse is the "painful feeling aroused in us by the present or future effects of our passions." If the effects are useful to us, we have no remorse. But we become worried, dissatisfied with ourselves, and feel shame, if we fear the hatred, scorn, or punishment of those whose esteem, favor, or affection we need.[43] Here d'Holbach's conclusion is like that of the moralistic Diderot and unlike that of Helvétius. There is no wicked man who is not ashamed of his conduct and who does not suffer more than he

---

[40] *Oeuvres,* V, pp. 295–96.

[41] *De l'Homme,* pp. 83–84. All supposedly psychic phenomena are only physical.

[42] *Système de la nature,* I, pp. 254–58.

[43] In *Le Système social,* d'Holbach describes conscience as putting ourselves in the place of others and judging ourselves from their viewpoint. "Thus conscience is in man the knowledge of the effects which his actions produce on others." (I, pp. 155–56.)

gains. He feels shame, despises and hates himself, and is always ashamed in his conscience. (On this point Diderot's speculative nihilism is far more radical.) But there is an important reservation: all this depends on what our society approves or blames; we do not blush for actions which are not disapproved. Conscience is, then, purely a function of the cultural milieu. In a licentious country, no one is ashamed of adultery; no thief has remorse in the company of thieves—we may add, no murderer where murder is condoned.[44] However, d'Holbach makes still another qualification: all men necessarily approve useful actions and disapprove harmful ones, which are called vices. This last statement does not fit very well with the preceding ones. Nor does what follows: that even in the most vicious and corrupt societies, the fundamental distinctions remain alive in each conscience; so that once more we may say, no wicked man can be happy. D'Holbach returns, indirectly, to universals and formal values of acts, although he has sought to evade the a priori conscience by a utilitarian determinism. "Thus the system of determinism," he concludes, not very convincingly, "establishes morality on an unshakeable basis."

D'Holbach's theory is further rationalized in *La Morale universelle,* where he writes: "Only profound and persistent reflection on the immutable relationships and duties of morality can enlighten the conscience and show us what we ought to do, or avoid, independently of the false notions which we find established."[45] It seems that we can, then, after all, rise above the empirical formation of our conscience, to the rational perception of objective truths. But what is the motivation for such reasoning? Only the necessarily determined results of an education which has instilled the desire to please and be approved (elsewhere d'Holbach considers these motives as necessary constituents of human nature). Thus d'Holbach seems to have trapped himself in a circle. One may nevertheless conclude that for d'Holbach conscience is a hybrid. It is not in itself natural or innate, but rises necessarily out of other natural feelings and social experience. It is irrational, since it absorbs contrasting and contradictory values from the

---

[44] In *Le Système social,* he puts the same idea this way: "A collective shame, or one which is spread over many heads, becomes a light burden for each one of those who bear it. When public opinion is vitiated, we end up by glorifying vice and infamy." (*Ibid.,* pp. 155–56.) For similar ideas in *La Morale universelle,* see I, pp. 58–59.

[45] *Ibid.,* I, pp. 59–61.

milieu; but the intellect can enlighten it and make it autonomous and critical. Objective values exist, but conscience is not necessarily a perception of those values.

The chief weakness and danger of the eighteenth-century empirical view is brought out most clearly in d'Holbach (and in Helvétius). The conscience and its operations can no longer be spoken of as a moral experience. It is reduced to a calculation of self-interest, more or less habitual or reflective. It leaves the door wide open to the rebellious amoralist. And in fact, the foes of the new philosophy were quick to seize on this deficiency in their refutations of d'Holbach. Holland denies that remorse and shame are "reasonable ideas after a disadvantageous act." We have none for involuntary disadvantageous acts, or for acts committed by error or ignorance, but only on the feeling of freedom, of the possibility of having acted otherwise.[46] Richard insists on the conscience's power of autonomous judgment, regardless of approval or the absence of social disapproval.[47] Le Franc de Pompignan also asserts that self-reproach is based on a different principle, on a predisposition antecedent to experience and reflection. The opinion that our actions are necessary would obviate remorse. D'Holbach's "morality," he concludes, is only calculation of self-interest.[48]

Sabatier de Castres, Sade, and Rivarol, despite vast differences, are related by their opposition to a liberal, humanistic philosophy. The young Sabatier was associated with the philosophic group. At that time he could write: "One does not stifle at will the lights of reason, nor in consequence the voice of conscience. Love of order is and will always be written in all hearts. If man were naturally wicked, as some philosophers have claimed, he would never have remorse."[49] Sabatier, the cynical and opportunistic counter-Revolutionary exile, expressed a different opinion. Conscience now is only conformity with established opinions. There is no "Silver

[46] *Op. cit.*, pp. 179–80.
[47] *Op. cit.*, pp. 142–47, 251.
[48] *Op. cit.*, pp. 209 ff., 281–92. Saint-Lambert's analysis of conscience is, in practically all respects, extraordinarily close to d'Holbach's. There are similar gaps in logic. He assigns happiness as the functional goal of conscience, but assures us that it cannot be reached by one who separates his own happiness from others'. However, according to his own reasoning, this is so only if a person's experience, and the kind of generalization he has developed the habit of inferring from it, have led to the formation of that type of conscience. See *Catéchisme universel*, II, pp. 18–19, 51; *Analyse de l'homme* (written 1788, publ. 1797), I, pp. 133–36, 159.
[49] *Dictionnaire des Passions*, 1769, II, pp. 349–50.

Rule" written in all hearts. Is it not all too clear that neither
natural nor civilized man follows it? "Virtue is so little natural
to man that its very name designates an effort." As for the Golden
Rule, it is so positively contrary to Natural Law, that compliance
can be obtained only at the price of violence and threats.[50]

Sade's principal target, like La Mettrie's, is remorse (and honor
and reputation), the great difference being that he is a practicing
nihilist, in open revolt against society. In his early and superficially moderate *Les Infortunes de la vertu* (1788, unpublished),
he puts into the mouth of the first of his line of female corrupters
of virtue an exhortation to her victim to recondition herself
against remorse. "Repeat often what gives you remorse and you
will soon dissipate it." [51] Since the prohibition of crime is against
nature, there is no crime; consequently remorse comes only from
the prohibition and not from the act. Elsewhere he analyzes conscience as flexible, molded by education, and denounces "the
heart" as the "falsest guide we have received from nature." [52]
Curiously, but logically, the terminus of Sade's nihilism is also
remorse, but in reverse.

> That is, then, an enjoyment lost (*une jouissance manquée*), for
> those of crime do not tolerate restrictions. I know them; if the
> imagination has not conceived everything, if the hand has not
> executed everything, the delirium cannot have been complete,
> because there always remains the remorse: *"I could have done
> more than I did."* [53]

Antoine de Rivarol's evolution was not unlike that of Sabatier.
Before the Revolution he was an independent thinker who rejected both traditional Christianity and systematic deism. In his
early work, written in refutation of Necker's *Importance des
idées religieuses* (1787), "he preaches a life attuned to the order
of nature as revealed by reason; a religion independent of the
institutions of God and man." [54] At this stage, he is closer to
Rousseau and declares that "through direct communion with the

---

[50] *Pensées et observations* . . . , Vienne, 1794, pp. 36–37.

[51] *Les Infortunes de la vertu*, 1930, pp. 171–73.

[52] *La Philosophie dans le boudoir*, 1948 [1795], pp. 204–5. See also *Histoire de Juliette*, 1954 [1796], I, pp. 19 ff., 195; II, p. 181.

[53] *Juliette*, III, p. 16. Cf. Westermarck: remorse is not necessarily moral—an egoist may reproach himself for having yielded to benevolence or conscience. (*Op. cit.*, p. 108.)

[54] R. G. Law, "Rivarol's 'Morale indépendante' and Pascal," p. 251. Rivarol's book was called *Lettres à M. Necker* (1788).

inner forces of nature, an individual may discover moral laws which have been distorted or subverted by institutions." [55] Conscience "is the light which instructs each man coming into the world," though it must be developed like all our faculties.

Later on, however, Rivarol's attention became riveted on the need of controlling the masses and the dangers of "philosophy." [56] Then he writes that conscience derives from education and easily withers away, so that "men and entire peoples may be brought to a frightful point of immorality." Rivarol is of course thinking of the Reign of Terror, but we can find twentieth-century analogues. "There are examples of men who have lost their remorse, and of men who have never had any." Nature cannot be trusted; it is not she who teaches men that it is better to be unhappy because of misfortune than because of remorse. There is no absolute justice. There is only usefulness, need, fear. Our justice cannot therefore be God's, and we are free "to turn our reason and our conscience to our own profit. There is no morality except from man to man." Nature is a jungle, war is its law and victory of the strong is its only code. "If nature suddenly produced a race superior to ours, we should at once be as guilty as sharks and wolves." Under these conditions, there is only one safeguard. Without the conditioning of small children, who could say what would become of the human race? In all this we can already see the seeds of totalitarian nihilism (as opposed to Sade's anarchistic nihilism).

The empiricists, then, for the most part saw moral experience as a question of expediency, with conscience as variable and as flexible as any other human reaction, although objective needs and relations, when related to the goals of self-interest, provide some consistent tendencies. A few extreme immoralists denied not the existence of conscience, but its validity. Both viewpoints have been carried forward into the twentieth century, a succession of nihilists representing the latter, and the main body of psychology supporting the former.

The most important figure in modern psychology is Freud. He accounts for conscience in terms that are in some respects a newer version of eighteenth-century theories, the great difference being

---

[55] *Ibid.*, p. 252.

[56] *De l'Homme*, 1800, pp. 175–76, 143–44, 211 ff. R. G. Law's article ignores this aspect of Rivarol's thought. He does not note how the statement "We may train a child for virtue as a falcon is trained for the hunt" follows in the radical philosophical line. (*Op. cit.*, p. 253.)

the concept of the unconscious or subconscious mind. In Freud's
theory, conscience is something quite irrational and a complex
phenomenon. Its origin lies in resistance to the Oedipus complex
in "instinctual deprivations," and its torments "correspond" to the
child's dread of losing his parents' love. It includes characteristics
and traditions of the race, "repetitions of some primeval phylo-
genetic experience," and an inherited cultural deposit in the id.[57]
Freud thus apparently admits some universals. In its individual
genesis, the conscience is the internalization of the super-ego, an
identification with the father or father-substitutes.[58] For the most
part, the content of conscience varies with that of the superego, that
is, with the age and the culture, and therefore reflects folkways.
"During the whole of a man's later life it represents the influence
of his childhood, of the care and education given to him by his
parents. . . ." [59]

One may question whether Freud's theory really accounts for
the existence of moral experience, for the jump, which he presupposes, from *fear* to *wrong*, from *must* to *ought*. There are many
actions which follow Freud's pattern and produce no moral experience. A child is told not to touch a hot iron, and perhaps he
does. The result of the experience is a "must," or a fear, but not an
"ought," or a wrong. Or we may suppose that the child has been
told not to torment a dog; he does, is bitten, and the same result
ensues as with the iron. But suppose the mother explains to the
child that "it is not nice," or right, to torment a dog, because the
animal has feelings, too, and "you would not like someone to do
it to you," etc. Then the result eventually is different. Eventually
—because this type of experience cannot take place in a very small
child. Why is this so? It cannot take place until the child has
reached a stage of mental development at which he is capable of
objectifying the world—of treating other beings as subjects, existing in and for themselves, and not only as objects, related to his
own subjectivity.[60] It is this, and the power of abstraction, which

[57] *An Outline of Psychoanalysis*, New York, 1949, pp. 121–23. *Civilization and its Discontents:* "Conscience is the result of instinctual renunciation, or: Renunciation (externally imposed) gives rise to conscience, which then demands further renuncia-tions" (p. 114).
[58] *Civilization and its Discontents*, pp. 120, 114 ff.
[59] *Outline, loc. cit.*
[60] Jean Piaget has shown that the small child lives in a purely subjective world of space, time, and cause. Piaget holds the moral experience to be associated with the development of the imagination, which creates the power of projection or empathy. (*Op. cit.*, pp. 417–35.)

lead to the suprapersonal view which characterizes the uniquely human moral experience—judgment (or indignation) on "the principle of the thing," concern for values which we would not like to see disappear from the face of the earth. The empirical explanation leaves no room for "the sense of fairness" which we see even in a child, for the difference between the cry of the child who is punished and the cry of the child who is punished unjustly, for the distinctive reaction of the human spectator who says, "This is not fair, not right." Digestion cannot take place without eating, but this does not make eating an explanation of digestion; so it is with Freud's description of the formation of the conscience.

More recently, some new schools of psychology, including the Existentialists, have thrown off or gone beyond the Freudian analysis. Erich Fromm is dissatisfied with the reduction of moral experience to "a reaction-formation against the evil inherent in man." [61] He dubs Freud's concept "the authoritarian conscience." It exists, to be sure, but it is not the only moral conscience. "Properly speaking, these people do not feel *guilty* but *afraid*"— the repetition of the eighteenth-century radicals' view is striking.[62] The authoritarian conscience represents an arbitrary, repressive tyranny. Fromm makes a convincing case for a "humanistic conscience," one based on the positive potentialities for good, on our reaction to ourselves, on being true to ourselves. This conscience is characteristic of a productive person living at a higher level than mere social adjustment.

Eighteenth-century theories of conscience correspond, in general, to the a priori and empirical views of moral experience, but the analyses offer sufficient variation to justify the further examination we have undertaken. Eighteenth-century thinkers essayed the first serious exploration of the origin and nature of conscience. Many of their conclusions, transformed by modern psychology, can be recognized in twentieth-century theories. The empirical view was an important step forward to a scientific understanding and methodology. Nevertheless, the fact that conscience originates in childhood conditioning is not a complete explanation of conscience, but rather a description of the process of its forma-

[61] See *Man for Himself*, New York, 1947, pp. 54 ff., 142 ff.
[62] Note also: "Guilt feelings have proved to be the most effective means of forming and increasing dependency; herein lies one of the social functions of authoritarian ethics throughout history." (P. 155.)

tion. Guilt and remorse are indeed forms of fear, induced by external authority; but they are also self-generated reactions toward the functioning of our self. Often they are weakness, leading to crippling guilt neuroses; but they are also the mechanisms whereby we develop the distinction between right and wrong.[63] We can understand the materialists' concentration on reducing conscience to remorse, and remorse to fear and habit, in the light of their desire to deny the existence in men of any a priori, or of any special psychic faculties that would separate them from the universal kingdom of nature.

To ask *why* in ethics is frequently useless, at least in regard to subjective moral experience; to find an explanation, we have to leave the field of moral experience, and then we are not really explaining. Why do we have esteem for ourselves and a feeling of pleasure when we satisfy our conscience (and shame or guilt when we do not)? To reply: because we were given approval or praise when we were helpless, irrational children, and this gave us pleasure (and the reverse, pain) may be the psychological explanation of the genesis of conscience; though it is perhaps insufficient, since we must go back a step further and account for the need for approval and the aversion to blame, as products of the insecurity of our being. These steps describe our development. But would there be such a development if man were not first, *in essentia,* a moral being? To offer as an explanation of conscience the fact that we are moral beings is of course tautological. And yet, is there another satisfactory answer?

A final word on the relation of conscience to moral nihilism. The standards of the group never become ethical standards merely by being required or approved by others, but only when we personally experience them as morally right. A person may say, "I am not interested in honor, duty or virtue. I find my happiness, without remorse or guilt, in so-called immoral actions. I make no apologies, for this is the way nature has made me." Such a person would seem to be in a fairly impregnable position. Perhaps there is no reply, other than the arbitrary punishment justified by La Mettrie. Or perhaps we may say that the self is not entirely self-sufficient, but depends, for its very existence as well as for its happiness, on the whole of which it is a part. Our acts take place

[63] See J. Huxley, *Touchstone for Ethics,* New York, 1947, p. 121.

in a context of institutions and relations from which it cannot, even if it will, dissociate itself. Even if we proclaim an anarchic right to happiness, we cannot conceive of happiness except in the framework of social existence.

II. Justice and Law

An important question which was debated throughout the seventeenth and eighteenth centuries concerns the relation between justice and law, and especially a particular aspect of that relation, that of logical priority. We shall not investigate the concept of justice itself. On that score there was general agreement that justice is giving to each his due—though Meister once queried whether the predicate of the definition was any clearer than the subject.[1] There was agreement, too, that justice was the cardinal virtue, the source of duties, though benevolence, humanity and "public spirit" gradually became its rivals. Some, it is true, associated justice with the principles of equality and reciprocity, while others, following Locke, held to the narrower view that it was bound to the right of property. The question of priority, however, is of particular interest, because of the highly significant division of thought which it evoked. It is closely related to the theory of the genesis and nature of moral experience, and has political implications, as well. The latter will be manifest in our discussion. As for the former, we may briefly say that precedence should be accorded to justice by those who hold an a priori theory, like Voltaire's, which makes experience a mere occasional cause for the development of latent judgments. Priority should logically be given to law by those who consider experience as effectively formative, since there are no predetermining abstract truths in the mind. Another way of posing the question might be this: does unfairness come from rules, or do rules derive from notions of unfairness? [2]

In general, the expected pattern is followed. Partisans of Natural Law, or, those who claimed mathematical demonstrability for

---

[1] *De la Morale naturelle*, p. 157.

[2] Sumner, Westermarck, and other modern relativists hold to the first thesis. In actuality, there is no either-or; the two propositions are complementary.

ethical laws, maintained the priority of justice. Locke, Cudworth, Cumberland, and Wollaston were among this group in England.[3] "To pretend by a law," writes the latter, "to make that just which before and in itself was unjust" is to ordain that what is true shall be false. In France, Meslier pointed out that if there are immutable moral laws, like mathematical truths, no one can change them.[4] Montesquieu was deeply concerned with this problem. In his *Pensées* he notes, about Hobbes's making law the source of justice: "I am sorry for it; for, being obliged to live with men, I should have liked there to be in their hearts an inner principle which would reassure me about them. . . ." [5] A review of the lost *Traité des devoirs* informs us that Montesquieu "shows that justice is not dependent on human laws, that it is founded on the existence and sociability of reasonable beings, and not on the personal inclinations or will of those beings." [6] The same viewpoint is apparent in the *Lettres persanes*.[7] However, the ardor of this faith does not quite coalesce with Montesquieu's political realism, which is far more concerned with the "is" than with the "ought." The theory is fine; but in practice, the conservative holds laws sacred. It is a *"bisarrerie"* of human nature that, unfortunately, sometimes makes it necessary to change them, but then only with the greatest precautions and solemnity. And then, the remedy is likely to be worse than the ill. "Whatever the laws are, we must always obey them, and regard them as the public conscience, to which private consciences must always conform." [8] This does not effectively coincide with Pensée 1906: "A thing is not just because it is a law, but it should be a law because it is just."

In a paper read before the Academy of Berlin in 1745, the indefatigable Samuel Formey took up the question, starting from the disagreement between Grotius and Pufendorf. Grotius had said that justice is independent of law, and prior to it. His successor had asserted that, on the contrary, actions are morally indifferent without law. Formey tries to conciliate the two views. The dispute, he claims, is only a logomachy. Taking "just" to mean

---

[3] Locke, *Essay*, IV, III, p. 18; Cumberland, *Treatise*, pp. 88–89, 198; Wollaston, *Religion . . . Delineated*, pp. 148–49; Cudworth, *Treatise*, I, p. i.
[4] *Testament*, II, pp. 340–46.
[5] *Oeuvres*, ed. Masson, II, pp. 343–44.
[6] *Ibid.*, III, p. 160.
[7] Lettre LXXXIII.
[8] *Ibid.*, Lettre CXXIX.

the morality of actions, then it is indisputably prior and fundamental to law. Taking the term to signify the obligation to conform our actions to moral qualities which have been established by rules and laws, then it is of course posterior to law. In fact, "equity," and not "justice" is the term Grotius should have used; but in all other respects he is right and Pufendorf is wrong. A law can most surely be inequitable, even if it cannot be unjust. Formey's reasoning leads one to wonder whether a law can, then, make what is inequitable "just." He sees the difficulty and replies in the negative, but does not dispose of the logical problem which grows out of the separation of the two terms.[9]

Voltaire's thinking on this question is once again characterized by the coexistence of Natural Law and utilitarian tendencies. In the *Traité de métaphysique* (1734), he denies an absolute justice, one unrelated to men; "we have no ideas of justice other than those we have formed of any action useful to society, and in conformity with *the laws established by us* for the common good."[10] But in the same chapter (IX) in which this empirical relativism of fact is expounded, Voltaire also affirms an immutable justice founded on Natural Law. We have seen that he expresses this view frequently throughout his life. He declares specifically that laws properly depend on a prior, immutable justice.[11] However, he constantly defines virtue, in the *Traité* and elsewhere, as conformity to established laws. The difficulty is obvious to the reader, if not to Voltaire. If justice, or being just, is a virtue, and justice is prior to law, then obedience to law cannot be a universal virtue, for obedience to an unjust law will make a man unjust, although, according to the definition of virtue, he is just. To obviate the dilemma, we must either make the further assumption that laws do, in actual fact, establish the justice demanded by Natural Law— an assumption which is empirically false or unverifiable, as Voltaire's own battles testify; or else make the definition conditional upon the fact. Voltaire does neither. As a pragmatical conservative,

---

[9] *Histoire de l'Académie de Berlin,* Berlin, 1746, I, pp. 97–101. A similar distinction had earlier been made in the anonymous ms. *Difficultés sur la religion,* fol. 63. When Toussaint, however, asserts the independence of laws and justice, he means only that laws may be in contradiction with the immutable Natural Law and, like religion, may push people to barbarities. (*Les Moeurs,* [1748] 1749 ed., pp. xxiii–xxxv.)

[10] *Traité de métaphysique,* ed. H. T. Patterson, p. 16. (Italics added.)

[11] "Loi naturelle," *Oeuvres,* Vol. 19, p. 606, *Le Philosophe ignorant,* Vol. 26, pp. 78–81.

he believes in obedience to laws. As a crusading reformer, he strives constantly to make laws conform to an ideal of justice which they did not represent. There is no contradiction whatsoever in his mind; both are requisite for the good of society, which remains his immutable lodestar.

The *Encyclopédie* defends the priority of justice.[12] The Physiocrats, believing in an absolute justice and "an order of duties and rights which are physically necessary, and consequently absolute," adhered strongly to this group.[13]

We have reserved for separate mention two men whose theory of moral genesis would have led us to expect their adherence to the opposite camp, La Mettrie and d'Holbach. La Mettrie is the objective observer of the world. Speaking from the viewpoint of relativism, he takes the opposite stand from most of the apriorists: there is no absolute justice, equity, vice, or crime, but only in relation to society—"beautiful arbitrary relations" he calls them.[14] This statement may seem to eliminate the priority of justice. But let us observe how La Mettrie works back to it. "What belongs to the law produces legal right" (*droit*); but this right in itself is neither rational right nor the right of equity; it is a "right" based on force, "which often crushes a wretch who has reason and justice on his side." [15] How can La Mettrie, who does not believe in any objective or abstract right, bring the law before the tribunal of "reason and justice"? The concealed motive is his nihilism, his desire to show the unjustifiability of society's restrictions on the individual—though, with characteristic clear-sighted honesty, he recognizes fully that society must protect itself, with or without

---

[12] See Jaucourt's "Equité" and Romilly-fils' "Vertu." In "Relation," however, Jaucourt, who was more a copyist than a thinker, expresses the contrary opinion. "It is the conformity or disconformity of our actions to some law (to which the legislator has attached, by his power and will some good or evil which we call reward or punishment) that makes these actions morally good or bad."

[13] E.g., Le Mercier de la Rivière, *L'Ordre naturel*, p. 8, and especially pp. 55–61. He points out that we would discriminate between two laws imposing death, the one for murder, the other for walking at a certain hour. Also Mably: "What! . . . is it possible that laws made by tyrants can be just! What! If the thirty tyrants had wanted to prescribe [such laws] to the Athenians, or if the Athenians had declared themselves in favor of those laws, would that be a motive to submit to them? Absolutely not." (*Droits et Devoirs du citoyen, Oeuvres*, XI, pp. 332–43; also, XI, pp. 256–57.) Christian apologists of course adhered to the traditional Natural Law view. See also, as defenders of prior justice, Linguet, *Théorie des loix civiles*, Londres, 1767, I, pp. 230 ff.; Condorcet, *Observations sur le 29ᵉ livre de l'Esprit des lois*, chap. XVIII.

[14] "Discours préliminaire," pp. 13–32.

[15] *Ibid.*, pp. 57–59.

moral justification. "What protects the weaker against the stronger," he adds in a loaded sentence, "may therefore not be equitable." Laws may, consequently, need to be rectified; not according to an abstract or absolute justice, in which La Mettrie does not believe; but only according to the interest of the group: "for that is the fixed point from which one can judge the just and the unjust. . . . One may say of [the laws] and of all human actions, that they alone are just or equitable which favor society, they alone unjust, which hurt its interests." In a word, there is really no inherence of justice or equity in law; "what is in the province of legality absolutely does not presuppose equity, which is recognizable only by the sign and characteristic I have mentioned," that is, the interest of society. La Mettrie thus offers a redefinition of justice, in terms of the community welfare, which becomes an abstract or objective criterion replacing Natural Law, and so the criterion having priority to law and entitled to judge the law. Law does not create justice, because it does not necessarily guarantee general interest, which *is* "justice." It is clear that if my own interest were to conflict with the general interest there would be no higher tribunal, no abstract, eternal, or certain right or wrong to which the dispute could be referred; there is only a contest of interests, a play of force, in which the community has, among other advantages, that of calling its interest "justice." With one blow, La Mettrie has undermined both the validity of law and the belief in a moral justice divorced from interest.

D'Holbach exalts justice as the basic virtue and social link. No relationship, no power has the right to force us to be unjust, "because justice is the support of the world . . . the true counterweight to the love we have for ourselves," the control of personal interest in favor of the permanent and larger, on which happiness depends.[16] Like La Mettrie, d'Holbach, by telling us that the law, to be just, must favor the "general interest" of society, identifies justice with "general interest"—whatever that phrase may mean.[17] He, too, sets up reason as a criterion higher than law. Reason's power to discern the general interest makes it a touchstone for the prevailing mores, which is always a system that tends to perpetuate itself by introjection into the individual conscience.[18] Justice, then, is prior to law.

[16] *Système social*, I, p. 105. See *La Morale universelle*, I, pp. 83, 92–95.
[17] *Système de la nature*, I, p. 154.
[18] *Ibid.*, I, pp. 157–58, 253.

It is not then the frequently irrational *will* of a people, it is not its special interest, it is not its laws and usages which make just what is not just *by its nature;* there is nothing really just except what is in conformity to the rights of mankind. Violence and conquest may be in conformity with the interests of an ambitious people; those who satisfy its passions may be in its eyes estimable and virtuous persons; but such a people is only a mass of evil-doers and murderers to anyone who has *healthy ideas* of international law, insolently violated by a nation which is an enemy of all others. The *permanent interest of man in general,* of the species, of the great world society, demands that one people respect the rights of another, just as the general interest of a particular society demands that each of its members respect the rights of his associates.[19]

In this sincere and eloquent passage, we can see how fundamentally different d'Holbach's thought is from La Mettrie's, and why he detested the earlier materialistic atheist, despite all they had in common. La Mettrie was the disillusioned, detached observer, stripped of ideals, the egoist concerned with personal pleasure, the scientist aware of the individual and social mechanisms engaged in a natural struggle of power. D'Holbach, as the italicized words reveal, was a moral idealist. For him will should submit to reason, things are right or wrong by their nature, an abstract norm exists. As a sensationist and materialist, as a proponent of scientific method, he recognizes the empirical character of moral and legal codes and also identifies justice with the "general interest." But it is clear that that much used and rarely defined phrase has a different meaning and stands for a different outlook than it did for La Mettrie. The "permanent interest of mankind in general," taken in combination with the other key words of the quotation uncover, beneath the frequent appearance of pragmatic utilitarianism, a belief in rational ideals and moral absolutes which identify d'Holbach in substance, though not in form, with the most idealistic of the Natural Law thinkers.

While not all empiricists place law before justice, only those who are empiricists, with a rare exception or two, do take this stand. As one view always seems to evoke its contrary, so we find this position expressed early among the Greeks. In the ideas of Thrasymachus, in Plato's *Republic,* we already find what is and will remain the essential of this position, as its adherents might

---

[19] *La Morale universelle,* I, p. 92. Italics added.

express it: the abandonment of an imaginary "ought" for a *de facto* acceptance of the world as it is. In all societies, he argues, those who seize power dictate the laws, dominate education and religion, manipulate rights, privileges, and conventions in favor of themselves and their class. The resultant code becomes what is accepted as justice, and in that name wins the allegiance of the masses. A really strong man will rebel and seize power; becoming a hero in his turn, his will is then the source of conventional morality.[20] In this doctrine, we can recognize seeds of nineteenth-century theories of class exploitation and of hero worship, as well as the empirical formulations of conscience and moral genesis.

Much closer to the period we are studying, Montaigne rallies to a similar kind of reasoning. "Now the laws maintain their credit, not because they are just, but because they are laws: this is the mystical basis of their authority; they have no other, and this serves them well. . . . Whoever obeys them because they are just does not obey them for what he justly should." [21] This view was approved and expanded by Pascal, although with a different aim. Not only is the justice of man a mere synonym for the existing customary and power establishment, but to speak of a justice which does not have the power to make itself real and effective is meaningless.[22] It is probable that Gassendi was also sympathetic to this general position.[23]

More influential than any of these writings was the repeated and detailed exposition of Hobbes. It is clear, for Hobbes, that civil laws are not founded on a prior definition of right and wrong. Quite to the contrary, it is law which defines the notions of justice, of right and wrong, and confers on them their power or quality of obligation. One cannot speak of justice or injustice prior to the existence of civil laws. Nor can one speak of an unjust law: the law, by definition, is always just.[24] Hobbes's influence is evident not only on those who adopted his ideas, but even more, in the continuous thunder of refutations and denunciations which they aroused in England and France. Among his chief followers we may, on this matter at least, count Spinoza. Before civil law, writes

[20] *The Republic*, 344A–344C. There is some contradiction in Thrasymachus, since he condemns tyranny as an injustice.
[21] *Essais*, III, p. xiii, "De l'Expérience."
[22] *Pensées* (Brunschvicg), 298, 312.
[23] Cf. J. S. Spink, *French Free Thought*, p. 101.
[24] Cf. R. Polin, *Politique et Philosophie chez Hobbes*, pp. 198–99.

Spinoza, there were only "the general laws of nature, there being no difference between pious and impious . . . because there was no possibility of justice or charity." Not until *droit* exists as an effective formulation "does it dawn upon us what is justice and what is injustice, what is equity and what is inequity . . . justice is dependent on the laws of the authorities, so that no one who contravenes their accepted decrees can be just. . . . Wrong is conceivable only in an organized community; nor can it ever accrue to the subject from any act of the sovereign. . . ." [25]

Among the Natural Law doctrinaires, Pufendorf stands alone in his attraction to this point of view. Rightness, he declares, is only "the conformity of the action with the law." [26] Since this position belongs more properly to empiricists, we are not surprised to see it strongly upheld by Hume, although the other British empiricists did not, in the main, follow him. Justice is ranked by Hume among the "artificial virtues," not among the "natural virtues." After conventions are entered into, "there immediately arise the idea of justice and injustice; as also those of *property, right,* and obligation." [27]

Among the French writers of our period, it is somewhat surprising to note Father Buffier's acceptance of the legalistic thesis. In his *Traité de la société civile* (1726), he admits, rather obscurely, a "limited kind of equity which may correct law," but asserts that "equity in general is manifestly the conformity of our judgment and of our will with the Law, or with the spirit of the Law." [28] With Helvétius, on the other hand, this position is obviously a part of his system. Justice and injustice presuppose a society and laws. They are invented by men in order to live together. If men had not made conventions, "there would not have been any general interest, consequently no just or unjust actions." [29] Thus there is no universal probity, for it would have to

<hr/>

[25] *Tractatus theologico-politicus,* in *The Chief Works of Benedict de Spinoza.* London, 1909, I, pp. 246–47, 207–8, 260. See also chap. 2 of the *Tractatus politicus.* "justice and injustice cannot be conceived of except under dominion." See also *Ethic,* Pt. IV, Proposition XXXVII, schol. 2.

[26] *Op. cit.,* I, p. 133.

[27] *Treatise of Human Nature,* ed. cit., pp. 59–60, 82–97, 133–34. The objection was frequently made that without a prior notion of obligation and justice, there was no obligation to be faithful to the first convention.

[28] Pp. 179–80. Similar views are found in the anonymous *L'Anti-naturaliste,* 1756 pp. 13–14, and in Morellet's "Sur la Liberté de la Presse," *Mélanges,* 1818, III, pp 41–42.

[29] *De l'Esprit,* p. 276. Prior to conventions are personal interest and physical sensation. Therefore physical sensation is the author of all justice!

consist in "the habit of actions useful to all nations," and there are no such actions. However nations could create universal probity by agreeing to laws and conventions.[30] In general, we may define injustice as "the violation of a convention or a law made for the advantage of the majority.[31] Therefore injustice does not precede the establishment of a convention, a law and a common interest." [32] Helvétius thus leaves the social culture free to set its goals and standards and to mold men's minds and characters in the selected direction.

Another unexpected proponent of legal priority was the anarchistic monk, Dom Deschamps. According to his theory, we have no conscience, or notion of right and wrong, just or unjust, before positive laws, from which they are derived. He concedes that the critic may inquire, Would laws have given us such notions if they did not find in our hearts this prior principle: "it is just to obey a law emanating from legitimate authority"? "Yes," replies Deschamps, "if it is true that this supposed prior principle is and can only be a subsequent principle, consequent to already existing law. And that is what it really is; for alone Law could enable us to know what a Law is . . . and it is only inasmuch as we are under Law that we can judge whether or not it is just to obey the Law." [33] This is quite peculiar reasoning, and one should really like to ask the friar how the first law came about, without a notion of law. Searching a bit further, we can discover the motive of this bizarre reasoning in Deschamps' ultimate purpose, the promotion of anarchism. Disentangling some involved sentences, we find that his final cultural stage, "the state of morals," excludes all laws, and any idea that there is a law which we must obey.

[30] *Ibid.,* pp. 240–41. Contract d'Holbach.

[31] Note the significant implied identification of general interest with the interest of the majority.

[32] *De l'Homme,* p. 251 ff. Helvétius' explanation for this refers back to his general system: we have no natural impulse to justice, no love of justice for its own sake. People lived together for centuries with no notion of right except that of might, "which is nature's right." (Men surpass this law, reach a moral level, but not for moral reasons.) Consequently laws are essential: "The abuse of power is tied to power as the effect is to the cause."

Helvétius' ideas were attacked by Hayer (*op. cit.,* VII, pp. 25–33): we ask ourselves about the justice of an act we are about to commit, not only about our interest, "or else I should have to have as a principle that everything which is to my advantage, or to that of Society, is, by that fact alone, just and equitable." Hayer then shows how this principle would lead to anarchy in human affairs. Sylvain Maréchal tried to defend Helvétius by a compromise view. (*Examen des critiques du livre intitulé "De l'Esprit,"* Londres, 1760, pp. 17–19.)

[33] *La Voix de la raison,* Bruxelles, 1770, pp. 11–18.

From a still more radical viewpoint, Sade espoused the priority of law over a so-called justice. With keen cynicism he points to one of the chief weaknesses in the thinking of Helvétius and other *philosophes,* a fault which Hayer had also denounced, and which we shall have occasion to mention again.

> Almost always, moreover, the laws of government are our compass for distinguishing just and unjust. We say, the law forbids such an action, therefore it is unjust. Nothing is more deceptive than this way of judging, for the law is directed towards the general interest; now nothing is in greater contradiction with the general interest than individual interest, and at the same time, nothing is more just than individual interest. Therefore nothing is less just than law, which sacrifices all individual interests to the general interest. But man, you say, wants to live in society, and so he must sacrifice a part of his personal happiness to the public happiness. All right; but how can he have made such a pact without being sure of getting back at least as much as he gives? But . . . you burden him much more than you satisfy him. . . .[34]

Indeed, if one were to adopt such a viewpoint, one could identify justice with individual welfare as readily as with "general welfare." In the first case, as for Sade, it becomes an impulse of nature, in the second, an adjunct of culture. But in neither case is the equivalence meaningful, from the ethical point of view.[35]

With this background, we may now retreat one step chronologically and examine the undeclared contention between Diderot and Rousseau, which is the most important nucleus of the eighteenth-century controversy on the matter of justice and law. In dealing with Diderot's opinions, we may disregard the occasional pronouncements of his more radical moods, in which he declared justice to depend on law, since these were unknown to Rousseau.[36] Diderot, insofar as Rousseau knew his thought on the matter, believed that men naturally form judgments of right and wrong.[37]

[34] *Histoire de Juliette,* IV, pp. 178–79.

[35] Sabatier de Castres' opinion fits the general outlook of his post-Revolutionary writings. "The words justice and injustice, good and evil, goodness and wickedness, express only ideas relative to the established laws and customs." (*Pensées,* pp. 18–19.)

[36] See *Introduction aux grands principes,* II, pp. 85–86. On p. 98 *ibid.,* he denies that men had notions of justice before laws were made. Conventions came from property, and presupposed no idea of justice but only of common interest. [The distinction between justice and common interest is to be noted.] The idea of justice grew out of the observation or infraction of the rules.

[37] Antoine Adam's interpretation of a passage in the *Apologie de l'Abbé de Prades* is most dubious. Diderot writes (I, p. 455) that in the state of nature men, living

This belief permeates his articles in the *Encyclopédie,* which are his most significant pronouncements on the subject.

It was the article "Droit naturel," we recall, which evoked Rousseau's disapproval. Diderot begins his discussion with an empirical statement. Rights are the foundations of justice, but in the state of nature, in which everything belongs to everyone, there may be no "distinct idea" of rights or obligations. However, whether the idea of justice is distinct or indistinct at that stage, it develops promptly in association.[38] At any rate, Diderot does not here pursue the question of genesis which he has raised, but proceeds at once to a theoretical analysis. The essential point is the implicit acceptance of Grotius' viewpoint, although with a technical correction: ". . . that equity is to justice as cause is to effect, and that justice can be nothing but equity declared." This point is made clearer in the article "Juste," in which Diderot amends Grotius' terminology: there is indeed no justice or injustice before laws, but there is equity prior to all law; equity and laws together constitute justice. Consequently, "justice," in the sense of "right," precedes law.[39] Justice, in the sense of an enforceable legal command, is subsequent to law, provided that law does not violate equity, by which is meant our rational approval of ends and means. With law, we have positive (in scholastic terms, "perfect") obligation. But no law can be the source of moral judgment, nor can a legislator's will change moral relationships, which inhere in the needs of self-preservation within an association. The law, then, is not *per se* the test of the rightness or wrongness of an action.

We need not discuss each instance that Diderot reiterates this opinion.[40] Its recurrence in two of his works is worthy of brief

---

in herds, had neither conventions nor authorities, and that, in consequence, resentment was "the only brake to injustice." Now this does not signify, as Adam asserts, that men had no idea of justice, since their resentment was for injustice (although they might not have been willing to *practice* the reciprocity implied by justice); but there was nothing else to prevent injustice. The ensuing analysis will confirm this interpretation. ("Rousseau et Diderot," *Revue des Sciences humaines,* 1949, pp. 25–26.)

[38] ". . . in the social acts of savage and barbarous peoples . . . and even in indignation and resentment. . . ." (XIV, p. 300.)

[39] "If we understand by *just* and *unjust* the moral qualities of actions which are the foundation [of those terms], the propriety of things, natural laws, without contradiction all these ideas are quite antecedent to law, since law builds on them and may not contradict them." (XV, p. 400.) Pufendorf is rejected. This point of view is obviously similar to Formey's.

[40] See article "Loisir," XVI, p. 3; and Moi's statement in *Le Neveu de Rameau,* ed. J. Fabre, p. 10; *Supplément au Voyage de Bougainville,* ed. G. Chinard, pp. 142–43.

mention. In the *Entretien d'un père avec ses enfants,* it is the basic question at issue, in the concrete form of an individual's decision. Is it right, and also more prudent, to follow the law's prescriptions, even when a heartbreaking inequity results, or may the individual "take justice into his own hands"? Without the law there is no theft, argues Diderot's sister, and no property, claims his brother. Rights and therefore justice inhere in the law. And Diderot contradicts both arguments. Reason, conscience, natural equity—all pre-date law. Man came before the legislator.[41] As a matter of practical prudence, however, Diderot is more often inclined to protect society against anarchy by upholding the duty to follow the law.[42] It is in his *Réfutation d'Helvétius* that Diderot repeatedly hammers at the theory that law creates the distinction between just and unjust. Even the savage knows that his stealing the fruits of another's labor is unjust. "Laws do not give us the notions of justice; it seems to me that they suppose them." The idea of justice is born of resentment, not of law, and of the danger of retaliation.[43] There is an objective and absolute basis for the judgment of just and unjust, in our needs, our life, our sensitivity, a basis "whose notion private and general interest vary in a hundred thousand different ways." But "the essence" is independent of self-interest. We must go beyond the superficial phenomenon of relativism to the universals in moral judgment, which constitute, contrary to Helvétius' argument, a "probity relative to the whole universe." [44] The savage may own no words to designate right and wrong, but his cry is not an animal cry, devoid of meaning.[45] Consequently, the first legislator had the notion of justice before he made his laws.[46]

Rousseau's thinking deliberately and sharply opposes Diderot's. For Rousseau, we remember, moral notions do not exist in the

[41] *Oeuvres,* V, pp. 296–97, 301.

[42] See *Salon de 1767,* XI, pp. 121–23. "My good actions will be mine; the law will be responsible for my bad ones. I shall submit to the law, but protest against it." If an individual defies bad laws, he encourages "the insensate masses to challenge good laws." Virtue is obedience to the certainties of law, not to a criterion of "public interest." See also *Supplément au Voyage de Bougainville,* II, p. 249, *Diderot et Catherine II,* pp. 320–23, *Lettres à Sophie Volland,* I, p. 219.

[43] II, pp. 355–56.

[44] II, p. 270.

[45] II, p. 388.

[46] II, p. 396. To the argument that laws may simply have sprung out of common interest, Diderot replies that each must have realized that it was just to follow the general interest. This is analogous to Hume's "benevolent impartial spectator."

state of nature. Justice is man's creation, a result of adherence to the general will, which is legitimized by the voluntary (and revocable) social contract.[47] The humanistic theorists of Natural Law had combatted Machiavelli and Hobbes, citing an eternal justice prior to law and the reasonable nature of the human species. The general will, for Diderot, was an act of the understanding, and nothing more, in reality, than a "universal Reason." While Rousseau supposes rationality and moral capacity, he makes the general will, in "Economie politique" and later writings, precisely what the second word of that phrase indicates, an act of will, and not an inevitability of nature or of reason. The State is an artificial "body," forming a *"moi commun,"* a "moral being" possessing a will, which may be called the general will. This will *is* "the rule of just and unjust"; it is the source of law, and therefore everything which the law orders is legitimate.[48] The law is "that celestial voice which dictates to each citizen the precepts of public reason, and teaches him to act according to the maxims of his own judgment, and not to be in contradiction with himself." [49] In the *Contrat social* he grudgingly concedes a universal justice emanating from God and from reason alone.[50] But this justice is (as Pascal had said) a vain word, lacking natural sanctions, and inexistent in the state of nature. Only conventions and laws effectively "unite rights with duties and set justice towards its object." And this is the work of the general will. We can no longer ask, then, "whether the law can be unjust, since no one can be unjust to himself." [51]

What is the significance of this disagreement? Antoine Adam, in the article referred to above, has interpreted it to mean that Rousseau had a liberal, progressive philosophy, and Diderot a

[47] The sources are in Hobbes and Spinoza. We recall that Rousseau will present a different story in *La Profession de foi.*

[48] Vaughan, *op. cit.,* I, pp. 241–42. This is so because the general will cannot err, but always tends to the "welfare of the whole and of each part." Moral judgment is thus "freed" from the limits of the subjective conscience.

[49] *Ibid.,* p. 245.

[50] Livre II, chap. VI.

[51] In the first version of the *Contrat social,* Rousseau had written: "For Law is prior to justice, and not justice to Law. And if the Law can never be unjust, it is not because justice is its basis, which may not always be so [in such a case, then, it is still, for Rousseau, just; but the statement is self-contradictory, since it admits a prior justice outside of law]; but because it is against nature that one should want to harm himself. . . ." (*Ibid.,* p. 494.) He also affirms that there was no "society of the human species," and consequently, no common moral will, no right before legislation, no equity before law. (P. 447 ff.)

reactionary, static philosophy. The truth seems to me to be exactly the opposite. For one thing, Diderot, according to Adam, believing that society is based on a universal human nature, leaves us no hope, in view of the evil in us. Rousseau, on the other hand, considers society an accident, so that vices result from men being badly governed; the evil is political, and has a remedy. This is to misinterpret both writers. Leaving aside as irrelevant the absurdity of considering society (as Rousseau does) as an accident, it is necessary to understand that the contingency involved is only a metaphysical one, not a historical one: the "original men" could not have remained forever in the state of nature. More important still, the evil, for Rousseau, is far more than "political"; it involves all human relationships, and *human nature* itself: for once the social relationship is embarked upon, the depravation of man becomes inevitable. Innocence is lost, and the moral state of good and evil begins. To say, as Adam does, that Rousseau believed that vices belong to "man mis-governed" and therefore liberation is possible, is to misinterpret the essence of his thought. For Rousseau evil is necessary and inevitable in any *naturally developed* society. Evil is indeed remediable, but it will not be expunged by political reforms. It can be remedied only by an artificial society and artificial men, subject to the statics of control. It can be overthrown only by revolutions, socio-political and individual, whose effect is, in Rousseau's words, to "denature" man, that is, to change his nature. "Liberation" from evil is possible, but not in a way which "liberates" men!

Diderot, on the other hand, admits the evil in human nature. However this does not necessarily lead, as Adam thinks (limiting his view to Hobbes) to absolutism. There is inherent evil in human nature, but human nature is not *all* evil. It remains possible to struggle for a better order. And let us not forget this: it was Rousseau who declared that society necessarily and universally depraves man. Diderot and the other *philosophes* held that it does not always or necessarily do so. Thus the very form of men's existence together permits a measure of change and improvement. Society, which is an expression of human nature, may emphasize the evil, or may tend to correct it.[52]

[52] Adam also asserts that Diderot's determinism makes progress impossible, which is to confuse determinism and fatalism. He also confuses the notions of progress or change with the attainment of an ideal state (which terminates progress). Conceiv-

The second issue is Adam's claim that the thesis of the priority of justice to law (as well as Diderot's concepts of human nature and society) involves an immutable absolute which is static and not progressive. This was the motive, according to Adam, for Rousseau's attack on Diderot's ideas. It is indeed correct to state that Rousseau's system was not congenial to Natural Law, but for a reason which is not given by Adam. His thesis in regard to justice and law is a coherent part of an abstract system whose goal is the remaking of society and of man in society. It is necessary for him that sovereignty be absolute. "But sovereignty, which is only the exercise of the general will, is free, like it, and is not submitted to any kind of prior engagement." [53] It is also necessary that men, in order to be made over from natural beings into social beings, should be susceptible to a complete conditioning process. "If it is good to know how to use men as they are [Diderot's viewpoint], it is much better yet to make them such as we need them to be; the most absolute authority is that which penetrates inside of man, and influences his will as well as his actions. It is certain that in the long run people are whatever the Government makes of them." [54] In the words of Paul Léon, Rousseau abandons "the absolutism of morals, creates an absolute juridical monism"; the conception of the totalitarian State is "in direct filiation with the Rousseauist monism." [55] Or, as d'Entrèves has expressed it, "There can be little room left for old-fashioned discussions about the nature of justice and the essence of law when human will is made the supreme arbiter of all human values." [56] It is, then, a complete misunderstanding of Rousseau which leads Adam to state that his was "a philosophy of liberty." [57]

On the other hand, Diderot's refusal to accept the thesis that justice is, by definition, what the law orders us to do reserves to minorities and to individuals the freedom to oppose the law. It is this opposition which is progressive and productive of change; it can properly be made in the name of justice, which is held to be *logically* (not chronologically or statically) prior to law. The con-

---

ing the latter, Rousseau rejects the former. Diderot did the contrary. Also, after presenting a simplified view of Rousseau's theory of the empirical formation of conscience, Adam declares that he "saw the peril of empiricism" (pp. 33–34).

[53] Vaughan, I, p. 311.
[54] "Economie politique," *ibid.*, p. 248.
[55] *Op. cit.*, pp. 237–38.
[56] *Op. cit.*, p. 75.
[57] P. 28.

cept of a universal human nature and the priority of justice is not static, but a guide for progress. Rousseau, however, was really aiming at the end of change and at the abolition of history, which has produced man's depravation.[58] According to Franz Neumann, Diderot's distinction in "Juste" is more than a logomachy. It is a sensible answer to legal positivism which, "with its thesis that law is nothing but the sovereign's will, had exterminated all attempts to measure the system of positive law on some normative standard." [59]

We can now begin to see the true significance of the contention over the priority of law and justice. Ethically, the priority of justice establishes values, gives a meaning to life, and allows for a moral criterion of judgment. The contrary view is pragmatic and utilitarian and denies any significance to the means which are chosen to achieve ends. Politically, the priority of law signifies that whatever is, or is willed, is right. There are no limits to the power of law and government (will may or may not decree limits), and to the crushing of dissension. The priority of justice, on the other hand, involves the priority of rights, the illegitimacy of pragmatic power decisions which violate rights.

Similarly, the admission of a universal human nature—or, more exactly, of universals in human nature—does not, as Adam thinks, imply the justification of whatever is, as "natural." Adam confuses, as is so commonly done, two senses of the word "nature"— nature as empirical description and nature as norm of right. Everything in human nature is natural, but not everything is good or right. There are instincts in men which may be said to violate the moral imperatives of human nature (as well as those of culture, which transcends nature). Quite to the contrary, it is the denial of universals that makes anything that is, right. If there is no "human nature," anything you do to men is legitimate. The concept of a "human nature" only establishes universal values, it does not mean that institutions are in accord with those values. Progress consequently becomes legitimate and necessary; on the other hand, when there is no criterion for critical judgment, there is no justification for change.[60] Diderot's policy, then, was liberal and

[58] See J. Starobinski, *Jean-Jacques Rousseau, la transparence et l'obstacle*, p. 22
[59] *Op. cit.*, p. 69.
[60] The idea of a "human nature" also constitutes a "human reserve" which is a barrier or limit to the power of thought control and conditioning, and such a limit does, in fact, exist. This view coincides with Diderot's theory of heredity as a limit to "education," and with his refutation of Helvétius.

progressive. Rousseau's was the absolute of totalitarianism, allowing each State to create its own values without hindrance from what is called "just" or "true." It is an arbitrary dynamism with no root or point of reference, and whose goal is a power-enforced stability. Diderot's dynamism aims at an ideal regarded as certain, but never conceives the possibility of an ideal State, in which a re-made man is frozen into the status of a mechanical unit of an organic whole.

If law determines justice, then, writes A. C. Garnett, we fall into the confusion of primitive ethics—the failure to distinguish between law as it is and law as it ought to be.[61] Human will is considered to be prior and paramount to human rationality.[62] The law "ought to be" whatever we will it to be. Those who have distrusted human rationality and considered men unworthy to be treated with dignity have frequently espoused the priority of law. Their mental outlook is typified by characters like the captain in Melville's *Billy Budd* or Hugo's Javert. The Renaissance writers who revolted against Natural Law, like Machiavelli, Luther, and Hobbes, favoring the individual and the empirical, were political absolutists. On the other hand, the priority of justice has been argued by men of widely differing political views, but all opponents of absolutism of the left or right. They include *philosophes* like d'Holbach and the framers of the *Déclaration des droits de l'homme,* but also Burke who decried arbitrariness of will in government and held law to be, in its nature, a rule of reason, and not something which derives its authority merely from its institution.[63]

The priority of law, in its absolutist forms, may be considered an abdication of nature in favor of culture, just as nihilism and anarchism are denials of culture in favor of nature. The priority of justice implies a middle ground of control by rational directives which are inherent in human nature, and which define the propriety or impropriety of our acts.[64] But our acts, as we have said,

---

[61] *The Moral Nature of Man,* p. 32.
[62] Justice, of course, in its concrete forms, is never entirely rational.
[63] See Parkin, *op. cit.,* p. 54. Burke, to be sure, interprets "reason" and Natural Law in the way which pleases him. He considered the *Déclaration* an act of will, while its authors thought they were formulating the objective, absolute (unalienable) laws in the nature of things.
[64] Cf. R. Hubert, on Diderot's theory of moral genesis: "Men's needs divide and oppose them. But their reflection on those needs draws them together and unites them. . . . Law transforms into a definite notion what was primitively only a latent aspiration; it gives to acts the character of just or unjust, only under this condition,

take place in a context of institutions and relations; these evolve and thus may require new definitions and new laws. An American philosopher recently noted: "A moral law does not imply the existence of a lawgiver. We can derive a moral law from a law-giver only if the lawgiver is moral. To know that he is, we would already have to possess prior knowledge of moral law independent of his example. If the enforcement of legal obligations had no reference to moral obligation, how could we condemn the infamous laws of Hitler and Khrushchev, or punish Eichmann and his spiritual kinsmen for executing their legal orders?" [65] In other words, respect for law depends on the sense of its close relation to moral law, on the fact that it embodies the ethical minimum necessary to social life. Of course it is always possible to deny this; to agree with Montaigne and Pascal, or with Sumner in our own century and hold that law is only the product of custom sanctioned by force; that its power and compulsion, not its rightness, constitute our obligation to respect and obey it. Then ethics and politics, as Helvétius claimed, become identical—that is, there is only politics. The law and its makers, on this view, have the power to change the worth of an act, to create or destroy moral values.[66]

III. Reason and Feeling

Although the problem of the role of reason and feeling in moral experience has been involved in the discussion throughout the preceding chapters, a brief summary and some additional comments may be useful. We have noted anti-rationalism, in relation to morals, in Montaigne and Pascal—although for Pascal reason "makes [man's] being." We may say as much for Fontenelle and even Malebranche;[1] however they are not, like many eighteenth-

that it is in itself in conformity to the general good, and so to reason." (*Op. cit.*, pp. 276–77.) Diderot had said, "It is then from human nature that the propriety of our acts results, which, in this sense, allow no variation." For Rousseau, it was the will of the social organism which was always and necessarily in conformity to the general good, and so to justice

[65] Sydney Hook, in a letter to a newspaper.

[66] Bergier thought that men could not live if notions of good and evil could be changed at will. It would not be possible to have a society in which lies, ingratitude, cruelty, perfidy and crime were in honor. (*Principes de métaphysique*, pp. 95–97.) This is an assertion which we may evaluate in relation to historical events of the twentieth century.

[1] *Recherche de la vérité*, II, p. 504.

century writers, anti-rationalists, but are rather impressed by the overwhelming force of passions in men. As the Protestant writer J.-Fr. Bernard put it, man has reason but abuses and betrays it.[2] Even in 1687, Father Bouhours had been struck by the prevalence of anti-rationalism in society, and the preference for *coeur* to *esprit*. According to Spinoza, it is plain "that we neither strive for, wish, seek nor desire anything because we think it to be good, but, on the contrary, we adjudge a thing to be good because we strive for, wish, seek or desire it." [3] This opinion refers to moral experience itself.

There is, then, a certain amount of confusion in the issue. The function of reason in moral judgment is one thing, its function in our acts (such as our refusal to follow it—a subject we discussed earlier), another. Furthermore, reason may be taken in the discursive sense, or as immediate intuition. The moral sense of Shaftesbury's school has affinities with sentiment, but is really a sublimation of reason, the purpose of which is to make it "natural" and immediate. And this, as we saw in discussing conscience, is precisely what Rousseau did, though in him the link between reason and feeling is even tighter.

The Natural Law school emphasized reason as the power of perceiving moral truths. Grotius, Pufendorf, Burlamaqui, all leave no doubt about this. Obligation inheres in a rule, based on a relation, and the rule derives from man's reasonableness. Chubb, Clarke, Wollaston believe reason to be the judge of actions. Locke's sensationism halts before ethical truths. He thinks that a complete morality can be derived by ratiocination from general a priori principles, without reference to concrete circumstances.[4] Swift's Houyhnhnms, on the other hand, are governed by reason, but it is a reason which "strikes you with immediate conviction; as it must needs do, where it is not mingled, obscured, or discolored by passion and interest." [5] It does not lead to disputation. This again is Rousseau's "lumière intérieure."

The first great defender of sentiment, as the essential component of moral experience, was David Hume. Morality, in his view, consists of impressions, is felt, not judged of. Virtue and vice are feelings of pleasure or uneasiness of a peculiar kind, peculiar

---

[2] *Réflexions morales*, Amsterdam, 1716, p. 1. See *An Age of Crisis*, chap. 9.
[3] *Ethic*, Part III, Prop. IX, Schol.
[4] Kaye in Mandeville, I, p. 49, n. 1.
[5] *Gulliver's Travels*, Part IV, chap. 8.

because divorced from self-interest.[6] Hume does give a role to
reason. It mediates between passions and their goals; but it is
neither the traditional enemy of the passions and appetites, nor
their master. *"Reason* and *sentiment* concur in almost all moral
determinations and conclusions," though the final judgment "depends on some internal sense or feeling which nothing has made
universal in the whole species." [7] Hume was severely criticized by
both Price and Reid. Hume had said, for instance, that it is not
the office of reason to determine ends. Reid argued that there are
rational principles of action.[8] Hume has been criticized by twentieth-century philosophers, one of whom accuses him of confusing
the justifiable notion that any value statement *expresses* a feeling
with the unjustifiable notion that we do not have a value statement until we have a statement which *indicates* a feeling.[9] Nevertheless, as with Hobbes and Mandeville, the attempts to refute
Hume, valid or not, are witnesses to the revolutionary depth of
his thought and the permanence of his influence. Before Hume,
comments Basil Willey, nature was linked with reason; after
Hume, it is linked with feeling, and morality is reduced to the
sentiment of approval or disapproval.[10] Reason, moreover, is rejected in favor of nature. Despite certain reactions, this statement
is true for England; but it is far less true for France.

In the eighteenth century, wrote Lanson, there were two tendencies, one toward an intellectual ethics of geometric precision,
the other toward an ethics of immediate sentiment, and at the
beginning, they were fused in the notion of rational morality.[11] It
is not certain that the two attitudes were really fused in many
cases. The essential matter, for thinkers of that early period, was
to be free from theological dogma, and to bring ethics closer to
the realities of human nature and motivation. It is in this sense
that we may interpret the statement of a *libertin,* the Marquis de

---

[6] Aiken, *op. cit.,* pp. 42–45.

[7] *Ibid.,* p. 177. Hume criticizes men like Malebranche, Montesquieu, Cudworth,
and Clarke for founding right on relationships. (Aiken, p. 196n.) For a fuller statement of Hume's views on this subject, see *ibid.,* pp. 219–21, 262–68 (Appendix I to
the *Enquiry*).

[8] *Essays on the Active Powers of the Human Mind,* in *Works,* ed. by D. Stewart,
New York, 1822, III, pp. 135–39.

[9] J. W. Smith, "The British Moralists and the Fallacy of Psychologism."

[10] *Op. cit.,* p. 111.

[11] "Le Rôle de l'expérience dans la formation de la philosophie du XVIII⁰ siècle,"
R. C. C., 1909, p. 857.

Lassay, written in 1717: "I believe I feel in myself admiration for virtue and horror for vice, independently of all prejudices; . . . not being able to enlighten myself by my intelligence [on free will and other moral questions], I act upon the sentiment which is engraved in the bottom of my heart." [12]

Marivaux describes a simple and good way of living, then asks:

> What do you say to my ethics? It is not very reflective, that's because it is natural. There are people who moralize in such a sublime manner, that what they say is good only to be admired, but what I say is good to be followed, and that's real morality, the rest is only vanity, folly. Intellectuals spoil everything. They look for everything they say in the land of pipe-dreams. They make Virtue a *précieuse* who's always worried about how she can be haughty enough, to distinguish herself. So they think that's virtue, and I teach them from my stool that there's nothing so simple as virtue, good morals, or reason. We don't need to think hard to act reasonably; reason comes naturally when we want to follow it—I mean real reason, for the one you've got to think about . . . is not the good reason; we're the ones who make that one, it's our pride that invents it.[13]

While it is difficult to determine whether de Lassay and Marivaux really mean reason or sentiment, some writers leave no room for doubt. Vauvenargues tells us that the voice of nature is the voice of morality, and that it has grown fainter as the voice of reason has increased.[14] Asking what principle enlightens us about good and evil, he replies, "the heart." Reason is unable to draw such ideas from itself and to engender virtuous acts. But he is really aiming at the exclusion of rational calculation of self-interest: "Magnanimity owes no account of its motives to prudence." (Maxim 130.) The confusion enters when we see him excluding conscience as "the most changeable of rules," one which obeys the feelings that dominate us. Which, then, is the feeling that gives us moral knowledge, and which is the feeling that conscience obeys? Jules Barni writes that for Rousseau conscience is a special instinct which judges other instincts, while Vauvenargues "leaves it up to the instincts themselves." Reason is thus opposed to nature.

Morelly, a communist, and Dulaurens, an amoralist, both warn

[12] *Ibid.*
[13] *L'Indigent philosophe*, in *Le Spectateur français*, 1728, II, pp. 10–11.
[14] Vyverberg, *op. cit.*, pp. 205–6.

against the deceits and vices of reason.[15] So does the sentimental
primitivist, Bernardin de Saint-Pierre. A disciple of Rousseau, he
attacks discursive reason as the slave of self-interest: ". . . those
maxims which are drilled into us from childhood: *get rich, be on
top,* are enough to upset our natural reason; they show us just and
unjust only in relation to our personal interest and to our ambition." There is a nobler, more constant, wider faculty in us. "I
feel, therefore I am." We have a moral feeling, a "sentiment,"
which is quite different from physical feeling. It is always pure;
"by subjugating our reason it becomes the most noble and delightful instinct of human life." [16] To this motley company we
must add the atheist Sylvain Maréchal, and two future reactionaries, Sabatier and Rivarol.[17]

But the larger number of writers in France still unite reason
and nature, and make reason the essential element in moral experience. A manuscript which probably dates from the late seventeenth century already takes essentially the position that was to be
Bayle's. "If there are certain and immutable rules for the operations of the understanding, are there not also rules for the acts of
will?" As it is wrong to reason in a way opposite to syllogisms, "so
it is a fault of [   ] [18] something without conforming to the
rules for acts of the will." The most general rule is to act according to right reason.[19]

Bayle also makes it clear that the general principle of obligation
is reason, and he, too, declares that there are rules for the will as
well as for reason.[20] Throughout this passage Bayle uses practically
the identical words that were used by the author of "De la
Conduite." He says that the rules are not arbitrary but emanate
from the necessity of things; that, as it is wrong to reason against
rules of syllogism, so with will; and that the most general rule is

---

[15] Morelly, *Code de la nature,* pp. 257–59. In an earlier work, however, Morelly
upholds reason as the instrument for perception of moral truths, that is, the conformity of acts with the public weal. (*Essai sur le coeur humain,* 1745, pp. 169–72.)
Dulaurens, *Le Compère Mathieu,* Londres, 1770, II, pp. 184–87.

[16] *Etudes de la nature, Oeuvres,* 1818, V, pp. 4–32.

[17] Maréchal, "Essai sur les passions," *Mélanges,* Avignon, 1782, pp. 22–23; Sabatier,
Dictionnaire, 1769, II, p. 502; Rivarol, *De l'Homme* [1783], 1800, pp. 1–14.

[18] Break in the ms.

[19] "De la conduite qu'un honnête homme doit garder pendant sa vie," Maz. 1194,
fol. 130–32. A reference to Mathias Knuzen, the notorious atheist, as a contemporary, is an indication of date. Knuzen disappeared about 1675.

[20] *Continuation des Pensées diverses sur la comète, Oeuvres diverses,* III, p. 406.
The conscience, for Bayle, is "a judgment of the mind which impels us to do certain things."

to act in conformity with right reason. This is so because a reasonable creature must conform to reason, or he betrays his nature. There can be no doubt about Bayle having known the manuscript, "De la Conduite." [21]

Other writers in the first half of the century who hold similar views are Buffier, Lemaître de Claville, Levesque de Pouilly, and Toussaint. Among these, Father Buffier is the most interesting. Two sorts of persons, he explains, say that reason is not a sufficient rule for morals, some for the sake of religion, others out of opposition to religion. He refutes both. Revelation can add nothing to the natural rights of reason. As for the argument of moral relativity advanced by the second group, Buffier counters it by upholding universal judgments, which are, therefore, natural.[22]

In the second half of the century, Diderot, as we have seen, and Voltaire, both believed the moral experience to be essentially rational, though not dissociated from affective elements. Diderot puts it this way: "Some may think that a knowledge of history should precede that of morality; I am not of that opinion. It seems to me more useful and expedient to possess the idea of the just and the unjust before possessing a knowledge of the actions and the men to whom one ought to apply it." [23] Virtue, writes Voltaire, requires "enlightenment, reflection, philosophy, although according to you [Rousseau], any animal who reflects is a depraved animal, from which it would logically follow that virtue is impossible. An ignoramus, a complete fool, is no more susceptible of virtue than a horse or a monkey." [24] The Physiocratic school would all adhere to the rationalistic thesis. Moral choice, declares Turgot, is a rational act, based on abstract principles derived from our desires and feelings.[25]

Like some of the writers we have mentioned, Kant believes that the universal quality of moral laws indicates their source in the reason. Man is above all a creature of reason; a "reason" that, as

---

[21] What distinguishes moral reason from reason is its universality. See Delvolvé, *Religion, critique et philosophie positive chez Pierre Bayle*, 1906, pp. 99–110.

[22] *Traité de la société civile.*

[23] *Plan d'une université*, Oeuvres, III, p. 493.

[24] "Lettre au Docteur Pansophe," Oeuvres, XXVI, p. 21. Voltaire has, to be sure, misunderstood Rousseau.

[25] "Sur le mot amour et sur l'amour de Dieu," Oeuvres, I, p. 362. However Turgot expresses exactly the opposite view, and upholds the primacy of feeling, in his second "Discours en Sorbonne" (1750), I, p. 224. Many other writers adhered to this position, including the Christian apologists, Mably, Bonnet, Boufflers, Delisle de Sales, etc.

distinguished from understanding and judgment, seeks to appre-
hend certain totalities which are not the objects of experience.
Man is a being of nature, insofar as he is subject to universal natural laws; but also a distinctive being, inasmuch as reason, whose
operation is spontaneous and different from physical nature, can
have a determining influence on his acts. That is, man can make
himself into a being bound by principles. Character is that "peculiar property of the will in accordance to which the subject binds
himself to definite practical principles which he has unalterably
prescribed through his own reason." [25a] Kant declares it impossible
to derive an ethics from a naturalistic analysis of human nature.
Like the modern Existentialist, he says that we must construct
our character by ourselves. The self is fundamentally a possibility
of existence which can realize itself through freedom. With reason,
however, the self can discover the moral principles which should
guide it.[26]

It is curious to see Sade superficially taking the same side as
Kant, and attributing moral judgments to reason. But the purpose
and the substance are quite different. Sade, too, separates reason
from nature. "Nature" is our feelings and instincts, and these, he
repeats, lead us to what is called vices and crimes. Laws, which
demand repression and sacrifice, are the children of reason.[27]

The rationalist view makes of moral experience a form of
knowledge, usually of objective facts and relations and of normative rules derived from them, and so of a class of truths. (It was
only extreme relativism, or nihilism, postulating the validity of
all judgments, or of none, that denied moral knowledge.) Such
knowledge may be intuitive, and is not necessarily provable. There
was, however, a considerable group of rationalists, and even some
empiricists, who thought ethics could be an exact science. Many
of this group went so far as to envisage mathematical proof, and
the comparison with geometry was frequently made.[28]

[25a] Kant, *op. cit.,* pp. 105–7, 332–33n.; J. E. Smith, "The Question of Man," in
C. W. Hendel, *The Philosophy of Kant and our Modern World,* New York, 1957,
p. 12 ff.

[26] According to G. Schrader ("The Philosophy of Existence," *ibid.,* p. 40 ff.) Kant
holds that through the exercise of freedom, the self becomes objective and alien to
itself. There is perhaps an influence of Rousseau here.

[27] *Histoire de Juliette,* VI, pp. 174–75.

[28] In favor of scientific or mathematical demonstrability were Pufendorf, Sir Wil-
liam Patty, Locke, Cumberland, Hutcheson, Benjamin Franklin, and Ferguson.
Hume mentions analogical proof from science and mathematics (Aiken, p. 225). In
France, Maupertuis, Father André, Vauvenargues, Le Guay de Prémontval, Morelly,

It is one of the characteristics of the eighteenth century that it most often considered man to be definable by his reason, but not reasonable (or motivated by his reason); that it held reason to be limited, fallible, or even erroneous, yet relied on reason for explanations and solutions, indulged and delighted in abstract thought and not infrequently in the spinning of systems. It is reason—in its various modes of functioning—which criticizes abuses, wrongs, prejudices, ill-adapted or outgrown social structures, which plans a reconstructed society and ethics, and the reconditioning of man. In ethics, however, the reason which was favored, with a few exceptions, was that of intuitive immediacy, not of ratiocination; and it is another characteristic trait of the period that its reluctance to draw a sharp distinction ofttimes makes it difficult to be sure whether its writers have intuition or feeling in mind. They certainly did not have in mind reason in Hume's narrow acceptance; but rather a judgment of propriety for beings such as we, with our needs, drives, and goals, both natural and social. An intuitive perception such as this could, by some, be considered an a priori, by others the result of earlier experience, habituation, or reasoning. Later, the frequent distrust of abstract, logical reasoning (or intellect) seemed, to many conservatives, amply confirmed by the events of the French Revolution, which they held to have resulted from the systematic political theories of Rousseau, Mably, Babeuf, and their disciples. The result was the anti-rationalism of reactionaries like Sabatier de Castres, Rivarol, and various Catholic writers of the Romantic period—an attitude which was renewed later in the nineteenth and twentieth centuries by proto-totalitarians and totalitarians. Burke, however, though a leader of the "anti-*philosophe*" movement, was not an anti-rationalist, despite his distrust of abstract and systematic reasoning. "Politics," he wrote, "ought to be adjusted, not to human reasonings, but to human nature; of which the reason is but a part, and by no means the greatest part." [29] In

---

Helvétius, d'Holbach, the author of "Connaissance" in the *Encyclopédie*, Condorcet and Rivarol all held to this view. The Académie de Berlin held an essay contest on the question, "Can moral truths be proved?" in 1752–53. Among those who openly opposed this view were Reid, Camuset, and Mably. There is no doubt that the mathematical approach reflected a misunderstanding of the nature of ethical experience. A. Cresson (*op. cit.*, p. 194) writes: "Ethics is not a mathematics. It cannot be constituted outside of experience, in a world of pure abstractions." See also A. Schweitzer, *op. cit.*, p. 201. This subject merits further specialized investigation.

[29] Quoted in Willey, *op. cit.*, p. 243.

this statement Burke is pointing out what he considered to be the great error of the "philosophic" movement. However his phrase is an exact description of what the *philosophes* did actually try to follow, and of their analysis of human nature. What happened was that their analysis, which was completely rationalistic, led to rationalistic solutions of the ethical and socio-political problems—even to the point where they thought that irrational (or unreasonable) man would behave rationally and reasonably if reason (in the sense of what was deemed to be culturally desirable) were indissolubly linked with the irrational element of self-interest. This led to systems such as those of Helvétius, d'Holbach, and Rousseau—though in Rousseau, as in Morelly and others, repression was an important added element. Formulations of a universal order, of abstract truths with absolute validity were the outcome. Even unsystematic thinkers, Voltaire and others, believing in immutable natural laws (a conception of abstract reason), thought them to be discoverable by the individual reason, intuitive or discursive. It is this belief which Burke thought a dangerous folly, because of its willful ignoring of another order of truth, that of history and custom, or the accumulated wisdom and traditions which are the life-blood of any culture.

Actually, nothing was more abstractly rationalistic than the debate itself, as to the roles of reason and sentiment in moral experience. They are, in fact, indissoluble in the wholeness and multiple functioning of the self. Reason, by itself, has no necessary relation to morality. As the novels of the time showed—and there is no more faithful reflection of the culture and prevailing ideology—reason may be used for evil.[30] On the other hand, without reason, there could be no moral life. "Valid ethical norms," writes a modern psychiatrist, "can be formed by man's reason and by it alone." [31] A. O. Lovejoy has shown, from a philosophical viewpoint, that while rationality may not determine choice, it is involved in moral judgments as self-consciousness, generalization, the truth of propositions, and "adjectival values." [32] A contemporary anthropologist draws a clear distinction between values ("ideas formulating action commitments") and sentiments, emotions, drives, or needs. Values are rationally justifiable, for they

---

[30] See especially Laclos' *Les Liaisons dangereuses*. Cf. *An Age of Crisis*, chap. 14.
[31] E. Fromm, *op. cit.*, p. 6.
[32] "Terminal and Adjectival Values," pp. 594–96, 602–3.

are "normative statements as contrasted with existential propositions." [33] It is clear that men could not have been intelligent beings without having moral judgments and sentiments, nor could
they have experienced the latter unless they were intelligent beings. Whether, as Clarke, Kant, and many French writers thought,
moral values, based on relations, must appear the same to the
understanding of all intelligent beings is a different question, one
which we have endeavored to clarify in regard to the Age of Enlightenment.

[33] C. Kluckhohn, "Values and Value Orientations," pp. 397–401.

Moral Values

Five

THE UTILITARIAN SYNTHESIS

THERE ARE two principal questions in ethical theory. One is psychological and refers to the genesis and nature of moral judgments: what elements of our constitution, what factors in our lives lead us to form distinctions of this kind, and what processes are involved? This question, with which the Ancients were scarcely concerned, was dominant in the eighteenth-century intellectual climate. It frequently involved a confusion between two different problems, the genetic factors of moral judgment and the justification of such judgments. The second question is substantive. It addresses itself to the objects of moral approbation and disapprobation, inquiring into the common quality (or qualities) of the modes of virtue (benevolence, rational self-love, proper action in a given situation, etc.)—in other words, into what makes something right or wrong, good or evil. This will be the subject of the concluding part of our inquiry.

The essential elements which gave impetus to the review of moral values in eighteenth-century France were the secularization of ethics and of the general outlook and the naturalistic analysis of human nature and motivation. "Man in revolt," writes Albert Camus, "is man situated before or after the sacred, and applied to demanding a human order in which all responses are human, that is to say, reasonably formulated . . . revolt is one of man's essential dimensions. It is our historical reality. Unless we flee from reality, we must find our values in it. Can we, far from the sacred and its absolute values, find the rule of conduct? Such is the question posed by revolt." [1] And such is the question which eighteenth-century moralists undertook to examine and to solve.

[1] *L'Homme révolté,* 1951, pp. 34–35.

In the first part of this study, we investigated the relation of God and of revealed religions to the foundations of ethics.[2] A belief in either or both enabled many people at that time to find a firm and convenient solution in the form of standards of conduct in conformity with the pronouncements of a superior and all powerful Being. In the eighteenth-century climate, however, deists, and even nominal Christians, were often swept by the tide of "revolt" to a re-examination of ethics in purely secular terms. In such cases, the existence of God also becomes nominal, in the sense that it is allocated to a metaphysical plane of reality which is not considered as an immediate causative or determining factor in the human order. This secularization is even more certain in the case of the relatively few atheists who led the vanguard of the "rebels." We may pose the problem, as it presented itself, in these terms: Is there a universal, general notion of moral value that will subsist by itself, with no support but that which belongs to human beings and sufficient to constitute moral law or obligation?

The general (though not exclusive) direction will be toward a social norm of value. The process of cultural evolution, in addition to the previously mentioned factors, led to a reaction against "that systematic morality which, attaching itself only to the salvation of the soul, neglected social welfare." [3] Fundamental to the social focus and of broader perspective was the underlying assumption that a valid, workable ethics would have to be human in its terms of reference and human in its goals. Such a framework returns us immediately to the dilemmas of human nature, to which we have given ample consideration. Awareness of these dilemmas led to a number of ethical problems. Does the rule of virtue, for instance, hinge on what the Stoics called the *honestum,* as contrasted with the *utile?* Is the rule of nature an abstract, inner standard? Or should we rather, like Cicero, admire the Stoics but reserve our adherence for a more realistic view, one whose criterion would be appropriateness, looking at men in their actual functioning as social and political animals? Shall virtues be inner-directed, with internal sanctions, or the reverse? Which is paramount, the individual, his obligation to other individuals, or the social group?

[2] Crocker, *An Age of Crisis,* chap. 1, chap. 13.
[3] Barni, *Les Moralistes français,* III, p. 39.

The dominant trends are utilitarian—that is, a theory which holds that the right action is the one which will probably produce the greatest amount of pleasure or happiness in the world. In France, however, this theory emerges out of a prior stage, in which "utility" is understood as being primarily and fundamentally utility to oneself. Utilitarianism involves the replacement of "the nature of things" as the support of value (as in Natural Law) by human nature. It implies (*consequently*, it was thought) replacement of "Virtue for its own sake" by virtue for reward, or satisfactory consequences. The eventual sequel was the idea of "virtue *as* its own reward," an almost desperate resort in order to conserve the moral component of value. This was an essential element in the situation as it evolved in France. It resulted from the naturalistic view of human nature in its prevailing form and the founding of ethics upon it, and from the end of heaven and hell. It was also one outcome of relativism which, denying absolute standards and inherent value, left utility as a touchstone. As Vauvenargues expressed it, "there is nothing which cannot be good or bad, useful or harmful, according to the occasion and the circumstances." [4] The atheist, in particular, found all acts to be equivalent and without meaning in Nature, or in themselves. However, we shall see that many proponents of Natural Law were also permeated by the same criteria.

While one of the chief weaknesses of eighteenth-century value theory is the confusion of "good" and "right," we must make that distinction, or else we cannot understand the nature of utilitarianism, or its major fault. For that theory the good is prior to the right, and right may be defined as what is productive of good. In contrast, the traditional moral philosophies had said, "Act out of respect for principle." Good (advantageous) results may be expected to follow, but they should not determine motivation. In short, other ethical theories do not deny that virtues are useful to mankind; on the contrary, it may be assumed that the original approbation of an act or attitude was related to its value as a universal, for mankind, and indeed, this is not excluded from Kant's categorical imperative. What is excluded is the judgment that what is useful, to the individual, the majority, or the whole community, is *ipso facto* right or virtuous. What is included is the

[4] *Oeuvres*, III, p. 250 ("Réflexions," p. 453).

supposition that moral imperatives might, in particular situations, be disadvantageous to individuals, the majority, or the whole community, and nevertheless be right and virtuous. Right and utility, in other words, are distinct, though not unrelated principles, and the former is not exclusively definable and justifiable in terms of the latter. For the utilitarian, acceptance of moral truths and values depends on proof of their validity in the form of evident social welfare or personal happiness. This is expressed most clearly by a utilitarian theologian, Father Castel: "Utility is an inseparable companion of virtue. The rules of morality are always advantageous to him who follows them; and they would cease to be rules, if they ceased to be useful. That is why some great men have taken happiness for the principle of morals." [5]

Another consequence of utilitarianism is evident in the last quotation. This is the shift in the object of judgment from intention to result. The utilitarian view has its source in the reduction of all motivation to self-love (or self-interest), and it finds this reduction convenient for its purposes.[6] The whole problem of moral judgment is—or rather appears—simplified. The difficulty of judging intention is obviated—as indeed it must, since there is only one form of motivation and that one nonmoral. We are left only with the value of the act, in terms of that same motive. Benevolence is, on this view, a kind of act which happens to satisfy selfish desires in a way that is useful to others. Motive is not involved in the term. To take care of a child, or to neglect him (to use Ferguson's example), derives from the same intent of self-gratification, but the results of the act are distinct. Or, to state the matter in a different way, Adam Smith agreed with Mandeville's analysis (which was that all acts result from self-interest, or "vice"), but concluded that the meaning of terms must be altered. "If it be vice that produces all the good in the world, then there is some-

---

[5] In Sabatier de Castres, *Dictionnaire*, II, pp. 394–95. Augustine had faced a similar dilemma. He opposed the Gnostic heresy because he realized that its demand that Christianity bring about the kingdom of God on earth could lead to the view that Christianity is justified by its utilitarian values, or else must be considered false.

[6] This is certainly not true for Shaftesbury or Hume, both of whom think in terms of social welfare. However, neither one is a categorical utilitarian. The analysis in this chapter is concerned essentially with the development of French thought, even though English moralists are brought in for analogical and comparative purposes. We should note, in this regard, that the great British utilitarians, Bentham and Mill, were not primarily concerned with motivation.

thing the matter with our terminology; such vice is not vice but good." Rejecting the rigorism that gave rise to his paradox, Mandeville "set up instead a utilitarian scheme of ethics." [7]

The evolution of thought in the eighteenth century which issues in utilitarianism reveals a definite pattern. The revolt against traditionalism begins with the assertion of egoistic hedonism, that is, with the demand for self-gratification. Then a major change of emphasis takes place when the locus of value is shifted to social utility: virtue, or duty to others becomes supreme, but conceived only as a function of duty to oneself. Identity of self-interest and the general interest is usually implied. Finally, love of virtue, in some instances, becomes transformed into an end, and the meaning of virtue into sacrifice of individual interest. Thus, what begins in self-centered egoism terminates at the opposite pole, in other-centered altruism, after passing through the major phase of a general theory of utilitarianism. In all of these developments, the emphasis is on the criteria of good acts rather than on motives.

This statement of evolutionary pattern must, however, be qualified. Altruism receives limited expression among philosophical writers, and is to be found mostly in sentimental middle-class literature. The movement from one phase to another is a matter of emphasis and diffusion, but is not exclusive; on the contrary, all three phases may be said to exist simultaneously, to some extent, at any and all moments. Finally, the utilitarian patterns, which are dominant and characteristic, do not exhaust the phenomena. The traditional ethics remains alive, especially among religious writers; since it contains no novel elements, before Kant, it is not of great interest. On the other hand, the original assertion of egoistic hedonism refuses to become completely sublimated into the socially centered developments. It not only persists in its original form of moderate epicureanism, but becomes transformed into a movement of extreme rebellion, nihilism, which is of great significance in the history of our culture. Such was the actual complexity of eighteenth-century intellectual history.

When we speak of utility, we must have an object in mind, which is the definition of the useful. For the vast majority of men in the eighteenth century, there is no doubt what this object was—happiness. It is therefore improper to study utilitarian ethics and

[7] F. B. Kaye, in *The Fable of the Bees*, CXXX.

the question of happiness as separate phenomena. In view of the near-universality of psychological hedonism (which we examined in the first part of this work),[8] happiness seemed the only justifiable value, since it was the only natural motive and goal of action. The whole psychology of the period—sensationism, association of ideas, pleasure and pain, the natural laws of conduct—plus the prevailing mores and social atmosphere, led to formulations such as that of John Gay: "obligatory acts are those which lead to happiness." [9] Or as Diderot put it, "there is only one virtue—happiness." A large part of French philosophy and literature became the expression and validation of egoism and the search for pleasure, with particular emphasis—in both forms of writing—on sexual excitement and satisfaction.

One may appropriately speak of a universal, omnipresent preoccupation with the question of happiness—its justification, its relation to ethics, its nature, and the ways of realizing it. In 1759, for instance, two tales were published in which happiness is the basic theme. One was *Candide*, the other Johnson's *Rasselas*. Both may be summarized (though *Candide*, of course, is far more complex), in the phrase which is the *leitmotiv* of *Rasselas*, "Surely happiness is somewhere to be found." From one viewpoint, then, the eighteenth century is a prolonged quest for happiness. Now, happy people are not obsessed by the search for happiness. Behind the search lies an anguished soul which is really seeking a meaning for its life.[10] In most writers there is an uncertainty, an ambiguity about happiness which underscores the moral crisis.[11]

The crisis of ethics had two components. The first was the secret menace of frustration and futility. Could one hold up as the highest value and devote his life to a goal which might be only a delusion, a phantom, a will o' the wisp? If this were so, all other values having been subordinated to it, there could only be a total

---

[8] *An Age of Crisis*, Section III, "Human Nature and Motivation."

[9] Quoted in Halévy, *op. cit.*, p. 4.

[10] The malady lies in the loss of a clear sense of meaning and purpose in life, in a feeling of being adrift and alienated in a world without center or boundaries in place or time, and most of all, perhaps, in the loss of values to direct action and give it meaning. See *An Age of Crisis*, chaps. 1, 2, 3, and my article, "*Hamlet, Don Quijote and la Vida es Sueño:* The Quest for Values." Boredom, melancholy, restlessness, libertinism are the symptoms. Paul Hazard simplifies the true picture and paints only the optimism (*La Pensée européenne au XVIIIᵉ Siècle*, 1946, I, chap. 2).

[11] The metaphysical doctrine of optimism for a time acted as a partial sedative to the inner disquiet. Although its overthrow increased pessimism, this only added to the intensity of the preoccupation with happiness.

collapse into nihilism. We shall return to this problem in the course of our analysis. The first component of the crisis was psychological. The second was ethical. If happiness is, naturally, the highest value, what becomes of moral virtue? To establish and validate moral values, it seemed necessary, in this situation, to follow one of three courses: to accept as absolute the supernatural commands of Revelation, to validate supranatural and "contranatural" criteria of reason and culture, or, remaining within the natural, to forge an inseparable link between happiness and virtue. The first solution had lost its force. The second might defeat the very object of individual happiness. As Victor Riquetti de Mirabeau wrote, "Virtue, which some want to make the spring of republics, is a prejudice against nature, one which dedicates the individual to the maintenance of public security against the extension of his personal property." [12] The third solution had as its flaw the subjectivism of happiness. It might also lead, like the second, to a social tyranny, which is a confession of nihilism.

In an association of virtue and happiness, it is possible to emphasize one term or the other. Virtue frequently becomes the dominant consideration, and happiness its support or substantiation, replacing the traditional imperatives. But very often, too, happiness remains paramount, and virtue is only a useful means. The difference is tenuous, and ambiguity is constant. "If all men were capable of possessing a virtue in all its perfection," writes Mably, "it would be unnecessary to ask what is the virtue which, by its nature contributing most to our happiness, should be placed first in order and in dignity." [13] D'Holbach is certain that "it would be idle to speak to men of morals and virtue, if the greatest good for them did not result; a totally gratuitous virtue is not a seductive chimera for beings who desire happiness by a constant compulsion of their nature." [14] Or, to take another out of an endless possibility of examples, there is Meister's definition of ethics as "the science of habits which can perfect our being and lead us to the most constantly happy state." [15] We are reminded of Kant's description of the two "ancient Greek schools," both of which "did not allow virtue and happiness to be regarded as two distinct elements of the *summum bonum*," but which differed "as

[12] Quoted by Weulersse, II, p. 94.
[13] *Principes de morale, Oeuvres*, pp. 282–83.
[14] *La Morale universelle*, III, p. 207n.
[15] *De la Morale naturelle*, Londres, 1788, pp. 10–11.

to which of the two was to be taken as the fundamental notion. The *Epicurean* said: To be conscious that one's maxims lead to happiness is virtue; the *Stoic* said: to be conscious of one's virtue is happiness." [16]

The contrast with the traditional ethics is obvious. As one eighteenth-century priest wrote, "A Christian must posit as a principle that he is on earth only to prepare his salvation." [17] This was the official view which had prevailed in the seventeenth century—whether it was practiced is another matter. In Guez de Balzac, Pascal, Bossuet, Fénelon, happiness is recognized as the prime human motive and desire, but its locus is in the next life, where (if paradise be gained) it is surer, more lasting and more perfect than any earthly simulacrum. From Pascal on, Christians were warned that the quest for happiness could not find its fruition here, and that man's merit and greatness lay elsewhere. "There is nothing so common among men," admitted Ameline, a Swiss pastor and theologian, "as the desire to live happily in this life: that is the aim and end of all their acts." But the fact is, he continues, that despite all their efforts, they are not happy. *Radix malorum cupiditas.* We have a limitless power of desire, but limited powers of realization. The end of our actions should therefore be the divine and infinite goods, but this is too much to ask of men ("man is always man, and by himself he can do nothing which is not human") without God's grace.[18]

It is easy to see why so many revolted against the Christian ethics as a fraud and a hypocrisy. Not only does it ask men to give up the reality of pleasure for the uncertainty of election to an unprovable paradise. Far more important, it admits—as Ameline does quite frankly [19]—that all good is valuable only for the pleasure it gives, or will ultimately give us. If this is so, why turn aside from the pleasure at hand, and on what grounds condemn pleasure, when it is the motive and reward used by God himself? Christianity, it is true, at other times lauded suffering as humiliation of the ego, acceptance of God's will, and the path to heaven. But few Christians dared to advance this thesis in a climate which

---

[16] *Critique of Practical Reason*, pp. 207–8. Kant goes on to show that virtue and happiness are "two extremely heterogeneous notions."

[17] Collet: *Traité des devoirs des gens du monde*, 1763, chap. 1.

[18] *L'Art de vivre heureux*, 1667, pp. 1, 17 ff.

[19] *Ibid.*, p. 62–63.

would have rejected it out of hand, which was in rebellion against needless suffering on earth, and thought that the reasonable way to live was to enjoy life as much as possible.[20]

The demand for happiness here and now produced a moral crisis which involved Christianity, even as Christianity, in its early centuries, had been obliged to fight a similar demand for happiness and justice on earth. The seventeenth-century Christian and the uncontaminated eighteenth-century Christian, by admitting and emphasizing that the quest for happiness here was an illusion and an inevitable frustration, avoided this crisis. Virtue, even when it thwarted happiness, was the only way to eventual happiness. It was not only right; it was worth-while. The widely read Abbadie, for instance, though not a Jansenist, followed and developed Pascal's analysis of man. Man is a low being, he says, incapable of virtue or happiness, "a phantom that walks amongst such things as have only appearance," the dreams and fictions of self-love, everywhere encompassed by Nothingness. "In time past he is no more, in the future he does not yet exist, in the present he partly is and partly is not. In vain does he endeavor to fix the past by memory, to anticipate the future by hope, that he may stretch the present to a greater length." Everything around him puts him in mind of his end and evokes the dread of death. " 'Tis a very grievous thing to a creature that loves itself so well, to behold itself continually dying." Fortunately men are not alone, but have their support in God.[21] There is no doubt, and no alternative.

We may compare this outlook with that of another Christian some sixty years later. Romilly-fils, writing the article "Vertu" for the *Encyclopédie,* declares that virtue lies in seeking happiness, and that conversely, virtue is the source of happiness. However, the virtuous are not happy on earth—in fact, the contrary is obvious. Religion alone makes the second statement true, because it gives the hope of later reward and recompense, without which virtue has small attraction, since happiness is the universal motive.

---

[20] In this regard, cf. the following dialogue from a twentieth-century nihilistic novel:

"Oh, you! naturally! You venerate suffering, you Christians!"
"We do not venerate it, we try to accept it."
"That amounts to the same thing."

(R. Merle, *Week-end à Zuydecoote,* p. 148.)

[21] *L'Art de se connoître soi-mesme,* p. 13 ff.

"If virtue is lovable, it is surely because it works for our happiness." Were this not so, what would virtue, order, universal harmony matter to *me?* To sacrifice for duty, if we have only this life, to give up all we have, and present happiness, would be the height of stupidity. But is there merit in loving virtue in this fashion? Yes, replies Romilly, "the rather rare merit of recognizing one's true interests." [22]

As we have seen so often before, Romilly, in his eagerness to defend his faith and his cause, undermines the cause of morality. If there is no heaven and hell, the materialist and the nihilist are right, and we must seek happiness in whatever way we can. In any case, virtue is no value or obligation in itself. Of course, we must recognize the fact that the concessions made by apologists were simply a change in tactics, not in substance or goal. Moreover, this dilemma into which many Christians drifted was certainly equalled by that of their opponents. In fact, for the *philosophes* there was not only the problem of virtue and happiness, but this other dilemma: men, most agreed, are unhappy; and yet the *philosophes* proposed happiness as the goal and highest value. Without God and a future state of bliss, how could this be justified?

The penetration of the dream of happiness was wide and deep. While the Jansenist Arnauld warned men to flee the pleasures of the senses, Malebranche defined happiness as a pleasurable feeling and affirmed that pleasure was God's way of making us happy. "Pleasure is always a good, and pain is always an evil; but it is not always advantageous to enjoy a pleasure, and it is sometimes advantageous to suffer pain." [23] Natural Law theory was to become similarly warped. The search for happiness, writes de Vattel, is "our first and most general obligation; since self-love is our first motive, and obligation is only the connection of the motive with the action, the obligation of working for our happiness . . . is the foundation of all the others." [24] Following this admission, we can

---

[22] Le Franc de Pompignan provides another example. Right would be a meaningless term, he declares, "if it were indifferent, for the happiness or unhappiness of those it obliges, to accomplish it or to thwart it." There would be no reason to prefer virtue (*La Religion vengée*, p. 207). Cf. Leibniz, *Monadology*, pp. 89–90. Cardinal Polignac also defends the same viewpoint, concluding: "Yes, I shall freely admit it; the sovereign good is pleasure; but pleasure taken in its true source." (*L'Anti-Lucrèce*, I, p. 64.)

[23] *De la Recherche de la vérité*, ed. Fr. Bouiller [1880], I, pp. 425–32.

[24] *Questions de droit naturel*, pp. 4–9.

take the next step, says de Vattel, and show that our happiness depends on our perfection and virtue; but happiness is the end and the obligation.

I. Hedonism

Utilitarianism is indissociably tied to happiness, but it is not—as Mill was later to protest—necessarily linked to sensual pleasure. Historically, however, its seeds lay in the hedonistic revolt of the seventeenth-century *libertins* (continuing certain currents of the Renaissance) against an ethical ideal which, in its other-worldly orientation, required limitation of the ego and its enjoyments, especially in regard to physical and sensual pleasures and the desire for greatness. Lanson, in an article already referred to, has studied the movement for a "secular morality" which gained wide momentum during the latter part of the seventeenth century and early eighteenth century. It was a movement which asserted the legitimacy of our natural demands and satisfactions, and expressed a hatred of suffering, which Christianity was accused of justifying and sanctifying. And so we have the open proclamation of hedonism, an empiricism which locates "good" in a universal form of experience—pleasure.

Some Christians moved rapidly to meet the challenge in a way which was to become widespread in the eighteenth century, by admitting the legitimacy of moderate sensual pleasures. As early as 1667, Ameline conceded that "voluptuousness, or sensual pleasures, are only feelings of love or joy excited in our soul by movements which it knows to be favorable to the constitution of the body." In fact, Ameline goes even further. Although the surest happiness comes from virtue, he admits that Epicurus was right in saying that nothing, not even virtue, is good except for the pleasure it gives us.[1] Malebranche, though he insists on the qualitative difference between pleasures, also grants that "any pleasure is a good, and at the moment makes the person who enjoys it happy. . . ."[2] The Jansenists, however, remained firm in their refusal to compromise their rigoristic position.

[1] *Op. cit.*, pp. 62–65.
[2] *Op. cit.*, I, pp. 427–28 [1675]. See also Abbadie, *op. cit.*, pp. 299–300. There were similar tendencies in the Quietist heresy.

The hedonistic movement was from the first, and in general remained, a moderate one. There were, to be sure, many exceptions, as is evidenced by *libertin* verse from Malherbe and Saint-Amant on.[3] But the principal *libertins* placed themselves under the aegis of Epicurus, that is (as they understood him) of moderate indulgence in all forms of pleasure. Rémond le Grec, Rémond de Saint-Mard, the marquis de Lassay, Baudot de Juilly all belong to the early eighteenth-century group.[4] The latter's *Dialogues sur les plaisirs* (1701) is a delightfully ironic work. One of the interlocutors, d'Ablancourt, protests against the thunder of the preachers:

> I am sorry, in truth, that a thousand gentlemen who are friends of mine, who are very virtuous, and who nevertheless carelessly enjoy the delights that life sometimes offers them are in danger of being damned for that. Isn't there any way of extending them a little mercy? Right now I am trembling for myself. I received a present today of two nice-looking melons, and some splendid strawberries. They're not really bad, you know, and it is pleasant to eat them. If every pleasure is a crime, as your Preacher says, I have a grievance against the person who in sending me those fruits . . . thought me wicked enough to enjoy something criminal. . . .

Patru disagrees. All voluptuousness degrades man and destroys the Christian by awakening the passions, the greatest enemy of reason. We are born for virtue, and for its recompense, Heaven, and nothing in pleasures leads to God. With women, especially, nothing is innocent, except flight. D'Ablancourt replies that pleasures are made for man, and that man needs them. Virtue and pleasure are not exclusive choices, and only the abuse of pleasure is evil. "It is permissible to live according to nature, which is only God himself." Pleasurable desires are "sacred rights, which one may and should follow. . . . We cannot so easily forget we are men, though it is easy to declaim against humanity." [5]

---

[3] E.g., the following verses, popular in the secret society, "Ordre de la Félicité":

> "L'Ile de la Félicité
> N'est pas une chimère.
> C'est où règne la Volupté
> Et de l'amour la mère;
> Frères courons, parcourons
> Tous les flots de Cythère
> Et nous la trouverons."

(Paul Hazard, *op. cit.*, I, p. 21.)

[4] See Lanson, *op. cit.*

[5] *Dialogues sur les plaisirs*, I, pp. 36–77, 154–81, 248. By the end of the second volume, Patru is convinced, or, as he says, "perverted." For Rémond le Grec and other early writers see Thémiseul de Saint-Hyacinthe, *Recueil de divers écrits*, 1736.

One of the most important propagandists for the new epicurean-ism was Saint-Evremond. To Pascal who had said that man's need to forget himself by means of entertainment is part of his wretched-ness, Saint-Evremond replied that it cannot be wretchedness, since it is a way of forgetting it.[6] He candidly says that virtue is a painful state, against inclination; that he prefers *sagesse,* or classical "pru-dence," indulgent and tranquil, a careful governance of pleasures, the avoidance of passions and commitments. "To live happily, we must reflect little on life, and leave our selves often." Solitude is fatal to happiness. Fame (prestige), wealth, power, love, volup-tuousness, "properly managed," are our refuge from the un-happiness which belongs to life. "But only the enjoyment of pleasure, voluptuousness, in a word, is the true end of all our acts." To avoid anything annoying, to be free and master of oneself— these maxims complete Saint-Evremond's prescription for obtain-ing what modicum of happiness life has to offer. He wagers against Pascal, and accepts the quest for happiness, imperfect though it is, in this world.[7]

For Fontenelle, too, happiness is an uncertain state. Only illu-sions make life bearable; thought and truth lead to sadness. New pleasures become new needs. Nature, nonetheless, wants us to live, and to seek pleasure, to strive constantly to make life bearable. But the best we can hope for is a balance of enjoyment and suffering.[8]

Bayle was another pessimistic defender of hedonism. No man is satisfied with his condition, he notes, none, therefore, perfectly happy. Happiness is not in our power, for what life does to us is too important. (Kant will uphold the opposite.) "Are galley slaves, prisoners, sick men happy?" Those whom we think happy, because of outer signs, generally are not. "There are few days when they are not envious of the contentment of mind which they suppose peasants enjoy." [9] But this is all the more reason, according to Bayle, for pursuing pleasure. The only happiness is on earth, so

[6] Pascal, however, does not deny the *efficacy* of diversion, but only condemns its betrayal of our true condition. Cf. Pensée 171 (Brunschvicg).

[7] *Oeuvres mêlées,* Amsterdam, 1706, III, p. 47; I, pp. 148–53; *Oeuvres,* ed. de Planhol, 1927, I, pp. 9–25; Barnwell, *Les Idées morales et critiques de Saint-Evre-mond,* pp. 65–90.

[8] *Dialogues des morts,* especially "Parménisque et Théocrite de Chio," "Sénèque et Scarron," "Lucrèce, Barbe Plomberge." See also Vyverberg, *op. cit.,* p. 43.

[9] *Oeuvres diverses,* III, pp. 669b, 669–70. The best of men have had a hard job at times "not to curse the day of their birth. . . . There are more evils than goods." (P. 831.)

God has willed, and all pleasures come from him. "Every pleasure is a good. . . . Sensual pleasures make us happy." God, the sovereign good, is not enough to make us happy. Therefore sensual pleasures do not have

> any stain, or any fault, which prevents them from making us truly happy. . . . A voluptuary's love of voluptuousness is only the result of the natural tendency of our soul to happiness. Every mind seeks its own good. The soul of a voluptuary finds its good in union with certain bodies. . . . It would seek virtue and piety no less ardently if it found the same pleasure in them. In a word, its disorderliness and crime do not consist in its taking for a good what is not a good, but in its not sacrificing to God its passion to be happy. . . .

The fact is that God has united, for a time, happiness and crime; and a voluptuary will say, "if I were to be eternally in the state in which I am when I enjoy, I should be eternally happy." One cannot deny, then, that any kind of pleasure is a good, and that it gives us happiness, whether it is legitimate or forbidden. Even Paul seems to admit this, since he says that if there were not another life, Christians would be the unhappiest of all men.[10]

It is obvious, from these lines, that if one did not choose to wager on the next life, any activity which brings pleasure is as good and valid as any other. Bayle denies that there are any qualitative differences in pleasure and happiness.[11] In fact, his reasoning could easily be transposed into one of La Mettrie's or Sade's writings.

The hedonistic movement swells during the first half of the century and continues strongly until its very end. Once again, we may find in the concessions of Christians significant evidence of its pervasiveness. Pleasures, writes the abbé Pluche, "do not dishonor men, since they are the work of God." Only excess or abuse is blameworthy. However, pleasure, he adds, is not the end of man, and he should not live as if it were.[12] In fact, the very pessimism about the possibility of obtaining happiness was much to the apologists' liking, and supplied them with a persuasive argument for what they had to offer. These views summarize the defensive stand of Christian apologists, and there is little need to examine the variations of tone.[13]

---

[10] *Ibid.*, I, pp. 450–57.

[11] See also, *ibid.*, III, p. 831.

[12] *Le Spectacle de la nature*, 1746, V, pp. 110–17.

[13] Cf., among many others, Trublet, *Essais*, 1749 ("He who knows how to be happy knows everything. . . . The circle of pleasures cannot be extended too wide. . .

Two or three Christian writers, however, deserve particular mention. The *Traité des premières vérités* (1724), a popular work by Buffier, defines good, or goodness, as "nothing but what makes us happy or contributes to it." [14] He admits that any good is useful, since it satisfies us in one way or another, for the moment or for eternity. Every man thinks of himself first and has his own good, corresponding to his own happiness. This must be admitted, although we really ought to reserve the term to "what contributes to the general happiness of all men, or what benefits or seems good to all." We should note, too, Yvon's article "Bien," in the *Encyclopédie*, in which he declares that the argument about sensual pleasure being "false," is itself false; surely, a man knows when he is feeling pleasure. It is also useless to argue that this kind of pleasure is contrary to order; such a person need only reply that he is only seeking his own contentment. The only *valid* argument is that sensual pleasures are not consistent with happiness because of their consequences; but there is no *moral* argument against them. The happiness argument is valid, because if the voluptuary answers that he cares only about the present, "I'll say to you that you are not a man in that," for man lives at once in past, present, and future.

Samuel Formey wanted to reconcile Christianity with reason and science. Like so many others, he agrees that "ethics is nothing, or it is the science of happiness." Virtue can best be practiced when one has proper comforts; their lack is an obstacle to morals. [15] He dwells on the relation between intelligence and happiness. Intelligent people have stronger perceptions. They are therefore capable of being both happier and unhappier than others. [16] We are reminded of Fontenelle, and of Voltaire's later tale, *Histoire d'un bon bramin* (1768). This relation obtains because "the feeling of our state is linked with the ideas we have of other possible states." Thus, too, it is possible to be happy, but not content. "Man's will impels him towards something better, so that contentment is the rarest of states." [17] Nevertheless the fact is that man can act by

---

Nothing matters but happiness."), I, p. 352 ff.; III, pp. 228 ff., 372–79. Holland writes: "My nature obliges me to love my well-being; I can therefore regard virtue as my duty only as far as I am convinced that it makes me happier than the pursuit of my personal interest." (*Réflexions philosophiques*, 1773, p. 197.)

[14] Chapter XV.

[15] "Discours sur l'obligation de se procurer toutes les commodités de la vie," in Bartholmess, *Histoire philosophique de l'Académie de Prusse*, 1850–51, I, p. 385 ff.

[16] *Le Bonheur*, Berlin, 1754, p. 37 ff.

[17] P. 58 ff.

himself only toward happiness and away from unhappiness. It is evident, then, "that all man's duty consists in augmenting his happiness, in preferring the states which will give it to him. . . . Thus moral duties are all the actions which a man should do for the sole reason that his happiness is involved in them." [18] And in this way we see how Formey, a Protestant defender of Christianity, is led by his desire to absorb the new currents to reduce moral duty to selfishness.

In many of these writers, there is a continued nuance of pessimism. Thus the abbé Trublet writes: "We are not happy; we hope to be. Everybody has in mind a certain situation for himself in which he flatters himself that he will be happier than he is now. Thus happiness is only in the waiting; not only for those who are awaiting it in the next life, but even for those who admit only the present life." As a result, we are all *working* for happiness to come (which is mainly work for acquisition), and how painful that is! [19]

Among the deists, Shaftesbury and Collins both defended sensual pleasures.[20] Collins, like Formey later, defines virtue and morality as "such actions as are in their own nature, and upon the whole, pleasant," immorality and vice as actions which are painful. Without pleasure or pain, one neither knows right from wrong, nor has any motive to practice it—for there are no other motives.[21] In France the *libertin* tradition was continued and strengthened by such writers as Fréret and Meslier. Fréret affirms that there is no happiness other than "the enjoyment of pleasures attached to our needs." [22] Meslier attacks the moral doctrine of Jesus and evangelical Christianity, confusing it (as was frequent) with the Christianity of the eighteenth-century Church. It reverses justice and equity, he charges, and favors the wicked; it perverts the natural maxim: "conquer in order not to suffer," into "suffer in order to conquer."

D'Argens, Toussaint, and Ladvocat all maintained the necessity of pleasure for happiness and defended sensual pleasures taken in moderation.[23] Christian Wolff asserted that happiness is our

---

[18] P. 80.

[19] *Op. cit.,* pp. 323–28. Cf. Polignac: man constantly pursues a happiness which he never finds; "he finds in himself only a dreadful emptiness." He must seek happiness outside of himself, in God. (*Anti-Lucrèce,* II, p. 291 ff.)

[20] Accompanied by right use, says Shaftesbury, *op. cit.,* II, pp. 173–74.

[21] *A Philosophical Inquiry Concerning Human Liberty,* London, 1717, pp. 90–91.

[22] *Oeuvres,* III, p. 110.

[23] D'Argens, *Lettres juives,* La Haye, 1738, Lettre L.; Toussaint, *Les Moeurs,* 1748, pp. 84–87; Ladvocat, *Entretiens,* 1721, pp. 55–59.

"capital obligation," and defined it as "the state in which we enjoy true and enduring pleasure." Passing pleasures are allowable if they do no harm.[24] Hume went further: "No gratification, however sensual, can of itself be esteemed vicious. A gratification is only vicious when it engrosses all a man's expense, and leaves no ability for such acts of duty and generosity as are required by his situation and fortune." [25] Boulanger declared that all happiness is equal, and that knowledge and unsatisfiable desires are its greatest enemies; men who think are "melancholy and thin." [26]

Maupertuis' *Essai de philosophie morale* (1749) is one of the more important works of the first half of the eighteenth century. As a scientist, Maupertuis wishes to reduce qualitative to quantitative differences. He defines a happy moment as the time of duration of the perception of a pleasure. There are only two elements in pleasure: duration and intensity. Greater intensity compensates for shorter duration, or the reverse. This leads to Maupertuis' famous hedonic calculus, or moral arithmetic, which had great influence on later utilitarians: happiness can be calculated as "the product of the intensity of pleasure or of pain and the duration." [27] This calculus, though not exact, is one that is naturally performed by every man. Good is "a sum of happy moments," evil a sum of unhappy ones. Happiness is "the sum of goods which remain after one has subtracted all the evils." Our action should be aimed at preferring the greatest good, thus understood, but everyone must do this in his own way, according to his own tastes.

Despite all this, Maupertuis is pessimistic about the chances. Our search for happiness, necessary and justifiable though it is, cannot be successful. In the average life there is more suffering than pleasure. Pleasure diminishes with its duration, but pain increases. All parts of the body can give us pain, only a few, pleasure. Excess of pleasure produces pain, but the reverse is not true. What is worse, life is a constant series of new desires, and we are always wishing to annihilate the time that separates us from their realization. We should, indeed, if this could be done, live only a few hours. All this time we would wish to annihilate is not

---

[24] *Op. cit.*, p. 28.

[25] "Of the Refinement in the Arts," in *Philosophical Essays*, Georgetown, D.C., 1817, I, p. 297.

[26] "Du Bonheur," *Oeuvres*, En Suisse, 1791, III, p. 326 ff.

[27] The idea of a calculus had already appeared in Wollaston's *Religion of Nature Delineated*, 1722, Sect. 2; it was not translated until 1756 (P. Hazard, I, p. 25n.).

a happy time. For confirmation, Maupertuis points to the pursuit of entertainment (a flight from the self), and to the use of alcohol and tobacco. Everywhere and at all times, "men have sought remedies for the ill of being alive." And who would consent to reliving his life? Notwithstanding these dour facts, Maupertuis defends the possibility, through the use of reason, of increasing the proportion of pleasure. Above all, we must dismiss as nonsense the idea that the pleasures of the senses are less noble than others. There is no difference between pleasures except duration and intensity, and "the most noble pleasures are the greatest ones." [28] Finally, there is no difference among the various ethical systems, Maupertuis maintains, except their method of calculating happiness—all seek the greatest pleasure in one way or another. In the Preface, Maupertuis defends himself against critics of his radical naturalism, claiming that calculation would show that greater happiness comes from the pleasures of virtue. The theory is nonetheless devastating.[29]

Montesquieu's ideas about happiness are variable. He is not a hedonist, but recognizes the value of pleasure. At times he is inclined to a mild pessimism. "We must set down the limit which happiness can attain through human nature, and not begin by demanding the happiness of angels," he notes in his *Spicilège*. But "everyone throughout life must get as many happy moments as possible." Business should wait on pleasure, and not the contrary.[30] How shall we find this happiness? In several places, Montesquieu insists that happiness comes from virtue; sobriety, prudence, the good will of others are essentials.[31] But religious notions are excluded; nature and reason are the only resources for man on earth. They may not be sufficient. Much depends on the inherited "disposition of our organs, favorable or unfavorable," and on the accidents of life, such as wealth. Different people will be happy or unhappy in the same situation. Some are always un-

[28] *Oeuvres*, I, p. 194 ff. In another piece, "Sur le Bonheur," Maupertuis asserts that the happiness each individual may have is a given constant (II, pp. 93–96).

[29] For Kant's criticism of Maupertuis, see Cassirer, *op. cit.*, pp. 150–51. Another criticism is to be found in M. Mendelssohn's *Recherches sur les sentimens moraux*, Genève, 1763, pp. 24–25. For Maupertuis' theory to be defensible, he charges, we should have to make two suppositions: 1. that all our feelings give us a pure, unmixed pleasure, 2. "that absolutely every displeasure diminishes the sum of happiness."

[30] *Pensées*, 206, *Oeuvres*, ed. P. M. Masson, Vol. II.

[31] *Lettres persanes*, X, XII; *Pensées*, 496: "Let us try to adjust ourselves to this life; it is not for this life to adjust itself to us."

happy: those who are bored and want nothing, those who want what they cannot have. Some are almost always happy: those who desire keenly and enjoy what is accessible, those "whose machine is so constructed that it is gently and continuously titillated," even by the little things of life, such as a book or a conversation. On the one hand, Montesquieu warns us that joy is fatiguing in the long run, and continual pleasure is incompatible with keen pleasure. On the other hand, he reassures us that pleasures are everywhere available: "they are attached to our being, and suffering is only an accident. All objects seem to be set out for our enjoyment." Art completes nature in this regard. The essential thing is to be open and ready to receive these happy moments; happiness consists less in pleasure than in "the readiness to receive pleasure." Even pain (contrary to what Maupertuis had said) may increase pleasure, as hunger sharpens appetite. We also have the great resources of pride and vanity, and that of hope. In fact, most of our life consists of pleasant hoping—far more than of pleasant possession. This argument, too, contradicts Maupertuis. A simple calculation, then, shows that we are mostly happy. The great enemy of happiness is wanting to be happier than others, "because we believe others are happier than they [really] are." Maupertuis also erred in his calculus, Montesquieu affirms, by including only pleasures and pains. "He overlooks the happiness of existence, and the habitual felicity which does not obtrude itself, because it is habitual." It is wrong to say, happiness is that moment which we would not exchange for another. "Let us rather say, happiness is that moment which we would not exchange for non-being." [32]

With La Mettrie we return to one of the most radical figures of the century. Having disposed of other values, his analysis leaves us only happiness. In *L'Homme machine* (1747) he declares, as others had, that man is "made to be happy," and so are all creatures, "yes, all, from the worm that crawls to the eagle who is lost in the cloud." Maurice Solovine comments: "To be happy! this idea alone dominates his thinking about human behavior. It is the cry so often uttered by those who find it hard to support the weight of obligations which so-called civilized society thrusts upon them, without offering them an equivalent individual compensation." [33]

La Mettrie does not deny that we may derive pleasure and

[32] *Pensées*, 157, 871, 274, 479, 620. The last thought is similar to one of Formey's.
[33] *L'Homme machine*, pp. 31, 103.

happiness from virtue and humanitarianism; the contrary is true.[34] But he makes no distinctions among pleasures other than their quantitative values. If one finds happiness in virtue, then all we can say is that he is "fortunately born." In his first important work, the *Histoire naturelle de l'âme*,[35] La Mettrie had asserted that happiness depends entirely on sensations, of which we are not the masters. It follows that we cannot create our happiness, or determine what will give us pleasure. But he then asserts that to look for happiness in thought, or in the pursuit of truth, is vain, for it depends on "corporal causes." People of quiet and moderate temperaments are most likely to be happy.

La Mettrie's most important piece on the subject, and his most notorious work, was his *Discours sur le bonheur* (also titled *Anti-Sénèque,* and sometimes referred to in the eighteenth century as *Discours de la vie heureuse*), published in 1748. Boissier summarizes La Mettrie's thesis in these words: "It is, then, finally, in sensual satisfaction, in the normal accomplishment of organic functions, under the imperious call of needs in a kind of perpetually unstable equilibrium between their requirements and their satisfaction, that happiness lies." [36] La Mettrie divides pleasurable "modifications" of our organs into three kinds: pleasure (those of short duration), voluptuousness (longer sensations), happiness (permanent pleasurable feelings).[37] He appeals to us to discard illusions; happiness does not come from perfection, virtue, honor, detachment, or serenity. Let us admit "the empire of the senses," and let us be happy. "The first condition of happiness is to feel." Feeling is natural to man, but not wisdom or virtue.[38]

This is the only truth that matters—happiness; it belongs to all, wise and ignorant, rich and poor, good and wicked. "Who has found happiness has found everything"—there is no other value.[39] Happiness may come from the organism itself (and this is best), or from such externals as voluptuousness, wealth, prestige. It may

[34] *Ibid.,* pp. 103, 141–142.
[35] La Haye, 1745, pp. 160–62.
[36] *La Mettrie,* p. 152.
[37] *Discours sur le bonheur, Oeuvres,* Amsterdam, 1774, II, p. 98.
[38] Ignorant people miss some pleasures, but avoid greater suffering. They do not fear happiness-giving illusions, nor care whether the earth turns around the sun or vice versa. "He is clever enough, who is happy enough." Again, we have the problem which will torment Voltaire in the *Histoire d'un bon bramin.* Thinking "is the poison of life. Reflection is often almost a remorse. On the contrary, a man whose instincts make him happy, is always happy . . . and cheaply." (*Ibid.,* p. 105.)
[39] *Ibid.,* p. 110.

also come from inculcated habits (by which term La Mettrie designates moral reactions and conscience). Hedonism, then—although La Mettrie is not consistent on this point—does not exclude virtue, which may, indeed, increase happiness. The virtuous man is happy "with that kind of happiness which belongs to virtue." [40] It is one kind of happiness. In this regard, however, to be taken for virtuous is just as good as to be virtuous. "What does it matter . . . if a man is vicious, if he passes for virtuous?" On the other hand, real virtues that do not bring the desired rewards and satisfactions are useless. The immoralism of La Mettrie's philosophy is evident. We should note his priority of values when he summarizes: "We make the happiness of society with our own." [41] Most of all, we do not have to be good to be happy—the wicked are equally happy, perhaps more, provided they are free from remorse. "It is then very clear that in regard to felicity, right and wrong are quite indifferent; that a person who gets greater satisfaction from doing wrong will be happier than anyone who gets less from doing good . . . there is a special kind of happiness which can be found in vice, and in crime itself." [42] This statement contains the kernel of Sade's philosophy.

Later in the essay, La Mettrie admits his preference for moderation, for the mere satisfaction of needs. Sensual pleasures are too brief, too infrequent, to constitute the permanent state which is felicity; but he insists that there can be no happiness without them.[43] "Let us give to nature what belongs to nature." We have, for instance, an urgent, even a daily need for coitus, and this need must not be frustrated. The modification of La Mettrie's extreme sensualism is therefore slight or inexistent. And soon after we find him telling the voluptuary to forget all else:

> . . . nonsense for you, all the stoic virtues; think only of your body. That part of you which is soul is not worth being distinguished from it. . . . Enjoy yourself whenever you can; enjoy the present, forget the past which no longer is, and do not fear the future. . . . Let pollution and orgasm (*jouissance*), lascivious rivals, follow each other in turn, making you melt day and night with voluptuousness; let them make your soul, if it is possible, as sticky and lascivious as your body . . . or if, not satisfied with excelling in the great art of voluptuousness, if debauch and

[40] *Ibid.*, pp. 120–21.
[41] *Ibid.*, p. 116.
[42] *Ibid.*, p. 139.
[43] *Ibid.*, pp. 169–70.

lechery are not strong enough for you, then filth and infamy
are your lot; wallow, like pigs, and you will be happy as they
are. . . . Let it not be said that I urge to crime; for I urge only
to peace of mind in crime.[44]

This "invitation" is repeated, in milder form, in *L'Art de jouir*
(1751), which is a hymn to pleasure. By severing happiness from
right and wrong, by rejecting moral values as inexistent or as
untenable compared to pleasure, by legitimizing and equalizing
all sources of pleasure, La Mettrie has, in effect, developed the
first theory of nihilism in the eighteenth century, and opened the
path to Sade.

Buffon is rather less optimistic than Montesquieu, but much
more proper than La Mettrie. In the chapter of the *Histoire
naturelle des animaux* (1749), entitled "Homo duplex," he distinguishes the soul, which is the source of calm and serenity, of
knowledge and wisdom, from the material, animal principle, "a
false light which shines only in the tempest and the darkness, a
murky torrent which rolls and carries passions and errors with
it." [45] But this qualitative distinction has little to do with felicity.
We are happy in both states. "In the first, we command [ourselves]
with satisfaction, in the second, we obey with still more pleasure."
The main point is that there should be no conflict, no tearing in
two directions. "It is in this unity of action that our happiness
consists: for if by reflection we start to blame our pleasures, or if
we try to hate our reason out of violence of passion, we at once
stop being happy." Doubt, worry, remorse follow the destruction
of unity. Thus far, Buffon's analysis bears a resemblance to La
Mettrie's evaluation, especially of remorse. But then he goes off
on an original tangent. We are most unhappy, he continues, when
both forces are strong and in balance. Then we are subject to
boredom and distaste for ourself and for life, and even the body
receives injury from the mental anguish. Therefore we are happiest in childhood, when the material principle rules exclusively.
Youth is next best, for although the spiritual principle is by then
awakened, it is completely overwhelmed by the new surge of
material force embodied in the sexual energies, so that unity is
conserved. We are far worse off in middle age. By then the dream

---

[44] *Ibid.*, pp. 175–76.
[45] *Oeuvres*, ed. Piveteau, pp. 337–40.

and the charm have vanished, leaving indifference [*dégoût*] and a sickening emptiness. The soul, too weakened to command, seeks another master; one master follows the other, producing ever new disillusionments. Melancholy and depression set in. Perhaps we run after the pleasures of youth; but, as it happens more and more frequently "that we experience pleasure less than our impotence to enjoy it, we are in contradiction with ourselves, humiliated by our weakness," with the result that we end in self-reproach and self-condemnation. Eventually the heart is healed, and a state of apathy follows. Worries about our career, injustices, the fading of the shining goal of glory into "a vain and deceitful phantom" complete the story, and we are left with—boredom, "that sad tyrant of all thinking souls, against which wisdom is less effective than folly." [46]

Voltaire had only wrathful scorn for La Mettrie. Yet he, too, began as a pure hedonist, though of the more usual, moderate variety, and he will reiterate La Mettrie's tri-partite division of pleasure, happiness, and felicity.[47] In 1722 he wrote to Mme de Bernières, "The main business of life, and the only business, is to live happily." [48] He quotes the libertin Bernier as saying that "abstinence from pleasure is a sin." [49] In even earlier verses he had heaped scorn on "insane mystics." [50] The famous poem, *Le Mondain* (1736), continues this hedonism and faith in happiness.

With increasing maturity and schooling in life's disappointments, injustices, and follies, and with the lessons garnered from his study of history, Voltaire's outlook evolves in two ways. He develops a social consciousness which to a considerable extent subordinates his egoism; in this way he may be taken as a model of the general evolution of moral feeling in the eighteenth century. And his optimism gradually wanes. In the 1750's, he undergoes a crisis of pessimism (for personal, political, and metaphysical reasons), from which his later recovery is only partial.

In the well-known *Discours en vers sur l'homme* (1738), he

---

[46] For a physical analysis of sensual pleasure, see *ibid.,* p. 329.
[47] "Heureux," *Encyclopédie.*
[48] *Oeuvres,* XXXIII, p. 62.
[49] *Ibid.,* XXXII, p. 544. See also *Samson,* III, p. 9.
[50]   ". . . Qui, dévots fainéants et pieux loups-garous,
        Quittent de vrais plaisirs pour une fausse gloire?
        Le plaisir est l'objet, le devoir et le but
        De tous les êtres raisonnables. . . ." (*Ibid.,* X, pp. 231–32.)

still maintains the possibility of happiness, and its equal availability to all classes. But this goal of life is already only an evanescent quality:

> Hélas, où donc chercher, où trouver le bonheur?
> En tous lieux, en tous temps, dans toute la nature,
> Nulle part tout entier, partout avec mesure,
> Et partout passager, hors dans son seul auteur. (*Ier Discours*)

It is easy to see that Voltaire is already engaged in what will be a great inner struggle for faith in life and in man. A large part of the other discourses in this poem is devoted to prescriptions for happiness, which may be summarized as enjoyment tempered by moderation. Pleasures are like flowers:

> Chacune a sa saison, et par des soins prudents
> On peut en conserver pour l'hiver de nos ans.
> Mais s'il faut les cueillir, c'est d'une main légère;
> On flétrit aisément leur beauté passagère. (*IVe Discours*)

It is not our task here to trace in detail the gradual deepening of Voltaire's pessimism, which one may follow in many studies devoted to him. We need only note several outstanding statements. *Zadig* (1747) shows thematically the difficulty of finding happiness even with the best intentions and the greatest care. The article "Félicité" in the *Encyclopédie* sounds like a mockery of his tripartite definition: "Felicity is the permanent state, at least for some time, of a contented soul, and that state is quite rare." In the article "Bien, Souverain Bien" (*Questions sur l'Encyclopédie*, 1756), happiness is now merely "an abstract idea composed of a few sensations of pleasure. . . . If we give the name of happiness to a few pleasures scattered throughout life, there is happiness indeed." The year 1756, with the Lisbon earthquake, marks the nadir of his faith in happiness—in God and in man, too—a period which continues until the early part of the next decade. The *Poème sur le désastre de Lisbonne* pictures all as sighing and dying in a "fatal chaos of misfortunes."

> Ce monde, ce théâtre et d'orgueil et d'erreur,
> Est plein d'infortunés qui parlent de bonheur.
> Tout se plaint, tout gémit en cherchant le bien-être. . . .
> Quelquefois, dans nos jours consacrés aux douleurs,
> Par la main du plaisir nous essuyons nos pleurs,
> Mais le plaisir s'envole, et passe comme une ombre,
> Nos chagrins, nos regrets, nos pertes, sont sans nombre.

Voltaire's masterpiece, *Candide,* broadens the picture to paint a world of rampant evil, cruelty, and misery. Happiness exists only in the unattainable realm of El Dorado; [51] all others struggle for a taste of it. Another jewel among his tales, *Histoire d'un bon bramin* (1761), poses a great humanistic note of doubt, and reveals the intensity of Voltaire's anguish.[52] Indeed, this apologue is of exceptional importance because, beyond Voltaire's personal torment, it reaches and lays bare the great weakness of the eighteenth-century eudaemonistic value system. As several writers had already suggested, thought is the enemy of happiness. With his usual facility for making abstract ideas vividly concrete, Voltaire pits the unhappy, thoughtful brahmin against the ignorant but happy old woman, more beast than human. But he, and everyone Voltaire consults, would rather be the unhappy brahmin than the old woman. How can this be? "For after all, what matters in life? to be happy." Yet we prefer being a man to being happy. "But, after thinking about it, it seems that it is very crazy to prefer reason to felicity." And Voltaire finds no way of explaining the contradiction. He can discover no issue from the dilemma, despite his perception of other values, for he could not quite transcend the value system of his time. Here we see the impasse of eighteenth-century hedonism, its self-defeating character, its ethically unacceptable terminus, the judgment of an act on a quantitative scale of pleasure, subjective and (openly or implicitly) amoral. Voltaire's problem had in fact been solved by Pascal, that great adversary with whom he wrestled for many years, and whom he never completely understood. Pascal had said that happiness is the natural motive of our acts, but he scorned it as the goal of life; man's greatness and dignity lie in his thought which, because it reveals his true position to him, creates anguish in him—the very anguish of Voltaire's brahmin. But without that anguish, one is not fully a man. Voltaire's animosity prevented him from separating the humanistic import of Pascal's genius from his mystical conclusions.

It would be futile to cite the innumerable epigrams in which Voltaire continued to express his disillusionment. They may themselves be epitomized by a line in *Il Faut prendre un parti*

---

[51] Perhaps (among other things) an ironic commentary on the Marquis de Lassay's kingdom of the Féliciens; see P. Hazard, *op. cit.,* I, pp. 20–21.

[52] XXI, pp. 219–21.

(1772): "Man is a very wretched being who has a few hours of relief, a few minutes of satisfaction, and a long series of sorrows in his short life." [53]

However, Voltaire's value outlook does evolve, in the displacement of its locus from the self to society, and from hedonistic satisfaction to altruistic beneficence. This change is evidenced in his own life, in his ever-expanding involvement in social problems, cases of injustice, and the welfare of the community in which he lived. It is visible in his increasing emphasis on virtue, and in his constant definition of that word as obedience to law. Typical of his mature outlook is the revulsion he felt for La Mettrie and d'Holbach (though the two should not be coupled). In the *Système de la nature* he had read these lines: "If man, because of his nature, is forced to love his well-being, he is forced to love the means to it. It would be useless and unjust to expect a man to be virtuous if he cannot without making himself unhappy. If vice makes a person happy, he must love vice." Execrable! cries Voltaire. "Even if it were true that a man could not be virtuous without suffering, we should still encourage him to be virtuous. The author's proposition would be the ruin of society." But the supposition, he adds, is not true; and indeed, d'Holbach's purpose was only to give a new proof of the necessity of being virtuous.[54]

For Helvétius conduct is "the art of happiness," [55] and ethics "the science of the means invented by men to live together in the happiest way possible." [56] Like Maupertuis and La Mettrie, Helvétius tried to supply a mathematical measure of happiness and suggested the possibility of a calculus based on the assumption that all pleasures are qualitatively equal. This view was all the more appealing to him, since a central idea of his system was the reduction of all psychic phenomena to physical. Pleasures, then, "are indistinguishable except in terms of their location, their velocity and direction, and their size." [57] Although Helvétius is one of the leaders in the swing to social utilitarianism, he conserves a large measure of egoistic hedonism. In a dull allegorical

---

[53] XXVIII, p. 535.

[54] To understand fully Voltaire's aversion to d'Holbach, we must therefore add the moral question to the political and the religious, and to their division on the question of strategy. He would surely have felt the same aversion to Diderot, had he known the latter's unpublished writings.

[55] *De l'Esprit*, p. 585.

[56] *De l'Homme*, IX, pp. 140–41.

[57] Charles Frankel, *op. cit.*, p. 60.

poem, "Le Bonheur," he gives his prescription for happiness. Love and ambition are pleasurable, but dangerous; riches may be quite useful. Most important are independence, tastes that can be satisfied, and intellectual pursuits, together with a controlled indulgence in sensual pleasures. The progress of knowledge is necessary to both private and public happiness. When men become enlightened, they will find happiness in unselfish good deeds. But, until the yoke of kings and priests is thrown off, the wise man will enjoy the arts, women, and the pleasure of enlightening others as much as possible. In being virtuous, however, Helvétius makes it clear, in *De l'Homme*, there is no question of sacrificing one's pleasures or passion; virtue is merely another passion which happens to conform to the general interest. As Hayer pointed out in criticizing him, virtue, like all else, is reduced to physical sensitivity.

Ethics, writes d'Holbach, "is the art of making man happy by the knowledge and practice of his duties."[58] From this opening sentence, one might expect a nonhedonistic theory, and we shall later see d'Holbach's emphasis on virtue. Individual happiness, however, remains an ever-present preoccupation. In one place, he defines happiness as "enduring, continuous pleasure."[59] In another, he warns that pleasures, especially sensual, are only momentary and cannot provide "the permanence necessary to happiness."[60] D'Holbach recognizes the subjectivity of happiness; it "cannot be the same for all beings of the human species, but depends on their particular temperament and conformation."[61] There is a fundamental contradiction here with two other theses advanced by d'Holbach: that morality is possible only if it brings happiness, and that moral laws and duties are universal.

In another work, d'Holbach declares that man seeks happiness "in all moments of his duration," and he defines happiness as "the continuous enjoyment of the objects of our desires."[62] There is no happiness without desires and passions. The question then becomes our ability to satisfy our desires. Consequently, happiness

[58] *La Morale universelle*, III, p. 207. Also: "As soon as there exist beings essentially lovers of happiness . . . and necessary to one another in procuring it, duties are established among them." (Quoted by Palmer, p. 189.)
[59] *Ibid.*, I, p. 12.
[60] *Ibid.*, III, p. 208. Cf. *Système de la nature*, I, p. 146: the keener the pleasure, the more fugitive, and the more likely to become pain.
[61] *Système de la nature*, I, p. 147. See also pp. 338–40 for a more detailed analysis.
[62] *Système social*, I, pp. 58, 167–70.

depends on our limiting desires to those we can easily satisfy. It is especially important to limit "artificial needs," which have a tendency to lead from one to another, as each is satisfied, until we have nothing left to desire and find ourselves in a miserable condition. "A pleasure demands to be followed by a still keener pleasure." [63] We must beware of this enslavement, which can only give us constant torment.[64] By prudent conduct of our lives we can do much to avoid this danger; but there are some men, "unfortunately born," whose temperament and imagination are uncontrollable and lead them to seek satisfaction in ways which threaten their welfare and even the security of society. Philosophers are the most "fortunately born" of men.[65] D'Holbach then contradicts his earlier statement that desires should be of a kind that can be easily satisfied. Such facility makes the objects of desire insipid; "to find charms in enjoyment, desire must be irritated by obstacles" and require effort and anticipation. "Action is the true element of the human mind; as soon as it ceases to act, it falls into boredom." Happiness therefore cannot be continuous.

D'Holbach, it seems, has presented an inconsistent and chaotic picture. We are not surprised by his conclusion. "By an irrevocable law of fate, men are forced to be discontented with their destiny, to make efforts to change it, to envy each other for a felicity which none of them enjoys perfectly." In a way, this is all to the good. If men were perfectly happy, there would be no activity. Society could not endure nor could a man's body remain healthy, without endless restlessness and the creation of new needs, even though the end of the circle for each individual is *dégoût*. The artificial needs, which d'Holbach elsewhere says lead to satiety and unhappiness, are therefore necessary and beneficent. Unhappiness, it seems, is the necessary and healthy condition of our existence, at the same time that happiness is the universal goal and the highest value! [66]

---

[63] *Ibid.*, I, pp. 172–73.
[64] *La Morale universelle*, I, pp. 17, 21–22.
[65] *Système social*, I, pp. 303–4.
[66] *Ibid.*, p. 34 note 1.
An assessment of the minor writers of the century would provide little of interest that has not already been brought out. For more detailed analysis, see R. Mauzi, *L'Idée du bonheur au XVIIIᵉ siècle,* especially chap. X. It is worth mentioning that Mme du Châtelet stresses illusions, among other factors, and the proper goal of seeking pleasant sensations (*Réflexions sur le bonheur*). Her approach to happiness is rationalistic and calculating; but this rationalistic woman is a romanticist and

There was one special kind of pleasure that was distinguished by several writers as constituting the purest, or most basic, kind of happiness. This may be called the feeling or experience of our own existence. We find a trace of it in Abbadie. While on the one hand, he notes, we strive to forget our existence (as Pascal had said) because of its wretchedness, at the same time we turn in upon ourselves and build an imaginary felicity composed of illusions.[67] We have noted his awareness of man's anguish at the nothingness which surrounds our being on all sides, ever threatening it.

Morelly, in his *Essai sur le coeur humain* (1745) asserts that God made the feeling of our existence a good, for "he has attached pleasure to whatever can make that feeling keener. Thus . . . pleasure makes us love our existence, because this pleasure cannot subsist without it." [68] Morelly is perhaps guilty of some confusion. Do we love our existence for the sake of pleasure, or do we love pleasure because it makes us experience and enjoy the feeling of existing?

In the *Encyclopédie,* the article "Homme" (signed "D.J.") links happiness to the existence feeling. According to the author's view, this need leads to restlessness, because it requires constant renewal by ever keener experiences, inasmuch as prolonged sensations become dulled. "We are therefore forced, in order to be happy, to change objects continually, or to exasperate a single kind of sensation. This is the cause of our natural inconstancy, which does not permit our wishes to remain firm, and of that progression of desires, which, always annihilated by enjoyment, rush forward towards infinity." In this analysis we can see, unrecognized, the

---

feels the emptiness of life. Beneath her apology for the passions and licentiousness, we can glimpse an emotional aridity; in her hunger for happiness, a desperate emptiness.

A note of quiet desperation and preoccupation with death are also evident in Roucher's verses:

> Quoi! Parce que la nuit finira la journée,
> J'irai, traînant partout une âme consternée,
> Détourner mes regards de la clarté des Cieux,
> Je croirai les plaisirs défendus par les Dieux,
> Et follement épris des vertus d'un faux sage,
> Je n'oserai cueillir des fleurs sur mon passage?
> . . . . Mortels! goûtez la vie:
> Hâtez-vous, saisissez le jour qui vous a lui;
> Et demain au tombeau, jouissez aujourd'hui.
> (*Les Mois,* Chant XII.)

[67] *Op. cit.,* 1710, pp. 19–20 (Part 2, chap. 3).
[68] Pp. 4–5.

germ of the Sadian psychology, or of that of other nihilists from Nero and Caligula on.

D'Holbach comments on the same need to seek ever keener sensations, despite the unattainability of a satisfactory object or the harm to our organism. "Man always wants to be made aware of his existence as vividly as possible, as long as he can do it without pain. What do I say? He often consents to suffer rather than not to feel." [69]

C.-G. Leroy approaches the same phenomenon in his analysis of the principles of human action. We are tormented by the need to experience a keen sensation of our existence; since only immediate sensations can make us present to ourselves, they must be renewed. Several of Leroy's sentences are lifted textually from the article "Homme." But he finds a contradictory principle of equal strength in man: lethargy and love of rest, so that we oscillate between the two contraries, the need to act and the desire not to. With the savage, the second principle is dominant. The flowing of a stream is enough to enchant him, and "the ignorance of a stronger emotion allows him to enjoy this peaceful situation neighboring on sleep." [70] Leroy is also a pessimist. The imperfection of social organization and the progressive blunting of sensation give us constant regret for an existence "which is constantly escaping from us, and which we are constantly trying to bring back." A frequent result of the dulling is the perversion of natural impulses, until actions which once would have made us shudder become necessary to us—witness the increasing cruelty of circus games devised to satisfy Roman ladies. "We may conclude that what is called pleasure consists only in the feeling of existence, intensified to a certain degree." Indeed, a close examination of our sensations and emotions "tempts us to believe that pain and pleasure, so essentially different, really differ only by nuances." The mystic, finding prayer insufficient, graduates to chains, hot coals, spikes. "By these different kinds of rigors against himself, he is made aware of his existence in a closer and stronger way than the person who simply performs the duties of civil life and charity." [71]

Rousseau, who was not a hedonist, gave this existence-feeling

---

[69] *Système de la nature*, I, p. 338.
[70] *Lettres philosophiques*, pp. 174–77. We have seen how the other impulse, according to Leroy, develops into the drive for power (*An Age of Crisis*, p. 315).
[71] *Ibid.*, pp. 194–200.

its most meaningful expression in his last work, the *Rêveries d'un promeneur solitaire,* taking it from the realm of philosophy into that of literature and concrete experience. In his case, however, that experience is obtained through isolation, inner concentration, and reverie, which exclude all hindrances to full and immediate self-experience. No longer is it a question of a Faustian up-reaching of will, insatiable, restless, coursing after an ideal usually recognized as beyond reach; it is, instead, a Platonic autarchy and the withering away of desire, as consciousness of the self fills the entire emptiness of the self. But this is only one pole of the Rousseauist ideal. As through all his life and work there is a profound split which he never succeeded in unifying, so in this matter he also conceives of the deepest fulfillment of the existence-need in the loss of isolation. In the fusion of the open self with other open selves, in the fragile happiness of the little circle centered around Julie, in *La Nouvelle Héloïse,* or in the wider communion of the spontaneous village festivals, the self experiences itself most deeply, even as its protective walls of isolation, made necessary by the normal course of artificial social life, are for a while demolished, like the walls of Jericho, allowing the "natural" feelings to take their course, immediate and unhindered. But this is literature. It was Rousseau's dream, which he never succeeded in realizing in life, except—he thought—with Mme de Warens. That is why, for him, there remained only reverie and isolation.[72]

While occasionally Rousseau may seem to place virtue above happiness, he more generally considers it as the path to happiness.[73] He eschews self-indulgence, as in *La Nouvelle Héloïse,* and at times even sounds Cartesian, as when he writes, in *Emile et Sophie:* "I learned that the first wisdom is to want what is, and to rule one's heart according to one's destiny." His concepts of happiness assume three forms, reflecting aspects of his general philosophy. For the individual, in addition to reverie and concentration on existence, he envisions simple pleasures such as the contemplation of nature, walking, herborizing. But we must emphasize that to a large degree this is really the expression of his

---

[72] Other brief references to "existence" may be found in Barbeu du Bourg, *Petit code* [1774], s.l., 1789, pp. 26–27, and Béguelin's "Réflexions sur les plaisirs et les peines de la vie," 1787, summarized in Bartholmess, *op. cit.,* II, pp. 27–29. The entire subject would doubtless repay deeper study.

[73] See *Discours sur les sciences et les arts,* ed. Havens, pp. 102–3, 114, 157.

own defeat and withdrawal. His preference, as we have seen, is for the small, intimate group, the self-sufficient and perfectly united little community. At this stage, the self is fulfilled through a surpassing of the self. The little group stands in contrast to the sophisticated society he condemns; the latter prolongs the "personal usefulness is all" of the state of nature, and, in fact, even exacerbates the evil, since interdependence (in contrast to dependence) involves doing one's own good through the hurt of others. In the perfect unity of Clarens, there is no dissonant private will. We may speak of both a submergence and a sublimation of the self. There is both a renunciation of individual will, that is, of the quest for personal good in any way distinct from that of the group, and an opening of the self to the immediacy of true contact. Rousseau constantly celebrates the result as joy and happy contentment. Finally, there is the abstract whole of the corporate self. In the macrocosm of the abstractly conceived ideal State, as in the ideal microcosm, there is no dissonant private will, but the harmony of sublimation in the organic whole.

Virtue in the *Contrat social, Emile,* and *La Nouvelle Héloïse* is exalted. It is exalted because it is defined as a sacrifice for a larger whole. In this sacrifice, Rousseau sees the way to happiness, which can come only from the elimination of the conflict between nature and culture, between the natural man and the artificial man. To speak of giving the natural man full sway, as Diderot sometimes does, is a folly which Rousseau never considers. The conflict must be eliminated by going in the other direction. In giving themselves up, in surrendering their egoistic atomism to the collective organism, men will find happiness and the expansion of their selves, because the mutuality of the sacrifice makes a new world, a unanimous world of harmony and open consubstantiality.[74]

Rousseau defines, then, two kinds of happiness, the sufficiency of the self and the surpassing of the self. And yet he, too, is fre-

---

[74] See the whole development at the beginning of *Emile,* e.g.: "Good social institutions are those which are best able to denature man, to take away his absolute existence for himself and give him a relative one, and transport his self into the common unity, that is to say, into the social self; so that each no longer thinks of himself as an individual, but as part of the unity." Otherwise, "always in contradiction with himself, he will never be either a man or a citizen."

This also explains why Rousseau expresses opposite views about ignoring or submitting to the opinion of others. The first represents the independence of the self, the second, its integration.

quently dubious about the very possibility of happiness, when he considers the various aspects of human nature and the human condition, and especially his own life. Men cannot be happy, he tells us in the fifth *Rêverie,* for they live in the past and the future more than in the present—a present which brings at best only fleeting pleasures and which no one would wish to last forever. "As for happiness, I doubt that it is known here." Happiness would require no regrets for what has gone before, no longing for something else to come, for a filling of the vague emptiness of the heart. In the last, unfinished *Rêverie,* he declares that happiness in this world is not for man, because everything changes, including ourselves; so that "all of our plans for happiness in this life are chimeras." As there are fleeting pleasures, so there is, too, a contentment of resignation. But as for happy men, "I have seen few, perhaps none." This was the Rousseau who had written, in the second "Lettre morale": "The object of human life is man's happiness." At the close of his own life, then, he admits that the goal is well-nigh unattainable.[74a]

From the standpoint of the question of happiness, the two tales which we mentioned at the beginning of our investigation stand out, it should now be clear, in one important way as most representative of the eighteenth century. In *Candide* and *Rasselas* we see the consuming dedication to the quest for happiness which characterizes the period (in thought, as well as in life), and the pessimism and frustration which frequently accompany it. That the frustration was also a part of life is evident in the personal correspondence, as well as in much of the fiction, of the time. The purpose of life is happiness, the highest value in life is happiness, and yet the conditions of life do not permit its realization—such is the content of the consciousness of many sensitive, thinking people. The mating of these apparent contradictories in the eighteenth century, together with the undying residue of hope for some better future on earth (whence so many books offering prescriptions for happiness) form a peculiar psychological syndrome which rises out of the uncertainties and anguish of a changing—in some ways, a dying—culture, and which contributes, by a reverse influence, to the intensification of those feelings. At the same time,

---

[74a] In the *Discours sur l'inégalité* (1755), he had said men are unhappy because they prefer appearance to reality. In the *Profession de foi,* he had written, of man, "The Universe is not big enough for you."

it was an intellectual defeat; thinkers were boxed in a corner by the sensationist reduction of behavior to pleasure-pain reactions and self-interest motivation.

The first, most spontaneous expression of the eager rush to happiness naturally took the form of a legitimizing of all pleasures.[75] This defense of pleasure, or defiant encouragement to it, will continue unchecked throughout the century. "The chief business of my life has always been to indulge my senses. I never knew anything of greater importance," wrote Casanova; and we may almost take these words as a motto for the age. The *philosophes*, of course, did know of other things, despite their defense of pleasure. But the novels of the time hold the mirror to life. A considerable part of them are obsessed with seduction, lasciviousness, and the search for sensation by characters whose senses have been dulled by pleasure (even as the philosophers said); and the spiritual dimension of love, or even real passion, is lost.[75a] If we think of Descartes' propositions: that the reasoned use of will gives the greatest pleasure, that we should estimate pleasure by a rule of reason, that pleasure should be independent of bodily passion, because dependence on body introduces an imperfection—if we think of these, we shall realize that the eighteenth century has both a feeling of existential realities and a disillusionment with ideals which have carried it very far.

The eighteenth-century commitment to happiness-seeking, and in simple fact, to pleasure is heavy. Perhaps this may be considered normal and unobjectionable. The difficulty is that it became involved with moral theory. Starting as a humanistic, antireligious reaction, it led down a very long road. On the one hand, ethical theory was used to justify pleasure; conversely, upholders of hedonism strove to reconcile their *summum bonum* with morality. The resulting moral confusion is disastrous.[76] That pleas-

---

[75] Pleasure, it has been made clear, could take many forms, from sexuality and an epicurean cuisine to friendship, benevolence, or the solitude and simplicity of a contemplative country life. But wherever revolt is involved, the accent is on the former.

[75a] Doubtless eroticism was also an expression of a vaguely felt feeling of the absurd, of a *malaise*, an emptiness, a loss of meaning and destiny. The many moralizing novels are a reaction to the prevailing hedonism; they express both the middle class taste and the increasing sentimental intoxication with virtue which (as we shall shortly see) was itself called forth by its contraries. For still another view on this phenomenon, see Mauzi, *op. cit.*, p. 428.

[76] "Finally happiness became a rite, whose idea was substituted for that of beauty. Since it was the purpose of all intelligent beings, the center to which all their ac-

ure is a good is undeniable. That it is a moral good or value is something else. It is evident that some pleasures are not morally good, and that others, such as malice, are evil; to pretend otherwise is nihilism, the assertion that the fact of my pleasure is the sole value. But graver still was the conception of happiness in elementary terms of physical sensation, because such a conception betrays the complexity of the human psyche and human needs. Isolation of the affective aspect of our activity, of what may be the common factor of our acts, but not their distinguishing factor (pleasure is common to both eating and creativity) falsifies our experience.

The psychological analysis of motivation into its pleasure component, the proclamation of pleasure as guide and goal for life, its denomination as the highest good, and its influence on moral philosophy all make the establishment of objective moral values extremely difficult and problematical. Happiness and of course pleasure are in their essence, as Sartre has said, subjectivity; they cannot exist in the kingdom of objectivity. But if we are to say that all pleasures are good and all pains evil, no moral distinctions remain. As Albert Schweitzer has said, "As soon as the notion of pleasure is brought into connection with ethics, it shows disturbances, as does the magnetic needle in the neighborhood of the poles. Pleasure as such shows itself incapable in every respect of being reconciled with the demands of ethics. . . . Reflection upon the ethic which is to produce happiness is compelled at last to give up the positive notion of pleasure in any form. It has to reconcile itself to the negative notion which conceives pleasure as somehow or other a liberation from the need of pleasure. Thus the individualistic, utilitarian ethic, also called Eudaemonism, destroys itself as soon as it ventures to be consistent." [77] Respon-

---

tions were directed; since it was the initial value; since this affirmation, *I want to be happy*, was the first article of a code prior to any legislation, to any religious system; people no longer asked whether they had deserved happiness, but whether they were getting the happiness to which they had a right. Instead of, 'Am I just?', this other question: 'Am I happy?'." (P. Hazard, I, p. 31.)

[77] *Op. cit.*, pp. 35–36. Cf. E. Fromm: "How can our life be guided by a motive by which animal as well as man, the good and the bad person, the normal and the sick are motivated alike? Even if we qualify the pleasure principle by restricting it to those pleasures which do not injure the legitimate interests of others, it is hardly adequate as a guiding principle for our actions. . . . Psychoanalysis confirms the view, held by the opponents of hedonistic ethics, that the subjective experience of satisfaction is in itself deceptive and not a valid criterion of value. . . . All masochistic desires can be described as a craving for that which is harmful to the total

sible ethical thinking could not stay at the level of pure hedonism. Its attempt to create bases for moral laws which would not conflict with personal interest led to a wider utilitarianism.

II. Social Utilitarianism

Despite the power and persistence of hedonism, then, a tendency begins which will end by outweighing it, and even, in some cases, submerge the individual and his subjective satisfactions in an abstract social whole. The focus of individual good is diverted toward social good. This change was facilitated by the concept of good as happiness, rather than as self-perfection. Hedonism, remarks Reinhold Niebuhr, ostensibly has no criterion of good except pleasure, but it manages to introduce the criterion of the "greatest good to the greatest number" into its estimate of moral value, "thereby proving that moral theory is practically unanimous in preferring the general to the particular interest," however interest may be defined.[1] There is a tide, growing stronger across the years, which shifts the locus of happiness and, *pari passu,* the criterion of moral value, to the impalpable entity called the group or the whole. In this way the eighteenth century was to reach an ethical attitude corresponding to its great effort for political and social reform, and which is therefore characteristic.

A social morality had been proposed by Descartes, but its metaphysical basis and content were different, its tone static.[2] With the *philosophes* it was something entirely distinct. They, remarks Henri Peyre, "were fired by a passion for man's better future, for his happiness and for the progress of the race. They offered their contemporaries a new faith to replace an outworn creed. Man would be happy in this world, not in another one, and not individually happy working out his own salvation in fear and trembling, but through saving other men in fraternal charity along with him."[3] The connection with the decline of religious au-

---

personality. To crave that which is harmful is the very essence of mental sickness. Every neurosis thus confirms the fact that pleasure can be in contradiction to man's real interests." (*Man for Himself,* pp. 173, 179–80.)

[1] *Children of Light,* New York, 1949, pp. 72–73.

[2] Bréhier, *Histoire de la philosophie,* II, pp. 111–12.

[3] Henri Peyre, in a paper read at the Weil Institute.

thority is obvious. "With the rejection of the Church, and of transcendental justice," comments J. L. Talmon, perhaps with some overemphasis, "the State remained the sole source and sanction of morality." [4]

We have seen the extensive pessimism about the possibility of happiness (somewhat less strong for the future than for the present), and commented on the fact that a great effort for personal happiness persists nonetheless. The intellectual infatuation with social happiness was even stronger, for the goal was nebulous and undefinable, and not subject to immediate personal feeling, and so more difficult to disprove or be disillusioned about. It became more and more clear that if each sought his own pleasure or happiness as the highest good, regardless of all else, society would become a battlefield and end in chaos, in addition to morality itself being destroyed. (There were important exceptions. Mandeville, the Physiocrats, and Adam Smith thought that if each worked exclusively for his own selfish good, the general good would *naturally* ensue.) [5] But if the locus of value were shifted from the individual to the group, then, it seemed, selfishness would be surpassed (but not destroyed); morality and society would be saved. This was the grand solution. Even religious people could concur in this utilitarianism. Bishop Berkeley, for instance, is almost an epitome in this regard. Starting from a naïve form of egoistic hedonism (good and evil are what satisfies our self-love), he then posits the existence of God and the rational obligation to obey his will, and finally concludes that God's will is not "the private good of this or that man, nation or age, but the general well-being of all men . . . which God designs should be procured by the concurring actions of each individual." [6] Secular moralists could not help realizing that their own criterion for judging conduct, the amount of pleasure or pain which results from an act, led to the inference that the act which produced the greatest amount of pleasure (the most pleasure for the most people) was the best. The many who did not really believe in a state of nature, but thought man naturally social, could also conclude that since values are to be founded on man's nature, and he is a

---

[4] *The Rise of Totalitarian Democracy*, p. 4.

[5] Halévy erroneously states that the theory of natural identity of interests begins with Adam Smith. *La Formation du radicalisme philosophique*, I, p. 21.

[6] *Passive Obedience*, in Berkeley, *Essay, Principles, Dialogues*, p. xxxiv–xxxv.

social being, then the good of society is his good. At any rate, be it by nature or by will, men were fated to live together and share a common destiny. The facts of dependence and interdependence made it impossible, according to optimists like Shaftesbury, Pope, and d'Holbach, to dissociate one's own happiness from that of others (a thesis which was denied or even reversed by pessimists and amoralists).

We can perceive the drift to social utilitarianism early in the century. Shaftesbury seems to have it in mind in his theory of symmetry: "the proportionate and regular State is the truly *prosperous* and natural in every Subject." [7] For Hutcheson, the foundation of moral sense is benevolence, or usefulness to the public.[8] Butler conceives of justice, veracity, and the common good as comprehensive ethical ends. Wollaston affirms that happiness is the end of society, and what makes most men happy is best. Any act that favors self over everybody else is wrong.[9] "It is manifest," proclaims Mandeville, "that when we pronounce Actions good or evil, we only regard the Hurt or Benefit the Society receives from them, and not the Person who commits them." [10] In fact, a government may commit evil in order that good may come of it—the "evil" then *is* good. Nothing beneficial can be wrong.[11]

In France, Rémond de Saint-Mard asks, "What do the motives we impute to men's actions matter, provided they are good, that is, useful to Society?" [12] Father Buffier warns us that the command, "Do unto others," is not so simple as it seems. A judge condemning a criminal to death would want mercy himself. Justice and right are above this maxim, form a higher maxim, which is "to seek our own advantage in everything, united with that of the men with whom we have to live." What furthers the common good is right.[13]

The superior validity of social over personal welfare (and the latter's dependence on the former) is the object lesson of the story of the Troglodytes in Montesquieu's *Lettres persanes*. Virtue, he

---

[7] *Characteristicks*, III, pp. 180–85.

[8] *Op. cit.*, p. 199. However Hutcheson holds pleasure-pain reactions to be immediate, and so not strictly dependent on advantage or detriment (p. 4). According to Halévy (*op. cit.*, pp. 16–17), moral sense theorists may be considered as utilitarians, because the principle of sympathy involves a spontaneous identification of private and general interest in the consciousness.

[9] *Op. cit.*, pp. 128–29.

[10] *Op. cit.*, I, p. 244.

[11] *Ibid.*, I, p. lx.

[12] *Oeuvres*, Amsterdam, 1750, I, p. 337.

[13] *Traité de la société civile*, 1726, pp. 27–32.

states simply in the *Esprit des lois,* in a republic, is love of the republic. His explanations make it clear (although he claims not to be speaking of moral virtue) that he means the preferring of the general interest to the particular.[14]

Vauvenargues is a somewhat contradictory writer. There are times when he sounds like a firm utilitarian, as when he declares that nothing is good or evil unless it tends to the advantage or disadvantage of society as a whole. "Who says 'society' says a body which subsists by the union of its divers members and fuses the private interest in the general interest; that is the foundation of all morality. . . . By what reason does an individual dare to sacrifice so many others to himself, without society being able by his ruin, to secure public peace?" [15] No one could have put it more clearly than Voltaire: "Virtue and vice, moral good and evil, is then in any country what is useful or harmful to society. . . . Virtue is the habit of doing those things which please men, and vice the habit of doing those things which displease men." [16] The passage is noteworthy for two reasons. The second part of it anticipates Hume. And, at this early period when Natural Law is strongest in Voltaire's thinking, we can see its fusion with utilitarianism: if there are certain universals, it is only *because* they are universally useful.[17] We should also note Voltaire's line in the seventh *Discours sur l'homme:* "To be good only for oneself is to be good for nothing." Good acts are those which lead to pleasure or to other advantages for our fellow citizens. All our ideas of justice, Voltaire explains, arise from the social utility of acts, in

[14] Bk. V., chap. II. Later, Montesquieu makes an important restriction for property (Bk. XXVI, chap. XV), and we must also take into consideration such factors as his belief in Natural Law and his attack against slavery. Maupertuis, in his "Eloge de Montesquieu," rejects the "obscure" principle of Natural Law and suggests a calculus of individual sacrifice according to the amount of happiness lost and gained. (*Oeuvres,* III, p. 401 ff.)

[15] *Oeuvres,* I, pp. 76–77 ("Du Bien et du mal moral"). He also says that "preference of general to personal interest is the only definition worthy of virtue and which should determine its meaning. . . . It is equally clear that humanity is better than inhumanity, that it is more likable, more useful, consequently more estimable." (*Ibid.*)

[16] *Traité de métaphysique* (1734), ed. H. T. Patterson, p. 57.

[17] We have already commented on the dilemma of Natural Law and utilitarianism in Voltaire. For another interesting example of a combination of formalism and utilitarianism, see Elie Luzac, *L'Homme plus que machine* (in La Mettrie, *Oeuvres philosophiques,* Amsterdam, 1774, III, pp. 190–92). The persistence of the dilemma in Voltaire can be seen in his *Philosophe ignorant* (1766). Certain acts are always, inherently, right or wrong. Then he asks: "but if I know for sure that the man to whom I owe two million will use it to enslave my country, am I obliged to return this fatal weapon to him? . . . in general, I need keep an oath only when no harm results." (XXVI, pp. 49–81.)

conformity with the laws we have established to this end. No act has an intrinsic or formal value; its effect on men alone confers value on it.[18] But suppose some men decide that what is of value to them is precisely what a society forbids? In these cases, force alone decides that the general good must be respected above personal good. Such men will be hanged, even as we shoot wolves. Voltaire thus seems to admit an ultimate arbitrariness in the morality of social good, or virtue, since there are elements in human nature which deny it and which it must deny by will or force. However, as a believer in Natural Law, he would call these "pathological deviations."

Hume considers utility the standard of all ethical values, in virtue of the fact that this is what the impartial benevolent spectator would approve; but he is referring to the general utility rather than self-interest. Like Voltaire, he endeavors to avoid moral skepticism by claiming an empirical basis for the preference of social virtues. Unlike most of the French philosophers, he attributes our approval of utility not to self-interest, but rather to disinterested benevolence, or the desire for the happiness of society, a feeling which is innate in all human beings.[19] But Hume holds utility to be superior to justice, and in fact, its only basis.[20]

The abbé Yvon's article "Bon," in the *Encyclopédie*, distinguishes three kinds of good. There is "animal good," or proper adaptation to function (an idea which Diderot will incorporate into his aesthetic theories); "reasoned good," or virtue, "the good which is beautiful," that is, the accordance of conduct with essential, immutable rules (Natural Law); and the useful, which is "the only good that has ascendency over our hearts." [21] In "Ac-

---

[18] This was the common opinion of partisans of a secular morality, throughout the century. Cf. Rivarol: "What we must especially avoid in morals, is to place virtue in indifferent acts, such as fasting, hair shirts, austerities: none of that can be useful to other men." (*Pensées inedites*, 1836, p. 13.)

[19] *Enquiry concerning the Principles of Morals*, Aiken, p. 208 ff. Hume's theory combines many elements, and he also claims, like Hutcheson, that some qualities are immediately agreeable, without regard to utility (p. 144).

[20] *Ibid.*, p. 182 ff. Unlike others, however, Hume, while considering utility to be the basis of value, makes moral judgment rest on intention—the sentiment which causes us to prefer what is useful (pp. 263, 266, 207n.). Moral goodness, then, cannot be identified with whatever conforms to the greater happiness principle (p. xxxiv). For a similar distinction made by Marmontel, see *Leçons de morale, Oeuvres*, XVII, pp. 210–12.

[21] Both Yvon and the abbé Mallet ("Charité") agree that it is chimerical to speak of loving God except in our own interest, that is, inasmuch as he has power to benefit or hurt us.

tion," Yvon writes: "Moral actions are nothing but men's voluntary actions considered in relation to the imputation of their effects on the common life." Like Hume, however, he keeps the moral "quality" in the will. Also in the *Encyclopédie*, Faiguet, in the article "Usure," puts forward utility as the touchstone of justice: "what is reciprocally useful is necessarily equitable. . . . The reciprocal advantage of the contracting parties is the common measure of what should be called 'just'; for there can be no injustice where there is no damage." And the author of the article "Philosophe" writes: "Civil society is, so to speak, the only divinity which he [the *philosophe*] recognizes on earth; he worships it, he honors it . . . by a sincere desire not to be a useless or harmful member."

Even La Mettrie may be spoken of as a utilitarian! True, everything is arbitrary, made by men, and there is no moral right or wrong, vice or virtue in itself. But society, arbitrarily if you will, does impose its standards. From society's own viewpoint, "Everything that is useful to society is [a virtue], the rest is its phantom." [22] Burlamaqui, a Natural Law theorist, claims to distinguish the just from the useful; but he also says they are related and derive from reason's approbation of whatever leads to real happiness. Little interested in good will, he defines virtue as the *habit* of actions in conformity with laws and duty.[23] For Morelly, what is useful to society is all that matters.[24] Condillac asserts that the morality of our acts consists of only one thing, conformity with the laws.[25] "It seems," writes d'Alembert, "that we can define injustice, or moral evil, which is the same thing, very exactly, as what tends to hurt society by disturbing the physical well-being of its members." [26]

Diderot is one of the most complex figures of the century. He is not fundamentally (that is, in the context of real life) a hedonist

---

[22] *Discours sur le bonheur, Oeuvres*, II, p. 127. Also: "Education alone then has improved natural tendencies; she it is who has turned men to men's profit and advantage. . . . Such is the origin of virtue; the public good is its source." La Mettrie's nihilism again lurks underneath: virtues and vices are politically instituted; otherwise "the edifice could not stand up and would fall into ruins. . . . Besides, convention and arbitrary value constitute the sole merit and demerit of what is called vice and virtue." (*Ibid.*, pp. 18–20.)

[23] *Op. cit.*, II, pp. 152–55; I, pp. 180–82.

[24] *Code de la nature*, I, III, pp. 64–65.

[25] *La Logique, Oeuvres philosophiques*, II, pp. 383–84.

[26] *Elémens de philosophie, Oeuvres*, I, p. 209. He also proposed drawing up a catechism of utilitarian moral responsibility (I, p. 234).

in ethical theory, though in his radical speculative works he extends hedonism into the zone of nihilism; we shall return to that aspect of his thought in the next chapter. Fundamentally he is a social utilitarian. Social experience, he holds, makes moral beings of us; and it is the task of education "to perfect the natural aptitude, if it is good, to stifle or lose it, if it is bad." [27] In *Le Rêve de d'Alembert,* Diderot's spokesman, Bordeu, declares that the idea of virtue must be changed "into the idea of beneficence," as determined by society; consequently, one can judge people only as "fortunately or unfortunately born." [28] "Good" and "right" refer then to the generality, surpassing the natural demand of dissonant individuals for happiness. Diderot knew, however, as did Rousseau, that the natural is never (or has never been) replaced by the cultural, and that men suffer a constant struggle between two coexisting urges or laws. In this struggle, society is right. Like Voltaire, La Mettrie, and many others, he makes it clear in his letter to Landois that vice and virtue do not exist, except as society may decide; and he who will not conform must be severed, like the gangrened limb.[29] What remains is to provide as strong a motive as possible to induce men to behave in the desired way. "It is not thoughts," he writes to Mme Necker, "it is actions that distinguish the good man and the wicked." While Diderot's utilitarianism stands in clear opposition to his moments of hedonistic nihilism, it is in equal if less dramatic disagreement with the apriorism of his Natural Law thinking which we examined earlier. According to Cassirer, Diderot underwent an evolution from apriorism to utilitarianism. Reference to our previous discussion would indicate rather a persistence of parallel currents, with the more frequent emphasis on the empirical and "scientific" approach.[30]

Happiness, for Jean-Jacques Rousseau, is the goal of activity.[31]

[27] *Oeuvres,* XVIII, p. 103; II, p. 410.

[28] II, p. 176.

[29] XIX, p. 432 ff. Diderot also extends this utilitarianism to smaller collectivities and condones a woman's infidelity for the purpose of improving her family's position. (*Correspondence,* ed. G. Roth, IV, pp. 120–21.) It is true that his attitude towards sexual morality is also involved here.

[30] See Cassirer, *op. cit.,* pp. 246–47. Cassirer seems unaccountably to confuse Diderot's dictum, "Let nature rule . . . without conventional hindrances" with social utilitarianism.

[31] See Note 32, pp. 171–72, in G. R. Havens' critical edition of the *Discours sur les sciences et les arts.* Rousseau probably values virtue above happiness, but he always considers it as the instrument of happiness.

Because of his concept of happiness, he places the locus of value (when he is not concerned with himself) in the group, large or small, rather than in the individual. The essential problem in the State is to make particular wills bend to the general will: "as virtue is only this conformity of the particular will to the general, to say the same thing in a word, make virtue reign." [32] In a fragment he writes:

> When we contemplate with a philosophical eye the interplay of all the parts of this vast universe, we soon perceive that the greatest beauty of each of the pieces which compose it does not lie in itself; and that it was not formed to remain alone and independent, but to concur with all the others to the perfection of the whole machine.
>
> It is the same in the moral order. The vices and virtues of each man are not relative to him alone. Their greatest relation is with society, and what they are in regard to the general order constitutes their essence and their character. [33]

Rousseau was in fact, as Schinz once noted, that kind of a utilitarian we now call a pragmatist. Thus in *La Nouvelle Héloïse*, he is entirely willing to compromise with his principles of equality and truthfulness in order to achieve the desired ends of a co-operative society, through the illusion of equality and the willing surrender of egoism. Truth is of value, but only insofar as it is conducive to happiness for men. [34] The civil religion of the *Contrat social* is a matter of utility, not truth. If virtue is relative to the welfare of the social group, so also is the happiness of individuals who have lost their natural independence. Just as the individual will is absorbed into that of a social "body," so the evanescent subjectivity of his happiness is replaced, as a criterion of judgment, by something more solid and objectively verifiable, public happiness, which, however, will necessarily reflect that of its components.

Where is the happy man? If he exists, who knows it? Happiness is not pleasure; it does not consist in a passing modification of the soul, but in a permanent and entirely internal feeling, which can be judged by no one except the person who experi-

---

[32] *Economie politique*, Vaughan, *The Political Writings of Jean-Jacques Rousseau*, I, p. 248. Also: "Wickedness is at bottom only an opposition of the private will to the public" (p. 278).

[33] *Ibid.*, I, p. 338.

[34] See L. G. Crocker, "The Problem of Truth and Falsehood in the Enlightenment," *Journal of the History of Ideas*, XIV, pp. 586–87.

ences it. No one then can decide with certainty that another is happy, nor consequently establish definite signs of individual happiness. But it is not the same with political societies; their good and their harm are all apparent and visible; their internal feeling is a public feeling . . . and one can without temerity judge their moral being. . . . Make man one, and you will make him as happy as he can be. Give him all to the State, or let him be completely himself.[35]

Rousseau's thinking on this matter is entirely consistent with the structure of his general system.

The most thorough-going and systematic utilitarian, and the most influential, was Helvétius. Speaking of ethics, he avers that "the true object of that science is the happiness of the greatest number." [36] This is purely a calculus of the greatest amount of good, for he had started with physical sensation and the egoistic pursuit of self-interest as the criteria of moral judgment.[37] Helvétius decisively eliminates intention as the basis of judgment, since no moral intention can exist.[38]

Helvétius, we know, considers justice as subsequent to law; and law is a utilitarian formulation.[39] The summary of Discours II of *De l'Esprit* speaks of "the same *self-interest,* which presides over judgments we make of actions, and makes us look at them as *virtuous, vicious* or *permissible,* according as they are *useful, harmful* or *indifferent* to the public. . . ." [40] The public weal is more important than any so-called morality. "The same actions may then become successively useful and harmful to a people, and deserve in turn the name of virtuous or vicious, without the idea of virtue changing. . . ." [41] For laws to be good, they must con-

---

[35] *Fragments,* Vaughan, *op. cit.,* I, pp. 325–26.

[36] *De l'Homme,* IX, pp. 140–41.

[37] *Ibid.,* VIII, pp. 56–57, *De l'Esprit,* Discours II.

[38] *De l'Esprit,* pp. 240, also 374–75: "The virtuous man is not then he who sacrifices his pleasures, habits and strongest passions to the public, since such a man is impossible; but he whose strongest passion is so much in conformity with the general interest, that he is almost always necessarily determined to be virtuous."

To this Hayer replied that, according to Helvétius, for an action to be virtuous it would have to conform both to personal and to public interest. If there is opposition, personal interest necessarily wins out. (*Op. cit.,* VII, pp. 65–69, 264.) The weakness in Helvétius' system which Hayer here implies was the one which Sade was to seize upon and to exploit: he does not justify (i.e., legitimize in moral terms) the supplanting of the private interest by the general, nor, consequently, any sacrifice in favor of others of the real good experienced by the sentient and self-centered individual.

[39] *De l'Homme,* p. 202 and discussion in preceding chapter.

[40] For a defense of utility, and definitions, see *De l'Esprit,* pp. 45–46, 73–80.

[41] *Ibid.,* pp. 154–58. This does not exclude, for Helvétius or other utilitarians, the possibility of universals (pp. 185–86).

form to the principle of public welfare, that is to say, the happiness of the greatest number, "a principle which contains all of
ethics and legislation." [42] The universal principle of self-interest
operates, then, on the three levels of organization: the individual,
the group, and the whole community. The last, being the most
inclusive, is the final criterion.

Helvétius pretends to scientific method and is seeking an objective, measurable unit of value. However he constantly confuses
subjective moral judgment with objective moral value. To quote
only one instance: "No matter where we look, we shall always see
self-interest presiding over the distribution which the public
makes of its esteem." [43] It is obvious that even if utility is the sole
criterion of value, the public is not always the best judge of that
value, and that, assuming it were the best judge, it does not always
accord its esteem and rewards in the light of the principle of
utility. But according to Helvétius, we have only to agree on what
is useful, and then we shall have agreement on morals and jurisprudence, and the happy society will ensue by the very necessity
of natural law.

With d'Holbach we again have the juxtaposition or unification
of the private and the public in virtue and in happiness.

> The virtuous man is he whose actions tend constantly to the
> well-being of his fellows; the vicious man is he whose conduct
> tends toward the unhappiness of those with whom he lives;
> from which his own unhappiness usually results. Whatever gives
> us true and permanent happiness is reasonable.[44]

D'Holbach, as we shall see, justifies the imposition of general
utility by making personal happiness dependent on it—since no
real sacrifice is possible to beings necessarily motivated by self-
interest. For the same reason, actions which tend to public happiness necessarily excite approbation—except in those "whose
passions or false opinions force them to judge them in a way which
does not conform to the nature of things. Everyone acts and
judges according to his own nature and his own true or false ideas
about happiness." [45] Both the good man and the bad are necessarily
determined by their differing natures, and so we have no way of
distinguishing between them except by society's judgment of the

---

[42] *Ibid.,* pp. 161, 175.
[43] *Ibid.,* p. 122.
[44] *Système de la nature,* I, p. 145.
[45] *Ibid.,* I, pp. 256–57. See also I, p. 337.

utility of their acts. There is no "moral" criterion, except this.

Little of significance is added during the rest of the century, though there are innumerable repetitions and confirmations.[46]

It is clear that in essence the utilitarian position is quite opposed to that of Natural Law. It does not bind us to ask "whether we are obligated to avoid legislation which violates the convictions of mankind," that is, ultimate principles of right and judgment.[47] If the criterion of virtue is social good, it is an empirical criterion, except insofar as we consider social living to have essential qualities and relationships. There can be, on this view, no virtue before society, nor in any "essential" human nature, nor in a so-called Natural Law (unless Natural Law is conceived of as meaning necessary social drives plus necessary experiential development in universal forms). We may speak of a gradual invasion of Natural Law theory by utilitarianism. Its viewpoints, by infiltration, transfuse and transform Natural Law, without its adherents being aware of it, with a resultant hybridization.

Utilitarianism was also a logical result of Newtonianism and the new science that arose in the seventeenth century. No longer did one seek the intelligibility of a law, but its constancy and predictability, with the aim of a practical science in mind.[48] By applying this method to the individual and society, eighteenth-century moralists proposed to determine the simplest and most

---

[46] Some additional references follow. Terrasson places moral duty above personal interest, but beneath the welfare "of States or the Public" (*op. cit.,* p. 51). L. de Beausobre, in *Le Pirrhonisme du sage* (Berlin, 1754): "The truly virtuous man considers only the choice of the best, and that best is always the good of the State" (p. 81). Cardinal de Polignac (*op. cit.,* I, pp. 57–58): "Since the universe is neither the dwelling nor the inheritance of a single man, and all have an equal right to enjoy it, the public interest is preferable to the private, and the happiness of all to that of one." Duclos, in one of the most interesting French attempts at establishing a scale of values (*Considérations,* pp. 333–48), speaks of the "extent of utility." Something whose utility "is common to a greater number of men merits greater esteem." Right and wrong are merely matters of public interest. "It is personal interest which makes crimes, when it is opposed to the common interest." Naigeon decrees: "I consent to name virtue only what procures real advantages to society (Discours préliminaire, 1782, pp. 87–88, *Le Militaire philosophe,* Londres, 1768, p. 165). Saint-Lambert praises Helvétius for having demonstrated that morals have been retarded by the habit of attaching virtues to actions "which are useful to no one," and of separating "private for general interest" (*Analyse de l'Histoire,* Discours préliminaire, in *Oeuvres philosophiques,* An IX, I, p. 35). Justice, Rivarol avers, is only the means to the end of self-preservation: "the end always has priority over the means; since indeed there are occasions when the State might be ruined if it consulted justice." (*Pensées inédites,* pp. 51–52.)

[47] Bredvold, *op. cit.,* p. 125.

[48] Philosophers did continue to seek the intelligibility of psychological, moral and political laws.

general basic law or laws which would explain the phenomena and permit their control. It was still a matter of extending our power over nature, into which man was completely integrated— without transcendence, we should note, although the very possibility of conceiving and accomplishing such a task is itself the sign of transcendence. Thus the constitution of a moral and political science is undertaken, analogous in its experimental method and exactness to the Newtonian physics. Utilitarianism is a Newtonianism, with the law of universal gravitation replaced by sensualism, determinism, association of ideas, and the principle of utility.[49] The principle of utility (welfare, happiness) was at first considered chiefly in regard to the individual. To repeat what Gay—and so many others—wrote, "Obligatory acts are those which lead to happiness." Approbation was reduced to "indications of reason relative to personal happiness." [50] The essential step, as we have seen, was the displacement of the locus of value from the individual to the community. It was essential for two reasons. It made possible the creation of a social utilitarianism, as distinct from egoistic hedonism. To those for whom morals and virtue were themselves vital, as distinguished from the goal of happiness, it seemed the sole possibility of preserving those values against the corrosion of nihilism.[51] For without this interposition, the other operative factors in the ethical climate—the weakening of Natural Law and of the belief in future rewards and punishments, plus the legalization of natural necessity for seeking pleasure— were headed in the direction of moral anarchism.

III. Virtue and Happiness

The philosophies of hedonism or eudaemonism, and of social utilitarianism, sometimes held conjointly by the same men, constitute a dichotomy which the eighteenth century was compelled

[49] The necessity of embracing psychological determinism is evident. In order to arrive at constant, universal principles of human nature and conduct, the constancy and predictability of causation is required.

[50] Others will replace or supplement reason by feeling or association of ideas (conditioned reflex), but Helvétius and Bentham will propose the direction of men by reason, and consequently, the liberation of ethics from sentiment.

[51] The preceding paragraph is based in part on Elie Halévy's classic work, *La Formation du radicalisme philosophique.*

to resolve. If self-interest is the only motive and happiness the only goal of conduct, and if, simultaneously, the locus of value is placed outside the particular sentient individual, a reconciliation becomes urgent. Moreover, if virtue is defined in terms of happiness, and if it is assumed that there is no natural impulse or reason to prefer the interest of others to our own, the amoralist must perforce triumph, unless it can be shown that there is an indissoluble, invariable identity between the two terms, virtue and happiness. This was the central problem of ethics for eighteenth-century thinkers, one with which they were faced as a result of their analysis of human nature and their reduction of moral experience to reactions of pleasure and pain. "It seems reasonable," writes a modern philosopher, "and in accord with common sense to maintain that each person, when faced with alternative courses of action, should calculate his own good and choose accordingly. But it also appears reasonable that he should take account of the good of others and choose the alternative which promises that greater good to all the world. The attempt to reconcile these two points of view has led to endless subtleties and sub terfuges. So astute a moral philosopher as Henry Sidgwick concluded that the only reconciliation of these two methods lay in divine sanctions. The dispute is settled if we have faith in God's justice." [1] Many eighteenth-century writers, however, believed they could solve this problem in secular, naturalistic terms.

Two approaches, related but not identical, were followed by them: enlightened self-interest, and what we shall call the virtue happiness equivalence. The similarity is obvious. In both cases we are summoned to make an apparent sacrifice of immediate good which turns out to be a gain. The difference, though less obvious is significant. The virtue-happiness equivalence assumes that an act of virtue possesses a quality which is in itself happiness-produc ing, and immediately so. Enlightened self-interest calls for a rational calculation of ultimate gain; it concedes that the virtuous act may not itself produce happiness.

Enlightened self-interest impressed many thinkers as the logica and effective solution to the dichotomy of self-interest and social interest, and as the gateway to an effective naturalistic ethics Social utilitarianism by itself was insufficient. If we expected men to act for the benefit of others, and particularly that of the com

[1] E. T. Mitchell, *A System of Ethics*, New York, 1950, p. 77.

munity as an abstract whole, we should then be returning to an intentional and altruistic morality. Such abnegation could not be expected of men, without having recourse to divine sanctions, which were held to be neither true nor efficacious. Enlightened self-interest seemed like the magic door which avoided all this. We have only to make men realize that when they choose the act that is best for all (or for most), they are acting in their own interest. Perhaps that is not always true, some conceded, but it could be made to be true if legislation and society were properly reformed, so as to be in accord with human nature, desires, and needs. The utilitarians, writes Albert Schweitzer, became convinced "that nature itself has bound up together what is ethical and what is advantageous both to the individual and the community." [2] If the self is a social self, is it not clear that its good could not be secured at the cost of the social unit of which it was a part? However, although nature may have made this link, it was certainly not a law which was naturally or spontaneously operative. The work of reason was required, as the phrase *"enlightened self-interest,"* or the French equivalent, "interest properly *understood,"* indicates.

Leibniz had a concept of enlightened self-interest which was quite different from that of the eighteenth century. He believed that if we loved ourselves in an enlightened way, then, by realizing our own perfection, we would also realize that of others; the more enlightened our self-love becomes, the more disinterested it becomes.[3] The eighteenth-century idea differed in two ways: a sacrifice was involved, and that sacrifice was motivated by interest rather than by disinterestedness. However the act itself was a "disinterested" one, and in the eighteenth-century view, that alone mattered. The roots of this concept are found in the seventeenth century, although it did not then achieve significant acceptance. Curiously, we find it in religious writers who despaired of human nature, and especially in the Jansenist, Nicole:

> We may conclude from all that has been said that to reform the world entirely, that is to say, to banish all vices and coarse disorders, and to make men happy in this very life, it would only be necessary in default of charity to give them all an enlightened self-love, which will enable them to discern their true interest,

[2] *Op. cit.*, pp. 56–57.
[3] *Monadology*, ed. Latta, pp. 148, 285.

and go towards it in the ways that right reason would reveal. However corrupted that society might be within and in the sight of God, there would be nothing better regulated from the outside, nothing more civil, more just, for, being animated and moved by self-love, self-love does not show itself; being entirely void of charity, one would everywhere see only the forms and traits of charity.[4]

It would not be possible to state more perfectly the illusion of so many eighteenth-century writers that men can be made to behave morally through a rational understanding of their true and ultimate interests; nor to reveal more dramatically their renunciation of the hope for a moral existence, except from the external viewpoint of the conformity of action.[5]

The doctrine of enlightened self-interest was developed in England, as well as in France, but received considerably less emphasis there. As early as 1672, Cumberland, making of the common good "the measure of every lesser good and evil, and of their comparative value," declared that this end would provide the "greatest practicable individual happiness." [6] We find the theory threading itself through Shaftesbury; though in a way it betrays the moral sense theory, the resultant happiness for him is more an accompaniment or sequel, an added factor, rather than the incentive itself. Shaftesbury lays especial emphasis on a refutation of the apparent opposition between self-interest and the general interest. His purpose is to show that "to be well affected towards the public interest and one's own is not only consistent, but inseparable." [7] Nevertheless, such dependency on reason does not accord with the *natural* tendency to virtue of the moral sense theory, although, as he usually does, Shaftesbury so interprets human nature that nature and reason coincide.[8] Butler's theory, as we can see in the first Sermon, at one point entertains the notion of enlightened self-interest.[9] Chubb accepts the hypothesis

---

[4] *Essais de morale*, 1713, p. 177.

[5] Cf. Ameline (1667): "Those who think only of themselves and their own interests hurt both themselves and others"; reason shows us that if we consider ourselves as part of the social body, we also share in "all the goods which are common to that body, without being deprived thereby of any of the goods which belong to us." (*Op. cit.*, pp. 217–20.)

[6] *A Treatise of the Laws of Nature*, London, 1729, pp. 62, 214, 224, 273–74, 277, 342.

[7] *Characteristicks*, II, p. 77. See also II, pp. 80–81, 175–76.

[8] Cf. B. Willey, *op. cit.*, p. 71 ff.

[9] He holds, however, that even if enlightened self-interest cannot be substantiated, altruism is still right.

warmly.[10] Priestley adopts it as a basic part of his theories: "when our interest is perfectly understood, it will be found to be best promoted by those actions which are dictated by a regard to the good of others. . . ."[11]

The enlightened self-interest theory developed slowly but substantially in France. Its essential theme was always the same. "Virtue seems to be a preference of others to oneself," wrote Abbadie. "I say that it seems to be, because it is really certain that virtue is only a way of loving oneself, much more noble and sensible than all others."[12] The social and economic decadence of the country pressed home on open-minded, responsible thinkers the organic quality of social welfare. Boisguillebert showed that even the privileged classes suffered from the general impoverishment, and he urged that, in their own interest, they give up some of their tax advantages. The privileged classes, significantly, were not sufficiently "enlightened." Saint-Evremond also urged an intelligent calculation: "To make oneself happy with less trouble, and to be happy with security, without fearing to be disturbed in one's happiness, we must, milord, act so that others are happy with us."[13] Many, apparently, would not make this calculation, although they were urged to it by writers of quite different outlooks and opinions. Le Maître de Claville recommends it to his readers.[14] Fréret defines virtue as "habitual tendencies toward the happiness and utility of those with whom we live in society, by the practice of which we engage them to care about our welfare in return."[15] Vauvenargues expressed it in a cynical maxim, "The

[10] "Some Short Reflections on Virtue and Happiness," in *A Collection of Tracts*, L., 1730. Man is designed for happiness, but in society "when he pursues his own happiness with strict regard to the common good, then he is in the most proper and likely way to obtain it," etc.

[11] *Institutes of Natural and Revealed Religion*, Birmingham, 1782, I, p. 94. The rewards are both those of conscience and the "good offices of others in return" (p. 107). Hume could not accept this theory because he believed in the multiplicity of motivation; people do have benevolent motives. Hume, moreover, like Butler, did not use happiness as a definition of good, but as a necessary condition. Good is what the disinterested benevolent spectator would approve; we may assume that he would approve what leads to happiness, but this is only an empirically corroborated supposition derived from reflection on our conduct.

[12] *Op. cit.*, p. 204.

[13] Quoted by Lanson, *op. cit.*, p. 719.

[14] *Traité du vrai mérite*, 1737, II, p. 192.

[15] *Oeuvres*, III, p. 2; also *ibid.*, pp. 9–10. This is what he terms a universal ethic based on reason and human nature. With good laws, "Every man who reflects about himself will be forced to recognize the necessity of virtue in order to be happy in this world," since he himself needs justice and esteem and protection. (Pp. 85–86.)

usefulness of virtue is so manifest, that the wicked practice it out of self-interest." [16]

Montesquieu, like Shaftesbury, considers altruistic motives insufficient. His allegory of the Troglodytes shows that self-interest cannot be avoided; while every action should not be a matter of cold calculation, self-interest, properly directed, is the practical basis of society.[17] The good survivors of the holocaust of selfishness teach their children "that the self-interest of individuals is always identical with the common interest; that to want to dissociate oneself, is to want to ruin oneself; that virtue is not something that should be hard for us; that we must not look upon it as a painful exercise; and that justice to others is charity to ourselves." [18]

Morelly makes the enlightened calculus an instinctive reaction, which only our unnatural society, with its vicious institution of property, has perverted.[19] Duclos is optimistic. What we need, he assures us, is to prove to men "that their own happiness depends on their loving each other. They can be shown that their glory and interest lie in the practice of their duties." [20] D'Alembert, in a systematic exposé of his moral theory and scale of values, defines virtue as the sacrifice of one's own welfare to the needs of others. But isn't this against nature? he asks. "Of course," he replies, "no natural or positive law can oblige us to love others more than ourselves; that heroism, if such an absurd feeling may be so termed, cannot be found in the human heart; but the enlightened love of our own happiness indicates as goods preferable to all others peace with ourselves and the favor of our fellows. . . . Thus the enlightened love of ourselves is the principle of every moral sacrifice." [21] D'Alembert proceeds to calculate the extent of sacrifices that are necessary or advisable.

The Physiocrats did not follow this theory, holding instead that the unrestricted promotion of one's own good, limited by the

[16] *Oeuvres morales*, 1874, III, p. 96 (Maxime 403). See also, among the earlier writers, Richer d'Aube, *op. cit.*, xxviii–xxix; Varennes, *Les Hommes*, pp. 16–19; Paradis de Moncrif, *Oeuvres*, 1751, II, pp. 308–16.

[17] See A. Crisafulli, "Montesquieu's Story of the Troglodytes," *PMLA*, 52:372–92, 1943.

[18] *Lettres persanes*, Lettre XII.

[19] *Code de la nature*, pp. 173, 262–64.

[20] *Considérations*, p. 9.

[21] *Elémens de philosophie, Oeuvres*, I, p. 212 ff. When D'Alembert says that "disinterestedness is the highest moral virtue," he is referring, of course, to action and not to intent. See also, pp. 207–8.

natural laws of free competition, would best further the public weal. Adam Smith also entertained this reverse notion, but conjointly makes moral demands in the name of enlightened self-interest.[22] Turgot averred that morals depend on "self-love regulated by justice, which is itself only a very enlightened self-love," but on the whole he is closer to the Physiocrats.[23]

The penetration of enlightened self-interest theory among religious apologists is insignificant. Although it corresponds to the theory of exclusive motivation by self-interest, which certainly had its antecedents in the Christian doctrine of depravity, Christian writers felt they were on safer grounds by promising the rewards in heaven rather than on earth. One does meet with occasional references. We must persuade men, wrote Marie Huber in 1738, that their duty is their interest; true spirituality's purpose is intelligent self-love, and religion and virtue are justified by their usefulness.[24] If only we reflect, says Boudier de Villemaire, we realize that our legitimate self-love must not interfere with that of others.[25]

Voltaire, too, pays little attention to this theory, preferring Natural Law as an exhortation and positive law as a compelling motivation. Yet it is to some extent implied in his concept of virtue as obedience to law, which he does not assume to be a form of devotion or altruism. It is also implicit in his drive to enlighten men. Voltaire, however, does not really attempt to set forth any clear statement of the moral problem and its solution. While this may be due in part to his aversion to systematic thinking, the fundamental reason, in greater likelihood, is his pessimism. Unlike the systematizers and revolutionaries, he does not really believe that enough social reform and enough enlightenment can be achieved to offset men's ferocious egoism. Sometimes he likes to say that evil comes from what society has done to men, especially when he is attacking the Christian dogma of original sin. But he knows better; he knows that men have made society in their own image.

---

[22] *The Wealth of Nations*, Bk. V, chap. 1, part 3.

[23] *Oeuvres*, I, p. 311.

[24] *Lettres sur la religion essentielle à l'homme*, quoted by A. Monod, *De Pascal à Chateaubriand*, 1916, p. 326. See also Terrasson, *op. cit.*, p. 42.

[25] *L'Irréligion dévoilée*, pp. 112–13, and by same author, *L'Andrométrie*, 1753, p. 20. See also Para du Phanjas, *Principes*, II, pp. 185–86; Gérard, *op. cit.*, I, pp. 283–85; Chiniac, *op. cit.*, I, p. 120.

Voltaire's cynical friend, Frederick the Great, does claim allegiance. Asking what virtue is, he replies: "It is a fortunate constitution of the mind which leads us to fulfill society's duties for our own advantage. . . ." [26] Men are evil, he writes elsewhere, but virtue is necessary to society. Self-love is the only possible solution. "What can be more beautiful . . . than to draw, even from a principle which can lead to vice, the source of public welfare and happiness?" All we have to do is to show men that it is in their interest to be virtuous, and they will be. The royal philosopher notes an apparent contradiction. Virtue is "an attitude of the soul which carries it to the most perfect disinterestedness." How can one reach disinterestedness through self-interest? And Frederick goes on to explain the wide powers of self-interest, especially when stimulated by the fear of blame and shame, and by the desire for esteem and glory. It is a matter of fact, he assures us, that disinterestedness always springs from self-love.[27]

The staunchest and most doctrinaire supporters of enlightened self-interest were among the Encyclopedic coterie. For Helvétius, there could indeed be no other way. Virtue is both social in locus and motivated by personal interest. This interest may be either immediate or calculated for the future. "Without interest in loving virtue, no virtue." When virtue is without credit, we despise it, and rightly so, for it answers no need. Why does virtue always triumph in the theater? Because we want it to be rewarded and so justify being virtuous. Virtue can be cultivated in men, because it becomes the expression of the desire for power, esteem, and wealth. Consequently, in any sound education, "the idea of my own happiness will always be more or less tightly linked in my memory with that of my fellow-citizens, and the desire for one will evoke in me the desire for the other. From which it follows that in each person love of his neighbor is only the effect of love for himself." [28] Thus Helvétius emphasizes education as a conditioning process, bent to produce a desired kind of thinking and feeling. Men, left to themselves, will not be enlightened enough to avoid the kind of behavior which Hayer had accused

[26] "Dialogue de morale," *Oeuvres*, Berlin, 1846–57, IX, pp. 101, 105.
[27] "Essai sur l'amour-propre envisagé comme principe de morale" [1763], *Oeuvres*, IX, pp. 87–98. This paper was later read to the public assembly of the Academy of Berlin.
[28] *De l'Homme*, IX, p. 137 ff.; X, p. 193. See also *De l'Esprit*, p. 374n.

Helvétius' theory of justifying; they must be compelled to be "enlightened."

With d'Holbach, similarly, enlightened self-interest is a constant theme. On this score his thought is scarcely distinguishable from that of Helvétius. We love virtue only for what selfish good it can bring us. But if we calculate our real self-interest, we must be virtuous, that is, favor other people's happiness in order to induce them to favor ours. Thus duty and obligation are related to happiness in a certain rationalistic view of happiness.[29] A key statement is this one: "Moral obligation is the necessity of using means suitable to making us happy."[30] And elsewhere: "The object of morals is to persuade men that their greatest self-interest requires them to practice virtue. . . . Virtue is lovable only because it is useful. . . . Virtue consists in making oneself happy by giving happiness to others."[31] We must not forget that alongside this doctrine of egoism, d'Holbach (like Helvétius) *defines* virtue as actions which tend to the well-being of others.[32] We are virtuous when we consider not ourselves but others; however, if we are virtuous, it is because we have no consideration for others, but only for ourselves. This is precisely the ultimate meaning and import of the enlightened self-interest theory in its pure form. Its primary assumption is that of a reciprocity insured by the interdependence of interests—a theory which a modern Spanish dramatist, Jacinto Benavente, has deftly satirized in his comedy, *Los intereses creados*.[33]

Where d'Holbach differs from others is in relating the pursuit of happiness and the necessity of "using" others to a formalistic concept of eternal relationships which contradicts the purely relativist and conventional theories of other materialists. He consistently stresses "the eternal and invariable relationships" be-

[29] *Morale universelle,* I, pp. 2, 75–81.
[30] *Système de la nature,* I, p. 150.
[31] *Système social,* I, p. viii.
[32] *Système de la nature,* I, p. 145, etc.
[33] For a modern version of d'Holbach, compare the philosophy of John Dewey. "Why be moral?" he asks. "The answer to the question 'Why not put your hand into the fire?' is the answer of fact. If you do your hand will be burnt. The answer to the question Why acknowledge the right is of the same sort. For right is only an abstract name for the multitude of concrete demands in action which others impress upon us, of which we are obliged, if we would live, to take some account. Its authority is the exigency of their demands, the efficacy of their insistencies." (*Human Nature and Conduct,* p. 326.)

tween human beings in society, and the eternal and invariable moral laws which result from them. The individual, in his system, is just as much bound to moral imperatives as under the rule of his detested Christianity, although they are supposedly based on natural rather than supernatural laws. He admits of no separate or real realm of moral experience; and yet this is precisely what he wants. When he says that "our duties are the means the necessity of which is shown to us by experience and reason in order to reach our proposed end," he is not suggesting nihilism, but a formalistic relation between a legitimate end (happiness) and the fixed, necessary means (virtue). "When we say that these duties *oblige us,* it means only that without taking these means, we cannot attain the end our nature proposes. Therefore *moral obligation* is the necessity of using means calculated to make the beings with whom we live happy, in order to determine them to make us happy. . . . Morality, like the universe, is founded on necessity or on the eternal relations of things." [34] Thus d'Holbach endeavors to make *natural* (that is, identical with physical nature) what serves the needs and ends of culture, and what a culturally conditioned reason approves.[35] We recall that d'Holbach had argued, in similar fashion, that conscience is entirely acquired, but that when it was formed *in conformity with the nature of things,* it was universal—thus in effect establishing an objective good and evil independent of subjective pleasure and pain reactions. D'Holbach wants desperately to be a moralist, but on the basis of selfishness and unmoral tendencies. His "self-love" and "self-interest" are shorn of all subjective or relativistic realities; they are declared to be universal and satisfiable in only one way—except for "monsters."

In Diderot's ethical theories (in regard to Diderot we cannot properly use the word in the singular), enlightened self-interest plays an important role. Although he sometimes exclaims that men love virtue, he also, in his radical speculations, recognizes (and sometimes approves of) their complete selfishness. Approval leads to nihilism; but recognition without approval leads to enlightened self-interest. And so this theory winds its way through

[34] *Système de la nature,* I, pp. 145–46, 392–93. These necessary ideas are not innate, nor instinctual, but are mechanically formed by the expression of pleasure and pain (pp. 182–83).
[35] See especially, *ibid.,* I, pp. 48–54; here, as on some other occasions, d'Holbach emphasizes the element of self-preservation within the context of self-love.

his works from beginning to end. Unlike some others, he never deludes himself about the difficulty of virtue. "What is virtue?" he asks in the *Eloge de Richardson*. "It is, no matter how you consider it, a sacrifice of oneself." [36] But the sacrifice does not involve an ultimate loss. In the *Essai sur le mérite et la vertu* (1745), he defines virtue as a constraint of passions so that they conspire to the general good, "a heroic effort, and yet one which is never contrary to one's personal interests." [37] This is a moralistic work. In a piece of a different temper, the *Introduction aux grands principes* (1763), his "proselyte" affirms it our duty to be happy; "whence derives the necessity of contributing to the happiness of others, or in other words, of being virtuous." [38] On the virtuous isle of Tahiti, the word "virtue" is dismissed as a "vain display" (*fanfaronnade*), and has been replaced by self-interest.[39] In the *Entretien d'un philosophe avec la maréchale* (1774), Diderot argues that education and experience can direct the natural pleasure motive toward virtue (reinforcing a natural tendency to beneficence).[40] The esteem of others, both now and in future generations, seems to him a most powerful reward and incentive. Thus Diderot, at times, thought that by advancing a doctrine of rational, intelligent selfishness, it might be possible to end the struggle in man, to heal the schism between his selfish nature and his social nature.

The many writers who embrace the enlightened self-interest theory in the later years of the century do not add anything new. They are, to be sure, testimony to the diffusion of that idea. We need only list some of the most important references.[41]

"Enlightened self-interest" is basically an attempt to unify nature and culture, through reason conceived of as culture's weapon rather than as "the slave of the passions." The essential natural

---

[36] *Oeuvres*, V, p. 214.

[37] I, p. 13.

[38] II, p. 85.

[39] *Supplément au Voyage de Bougainville* (1772), in *Oeuvres philosophiques*, ed. Vernière, p. 499.

[40] *Oeuvres*, II, p. 510.

[41] E. Beaumont, *op. cit.*, pp. 47–48; Dom Deschamps, *op. cit.*, p. 156 and n.; Mirabeau, *Essai sur le despotisme* (1772), *Oeuvres*, 1835, VIII, p. 11; Mably, *De la Législation*, p. 30 ff.; *Principes de morale*, *Oeuvres*, X, p. 279 ff.; Robinet, *Dictionnaire universel*, arts. "Amour de soi-même," "Droit naturelle," "Morale"; Condorcet, *Esquisse*, 2e Partie, Xe Epoque; Saint-Lambert, *Catéchisme universel*, *Oeuvres philosophiques*, II, pp. 19–20, 129; Delisle de Sales, *Philosophie de la nature*, I, pp. 20–21; *Philosophie du bonheur*, I, pp. 187–97, II, pp. 131–32; Barbeu du Bourg, *op. cit.*, pp. 34–36; Sabatier de Castres, *Pensées*, pp. 51–52.

drive is safeguarded, but its "bad" aspects are curbed. Those among its adherents who were naturalists were thereby introducing value distinctions among the several natural impulses and desires, and their varied modes of satisfaction. They were in effect, if not in deed, admitting that culture creates values, too, and that these take precedence over merely natural values (that is, over natural values which are not also sanctioned by culture). Virtue, wrote a nonnaturalist, is not nature, but a correction of nature; [42] and this definition applies strictly to all but the nihilistic writings.

Nevertheless this fine nostrum had its opponents in the eighteenth century. Their objections were various. Boufflers saw a limit. "One may also be just, it is said, out of intelligent self-interest; but self-interest is concerned only with duties that are seen and judged by [other] men; remove men's look and self-interest will again think only of itself. Therefore one is really just not out of fear or self-interest, but out of love of justice. . . ." [43]

Among the apologists, Bergier was the principal enemy of this theory. He doubts the power of reason to control passion and direct action. "There is, in this life, no interest general and strong enough, no reward so certain, no punishment so infallible, as to persuade us to virtue when it is opposed by a violent passion or present advantage." [44] In this argumentation, Bergier was being far more consistent with the analysis of human nature and motivation accepted by most of the *philosophes* (and many others, besides) than they were themselves—we need only mention the analyses of Bayle, Fontenelle, and Hume.[45] Elsewhere he proffers a satirical barb: "[a man's] enlightened self-interest is therefore to get as much advantage for himself as possible, and to contribute as little as he can." [46] If a man is powerful or clever enough to get the help and esteem of others without giving them his, he will reach the perfection of morality: "virtue's heroism is to make dupes." It is obvious that Bergier is keenly aware of the nihilistic opportunities offered by an ethics of self-interest. This is most clear when he repeats d'Holbach's leitmotif with only a slight change of accent: "Since man's sole purpose is to make his existence happy

[42] Le Maître de Claville, *op. cit.*, I, p. 95.
[43] *Discours sur la vertu* (Académie de Berlin, 1797), 1800, p. 45.
[44] *Principes de métaphysique*, pp. 162–63.
[45] See *An Age of Crisis*, chap. 9.
[46] *Examen du matérialisme, ou Réfutation du système de la nature*, 1771, II, p. 394.

. . . he should work for others only insofar as he has good reason to hope that it will be to his own advantage." [47] (Obviously, if everyone did this, no one would do anything at all for anyone else.) This is a reversal of morality, exclaims Bergier; it makes virtue identical with something else that is not virtue.

Among the secular writers, the most determined foe of enlightened self-interest was Rousseau. As early as 1743, in his *Jugement sur la Paix perpetuelle* of the abbé de Saint-Pierre, he pointed out a fatal flaw. The conditions required for the adoption of Saint-Pierre's plan were those anticipated by the proponents of enlightened self-interest, and Rousseau declares them to be impossible: "for it would be necessary that the sum of private interests be less than the common interest, and that each should believe he saw in the good of all the greatest good that he could hope for himself. Now this requires a concourse of wisdom in so many heads, and a concourse of relations of so many interests, that one cannot hope that chance would bring about the fortuitous accord of all the necessary circumstances." And he adds—very significantly for his own political thinking and for the logical implications of eighteenth-century ethical thought: "however, if accord does not take place, only force can take its place; and then it is no longer a matter of persuading, but of compelling. . . . What is useful to the public is scarcely ever introduced except by force, since private interests are almost always opposed to it." [48]

In the *Discours sur l'inégalité*, Rousseau's picture of human nature in society is in fundamental opposition to the theory of enlightened self-interest. His derision breaks out in Note i.[49] In present societies, men, inevitably and in all duty, hate and hurt each other. There is no way of reconciling their interests.

> If you answer that society is so constituted that each gains in serving others, I shall reply that this would be very well, if he did not gain still more in hurting others. There is no legitimate profit which is not exceeded by the profit we can make illegitimately, and the wrong we do to others is always more lucrative than the services. It is only a question of securing impunity; and that is what the powerful use all their force to do, and the weak all their ruses.[50]

---

[47] *Ibid.*, p. 227.
[48] Vaughan, *op. cit.*, I, p. 392.
[49] Vaughan, *op. cit.*, I, p. 203.
[50] The same idea is again baldly stated in the *Lettre à d'Alembert* (ed. Fuchs, pp. 31–32).

The basis of Rousseau's central idea in the *Contrat social,* the total sovereignty of the general will, is precisely the impossibility of enlightened self-interest.

> Indeed, each individual as a man may have a particular will contrary to or different from the general will which he has as a citizen. His private interest may speak to him quite differently than the common interest; his absolute and natural independent existence may make him look upon what he owes to the common cause as a gratuitous contribution whose loss will be less harmful to others than the payment will be onerous to him . . . an injustice whose progress would cause the ruin of the body politic.

The conclusion, foreshadowed by his criticism of Saint-Pierre, follows: "we shall force him to be free." [51]

Rousseau's ethics alternates between the sufficiency of intuition, conscience, and common sense, when he is considering the individual as an independent, self-guiding entity, and the constraint or indoctrination imposed by "guides," when he is considering the individual as a part of the communal totality or *"moi commun."* Not only is Rousseau's moral and social thought hostile to the enlightened self-interest theory; his personal hostility to the Encyclopedists enabled him to feel considerable satisfaction in the opportunity for "unmasking" them which that theory gave him. For these self-styled benefactors and lovers of mankind also proclaimed that we could act only out of self-interest, told men that the right and best thing for them to do was to pursue their own interest. They are really arguing, he charged, for the denial of all values in order not to be hindered in the pursuit of their pleasures —of all pleasures.[52] Only he, Jean-Jacques, was the true lover of virtue, the true moralist.

Diderot, too, when he is not intoxicated with virtue, or attempting to defend it, was perfectly aware of the same facts. In his *Observations pour la confection des lois,* written for Catherine the Great, he notes: "It is evident that in a well-ordered society, the wicked man cannot hurt society without hurting himself. [How many times had Diderot written this?] The wicked man knows this. But what he knows even better is that he gains more from his wickedness than he loses as a member of the society

[51] Livre I, chap. VII; also II, chap. VI.

[52] Cf. J. Starobinski, *op. cit.,* pp. 89–90 (with caution, since Starobinski does not point out the injustice in Rousseau's reasoning, especially the affirmation that the Encyclopedists condemned self-interest), and the references given to the *Dialogues*

which he is harming." As we shall see in Chapter 7, Diderot is essentially a "liberal." He refuses to draw Rousseau's political conclusions. He rejects the inculcation of "patriotism," the imposed discipline of personal pleasures, and the demand for sacrificing them to the social welfare. "I want society to be happy; but I want to be happy, too; and there are as many ways of being happy as there are individuals. Our own happiness is the basis of all our true duties." Consequently, the sovereign, or general will—contrary to Rousseau—is limited by unalienable rights, and government's role should be minimal. It is clear that Diderot is torn between the desire to make men virtuous through social organization and the desire to leave them as free as possible to realize their happiness, each in his own way. He does not really believe in his own rational solutions, as much as he would like to. And so, in Diderot's dilemmas, we can see in sharp focus the dilemmas of ethical thought in his time.

It is noteworthy that Sade opposed enlightened self-interest on the same grounds as Rousseau, though with different motives and conclusions. We recall, from our discussion of Justice and Law, that he denies the general interest any prerogative.[53] In the earlier *Les Infortunes de la vertu,* Sade had tried, somewhat more subtly, to point out a possible contradiction between virtue and public interest. "When the general interest of men leads them to moral corruption, he who will not want to be corrupted with them will fight then against the general interest." [54]

There were even more weaknesses and flaws in the argumentation for enlightened self-interest than its eighteenth-century opponents specified. Chubb, for instance, in his *Reflections on Virtue and Happiness,* had proposed that while it is reasonable to prefer my own happiness to another's when we both cannot be happy at the same time, the "public felicity" must be preferred to mine because the greatest good should be preferred to the lesser. Now there is obviously a logical gap between the first statement and the second, because the quantity of good measured by the word "greater" involves a different kind of evaluation, the first being subjectively experienced, the second rationally conceived. If the second standard were to be uniformly applied, then the first proposition would no longer be true, for we should often, on that

[53] *Histoire de Juliette,* IV, pp. 178–79.
[54] *Ibid.,* pp. 168–69.

ground, have to prefer the happiness of another individual to our own. And conversely, if we are to prefer our *feeling* of happiness to another person's, then we are entitled to do so in regard to any number of persons. (Even weaker is Chubb's asseveration that to get pleasure out of doing harm to others is unnatural, because it introduces evil into the world.) In strict terms, as d'Alembert admits, there is opposition between personal and social interest; if a sacrifice or "renunciation" is demanded, this must be so. The imposition of *identity* depends on an "ultimate" self-interest which, as Rousseau and Sade pointed out, is not experienced or certain. But the proponents were so convinced of its certitude that d'Holbach could confidently admit that "if vice makes a man happy, he should love vice." [55]

There were several other flaws in the theory. The assumptions most open to challenge were the interpretation of the "best satisfaction" of self-interest, and what Halévy has called "the artificial identification of interests." Reason was called upon to accomplish a most difficult task, perhaps in many instances, one beyond its powers: that is, to dispossess original instincts by a rational vision of ultimate good and a theoretical ideal which often involves a partial or complete sacrifice of the original good—even, in extreme cases, of self-preservation. Is the motivation involved strong enough to overcome instincts and passions? Christian virtue was a formalism dependent on conscience and divine commands. Enlightened self-interest was an eudaemonistic teleology which in some cases —as with d'Holbach—ended up with a very similar formalism (excluding differences of detail). But the immediate implication

[55] The theory of enlightened self-interest also runs counter to the psychology of the Enlightenment, as Cassirer describes it: that the moving power comes from the will, from uneasiness, not from the idea of "a future good towards which the act is supposed to serve as a means." (*Op. cit.*, pp. 102–3.) Albert Schweitzer writes: "But it does not follow that the individual becomes more moral the better he understands his own interests. The mutual relation between him and society is not of such a character that he derives benefit from the latter just in proportion as he himself by his moral conduct helps to establish its prosperity. If the majority of its members, with short-sighted egoism, are intent only on their own good, then the man who acts with wider outlook makes sacrifices from which there is no prospect of gain for himself. . . . If, on the other hand, through the moral conduct of the majority of its members the condition of society is favourable, the individual profits by it, even if he fails to behave towards it as morality demands . . . he will carve out for himself an unduly big share of personal prosperity out of the prosperity of the community." Therefore rightly understood egoism will not oblige the individual to activity for the common good. (*Op. cit.*, pp. 72–73.) In truth, each person feels the risk of being taken advantage of, if he sacrifices for the common interest and others do not. Schweitzer's arguments are precisely those of Rousseau.

of radical materialism is an "evolutionary morality" of the strong. The other outcome requires the intervention of a moralizing intelligence operating in a social medium. Furthermore, the supporters of the theory all claimed that men are virtuous, not out of esteem for virtue, but only to win esteem and praise (and to avoid their opposites). However, if men did not esteem virtue, how could one win esteem by practicing it? On the other hand, the criticism that enlightened self-interest proposes an immoral basis for moral action does not point to an inconsistency (although it may be a valid objection), since it rests on a definition of "moral" as intentional, whereas, as we have seen, the utilitarians place moral value in the act.

In reading some of the moralists who supported enlightened self-interest, with heuristic emphasis, one sometimes gets the feeling that they were uneasy, and entertained unavowed mental reservations. Diderot, and doubtless others, never really forgot that men, subject to emotions, prejudices, and impulses, are very little swayed by reason, even in their own interest; and that the motive of their choice is not, most often, the ultimate results of an action, but the relative pleasantness of the *idea* of several possible courses of action. Perhaps they were vaguely aware of the type of criticism Lord Keynes once made of Bertrand Russell, and which we may aptly fit to them: Russell, points out Keynes, argues that our troubles are due to the fact that men have not lived rationally; therefore the remedy is to start living rationally.

Because of these shortcomings and these misgivings, many moralists turned for a supplement to the virtue-happiness equivalence, which offered the advantage of an immediate and certain fulfillment of the egoistic demand for happiness. The goal was still the same. If men have to pursue their happiness above all else, and society needs virtue above all else, a reconciliation must be affected. The problem was eternal, and the Christians faced it with the promise that the reconciliation would take place in the life to come. "Be just, be happy," writes the abbé Pey. "That is what the law of nature says to all men; and as under a just God justice must lead to happiness, these two laws may be reduced to this unique precept: Fear God and observe his commands."[56] The

---

[56] *La Loi de nature*, Montauban, 1789, pp. 16–17. Cf. Leibniz (ed. Latta, pp. 292–93): "But in order that it may be concluded by a universal demonstration that everything honourable is beneficial and that everything base is hurtful, we must assume the immortality of the soul and the Ruler of the universe, God."

secularists did not have this evasion. Their answer had to be one akin to the Stoic doctrine that virtue is its own reward, that happiness lay in the virtuous act itself. Obviously this involved an idea of happiness which was divorced from the sensual pleasure of hedonism. It was happiness conceived of as contentment, good conscience, self-approbation flowing from the contemplation of an ego-image which the person could look upon as satisfactory.[57] It was nonetheless in harmony with the general utilitarian view, as we can see by Crousaz's objection that if virtue were always rewarded, it would be a simple matter of interest to be virtuous.[58]

On the thesis of virtue-happiness there was, with some exceptions, little quarrel between the pious and the free-thinkers. It was good Christian doctrine. As Ameline had said in 1667, "Good conscience is the Paradise of man on earth . . . it makes the most painful and grievous life sweet and contented." [59] This litany is repeated in countless sermons as well as in the writings of the apologists. Virtue "can make our happiness in this world," Bergier assures us, "never is crime really advantageous."[60] No power on earth can frustrate this reward, adds Paulian. "Even if the entire universe were unjust towards the man of good, he still has the advantage of loving himself, of esteeming himself, of turning within his own heart with pleasure, of contemplating his actions with the same eyes with which others would see, were they not blind." [61] How Jean-Jacques would have approved and echoed these words, with himself in mind!

Among secular moralists, the virtue-happiness equivalence does not appear to have been a dominant theme in the early part of the century, although brief references are not infrequent. Perhaps it sounded too much like a preacher's discourse to be palatable at a time of hedonistic indulgence; moreover, the issues and difficulties of a secular ethics had not become sufficiently sharpened to create an awareness of the need for it. Bayle, who was not at all attracted by the calculus of enlightened self-interest (not believing men to be rationally motivated), at times found this alterna-

---

[57] Most eighteenth-century moralists would have affirmed that an ego-image is selected because its contemplation gives pleasure; but it is equally possible to argue that it gives pleasure because of admiration for or approbation of virtue, the approbation being the prior and determining factor.

[58] *Op. cit.,* pp. 180–84.

[59] *Op. cit.,* pp. 46–47.

[60] *Examen,* p. 220.

[61] *Le véritable système de la nature,* Avignon, 1788, pp. 209–13.

tive appealing. At least he is aware of the powerful effects of remorse. "Nature has so tied together sadness with reflection on an unjust act of which one feels guilty, that even those who have feared nothing from God have been downcast in recalling their evil deeds." [62] Bayle, however, as Voltaire was to say, *se combat lui-même,* and we shall return to him later. Pope assures us that happiness, "our being's end and aim," cannot be had alone or by seeking more than one's share.

Oh blind to truth, and God's whole scheme below,
Who fancy Bliss to Vice, to Virtue Woe! (*Essay on Man,* IV, 93–94)

Pope does add a word to take care of scoffers (like Bayle, as we shall see):

> "But sometimes Virtue starves, while Vice is fed."
> What then? Is the reward of Virtue bread? (149–50)
> . . . Nor is his claim to plenty, but content. (156)
> . . . That true *self-love* and *Social* are the same;
> That *Virtue* only makes our Bliss below. . . . (396–97)

Among early French writings, the *libertin* piece, "Réflexion sur l'existence de l'âme," while upholding this view, cautioned that it was only for "honnêtes gens," and would be dangerous for the rabble, who are not open to such delicate feelings.[63] The high-minded, though not always consistent, Vauvenargues defines small men as those who are easily discouraged by what life does to them. Greater souls keep their feeling of worth despite injustice or persecution. But Vauvenargues' virtue is the antique strength of character rather than a general idea of moral virtue, and he is basically a pessimist, saddened by the cruelty of life and men's indifference to merit and virtue.[64] Montesquieu's Troglodytes learn the joys of virtue, and Usbek later exclaims, "When a man examines himself, what a satisfaction for him to find his heart is just! This pleasure, as severe as it is, must delight him; he sees his being as far above those who do not have it as he sees himself above tigers and bears." [65] Here the pleasure is clearly egoistic and comparative. Hume, too, believes that virtue, in a practical way, is productive of happiness, but does not dwell on the matter.[66]

---

[62] *Oeuvres diverses,* III, p. 320. Then how do some who kill feel no remorse? "Those people imagine that everything considered, their act is not wrong."
[63] Printed in the *Nouvelles libertés de penser,* Amsterdam, 1743, pp. 170–71.
[64] *Op. cit.,* I, pp. 141–42, 128–29, 138; II, pp. 140–43.
[65] Lettre LXXXIII.
[66] *Enquiry,* p. 169.

Voltaire was, in general, an adherent. In an early poem he writes that all the glories of earth mean little if we do not have a just heart and are not pleased with ourselves, liked by the good and approved by the wise.[67] These sentiments are repeated in a much later play, *Les Scythes* (1767).[68] This is poetry. But in prose, too, Voltaire, fulminating against d'Holbach, asserts that it is "proven by experience that the satisfaction of having conquered [vices] is a hundred times greater than the pleasure of having succumbed to them." [69] However Voltaire was too much the realist, and the pessimist, to make a major commitment to so optimistic a theory as the virtue-happiness equivalence. *Zadig* and *Candide* show us the practical "rewards" of virtue in this world, in almost nihilistic terms. In the article "Souverain Bien," he notes dryly, "The virtuous man with kidney stone and gout is very unhappy"—but then adds, "less than the evil man in the same situation." The insolent persecutor caressing a new mistress is very happy. And Voltaire here reaches a nonutilitarian conclusion, one which harks back to his fondness for Natural Law: "Virtue is not a good, it is a duty; it belongs to a different class, of a higher order. It has nothing to do with painful or pleasant sensations."

Voltaire again brings to mind Samuel Johnson's *Rasselas*, whose hero starts out in the world, from the prison of his El Dorado, confident that virtue will bring happiness and "the benediction of gratitude" of men. He is disinclined to believe the warning of Nekayah: "But this, at least, may be maintained, that we do not always find visible happiness in proportion to visible virtue. All natural and almost all political evils are incident alike to the bad and good. . . . All that virtue can afford is quietness of conscience and a steady prospect of a happier state; this may enable us to endure calamity with patience; but remember that patience must suppose pain." [70] Rasselas learns that the warning is true and retreats to his El Dorado.

It is toward the middle of the century that the virtue-happiness equivalence begins to be looked upon as a valuable factor in the

[67] Epitre XVI (1718), *Oeuvres*, X, p. 244.
[68]   ". . . le secret témoignage
            Que la vertu se rend, qui soutient le courage,
            Qui seul en est le prix, et que j'ai dans mon coeur,
            Me tiendra lieu de tout, et même du bonheur." (VI, p. 308)
[69] XVIII, p. 371.
[70] *Rasselas*, p. 51.

support of secular morality. It progresses simultaneously on two fronts; clarified in the speculative thinking of moralists, it obtains ever wider diffusion on the wings of the increasing vogue of sensibility. In 1748, Burlamaqui's *Principes du droit naturel* insists on this relation.

> Everything contrary to the lights of reason and conscience can only win the secret disapprobation of our minds and cause us chagrin and shame. The heart is wounded by the idea of crime, and its memory is always sad and bitter. On the other hand, any conformity with right reason is a state of order and perfection which the mind approves; and we are so made that a good action becomes for us the germ of a secret joy; it is always recollected with pleasure. And truly, what is sweeter than to be able to bear witness to oneself that one is what one should be, and that one is doing what one should do and what one should reasonably do, what befits us best, what is most in conformity to our natural destination? Whatever is natural is pleasant; whatever is within order is satisfying.[71]

Burlamaqui, however, is unable to stay within the bounds of secularism. He undertakes a lengthy examination of the objections to this theory.[72] Some of these he believes he can refute. While it is true that injustice and passions sometimes afford pleasure or advantage, virtue is surer, its results are more real, pure, and enduring, since man is a reasonable and social being. As for natural ills, virtue helps to avoid them, and gives greater strength to bear them. "There is a contentment inseparable from virtue, which can never be taken away from us; and our essential happiness suffers but little damage from the passing, external accidents which sometimes bother us." [73] Nature links the physical and the moral, in good and in evil. But then Burlamaqui admits that life does not work out that way. The goods and ills of nature and of fortune are not distributed according to merit. The wrongs of injustice fall upon the innocent as often as on the guilty; even more, virtue itself frequently attracts persecution, and the good man becomes "the victim of his own virtue." In such cases, what argument do we have? "Will the inner satisfaction given by the testimony of good conscience suffice by itself to determine a man to sacrificing his goods, his security, his honor and even his life?"

[71] II, pp. 224–25, 227–30.
[72] *Ibid.*, pp. 230–41.
[73] A long quotation from Isocrates follows, to the effect that virtue promotes our self-interest.

This is a question of widest import to the welfare of society. On the one hand, only the observation of natural moral laws can preserve social order and make men happy. On the other hand, virtue and vice are not sufficiently distinguished by their consequences to induce men to follow these laws. Every law must have a sufficient sanction to determine a reasonable creature to obey it for the sake of his own self-interest, which is the motive of action. While the moral system is generally advantageous, it does not recompense particular individuals in particular instances for the required sacrifice. It is for this reason that civil law exists, to back up Natural Law. But civil law, though a help, "still leaves a great void in the moral system," and vice is frequently better rewarded than virtue. It is at this point that Burlamaqui, with his back to the wall, slips out of the noose and finds the answer in God's rewards and punishments in the life to come.

Diderot was an ardent champion of the virtue-happiness equivalence. "The happiness of the good, 'the peace of soul' found in *bienfaisance*," writes Jean Fabre, "is one of the themes developed by Diderot to the point of dizziness." [74] Pierre Hermand declares that the coincidence of virtue and happiness is "the keystone" of Diderot's ethics. After all, if happiness, as he declares, is the highest end and duty, there is no way of justifying moral virtue unless it produces that result. Only the vicious man would be wise, or indeed, moral, and thus nihilism would be entirely justified. The inevitable consequences of virtue and vice form the refrain of Diderot's *drames*, of much of his criticism and theorizing in aesthetics, and of many of his letters. We need refer to only a few of his statements. By virtue, he declares, most significantly, we can transcend nature.

> Thus you will raise yourself, so to speak, above her, by the excellence of a system which repairs its disorders. You will be happy in the evening, if you will have done more good than it has done harm. That is the only way of reconciling yourself with life. How can you hate an existence which you make sweet to yourself by its usefulness to others? . . . The heart of man is sometimes serene and sometimes covered with clouds; but the heart of a good man, like the spectacle of nature, is always great and beautiful, whether tranquil or agitated. . . . The habit of virtue is the only one which you can contract without fear for the future. Sooner or later the others bring regret. [75]

[74] *Neveu de Rameau*, ed. J. Fabre, p. 186.
[75] *Le Père de famille*, "Epitre dédicatoire," *Oeuvres*, VII, pp. 183–84.

No reward is needed, writes Diderot to his mistress, for beautiful actions, and wickedness is its own punishment.[76] In the *Introduction aux grands principes* (1763), he openly declares that the paths of virtue and happiness must be identical, or else it would be folly to be virtuous. Here it is quite clear that happiness is placed first in the scale of values; but Diderot really loves virtue at least as much as happiness, and if the intellectual framework of his time and of his own materialism had permitted it, he would doubtless have reversed the order. The least he can do is to assert their equivalence. "No; the path of happiness is the same path of virtue. Fortune may bring reverses upon it, but it cannot take away that sweet delight, that pure voluptuousness which accompanies it." Conscience, the testimony of one's inner self—"that is the source of true goods and ills; that is what makes the happiness of the good man amidst persecutions and misfortunes, and the torment of the wicked, amidst fortune's favors." [77] In the *Encyclopédie*, Diderot tries to substantiate his thesis by a pseudo-scientific analysis of temperament.[78] In both his first work and his last, in the *Essai sur le mérite et la vertu* and the *Essai sur Claude et Néron*, he uses the same phrase: "No happiness without virtue." He risks all on that proposition.[79]

For d'Holbach, as for Diderot, the virtue-happiness equivalence becomes a mainstay of his system. Like Diderot, he desires virtue more than anything but knows that men desire happiness more than anything. His thought, like Diderot's, contains pronounced formalist elements, despite its announced teleology of happiness. He also agrees that it would be folly to be virtuous, if evil-doing were the path to happiness. But he is more convinced than Diderot of the certainty of the argument. "It is only by virtue that [man] can make himself happy." [80] D'Holbach is aware of the objections. Like Burlamaqui, he knows that often virtue, far from being esteemed and rewarded, is "in almost all countries hated, persecuted, forced to sigh for the ingratitude and injustice of men." How can d'Holbach, the atheist, escape the noose? His recourse is

---

[76] *Correspondance*, ed. G. Roth, II, p. 225; III, p. 118.
[77] *Oeuvres*, II, p. 88.
[78] Article "Plaisir," *Oeuvres*, XVI, pp. 297–99.
[79] *In Claude et Néron* he repeats again: "there is only one duty, to be happy; there is only one virtue, justice." Since duty is to be virtuous, happiness and justice are made synonymous. (III, p. 312.)
[80] *Système de la nature*, I, pp. 342–47. Here enlightened self-interest is inseparable from the virtue-happiness equivalence.

to betray the materialist-sensualist philosophy, which allowed of no difference between pleasurable sensations except the quantitative (intensity and duration), and to affirm an arbitrary definition of happiness that is in accord with his formalism of virtue, and is therefore a *petitio principii.*

> I answer by admitting that as a necessary consequence of mankind's errors, virtue rarely leads to the objects of which the rabble makes happiness consist. . . . But the good man does not desire either the recompenses or the suffrage of a society so badly constituted; content with a domestic happiness, he does not seek to multiply relationships which would only multiply dangers; he knows that a vicious society is a whirlpool with which the virtuous man cannot coordinate himself; he steps aside, away from the beaten path, in which he would inevitably be crushed. He does the good as much as he can, in his sphere; he does not interfere with the wicked who wish to go down into the arena; he sighs at the blows they give each other, he congratulates himself on the mediocrity in which he places his security.[81]

Regardless of how life treats good and evil men, d'Holbach steadfastly maintains that the evil man is odious, is hated and despised, and therefore must be insecure and unhappy, and that he blushes at the bottom of his heart. "The least reflection proves to us that there is no wicked man who is not ashamed of his conduct, who is really satisfied with himself, who does not envy the fate of the good man, who is not forced to admit that he has paid very dearly for the advantages which he can never enjoy without unpleasant reflections about himself." [82] And so, on and on. The good man has a different fate. He "consoles himself by looking within himself, approves himself on finding in his heart a pure joy, a solid contentment, the right to expect the affection and esteem of those whom his fate allows him to influence." [83] On the one hand, then, d'Holbach proposes to us that we should be unselfish out of selfishness and assures us of a rigorous formal relation, an inevitable result. Conscience takes the place of the paradise of the Christians. On the other hand, he admits at other times that this universal truth is not operative in our society, in which the wicked reap rewards without corresponding penalties

---

[81] *Ibid.*, I, pp. 347–48.

[82] *Ibid.*, I, p. 255 ff. See also the emotional passage at the end of the volume (I, 397), and *La Morale universelle*, I, p. 62 ff.

[83] *La Morale universelle*, I, pp. 82–83, 26; III, pp. 207–10, 214, 218, 233–35.

from their warped conscience. Ethics now veers to politics: we must reform society so that this great truth becomes true. D'Holbach's ethics are built on sand.[84]

Rousseau was not a partisan of enlightened self-interest for the reasons we have seen, but the equivalence theory appealed to him strongly. It had the virtue of the immediate, and of not depending on rationality. The Savoyard Vicar summarizes his view:

> The wicked man fears himself and runs from himself; his joy comes in throwing himself outside of himself. He casts worried looks about him and seeks an object that will divert him; without bitter satire, without insulting mockery, he would always be sad; the mocking laugh is his only pleasure. On the contrary, the serenity of the just man is inner; his laughter has no maliciousness, but joy; he carries its source within himself; he is as gay alone as in the midst of a group. . . .[85]

Julie, in *La Nouvelle Héloïse,* is the incarnation of this theory. Worried, furtive, and unhappy when she sinned, the return to virtue liberates her heart from its oppressive weight, and she exults in her release. Unfortunately, as the novel proceeds, it becomes less certain that she is really happy. Rousseau, too, makes a clear distinction between the material and the moral rewards. Not an upholder of enlightened self-interest, he can admit without inconsistency that virtue is not rewarded by the world, but only in our hearts.

Once more we may speak of a refrain, of a chorus of ayes, which continues to the end of the century, and it is sufficient to list some of the principal references.[86] We must also reckon into the account

---

[84] Holland pointed out that the phrase, "Man cannot be happy without virtue," is meaningless in d'Holbach's mouth. If we are so constituted that we have impetuous desires, necessary to our happiness which, as d'Holbach admits, can be satisfied only at the expense of others, one cannot say that virtue produces happiness. Holland emphasizes the trials of virtue but, instead of showing that virtue and happiness are different things, he claims that virtue gives us a different and better kind of happiness! (*Op. cit.,* I, pp. 256–65.) The same point is well argued by Bergier (*Examen,* I, pp. 414–22); part of his argument is given in R. R. Palmer, *op. cit.,* pp. 189–90, 215–16. See also d'Holbach's *Système social,* I, pp. 58–65.

[85] *Emile,* p. 351. See *La Nouvelle Héloïse,* ed. Pomeau, pp. 199–200, 344, etc.

[86] Frederick the Great (*Anti-Machiavel, Oeuvres,* VIII, p. 89), amusingly writes that the tyrant will always be unhappy: "he will not escape that fatal melancholy which will strike his imagination, and which will be his executioner in this world." Toussaint pens a naïve piece to show that the wicked are always unhappy, virtue always rewarded, "Discours sur les Avantages de la Vertu" (*Histoire de l'Académie de Berlin,* 1766, pp. 461–66). Mirabeau is equally naïve, asserting, together with the usual themes, that no man conceives himself as the center of the world (*Des Lettres de cachet, Oeuvres,* VII, pp. 40–56). See Naigeon, *Discours préliminaire,* pp. 92–98;

the innumerable moralizing novels and short stories whose lesson
is the same; the outstanding example is Bernardin de Saint-
Pierre's *Paul et Virginie.*

Like the theory of enlightened self-interest, the virtue-happiness
equivalence had its critics in its own time. As it became increasingly diffused and more important, the attacks on it also increased.
We hear very little against it in the first half of the century. We
shall note Bayle's devastating scrutiny under another head. One of
Rémond de Saint-Mard's characters declares: "You have no idea
how many impudent people I have seen who were very happy
despite it." [87] Mandeville criticized it by implication, when he
wrote that there are few men of virtue, "because all the Recom-
pence a Man has of a virtuous Action is the pleasure of doing it,
which most People reckon but poor Pay."[88] J.-Fr. Bernard brings
out the very arguments to which Burlamaqui and d'Holbach
later attempted a reply.[89]

Subsequently, the virtue-happiness equivalence and its attempted synthesis of nature and culture were attacked principally
by two groups, both of whom were interested in marking the
separation between nature and culture. Although both groups
were of lesser importance (in regard to diffusion, but not in regard
to cultural history), they gathered strength in the second half of
the century. The first were the nihilists, the second the altruists.
We may advance the hypothesis that the development of utilitarian
thinking called forth these two opposing outlooks, in a way that
Natural Law and simple, prudent hedonism, which dominated
in the early part of the period, had not.[90]

La Mettrie was the first nihilist to issue an open challenge.
Virtue, he contends, is not natural to man and has no relation to
happiness. Men are blissfully happy in the midst of vice, and many
virtuous people are solitary and dour: "people respect them and
run from them, that's the fate of virtue; while everyone seeks out
likable people with vices which are despised." Happiness comes
from the art of pleasing, not from virtue. There are instincts by

Du Pont de Nemours, *Philosophie de l'univers,* pp. 110–17, 222; Delisle de Sales,
De la Philosophie de la nature, II, p. 161; Marmontel, *Leçons de morale,* p. 422 ff.
    [87] *Oeuvres,* Amsterdam, 1750, I, pp. 304–5.
    [88] *Fable* (1714–1729), I, p. 246.
    [89] *Dialogues* (1730), pp. 72–88.
    [90] The chief current of criticism of the virtue-happiness equivalence is probably
in the novel. See *An Age of Crisis,* chap. 14. Virtue is shown to be a handicap in
the world.

which every animal is led to happiness; virtue is not among them. "It is the same with all the wicked. They can be happy, if they can be wicked without remorse. I dare to say more: he who has no remorse, in such familiarity with crime that vices are virtues for him, will be happier than such another who, after a fine action, is sorry he has done it, and so loses all the gain." [91]

Not many men have had Diderot's intellectual courage—or versatility. In *Le Neveu de Rameau* he challenges the basis of his own moral philosophy, in the person of the protagonist of the dialogue, "Lui" (Rameau's nephew). When Lui's antagonist ("Moi") declares that one must be virtuous to be happy, he retorts, "And yet I see an infinity of honest people who are not happy, and an infinity of people who are happy without being honest." Moi's only reply is, "You think so." How close are some of the following lines, spoken by Lui, to La Mettrie's:

> *Lui:* And since I can make my happiness by vices which are natural to me, and which I have acquired without work, and keep without effort, which fit with the morals of my nation . . . it would be very strange for me to torment myself like a damned soul, to castrate myself and make myself into something else; to give myself a character foreign to mine; very estimable qualities, I admit, without argument; but which would be hard for me to acquire, to practice, would lead me nowhere, maybe worse than nowhere. . . . They praise virtue, but they hate it; but they run from it, but it freezes you with cold, and in this world you've got to have warm feet. And then, it would make me sour-tempered, infallibly; for why do we so often see the pious so harsh, so ill-tempered, so unsociable? It is because they have undertaken a task which is not natural to them. . . . And to cut the matter short, I won't put up with your happiness, nor the happiness of some visionaries like you.
> *Moi:* I see, my friend, that you don't know what it is, and that you are not even made to learn it.
> *Lui:* So much the better, blast it! So much the better. It would make me die of hunger, of boredom and perhaps of remorse.[92]

Diderot's character, Lui, reminds us of those Helvétius and d'Holbach write about, the ones who are so naturally disposed ("unfortunately born") that they cannot find happiness except in vice. And Diderot himself, in his *Réfutation d'Helvétius*, later takes Lui's view in a broadside against Helvétius' thesis that education

[91] *Discours sur le bonheur*, pp. 172–73.
[92] *Neveu de Rameau*, ed. J. Fabre, pp. 43–46.

can change men. "Isn't the practice of virtue a sure means of being happy? . . . No, indeed! There are men, so unfortunately born, so violently moved by avarice, ambition, disorderly love of women, that I would condemn them to unhappiness if I prescribed to them a constant struggle against their dominating passion.[93] But won't that man be unhappier as a result of his passion than because of his struggle against it? I'm sure I don't know, and every day I see men who prefer to die than to change their ways." [94] Diderot cannot escape from the noose, as long as happiness is the end and virtue the means.

A few apologists also stood up in opposition to the virtue-happiness equivalence. They refused to abandon the traditional notion of virtue as a sacrifice of egoism, rather than as its fulfillment. Bergier pointed out that the theory made of Natural Law only a tendency to pleasure and the avoidance of pain. Why do the materialists complain that there is no Providence because vice is triumphant in the world? Isn't this complaint the very refutation of their virtue-happiness theory? [95] Men's nature being what it is, society must be what it is; virtue cannot be happy in this world, and any planning for such a world is "ideal and chimerical." [96] The monk, Jacob (Bernard Lambert), ridiculed the idea that virtue is its own reward. Happiness is the sovereign good, and virtue can't give us that, "because it often imposes the most painful sacrifices on us." Its reward will come later, but it is a pretty poor reward by itself, for a creature who wants happiness above all else and who is incapable of disinterestedness.[97]

It is clear that the virtue-happiness equivalence (like enlight-

---

[93] For the theory of "the dominating passion," see *An Age of Crisis,* p. 239.

[94] *Oeuvres,* VI, pp. 438–39. See *Rêve de d'Alembert,* II, p. 176. This is the same Diderot who defied d'Holbach (as he writes to Sophie Volland) "to find me in history a scoundrel, however perfectly happy he may have been, whose life did not offer me the strongest presumption of unhappiness equal to his wickedness; and a good man, however perfectly unhappy he may have been, whose life did not offer me the strongest presumption of a happiness proportionate to his goodness. My dearest, what a beautiful task [to write] the secret and unknown history of those two men! If I could do it according to my liking, the great question of virtue and happiness would be far advanced; we shall have to see. . . ." But d'Holbach, laughing, found it easy to pick up any volume of history as an answer, and Diderot, despairing, is reduced (as Jean Fabre notes) to Rousseau's postulate: "it is bad education, bad example, bad legislation which corrupt us. If that is an error, at least I am glad to find it at the bottom of my heart. . . ." (*Ibid.,* pp. 187–88.)

[95] *Métaphysique,* pp. 162–63.

[96] *Examen,* I, pp. 422–23.

[97] *Essai sur la jurisprudence universelle,* 1729, pp. 318–28. See also Pey, *op. cit.,* p. 127.

ened self-interest) is a secularization of Christian morality in regard to motivation, and was therefore bound to be opposed by some sharp-thinking theologians.

Man's moral history is an unending struggle to surpass the instinctual egoistic drives, to harness their libidinal energy to creative and co-operative social purposes. Freud, who in many ways was a spiritual child of the Enlightenment, wrote, "I should imagine that as long as virtue is not rewarded in this life, ethics will preach in vain." [98] That is precisely why the major group of eighteenth-century moralists tried so hard to convince their readers that it is rewarded, inevitably and handsomely, far more than vice, whose visible rewards are delusive and whose hidden punishments are cruel.

Duty and pleasure, they urged, coincide; morality asks nothing more of us than that we should be happy. The secularism which had been saying that happiness comes from following nature, now said that it followed virtue—but without violating nature. This, according to Robert Mauzi, constitutes a *"double mauvaise foi."* How true this judgment is can be seen in a phrase of Delisle de Sales: "the purest soul is ready to go astray, when one is clumsy enough to put into conflict its inclination to happiness and its virtue." [98a]

Finding themselves unable to avoid the question of what actually happens in real life, the moralists were forced to retreat to the inner sanctum of conscience, and its rewards and punishments. They overlooked the fact that while virtue does have its rewards, they are not necessarily greater than those of vice, nor are the pangs of remorse more cruel than the deprivation of other satisfactions and pleasures. The idealistic thinkers tried to make men believe that they are not really happy, when they act and live in certain ways, even though they feel happy. Give up these pleasures and satisfactions, they urged, like religious apostles, and you will know real happiness. These supposed "experientialists" in ethics turned their backs to experience, which belies their doctrine. Is it any wonder that rebellious spirits reared their heads and declared all this to be nonsense or bad faith—an arbitrary imposition on fools?

This was not the only way in which the virtue-happiness

[98] *Op. cit.*, p. 140.
[98a] *Philosophie du bonheur*, I, p. 145.

equivalence ran counter to other beliefs and attitudes of many of its proponents. To say that virtue is its own reward and wickedness punishes itself implies that virtue is part of human nature, of its essence and natural function—an idea that many adherents of the theory did not accept.[99] The virtue-happiness equivalence, moreover, like the optimism of Leibniz, Pope, and their disciples, was a philosophy inimical to social action and reform. If one can be happy in any situation, it is scarcely worth while trying to change the world. (However d'Holbach said that if we did change the world, virtue would also receive material rewards.) Finally, the equivalence proposed is, as Kant shows, a disguised form of the moral sense theory, which had also been rejected.[100]

In sum, we may recall that ethical systems fall into two main groups, according to their choice of the ultimate ends of life: those which embrace pleasure or happiness, and those which hold up virtue or character. If the selected end is virtue, happiness is often thought to accompany it. If happiness is the end, then virtue is sometimes recommended as the means to achieve it. This was the eighteenth-century utilitarian choice.

In Plato's *Republic*, Glaucon, dissatisfied with Socrates' refutation of Thrasymachus' arguments, asks him to prove that justice is a good; that it is, as Socrates claims, in the highest class of goods —those which have both intrinsic and instrumental value. Most people, he says, reckon justice in the troublesome class, among goods which are to be pursued for the sake of rewards and reputation, but in themselves disagreeable. Men who practice justice do so of necessity and against their will. Glaucon sketches this theory of the origin of justice: to do injustice is by nature good; to suffer injustice, evil; but the evil is greater than the good and so men establish laws and what is ordained by law is termed just. He then cites the story of the ring of Gyges, which made a man invisible and beyond punishment, in order to show that no man, having this godlike power, would be just: "wherever any one thinks that he can safely be unjust, there he is unjust . . . for all

[99] *Cf.* Kant, *op. cit.*, p. 128: "In order to imagine the vicious man as tormented with mental dissatisfaction by the consciousness of his transgressions, they must first represent him as in the main basis of his character, at least in some degree, morally good; just as he who is pleased with the consciousness of right character must be conceived as already virtuous."

[100] "It is, therefore, impossible to feel this satisfaction or dissatisfaction prior to the knowledge of obligation." (*Ibid.*) For Kant's argument against the equivalence, see p. 221. See also Lecky, *History of European Morals*, I, p. 61.

men believe in their hearts that injustice is far more profitable than justice." If, on the other hand, we take an equally extreme example of the just man, one who is so despite the fact that everyone takes him to be unjust (an assumption which is necessary so that no reward is involved), it is clear that he is the unhappier of the two.

In the actual development of the dialectic, neither Glaucon nor Socrates remains on the level of intrinsic good.[101] Glaucon's challenge becomes an insistence that Socrates prove that justice is an instrumental good. The crucial point of his argumentation lies in this demand; "When both have reached the uttermost extreme, the one of justice and the other of injustice, let judgment be given which of them is the happier of the two." It is the same demand which the eighteenth-century philosophers were trying to satisfy. Like the Greeks, they were not asking, "What ought I to do?" but "How should I live in order to achieve happiness?" Virtue is valued for the good it secures: ostensibly the happiness of the individual, in reality, the welfare of society—which is the reason they were so desperate to prove that it does also make the individual happy. But in fact, moral virtue and right action can never be justified, adequately or entirely, in terms of self-interest. Self-interest can be an inducement, but not a moral reason. For if self-interest is plainly served by immoral action, then either there is a moral reason to be moral, or no reason at all and the nihilist has won the day. The only pertinent reason is one which the skeptic will not recognize and which the moral person does not require: that our unique power of making moral distinctions and of being moral is also, by its very existence, a duty so to do. But as Hume knew, moral skepticism cannot be countered by providing reasons to persuade those who are not moral to become moral. This is one of the reasons why the eighteenth-century enterprise was bound to fail.

IV. Altruism and Anti-utilitarianism

Under the influence of sensationism and naturalism, hedonistic ethics—or, to be exact, one branch of it—had evolved through

---

[101] Adeimantus tries to bring it back to grounds of intrinsic good. See also *Gorgias*.

social utilitarianism to enlightened self-interest and the virtue-happiness equivalence. The moralists, frequently omitting such notions as freedom, right, and motive, and confining themselves to those of good, usefulness, self-interest, and society, had nevertheless reached the same terminus as the traditional morality: virtue is, or involves, self-sacrifice. Whether virtue is conceived of as prudential wisdom or as renunciation, it is taken as a value instrumental to the end or intrinsic value, happiness. (Happiness, secularized, is returned to earth.) Virtue is an evaluation made in reference to the useful result of an act, not to good will, or the performing of one's obligations out of the desire to do just that.

Inevitably, however, the sign is often taken for the thing. By a natural psychological process of association, the act or idea of sacrifice itself, rather than the end it was supposed to serve, often becomes the thing of value, the object of praise.[1] In like fashion, by a kind of mental shorthand, the general welfare (virtue, public spirit, patriotism) which was justified in terms of intelligent self-interest attracted to itself the characteristic of value. We may say that in this sense egoistic utilitarian thinking bred its own antithesis. At the same time—since no part of an inherited cultural complex is completely left behind—persistent voices of the traditional altruistic concept of virtue, never entirely stilled, lashed out in criticism of the new naturalistic utilitarianism. Sympathy, it was claimed, is as much a part of our original endowment as egoism, since we are social beings; and individual reflection aided by social influences transmutes egoism into self-sacrifice.

The anti-utilitarian currents merged, and flowed on, indistinguishable. In truth, the confusion was even deeper. *Bienfaisance,* we have just seen, was often lauded, from a utilitarian viewpoint, as the immediate means to happiness. But at other times it was the element of self-sacrifice in *bienfaisance* which won the highest esteem and the most abundant tears. Except in specific cases it would be difficult to distinguish the two. Certain it is that the rising tide of pre-romanticism favored this confusion. The lachrymose sentimentalism of the middle classes, conjoined to the praise of virtue-sacrifice, produced in the last decades before the Revolution an emotional intoxication with virtue which functioned as an

---

[1] Robert Mauzi distinguishes three concepts of virtue: (1) internal plenitude and good conscience ("*la volupté du sage*"), (2) social action and *bienfaisance,* (3) internal struggle and sacrifice, which bring their own *voluptés.* (*Op. cit.,* pp. 602-3.)

antithesis to the arid, rationalistic skeptical facets of the age. The Revolution was to profit from it, and turning it to its own uses, augment it.

We may first note very briefly the persistence of altruistic currents in England. This chiefly concerns the opposition to Hobbes and to Mandeville. Cumberland had asserted, in 1672, that "It cannot be proved that animals, in those voluntary actions by which they actually promote the good of others, as well as themselves, do not alike intend and will both." [2] Shaftesbury holds up several criteria: actions are intrinsically good or bad, intention is the moral touchstone, the natural "affection of a Creature" is toward the good of the species; he defines virtue as "a certain just disposition, or proportional affection of a rational creature towards the moral objects of right and wrong." [3] Among the first, he raises the standard of benevolence.[4] Wollaston distinguishes right, or obligation, from good.[5] Hume makes natural sympathy, an original component of human nature, one of the bases of his moral philosophy, though he associates it with the pleasure it gives us. Hartley declares that self-interest should not be a primary pursuit, neither "gross self-interest" nor "refined self-interest." The latter, worse than the former, shelters itself under an assumed ideal. Even "rational self-interest"—the pursuit of the best means for happiness—is dangerous; by augmenting ideas and desires which center in the self, it extinguishes other motives: love of God and neighbor, sympathy, the moral sense.[6] Kames, following Hume, deems benevolence a principle of action in man; the happiness of others is an object agreeable to the mind.[7]

There is scanty evidence in France of similar attitudes, during the first decades of the century, outside of homiletics. The manuscript, "Difficultés sur la religion," does mention that part of the virtue of a duty lies in its difficulty and the efforts it requires.[8]

---

[2] *Treatise*, p. 129.

[3] *Characteristicks*, I, p. 352; II, pp. 77–81, 40, 24–30. However Shaftesbury does not discard enlightened self-interest or virtue-happiness.

[4] Wm. F. Alderman notes that Fielding, in *Tom Jones*, derides Shaftesbury's benevolence; he shows that it is destructive to the Christian belief in merit, and that the virtuous hero is not happy. Dr. Johnson, Berkeley, Swift, and Wesley agreed. ("Shaftesbury and the Doctrine of Benevolence," *Transactions of Wisconsin Academy of Sciences*, XXVI, p. 143.)

[5] *Op. cit.*, p. 35 ff.

[6] *Op. cit.*, II, pp. 271–80.

[7] *Essays*, pp. 82–83.

[8] Fol. 34 (Mazarine 1163).

The abbé Desfourneaux writes that morality has two ends, self-advantage and the advantage of others; the highest virtue is magnanimity, or greatness of soul, "a trait of the soul which raises it above that low self-interest which attaches almost all men to little things and to themselves." For most, "self-interest is the heart of all their actions"; but it is possible to want to do good to others without any thought of self.[9] Mme de Lambert advises her son not to neglect legitimate self-love, but to surpass it in the love of justice, and of others.[10] In a recently published maxim, the abbé de Saint-Pierre inveighs against nonmoral motives of success or reputation; one should rather "try to make himself worthy of it by his good actions."[11] Fréret, after developing a philosophy of hedonism and enlightened self-interest, declares: "Sublime virtue will consist in procuring the happiness of others at the cost of one's own."[12] It turns out that this, too, may be a calculation. But when he writes, "by 'virtues' we should understand habitual tendencies to do what makes our fellows happy,"[13] and omits what is *sous-entendu*, namely, in order that they should make us happy, it is easy to see how the locus of value came to be displaced. The high-minded Vauvenargues asserts that "humanitarianism is the first of virtues."[14] Pity is not merely "a return upon ourselves," he insists; "isn't our soul capable of disinterested feeling?"[15] Father André also lashes out at the theory of exclusive self-interest motivation and insists that there is no virtue without a real sacrifice, over and above any satisfaction. The source of disinterestedness is compassion, an immediate impulse to help others.[16]

To be sure, these are only inchoate reactions. But they begin to grow in number around the middle of the century. Levesque de Pouilly emphasizes sympathy.[17] Toussaint makes love (rather than self-interest) the basis of ethics. "Only love can make us faithful to our duties; it is the foundation of our relations, and the only knot which maintains them." We should love men, treat them with

[9] *Essay* (1724), pp. 358–68.
[10] *Avis d'une mère à son fils* (1728), p. 53.
[11] Perkins, "Unpublished Maxims," p. 502.
[12] *Oeuvres*, (1722), IV, p. 115.
[13] *Ibid.*, III, p. 76.
[14] *Oeuvres*, III, pp. 174, 219 (Maxims 98, 322).
[15] *Connaissance de l'esprit humain*, chap. XXXVIII.
[16] "Discours sur l'amour désinteressé," *Oeuvres philosophiques*, 1843, p. 370; "Discours sur les passions," *Oeuvres*, 1766, II, pp. 24–26.
[17] *Op. cit.* (1747), pp. 133–35.

kindness purely out of consideration of the fact that they are men.[18]

Morelly, though allowing for natural self-interest, considers an egoistic motive as annulling virtue, which is the love of good itself.[19] Fraternity and co-operation are emphasized in his epic poem, *La Basiliade* (1753), and take the place of enlightened self-interest.[20] The *Code de la nature* (1755), with its totalitarian, controlled society, is one of the first works to stress *bienfaisance*. Morelly calls it the highest of our moral ideals and names love as its basis. Morelly also follows enlightened self-interest and advises *bienfaisance* because it is "the first and surest means to present happiness"; nevertheless, he considers *bienfaisance* to be prior, in the natural order, to any other idea.[21] It is the nefarious institution of private property which has upset the beautiful order of nature.

Buffon in a way puts compassion prior to interest, by making it a physical reaction, one which he claims is shared by animals.[22] Formey, who indulges in a mélange of theories, denies that the advantageousness of an act suffices; it is not virtuous "if it does not really have as its goal the good of others, or universal good." [23] In 1759 the *Journal de Trévoux* reviewed a "Discours moral sur le plaisir de la bienfaisance," qualifying it as a sound but tiresome work.

Voltaire praised the abbé de Saint-Pierre for inventing the word *bienfaisance*. Himself a utilitarian with an invincible tendency to Natural Law and formalism, and with little faith in the virtue-happiness equivalence, he nonetheless makes *bienfaisance* the highest virtue and the central theme of his practical ethics. A deist, he exclaims:

> Ah! si vous êtes son image,
> Soyez comme lui bienfaisants.[24]

[18] *Les Moeurs*, Amsterdam, 1748, pp. 258–59, 340–45. In 1768, Toussaint read a paper on "Bienfaisance as an Active Principle" to the Academy of Berlin.
[19] *Essai sur le coeur humain* (1745), pp. 198–99, 20–22.
[20] See comment in Chinard's ed. of *Code de la nature*, pp. 59–60.
[21] *Code*, pp. 244–46, 263–64, 270–71, 173, 213–15.
[22] *Oeuvres*, ed. Piveteau, p. 367 (1758). For other references to compassion, see H. Hastings, *Man and Beast*, Baltimore, 1936, p. 232–42.
[23] *Mélanges philosophiques*, II, pp. 70–71. Also, *Le Bonheur* (1754), pp. 88–89, where he emphasizes motive.
[24] *Oeuvres*, VIII, p. 544.

And in an ode:

> L'homme n'était pas né pour égorger ses frères . . .
> La nature en son coeur avait mis la pitié.
> De tous les animaux seul il répand des larmes,
>   Seul il connaît les charmes
>   D'une tendre amitié.[25]

In his important article, "Vertu," he considers force, prudence, and temperance to be "useful qualities," but inferior to justice. However, "it is still not enough to be just, you must be beneficent: that is what is really cardinal." He also dismisses faith and hope as virtues. As for charity, it is what the ancients called love of our fellows. "That love is nothing, if it is not active: *bienfaisance* is therefore the only true virtue." If it is argued that nobody can follow virtue if you take away the reward, Voltaire will answer, "Then you have only your own interest in view." God and virtue should be loved for themselves.[26] Voltaire's life is the great testimony to the sincerity of his words. It was Rousseau whose love of man was abstract, and did not extend to men.

Bienfaisance, as an ethical absolute, was not favored by the apologists. Le François, in fact, severely criticized Voltaire's article, "Vertu." He insists that we must consider the motive of any act of *bienfaisance,* and that virtue is love of order, i.e., of the hierarchy of values according to God's plan.[27] Ilharat de la Chambre identifies virtue with the accomplishment of duty.[28] This is also the dictate of Para du Phanjas, who adds that the motives must be self-control and the desire to do one's duty, but not pleasure.[29]

The enthusiasm for virtue and benevolence, nevertheless, reaches a point at which sensibility and virtue are confused, and the ready flow of tears is taken for a sign of virtuous character.[30] As the article "Sensibilité-Morale" in the *Encyclopédie* puts it: "Reflection can make an honest man; but sensibility makes the virtuous man."

Thus the primary virtue was benevolence, and it . . . of course, was an old Christian virtue. The *philosophes* some-

---

[25] VIII, p. 489 (1768).
[26] XX, pp. 572–74. See also XXXII, p. 555; *Notebooks,* I, pp. 23, 219, 221.
[27] *Observations sur le Dictionnaire philosophique, Oeuvres,* 1856–57, I, pp. 818–20.
[28] *Op. cit.,* II, pp. 80–85.
[29] *Op. cit.,* p. 266.
[30] For a brief discussion, and references not given here, see Mornet, *Les Origines intellectuelles,* pp. 109–12.

what altered the idea, making it not a commandment but an
inclination, and teaching, for the recalcitrant, that men in particular *should* be humane because men in general *were* humane,
thus keeping up the appearance of deducing values from facts,
and duties from actual behavior.[31]

The anonymous article "Généreux," in the *Encyclopédie,* can
only be described as a hymn to virtue. "What happiness for man
to be able thus to become superior to his own being. . . ."

Rousseau, too, becomes emotionally excited on thinking of
virtue, though for him it is less the benevolence which moves him
than the heroic quality of victory over self. "The soul becomes
heated, the spirit rises, in speaking about virtue. Even the most
perverse sometimes feel its divine transports; and there is no man,
however wicked, who has not felt in his heart some sparks of this
celestial fire, and who has not been capable of heroic feelings and
actions, at least once in his life." [32] The very meaning of virtue—
as Rousseau distinguishes it from "goodness"—is the discipline
or suppression of the instinctual ego; it is a renunciation or turning away from nature, rather than a yielding or a compromise.
Nature and culture are not parallel lines. Virtue belongs to culture
only. And culture is a human construction, partly a rational construction, a new order of things, a new way of being, to which the
natural, as a self-justifying order, is inimical. Happiness is still
the aim of the cultural order, but the conditions and the road are
different. Virtue is its way, not the drive to happiness in its "natural" forms.

Diderot's virtue is really altruism, and *"bienfaisance*-sacrifice"
is its concrete form. What matters if in *Le Rêve de d'Alembert* he
had argued that determinism voids merit and annuls good and
evil, other than mere convention, and that he had derided shame
and remorse; or that in *Le Neveu de Rameau* he paints a world
where selfishness and happiness coexist? There is a love of virtue
innate in all men, prior to all convention. It may involve sacrifice
and unhappiness, he admits in the *Réfutation d'Helvétius*—so
much the better. "What is virtue?" he asks in his *Eloge de Richardson.* "It is, no matter how you look at it, self-sacrifice." [33] In *Le
Fils naturel,* the hero and heroine are quite ready to destroy the

[31] Palmer, *op. cit.,* pp. 191–92.
[32] *Fragments,* Vaughan, I, p. 337. See *La Nouvelle Heloïse,* ed. Pomeau, pp. 97, 142,
etc., etc.
[33] *Oeuvres,* VII, p. 214.

happiness they had planned for themselves. A phrase of Dorval's bears witness to the confusion we noted near the outset of this section, between *bienfaisance* conceived as the immediate source of happiness and as a difficult sacrifice. "Virtue," he exclaims, "sweet and cruel idea, dear and barbarous duties! . . . O virtue, what are you, if you demand no sacrifice?" But the sacrifice does —immediately—fill their souls with well-being. How often in his letters, plays, and art criticism does Diderot become exalted, or weep, at the hearing or sight of a noble, virtuous deed! Or enraged by a tale of wickedness, which seems to lower all mankind!

In a more analytical way, Leroy considers benevolence a basic reality, one which speaks when it is not hindered by self-interest, and which grows stronger with use. Compassion is the one absolute which distinguishes man from beast, writes this close observer of animals.[34] He suggests that it should be the major objective in the education of children and advises the use of pathetic stage spectacles—a technique which the *comédie larmoyante* and the bourgeois *drame* of the period, fathered by Nivelle de la Chaussée and Diderot, were exploiting amply.[35] As for d'Holbach, while he joins the chorus in praise of *bienfaisance,* he will not admit it as anything but a form of self-interest, and deems pity a result of our weakness and the desire to avoid discomfort.[36]

Delille sings of *bienfaisance* in his long poem, *Les Trois règnes de la nature:* "And the beneficent man is the image of God." [37] A lesser poet, Nougaret, fulminates in 1769 against the lack of grain and its high cost, which he attributes to selfish profiteers. But this is hard to believe, for men are not evil.[38] Pity, writes

[34] The sharing of feelings, he claims, is the foundation of sociability, and of virtue. Compassion is independent of self-interest.

[35] *Op. cit.,* pp. 202–4, 264–70.

[36] *Système social,* I, pp. 111–12.

[37] Chant VIII.

[38]   "Mais à l'humanité c'est assez faire outrage.
Non, des coeurs aussi durs n'existèrent jamais;
Non, de la Calomnie émoussons les traits.
Quoi, séduit par l'amour d'une vaine opulence,
On peut des malheureux ravir la subsistance,
L'on entend sans douleur ses sanglots et ses cris,
Et du bien qu'il souhaite on double encore le prix!
Le féroce lion respecte la Nature;
Va-t-il à son semblable arracher la pâture?
Et l'on voudrait qu'un homme, artisan de nos maux,
Surpassât la fureur des cruels animaux!"
Pensons mieux des humains; non, la soif des richesses
Ne fit naître jamais tant de scéleratesses. . . .
          (*La Voix du Peuple,* Amsterdam, 1769)

Sabatier de Castres in an early work, is the first feeling of the heart and the source of all virtues.[39] Chamfort, high-minded yet cynical, also breaks into verse to celebrate virtue. This, he says, is worthier than any human accomplishment.

> O prodige plus grand! ô vertu que j'adore!
> C'est par toi que nos coeurs s'ennoblissent encore:
> Quoi! ma voix chante l'homme, et j'ai pu t'oublier!
> Je célèbre avant toi . . . Pardonne, beauté pure;
>   Pardonne cette injure. . . .
> Là, tranquille au milieu d'une foule abattue,
> Tu me fais, ô Socrate, envier ta vigueur;
> Là, c'est ce fier Romain, plus grand que son vainqueur;
> C'est Caton sans courroux déchirant sa blessure:
>   Son âme libre et pure
> S'enfuit loin des tyrans au sein de son auteur.[40]

Are these mere words? We will not think so if we remember how Chamfort took his own life, with razor and revolver, to escape imprisonment by agents of committees of Public Safety.

The vogue of the pastoral, in poetry and fiction, can be explained by its uniting two high fashions—nature and virtue. Bernardin de Saint-Pierre's *Paul et Virginie* and Marmontel's *Annete et Lubin* are two of the most popular examples.[41] Marmontel's *Moral Tales* carried on the mode and furnished the antithesis to the *Immoral Tales* of the Prince de Ligne and countless others which merited the same title.

But let us return to the philosophers, several of whom are worthy of mention. The eccentric, Rouillé d'Orfeuil, decries the universal bandying about of the word, *bienfaisance,* and anathematizes all the books being written about it. Burn them! he cries. It is enough to follow the Golden Rule, to right wrongs, to solace the innocent who are suffering, to make others happy—there is no need to write books. Of course disinterestedness is an essential, for self-interest is the vice of low born churls; "every gentlemanly heart must despise it." [42] Saint-Lambert urges benevolence, but, although it has some roots in our being, it is, in his opinion, largely a matter of selfish calculation; however he recommends that it be

---

[39] *Dictionnaire des passions*, II, p. 257.
[40] *Oeuvres Complètes*, I, pp. 444–47.
[41] See Jean Fabre, "Une question de terminologie littéraire; *Paul et Virginie,* pastorale," *Annales publiées par la Faculté des Lettres de Toulouse*, 3:168–200, 1953.
[42] *L'Alambic moral*, Maroc, 1773, pp. 84, 198, 535.

taught to children, even with the use of trickery. Saint-Lambert nevertheless claims that "love is the source of all virtues." [43] Delisle de Sales exclaims: "Oh virtue! all beings are annihiliated before you; you alone, you take the place of all goods given by nature, or created by opinion; you exist, and evil is no longer on earth." [44]

The 1780's show no diminishing of fervor. Sylvain Maréchal, refusing to accept the sensationist analysis, places "that natural impulse which carries us to our fellows" alongside of the desire for happiness. We love to do good, and not out of hope for a return. "I appeal to your heart, I appeal to mine, I appeal to all worthy hearts; this pleasure which we take in doing good to our fellow men is not the effect of a vile calculation; that inner satisfaction which follows a service is not degraded by the hope of a reward. What man, traversing a deep forest at night in a country he will never again see, would fail to succor the unfortunate man who would call upon him?" [45] In Sylvain Maréchal we can see a concrete example of another phenomenon connected with the intoxication of virtue. In the years preceding the Revolution, self-sacrifice and benevolence take still another step, and become particularized as patriotism, which Robespierre later embodied, and which he tried to propagate among the people. We get a taste of it in another piece by Sylvain Maréchal, written after the Revolution, and expressing the bitterness of disillusion:

> Virtue rewards those who are faithful to her; virtue is not a beautiful and sterile theory. . . . Virtue sometimes ignores or disdains conventions. Considerations touch it little; harsh, fierce, brusque like truth, she does not know the use of circumspection. There is no compromise with her, she wants everything or nothing. . . . There is something above a good citizen, an excellent patriot, that is the man of virtue. . . . The man of virtue lives as if there were no laws. . . . Man complains of the limits to his faculties: ungrateful atom! has he then forgotten that he can reach virtue? eh! what is there beyond that? [46]

[43] Note to "Hiver," in *Les Saisons*, p. 242; also *Catéchisme universel, Oeuvres*, II, pp. 21, 152–53; *Commentaire sur le Catéchisme*, III, pp. 4–8.

[44] *De la Philosophie de la nature*, III, pp. 404, 244–46.

[45] "Essai sur les passions," *Mélanges*, Avignon, 1782, pp. 118–23.

[46] *De la Vertu*, 1807, pp. 88–91. Cf. M. Dumas, *L'Esprit du citoyen*, Neuchâtel, 1783: "Every man must work for the public." It is not only our obligation, but part of the nobility of man's nature, of "the grandeur of his destiny." Virtue makes him like God.

Lamourette writes: "Virtue supposes effort and resistance. If man were necessarily just, or if nothing of what he owed to God and Society were difficult for his weakness, he would have *Innocence*, without having Virtue, which signifies a determina-

A related and somewhat broader version of benevolence went under the name of *humanité*. This word, however, which the sentimental currents appropriated and absorbed, had had an earlier history. More than charity, or humanitarianism in the narrow sense, it had already come to signify the unity of the human kind, and the duty of each to all. Its root, so it was thought, is our universal likeness, embodied in our needs and reactions, and particularly in our need for each other—not only as a survival mechanism but also as a natural inclination, call it pleasure or sympathy. These themes, which we have encountered throughout our study, lead to the conclusion that no man can think anything human alien to himself. The word and idea of *humanité* were destined to spread and gradually engulf all but the most skeptical, cynical, or nihilistic of eighteenth-century souls. The most optimistic grounded it on a supposed original goodness in men. Atheists attributed it to biological, psychological, or calculated utilitarian requirements. Deists and Christians—who constitute the bulk and the average—saw it as an aspect of Natural Law, immediately intuited by right reason. In any case, human nature and human welfare on earth, openly or implicitly, with or without an ultimate sanction of divine command, were to be the guideposts of proper moral action—an ethical view that stands in contrast with the moral writings of the seventeenth century. Such a faith, if charged with emotion, and made into an all-inclusive, sufficient virtue, might almost become a secular religion, rivaling the Christian dependency on the supernatural for salvation and for direction. It became, as we know, the religion of the *philosophes,* and spread beyond them to wider segments of society.

Although the development of an ideal of "humanity" had already been evident in the first half of the century, it was then rational rather than sentimental. It may be described as a peculiarly eighteenth-century development of Natural Law doctrine. It was taken as a rationally intuited truth and law, God-implanted or simply natural, whose function is the socialization of the self-centered individual. Pufendorf, Bayle, Montesquieu, and many others proclaimed "humanity" in its multiple senses, or defined it as the epitome of all virtues, as a moral imperative inseparable

---

tion of the will to prefer justice to personal tastes and enjoyment. (*Pensées sur la philosophie de la foi,* 1789, p. 5.) Many other references could be given.

from order and justice, and from social well-being. At the same time, it was considered in one of two ways, either as the counterpoise to self-love, in *homo duplex,* or else as the sublimation and fulfillment of self-love, not its sacrifice. In either case, "humanity" substitutes natural love (not necessarily excluding natural self-love, then) for the Christian emphasis on original sin, on the corruption of self-love, on grace and ritual as ways to salvation or happiness in another life. Humanity, a rational claim, rivals with Christian charity as a social duty which is rightfully expected of men.

In the second half of the century, the spread of sentimentalism, *sensibilité* and enthusiasm for virtue gradually transforms the ideal of "humanity" into an emotional war-cry. The emphasis is on the joy, the outpouring of the heart which accompany participation in the happiness of others and (even more) in their sorrows. *"Humanité"* is spoken of now as a passion, a sweet, good passion, not as a rational calculation or conviction. Diderot, Bernardin, Marmontel, and many others celebrate it and preach it. To all intents and purposes, it accompanies or fuses with the movement of sentimental benevolence.

The ideal of "humanity" was upheld not only by the minority of writers who considered men to be naturally good, but also by the majority who deemed them either evil or an indifferent mixture. Philosophers such as Diderot and Rousseau do not consider this natural impulse to be strong, in comparison with the selfish impulses. They emphasize the need to inculcate and to strengthen it, at every step, by education and the power of legislation. For the rationalistic adherents of Natural Law, "humanity" was a *droit* that men would follow, if they were all rational and good—which they are not; for the sentimentalists, it was a natural sympathy and impulse that would bring men their deepest happiness, if they were unspoiled by the struggle for existence, power and prestige—which they are not. For both groups, then, only a few "well-born souls" actually did find their intellectual or emotional delectation this way. A program of education and a political program were thus required, to induce or compel men to act as they *naturally* want to, or should. We shall see more of this in our final chapter.

At the same time, in accord with the shift of emphasis in *droit naturel* from the element of duty to the element of rights, the idea of humanity gradually acquired another political connotation. A social order which was unfavorable to *humanité,* it became evident, was not a good order, and but one to be changed. In 1776, in his *Ethocratie,* d'Holbach makes it clear that "humanity" presupposes equality of rights. The ideal of humanity, then, in association with developments in Natural Law theories, is the fountainhead of the "liberté, égalité, fraternité" of the French Revolution. We have tried to show, in summary fashion, in the concluding chapter of *An Age of Crisis,* how this virtue of humanity, "by a strange perversion, came to be the justification of violence and barbarism." [46a]

Although the ideal of "humanity" had its roots in Natural Law doctrine, and remained tinged with utilitarian associations, its great diffusion, in the second half of the century, depended on its association with the trend of benevolence and sentimental virtue. It was, moreover, though a noble and admirable ideal, subject to the weaknesses of the cult of benevolence, even as it benefited from the emotional strengths of that trend. It differed somewhat from benevolence in being more vague, general, and abstract, leading Palissot to charge the *philosophes* with "loving mankind, in order to love no man."

A few voices, but not many, dared to speak up against the new cult. Quite early, Crousaz had criticized Pope's exaggerated altruism, warning that we must be careful to choose the objects of charity, and not to overdo it to the point of ruining oneself and family.[47] In England, Price issued a similar warning. Benevolence, he notes, is not all of virtue. If it were, everything would be indifferent except the degrees of benevolence; there would be no distinction of persons involved, no other ground for disapproving injustice and falsehood. Most keenly, he points out that the doctrine is nothing but a disguised form of the greater happiness principle. If to make others happy is the highest value, we should be entitled to take the fruits of labor from one and give it to another whom it would make happier.[48] The theologian, Nonnotte, also criticized Voltaire's article, "Vertu." If a wife is unfaithful, he

---

[46a] P. Vernière, "L'Idée d'humanité au XVIIIᵉ siècle," p. 178, to which article I owe part of the preceding development. Vernière does not attempt to answer this question, or that of "the historical responsibility of the philosophy of the Enlightenment for the excesses of the Revolution."

[47] *Examen* (1737), p. 200.

[48] *Review* (1758), p. 131.

demands, but is charitable, does that make her virtuous? No, indeed; virtue is "conformity of our conduct with the prescriptions of reason, cause, and law." [49] In 1775, two more writers offered a protest. Charles Levesque, while conceding that it is our duty to do as much good as we can (citizens must be useful to the State), asserts that self-interest comes first. After all, it is in the interest of the State that each citizen takes care of himself and his family first.[50] The second writer was Marat. His words are helpful in reminding us that the current of egoistic analysis of human behavior continued to flourish. A doctor, with the pretension to a scientific analysis of man, Marat denies that compassion is a natural or innate feeling; it is unknown to children and to savages. It exists, to be sure, but as a product of culture. To pity others, we must know what it is they are suffering, but not be suffering at the time ourselves: "nobody gives to anybody else anything but the sensibility which he does not need for himself." Men can easily habituate themselves to dulling this feeling. Basically, there is a great reservoir of cruelty in men, as their love of cruel sports testifies.[51] And de Boismont, in 1781, lapses into irony: "Oh! Monsieur, we've made a great step forward! . . . Honesty, uprightness, integrity, all those old words which disturb nature, are now fortunately replaced by those of *bienfaisance* and *humanité;* with those two words you accomplish everything: glory, reputation, justice. You can corrupt . . . steal from half the human race; as long as fine tirades, or a little public act proves that you are concerned with the happiness of the other half, everything is fine." [52]

As if in illustration of de Boismont's words, one of the most striking scenes of Laclos' *Les Liaisons dangereuses* (which appeared the following year) offers a confirmation of the arguments of the proponents of the morality of benevolence (in regard to its innateness, its power, and its results in terms of happiness), and at the same time, the confirmation of the arguments of its adversaries. We recall that Valmont is the nihilist, the embodiment of

[49] *Dictionnaire philosophique de la religion,* Besançon, 1774, IV, p. 455. We should not forget Malebranche's earlier insistence that the moral criterion is duty, not a good, whatever it might be.

[50] *L'Homme moral,* I, pp. 182–84.

[51] *De l'Homme,* I, pp. 162–69.

[52] *Lettres secrettes sur l'état actuel de la Religion et du Clergé en France,* n.p., n.d., p. 3.

evil for evil's sake. Valmont walks to the village in order to succor a desperately needy family—this being a calculated plan to further his reputation so that, precisely, he may win some advantage in the heart of the woman he is planning to ruin. On the way, he takes sadistic pleasure in tormenting the spy who is following him. Then he reaches the cottage and succors the desperate family:

> After this simple action, you cannot imagine what a chorus of blessings from all those present resounded around me! What tears of gratitude flowed from the eyes of the old head of that family, and ennobled that patriarchal face which a moment before had been made hideous by the fierce imprint of despair! I was examining this spectacle when another peasant, younger, leading a woman and two children by the hand, rushed up to me and said to them "Let us fall at the feet of this image of God"; and, at the same instant, I was surrounded by this family, kneeling at my feet. I will admit my weakness; my eyes were damp with tears, and I felt within me an involuntary but delightful impulse. I was astonished by the pleasure that doing good makes you feel; and I would be tempted to believe that those whom we call virtuous people do not have as much merit as they tell us. . . . You will notice that my faithful spy was in the crowd. My purpose was accomplished. . . . When everything is calculated I can congratulate myself on my invention. That woman is without doubt worth all the trouble I am taking . . . and having in a way, paid for her in advance, I will have the right to use her according to my whims, without having anything to reproach myself for. I forgot to tell you that in order to put everything to a profit, I asked those good folk to pray to God for the success of my projects.

Valmont's machinations have the desired effect on his intended victim. She is convinced that he is on the path of reform, and weeps at the story of his benevolence. "Now tell me," she asks, "if M. de Valmont is really an unregenerate libertin, if he is only that and acts in this way, what is there left for good people to do? Can the wicked share with the good the sacred pleasure of benevolence?"

Despite the wave of enthusiasm, then, it appeared to many that altruism, like egoism, is a natural quality which can be moral or immoral according to the mode of exercise. The reaction against the Christian call to self-sacrifice had led to philosophies of hedonism and egoism, and thence, through the transfer of the locus of value to society and the sublimation of egoism in its so-called "enlightened" forms, back again to the spirit of sacrifice, but on a secular basis of love for man rather than of love of God through his creatures.[53] In this way moralists returned to that impulse to virtue-sacrifice and benevolence which is part of man's earliest biological and social heritage.[54] Simultaneously, they recaptured an indispensable element of the ethical experience. But the enthusiasts went too far and forgot that this element must itself be submitted to and ruled by general laws or principles of obligation, however they may be conceived. It is not surprising, then, that a few men, dissatisfied with the alternatives offered by utilitarianism, whether in the form of enlightened self-interest or benevolence (not to speak of the hedonism of the egoists or of the Physiocratic school) proposed an ethics of self-perfectionism. The current was weak, the traces few, but we cannot overlook them completely.

The ethics of self-perfection had been developed as a systematic philosophy by Spinoza. In the late seventeenth and early eighteenth centuries we encounter little more than isolated statements. Thus Abbadie had set it along with happiness as the two highest goods. Negatively, he explains, men want to get rid of their faults —unless it means giving up pleasure. Positively men want perfections that do not belong to their species. They often fail to think of the perfections they should have as *men*, rather than those attached to their careers and status. We should consider ourselves in God's eyes, rather than in men's. "Even men's passions become perfections when they have their proper extension in immortal man." [55]

"If glory and merit," asks Vauvenargues, "do not make men happy, does what is called happiness deserve their regrets? Would a courageous spirit deign to accept either fortune or peace of mind, or moderation, if he had to sacrifice to them the vigor of his feeling and lower the soaring of his genius?" Pleasure, then, is not for Vauvenargues the standard of value.[56] Perfection, writes Christian

<hr>

[53] Cf. Mornet on the Christian view: one must love nothing and no one except in God. Charity really means love of God, and if one helps one's neighbor it is for the love of God. (*Op. cit.*, p. 106.)

[54] Cf. E. Westermarck, *The Origin and Development of Moral Ideas*, p. 186 ff. Also, E. Dardel: "Whoever calls men to sacrifice is appealing, beyond the demonstrable and the reasoned, to psychic dispositions and inner impulses capable of engaging the person, and of the same essence as that which, among archaic peoples, takes the form of myth." ("Signification du Mythique," p. 70.)

[55] *Op. cit.*, pp. 287–97.

[56] *Oeuvres*, III, pp. 19 (71), 61 (272 "variants"), 195 (217).

Wolff, is our natural duty to ourselves. He defines the word as "the harmonious use of all the faculties of our soul, both higher and lower." To this is added the duty to develop each faculty to its maximum.[57] Yvon also mentions happiness and self-perfection as our two duties, but defines the latter term as the "perfect conformity of our will with order"—a reminiscence of Malebranche.[58]

Formey was particularly interested in the ethics of self-perfection, and seems to have been familiar with Spinoza. He defines perfection as "the accordance and harmony with which the diverse parts of a whole conspire to the same end." [59] The parts of man are two—body and soul. Therefore the goal of this composite being is "the maintenance and increase of the faculties of his soul and body, which he is obligated to procure with all the means in his power." As a free and moral being, there is much a man can do. "Perfection" applies to this moral life. But what is the purpose toward which all we do should tend harmoniously? It is the accomplishment of our natural functions: a mind that wants knowledge, a soul that desires moral good, a body to be kept vigorous. The result of the complete exercise of our faculties will be happiness. In summary, there are four golden rules that lead to perfection: first, to will it; second, to do nothing without relating it to the end, or a subordinate end; third, to harmonize the subordinate ends, so that one is always a means to the other, and the whole a means to our perfection; fourth, never to permit anything contrary to perfection.[60]

What is primary, according to Moses Mendelssohn, is not the pleasurable feeling but the effort toward perfection, which produces it. Our soul tends toward perfection, and no other choice has a sufficient reason. Perfection lies in unity. It is not true, as some argue, that this is a form of egoism. "Do you then imagine that the principle of perfection allows me to concentrate within myself, and to make a sad desert of everything that surrounds me?" No, Mendelssohn insists, this instinct, as natural to us as self-

---

[57] *Principes* (1758), pp. 21–23.

[58] "Amour-propre" (*Encyclopédie*).

[59] "Essai sur la Perfection," in *Mélanges philosophiques*, Leyde, 1754, II, pp. 109–19.

[60] See also the lengthy development in Formey's "Système du vrai bonheur," *ibid.*, II, pp. 53–105, against hedonism and self-centeredness, and in favor of self-perfection.

preservation, is a principle of inclusion, not of exclusion. The separation of the self from others is "moral death." [61]

In a way, the ethics of self-perfection was another form of the enthusiasm for virtue, one which refused to take the simple direction of benevolence. The enthusiasm for virtue, notes Jean Fabre, was more than an exaltation of sensibility, more than sentimental rose-festivals and the nauseating "literature" that went with them. The spiritual tension common to Charlotte Corday and Mme Roland, to Chénier and Saint-Just, and the virtue to which they were dedicated consisted in the will to devote their lives to an ideal which surpassed their lives. It was not a stoical virtue, but one which sought "a lever in the strength of passions. Implying the affirmation of the self, it is far from letting itself be enclosed in the self . . . [it] intoxicates itself on nobility and energy, but does not blush to lay down as a principle . . . to seek the happiness of the greatest number." [62]

The ethics of self-perfection, writes Schweitzer, falls into the optimistic-ethical world view. It lacks a content, and is not capable of so establishing the basic principle of the moral that it has a content which is ethically satisfying. The ethics of altruism "starts from altruism as content in order to conceive it as belonging to self-perfection"; the ethics of self-perfection "starts from self-perfection and seeks to conceive altruism as an item in its content which is a necessity of thought." [63] Kant also criticized this ethics as "empty and indefinite," and as unable to avoid "presupposing the morality which it is to explain." [64]

It need scarcely be added that the transcendental, Christian ethics continues its unbroken history throughout the eighteenth century. As the pious Protestant, Crousaz, writes, "we must give ourselves entirely to our Creator, live, think, act only to please and to obey him." [65] Le François agrees: "Man is made for God: the essential end of his being is therefore to attach himself to his God. . . ." He will incidentally be useful to men, and be happy.[66] "Man cannot propose his own goals," affirms Gauchat; he would

---

[61] *Recherches sur les sentiments moraux*, Genève, 1763, pp. 32–46. Cf. also, Robinet, *Dictionnaire*, "Bien," "Bon," "Devoir," and Bouchaud, *Principes de métaphysique et de morale* (1780).

[62] J. Fabre, *Chénier, l'homme et l'oeuvre*, p. 38.

[63] *Op. cit.*, p. 218.

[64] *Fundamental Principles*, *op. cit.*, pp. 61–62.

[65] *Op. cit.*, p. 182.

[66] *Observations*, I, p. 819.

"have neither author, nor master, nor rule but himself." Make man independent, say he exists for self-preservation and happiness —here is the whole philosophy of nihilism—is Gauchat's conclusion.[67]

The dominance of a utilitarian-type thinking is evident from its diffusion, the quality of the minds which embraced it, and its pervasive infiltration of other types of ethics. And yet, in a counter-movement, ethical formalism takes possession of an important phase of utilitarianism. The vogue of virtue-altruism-*bienfaisance* had happiness (of others) as its end, but the act itself became the bearer of value, often, as its critics complained, regardless of other moral criteria.

We have considered the criticisms of the various aspects or components of the utilitarian synthesis. There remains for us to examine some general criticisms of utilitarianism as an ethical philosophy.

There were some who refused to lose sight of the fact that an important object in moral judgment (some would say, the most important) is intention, or good will. Virtue, Malebranche had said, is the love of order, "an habitual, free and dominating love of immutable order." [68] The criterion of benevolent intention was the implication of Bayle's "impious paradox," that of the English anti-utilitarians and of Hume. It was upheld by a few apologists,

---

[67] *Op. cit.*, XVI, p. 88. For the Christian view, see also Maupertuis, *Oeuvres*, I, p. 232 ff.; Abauzit, *Oeuvres*, Genève, 1770, pp. 44–76; Bergier, *Principes*, pp. 159–60, 220–25; Para du Phanjas, *op. cit.*, p. 114 ff.; Jamin, *Pensées théologiques*, 1769, pp. 54–55; La Luzerne, *Instruction pastorale*, 1786, pp. 48–132; Gauchat, *op. cit.*, I, pp. 206–7; Dulaurens, *Portefeuille*, IV, pp. 148–54; Bernardin de Saint-Pierre, "De la Nature de la morale"; Marmontel, *Leçons*, pp. 208–10. See also the previously cited works by A. Monod and R. R. Palmer.

Para deduces the existence of God from the existence of virtue. If there is no God, he argues, whose will binds men, each is his own ultimate end. Then there is no limit to his right or his conduct, and virtue is folly. But such conclusions are so revolting that they are patently false. "Therefore God exists. Q.E.D." We have noted several times that such a rigoristic approach advanced the cause of nihilism.

La Luzerne defends the Christian virtues largely on the basis of their usefulness. Like the nihilists, he implicitly denies the existence of moral feeling; religion is effective because men act only for rewards and to avoid punishment.

These are some examples of the failure of transcendental ethics in the eighteenth century. Suffused with new ideas, the notion of transcendental self-evidence is often forgotten and rules applicable to cases are almost never clearly given. Prudence and self-interest are given a wide role. This is a good distance from, for instance, the dictum of Malebranche: "For all our actions are good or bad only because God has commanded or forbidden them, or because of eternal law . . . or because of the written law. . . ." (*Recherche de la vérité*, I, pp. 426–27.)

[68] *Traité de morale*, chap. 3. The term "dominating" is similar to Kant's "practical."

although most agreed that men could not act out of pure love of virtue. Holland, for example, exclaims against d'Holbach's assertion that "virtue is everything which is truly and constantly useful to men living in society": "It follows from this beautiful definition that a fertile field is very virtuous. . . . Let us rather say that virtue, although very useful, is in itself different from utility. It consists of an invariable inclination to the right. . . . The good which results from an action is not what makes it estimable; it is the principle of generosity, affection, gratitude, humanity, from which it comes. We despise the vicious man, even when his bad actions turn to our advantage; the intention which accompanies them makes their moral worth." [69] Holland points out that d'Holbach is inconsistent when he writes that the virtuous man is one who *is inclined* to doing good. D'Holbach says that "virtues" relating only to the individual himself are not virtues but prudence. In this case, suggests Holland, his whole system is one of prudence and not of morals. Marmontel argued also that every act is pleasant or useful to someone, and on this basis, they are all good.[70] One of Kant's great distinctions was between the man of good morals and the morally good man.[71]

The main ground of criticism was the neglect by utilitarians of the distinction between right and good. "Even before the rise of this movement, Grotius had warned that "utility is not the mother of the just and equitable, and that men would not cease to seek for the right and to further it for right's sake, even if no use or profit were connected with it." [72] Pufendorf, following him, calls the useful and harmful a different science from the right and wrong.[73] Bayle's opinion may be summarized in the following lines: "Reason dictated to the ancient sages that one should do the good for the sake of good itself and that virtue (or truth) should stand as a recompense for itself, and that it belonged only to a wicked man to abstain from evil out of fear of punishment." [74]

A detailed scrutiny of the British anti-utilitarians would take us beyond the scope of this chapter. Yet we cannot pass them over

[69] *Op. cit.*, I, pp. 139–42.

[70] "Bonté," *Encyclopédie*, Supplément.

[71] *Critique*, pp. 337–38. Also: "We call a man bad, however, not because he performs actions that are bad (violating law), but because these are of such a kind that we may infer from them bad maxims in him."

[72] *Prolegomena*, Sect. 16.

[73] *Op. cit.*, I, pp. 47–48.

[74] Quoted by Pichon, *Les Argumens de la raison*, Londres, 1776, p. 97.

without brief consideration. Butler emphasized that approval and disapproval are unavoidable, and that their object is the desert of the agent, rather than the good produced by the act itself. The whole of virtue, he says,

> does not consist in promoting the happiness of mankind. For it is certain, that the sum of the most shocking instances of injustice, adultery, murder, perjury, and even of persecution, may, in many supposable instances, not have the appearance of being likely to produce an overbalance of misery in the present state; perhaps sometimes may have the contrary appearance. . . . Nay, farther, were treachery, violence and injustice no otherwise vicious, than as foreseen likely to produce an overbalance of misery to society; then, if in any case a man could procure to himself as great advantage by an act of injustice, as the whole foreseen inconvenience, likely to be brought upon others by it, would amount to, such a piece of injustice would not be faulty or vicious at all; because it would be no more than in, any other case, for a man to prefer his own satisfaction to another's in equal degrees. The fact then appears to be, that we are constituted so as to condemn falsehood, unprovoked violence, injustice, and to approve of benevolence to some preferably to others, abstracted from all consideration which conduct is likeliest to produce an overbalance of happiness or misery.[75]

Price distinguishes between right as fitness taken in the non-moral sense of means to an end, and in the moral sense, which leads to judgments of guilt or virtue. [76] If nothing can oblige but the prospect of pleasure and pain, then vice is only imprudence, and "nothing is right or wrong, just or unjust, any further than its affects self-interest; and . . . a being independently and completely happy, cannot have any moral perceptions." [77] This is precisely what Helvétius and d'Holbach were later to assert. But Price argues that on the self-interest principle, virtue in certain circumstances becomes vice (an action that is not fit). He supports the formal value of acts—such as the wrong of lying; if lying is once admitted as justified by its advantages to us, there will be no limit to deceit. "Can we, then, when we consider these things,

---

[75] "Of the Nature of Virtue," *The Analogy of Religion*, Appendix, pp. 340–48.
[76] Chapter VII of Price's *Review* is particularly important, showing in detail that the useful cannot be the criterion of the right. Raphael comments that the error of utilitarianism lies in saying that our obligation is to the happiness of others based on the nature of happiness alone; whereas it is an obligation to *them*, arising from our relation to them as personalities.
[77] *Ibid.*, pp. 106–7.

avoid pronouncing, that there is an *intrinsic rectitude* in keeping
faith and in sincerity, and intrinsic evil in the contrary; and that
it is by no means true, that veracity and falsehood appear *in themselves,* and *exclusive of their consequences,* wholly indifferent to
our moral judgment?" [78]

Reid declares that the rule of greatest good is not enough. The
correction of the tendency to immediate good by the good of the
whole is a purely rational principle. But men are not rational
enough and are too ready to make exceptions. A "disinterested
regard to duty" is also requisite. Others are only *trained* to a
certain discipline. Duty cannot be resolved into the notion of
interest, and obligation is a relation between the real quality of
the action and the person of the agent.[79] Ferguson, too, makes the
point that moral obligation is itself "an ultimate fact and principle of nature, not an appearance to be explained from any other
principle better known." [80] We are all the keepers of our fellow
creatures; and "what hast thou done with thy brother Abel?" was
the first expostulation in behalf of morality.[81]

In England, then, anti-utilitarianism was a strong movement,
and functioned as a reaction to Hobbes, Mandeville, and Hume.
In France, however, the protests were relatively insignificant.
Altruism, we must remember, operated within the utilitarian
framework of producing the greatest amount of good, or happiness. The opposition was concentrated in the theological group,
where it did not offer a secular alternative for those who had
broken away from orthodoxy. Denesle, for one, points to the lack
of a moral principle in utilitarianism. A son ought to kill his
annoying, gouty old father; this would put him out of a useless
life and would be good for the son and also for the public interest,
since the son would spend his money. After all, public interest
should prevail over the private, and the greater happiness principle (as well as self-interest) justifies the act.[82] Bergier takes a
different tack: utility is too inconstant and relative to serve as a
moral rule.[83] It may require the sacrifice of justice, equity, and of

[78] *Ibid.,* p. 133.
[79] *Active Powers,* pp. 137–53.
[80] *Institutes,* 1785, pp. 108–11.
[81] *An Essay on the History of Civil Society,* Edinburgh, 1814, pp. 57–61.
[82] Denesle, *Examen,* p. 5 ff.
[83] *Examen,* pp. 225–27.

civil laws, adds Hayer.[84] Virtue, says Bergier again, "pleases us independently of the advantage which it may bring us; crime can tempt us only insofar as it appears useful." We never feel regret for a noble deed, even if it produces only ingratitude and hatred.[85] The idea of social utility and the idea of right are essentially different, argues Richard; the latter is conformity to the divine or natural law of duty, which the former often violates. The moral law inheres in the essence of things, as the expression of our relations to others, which we are not free to change. Man has duties because he has reason.[86] Richard's analysis leads into the dilemma of the white lie, and of the legitimacy of lying in general. He, like Kant, erects truth-telling into a formal absolute. Much earlier in the century, Father André and Malebranche, in an exchange of letters, had devised ways of justifying the white lie, without (they thought) betraying their rigoristic formalism.[87]

As for criticism of utilitarianism from the secular point of view, there is little to be mentioned other than the animadversions, which we have already considered, against particular theories. Turgot, it is worth adding, was aroused by Helvétius' *De l'Esprit*, and he protested more than once against its exclusion of the independent ideas of justice and right. Helvétius, he complains, incorrectly reverses the proposition, "justice for all is to the interest of all." Nor does he ever understand men's need to love—other than sexual appetite. Philosophically, his maxim, "self-interest is the sole principle of human behavior" is stupid, and means only "man desires only what he desires." But moral judgments, affirms Turgot, are a real factor in decisions, alongside of self-interest.[88]

The great opponent of utilitarian and happiness theories in ethics was, of course, Kant. Like others before him, but with

---

[84] *Op. cit.*, VII, pp. 266–67. Also Camuset, *Principes*, p. 322; Para, *Saine Philosophie*, I, p. 240; Pey, *op. cit.*, pp. 94–109.

[85] *Principes de métaphysique*, pp. 155–59.

[86] *Défense*, pp. 24–27, 247–51.

[87] André, *Documents inédits*, 1844, 1856, I, p. 10 ff. (1706). On this subject, see L. G. Crocker, "The Problem of Truth and Falsehood in the Age of Enlightenment," *Journal of The History of Ideas*, 14:575–603, 1953. Further research has revealed considerable additional bibliography on this question.

[88] *Oeuvres*, I, pp. 362–63; also, letter to Condorcet, III, pp. 637–38. For other criticisms of utilitarianism, see Sénac, *Considérations sur l'esprit et les moeurs*, in *Oeuvres*, Hambourg, 1795, pp. 252–71; Marmontel, *Oeuvres posthumes*, 1806, XL, pp. 74–76. Honesty is useful, writes the latter, but everything honest is not useful.

greater logical cogency and system, Kant argues that if it is wrong
to lie, it is not in order to avoid a greater evil (such as loss of
credit), but because lying "must be regarded as evil in itself, so
that the imperative of the prohibition is categorical." He argues
that man is bound by laws of duty which are both universal and
of his own making. But on the interest theory (private or public),
man never acts out of duty, and the imperative, being conditional,
is not a moral command. We then have what Kant terms the
heteronomy of the will, which is the source of all spurious principles of morality: the will does not give itself the law (as the fitness of its maxims to be universal laws), but goes out of itself and
seeks the law in the character of its objects—"I ought to do something because I wish for something else." It is true that I ought
indeed to promote the happiness of others, "but simply because
a maxim which excludes it cannot be comprehended as a universal
law." Empirical principles are wholly incapable of serving as a
foundation for moral laws, for they lack the force of universality.
The principle of private happiness is most objectionable, because
it is false (experience denies the relation between virtue and prosperity), because it is not moral in principle, and because it positively undermines morality, by putting the motives to virtue and
to vice in the same class, teaching us "only to make a better calculation." Exactly like La Mettrie and Sade, Kant declares that
it is impossible to distinguish between higher and lower desires
by separating those which come from the senses from those which
come from the understanding, since "it is of no consequence
whence the *idea* of this pleasing object is derived, but only how
much it *pleases*." The feeling of pleasure is of one and the same
kind, and can differ only in degree. Only when reason of itself
determines the will immediately, not by means of an intervening
feeling of pleasure and pain, can we speak of moral law and conduct. To be happy is a wish which is a law that is subjectively
necessary, as a law of nature; objectively, however, it is a contingent
or relative principle, and can never furnish a universal law, "since,
in the desire for happiness it is not the form [of conformity to
law] that is decisive, but simply the matter, whether I am to expect
pleasure in following the law, and how much." On this basis,
"practical" principles [those determining the will] can never be
universally directed to the same objects; and even if they could,

the unanimity itself would only be contingent, only empirically and subjectively valid. From the erection of the desire for happiness into a universal "practical" law, the extreme opposite of harmony must follow, and the complete destruction of the maxim itself. "For, in that case, the will of all has not one and the same object, but everyone has his own [his private welfare], which may accidentally accord with the purposes of others which are equally selfish, but is far from sufficing for a law; because the occasional exceptions which one is permitted to make are endless, and cannot be definitely embraced in one universal rule." [89] With such empirical principles,

> each man makes his own subject the foundation of his inclination, and in the same subject sometimes one inclination, sometimes another has the preponderance. To discover a law which would govern them all under this condition, namely bringing them all into harmony, is quite impossible. . . . The principle of happiness may, indeed, furnish maxims, but never such as would be competent to be laws of the will, even if *universal* happiness were made the object . . . it can supply only *general* rules, never universal; that is, it can give rules which on the average will most frequently fit, but not rules which must always hold good and necessarily.

For man, as a sensible being, happiness is the only thing of consequence, "but it is not *absolutely the only thing* of consequence." He is "not so completely an animal as to be indifferent to what reason says on its own account, and to use it merely as an instrument for the satisfaction of his wants as a sensible being." Reason in that case would be only "a particular method which nature had employed to equip man for the same ends for which it has qualified brutes, without qualifying him for any higher purpose." But we do have this higher purpose—to take into consideration good and evil in themselves, as determined by moral law, and not as its determinants. All previous moralists have made the error of seeking for an object of the will which they could make the matter and the principle of a law; whether they placed this object in happiness, in perfection, in moral feeling, or in the will of God, "their principle in every case implied heteronomy," and must be determined by empirical conditions, "since their object, which

[89] We are here reminded of the reasons for Rousseau's preference of a general will to the pluralism of private wills.

was to be the immediate principle of the will, could not be called
good or bad except in its immediate relation to feeling, which is
always empirical." [90]

At this point, we may offer some further observations. A purely
organic view of man leads most logically to an evolutionary ethics.
To arrive at virtue in a sense that has moral meaning, man must
be considered as functioning also on a hyperorganic level. It is this
level which requires the overriding of biological instincts, a partial
or complete sacrifice of the original good (self-preservation, selfish
happiness) in order to fulfill *its* need, which is the satisfaction of
a rational ideal of good based on consciousness of the meaning of
our actions. The pleasure-happiness value, in its naïve form, makes
each individual the center of the universe and makes subjective
evaluation the rule. Such a rule eventually leads to anarchism and
nihilism by calling into question the function of society and
government. On the other hand, the effort to establish objective
value by social utilitarianism leads to the vague and indecisive
idea of "general welfare"—a phrase rarely defined by its proponents, but which generally seems to signify the happiness of the
majority, sometimes the happiness of all. On this view, the locus
of value vanishes entirely. The happiness of all can only be the
happiness of each, which from the viewpoint of moral law is contradictory in practical terms. If the happiness of the majority is
taken as the rule, then it is for the happiness of the other that I
am to sacrifice my own. The protest is inevitable: why is the happiness of another more valuable than my own, and why am I bound
to sacrifice my own to it? [91]

"Your head is so filled with the right," remarks a character in
some modern novel, "you can't see the good." We may reverse this
statement and apply it to eighteenth-century utilitarianism, which

[90] Kant, *op. cit.*, pp. 37, 51, 59–63, 105–16, 123, 125, 150–55, 163.

[91] Some would argue that the utilitarians were not consistent, that they made
moral judgment a function of maximum welfare, not realizing that the maximization of welfare is a prior moral principle. "Without natural moral perceptions we
should never have known that it was our duty to seek the happiness of mankind
when it diverged from our own. . . ." (Lecky, *op. cit.*, I, p. 69.)

Niebuhr maintains that the most naïve form of faith is that in the identity between individual and general interest. Utilitarianism extracts "a covertly expressed
sense of obligation toward the 'greatest good of the greatest number' from a
hedonistic analysis of morals which really lacks all logical presuppositions for any
idea of obligation, and which cannot logically rise above an egoistic view of life."
(*The Children of Light and the Children of Darkness*, New York, 1949, pp. 29–30.)
See also Schweitzer, *op. cit.*, pp. 39–40.

defined right as conduct productive of the greatest good, that is, well-being and happiness. Right, modern philosophers have argued, introduces an element outside of "good"—an exaction, demand, "ought" derived from claims, responsibilities and obligations inherent in our human relations and in our rational awareness of them. The right, in general, promotes the good, but is not determined by it, and is a claim *sui generis*. Either one may imply or demand denial of the other. We need only think of Socrates, and of military aggression.[92]

The eighteenth century faced this dilemma in the controversy over slavery. In this debate we can see how the separation between pure utilitarianism (which takes all ends in view) and expediency (which does not) tends in real situations to become fictitious and unrealizable, since good is defined in terms of general welfare, and the latter term is interpreted—as Helvétius would have been the first to admit—in terms of the self-interest of the dominant group, or "particular will." If the useful was right, then slavery was right—if it could be proven useful to the "general welfare," to the greater good of the whole. Its supporters argued that it was most useful and in fact absolutely necessary in the colonies, and therefore was morally right. Many of its utilitarian opponents, even though they actually spoke out of a feeling of its injustice, were forced to argue, in order to be consistent with themselves, that it was not necessarily or really useful. Some inconsistently asserted that it was unjust even though necessary and useful. Montesquieu, caught in the dilemma, hedges. Turgot says that slavery is unjust *but* sometimes useful; however he gives us no clear moral decision as to whether it is *justified*. Not so with Linguet. He went further and followed Helvétius' justification of public welfare above all else, which was the true course of eighteenth-century utilitarianism. The *philosophes* are right, concedes Linguet, in calling slavery an injustice. "But between them and me there is this difference, that they believe that injustice to be harmful, while I believe it necessary." [93] In American literature, Huckleberry

---

[92] If we reject the just claims of our fellows on the ground that such rejection will produce greater good, remarks E. T. Mitchell, we are on dangerous ground. It is arguable that the death of Socrates has produced more good in provoking reflection on the importance of free inquiry than would have resulted from his acquittal. Would this have justified a juror, who believed Socrates innocent, in voting for his condemnation? (*Op. cit.*, p. 516.) The right and the good are also involved in Socrates' decision not to escape.

[93] *Théorie des loix civiles*, II, pp. 280–82.

Finn intuited the right—that there is a human dignity, that men ought to be treated as ends, never as means only, that right and wrong depend on objective relations, not on subjective will— and thus he surpassed the criterion of naked usefulness embodied in the pressure of the social norm above which he had to rise. The good is, indeed, what satisfies our purposes; but to equate this with the right is to evade the moral question—are our purposes right, and what purposes are right for man? There is a world of norms, ends, and values, established by man's reasonable nature (which is aware of his sensible nature), that transcends the empirical sphere of desire. Moral judgment cannot be explained in terms other than itself (such as pleasant emotions, benevolent instincts, customs, usefulness) without "explaining it away and losing it." [94]

The preoccupation with "natural man" and the "natural," which was so powerful an element in eighteenth-century thought, also made it difficult for eighteenth-century moralists to realize that moral good involves a different *kind* of experience than that of happiness, the sole criterion of "natural man." It may be true that nature causes us to desire happiness above all else, but it is also certain that our nature makes judgments of right and wrong inevitable, and that it makes us need and prefer (if not always desire) the right. We cannot therefore say that because we have this paramount natural desire for personal satisfactions, right and wrong are to be judged solely in relation to their furtherance or hindrance of our happiness. To consider right and good as equivalents is a redundancy similar to that of might and right which Rousseau pointed out so tellingly in the *Contrat social*. It is also obvious that, as Kant said, there can be no general law of happiness, not even for one individual; and that we feel and judge it wrong for one individual to hurt another for his own pleasure. Enlightened self-interest and virtue-sacrifice were proposed in order to overcome these difficulties, but still and always as a means to happiness, even when, in extreme cases of heroic virtue, one's own happiness was sacrificed for that of others. Sacrifice, however, may be not only for happiness, and the ethical good may involve the surpassing of natural good (interpreted as happiness). But because of the desire to integrate man into nature as a wholly "natural" being, it was difficult for such a view to be accepted

---

[94] L. I. Bredvold, "The Meaning of the Concept of Right Reason," pp. 128, 127.

within the eighteenth-century frame of reference. It was not seen that man's uniqueness lies in the fact that, though he is wholly in nature, he transcends nature, because of his peculiar ability to contemplate himself and all else in nature objectively, and so to conceive of other beings as subjects. The difficulty, in sum, derived from the confusion of moral value and psychology, of the moral and the empirical. We can only desire happiness (it was thought), so everything else must be made compatible; there is no meaning in saying that we ought to value and desire something else or act in some other way.

But eighteenth-century utilitarian moralists desired, above all, to reconcile and unite nature and culture, or nature and reason. Happiness was to be safeguarded, and never given up as the highest value; but happiness could only be achieved, it was asserted, by submission to the cultural norms, and reason dictated the sacrifice of immediate or apparent happiness in order to achieve "real" happiness, or the greatest amount of happiness (according to the several views). Reason and culture were not distinct from nature and its great demand, but the servants of that demand— even as in any particular case they might be its master; so that this "nature" philosophy, which set up the natural happiness goal as the *summum bonum,* actually came to rely on reason to control or negate natural instinct in order to overcome hedonism and nihilism, and to preserve moral value and social order. Utilitarianism, comments John Dewey, "exaggerated the role of rational thought in conduct . . . it assumed that everybody is moved by conscious considerations and that all that is really necessary is to make the process of consideration sufficiently enlightened." [95]

We have examined the objections raised in the eighteenth century to this philosophy. We shall shortly see that its failure to convince, its inability to grasp either the realities of passion ("nature") or the contradictory realities of the moral (reason and culture) led nihilists to assert the first at the expense of the second. But it could also lead to the assertion of the second at the expense of the first. The centering of value in "society" (as an abstract entity) is obviously a form of moral absolutism, and it would be folly to expect that a political absolutism would not follow. There are many implications of totalitarian conditioning, control, and

---

[95] *Human Nature and Conduct,* pp. 221–22. Dewey adds that the rational element of conduct is nevertheless important.

repression in eighteenth-century thought.[96] Noting that the utilitarian spirit is reflected in attitudes toward the arts and science,
C. C. Gillispie points out that one aspect of it finds its way into
collectivist philosophies and into the Jacobin totalitarianism
"which found value in science only so far as its utility could be
demonstrated." [97] We may add to this the fact that utilitarianism,
or the greatest happiness principle, is destructive of the very natural rights which some of the utilitarians defended. "For if morality and social institutions are justified merely by their utility,
rights must be so too, and in consequence any claim to a natural
right is either nonsense or merely a confused way of saying that
the right does conduce to the greatest happiness." [98]

Let us summarize briefly. The eighteenth century found four
ways to make a bridge between the egoistic starting point of self-
interest (unique motive and end of behavior) and the ethical
termini of social conformity, general welfare, or altruism. Common to all four groups was the general value outlook of utility
(happiness). Some held the ethical termini to be a natural result
of a laissez-faire pursuit of self-interest. A few thought this statement was true, but only in the conditions of anarchical primitivism. Others went to the opposite extreme, and demanded a
rigidly controlled and highly conditioned society, either primitivistic or culturally advanced. In the middle stood the proponents
of enlightened self-interest and virtue-happiness as the justification
of the good of the greatest number, in preference to one's own;
and in some milieux a mode of altruistic benevolence, which apparently surpassed self-interest, was engendered. In this fashion
they answered the questions involved in establishing a secular
ethics: what is the good? why be good? how make man good? how
reconcile, or synthesize the two goals, virtue and the pursuit of
happiness (culture and nature)?

On the other hand, four arguments were proposed in the eighteenth century against the various solutions of utilitarianism. First,
it is more to our individual advantage to violate the general interest when we can get away with it. Second, each man finds happiness differently, and no rules or objective universals are possible.

[96] See Chapter 7 of this volume; also *An Age of Crisis, passim,* and Talmon, *The
Origins of Totalitarian Democracy.*
[97] "The Natural History of Industry," p. 402.
[98] Sabine, pp. 566–67.

Third, the criterion is a nonmoral one. Fourth, we have a non-egoistic moral "instinct" or need which is primary, not secondary. Modern philosophy has amplified this criticism, and today utilitarianism is an ethics held only by a small minority of philosophers.[99]

We must recognize the fact that utilitarianism had a valid function in the eighteenth century and that it made important positive contributions. The rise of utilitarian thinking was an accompaniment and a result of the rise of secularism, of a scientific attitude toward social problems, and of the economic changes that were ushering in the age of capitalism. For those who re-examined ethics from a naturalistic viewpoint, it supplied positive criteria which made supernaturalism superfluous or, in some cases, only a useful adjunct. It attempted to ground itself on the analyzable data of human behavior as psychology could supply it—a consideration which no ethical philosophy can ever ignore. For the purposes of the correction of governmental abuses and of a basic restatement about government itself, as well as for the new economic structures, it supplied a most valuable rationale which could justify the promotion of general welfare in a way that feudal institutions were no longer able to do. In a word, it responded to the needs of the time and seemed like the answer to the great problems. Its legacy to the nineteenth century is historically of great importance. In a more permanent way, eighteenth-century utilitarianism contributed to the independence of ethical and social thought from a prioris and absolutes. These positive values stand in need of no defense and are quite well-known. It is far more important for us to bring out the inherent weaknesses of utilitarianism as an ethical theory (especially in its eighteenth-century French formulations), and to uncover its actual role as a factor in cultural history. This role was determined partly by its weaknesses and partly by its strengths; and partly, also by the peculiar circumstances of the cultural context which caused its development and which determined its actual functioning within that context. This we have tried to do, partly in this chapter, and also in the two chapters which follow.

[99] For an interesting nineteenth-century criticism, see Lecky, *op. cit.*, I, pp. 36–40, 69–70, 98–100. For criticism of twentieth-century sequels, see E. Vivas, "Animadversions on Naturalistic Ethics," and M. C. Swabey, *The Judgment of History*, pp. 141–42. The reader is urged to consult these references, to get a view of later perspectives growing out of the eighteenth century.

Six

THE NIHILIST DISSOLUTION

I. The Seeds of Nihilism

THE WHOLE AIM of the utilitarians was to unite nature and culture in a harmonious synthesis. In order to make individuals happy, and to induce them to make their society ordered and happy, it was necessary that the apparently contrary pursuit of self-interest and of the general welfare be reconciled. This they endeavored to accomplish in the several ways we have examined. But there were other writers, many others, who suspected, feared, or believed that they had not succeeded, either theoretically or in a practical way. The dissenters may be classified in two groups. There were those who only took note of the shortcomings of ethical theory; some of these, like Voltaire, sank into pessimism (in this regard), and de-spaired of ever reconciling the two antagonists. A few others, however, tacitly or openly approved the failure. Denying the validity of culture's repression of the ego and its will (of nature, then), they revolted against culture in the name of nature, against the super-ego in behalf of the deep instinctual drives. Since they shared the same critical approach with the first group, we shall not try to treat them separately. Nor shall we repeat the many evidences of nihil-istic thinking we have already encountered in these two volumes; or the numerous instances of a type of anti-nihilistic thinking that because of its weakness or untenability actually strength-ened the alternative, which it moreover warned would be justified if its own position was impugned.[1] We shall rather inquire further

[1] Unfortunately it appears necessary to warn the reader again that the *philosophes* are not depicted in this study (with a few stated exceptions) as proponents or

into the three bases of nihilism which were present to eighteenth-century minds: the absurdity of the world, the power of hedonism, and the character of human life. First, however, some general observations are in order.

The confrontation with nihilism is peculiar to our Western civilization. It belongs to its very essence, and is the mark of its greatness. If, as some predict, it is also the cause of its doom, then our civilization will have turned out to be a tragic one—in the true sense of that word; but it will have been nonetheless great. Nihilism is not found in primitive or even in other relatively advanced cultures, because they are either authoritarian, or not centered on the primary value of the individual. Nihilism comes about when the individual revolts against the forces which tend to make him subservient to an end which is not himself.

Nature knows not the individual. In the life of social animals, such as bees, ants, or termites, everything is for the community, and the individual is sacrificed; nothing matters but the continuity of the species. Human societies, too, a modern philosopher points out, survive only by the repression and discipline of its individuals.[2] What is the object of this sacrifice? Is it not the same?

---

victims of nihilism. It is the contrary which is true. They had faith in their ability to impose limits on the ego. Their "tragedy" (a word which has been attributed to me) lies in the fact that their struggle against nihilism, which they undertook out of devotion to the moral life, did not succeed, and to a certain extent furthered its march. The rejection of authoritarian ethics and the effort to build anew—historically necessary though it was—involved a constant confrontation with nihilism, a confrontation which was in itself, as Diderot admitted, fraught with peril. Furthermore, the attitudes toward the nature of moral experience and the justification of moral values were often not unfavorable to nihilism, as they turned out. The "tragedy" was not that of the eighteenth century so much as that of the succeeding generations. The revolt of nihilism, writes Albert Camus, "appears in the history of ideas, in a coherent fashion, only at the end of the eighteenth century. . . . But from that moment on, its consequences unroll uninterruptedly, and it is not exaggerated to say that they have molded the history of our time." (*L'Homme révolté*, 1951, p. 43.) One of the purposes of our inquiry has been to determine *why* the crisis burst forth at the end of the "Age of Enlightenment." Like many others, the present writer is a devoted admirer of that age; but the historian's loyalty must be to impartial truth, as he conscientiously sees it. And we cannot understand the problem, the efforts or the legacy of the eighteenth century if we ignore this aspect of its intellectual climate.

We may speak of several varieties of nihilism, such as meaninglessness (the absence of value), and satanism (the inversion of morality). The two were confused in eighteenth-century thinking, and history shows that they often tend to coalesce in practice. The first produces the second when we add to it both the psychological assumptions of pleasure-pain and the belief that the libidinal energies are characterized by aggression and the assertion of self at the cost of the other.

[2] A. Cresson, *op. cit.*, pp. 111–12.

Are we, then, less blind than bees, and is not the whole notion of duty a cheat?

Only human beings, who are relatively free and not bound completely by instinct, have the possibility of this revolt.[3] But revolt is not universal in culture. It has taken place in our culture, because in it the objectifying of the world and of ourselves has reached the highest point. Our culture, more than any other, has challenged the commands of nature and its limits, inquired with open eyes into the meaning of our lives and of all that is. We have abandoned the safety of willing submission to natural rhythms, social customs, and metaphysical absolutes, for the highest and most perilous adventure that is possible—the quest for mastery over nature, the world, and our own destiny. This is the adventure of alienation and of uncompromising truth.

Camus has made it clear that the human revolt, which is the central meaning of our history, may (and should) be, in itself, the foundation of human solidarity and of moral value. An essential part of this history (both cause and product) has also been a revolt in favor of the worth and importance of the individual.[4] Consequently, part of its energy has been directed (or misdirected) in a path which is destructive to solidarity and moral value. Our examination of the world and of the human world has revealed the absence of a metaphysical ground for moral values, obligation, and ideals, which are limits to the self and the assertion of other priorities. From these factors comes the revolt of nihilism, which is not only against culture, but against mankind itself. It was only a constructive revolt which the *philosophes* had desired; but they were unable to halt the dynamics of revolution, even as the men of '89 could not prevent the coming of '93.[5]

[3] One great weakness of nihilism is that its revolt against culture, which in this sense is the human way of carrying out the "purposes" of nature, is made in the name of nature. But nowhere does nature sanction the supremacy of the individual. Culture, by its transcendence of nature, has made this possible, and thus bred its own antithesis or adversary.

[4] The fact that the greatest single impulse in this direction has come from Christianity is by no means contradictory, since Christianity is itself man's revolt against nature—both metaphysically and morally. But Christianity substitutes other dependencies. Secularism, or naturalism, carries the revolt a great step further, but accepts the dependencies of culture as a valid limit to the individual. Nihilism demolishes all structure and limit.

[5] Only in this figurative sense, and not literally, is the following statement about Sade true: "An insane libertine? Rather an outlaw, whose greatness springs from

The rational genius of Western culture matured early in ancient Greece. The basic problems of the individual and society, of the valuation of values, were soon brought into the open by Sophists and Skeptics. Carneades, as reported by Cicero, and Plato's Callicles and Thrasymachus denied the pretensions of culture and asserted the identity of justice with nature, that is, with the demands of the ego and the law of the strong. Other Greek and Roman philosophers exercised great ingenuity in the attempt to refute their reasoning and to justify social and moral law. The Christian centuries of the Middle Ages constituted a bulwark against corrosive thinking. A pacifying solution to human destiny and the weight of authority turned the rather limited number of inquiring minds to innocuous and sterile controversies. In the Renaissance centuries, the minds of men loosed their shackles, reopened the closed circle of their horizons and reclaimed freedom. In the sixteenth and seventeenth centuries in Italy, France, and England, many advanced thinkers refused to accept the orthodox views about the world, nature, the State, and man.[6] Disillusion and pessimism were prevalent in Protestant theology, in political thought (Machiavelli and his followers), and among men of letters, such as Montaigne and Donne. The optimistic Thomistic version of the world and of man's place in it, the optimistic Christian humanism of Pico, More, and Erasmus were no longer unchallenged. Universal rational law, the legitimacy of limits to the aspirations of individuals or of the species, the primacy of art over nature, all were questioned or denied. To sensitive and independent thinkers or poets, the world no longer seemed a moral order, the State no longer the instrument of justice, man no longer

---

his insubmissiveness and his philosophy from his temperament! . . . Did Diderot do otherwise? Consequently, a man of the eighteenth century, profoundly. He offers . . . an almost perfect model of the *philosophe*, fashioned as he was by the articles of the *Encyclopédie* and the works of Rousseau, the gluttonous and sometimes disparate curiosity of his mind, and the uncontrolled impulses of his heart." (H. Vallet, review of Lely, *Vie du Marquis de Sade*.)

[6] Cf. the statement of Lucien Goldmann concerning the seventeenth century: "Within the old ethical and Christian forms a radically amoral and unreligious philosophy is now developed." (*Le Dieu caché*, p. 39.) In the first chapter of *An Age of Crisis*, we touched on the influence of the scientific revolution. Charles Frankel has noted in a book review that the belief of Dostoevski's character ("If there is no God, then anything is lawful") is "one of the characteristic reactions to the world-view that appear to be implicit in the modern physical and biological sciences."

pre-eminently a rational being. Disorder and evil, they recognized, are not unnatural, though their universal existence in God's world remains baffling to the human mind. If there is a natural harmony, man upsets it by transgressing against his own nature. This is one of the dominant themes of Elizabethan tragedy. It is central to Shakespeare's great tragedies, and to *The Tempest*.[7] Shakespeare passed through the dark clouds and reasserted his humanism. In *Troilus and Cressida,* he foresees the consequences of submitting moral values to the natural law of force:

> . . . Then right and wrong
> Should lose their names, and so should justice, too.
> Then everything includes itself in power,
> Power into will, will into appetite,
> And appetite, a universal wolf,
> So doubly seconded with will and power,
> Must make perforce a universal prey,
> And last eat up itself. (I, 3)

This is a remarkable outline of much of the Sadian doctrine.

Despite efforts to re-establish authoritarianism in the seventeenth century, men continued to question and to rebel. An essential aspect of the history of Western thought and of political action since the Renaissance is the continuing confrontation between the supporters of moral laws as cultural limit, and those who either deny them or wish to impose limits as mere assertion of raw will and force. If there is no accepted objective standard, there is no basis for judgment or condemnation. We can then either accept this social tyranny, in which case the individual has no basis for protest; or we can reject it, in which case the individual decides for himself what is "right," that is, in conformity to his will. In the first case, nihilism, accepted (implicitly, if not openly) as true, is repressed. In the second case, it is accepted.

Hobbes, Spinoza, and Mandeville are three of the important figures who influenced eighteenth-century French writers. Hobbes, as we have seen, was understood as embracing the first of the two alternatives. Spinoza supplied much grist for the mill of nihilism. This is an injustice to him, but the historical process is not determined by justice—even assuming that men could agree on what constitutes justice. Most readers of the ascetic Jewish philosopher

---

[7] See L. G. Crocker, *"Hamlet, Don Quijote* and *La vida es sueño:* the Quest for Values."

were unable or did not bother to understand his system; and his works contain numerous passages which, taken in isolation, seem to go further than Hobbes.[8] For Mandeville the discipline of morals was only a deceit to make people believe that the sacrifice of self-interest is compensated; so men are tamed by imaginary compensations, such as praise and honor, while the strong unscrupulously exploit them "with greater Ease and Security." [9] Mandeville's ethics, writes the editor of his works, is a combination of philosophical anarchism with utilitarianism. The existence of such a combination is significant.[10] Because there are no objective criteria for action, thought Mandeville, all values are nothing more than what is arbitrarily desirable or imposed by whoever exerts power. Even if such ideal criteria existed, human nature would make them unrealizable.

Naturalistic ethical thought, in its radical and rebellious forms, follows these views. The great defensive weapon of the moralists was, as we have seen, the attempt to replace the individual by society as the locus of judgment and value. However, since happiness still remained the goal and the value, many refused to make this transition. They denied its justification. Had it, in fact, been justified? When writers, such as Gay, declared, "Obligatory acts are those which lead to happiness," whose happiness were men to think of? Enlightened self-interest and the virtue-happiness equivalence sounded, in the long run, like pious Sunday sermons, and (as was clear even to some of their proponents) did not tally with the facts of life.

Various factors in life and in thought contributed to this defeat. The mores of an important sector of French society, as Dom Deschamps and other critics pointed out, actually favored hedonism and amoralism, and made it difficult to practice moral precepts.[11] Perhaps people in other times had not lived very differently, but in the eighteenth century they were more careless about their self-indulgence, and even justified it. If it is true that the novel is

---

[8] "Spinoza . . . still uses the word *God* to develop the most radical refusal of transcendence and entitles *Ethic* a book in which all the considerations on behavior start out from the *conatus*, from the egoism of the modes which tend to persist in their being." (L. Goldmann, *loc. cit.*)

[9] *Op. cit.*, I, pp. 27–35.

[10] *Ibid.*, p. lvi. Also p. lix: "Indeed, anarchism in the realm of theory accords very well with utilitarianism in the world of practice, and always has so accorded." Kaye emphasizes the influence of Bayle (p. li).

[11] Dom Deschamps, *op. cit.*, pp. 136–37.

the mirror a society holds up to itself, or its way of talking to itself about itself, then we must surely take the prevalence and popularity of licentious literature as a sign of rebellion against the traditional value system, against culture itself and its restraints.[12] The view of Augustinian Christianity, as expressed by Pascal's "the self (or ego) is hateful" and seconded by Fénelon and others, was reversed, as we have had ample occasion to observe. With the narcissism of Rousseau, the self becomes the delectable object of contemplation and experience; he wants to "actualize all its affective powers." [13]

We have seen, too, how the reduction of experience to a single motivation led to a reduction of moral action to nonmoral motives.[14] If self-interest (pleasure and pain) is the sole and universal principle of action and is a necessary determination, then self-interest and not obligation is the law of man. We can only call acts pleasurable or useful (or the contrary) and judge them according to the amount of happiness they yield. To each individual nothing really matters but his own happiness; if he is benevolent, it is because he is so constituted that benevolence gives him pleasure.[15]

Right and duty, however, cannot inhere in our physical or "animal" nature, and it was to this that human experience and activity were reduced: ". . . there existed in the eighteenth century a widespread desire to equate the moral with the physical world: to see in it an order comparable with the order of Nature." [16] If self-interest was selected as the fundament for moral values, it was in part because pseudoscientific thinkers were seek-

[12] For a similar observation in regard to early seventeenth-century *libertins,* see Spink, *op. cit.,* pp. 42–43, 46. But there the anarchism was a revolt in favor of moral perfectionism.

[13] Marcel Raymond, Introduction to *Rêveries du promeneur solitaire,* p. VII.

[14] Cassirer considers this the culmination of eighteenth-century analytic method (*op. cit.,* pp. 25–27).

[15] A modern example of the consequences of this subjectivism, in pseudoscientific dress, is found in the work of Westermarck. If I say it is wrong to resist evil, argues Westermarck, and yet resistance to evil does not call forth in me an emotion of moral disapproval, then my judgment is false. There are no moral truths; ethics cannot fix rules for conduct, it can only study the moral consciousness as fact. That which appears to each man as right or good is what is right and good. Everyone has the right to follow his caprice and inclinations, and to evade the laws if he can. But society does not have to recognize this as his right. (*Op. cit.,* p. 108.)

[16] Willey, *op. cit.,* p. 137. See Helvétius, *De l'Esprit:* "physical sensitivity and personal interest have been the creators of all justice" (p. 276), and d'Holbach, *Système de la nature,* p. 2.

ing for the moral counterpart to gravitation. Hand in hand with all this went the campaign to rehabilitate the instincts and the passions (or "nature," so understood)—a dangerous course whose consequences were not at first foreseen. It was often accompanied by the exclusion of reason as a motivating force and even as a valid criterion of right and wrong. The denial of the existence or validity of norms available to reason, for which the partisans of Natural Law continued to plead, was also favorable to the cause of moral anarchism. In moral judgment, according to Hume, all we are dealing with is fact and experience, and not truth. Seeing the danger of emotional subjectivism, Hume tried to establish an objective norm in the "benevolent impartial spectator"—but could this, in effect, be anything except a process of reason and reflection? To be sure, Hume's revolutionary attack was not intended as an assault on culture, but by placing the validity of the limits and sanctions of culture on the basis of variable emotional impulses and an arbitrary right of the majority, it may well have been conducive to that result. While he did not envisage the really radical position that nothing makes value statements true, he nevertheless said nothing that could be construed as against this opinion.

Accompanying these developments was the desire for a total integration of man in nature, with refusal of any transcendence, even though it was admitted that his more complex physical organization gave him certain special abilities and ways of living. The important thing, as La Mettrie, d'Holbach, and others made clear, is that he is submitted to the same laws; everything is response to need—mechanically, some added, like a tree or a machine.[17] Man merely carries out natural forces—without any freedom whatsoever—in all he does, whether he loves or hates, helps or hurts, gives life or takes it. As Hume had said, in regard to suicide, whatever is, is natural, whether it follows nature's own operations or violates them. With theories such as these, it became easy for some to accept the view that "just and unjust according to law" is a distinction which cannot be justified in the face of a contrary demand on the part of nature—a demand which was even called "just according to nature," although it was simultaneously proclaimed that nature is amoral! Look beyond good and evil, they urged, to the complete fulfillment of the self. "And

[17] *Système de la nature*, I, pp. 76–87, 184, 263–64.

if, to do that, we have to trample on skulls, let us trample them without remorse." [18] An unbroken line of thought leads from such eighteenth-century views to Hitler's *Mein Kampf* and the Nazi infamies.[19]

At the beginning of the eighteenth century, "everything that is, is right" was a metaphysical judgment. By the end of the century, it could be argued that this maxim was often accepted also as a moral truth. What was natural in a descriptive sense took on the value of a natural norm. Good and evil were meaningless, except in relation to the pleasure principle. Men who are virtuous are merely following the necessities of a "fortunate nature"—fortunate, because, as Helvétius puts it, "the actions which are personally useful to these virtuous men are the actions which are just, [i.e.], in conformity with the general interest." But if I have another kind of nature, I must still follow the principle of self-interest; it would be wrong, wrote d'Holbach, to give up happiness for virtue.[20] Helvétius contradicts himself when he says that for the "honor of humanity" he mentions the few who are "fortunately born." No honor is involved, since they are following the same rule as the others. Moral distinctions are annihilated, in regard to persons. "Actions must be regarded as indifferent in themselves; it is up to the State's needs to determine those which are worthy of esteem and of scorn." [21]

Utilitarianism and naturalism, then, as they were developed in the eighteenth-century context—willfully or unintentionally, consciously or unconsciously—brought the concepts of nihilism into a stronger light. Both, working together, induced a revolt of the ego against the frustration of its demands, against sacrifice for others, and simultaneously a revolt against rationalistic ethics in favor of the instincts and the affective elements of the personality.[22] We have seen that the secularization of ethics (and of philosophy in general) led to open approval of the ego and its demands. The

[18] Cresson, *op. cit.*, p. 13.

[19] See H. Rauschning, *The Revolution of Nihilism,* as well as *Mein Kampf.*

[20] "It is unjust to ask a man to be virtuous, if he cannot be so without making himself unhappy; as long as vice makes him happy, he must love vice." (*Système de la nature,* I, p. 152.) Of course Helvétius thought society could be so organized as to make it to our interest to be virtuous, and d'Holbach believed that only virtue brought happiness. But we have seen how these palliatives were criticized.

[21] *De l'Esprit,* chap. XIV.

[22] Again we repeat that while people have always lived egoistically, divine command and Natural Law had prevented a conscious revolt, one that tried to justify itself in terms of theory or truth.

ethical theories developed during the eighteenth century represented a search for new ways to control those demands. The search had to take place within the prevailing intellectual framework of naturalism, sentimentalism, and utilitarianism. The utilitarian synthesis was the great effort of naturalism against anarchistic amoralism, against the revolt of the ego. It was a logical sequel to the rejection of rationalistic ethics, which had stressed immediate and eternal laws of right and wrong in an attempt to transcend both relativism and personal emotions (therefore, to transcend certain aspects of human nature). But utilitarianism, despite its naturalistic presuppositions and orientation, itself contained important rationalistic elements whch were undemonstrable—notably the identity of self-interest (the unique and universal motive and value) and the public interest. The unconvincing nature of its three main tenets—the social locus of value, enlightened self-interest, the virtue-happiness equivalence— added to the outgrowing of the medieval Christian world-view, left the European conscience with a deep disquiet and insecurity. It was no longer easy really to believe in an autonomous power to create the self in virtue of an intelligent vision of what it ought to be, or, indeed, that there was any such "ought" other than a sham or an arbitrary cultural pressure.

In the revolt of nihilism, as in all ethical thought, the view of the universe and of man's place in it—that is, the metaphysical fundament—is one important element. While we shall not attempt to duplicate our earlier analysis of this problem,[23] certain aspects may now receive further emphasis. Nihilism is a principle of disorder. It asserts the ego as a law in the absence of law. If the universe has no meaning, then all things and acts are reduced (from the viewpoint of the universe, or *sub specie aeterni*) to one level of indifference, and no significant moral action is possible.[24] The absurd, the inexistence of value, unchained egoism, disorder: such is **the** progression. As the result of an uncompromising final

---

[23] See *Age of Crisis*, chap. 1, 2, 3.

[24] Cf. Spinoza: "Nothing happens in nature which can be attributed to any vice of nature, for she is always the same and everywhere one. Her virtue is the same, and her power of acting; that is to say, her laws and rules, according to which all things are and are changed from form to form, are everywhere and always the same; so that there must also be one and the same method of understanding the nature of all things whatsoever, that is to say, by the universal laws and rules of nature. . . . I shall consider human actions and appetites just as if I were considering lines, planes or bodies." (*Ethic*, III, opening statement.)

cosmic defeat, man wins his freedom, permitting him to be first himself as a separate entity, and only by voluntary extension a member of an environmental unit.[25] The constructive, humanistic reaction will assert that there is more than the individual ego: there are men, and there is mankind. But we have examined the efforts in this direction and have seen the difficulty of establishing this viewpoint as a valid and effective criterion of law. When the world is no larger than man in general, it is very difficult to keep it larger than one's self in particular.

Both Fontenelle and Bayle, like Mandeville and their followers, were impressed by the idea that the social and physical order are alike brought about through the workings of evil. The problem of evil haunted all who believed in God. "The moral world," wrote Chamfort, "seems to be the product of the caprices of a devil who has gone mad." [26] Richardson's Lovelace boasts of his satanism; M. de Thou, in Duclos' *Mme de Luz,* justifies his satanism on the ground that he is following nature. Only optimists and providentialists continued to assert that nature is good. At best, it is indifferent and devoid of value, except biological survival. And yet, so many who thought thus about nature—and similarly about men —demanded an ethics that would not violate nature! Since immoralists also raised their standard in the name of nature, the concepts of nature, it is obvious, must have been very confused.

The men of the eighteenth century were equally impressed by the sad lot of the innocent and virtuous. This was, as we have noted, a constant theme in literature, as well as philosophy. The many novels on this theme testify, according to Robert Mauzi, both to the revenge of common sense against the illusions or bad faith of systems, and to the release of perverse instincts. Speaking of himself under the name of Clazomène, Vauvenargues writes: "If we search for some reason for such a cruel destiny, we shall have, I think, difficulty in finding it. Is it worth inquiring why very clever gamblers are ruined while others make their fortune? Or why we see years without spring or autumn . . . ?" [27] Painting the earth as ravaged by disasters, afflicted by the cruelty of one living being to another in a dog-eat-dog struggle for existence, he cries: "Oh earth! Oh earth! You are only a tomb and a field of

---

[25] Ironically, the freedom was surrendered to a mechanical theory of psychological determinism.

[26] *Maximes et pensées,* II, p. 14.

[27] *Op. cit.,* II, pp. 140–43.

corpses; you bring to birth only death. Who could have created you?" [28]

If the world is a world of evil, and if God permits evil (or even connives at it), why should we not find authorization in the model, asked Bayle, and follow suit? [29] Or if everything is morally indifferent to this God, then, said Crousaz, everything should be indifferent to man. If I can kill a sparrow, because it is to my interest, I can kill a man.[30] Should we not revolt against such a God, who plays with us as wanton boys with flies, and enslaves us to evil? No one realized the possibility of such dangerous thinking better than Christians, even seventeenth-century Jansenists:

> Mais, s'il faut ne te rien déguiser,
> Mon innocence enfin commence à me peser.
> Je ne sais de tout temps quelle injuste puissance
> Laisse le crime en paix, et poursuit l'innocence.
> De quelque part sur moi que je tourne les yeux,
> Je ne vois que malheurs qui condamnent les dieux.
> Méritons leur courroux, justifions leur haine
> Et que le fruit du crime en précède la peine.[31]

But how often have we seen these same Christians undermine the position of moral values, by asserting that without God, no right is possible, and that might, in all its hideous forms, would be right and proper? [32] "If God does not exist," cried Rousseau, "only the wicked man is wise." Rivarol, a protototalitarian, went so far as to assert that God is present in the physical universe, since all objects behave in accordance with strict law, but absent from the moral order. Consequently, men have had to invent religions, which are

---

[28] *Ibid.*, pp. 18–19.

[29] *Oeuvres diverses*, III, p. 307. God's laws, the infidels often argued, can only be those he has put into our hearts. If there are other laws, then God does not love men, and has no right to punish them. If revealed laws deprive him of pleasure, they are unjust, since pursuit of pleasure is a natural law. Therefore it is not necessary to observe laws. (Fréret, *op. cit.*, pp. 133–37.)

[30] *An Age of Crisis*, p. 29.

[31] Racine, *Andromaque*, III, p. 1.

[32] To the many examples we have already cited, others can be added. The abbé Duhamel attacks Pope for not believing in heaven and hell. Why be virtuous, then, "since having nothing to hope for in another life in recompense for the loss of your own advantage, you are your own enemy in depriving yourself." (*Op cit.*, p. 80.) And Chaudon: "There is no other God, says Spinoza, but blind, universal substance; consequently, no moral ruler except the force and desires of each individual. Nothing is commanded or forbidden. Everything is good if you can get away with it. . . . If everything is eternal, natural and necessary, why have laws, remorse or fear? There is no freedom, no vice or virtue, everything is indifferent." (*Op. cit.*, II, p. 34.)

useful falsehoods: "if all that had [really] existed, if there had been moral laws, like physical . . . the intervention of God, and consequently religion, would have been unnecessary." God punishes our mistakes (like falling out of a window), but crimes belong to human justice—which explains why crime, intelligently committed, prospers. Men are therefore compelled to engage in "a conspiracy for order." [33] Sisson de Valmire, a sincerely pious man, went even further and blamed God for creating a moral order. The physical order is good, but becomes corrupted when submitted to the moral. In the physical order, "man, I claim, was as perfect as he could be. The first man would never have committed an excess, never sinned, had God not imposed on him an accidental obligation foreign to his nature." [34]

If the irrationality and mystery of the universe, the longing for explanation and clarity and the reaction against the universe's refusal to supply them are one source of nihilism, the most compelling sign of irrationality (and of injustice, Unamuno was to say) is the existence of death. Moral values have no validity, it is often held, for a universe in which moral beings are ephemera. The annihilation of men destroys their status in being, which is their greatest desire, and simultaneously wipes out all their creations, including moral values and laws.[35] Death confirms the naturalistic view of man's total involvement in natural process, the same processes by which the other flora and fauna of the universe spring up, bloom, and perish forever. A man may then say, "I shall follow nature, it is the only noncontingent whole I am part of; but since there are no distinctions in nature, I need not think of others; since the universe is useless as a source of value, I am my own absolute." Such a denial of human relations and history is wrong, to be sure; it is not only to accept the absurd (that of the world), but to create the absurd (for man). Neverthe-

[33] *De la Philosophie moderne*, pp. 23–30.

[34] *Dieu et l'homme*, Amsterdam, 1771, p. 131.

Laya's play, *L'Ami des lois* (1792), produced at the same time that Sade was writing, supplies impressive evidence of the prevalence of the view that nihilism could be the logical conclusion to be drawn from the fact of an absurd universe. See Nomophage's speech, Act IV, Scene 1. The world belongs to the strong, and all is indifferent in a universe without values. There are no virtues or vices. Nomophage is in several regards a Sadian character.

[35] Cf. Albert Camus: "The absurd is born of this confrontation between the human need and the unreasonable silence of the world." Death is the ultimate injustice, and it is this which renders everything meaningless in the end. (*Op. cit.*, p. 21.)

less, the practical consequences are obvious in the writings and deeds of innumerable men. Why sacrifice pleasure to some ideal or moral principle, when death ends all? This is for some the most obvious conclusion.[36] If life is meaningless, it is without worth, and murder is no crime—there are no crimes.[37] Destruction is the only absolute available. In view of these considerations, the relative unimportance of the death-annihilation theme and of the dread of nothingness, in eighteenth-century literature, is rather striking.[38]

In sum, the situation may be characterized in Nietzsche's words: "the disappearance of the idea of God deprives the ideas of equality and justice of all justification." If there is not a moral order (it is commonly held), transcending the order of nature, then there is no tenable justification for these notions. The secular moralists sometimes believed they could find such an order within the realm of nature, in those special, anti-natural forms of nature denominated Natural Law and conscience; but increasingly they turned to the justification of moral values as the work of culture, in opposition to nature. The need to justify made it difficult for them to see what simply *is*, and needs no more justification than nature itself —the fact that man, transcending nature (even as he is in nature, and is a creation of nature), has himself created the moral order and added it to nature. This is the humanistic position they really held, and which they did not crystallize with sufficient clarity.

The anguish of uncertainty and despair before infinite but silent space and an enigmatic universe had been felt by France's greatest poet-philosopher of the seventeenth century. In an age when

---

[36] The following words were written by a prisoner, on his dungeon wall: "There is no heaven or hell. When you are dead there is an end of everything. Therefore, ye scoundrels, grab whatever you can; only do not let yourselves be grabbed. Amen." The *carpe diem* theme runs throughout libertine verse. Parny, "the French Vergil," urged his readers to enjoy life, which is all that matters.

> "Le temps s'en va, le temps s'en va, Madame,
> Las! le temps, non! mais nous nous en allons. . . ."

That is the best thing we can do "before the long night of the grave":

> "Cet abîme sans fond où la mort nous conduit
> Garde éternellement tout ce qu'il engloutit.
> Tandis que nous vivons, faisons notre Elysée."

This means casting off all religions and social brakes; follow nature. (H. Potez, *L'Elégie en France*, 1898, pp. 140–44.)

[37] In Christianity, men tried to convince themselves that death is objectively and subjectively escapable.

[38] However, a thorough study of this problem should be undertaken.

pessimism was shorn of its metaphysical dimension and expended its force in subtle analyses of human nature, Pascal, the outstanding exception, stands out as its most significant writer. Pascal was haunted by the fear of an absurd, meaningless world. He was fully aware of the nihilism which lurked in such a conclusion. All his life he had to fight himself, fight for the faith that would keep him out of the black pit of nothingness. The atheist whom his *Pensées* were written to convince may well have been the skeptic that he had been, and dreaded to become again. He was his own adversary in the argument. And who can say whether the maceration he inflicted upon himself was not, in part at least, a way of punishing and combatting the serpent of doubt?

The vital role that the theory of probability has come to assume in scientific work and in philosophic thought was foreshadowed in the work of Pascal. He began by applying the theory to gambling; he ended by applying it to God. Pascal stood at a turning point in history, at the time when the new science had begun to challenge vigorously the old faith. Like every thinking man of his century, he was impelled to take part in the conflict and to seek some resolving philosophy. Intensely religious by nature and yet a notable contributor to science and mathematics, Pascal felt the conflict more poignantly than any other man. Because he saw both sides so well his mind became a battleground and in a most appealing passage he openly declared his bewilderment:

"This is what I see that troubles me. I look on all sides and I find everywhere nothing but obscurity. Nature offers nothing which is not a subject of doubt and disquietude; if I saw nowhere any sign of a Deity I should decide in the negative; if I saw everywhere the signs of a Creator, I should rest in peace in my faith; but, seeing too much to deny and too little confidently to affirm, I am in a pitiable state, and I have longed a hundred times that, if a God sustained nature, nature should show it without ambiguity, or that, if the signs of a God are fallacious, nature should suppress them altogether: Let her say the whole truth or nothing, so that I may see what side I ought to take."

Pascal's wager was not a flippant remark. It was a cry of despair.[39]

[39] Kline, *Mathematics and Western Culture*, pp. 374–75. Cf. the words of Henri Peyre: "True it is, however, that Pascal may have felt intellectually closer to the *libertins* than to the conventionally devout . . . and it may be questioned whether Pascal himself was fully convinced by the famous sophistry of his Wager, meant to frighten the agnostic gambler into a posture of faith." [Paper read at Weil Institute Conference.] Unamuno, who in some ways was closer to Pascal than any other modern man, pictures him a pyrrhonist with a desperate will to believe. ("La Foi pascalienne,'" pp. 219–21.) Since I have written this, a similar viewpoint has been argued by L. D. Maher, in his review-article, "Pascal's Suicide."

Pascal's confrontation with nihilism takes place both on the metaphysical and on the human level. On the metaphysical level, his anguished "Thoughts" reveal a man obsessed with the dread of nothingness and the fear of dying in an indifferent universe. His anguish is not of the infinite, as it is usually said, but of the annihilation, the meaninglessness, which is its threat. For Pascal is, in France, the first modern man (as Shakespeare was in England): the first to make the confrontation with existence and the naked "I," to experience his alienation, lost in the dark spaces of an indifferent world, to feel the homelessness of his spirit. Man is not in harmony with the world; he is a stranger, aware of himself and of death, condemned to be able to know, and yet to be unable to know. With Pascal, awareness of death becomes the dominating aspect, the meaningful truth of life; he is constantly returning to it in the *Pensées*.[40] His earthly being grows to be detestable to him. Unable to identify himself with life and with man, he turns to death and to Christ as the only hope. If he cannot accept life, it is because of the absence of an absolute justification of death. But when life is anguished and negative, death becomes positive. Death is liberation from an absurd universe of apparent injustice. Death is the implicit subject of the *Pensées*, for it is both the destroyer of all meaning and the requisite for finding meaning. That is why Pascal's desperate attempt to convince others is the other face of his effort to convince himself and to surmount his own insecurity. His universe is meaningless without the God on whom he has wagered. There is within us "an infinite abyss," which "can only be filled by an infinite and immutable object" (Pensée 425). Through his own agony, Pascal pictures man, unable to attain to the absolutes he demands, perched between all or nothing.

Pascal's conception of man and of human life is equally impregnated with nihilism, though again he will never accept that outcome, but will cling desperately, pathetically, to his faith as

[40] Of a large number of pertinent passages, we may quote only two or three. "When I see the blindness and the wretchedness of man, when I regard the whole silent universe, and man without light, left to himself, and as it were, lost in this corner of the universe, without knowing who has put him there, what he has come to do, what will become of him at death . . . I become terrified, like a man who should be carried in his sleep to a dreadful desert island, and should awake without knowing where he is, and without means of escape." (P. 692.) "When I consider the short duration of my life, swallowed up in the eternity before and after . . . engulfed in the infinite immensity of spaces of which I am ignorant, and which know me not, I am frightened." (P. 205.) "The last act is tragic, however happy the rest of the play; at the last a little earth is thrown upon our head, and that is the end forever." (P. 210.)

the only possible source of meaning. Man is a paradox; he has reason and is irrational; he has majesty but is weak, wretched, insecure, unhappy. Thought forces upon him the despairing awareness of human finitude in the midst of an infinite universe. He runs constantly to entertainment, in order to forget his misery and fill the emptiness of his self. To confirm his existence, he aspires restlessly to absolutes and infinities, that is, to godhood.[41] Man is the creature of eternal contradiction between aspiration and reality, in the realms of truth, justice, and power (absolute status in being). Reason is hateful; though it gives man his greatness, it separates and alienates him from the world and is the source of the skepticism which wracks him. Pascal clutches at original sin as the justification for his hatred of man and of life. The ego is hateful. All men hate each other, naturally. Society is a state of war, life is Hobbes's state of nature. Only force or ruse hold men's brutality in check. Law *is* only the imposition of force, not the expression of reason. What passes for justice is arbitrariness and self-interest. All rule is usurpation.

There is no revolt in this. On the contrary, Pascal "was content that force should rule and tame the self-seeking impulses of the men subjected to it, lest anarchy destroy all. . . . There is more than the skepticism of a Montaigne or a Charron here, resigned spectators of the vagaries of human conduct; there is a bitter and positive denial of the existence of any justice among men based on reason or experience." [42]

Pascal, unlike the *philosophes,* cannot turn to nature for guidance. He sees evil forces disguising themselves in the most innocent

[41] "He wanted to make himself his own center . . . and on making himself equal to me by the desire of finding his happiness in himself, I abandoned him to himself." (P. 430.) Pascal's own pride, his unconscious hatred of the hidden God before whom he had to humble himself, are brought out by Robert Payne (*Hubris,* pp. 191–215).

[42] Spink, *op. cit.,* p. 72. Spink points out the similarities with Hobbes. Pascal is more pessimistic than Hobbes. What the Englishman attributed to the state of nature, the Frenchman applies to the existing social state. Hobbes found some hope, through the organization of societies, within this life. The social compact establishes laws and governments which men can accept not only as existent but as right. For Pascal, there is no hope for men, except in life to come, which is only a probability, a wager. Hobbes considers that the evil is partly transformed and surpassed, and that man reaches a moral level. Pascal tells us that he remains evil, and only wears a mask. There is no hope for man through himself, hope only for a capricious chance of grace. Culture is futile, or superficial. Blind faith is the only escape from nihilism.

According to Jean Ehrard, the *philosophes* were "fascinated and frightened by Pascal's nihilism." ("Pascal au siècle des lumières," p. 252.)

actions, in the most benign natural occurrences. His own humanity
frightens him with its cravings and its needs. Life and its finitude
terrify him. He turns instead to the irrational and the supernatural, abdicates life in favor of death. He turns to faith from complete lack of faith. He is forced to construct an abstract system of
certainties to allay his passions, to justify and protect his self-
loathing, fear, and despair. His self-abasement, which is the
rejection of self, is founded on the sight of our nothingness in the
universe and on the Christian revelation of original sin—"a lost
God and a corrupt nature" (441). Renouncing the challenge to
live in this world as a man, he becomes the humble, docile servant
of God. Faith is the link between the point where reason becomes
insufficient and the point where the awareness of God and truth
begins. But, in order to prove the existence of God, Pascal has
wrecked the entire moral structure of human life.

What is this God Pascal gives us? He is the realm of grace, but
also the realm of force. For the divine world, as well as the human,
as far as we can understand and experience it—is ruled by power
and arbitrary will. If in one there is no justice, in the other there
is no comprehensible justice. The arbitrary, not the rational,
everywhere prevails. There is no relation between this God and
our moral values, his justice is not ours. God is incomprehensibility
raised to the power of infinity. Thus, even if this God represents
truth, man is incapable of coming to know his truths. There can
only be a wager. Since the Absolute has no correspondence with
the human world, it can only solve the problem as an act of blind
faith.

Yet Pascal thinks that alone this God can protect whatever poor
pretense of a moral life we are capable of: "It is certain that the
mortality or immortality of the soul must make an entire difference to morality." Suppose, now, that we take away this God, what
is left? A vile creature who is utterly incapable by himself of any
moral life. Again it is all or nothing—immortality or immorality
are the only alternatives Pascal gives us.

La Mettrie, in another generation, was to give men a choice
between nihilism and arbitrary force. Pascal, too, seeing man
poised in dread anguish between the infinity he aspires to and the
nothingness which is his truth, incapable of escaping the vicious
circle of his self, incapable of knowing or practicing justice, would
have left us no other choice, were it not that his despair projected

him into the vision of God's world of grace, as dark and capricious and terrifying as our own, but which he willed to accept, in blind faith, as the only hope, and then laboriously endeavored to justify. Pascal's way out, Pascal's God, could not himself be accepted by many men as a principle of justice. For Pascal, it was otherwise. Intensely aware of the essential futility, suffering, and injustice of life, and of the chaotic, oblivious world in which this life struggles, if he had not convinced himself of God, and of immortality, there would probably have been no other recourse for this haunted man but the revolt of nihilism—the despairing cry of defiance shouted in the face of injustice and absurdity. Sade, it is so true, is only a "Pascal without God." And Chateaubriand was to exclaim: "What would that great man have become, if he had not been a Christian!"

A century later, Voltaire felt the grip of pessimism and despair. Most *philosophes* did not experience this anguish, partly, it may be, because the reintegration of man into nature diminished the feeling of alienation. Voltaire's torment, both metaphysical and human in origin, was in some ways very close to Pascal's. Yet he detested Pascal and wrote a work to refute him. He, too, refused the descent into the abyss and clung to God, albeit a shadowy one; but he was also a naturalist, a disbeliever in religion and immortality. He could not hate men, despite everything they had done, but continued to cherish some hope for them. Pascal recognized the gap between human aspiration and human reality, but did not understand that man must try to fill this gap, because he is man, and as man he must live. It is not necessary to know the beginning and the end, to conquer infinities and absolutes. What we must reconquer is the human, by revolting against the realm of the sacred. This was the spirit that animated Voltaire and the eighteenth century.[43]

But Voltaire felt a far greater anguish than any other writer of his time (excepting Vauvenargues, whose work does not have his reach). Although he thought that man might at least partly overcome his alienation by rational and co-operative action in history,

[43] Cf. C. N. Cochrane, *Christianity and Classical Culture*, pp. 451–52: "The Augustinian doctrine of sin and grace marks the acute breach between Classicism and Christianity: Aristotle thought that virtue and vice are both alike in our own power. "For Augustine, perfectibility through knowledge or enlightenment was wholly illusory; for the aberrations of mankind, he saw no remedy through education."

he did not really believe that man would ever be put to rest by the attainment of a just social state and remained deeply troubled by a world in which God was futile. He agreed with Pascal both on the limit and on the value of reason (which is superior to the universe), on the dualism of man's greatness and wretchedness, and on opposing the quixotic or the reaching beyond our proper place. But he refused the blind faith in a realm of grace and incomprehensible justice. He had no refuge but a meager faith in man's courage and intelligence. He could not retreat to original sin in order to justify suffering and death. God exists, but his creation is not a good one—a fact which always led Voltaire back to Bayle's paradox. Voltaire gives up the attempt to find a rational explanation for what happens here—cause and effect do not seem to work in the moral world, as Zadig finds out. Job's great cry of protest, echoing down the ages, sounds again in Zadig's immortal "But . . ." Despite its "happy ending," *Zadig* is suffused with a deep feeling of alienation from an absurd world whose "order" is disorder and whose justice is incomprehensible. We are even incapable of ascertaining what we are up against, in a world where God's plans are only Micromégas' blank page, where the innocent are punished and the wicked (who are strong) triumph.[44] Voltaire, too, finds man an alien in an incomprehensible world, one which has no consonance with his ideals and provides no support for his values or his hopes.[45]

[44] See *An Age of Crisis*, pp. 23–26, 63–67. Also the following description of man's fate in the ninth chapter of *Zadig*: "Then he imagined men such as they really are, insects devouring each other on a little atom of mud. This true image seemed to annihilate his misfortunes, by painting to him the nothingness of his being and that of Babylon. His soul projected itself into the infinite, and contemplated, liberated from its senses, the immutable order of the universe. But when afterwards, brought back to his self-awareness and looking within his heart, he thought that Astarte was perhaps dead for him, the universe disappeared before his eyes and in all of nature he could see only Astarte dying and Zadig unhappy."
William Bottiglia speaks of "a painful awareness of the unsolvable conflict between the clocklike order of a rational, mechanical universe and the mad confusion of an illogical, capricious actuality," and of the helplessness of the individual in an unhuman world. (*Voltaire's Candide: Analysis of a Classic*, pp. 89–92.)

[45] René Pomeau points out that Voltaire feels man to be lost in the divine immensity; in God's scale, good and evil disappear (XXIX, p. 341), and so do remuneration and punishment after death. "Such a philosophy is anti-humanistic." More than once, Voltaire calls man a prisoner awaiting his death sentence to be carried out, trying to amuse himself until the time comes. "And when the hour does arrive, it becomes clear that we have lived to no purpose. All reflections are vain, all reasoning on necessity and on human wretchedness are only wasted words." (XLIX, pp. 80–81; XLIII, p. 310.) Pomeau rightly characterizes this as "pascalian metaphor expressing the pathetic impotence of man in the hands of a jailer God."

Candide occupies a position in Voltaire's humanistic struggle against nihilism which is analogous to that of the *Pensées* in Pascal's mystical struggle against nihilism. It seems evident that he did not intend originally to examine this problem in *Candide,* or to make it the decisive battle. But in refuting "optimism," he was forced to do just that, because he was forced to paint a picture of the world as it is—the worst of all possible worlds. The problem is constantly brought to the fore by his ironic method, which is to oppose the *candid* attitude and life's realities. The candid attitude would be fine, if the world were, not the best of all possible worlds (which is meaningless in terms of "good"), but a decent world, one which corresponded in some degree to human needs as well as moral notions. But from the beginning, the candid attitude is defeated by existential realities, natural and human. Each episode brutally illustrates this truth, which is also symbolized, ironically and humorously, by Candide's search for an ideal in the form of Cunégonde, who corresponds to his aspiration as little as Dulcinea does to Don Quixote's. In *Candide,* Voltaire comes to the verge of nihilistic despair, but he does not submit. His answer is not a refutation, however, nor a vista of hope. It is a modest, humanistic response to the challenge, but a most courageous one. There remains the dignity of irony (equivalent to Pascal's superiority through awareness), and the co-operation of men in productive work. With good will, we can salvage the small amount of happiness which is man's lot.

God is no part of this solution. Voltaire is determined to reject both extremes; he refuses to choose between the sacred and revolt, between all or nothing. He refuses the either-or and seeks a middle way. He does accept God, but he refuses to justify God, or to make of that incomprehensible being an element in the pragmatic defense of values. He is not too far from Ivan Karamazov—or from Job: it is God's world, but he will not accept it as a good world. What is left? A human way: to avoid absolutes and in-

---

However we must also realize the implicit nihilism. Our questions have no answer. "Oh atoms of one day! Oh my companions in the infinitely small, born like me to suffer everything and to be ignorant of everything, are there any among you mad enough to think you know all that? No, there is none; no, at the bottom of your heart you feel your nothingness, as I realize mine." (XIX, pp. 425-27.) Pomeau depicts a Voltaire who is "emotional and irritable, subject to falling into astonishing depressions." Many texts speak of his horror for himself and for others [cf. Pascal]. But he rages against it and demands greatness. (*La Religion de Voltaire,* pp. 408, 418-19, 269.)

finities, to seek the pragmatically useful within our circumscribed view and field of action. The answer assumes that we must conduct our lives and base our justifications without reference to a supporting cosmos. Perhaps this is ineffective against the absurd. But it is our only way, unless we accept the realm of the sacred. Voltaire, it must be admitted, does not have a firm confidence in his own solution. The best we can do, he tells us, is to cultivate our garden. But is it not clear, from the picture of the world as Candide discovers it, that there will always be many who will not do this? Will there not always be those who live by raiding and exploiting the gardens cultivated by others, and live with impunity, power, and prestige, until they, too, are despoiled in the pitiless struggle for existence which he so powerfully portrayed in *Candide?*

Pascal showed man the wretchedness of his condition. But it was wretchedness only without God, and so he wagered on God. However this was an act of will. Rousseau tried to escape by attributing human suffering and injustice to men and society, rather than to the world. Voltaire urges us to constructive action against the world. He chooses the realm of justice, of enlightenment and co-operative social action, in the measure in which this is possible—the realm of the human. But he does not go so far as Malraux, Camus, or Sartre. He wishes to keep, somehow, his remote, nebulous, inscrutable, do-nothing God. He does not embrace nihilism as a starting point on which to build the human world. He sees it, is frightened by it, and dares not contemplate it too long and steadily, or without the defensive weapons of humor and irony.

The revolt of secular morality and the upsurge of hedonism testify to the fact that there were many who were unwilling to accept Pascal's wager on the possibility of eternal bliss against the enjoyment of a brief life. Nor would they acquiesce in his judgment that the *misère* was necessary in this world and that the *grandeur* was for the next. Serious utilitarians were not receptive to the current of Christianity which minimized works for faith or grace, or substituted election for responsibility—and they would not wait for eternity.

After the metaphysical disorientation, the tide of hedonism was the next wellspring of nihilism. Nature seemed the sign of God's wisdom and goodness, and in some minds was worshiped in God's place. Starting from the premise that pleasure and pain are the only motives, and pleasure-happiness the highest value, adding to it the widespread maxim, "nature is good," it is not difficult to reach the conclusion that the free expression of the self is justified as nature's law. Every creature tends to happiness—hundreds of writers said so, even Christians. The Physiocrats said, "Whatever made for the greatest pleasure in a world governed by natural law was justified by natural right." To be sure, a rational person would look to his ultimate interest, but what ground had the eighteenth-century analysis of man given for this assumption of rational behavior? Did the facts warrant it? Spinoza had put the matter clearly:

> Anything that exists in nature which we judge to be evil or able to hinder us from existing and enjoying a rational life, we are allowed to remove from us in that way which seems the safest; and whatever, on the other hand, we judge to be good or to be profitable for the preservation of our being or the enjoyment of a rational life, we are permitted to take for our use and use in any way we may think proper; and absolutely, every one is allowed by the highest right of nature to do that which he believes contributes to his own profit.[46]

To those who urged that there was no conflict between virtue and self-interest, no real sacrifice, that what is good for others is good for ourselves, the immoralists gave a categorical No. The ones who acted in accordance with such a belief were the dupes, while the clever gathered the fruits of not doing so. They would laugh at the naïveté of de Vattel: "Let us then work for the happiness of all; all will work for ours, and we shall establish our happiness on the most solid foundation." [47] The anonymous author of the early eighteenth-century manuscript, *Jordanus Brunus redivivus*, refused to accept the loss of freedom in exchange for the moral order. "Man, born free, independent, finds himself, as soon as he begins to feel the joys of his existence, in a confinement which shackles all his senses. He wants to know why his freedom is infringed on; and no one can tell him." [48] Setting the tone for many others, he charges that there are arbitrary customs, not moral laws; what is right here is wrong elsewhere. And after all, doesn't morality, as Morelly later said, have to be in accord with nature? [49]

---

[46] *Ethic*, IV, Appendix, VIII.
[47] *Op. cit.*, pp. 90–91.
[48] Fol. 100. Cf. the opening of Rousseau's *Contrat social*.
[49] *Code*, p. 257.

It is very simple; happiness is necessary to me, and *that* is necessary to my happiness. Since pleasure and pain are nature's mechanisms, argues de Chastellux, "it is easy to see that the happiness of everything that exists consists solely in accomplishing the wish of nature."

To the many references already cited in the course of this study, we may add several selected confirmations. The author of the manuscript *L'Âme mortelle* sees no limit. "Pleasure and pain are the natural and incontestable characteristics of good and evil; as we are not the absolute masters of our bodily impulses, it is not in our power to stop them. The weight which makes us lean and drags us to sensual good is natural to us. It is a modification of matter configured in such and such a way." [50]

Boulainvilliers follows Spinoza, according to the current interpretation. Having shown that the essence of existence is perseverance in being, he concludes from this fact, plus our sensitivity, that a man must necessarily seek "the means he esteems suitable to procure his preservation and well being," and reject the contrary. Nothing is good or evil except as we feel it to be so, desire it, or flee from it. "I call 'good' any kind of satisfaction and whatever means lead to it; I call evil, on the contrary, any kind of sadness, and especially that which is born of frustrated desire . . . so that anything is esteemed good or bad according to personal ideas." What gives us joy augments our being and "the reality" of ourselves. Anything which restricts our power (the free expression of desire) is evil. There is no question of moral value here, or of cultural imperatives; there is only nature. [51]

Two serious thinkers, d'Argens and the abbé Dulaurens, wrote licentious novels in which a similar philosophy is both defended and practiced. In the former's *Thérèse philosophe,* the heroine prefaces the story of her addiction to debauchery with this exordium: "Imbecile mortals! you think you are the masters to extinguish the passions which nature has put in you, [but] they are the work of God. You want to destroy these passions, restrict them within certain limits. Insane men! Do you then pretend to be second Creators as powerful as the first? Will you never understand that everything is as it should be, and that all is

---

[50] Fol. 78–80.

[51] *Réfutation des erreurs de Benoît de Spinosa,* Bruxelles, 1731. For Spinoza, power exists in reason, as adequate ideas; his belief in the centrality of reason as the defining characteristic of man is far from the materialists' interpretation of his thought.

good . . . ?" [52] Thérèse proposes her life as proof of her philosophy. She had been carefully brought up, hearing only of virtue and the happiness it inevitably brings, and of the scorn, shame, and remorse which follow vice. When adolescence came, all that melted away, like snow under a hot sun. The passions of the flesh are surely sanctioned by God—or else the devil is the stronger. After expounding a Spinozist doctrine and rejecting Christianity as a hoax and as anti-natural, one of the characters summarizes: "Let us conclude, then, dear friend, that the pleasures you and I are enjoying are pure and innocent, since they offend neither God nor man, because of the secrecy and decency of our conduct." Everyone must be happy in his own way; "each must seize the kind of pleasure which is suitable to him," remembering, however, that our happiness depends on that of others. Then isn't it our duty to spread this doctrine and make others happy? No, is the reply, this is not a doctrine for the common people. For them, religion and the fear of punishments are necessary. D'Argens, then, does not embrace nihilism, but tends toward it, especially for an élite of superior men and women. He also tends toward a protototalitarian tyranny—which is but the other side of the coin.[53]

Dulaurens' *Imirce*, as the title says, is a daughter of nature. She has been brought up in isolation in a cave (together with a man, Emilor, whose child she has borne). When Ariste discovers her and brings her to his room, she spontaneously seeks his sex and his love. Then, learning about life, she is outraged at seeing people beg, instead of taking the food which is at hand. She condemns inequality and money. When she rebels against modesty and restrictions on sexual activity, the author adds in a footnote: "Doubtless Revelation will rectify these bad natural sentiments." Then Emilor condemns civilization. Ariste defends it: men would kill each other without laws and order. No, replies Emilor, man is naturally good, "he is a child whom [lawmakers] have bound and who struggles to break his chains." Without laws, men would not know crime and would not have found it necessary to satisfy their

[52] *Thérèse philosophe*, La Haye, n.d., p. 3. The attribution to d'Argens is probable. Similar ideas are expressed in the abbé Barrin's *Vénus dans le cloître*, a book which interested Diderot when he was a young man. Diderot's *La Religieuse* is a far less crude presentation of the same thesis. *Thérèse philosophe* also contains a strong defense of determinism and of the thesis that our organic constitution is all, education nothing.

[53] *Ibid.*, pp. 3, 16–23, 120–22; Part II, pp. 50–56.

passions.[54] "Abolish all laws, enlighten men, and you will expel crimes from the earth, where freedom should be the first law. . . . Throw your laws into the fire, imitate Nature; she has made none for man." [55] *Imirce,* then, belongs to the school of anarchism of the optimistic primitivists, not to the group of nihilists who thought man to be essentially evil, and accepted evil. The primitivists nurtured the illusion that man would be different in a nonsocial condition, and still be essentially man.

Still more radical, and entirely contrary in its judgment of men, was the same writer's *Le Compère Mathieu* (1766).[56] Here are some of the ideas expressed by the characters in this picaresque philosophical tale. Children owe no obligation to their parents (a favorite idea of Sade's): parents thought only of their own pleasure, and no other animal in nature mourns its parents. Laws are a tyranny, shackles which should be thrown off. There is only one valid law—"the right which nature gives to the strong over the weak." [57] Since we have no other life, we are entitled to our natural freedom, of which laws deprive us by establishing property and inequality. Property is the greatest injustice and source of evil. Moral distinctions are nothing more than "the opinions of those who have invented them to support their interests." [58] Conscience is the torment of the weak and of fools. Shame is not natural, or animals would experience it. Rape is a perfectly justifiable natural act: "to exploit a woman is an action which is good in itself, since it is Nature's purpose to procreate the species and relieve our needs whenever we have them; so there is nothing wrong in exploiting a woman in public." [59] Natural law is universal—the same for animals and for men, and there is no special "Natural Law" for men.[60] The prohibition of cannibalism is absurd and irrational; a dead human body is no different from a dead animal body. Dulaurens concludes, however, that true wisdom is to live tranquilly in the midst of a depraved society.

The discussion of these three novels has carried us forward

---

[54] Helvétius reasons in exactly the same way, concerning sexual satisfactions. Diderot similarly.

[55] *Imirce, ou la fille de la nature,* Berlin, 1765, *passim.*

[56] Londres, 1770.

[57] *Ibid.,* I, p. 15.

[58] *Ibid.,* I, p. 185.

[59] *Ibid.,* II, pp. 107, 7.

[60] *Ibid.,* II, pp. 118–20. But Dulaurens defends the right of suicide, which is unique to man (p. 233 ff.).

chronologically.[61] Let us now return to La Mettrie, to complete our earlier analyses of his thought. La Mettrie refused to man any transcendence over nature. We are in nature's hands, "like a clock in those of a clockmaker; she has fashioned us as she wished, or rather as she could. In a word, we are no more criminal, when we follow the imprint of the primitive impulses which govern us, than the Nile is for its inundations and the sea for its ravages." [62] In our "moral" philosophy, he holds, we should think of the body before the soul, for the body is prior. Our best guide is to follow the instinct of men and animals and cultivate the mind only to secure greater advantages for the body: ". . . if a man has sound taste, bread is a more solid food than reputation." [63] It is foolish to think that a savant is worth more than an ignorant man; better an ignorant man who has known how to get rich. "There is no vice or virtue, nor moral good or evil, nor just or unjust; everything is arbitrary and made by the hand of man. . . . Physical passions are the only real pleasures. . . . In regard to happiness, good and evil are indifferent, and he who gets greater satisfaction out of doing wrong will be happier than whoever gets less out of doing right." There are, then, only quantitative differences between actions. One type of action is probably most pleasurable quantitatively: "Nature . . . approves of crimes rather than of virtue, since she inclines us more to them, and since they are more useful to our happiness." We recall, too, how La Mettrie condemns remorse, which he describes not as a manifestation of moral life— since there is no autonomous moral life—but of social pressure and habituation. "In a word, we should not, on the pretext of avoiding remorse, refuse to nature what she demands, nor above all, repent for pleasure. . . . We may, then, rightfully conclude that if the joys derived from nature and reason are crimes, men's happiness lies in being criminals . . . he who has no remorse, because of so great a familiarity with crime that for him vices become virtues, will be happier than such another who, after a fine deed, is sorry he has done it, and so loses all its reward." The nihilistic rebel must also despise life: "Then, indeed, I maintain, parricide, incestuous, thief, scoundrel, villain, and just object of the execration

---

[61] For other pertinent novels, see *An Age of Crisis*, chap. 14.

[62] *Système d'Epicure*, *Oeuvres*, 1764, II, p. 162. Diderot and other materialists were at times appalled by this complete reduction, drawn from the logic of a materialistic system so like their own.

[63] *Discours sur le bonheur*, pp. 151–58.

of good people, you will yet be happy." You have only to watch out for the policeman, and fear the gallows more than conscience or the gods.

The similarities of La Mettrie's thinking to Sade's are so obvious that we can understand why the marquis called him one of his spiritual godfathers. He gives man a choice between anarchism and tyranny. Moral values are denied, and subjective happiness is affirmed. The two are declared to be, not linked, as the utilitarians suggested, but opposed. The refusal to admit self-transcendence over the machine, or the transcendence of culture over nature, the proclamation of unlimited sexual freedom and the destruction of remorse as a limit, these are cardinal tenets of a philosophy of nihilism. La Mettrie is unwilling to pay the price of civilization, which is the repression or suppression of instinct.[64] For La Mettrie, to be sure, nihilism is a speculative truth, to be limited to the *cognoscenti*. Alone even among nihilists, he is so perfectly consistent and logical, that he does not dispute the right of society to impose its notions and standards, and to punish and kill violators. This is merely the universal law of the strong and of self-preservation, which obtains for the group as well as for the individual. "The laws are there, with their escort of executioners, to assure the security of society, which has nothing in common with the practice of virtue." Society preserves itself by inspiring fear. Thus La Mettrie substitutes one fear to counteract the loss of another (remorse) and implies an eternal war between the individual and society, between nature and culture. "The punishment of crime is part of the social order to which the philosopher refuses any authority. The secret of happiness consists in rejecting any evolution towards the (morally) good; it is to be subservient to our needs such as they are, good or evil. Or rather there is nothing good, nothing evil. There are only organic forces which weigh on us and impel us to such or such an action: if we resist it, on the grounds of the false assumptions of education, we are unhappy." But will not this fear, which substitutes in function for the moral conscience, turn into remorse? Can man ever escape his moral self?

---

[64] According to Aram Vartanian, La Mettrie was one of the first to perceive "that one of the most besetting dilemmas of the modern civilizing process lay in the constant increase of the individual sense of guilt, which, emerging as a noxious by-product of cultural progress, actually threatened to nullify its many gains for humanity." (*L'Homme machine*, p. 53.)

Unlike La Mettrie, Helvétius was not a nihilist, and his utilitarianism was aimed at defending morals, properly understood. However, a poor defense—as Diderot knew—can be more damaging than an attack. If Sade considered Helvétius as another of his spiritual godfathers, it was for good reason. There is no difference, Helvétius tells us time and again, between a virtuous and wicked man, except the way in which their self-interest is modified —all are necessarily moved to seek happiness. We should be thankful if we are "fortunately born," and do not have "any of those tastes and passions which would have forced us to seek our happiness through the misfortune of others." If we did have them, there is nothing we could do about it, since we must, necessarily and justly, seek our happiness, in whichever way nature has directed us to find it. "For one always obeys his self-interest; whence the injustice of all our judgments, and of those names of just and unjust given to the same action, according to the advantage or disadvantage each one gets out of it." [65] In these lines we have the abdication of moral conscience and will, and the dissolution of moral judgment. As for virtue, "The highest virtue, just like the most shameful vice, is in us the effect of the greater or lesser pleasure we get out of indulging in them. . . . There is no use in pretending; one necessarily becomes the enemy of men when one can be happy only by their hurt. . . . The virtuous man is not then one who sacrifices his pleasures . . . to the public interest, since such a man is impossible." [66] In his eagerness to reduce the moral order to the physical, he "easily discovers" the source of human virtues in physical sensitivity, which produces self-interest, which brings about arbitrary social conventions, which create right and wrong.[67] Exactly like La Mettrie, Helvétius considers moral standards to be the law of the strong—a just and proper tyranny: "Indeed, if force resides essentially with the greatest number, and justice is the practice of actions useful to the greatest number, it is evident that justice is, by its nature, always armed with the necessary power to repress vice and force men to be virtuous." [68]

D'Holbach stands rather close to Helvétius. The two major

---

[65] *De l'Esprit*, pp. 52–53.

[66] *Ibid.*, pp. 372–74. The difference between Helvétius' naturalistic ethics and Sadian nihilism is made clear in the following line: "It is as impossible for him to love the good for its own sake as it is to love evil for the sake of evil." (P. 73.)

[67] *Ibid.*, p. 276.

[68] *Ibid.*, p. 229.

differences are his emphasis on the organism rather than environment, and the belief that moral values are not the creation of arbitrary convention but inhere in objective social relations. D'Holbach is also much more the moralist and preacher of virtue. Nevertheless, we find in his writings the same basic ambiguities, the theories which, designed to buttress a "natural" ethics, may also be interpreted to support amoralism. Since whatever we do is equally within the necessary order of nature, he assures us, we cannot call any acts "unnatural," or differentiate among them on any basis of objective natural values.[69] The needs of social living, then, constitute the sole differentia, and a man is "good" or "evil" only as his actions, which are all necessary, natural, and beyond his power to modify, favor or counter these criteria. Fortunately, self-interest motivates us toward conformity. But there is no moral world within us. This is the essential point; there is only the pursuit of happiness which is modified by awareness of the moral (i.e., approved) modes of action. There is nothing but complete egoism.

> Whatever procures us true and permanent happiness is reasonable; whatever disturbs our own happiness or those of beings necessary to our happiness is insane or unreasonable. . . . Our *duties* are the means of which experience and reason show us the necessity in order to reach our proposed end. . . . If man is forced by his nature to desire his well-being, he is forced to love the means to it; it would be useless and perhaps unjust to expect a man to be virtuous if he is unable to without making himself unhappy. If vice makes him happy, he must love vice. . . .[70] Every one acts and judges necessarily according to his own way of being, and according to the true or false ideas he has about happiness. . . . The good man and the wicked act upon equally necessary motives; they differ only by their organism. . . .[71]

It is not difficult to see that if something is our duty because it makes us happy, some men will also say, although it does not follow in logic: "That does not make me happy, therefore it is not my duty." D'Holbach, of course, believed that we can be happy only by being virtuous. But he never establishes this, other than as a supposition.

With the Benedictine monk, Dom Deschamps, we return to

---

[69] *Système de la nature*, I, pp. 69–70.

[70] "Il Doit aimer le vice." The word "doit" also includes the idea of obligation, and is not exactly translatable.

[71] *Ibid.*, I, pp. 145–46, 163, 257.

optimistic primitivism. Deschamps urges the complete dissolution of the social bond. Men, according to his argument, have always revolted against moral restrictions, and laws are a slavery. We live in a condition of contradiction, torn between the demands of nature and those of culture.[72] Because of laws, all men are in a state of war with each other, too, within the galley in which we are chained. If there were no laws, there would be no crimes, and we should still be in the state of innocence, for laws create vices and virtues.[73] (Where all is permitted, nothing is wrong!) Morals, then, must be abolished, along with laws and the tyrannical society which imposes them on nature—in short, men must be freed *from the very idea of right and wrong.*[74] Deschamps, like other primitivists, is not a nihilist in the sadistic sense of condoning or exulting in hurt to others. He has the sweet illusion that in the state of anarchy all artificial passions and depraved tastes would be unknown. Men would live in the wise and peaceful indulgence of their "natural appetites," live (as La Mettrie had suggested) a purely physical life.[75] Hume, interestingly, had made a supposition very close to this dream, but Deschamps dreamed that it could come true.[76] And indeed, nothing is needed to fulfill it, except a different human race!

Thus French philosophy in the eighteenth century becomes the pseudoscientific expression of egoism and the search for pleasure, at the same time that it sought to establish a new ethics. It is obvious from the data we have examined that the sexual activities were one of the foci of the revolt against cultural limitation. The sexual act, in the eighteenth century, was at the center of art, gastronomy, fashion, and literature. The large number of novels in which sexual license, expressed as open revolt, reaches incredible extremes, is a striking social and psychological phenomenon.

---

[72] "Our laws, by putting a brake on our most natural inclinations, constantly contradict them, and our inclinations constantly contradicted by our laws, revolt against them and want to have their way despite them. Now this cannot be the case without producing that violent state which puts us in continual contradiction with ourselves and with each other; which makes us always distrustful, masked and constrained; which makes us fear our fellows; which separates us from them and makes it requisite for us not only not to do the good which we could, but to hurt them, either out of revenge for their hurting us or to prevent them from so doing, or to achieve our good." Dom Deschamps, *Le Vrai Système*, pp. 140–41.

[73] *Ibid.*, pp. 14–43, 154.

[74] *Ibid.*, pp. 54–55, 83.

[75] *Ibid.*, pp. 160–61, 166–67, 207–8.

[76] *Enquiry*, Aiken, p. 186.

The *Histoire de Mlle de Brion,* for instance, urges women to yield without inhibitions and offers enticing examples. *Vénus dans le cloître* recommends lesbianism and all other forms of debauchery and flaunts the goal of physical pleasure in the face of tyrannical restrictions. It condemns "that inconvenient virtue of which our century is incapable," and assures its readers that "we are not responsible for the fantasies, penchants, inclinations which [nature] gives us . . . it is she who is guilty. . . . And we cannot reproach men for the vices they are born with. . . ." [77] D'Argens' *Thérèse philosophe* denies the applicability of so-called moral distinctions to expressions of the sexual urge. Duclos' *Mme de Luz* and many other stories and novels confirm the philosophers by showing us men and women driven beyond their power of rational control by their sexual drives, making moral rules and duties seem pitifully ineffectual and secondary.

Among the philosophical writings, there are several opinions which are worth adding to the evidence we have seen thus far. Bayle mounts an insidious attack on the concept of the fall of man through sex.[78] He makes three points. God said, Be fruitful and multiply; we would not be human if we did not already know good and evil; beasts have not fallen, and yet "what is called *libido,* and the most impure and unrestrained things that can be conceived under that term, are clearly seen among beasts when animated by love's fire." In the article "Hélène," Bayle affirms that reason is powerless to withstand sexual desire. Life is a fight between passions and conscience, "in which the latter is almost always conquered." A pagan, not knowing the Christian God, could only assume God's responsibility for all this.

Sexual license was also encouraged by innumerable reports of travelers to newly discovered lands with idyllic primitive cultures, in which there was unbounded interest. Lahontan, Bougainville, and the rest paint, more or less accurately, societies in which happiness and peace accompany the more or less free indulgence in sexual play.

Mandeville castigates convents and monasteries for their hypocritical chastity and hidden lubricity. There is not much use in trying to repress nature, he warns. The average man wants to be

---

[77] [Barrin], *Vénus dans le cloître, ou la Religieuse en chemise,* Nouvelle edition, Dusseldorf, 1746, pp. 138–39. (The original date of publication, 1683, is significant of the depth of the movement.)
[78] "Eve," *Dictionnaire,* II, p. 813.

bowed to by others and to be served with luxury in all his pleasures. "While thus wallowing in a Sea of Lust and Vanity, he is
wholly employ'd in provoking and indulging his Appetites, he
desires the World should think him altogether free from Pride
and Sensuality. . . ." [79] But artful moralists have taught us so to
disguise

> our darling Passion, Lust, that we scarce know it when we meet
> with it in our own Breasts; Oh! the mighty Prize we have in
> view for all our Self-denial! can any Man be so serious as to
> abstain from Laughter, when he considers that for so much
> deceit and insincerity practis'd upon ourselves as well as others,
> we have no other Recompense than the vain Satisfaction of
> making our Species appear more exalted and remote from that
> of other Animals, than it really is; and we in our Consciences
> know it to be? [80]

Mandeville, however, while lifting the mask, does not deny society's need "to render odious every Word or Action by which we
might discover the innate Desire we feel to perpetuate our Kind,"
and to brand innocent, unhypocritical submission to our most
"Furious Appetite," nature's most pressing demand, with the ig-
nominious name of brutality. For Mandeville, then, the division
between *any* so-called moral evaluation imposed by culture, and
what is natural in us, is complete.

Still in the early years of the century, Rémond de Saint-Mard
advocates what amounts to "free love." A wise husband, he urges,
will be charmed by his wife's infidelities and find her the more
vivacious. "Believe me, husbands sometimes owe greater obligation than they know to their wives' love affairs." [81] Moreover, nature's law commands us to be inconstant. The Protestant, J.-Fr.
Bernard, calls marriage "a country of absurdities," and a sure way
of killing love; many married couples would find that the secret of
loving each other lies in never seeing each other." [82] Such satirical
observations abound in memoirs and commentaries on the times.

To restrict sexual practices, asserts Meslier, would be to condemn nature and her creator—if she has any—for there is no urge
closer to the root of our nature. We need not return again to

---

[79] *Fable of the Bees*, I, p. 149 ff. The entire passage is worth reading, for its
satirical picture and tone of nihilistic insinuation.

[80] *Ibid.*, I, p. 145.

[81] *Oeuvres*, Amsterdam, 1750, I, pp. 125–27, 143, 264. He is somewhat more
prudent in his *Lettres galantes et philosophiques*, Cologne, 1721, II, pp. 161–64.

[82] *Réflexions morales*, Liège, 1733, pp. 430–31.

La Mettrie's rhapsodies, which may be epitomized in this line: "Pleasure, sovereign master of men and gods, before whom everything disappears, even reason itself, you know how much my heart adores you, and all the sacrifices it has made at your altar." [83] Morelly, in his heroic poem, *La Basiliade,* significantly makes the sexual act the sign of God within man, in the power to create. There is no "hypocritical modesty" in his utopia, where boys and girls copulate freely under the joyous eyes of those who watch them. "O love, these people submitted without fear or crime to your delightful transports." [84] The old sage in the poem warns the civilized: "You think you can reform Nature, *impose rules upon her;* you will make her furious by subjecting her to useless duties." [85] It is no less significant that Morelly, in devising a totalitarian communistic society, in his later *Code de la nature,* places such matters under rigid controls.

An examination of lyrical and light verse would carry us too far afield. A few lines from Dorat's *Abélard à Héloïse* will suffice to provide a typical sample:

> Il en appelle du Dieu de la religion au Dieu de la nature.
> "Vous montrez le bonheur, Héloïse le donne.
> Dieu veut qu'on aime. . . .
> Va, notre Dieu n'est pas un tyran formidable.
> Un feu qu'il alluma peut-il être coupable?" [86]

Helvétius is another apologist of free love, although he pretends not to be.[87] We should be better off, he maintains, if women were in common and children made wards of the State. If so-called debauchery were, then, authorized by the State and by religion, the corruption of morals and many "crimes" would be eliminated. The differing practices of nations prove that ours are not necessary, or the best. As the Siamese say, "it is pleasant for men to have desires, and for women to excite them. It is the happiness of both sexes, the only joy heaven mingles with the ills it inflicts on us. What barbarous souls would want to take this, too, away from us?" In the Indies, notes Helvétius approvingly, any woman who refuses herself to any man is punished by death. The Greeks practiced homosexuality without any harm to society. The fact is,

---

[83] *La Volupté, Oeuvres,* I, pp. 335–36.
[84] *Naufrages des Isles flottantes, ou Basiliade,* Messine, 1753, I, p. 16 ff.
[85] *Ibid.,* I, p. 47. Italics added.
[86] Potez, *op. cit.,* pp. 58–59.
[87] *De l'Esprit,* pp. 146–48, 150–51.

then, that culture cannot change nature [a nihilistic proposition in its implication that culture should not try to control, or regulate nature]. Why blame women for "vices" they cannot help, and which are vices only because of the laws? If we abolished all prohibitions against adultery and allowed women freely to satisfy all their whims, there would be no more "unfaithful women." [88] (That is to say, once again, if there were no laws, there would be no crimes.)

It is surely not surprising that Dom Deschamps includes sexual anarchy in his anarchistic utopia. The "cruel obstacles" of modesty, chastity, and especially marriage are responsible for endless crimes, he charges. Women as property can only have the effect of all property, that of making all men thieves. What kind of laws are these, that we are always violating them? [89] Polly Baker's notorious oration, in Raynal's *Histoire des Deux Indes* (in which Diderot may have had a hand), is a plea against the social frustration of legitimate natural demands, and a justification of bearing children out of wedlock.[90] And Brissot, the future revolutionary, argued that no man has property in a woman beyond his need. "Man of nature! follow your wish; hearken to your need, it is your only master, your only guide. Do you feel a secret fire enkindled in your veins at the sight of a charming object; do you feel those happy symptoms which tell you you are a man? Nature has spoken, that object belongs to you. . . . Love is the only title to sexual possession, as hunger is the only title to property." [91]

Not infrequently, as we have noted, do eighteenth-century writers condone or portray sexual perversions. This is an inevitable consequence of "naturalism" as it was understood. Diderot's defense of perverted practices, in the third section of *Le Rêve de d'Alembert,* is no different at all from that of Sade: "It is absurd to say that this mania outrages [nature], how could that be, since she inspires it in us?" [92] The confusion of the naturally descriptive with the naturally normative, or of nature and value, of what is and what ought to be, is a consequence of much of the thinking we have encountered. In fact, however, we have here an interest-

---

[88] *Ibid.,* p. 156.
[89] *Op. cit.,* pp. 121–28, 163–65, 207–8.
[90] 1770 ed., VI, pp. 257–62.
[91] Quoted by Morellet, *Mélanges,* III, pp. 303–4.
[92] *La Philosophie dans le boudoir,* n.p., 1948, p. 64–65. Sade, however, also wishes to "outrage" nature. But Diderot expresses the opposite opinion in a fragment (*Oeuvres,* VI, p. 453).

ing reversal of natural teleology. Instead of pleasure being the instrument of a purpose—procreation—the result becomes incidental (or unwanted), and pleasure usurps the role of end. There is only one step more to take, and Sade will take it: "if nature forbade sodomy, incest, pollutions, etc., would she allow us to get so much pleasure from them? . . . what is most filthy, most infamous, most forbidden, is what excites us most." [93] He does not realize that for nature—if we were to make its laws our only ones —the individual and his pleasure are in themselves totally unimportant.[94]

There are also a few instances, before Sade, of the realization that sexual urges are associated with cruelty, destruction, and the aggressive impulses, that is, the satisfaction which comes from hurting, exploiting, and victimizing others. Duclos, Diderot, Laclos, and Rétif all show this awareness.[95] In Saint-Just's lascivious poem, *Organt,* which details rapes and perversions, there appears an obsession with "the infernal power escaping from the human being. . . . Above all, the stress is placed on the pleasure felt in spite of [because of] the indignities to which the partner is submitted." [96]

From these observations on the connection of sexual revolt with perversion and aggression, it should be obvious that the persistent current of licentiousness and the ever-increasing attempts to justify it are more than a matter of frivolity or relativistic choice of mores. They are an intimate part of a general orientation toward morals and values, and betray the ultimate (if often only implicit and unrecognized) tendency of that outlook. A number of eighteenth-century writers were aware of such dangers, and warned against them. Wollaston, for instance, based the prohibition of adultery on its disruption of the family unit, the confusion of kinship and the damage to the general order and tranquillity.[97] Some writers protested against the reduction of the sexual relationship to the mere matter of physical pleasure. Chaudon and Vauvenargues, in

---

[93] *Ibid.,* pp. 73, 68.

[94] For a discussion of the psychological harm done by sexual restrictions, and of that done by perversions, see Brill in S. Lorand, *Psychoanalysis Today,* p. 178 ff.

[95] See *An Age of Crisis,* chap. XIV.

[96] A. Ollivier, *Saint-Just et la force des choses,* 1954, p. 50. "Sexuality is only a supplementary manifestation of the world's madness." The background of this image of love is humiliation. "The thirst for the absolute which possesses him will never be appeased. . . . It is curious that one of the last visions of Organt on the threshold of Hell is marked by an attraction towards Terror."

[97] *Op. cit.,* pp. 141–42.

addition to others we have noted,[98] resented this reduction of human emotion to animal sensation. One doesn't choose the prettiest woman, observes Chaudon: "Then it is the character which determines us; then it is the soul we look for. . . ." [99] Montesquieu questioned the attributes commonly given to the word "natural." It is not true, he insists, "that incontinence follows nature's laws; on the contrary, it violates them. It is modesty and reserve that follow those laws." [100] D'Holbach, who was truly concerned about virtue, steps out of line with respect to his group by upholding chastity, modesty, the sanctity of the family.[101] "Are these opinions only prejudices or arbitrary conventions?" he asks, and replies in the negative. "Their basis is experience." Experience proves that debauchery leads to deterioration of the individual and destroys his usefulness to society.

> The profligate, tormented by an exclusive passion, continually excites his lascivious imagination, and thinks only of ways to satisfy the needs it creates in him. A girl who has violated the rules of modesty, dominated by her sexual ardor, hates work detests all reflection, mocks prudence, is unfit to become an attentive and hard-working mother, thinks only of pleasure or, when by her dissoluteness it has become less attractive for her, she thinks only of the profit she can get from the traffic of her charms. . . .[102]

Those who govern are rendered unfit. Finally, all moral rules and values are destroyed:

> A nation is lost when the dissolution of its morals, authorized by the example of its leaders, and rewarded by them, become universal; then shameless vice seeks no longer to cover itself with the shadows of mystery, and debauchery infects all classes of society; little by little decency having become ridiculous, it forced to blush in its turn. . . . But debauchery, when it becomes habitual, annihilates all feeling in the heart, all reflection in the mind; the libertine stifles by new excesses the remorse which the first crimes might evoke in him.[103]

[98] See *An Age of Crisis,* pp. 101–6.
[99] Chaudon, *op. cit.,* I, pp. 35–37.
[100] *De l'Esprit des lois,* XVI, p. 12.
[101] *La Morale universelle,* I, pp. 251–59. The institution of the family has been aptly described as the "civilized means of blending man's animal drives with his social nature." (Bottiglia, *op. cit.,* p. 17.)
[102] *La Morale universelle,* pp. 250–51.
[103] *Ibid.,* pp. 251–52, 253–54. See also d'Holbach, *Système social,* III, pp. 125–3 He opposes lewdness in literature and the theater and suggests a "code of morals for the theater. The wicked should always be shown in a bad light and punished

D'Holbach's analysis contains far more truth than the rebellious theories of sexual license—provided one really opts for culture, not against it. Delisle de Sales also connects loyalty to family with the general concept of duty in society.[104] Charles Levesque calls an attempt against the morals of a family an attack upon the State, for it propagates vice, as well as ruining the happiness of the innocent. He excoriates the defenders of adultery, who are undermining a basic social institution.[105] And earlier, Toussaint had condemned libertines: "They love only for their physical pleasure, like animals, heedless of the partner of their pleasures. Nature's end is the birth of children; that is what they fear." Adultery is worse, adding injustice, perjury, and perfidy to debauchery, and is condemned *by nature*.[106] Indeed, it is significant that enemies of the family bond are either those with anarchistic tendencies, or supporters (but not all) of a totalitarian collectivism which would (like Communist countries today) substitute the primacy of the State for that of loyalty to family.

Rousseau's attitude toward sex is one key to an understanding of his system. Innocent in the state of nature, sex need not then be limited by any rules of decency or legality. But once men are within a culture, sex, like other natural impulses, becomes altered and perverted by artificial adjuncts, by competition, property, and so forth. However Rousseau—despite what he may on occasion say and what others have said about him—is the partisan of culture, not of nature. Once men are in society, sexual impulses must be severely disciplined to conform with ethical standards. What is natural is not virtuous, or social. In stark contrast to Diderot's *Supplément au Voyage de Bougainville,* Rousseau has his Julie exclaim, "I want to be chaste, because that is the first virtue which nourishes all the others." [107] Order and social utility condemn licentiousness. To affront these truths is to place one's own interest above all else, and to take the (nihilistic) attitude that nothing matters except one's own happiness, even if it has to be secured "at the expense of all other men." But by self-discipline, a person can

---

The effects of tyranny, injustice, ambition, and fanaticism should be driven home, and love should be excluded from tragedy. He ends with a plea to woman ("Enchanting sex! whom nature formed to exercise the sweetest empire, learn at last the worth of reason. . . .") and a sermon on the superiority of virtue to pleasure.

[104] *Philosophie de la nature, I,* p. 245.
[105] *Op. cit.,* pp. 101–110.
[106] *Les Moeurs,* pp. 240–44.
[107] *Nouvelle Héloïse,* III, pp. 66–68.

transcend nature, be "more master of himself, stronger, happier and wiser."

Rousseau's opinion remains consistent throughout all his works. If *La Nouvelle Héloïse* reveals the disastrous effects of premarital indulgence, the sequel to *Emile* does as much for marital infidelity. The *Lettre à d'Alembert sur les spectacles* might be called a letter on puritanism, in which society is opposed to nature as norm.

> Even if it could be denied that women are naturally modest, would it be less true that in Society their lot should be a domestic and retired life, and that they should be brought up on principles suitable to that end? If shyness, non-aggressiveness (*modestie*) and modesty (*pudeur*) which are appropriate for them, are social inventions, it is important to Society that women acquire these qualities; it is important to cultivate them in them, and any woman who disdains them offends morality.[108]

Rousseau's position is antithetical to that of the *philosophes* who sought the *natural* in order to reform society. For him culture *is* artificial, and its laws now obtain, transcending those of nature. And the essence of nihilism is the refusal to accept the transcendence of reason over instinct in man, and of culture over nature. Although the utilitarian synthesis asserted, on the contrary, the primacy of culture and reason, its basic psychology and definitions of moral value, as well as many more radical statements, did not, in fact, always tend to support that primacy.

The significance of control of the sexual drives thus becomes more evident. Human sexual relations have a psychic dimension which does not obtain among animals; it is not only physical pleasure which must be considered, but the involvement of the whole personality, both internally and in its relations to others. As Niebuhr has said, marriage "initiates an organic process of mutuality which outruns any decision which created it." [109] In the final analysis, to ask whether sexual controls are natural to mankind is to ask whether culture is natural to mankind, for they are indissociable; and to speak of mankind without culture is to speak of a prehuman being, and not of man. Actually, the family group and parental care are natural phenomena even among the anthropoids. And primitive societies of men, so far as is known, have all imposed some restrictions and taboos, although the degree of

[108] Ed. Fuchs, p. 117.
[109] *Op. cit.*, pp. 56–57.

license is often much greater, or apparently so because of the strange forms it takes.[110]

Morals are the instrumentality of culture. There can be no culture without the regulation, sublimation, or repression of certain egoistic, aggressive, destructive instincts or drives. The sexual drives are at once the most powerful and aggressive, and the most persistently refractory to discipline. Freud, in our own time, has confirmed the inseparableness of sexuality and the other aggressive instincts, and society's need to repress them.[111] Any morality, therefore, any culture, must begin with this. History, anthropology, and psychology all testify to the same fact. On the other hand, nihilism always includes and usually begins with a revolt against sexual restraints. From there it is only a step to the other egoistic aggressions. Consequently, to deny the legitimacy or the possibility of transcendence over nature in this field of behavior is, deliberately or unintentionally, to deny culture. This Rousseau realized more clearly than any of his contemporaries.

The third factor contributing to the emergence of nihilism was the analysis of human nature. Certain optimists continued to hold the belief that man is naturally guided by reason to seek the good, and that his nature impels him to sympathy, fellowship, and benevolence; this tendency was maintained, in certain milieux, by the increasing vogue of sensibility. On the other hand, the more vigorous thinkers of the day were swayed by the contrary view, that men (either because of nature or because of society, or both) are engaged in a pitiless struggle for survival; consequently, they are selfish, acquisitive, and aggressive, devoted only to their own interest and happiness; and their reason is a slave to these ends, not the master.[112] The essential point is this: the utilitarian synthesis merely endeavored to set up a perspective, within the framework of these suppositions, which would favor the demands of society upon the individual.

It will, however, be useful to emphasize still further that aspect of the analysis which revealed the natural urge to power, even to

---

[110] Some anthropologists believe that sexual limits were established in the New Stone Age, among Cro-Magnon men, but that they were unknown to Neanderthals.

[111] The reader is urged to consult, in particular, Freud: *Civilization and its Discontents*, pp. 86–87. See also Darwin, *The Descent of Man*, pp. 118–19 (chap. IV).

[112] See *An Age of Crisis*, Part III, "Human Nature and Motivation." In the Renaissance, the two currents are the neo-Platonic-idealistic and the naturalistic-pessimistic.

godhood, and to the hurt of others, since this is the ultimate reach, and the basic motive of nihilistic attitudes, and since it determines to so large a degree the conditions of life.[113]

Hobbes had seen that the need for approbation and importance turns into a compulsive power urge.[114] He had also submitted that according to nature's law (that is, prior to culture and morality) "every man has a right to everything; even to one another's body." [115] The "right of nature" is only the right of power. Although legal right arises from the compact, it, too, is only an assumption of power.[116] Pascal's analysis culminated in the self making itself the center of everything and striving "to be the tyrant of all others." [117] Spinoza developed similar views, laying emphasis on envy, vengeance, and cruelty—the satisfaction of hurting others. "It is by the highest right of nature that each person exists, and consequently it is by the highest right of nature that each person does those things which follow from the necessity of his nature; and therefore it is by the highest right of nature that each person judges what is good and what is evil, consults his own advantage as he thinks best, avenges himself, and endeavors to preserve what he loves and to destroy what he hates." [118] Spinoza, like Hobbes, also posits the cession of this natural right to society; nevertheless, this passage and similar ones, taken by themselves, had great impact on the drift of radical thought and could serve as an epigraph to the nihilist revolt. In both the *Tractatus Theologico-politicus* (Chapter XVI) and the *Tractatus politicus* (Chapter II), Spinoza insists that in nature right is coextensive with power, and that nature includes man. Nature forbids nothing. The following statement might well have come verbatim from the pen of one of the eighteenth-century extremists: "Whatsoever an individual does by the laws of its nature it has a sovereign right

[113] See *ibid.*, especially chap. 11.

[114] *Ibid.*, p. 286.

[115] *Leviathan*, chap. XIV.

[116] "To those therefore whose power is irresistible, the dominion of all men adhereth naturally by their excellence of power; and consequently it is from that power, that the kingdom over men, and the right of afflicting men at his pleasure, belongeth naturally to God Almighty; not as Creator, and gracious; but as omnipotent. And though punishment be due for sin only, because by that word is understood affliction for sin; yet the right of afflicting, is not always derived from men's sin, but from God's power." *Ibid.*, chap. XXXI.

[117] See *An Age of Crisis*, p. 287.

[118] *Ethics*, IV, Prop. XXXVII. Also, V, Prop. XLI, and *Age of Crisis*, pp. 288–89.

to do, inasmuch as it acts as it was conditioned by nature, and cannot act otherwise." [119]

Bayle stressed Carneades' opinion that, in the human condition, if men "want to be just, they act imprudently and foolishly; and that if they wish to act prudently, they are unjust." Therefore there is no justice, "for a virtue inseparable from foolishness cannot pass for just." [120] Bayle was, if anything, a disabused realist. Is the reward of conscience enough? he inquires. For one thing, virtue is not positively related to prosperity or success. Most often, it seems, the right side loses. Brutus' defeat and Mark Antony's triumph led the former to say that virtue has no reality, and that "if one did not wish to be a dupe, he had to regard it as a vain name, and not a real thing." [121] On this Bayle comments that such a conclusion was logical for pagans, who did not know that justice would be accomplished in the next life. The comment is—as so often with Bayle—engagingly ambiguous. Pagans who held virtue to be real were illogical; without future rewards, "we could put virtue and innocence among the things about which Solomon pronounced his definitive judgment, Vanity of Vanities, all is Vanity. To lean on one's innocence would be to lean on a broken reed which pierces the hand of him who wants to use it." Power is the basic law; it alone is real. Now Bayle's reasoning gradually becomes frankly nihilistic. Right, justice, virtue, upon reflection, do no harm, and if all other things are equal, it is better to have them on one's side; injustice may prejudice one's cause. Upon further reflection, however, it seems the side that is right is likely to be confident, strive less, and use only honest means. This puts it at a disadvantage in regard to the unjust man, who will use extreme activity and any expedient, or add iniquity to iniquity. In fact, the advantage for the evil is so great, that if they fail it is only because they have not dared to be wicked enough. Again, in the article "Saducéens," Bayle limits religion's influence to the supposition of eternal rewards and punishments. Certainly, it is useless to talk of God's justice on earth: "it is almost impossible to persuade people that they will prosper on earth by living honestly, and that they will be struck down by ill fortune if they live evilly."

[119] For the important contributions of Nicole, Malebranche, and Abbadie, see *An Age of Crisis,* p. 289 ff.

[120] *Dictionnaire,* II, p. 307 ("Carnéade").

[121] *Ibid.,* art. "Brutus." See also, *ibid.,* "Melanchton."

Experience shows quite the contrary to be true. But what about the virtue-happiness equivalence? What about deep down inside? Aren't the wicked punished by conscience, the good rewarded by virtue itself? Maybe. "They'll tell us a hundred fine things about that, they'll fill our ears, and in a way we'll be convinced. But the building won't be sound, it will be only an intermittent faith, they will always have to fear that in bad intervals we may call them false doctors, and make them the same reproach that Brutus made to virtue." And again, in the article "Spinoza": "It is quite evident that in this life good actions do not lead to temporal good, and that evil actions are the most ordinary and surest means of making one's fortune."

Saint-Evremond is striking in his anticipation of Diderot's *Neveu de Rameau*. He has one of his interlocutors say:

> . . . I find only two things which can prudently occupy a wise man; to acquire and to keep. Honor is only a stubborn prejudice of young men. . . . As for me, my mind has never been spoiled by fantasies. Duty, friendship, gratitude, obligation, and the rest of those errors which link fools and the weak, have never hindered me a moment. Nature made me be born with a real genius for self-interest, which I have cultivated by study and fortified by experience. . . . You will never be wrong if you take as a guiding maxim, prefer the useful to the honest, it is Nature's only plan. . . . As long as we have money in our coffers, we'll have devoted friends and servants. . . . As you have to live with people who have designs on you, it is up to you to take precautions against them . . . it is good to appear disinterested sometimes to cover a secret design of self-interest.[122]

Nihilism, then, advances beyond hedonism. Pleasure-happiness being postulated as the only motive and value, it is subsequently discovered that pleasure is often "immoral," or that the most intense pleasures are immoral, and involve hurt to others. The final step is to discover that the act of hurting and destroying is itself a source of pleasure. If we add to this the persuasion that men are determined by the senses, so that all values are relative; and that no one is responsible, since he cannot choose his values, then all obligation not "to seek our pleasure as we must" evaporates.

In England, unlike France, ethical writings were almost entirely

---

[122] *Oeuvres Mêlées,* II, pp. 357–77. The other speaker defends virtue, much as Diderot was to have his "Moi" do. A middle ground is taken in the third part, but somewhat to left of center.

justifications of morality, and it was generally admitted, as Hume put it in his *Enquiry,* that "absolute, unprovoked, disinterested malice has never, perhaps, place in any human heart." As much may be said of most eighteenth-century English novels, although out of the justification—especially in Richardson—arises a taste for evil. In France, however, just as the bases of moral value were submitted to corrosive analysis, so too there is an important current in the novel which translates the lack of justification, the uncertainty of a hierarchy of values (or the equivalence of values) into a plunge into evil. Realization of the evil (selfishness, aggression) in human nature and of the heartlessly competitive conditions of life is a frequent note in the first half of the century. Fougeret de Monbron, in his notorious *Margot la ravaudeuse* (1750) draws the conclusion that "it is very difficult to be an honest man when you are a beggar. . . . In this world there is only good luck and bad luck." [123] In another passage which unmistakably anticipates *Le Neveu de Rameau,* a character in the story summarizes the lesson of his travels:

> I have become completely convinced that uprightness and humanity are everywhere only conventional expressions which at bottom contain nothing real or true; that everyone lives only for himself, loves only himself; and that the cleverest man is really only a clever actor, who possesses the great art of being dishonest under an imposing mask of candor and equity; and inversely, that the most wicked and despicable man is the one who can least disguise himself. This is precisely the whole difference between honor and wickedness. . . . A vice or two more, I mean dissimulation and disguise, would have put me in step with the human race. I would be, to be sure, a little more scoundrelly; but what harm would there be in that? It's something I would share with all the decent people of the world. Like them, I would enjoy the privilege of duping the next fellow with a calm conscience. . . . I admit with complete frankness that I am a worthless scamp; and that the only difference between me and others is that I have the boldness to unmask myself, and that they do not dare to.[124]

We have seen elsewhere how, in certain important novels, the lust for pleasure becomes the lust to hurt, to triumph, and exult over another's being.[125] Someone has written, "The nature of evil

[123] Hambourg, 1800, p. 158.
[124] Pp. 44–47.
[125] See *An Age of Crisis,* chap. XIV.

is to create evil and to enjoy the successes of its art. Richard of Gloucester and Iago laugh . . . out of the exultation of Satan, creating deceits and stratagems designed to overthrow creation." This is what is illustrated in the world of Laclos and Rétif, in which to develop the self means to deny others.

Voltaire was frequently embittered by his awareness of this cruel aspect of life and its destructiveness to human moral values.[126] In the *Traité de métaphysique,* side by side with Natural Law, he traces an "evolutionary ethics" in which prudence is admittedly the only restraint to aggression.[127] Three times, in his *Notebooks,* he sets it down that the world is the house of the strong. There are the strong and the weak, the exploiters and their victims, "the asses who carry and the men who load." [128] Ironically, he notes in *Candide* that "Natural Law teaches us to kill our neighbor, and accordingly we find this practised all over the world." In *Il faut prendre un parti* (1772), Voltaire returns to the theme of the struggle for survival. The earth is a vast field of carnage, in which all life survives at the expense of other life. "And what is even more cruel is that in this horrible scene of ever-renewed murder we see clearly a definite design to perpetuate the species by the bloody corpses of their mutual enemies." [129] Voltaire writes these lines in order to prove that evil is relative, necessary, and approved by God. Then why not extend justification to men? Although Voltaire never does this, his ironic or bitter tales of human cruelty in *Les Voyages de Scarmentado, Zadig,* and *Candide* portray the world as being in fact exactly that scene of crime and carnage which the nihilist was dedicated to justifying.[130]

In *De l'Homme* Helvétius carries his underlying nihilistic analysis even further than in *De l'Esprit* by discussing at length the basic power drive in men and their desire to be despots over other men, a satisfaction which he considers necessary to their happiness.[131]

Quesnay set forth with frankness the materialists' objections to the idea of Natural Law.[132] According to them, he explains, force,

[126] For Voltaire's bitterness and scorn for man, see Pomeau, *op. cit., passim.*

[127] *Ed. cit.,* pp. 61–63.

[128] *Voltaire's Notebooks,* I, pp. 324, 382, 417. Also in *Dictionnaire philosophique,* "Egalité."

[129] *Oeuvres,* XXVIII, p. 534.

[130] See also XXI, *ibid.,* pp. 243–44, 577–94.

[131] See *An Age of Crisis,* pp. 313–14, and *De l'Homme.* Sect. IV, chap. 4–10, Sect. V, chap. 4. The theme is also touched on in *De l'Esprit.*

[132] *Essai physique sur l'oeconomie animale,* III, pp. 364–69.

ruse, and talents establish right, because that is the way things effectively are. Man, unlike other animals, tends to make himself master of all goods in order to make himself master of other men. Animals, when they have satisfied their needs, let others satisfy theirs, but men know no limit and seek the subjection of others. The natural order, therefore, and the constitution of men are hostile to the values which result from convention (that is, culture). Since no justice is possible without the sacrifice of self-interest, and we can never have confidence that others will reciprocally conform, men "may choose any way to satisfy their need." To all this Quesnay replies that these things merely correspond to the way people behave; that they are mere matters of fact, which do not change law or right, and that men would do better to follow a political order of law.

According to the apologist, Denesle, the idea that something is just or unjust in relation to each person's well-being is destructive of the word "justice." If, as the materialists claim, the justice of laws is based only on the desire to preserve what has already been grabbed, then I can "justly" swindle to satisfy my desires. The upshot of this philosophy, he continues, is that unless a man is a fool, he will be decent only insofar as it serves his purpose as well as or better than vice.[133] Many other apologists repeatedly pointed out the nihilistic potentialities and tendencies of the materialists.[134] Sometimes they were even accused of actually being moral anarchists, which, of course, was untrue for the most part. The popular opinion was epitomized by J. N. Moreau's story, in his sensational *Mémoire pour servir à l'histoire des cacouacs* (1757), of the man who returns home and finds everything stolen by a valet who had been studying the writings of the "cacouacs." The valet has left this note:

> My dear master: All living beings are by nature equal and have a right to the same goods; it is by a freak invention that men have obliged themselves not to strip each other. Justice is founded only on self-interest; the great and only motive of our actions is self-love, and the fundamental law of society is to accomplish one's own good with the least possible hurt to others.

[133] *Examen*, pp. 17–21; also, pp. 5–16, where we find the following: "And so, if one only loves pleasure, the most atrocious crimes, being only the necessary and inevitable action and reaction of bodies, put into action by universal motion, should not give us pause."

[134] See Gauchat, I, pp. 254–55; XVI, pp. 62–68, 91–92; Pichon, *Les Argumens de la raison*, pp. 77–81; Hayer, *op. cit.*, VII, pp. 25–33; Richard, *Exposition*, pp. 42–43; Bergier, *Examen du matérialisme, passim*.

[Cf. *Rousseau's Discours sur l'inégalité*.] Now, my dear Master, I need your money. . . . I am stealing it from you in your absence; I might have taken it and cut your throat; but a true Cacouac never hurts his fellow men except when he is forced to do so for his own good. . . .[135]

Deists were worried, too. Delisle de Sales protested (against Helvétius) that nature is not contradictory, does not tell one to help, another to hurt. We must deny this paradox, else all laws become unjust, as a man can always claim he is following nature.[136] In a later work he draws up a well thought out indictment of the materialists' ethics, based on six grounds: determinism, the law of the strong, the physical (blind) nature of moral experience, the unique and justified happiness motivation, the placing of nature above man, the doctrine that what is natural is good.[137] Sabatier de Castres, looking back on the Revolution, warns that culture cannot take nature as its model, since nature knows only personal interests, needs, and passions. "Civilized society is a second Nature, which has its needs, its ways, its particular motions, and which retains from the first [Nature] only the feeling which makes each prefer himself." [138]

Diderot's involvement with nihilism was greater, perhaps, and certainly more significant, than that of any other eighteenth-century thinker before the Revolution. The remarkable phenomenon which distinguishes him is the fact that he was also, as we have seen, one of the great defenders of morality, justifying it by Natural Law, by calculated enlightened self-interest, by the sentimental effusions of a heart enamored with virtue and tireless in preaching it. His awareness of this deep contradiction and his explanation for it are revealed in his famous cry, "I am infuriated at being entangled in a devilish philosophy which my mind cannot help approving and my heart cannot help denying." He wanted desperately to believe in the moral virtue he loved; but he could do so only by turning his back on the logic of his powerful reason. There were other times, however, when, in the stillness of his study, he gave free rein to rational analysis and the taste for paradox. Then, deterred by no extraneous considerations, he pursued his system of materialism to its furthest reaches. The dualism

---

[135] *Mémoire*, etc., 1828, pp. 50–51.
[136] *De la Philosophie de la nature*, II, p. 182 ff.
[137] *De la Philosophie du bonheur*, II, pp. 65–70.
[138] *Pensées*, pp. 54–60.

of Diderot is that of the moralist who follows his deep intuitions and emotions, and that of the detached thinker who, pursuing the bent of his abstract reason, reaches contrary conclusions. And it is true, writes René Hubert, that the extreme consequences of Diderot's materialistic naturalism are more logical than his deduction of a universal morality from an innate tendency to do good.[139]

Diderot had begun, in his translation of Shaftesbury's *Essai sur le mérite et la vertu* (1745), with the primacy of the moral, through which he viewed nature. In the *Pensées philosophiques* (1746), nature began to struggle with morality; in his consideration of God's existence, we can see him weighing moral against metaphysical arguments, while biology, too, enters into the contention. Starting from *La Lettre sur les aveugles* (1749), naturalism has expelled all other viewpoints. God and free will are discarded. A system of materialism is rapidly developed, reaching the fullest possible amplitude in the three dialogues of *Le Rêve de d'Alembert* (1769).

While Diderot at times attempts to escape the consequences of determinism, at other times he admits that a rigorous determinism destroys the basis of moral discriminations.[140] His naturalism shows him a universe empty of moral value, and also the relativity of moral judgments to the physical organism.[141] Sensationist psychology adds to the rigorous mechanism of the man-machine (who is "fortunately born" or "unfortunately born") the impulsion toward happiness or pleasurable experience, and aversion to its contrary. From all this it follows that we cannot look to nature as a source or support of morality.

That these factors led Diderot to an undimmed realization of the challenge of nihilism is clear in his article, "Droit naturel," which we have examined in some detail. The basic tenets of amoralism are forcefully stated in paragraph iii of that article. But in "Droit naturel" he is the defender of morality, and there is no reason to doubt his sincerity. However, the more usual form of his defense is not Natural Law, but enlightened self-interest. It is difficult to believe that Diderot, with his sharp intellectual dis-

---

[139] "La Morale de Diderot," p. 41.
[140] See *An Age of Crisis*, pp. 165, 170–72.
[141] E.g., "let us forgive nature who is blind. . . . Everything is indifferent (*égal*) for her. The good man and the wicked are indistinct parts of the universal order." (*Lettres à Sophie Volland*, II, p. 277.) For relativism to organism, see *Lettre sur les aveugles*.

cernment, did not perceive the nihilistic trap concealed in that theory whose weakness he more than once pointed out. Some apologists, we recall, had urged acceptance of Christianity, warning that if there were no rewards and punishments in a future life, it would be foolish and insane to be virtuous. The proponents of enlightened self-interest only transposed the same thesis to this earth. Virtue, they claimed, brings the sure reward of happiness, vice incurs inevitable punishment; it is because of this certainty that virtue is valid, and any so-called virtue which did not bring happiness would not be virtue. If happiness could be had through evil, or if it could be had only through evil, then evil would be justified; or rather, there would be none. "Eh! what would morality be, if it were otherwise? What would virtue be? We would be mad to follow it, if it took us away from the path to happiness; we should have to stifle in our hearts the love it inspires in us, as the most harmful inclination." [142] But Diderot knew that the virtue-happiness equivalence was uncertain and did not possess the validity of law; his Rameau's nephew makes this clear. He also knew that what people commonly called a "calculus of happiness" was infinitely variable, and could not form an ethical theory.

It was inevitable, then, that he should have been led to a deeper exploration of nihilism. Diderot, writes Mario Praz, carries materialism "to its logical consequence," and proclaims "the supreme right of the individual to happiness and pleasure in opposition to the despotism of morality and religion." [143] Actually, this was more than a purely intellectual exercise. In the complexity of Diderot's being, there was a persistent streak of rebelliousness and anarchism. Alongside the moralizing, prudent bourgeois was the defiant bohemian, dreaming of adventures. That is why Dom Deschamps' work struck a responsive chord in him. Deschamps' idea, he wrote to Sophie Volland, is that "the human spirit will be unhappy as long as there are kings, priests, magistrates, laws, a yours, a mine, the words 'vice' and 'virtue.' You can judge how much pleasure this work, badly written though it is, must have given me, since I suddenly found myself in the world for which I was born! . . . I did not see a line to cross out in his whole work, which is filled with new ideas and bold assertions. D'Alembert has read it, but doesn't agree with me." [144] Diderot is con-

---

[142] *Oeuvres*, II, p. 88n.
[143] *The Romantic Agony*, p. 97.
[144] *Lettres à Sophie Volland*, II, pp. 271–72.

vinced that there can be no real happiness for mankind except in a state such as Dom Deschamps describes.

This line of thought reaches its highest point in the *Supplément au Voyage de Bougainville* (1772), in which he imagines the natives of Tahiti living in an idyllic state of semianarchism. The dialogue, though it touches on a number of subjects, centers on this theme: "There existed a natural man; we have introduced within this man an artificial man, and there has arisen inside the cavern a continual war which lasts throughout life." [145] Here, then, nature is openly set against culture, and preferred—a position which is prudently attenuated at the end of the dialogue and which at other times is vigorously refuted by Diderot. The essential import of this view is that, as Darwin and Freud later emphasized, the price of civilization is conflict, between instinct and reason, between nature and culture.[146] Diderot, when he is engaged on this path, refuses to pay the price; he dreams of natural innocence and of happiness and condemns social law as denaturing man. His thinking is in sharp contrast with that of Rousseau, who also wishes to put an end to the conflict, and who also believes it useless to try to make the natural and the social coexist peacefully, like the lion and the lamb—as the theory of enlightened self-interest, precisely, pretended to do. Rousseau, in contrast to the primitivist, would accept and complete the "denaturing of man" by culture.

The *Supplément* is primitivistic in its thinking, rather than nihilistic. It does not enthrone individual egoism or accept the evil in men as valid because natural.[147] Nevertheless, any denial of the validity of culture and its repressions is conducive to nihilism. And the affinity becomes explicit on two issues. The first is the rejection of civil laws or moral codes when they contradict the demands of nature. "The empire of nature cannot be destroyed. . . . Civil law must be only the statement of the law of nature." [148]

---

[145] Ed. Chinard, p. 190.

[146] Cf. Darwin, *The Descent of Man*, p. 125: "As a struggle may sometimes be seen going on between the various instincts of the lower animals, it is not surprising that there should be a struggle in man between his social instincts, with their derived virtues, and his lower, though momentarily stronger impulses or desires."

[147] There is a curious point of contrast with Sade's *Dialogue d'un prêtre avec un moribond*. In the latter, the dying man presses the priest to enjoy a girl he offers, not so that the priest may taste pleasure, but so that he might have the spectacle of it. In the *Supplément au Voyage de Bougainville*, Orou makes the same offer, but appeals to the priest's goodness and generosity.

[148] *Ibid.*, pp. 189, 180.

It is obvious that such a criterion would make the work of culture superfluous and leave only nature. The second issue is the particular application of this general rule in which Diderot is interested —the free expression of the sexual libido. He rejects the role of society and morals in relation to an act which is "susceptible of no moral evaluation." He thereby reduces the sexual expression to an animal one (though elsewhere he is indignant at such a reduction). Society may pile up its taboos and punishments, but man's indocile drives will always revolt: "and you will not succeed in denaturing me." [149] Here Diderot considers nature as normative as well as descriptive of facts; he overlooks another fact, that social man (following this line of reasoning) is inevitably "denatured." Most important of all, he is under the illusion that one can free the aggressive sexual instincts, and yet have men live together in peace and harmony; he does not understand, as Sade and Freud were to do, the interconnectedness and inseparability of all the aggressive instincts, and the consequent need of any culture to begin by a discipline, or patterned expression, of the sexual urges. And indeed, when we look closely at his idyllic Tahitian society, we see that rules there are, and that, loose though they be, they are still violated. But Diderot nevertheless proclaims that to civilize man and to put order into nature is to become man's tyrant, to destroy his happiness and freedom.[150]

Nature, then, is exalted above culture. And yet, Diderot, in this work, pretends to offer us the bases of a valid, "natural" ethics. But he is unable to maintain any consistency or to stay within the natural framework. Nature *and reason,* he tells us, are the watchwords; and the criterion of good and evil is "the influence of your conduct on what is *useful to you* and on the *general welfare.*" [151] But here, surely, is another conflict as serious as the one between nature and culture—or rather, it *is* that same conflict! The eternal will of nature, he asserts, "is that good should be preferred to evil, and the general good to the private." But is this "the will of na-

---

[149] *Ibid.,* p. 189. In the *Additions aux Pensées philosophiques* (1762), Diderot again refuses to place a moral evaluation on the sexual act, regardless of circumstances. He reduces it to "the voluptuous rubbing of two membranes," that is, to animal terms, implicitly denying the psychic and social dimensions.

[150] *Ibid.,* pp. 192–93. The passage is reminiscent of Rousseau's "romantic" mood, in the *Discours sur l'inégalité.* Diderot elsewhere condones a wife's being unfaithful for the purpose of improving her family's position, and an unmarried woman's right to motherhood. (*Lettres à Sophie Volland,* I, pp. 279–80, 295.)

[151] *Supplément,* p. 143 (italics added).

ture"? Is it "natural" in the same sense that the sexual instincts are approved of as "natural"? Does it not rather lead to cultural restrictions of aggressive egoistic dynamisms? Diderot is obliged to evade the difficulty by asserting an ethical formalism which denies to culture the right of evaluating actions. "Is it up to [magistrates and priests] to call harmful actions good, and innocent or useful actions harmful?" [152] Nature, once and for all, determines these distinctions; reason's role is merely to distinguish them, culture's role to approve them. But it is obvious that man's nature is also a social and a moral nature; and that it demands limitations on instinctual nature which are, in essence if not in form, natural, and which are creative (that is, the work of culture), not given. Jealousy and possessiveness, moreover, are as natural as license, incest, and homosexuality. The imposition of structure, and so of limit, is natural. Shall we, furthermore, judge the "useful" in the light of immediate pleasure (fornication, stealing) or in the light of the total nature of man and his complete self-realization? Unless this is considered we fall either into the anarchism which is one facet of the *Supplément* or into the totalitarianism to which the unqualified preference of "general welfare" to individual welfare may easily lead. At one point, Diderot is driven back upon his basic naturalistic foundation of ethics: similarity of organization and of needs, attraction toward the same pleasures, aversion to the same pains.[153] But these raw facts, taken by themselves, may lead to and justify the struggle for survival and the law of the strong. It is only when we add the natural need for moral judgments (and perhaps certain universal judgments), which accompany the need for structure and pattern in social intercourse, that these facts become productive of morality. Certainly, Diderot knew that since "all actions are indifferent" in nature, nature (taken in this broad sense) cannot give us moral directives.[154]

The *Supplément au Voyage de Bougainville,* one of Diderot's weakest productions, is a work of optimistic primitivism which borders on, and at some points leads to, the denial of moral distinctions.

In the *Introduction aux grand principes* (1763), we have a

---

[152] *Ibid.,* p. 142. In places, the formalism reminds us of "Loi naturelle."
[153] *Ibid.,* p. 181.
[154] For a further critique of the *Supplément,* see H. Hinterhaüser, *Utopie und Wirklichkeit bei Diderot,* and L. G. Crocker, *Two Diderot Studies,* pp. 31–35.

dialogue written by an enemy of the *philosophes,* in which the author, with force and clarity, expresses the tenets of nihilism as he sees them implied by the materialism of his time.[155] Diderot angrily replies to the allegations and expresses a social ethics of enlightened self-interest. However, the same nihilistic tenets are expressed or explored in several of his own major writings.

The *Rêve de d'Alembert* (1769) is a complete system of materialism. Taking nature as standard, Diderot declares that "Whatever is cannot be either against nature or outside of nature." [156] In the third dialogue, this doctrine is applied to justify sexual perversions and incest. Everything, it has been established, is necessary; the "whole" contains no "evil" nor any moral discriminations. Good and evil are only relative to the individual, or to arbitrary conventions. These views imply that each individual will decide for himself, according to his own interest and pleasure, what is right and wrong. (Since each social unit will do the same, the struggle he condemns in the *Supplément* becomes inevitable.)

Once more, the words "nature" and "natural" are used with an ambivalence of questionable validity. "Man is only an undifferentiated effect, the monster only a rare effect; both are equally natural, equally necessary, equally within the universal and general order." [157] Although this is quite acceptable as a description of fact, it is not necessarily admissible as a prescription of value. But the clear implication in the *Rêve* is that everything is equally natural and *therefore* equally valid. This is especially so in view of moral determinism. Bordeu, Diderot's spokesman, admits that virtue and vice have no real status, that self-respect, shame, and remorse are "puerilities founded on the ignorance and vanity of a being who imputes to himself the merit or demerit of a necessary instant." [158] In view of all these factors, the useful and the pleasant are the only criteria for discriminating between actions. We must transform the notion of virtue "into that of benevolence, and its

[155] *Oeuvres,* II, p. 75 ff.

[156] *Ibid.,* II, p. 188. Therefore nature is indifferent to good and evil, and provides no basis for right and wrong—for a so-called "natural morality," as the *Supplément* maintains.

[157] Compare Sade: "They were monsters, fools object to me. Yes, according to our morals and way of thinking; but relative to the great views of nature towards us, they were only the instruments of her designs; it was to carry out her laws that she endowed them with those fierce and sanguinary characters." (*Histoire de Juliette,* quoted by M. Praz, *loc. cit.*)

[158] *Ibid.,* II, p. 176.

opposite into that of wrongdoing. We are fortunately or unfortunately born." The implication is that social utility takes precedence over individual will, and that an arbitrary code of behavior ("morality") is thus established by force; however there is no attempt to justify—nor, within this framework, would it be easy to "justify"—the precedence of the one over the other. Even more serious: there is good and evil in relation to our purposes, but it is not possible to inquire whether our purposes are good or evil— they are merely natural and necessary.[159]

In 1762, with *Le Neveu de Rameau,* and then again between 1770 and 1773, Diderot embarked on a remarkable series of works which may be considered as moral experiments, because in them he tests the validity of certain theories and the viability of certain types of characters. Following his own experimental theories, he selects characters and situations that are exceptional or extreme and taken from real life, and then puts them to the test, often in the joust of dialogue. Nihilistic characters and theories form an important part of this exploration. Always Diderot is interested in the character who has *greatness of being.* While he admires the person who is great in virtue and self-sacrifice, those who are great in evil are also admirable to him, and more fascinating, more provocative of ethical speculation.[160] One of his principal concerns is the relation of greatness in being to morals, and especially to evil.

Among the briefer experiments, several involve the problems raised by our study. In *Ceci n'est pas un conte* (1772), the relation between the sexes is represented as one of ruthless war and exploitation. The good person is destined by nature to be the hapless victim of the evil person, because goodness is weakness and evil is strength. This is nature's law; reason and culture are unable to change it. In the same year, Diderot wrote *Mme de la Carlière,* in which an extraordinary woman demands an absolute (of fidelity) and prefers self-destruction to compromise with life on its own

[159] "For no mere obligation," writes Cassirer about Diderot's theory, "can presume to annul or to alter fundamentally the empirical nature of men." (*Op. cit.,* p. 246.) True; but the real question raised by Diderot's analysis is rather, Can there be an obligation? Cassirer's conclusion, "Then Diderot finally has to found the superiority of natural law and natural morality over theological ethics principally in the nature of their effectiveness" is quite erroneous, since the "natural law" Diderot is dealing with is not a moral law.

[160] Cf. *Pensées philosophiques,* III (1746): "Constraint destroys the greatness and energy of the soul."

terms. In this tale, the emphasis is on the uncertainty of moral judgments, indeed, on their complete lack of validity—a lesson which is symbolized by the gesture of its male protagonist, who rips up his magistrate's gown. The masterful dialogue, *Entretien d'un père avec ses enfants* (1771) applies the problem of moral judgment to the anarchistic individual who sets himself up against law and order. The problem is complicated in interesting fashion. It is not a question of egoism or evil; Diderot and his supporters in the dialogue claim exemption from law for the exceptional individual in order better to realize an ideal of justice which the law, in its formalized rigidity, cannot, in certain cases, bring about. The result, however, is no less destructive to the necessary forms of social functioning. The exceptional individual, in his claim, puts himself not only above law, but above civilization. "Isn't the reason of the human race more sacred than the reason of a legislator? . . . It seems that we have to stumble about for centuries, from extravagances to extravagances and from errors to errors, to arrive at the place where the first spark of judgment, instinct, would have carried us immediately." [161] We are brought face to face with an agonizing dilemma: civilization and morality may find themselves in utter opposition. The accomplishment of right may require an act ruinous to the structures of organized society. The result of this experiment is therefore an impasse in which coexisting human requirements are found to be incompatible.[162]

Among Diderot's "moral experiments" are his two literary masterpieces, *Le Neveu de Rameau* (1762) and *Jacques le Fataliste* (1773). Both are complex, many-faceted works, involving much more even in regard to morals than can be discussed here.[163]

The central theme of *Le Neveu de Rameau* is that of the nihilist ("Lui," or Rameau's nephew) who fails of the greatness in being which the nihilist must have to be successful, and who is consequently reduced to becoming a pitiful clowning jester and parasite, whose perceptions about man and morals have the jester's wounding pointedness of truth. The essential mechanism of the

[161] *Ibid.*, V, p. 301.

[162] Cf. V. Hugo's Javert and Melville's Billy Budd. Diderot, it is well-known (like Voltaire and Rousseau!) frequently takes contrary positions. In a letter to Sophie Volland he had condemned the view which he supports in the *Entretien* (*Correspondance*, ed. Roth, III, pp. 318–19).

[163] For a fuller analysis, see L. G. Crocker, "*Jacques le Fataliste,* an 'Expérience Morale,'" and "*Le Neveu de Rameau,* une expérience morale." The discussion which follows is based on these two articles.

dialogue is the confrontation with another mediocrity ("Moi," who is at least partly identified with Diderot), who supports the love of virtue, enlightened self-interest, and the other semihypo-critical pablum (as it appears) which was in fashion. Although Lui does not win our admiration or support, he effectively routs the shallow conventionalism of his antagonist. While we cannot here indulge in a thorough-going analysis of this remarkable work, it is necessary to point out that Lui represents an experiment with nihilism, and that part of the drama comes from its confrontation with traditional moralism.

In his character, Lui stands for the refusal of conventions, of moral shame and traditional ideals; furthermore, he has made this into a philosophical system, which he applies with only a few in-consistencies. "Never false," he says, "as long as it is in my interest to be true; never true, as long as it is my interest to be false." He boasts of being "selfish, vile and perfidious." Others exist only so that he can live at their expense, and nothing has value except himself. Life is reduced by him to organic activity and pleasure. We have, then, a radical naturalism which considers culture a mask and lowers man to the level of the instinctive demands of the ego. No rational or social structure replacing nature and individual anarchism is admitted. All acts are equivalent, provided they bring ego-satisfaction.

All men, Lui holds, are essentially nihilists, seeking their own satisfactions at the expense of the weak. The rules imposed by society apply only to those who are too weak to attempt what they would like to do, and to those would-be "strong" who are not strong or clever enough to succeed. So-called moral people, he claims, are either scoundrels who have added hypocrisy to other vices, or are envious of those who are "free"; he, at least, is honest in his vices, as his adversary admits. Like other nihilists, Lui finds in cosmic disorder the justification for human disorder and re-fuses any transcendence.

When Lui turns on Moi and forces him to defend himself, the weakness of Moi's ethics of enlightened self-interest becomes clear. The highest value, for *both* men, is really the same: happiness. All that Moi can do is to affirm the superior efficacy of nonegoistic conduct. Thus the difference between them is reduced to a mere calculation, or even worse, to pure subjectivity, and does not desig-nate a moral superiority. Further, the truth of the equivalence is denied by Lui. "And yet I see an infinity of honest people who are not happy, and an infinity of people who are happy without being honest." On this point, and in other ways, Moi is unable to impose or to justify his moralism.

The picture of society, in *Le Neveu de Rameau,* tallies with Lui's views, not with Moi's. Morality is *against* men's real desires, and so they are always striving to evade it. "People praise virtue, but they hate it, and run from it; it freezes you, and in this world, one must have warm feet." Patriotism, friendship, sacrifices, and duties are vain gestures. "Gratitude is a burden; and every burden is made to be thrown off," and, "whatever you do, you can't be dishonored when you are rich" are epigrams which foreshadow Sade. Society, in short, is a jungle in which men devour each other like wolves, and in which it is necessary to be wicked to survive (exactly as Rousseau had said in his *Discours sur l'inégalité*).[164]

The strong man is the one who realizes that moral rules have no validity (that is, sanction or penalty) which can oblige him to respect them. Such rules are accepted, but only to violate them against others and to demand their protection for oneself. "In nature all species devour each other, all estates devour each other in society. . . . In the midst of all this, only the imbecile or the indolent is hurt without hurting others; and he deserves what he gets." The weak are nature's designated victims. In such a world, moral standards are not only vain and anti-natural; they are dangerous.[165] Even more: vice and virtue do not exist: "it may be that you call vice what I call virtue, and virtue what I call vice." Man has no dignity; he is always dependent on others and forced to play humiliating, hypocritical roles (*"la pantomime des positions"*). How can we speak of dignity or of values, when death makes everything and everyone equal? We are brought back to

---

[164] Cf. d'Holbach, who writes, however, from a political rather than a metaphysical viewpoint: "One cannot give morals to a nation whose sovereign is himself without morals and without virtue; where the great consider virtue as weakness; where priests degrade it by their conduct; which the common man, despite the fine harangues of his preachers, knows well that to pull himself out of poverty, he must lend himself to the vices of those who are more powerful than he. In societies so constituted, morals can only be a sterile speculation. . . . All who want to run to fortune, or make their fate more pleasant, let themselves be carried away by the general torrent, which will force them to break the obstacles raised by their conscience." (*Le Christianisme dévoilé,* 1761, pp. 18–19.)

[165] In the *Eléments de physiologie,* Diderot, discussing the necessity of adaptation to changing environment and the struggle for survival, will write: "The world is the house of the strong."

man's need to affirm his being which lacks status in an absurd world in which death is the definitive fact; to affirm it by feelings of superiority and power over others, and by hurting them and forcing them to recognize his place and power. "Everything that exists . . . seeks its well-being at the expense of whoever it may be. . . . I love to command, and I shall command."

Lui is the object of satire and scorn, because he is a rebel without the strength or the consistency to win. Nihilism is only for the strong, for whom moral and social laws are challenges to greatness. Lui can reach greatness only in the fantastic clownery of his pantomimes, which are in a world of pure artistry, protected from life. His performances, remarkable though they are, are devoid of dignity and moral value. Incorporating absurdity as their very essence, they define the absurdity of our values, of our acts, of our existence.

In *Jacques le Fataliste,* Diderot is testing theory in the main story, and character in the interwoven tales. Again the dialogue between Jacques and his master is supplemented by the test of events. A conclusion which was adumbrated in *Le Neveu de Rameau* is here fully developed: human moral life is too complex and inconsistent to be reducible to any abstract theory. This is seen both in the chaotic world which Jacques' adventures uncover (one which constantly belies the predictability of determinism) and in his own inability to live in conformity with his philosophy. Do we do something because it is our "destiny," or is it our destiny because we do it?

Jacques' extreme determinism is in itself a first link with moral nihilism. We are all automatons, he says, "thinking machines," and there is no self-transcendence. The efficacy of the human will and of rational foresight is repeatedly denied. There is, consequently, no virtue or vice, merit or blame, or moral responsibility. The maxim that all action is blind produces a feeling of the futility of all action, the feeling that we are aliens in this world, wandering blindly. "For heaven's sake, reader . . . do we know where we are going?" We are in a capricious and unreliable world, in which the results of our acts have no necessary correspondence with their supposed quality or their motivating intent: "good brings evil, evil brings good. We walk in the night beneath what is written on high, equally insensate in our wishes, in our joy and in our affliction." For it is a world in which "we never know what heaven wants or doesn't want, and perhaps it doesn't know either." And Diderot's book is itself the image of such a world, capricious and disordered. Through his own uncaused caprices as author and through Jacques, Diderot supplies the "proof" in action which cannot be given in terms of discursive logic, that life is arbitrary and not mechanical.

In order to explore the complexities and the moral capacities of men and women, Diderot interweaves the story of Jacques and his master with other anecdotes. In these he tests moral experience in the empirical world through the observation of unusual forms of human character and action. These are again concerned with the human capacity for evil, and with the relation between morality and greatness. The two principal tales are those of Mme de la Pommeraye and of Father Hudson. We cannot here analyze these in detail. Both protagonists violate conventional law and Natural Law; both take great risks and have the greatness of being which enables them to triumph. With both, the cause of their rebellion is the need for satisfaction of the ego in its basic demands of sex and domination; the weak are their victims. Vengeance becomes an all-consuming need, in order to re-establish the feelings of self-importance, power, and security.

Mme de la Pommeraye's greatness is not evident when she is a good woman. In this fact we penetrate to the heart of Diderot's ethical dilemma. Conventional virtue seems to be linked with mediocrity; it is in evil that Mme de la Pommeraye achieves greatness in being. From this episode, moreover, it also becomes apparent that moral values are acquired and secondary, whereas hatred, vengeance, the restitution of the ego's self-regard are primitive and primary. We are shown the cruelty and heartlessness of which human beings are capable when the ego is threatened or its primitive energy aroused, and the feeling of superiority which comes of hurting and ruining others, of using them as tools for ego-satisfaction. Moral acquiescence appears as a surrender of the self. It is obvious that the proposition is one of nihilism, and the picture of delight in evil, of admiration for evil greatly done, seconds the conclusion. It is further reinforced by the ironic peripeteia in which Mme de la Pommeraye's vengeance turns out to be the moral salvation and happiness both of her foe and of the prostitute she has tricked him into marrying. Again it appears that the results of our acts belie our intent, and there is nothing we can count on. In such a universe, ethical certainty becomes even more elusive.

The adventure of Father Hudson is the pendant to that of Mme de la Pommeraye. Hudson is a pre-Sadian character, one who knows no restraint to the egoistic vitalities. He considers himself the exception, by right of superiority—a "right" which extends to using other men and women as instruments or means to satisfy the ends of his ego. They are the victims through whom he obtains satisfaction for its instinctual power-demands for a godlike affirmation through the use and abuse of others. His acts involve the free play of power, not only beyond the right, but in pleasurable frustration of the right. Traditional morality, for him, consists of rules for the mediocre, which the superior person not only disregards, but uses as an instrument for domination. Like Mme de la Pommeraye, Hudson effectuates a poetic and satanic revenge. The good are defeated. Evil triumphs and goes on to further triumphs. Once again, greatness of will and of mind is destructive of moral laws and restraints, and reveals their weakness, their secondary or acquired status, indeed their nullity before the ego's demands. Again and again in other minor episodes, Diderot shows that to attempt evil without the necessary greatness is to court certain disaster, so that success in evil seems to be the very mark of greatness.

Throughout the novel, Diderot emphasizes the uncertainty of our moral judgments, and he discusses this problem openly in relation to his characters. So often, too, the ones who seem virtuous are really vicious (and occasionally, the reverse), so that the words "vice" and "virtue" as commonly used are made to seem meaningless. On scanning Diderot's picture of the world, one would say that morality exists only because men are evil; therefore it is, in a sense, a stranger to them. Contrary to Christian and Natural Law ethics, it is man's nature to return evil for evil, or worse still, evil for good. One character, M. le Pelletier, who does return good for evil is regarded as either a coward or a madman. In the final tale of the master's victimization by a group of cruel knaves whose actions are characterized by lust, greed, and heartless destruction of others, we perceive a central nihilistic proposition—that of Sade, or of Rameau's nephew—that man survives by feeding on others, by acts of cannibalism. This, it would seem, is our deepest nature. How feeble is the moral world by comparison! The whole picture is summed up near the end in Jacques' words: ". . . everything in nature thinks of itself and only of itself. What matters if it hurts others, as long as it does me good?"

On the one hand, then, the quality of human character and relations is corrosive to the ethical life. On the other hand, the refutation of determinism, a doctrine which itself eliminates ethical distinctions, is accomplished only through the uncovering of a chaotic world which yields the same result. Most despairing of all, perhaps, is our inability to judge the worth of persons and acts, our uncertainty in all borderline, complex, extreme cases. Inability to reach a moral judgment implies powerlessness to discover or to create moral truths, values, and standards anchored firmly in reality and satisfactory to the moral reason.

Among the motives which prevented Diderot from publishing his radical works was their ultimate nihilistic substance, their confirmation, as he contemplated human beings in the arena of the life-struggle, of a doctrine contradictory to what he felt were the necessary conditions for social life. The doctrine might be true. But it was a truth contrary to another aspect of his work and *faith,* as evidenced by his own efforts to promote virtue, and even by his cultivation of a legend about himself as the virtuous philosopher. And so the philosopher preferred to pull the blinds down about his private intellectual world.[166]

Diderot never convinced himself intellectually that nihilism was wrong, that moral values had any status other than as the power-enforced demands of the social group. But he knew that there was no safety in that road. Although he wrote frequently against falsehood and illusion, he had to accept this illusion (as it seemed to him), or at least, this "truth" of another order. If all men accepted it, then it would be as if it were true. Men would create their own tight little world of right and justice. Diderot's dilemma explains his violent aversion to La Mettrie's open and uncompromising nihilism. La Mettrie's principles, he declares, would end law, education, and morals, "would send to the insane asylum the courageous man who foolishly struggles against his disorderly

---

[166] Diderot reminds his reader "that there is a speculative doctrine which is neither for the multitude nor for practice, and that if, without being false, one does not write all he does, one is not inconsistent if he does not do all he writes." (*Jacques le Fataliste,* IX, p. 252.)

inclinations, and would assure immortality to the wicked man who would remorselessly abandon himself to them." [167]

On the other hand, Diderot was aware that the doctrine and the picture were also one-sided, and really too simple to account for the moral world. The latter, we find, does exist, despite doctrine; and moral good persists in life, even in the face of dominant evil. Perhaps we cannot explain the persistency of man's aspiration toward virtue and of his admiration for it, but neither can we explain them away. We must remember that even as Diderot was exploring, in this uncompromising fashion, the furthest reach of his materialism, he was also writing, or about to write, his great humanistic rejoinder to eighteenth-century materialism, the *Réfutation d'Helvétius,* a work in which he proclaims the distinctiveness of the human and the impossibility of accounting for it by reductive methods. Here Diderot places his finger on the error of the materialistic "evolutionary" ethics: while we must not take man out of nature, we must also realize his separate and distinctive place in nature, and its claims.[168] Ethics must be relative to man—not to all life and incidentally to man.

It is Diderot's view, in the *Réfutation,* that the human (moral) world will assert itself despite all "evidence" and "reasoning" (mostly fallacious) to the contrary. It is, moreover, the best world. However, it is not to be concluded that Diderot has reached a definite decision, and sees his way clearly. There are two indications to the contrary. The first is implicit. It is the great man, he repeats, who is the nihilist, or at least the successful one. Diderot finds reassurance in the fact that they are few. "There is a constant phenomenon in nature, to which Helvétius has not paid attention; it is that great souls are rare, and that nature has made scarcely any but common beings; and that this is the reason why moral causes subjugate the organism so easily." [169] The other indication is explicit, and of exceptional importance. It brings together both

[167] *Essai sur les règnes de Claude et de Néron* (1778–82), *Oeuvres,* III, p. 217. Jean Thomas comments, in regard to Diderot's thought in his later years: "It is the revenge of life against paradoxes, of experience against the optimistic spirit." He quotes a fragment of Diderot's: "Great knowledge, truly important knowledge, we get we know not where. Not in the book printed by Marc-Michel Rey or elsewhere, but in the book of the world." (*L'Humanisme de Diderot,* p. 72.)

[168] The same idea is expressed by the biologist, George G. Simpson, *op. cit.,* pp. 307–8, 310–11. Simpson adds that while man is in evolution, with him evolution takes a radically different course, of which ethical judgment is a chief characteristic.

[169] *Réfutation,* II, p. 393.

aspects of Diderot's ethical thought, his emotional and pragmatic commitment to morals, and the recognition of his intellectual inability to validate them. It clearly reveals his full awareness of the menace of nihilism, and the meaning of his work as a struggle against it.

> I will tell you even more; if there are apparently complicated questions which have appeared simple to me on examination, there are some apparently very simple ones which I have judged to be beyond my capacity. For example, I am convinced that even in as badly ordered a society as ours, in which vice which succeeds is often applauded and virtue which fails almost always ridiculous, I am convinced, I say, that everything considered, there is no better way of obtaining happiness than to be a moral person. This is the work which I feel is the most important and the most interesting to be written, the one which I would remember with the greatest satisfaction in my last moments. This is a question which I have pondered a hundred times and with all the mental concentration of which I am capable; I had, I think, the necessary data. Shall I make a confession? I have never dared to take pen in hand to write the first line of it. I said to myself: if I do not emerge victorious from this effort, I become the apologist of wickedness; I shall have betrayed the cause of virtue, I shall have encouraged mankind to vice. I do not feel myself qualified for this sublime task; I would devote my life to it in vain.[170]

On the one hand, then, Diderot preaches a social morality of enlightened self-interest, a rational theory in which esteem and happiness are the reward for virtue. Attached to this ethics, and supporting it, is a sentimentalism of virtue, a frequently lachry-

---

[170] *Ibid.*, II, p. 345. R. Mauzi calls this avowal "capital for the understanding of all Diderot's work." (*Cahiers de l'Association internationale des etudes françaises,* 1961, p. 257.) See also H. Dieckmann, *ibid.,* p. 398.

In 1769 Diderot had already made a similar avowal: "No, by Jove, there are men so unfortunately born, so violently impelled by avarice, ambition, a disorderly love of women, that I would condemn them to unhappiness if I commanded them to struggle continuously against their dominating passion. But won't those men be still more unhappy as a result of their passion than as a result of the struggle against it? My word, I don't know at all, and every day I see men who'd rather die than mend their ways. I was very young when the idea came to me that all of ethics consisted in proving to men that after all the best way to be happy in this world was to be virtuous; I immediately started to meditate on this question and I am still meditating." (*Oeuvres,* VI, pp. 438–39.)

And yet the statement, "I had never dared take pen in hand," is not quite true. He *had* tried once—in "Droit naturel." Doubtless he had been unable to go on believing in the validity of his solution; and this was inevitable because he posed the problem, as we see here, on the basis of happiness—thus confusing two realms of existence.

mose surge of the heart. There is some difference between the two. With the former, Diderot writes like d'Holbach:

—What, in your opinion, are man's duties?
—To make himself happy. Whence the necessity of contributing to the happiness of others, or in other words, of being
virtuous.[171]

With the latter, we have an immediate adherence, an effusion of emotivity. On the other hand, Diderot's private intellectual spec-ulation convinces him of the relativity of moral judgments, of their dependency on physical organism and on social conventions which lack any inherent "oughtness" or quality of obligation, and are only arbitrary and power-enforced. His ultimate explorations strip off the superficial moral coat which culture has put on man and emphasize the primacy of nihilism in his psychic needs, as well as its effective existence within social cultures. His view of nihilism also has a metaphysical dimension. Nature and the world contain no moral values, nor offer any basis for them in our lives. Insofar as man is a moral being, he is, then, anti-natural (though not anti-human). This coincides with the Christian view, and with the essence of Rousseau's position. But if one is a nihilist, he admits the legitimacy of nature only, and not of culture; and Diderot, in this context, declares that morality may not contradict the demands of nature in man. Then, reacting against his own theories, he later insists on the distinctive psychic and moral realities and demands of human nature. He is the defender of culture. He accepts the validity of life in preference to that of logic, the needs of society and culture as paramount to abstract truth. However there is no true reconciliation, no peace of mind. As with Zadig and the angel Jesrad, there is always the "but." If, as Carl Becker claims, the purpose of Diderot's speculative thinking "was to furnish a firm foundation for natural morality," then his effort was a failure.[172] The proof lies in his inconclusive struggles, and in his own candid confession. He was never able to establish moral values rationally. His reason led only to their destruction.

Diderot was an artist and best able to express himself artisti-cally, generating and developing an idea by means of different masks; weighing, considering, judging, sometimes leaving the problem unsolved, sometimes allowing an orthodox character to

[171] *Introduction aux grands principes*, II, p. 85.
[172] "The Dilemma of Diderot," p. 63.

resolve it, sometimes a radical one. In any event, he could voice the most extreme positions convincingly through personae without committing himself irrevocably to one side or the other. He was essentially a moralist trying to discover a basis for ethics within the human sphere, but committed to the moral life even if he could not succeed in this, his greatest hope. He was, without doubt, the greatest experimenter in morals in the Age of Enlightenment.

We come finally to Rousseau. Part of Rousseau's break with the *philosophes* was due to his opposition to their nature philosophy which, he believed, menaced morality and culture. Unable to see any sure ground for a secular ethics, he embraced the sacred as a necessary support for culture and a bulwark against the absurd. He was also shielded from his own despair by his clinging to a personal God, and so to providentialism and the belief that justice would be done (i.e., values restored) in the life to come.[173] Like Pascal, he too experienced a revulsion at the thought of an empty universe; it is apparent in Julie's horror at Wolmar's atheism which in the spectacle of nature sees only "a chance combination, a blind force, an eternal silence." [174]

However Rousseau's chief concern with nihilism inheres in his accusation that the societies of men—as they have *naturally* developed (that is, in the unplanned course of history)—are nihilistic and necessarily so. He does not, of course, use the word, since it did not exist; but the picture in the *Discours sur l'inégalité* is unmistakable. To the stark description of rampant nihilism which we earlier examined,[175] we may join the following lines:

> But with social man it is a quite different story: it is a matter of providing first for necessities and then for superfluities; then come delights, and then immense wealth, and then subjects, and then slaves—he does not have a moment's relaxation. The strangest thing is that the less natural and urgent needs are, the stronger the passions, and what is worse, the greater the power to satisfy them; so that after long prosperity, after having swallowed up many treasures and ruined many men, my hero will

---

[173] In his third *Dialogue*—to take one example—Rousseau thunders against the *philosophes* for destroying conscience and moral law, leaving only force, "leaving to the senses an absolute empire over man, and limiting everything to the enjoyment of this brief life, . . ." To their doctrine he opposes an innate conscience, "which nature engraves in all hearts."

[174] *Ibid.*, Part V, chap. 5.

[175] See *An Age of Crisis*, pp. 279–80, 308–12.

end up by killing everything until he is sole master of the universe. Such is in brief the moral picture, if not of human life, at least of the secret aspirations in the heart of every civilized man.

It is so, because society necessarily causes men to hate each other insofar as their interests are opposed, "to render each other apparent services and really to do each other unimaginable hurt." Each individual's reason must dictate to him maxims directly contrary to those of public reason.[176] Each finds his benefit in the *misfortunes* of others. We secretly wish for them and feel joy when they occur, for one's loss is another's prosperity. Even public calamities, like epidemics and wars, are hoped for and awaited by many individuals. "Let us then penetrate through our frivolous show of *bienveillance* into what goes on at the bottom of our hearts, and let us reflect on what a state of things must be in which all men are forced to caress each other and to destroy each other, and in which they are born enemies out of duty and crooks out of self-interest." [177]

Self-affirmation, or the power drive is, then, the result of endangering the ego's security by placing it in a situation of constant comparison and competition. The need for self-protection is deep, its manifestations varied, and its tendency is always to the hurt or destruction of others.[178] By the realization that such action is required for complete self-expression and protection, Rousseau's thinking in this regard becomes part of the pattern we have sketched.

Rousseau is also in agreement with the immoralists when he admits that if moral good is not in conformity with our nature, "and if man is naturally wicked, he cannot cease being so without corrupting himself, and goodness is in him only a vice against nature." [179] In his insistence that men should free themselves from "opinion"—that is, the judgment of others—and follow their own nature, Rousseau unknowingly indulges in an ambiguity which

[176] Whence the necessity of Rousseau's "guide."

[177] Vaughan, *op. cit.*, I, p. 203.

[178] Cf. *Les Confessions:* "I drew from it this great maxim of morality, perhaps the only one of practical use, to avoid situations which put our duties in opposition with our interests and which show us our good in the hurt of others, sure that in such situations, however sincere our love of virtue, we weaken sooner or later without realizing it, and become unjust and wicked in our actions, without having stopped being just and good at heart." (*Oeuvres*, VIII, p. 38.)

[179] *Emile, Oeuvres*, II, p. 258.

lends itself perfectly to nihilism and sadism.[180] His views are—
in form—close to those expressed by some of Sade's characters.
"The first principle of my philosophy," Mme Delbène explains to
Juliette, "is to defy public opinion. . . . Our happiness should
depend only on ourselves, on our conscience. . . ." [181] Even more,
Rousseau's autarchy of happiness in the fifth *Rêverie* is also a
striving to godhood: "one is sufficient unto himself like God."
Like the radical thinkers, he is under the influence of the line of
thought stemming from Spinoza, though he applies it differently:
"Everything that seems to extend or affirm our existence flatters us,
everything which seems to destroy or compress it afflicts us."

Nevertheless, there is beyond any doubt a rebellious, anarchistic-
primitivistic tendency in Rousseau which heightens the relevancy
of lines such as these. He has a fundamental hatred of man's rational powers, an aversion even to language—to all the *human*
work, the work of culture, that which is above and against the
natural, the spontaneous, the immediate. In his early writings,
and also in the last (when he had reached a psychotic state), and in
occasional outbursts, he is an anarchist at heart. He was not a
nihilist; he never denies the difference between right and wrong,
but praises a premoral state of innocence, seeing nihilism as the
product of society.

But it was precisely the underlying nihilism and anarchy of the
present social state which impelled Rousseau to seek refuge in the
opposite extreme (as extremists in religion or politics are often
seen to exchange places, passing over the middle ground). It was
also the conviction that man is evil (however much he may have
said the contrary). Only when men (conceptually) live in a presocial state of relative isolation are they governed by natural pity
and *amour de soi*. As soon as there is fixed intercourse, there is
comparison and reflection, which inevitably result in opposition
and competition, the desire for superiority and the hurt of others.
Yes, men would be good (but not virtuous, only not-evil) if they

---

[180] Not only in the *Discours sur l'inégalité*, but in all his personal writings. See
the long development in the first *Dialogue*, which includes the following ambiguous
statement: "All of nature's first impulses are good and right. They tend, as directly as possible, to our self-preservation and our happiness." Because of our
weakness, we do not persist in following the first impulse; the strong soul "does not
turn aside, but like a cannon ball, goes through the obstacle, or weakens and falls
on meeting it."

[181] *Histoire de Juliette*, I, p. 15. She continues with a discourse on the relativism
of conscience. See also *ibid.*, I, pp. 134–35.

expressed and followed their first impulses—like Jean-Jacques, of course—if they acted without prudence, calculation, reflection. But Jean-Jacques is unique (as he takes care to tell us); immediacy is lost in society—as the necessity for a "guide" in the new society of the *Contrat social* makes only too clear. In society, what is most needed, precisely, is *virtue*—something which is not the first impulse, but requires reflection, and conscience, and often the overcoming of the first, natural impulse.

He chooses then another absolute, the general will, and opposes an organismic theory of collectivism to the philosophy of nature. Rousseau's espousal of conditioning and repression exists only because of his persuasion that men are evil in their natural impulses toward each other, as those impulses are evoked and developed by social living. His protototalitarian type of political-social system (to which we shall return in more detail in the next chapter) rests on the assumption that a state of war and immorality, or a state of nihilism, is inevitable without draconian measures amounting to a total revolution. He does not believe that the rationalistic ethical philosophies of his time have solved the problem which Julie states in these words: "But what does all that matter to my personal interest, and after all, which is more important to me, my happiness at the expense of the rest of men, or the happiness of others at my expense?" (III, 18.) Natural man, in Rousseau's concept, was governed by id alone, and the present social state is an intolerable conflict of id and superego. His political theory proposes a state of almost complete dominance of the cultural superego, that is, the complete "socialization" of man. The nihilists and primitivists wished to eliminate the conflict in the opposite way, by denying the validity of the cultural superego and freeing the id. When Rousseau builds a rational philosophy, then he becomes the defender of culture. He refuses the proposed synthesis of nature and culture (of natural man and artificial man). Edmund Wilson, following Mario Praz, has said that Sade "appears as the opposite pole to Rousseau, and if we do not allow him his place, the picture remains incomplete." [182] The remark is an astute one and an important one, if it is interpreted correctly.[183] We must realize that

---

[182] *Eight Essays,* New York, 1954, p. 177.

[183] Wilson mistakenly makes the polarity consist in the simplified and inaccurate interpretation of Rousseau as meaning what his words literally say: that men are naturally good and society corrupts them. Rousseau means that man has left the

if Sade and Rousseau are at opposite poles, it is because at one point they touch each other; and also, that Rousseau's bitter indictment in the second *Discours* was food for Sade's reflections. Rousseau rebelled against evil and injustice, Sade embraced them; the one said No to the natural world, the other said Yes. In both cases, the attempted synthesis of nature and culture is dissolved.

The utilitarians had attempted such a synthesis. To obtain a better perspective on that attempt and on the difficulties involved, it will be helpful at this point to refer again to Freud's analysis of this problem.[184] After describing the processes of individual and cultural development, Freud further declares that the two are engaged in endless contention. The cultural group, like the individual, is subjected to a superego, consisting of ideals and standards, which are partly codified in systems of ethics. Ethics deals with "the sorest point" in any civilization, "the constitutional tendency in men to aggressions against one another." Our cultural superego demands that we love our neighbor as ourselves. This is too severe a command, one of which the ego is psychologically incapable, just as the individual superego is too severe, cares too little about the happiness of the ego and neglects the strength of the cravings of the id. "What an overwhelming obstacle to civilization aggression must be if the defence against it can cause as much misery as aggression itself!" [185]

From Freud's analysis it should be even clearer that the naturalistic-utilitarian ethics was essentially an attempt to overcome the eternal conflict which he describes, and that it hoped to preserve

---

premoral state of innocence and entered the moral state of virtue and vice, and that in existing societies, vice is by far dominant.

[184] *Civilization and its Discontents*, pp. 133–40. See chap. 3, above.

[185] For further commentary, see H. Marcuse, *Eros and Civilization*, pp. 3–18 Among other observations, Marcuse states: "The animal man becomes a human being only through a fundamental transformation of his nature, affecting not only the instinctual aims but also the instinctual 'values'—that is, the principles that govern the attainment of the aims." The conversion is from immediate satisfaction to delayed satisfaction, from pleasure to restraint of pleasure, from play to work, from receptiveness to productiveness, from the absence of repression to security. Repression of instincts "is imposed not by nature but by man. . . . The notion that a non-repressive civilization is impossible is a cornerstone of Freudian theory." Marcuse goes on to explain Freud's preference for a state where freedom and necessity coincide; this was, we remember, the dream of Rousseau.

We have already proposed the antithesis of Sade and Kant as termini of eighteenth century thought, due to the inability of the utilitarian synthesis to win the day (*An Age of Crisis*, p. 376). The reader is urged to refer to Kant's argument against nihilism, in *A Critique of Practical Reason*, ed. Abbott, pp. 15, 41–49, 52, 57, 74, 80, 109–113, 124, 149–50.

what was necessary for culture while loosening the grip of an excessively restrictive cultural superego, as it was embodied in supernatural Christian standards. The libidinal demands and satisfactions were, in several ways, given a larger scope. There were, however, two great weaknesses in the proposed synthesis. The first was theoretical. By denying the transcendence of the individual or of culture over nature and leaving only the goals of the id (which are to be manipulated), the supposed synthesis remained heavily committed to nature. On practical grounds, however, the actual commitment advanced more and more to the side of culture (progressing from hedonism to social virtue). If the happiness of the individual was, in one sense, given a larger scope, in another sense the real effort was to *cheat* or delude the id, by making the ego believe that happiness and ego-satisfaction would come best from virtue, or the sacrifice of the id to the cultural superego.

On the one hand, human reason is a principle source and instrument of culture. On the other hand, the prevailing analysis in the eighteenth century showed the individual to be dedicated to the satisfaction of the demands of the id; reason is its instrument, as it is also the ego's instrument for self-protection. Since reason occupies this mediating position and function, culture may attempt to use reason to delude the id. There have always been two streams of ethical thought: one is the justification of virtue in terms of obligation (dissociated from self-interest, often to its detriment); the other is the justification of virtue in terms of egoism (self-interest). In the first case, man is asked to transcend or deny basic aspects of his nature, in the name of transcendence and its values. In the second case, the purpose is the same, but reason is used to give the impression that no transcendence or real denial is being called for.

Hume had been consistent. But his self-denying ordinance in the matter of reason's function was not accepted by those moralists who nevertheless denied Natural Law. R. V. Sampson has observed that utilitarianism and Marxism are the two schools which appear within the main stream of the Enlightenment tradition. Both sought in different ways "to give a rational, non-subjective validity to their value systems. In the outcome, however, these attempts suffer alike from the fact that they rob the moral relation of all content of obligation," and render the very concept of duty meaningless. "The explanation that moral behaviour consists in the pursuit not of self-interest but of 'enlightened' or 'benevolent' self-interest does nothing to advance the inquiry as to the true source of moral obligation, since it leaves unexplained the grounds of 'enlightenment.' . . . The attempt fails ultimately because it seeks to reduce ethics to a branch of psychology." [186]

The utilitarian synthesis was thus doubly unsatisfactory. From the viewpoint of ethical thought, by remaining within the compass of nature, it fails to establish any obligation except to one's own self-interest. From the viewpoint of the cultural process, it becomes self-evidently improbable or false ("my interest is *not* to sacrifice my interest to virtue"). The demands of the cultural superego appear in the light of a tyrannical imposition and an unjustifiable fraud which actually violate the great "natural law" of self-interest. Despite the somewhat uneasy persistence of utilitarianism in the nineteenth century, there is no doubt that the currents of doubt and of nihilism accomplished the dissolution of the synthesis of nature and culture which it had sought.

The same forces which had led to the revolt against Christian ethics now revolt against bourgeois utilitarian ethics (somewhat analogously to the sequence of the French Revolution and the Communist revolution). The revolt has two faces. Nihilism is the rejection of the prevailing organization of instincts which is imposed by any culture, and *ipso facto* of all moral restrictions to the id (a revolt against repression of the instincts). Totalitarianism is a defense of culture based on the acceptance of the truth of nihilism; it pretends to nothing more than a tyrannical and arbitrary imposition of a superego and contemplates the remaking of the individual, through the pressures of total conditioning, so that the id is inhibited and the ego enslaved. If the effort toward humanistic self-control and voluntary co-operation does not succeed, culture is left with no other way to defend itself.

It is because hedonism represented the revolt against the limitations of Christian ethics to the happiness instincts that, when the force it represented did not become fully absorbed and satisfied by the utilitarian synthesis, its drive was turned toward the nihilistic revolt against morals, and so against culture. This was a logical relation under certain conditions, particularly in an intellectual framework in which psychological hedonism and hedonism as a method for determining choices were confused. If we were

---

[186] *Op. cit.*, p. 230.

to take hedonism and nihilism abstractly, it would be correct to say that there is no necessary progress from one to the other; to go from the description of man as motivated by egoism to the conclusion that his instincts should be free because they are natural is not—taken outside the total cultural context we have outlined—an unavoidable conclusion. But the fact is, we are dealing with complex cultural contexts and with history, not with isolated bits of abstract logic. The development of decadent and nihilistic movements in the nineteenth century, the rise of totalitarian philosophies, certain movements in all the arts, political events—all show that for many this did seem the logical step, and that the step was indeed taken.[187]

While the naturalists wished to substitute the realm of social justice for the realm of grace, their inquiries created the gravest doubts about the very existence of justice, about man's capability of attaining it, and his desire for it. The centrality of the individual, the reduction of the individual to pleasure-pain sensations, and the assertion of the natural vitalities led to this outcome. The achievement of order, within the artifice of culture, is impossible on the basis of the unconditioned natural demand for happiness, with its requirement of free self-expression. The nihilistic sectors of eighteenth-century thought contain the seed of modern irrational movements, such as Nazism. If there is only life and death, only the law of force, and happiness instincts, if we and the world are absurd and meaningless, then values have no standing. There is no reason not to live each for ourselves, individually and as national groups, according to our own arbitrary will—as far as the arbitrary will of our culture, or the world, allow.[188] Reducing man to the indiscriminately natural, to self-interest motivation, was

---

[187] "A hedonistic ethics had long been accepted, to a greater or lesser degree, by the Enlightenment; Sade merely extended and perverted a doctrine already prevalent in non-Christian circles." (H. Vyverberg, *Historical Pessimism in the French Enlightenment*, p. 225.)

[188] As Quevedo put it in *La Vida del Buscón:* there is no value except life; the important thing is to live (and it is difficult), and then, to live well, which can be done only at the expense of others. In the romantic revolt of nihilism, however, the objective of survival is replaced, as Nietzsche said, by the will to power.

"All of us carry some sort of Hitler in ourselves," writes Max Picard, "an inherent sickness of the soul . . . Hitler was far more than just an economic or a political phenomenon; he was the inevitable product of the inner chaos of modern man, of the disordered state of Western civilization." (*Hitler in Uns Selbst,* quoted by Alfred Werner, in "Germany's New Flagellants," p. 177.) See also Hermann Rauschning's *Revolution of Nihilism.* Marxist totalitarianism springs from the same dilemma, but is, in theory, less sadistic and more systematically rational.

thus a sure road to nihilism. And, as we have seen, "nature" tended to become assimilated to the "animal"; since it is impossible to draw a line of distinction between nature and culture, in man, this was the easy thing to do when one wanted to talk of nature in a specific sense. This is, indeed, a fundamental confusion in much eighteenth-century thinking, which frequently overlooks the fact that man is naturally a creature of culture.

Man, however, is the only animal who sets his own course, which may take him against the course of the rest of nature. This is his distinctiveness and the basis of his values—a "Natural Law" which is not "nature's law." It is what we do, what we work and die for, beyond self-interest, that justifies man, gives him meaning and dignity, rescues him from the absurd. Man alone lives simultaneously in a subjective and an objective world. From the viewpoint of objectivity, he shrinks to nothingness (his being, his works). From the viewpoint of subjectivity, his being is everything.[189] The antithesis produced by attainment of the objective level leaves him troubled and insecure, devoured by the need to affirm his being, at the same time that the basis of dignity and meaning are lost. Alone with foreknowledge of his death, he carries that haunting sentence with him every day of his life. All he accomplishes is in defiance of the mocking spectre of annihilation, of nothingness, an unconquerable refusal to accept futility and nonmeaning. Sometimes the defiance is heroic. More often it is an evasion into comforting dreams of immortality. But the dream is itself a response to nihilism. The very persistence of human life and culture are, in a real sense, a triumph over the challenge of nihilism.

II. Sade and the *Fleurs du mal*

Sadism is a dark pool formed by those streams of eighteenth-century philosophy which flow into it. There is nothing in Sade's nihilism which, in essence or in embryo, is not also found in the writings we have examined. The differences are great; but they are differences of degree, thoroughness, universality, consistency. Sade unifies the disparate elements of seventeenth- and eighteenth-century nihilistic thinking into a powerful revolutionary system

---

[189] We recall how Zadig realized this.

and carries it ruthlessly to the most extreme conclusions possible.

Two mainstreams of thought empty into the sadian pool: the idea that pleasure is the sole value in a wholly natural and valueless world; [1] and the idea that man must escape contingency (anguish, insecurity) by an affirmation of his own being. The sexual torture and murder associated with Sade's name are, in fact, the ultimate, exacerbated expression of these earlier findings. These two major propositions are synthesized through Sade's general concept of sex, which also had ample precedents. The major propositions are supported by a congeries of minor propositions, all of which the reader will recognize. Sade's originality lies in his discovery of the all-pervasiveness of the sexual libido, in addition to its previously recognized connection with aggression, and in the synthesis of these facts into a total nihilistic philosophy.

Sade was not a great philosopher or a good logician—quite to the contrary. It may also be argued that he was insane. But it is necessary to understand that these two facts are entirely irrelevant to his importance in the history of culture. And that is the concern of this study.[2]

Sade was the first to construct theoretically and to realize graphically, in the concreteness of literary character and actions, a complete system of nihilism with all its implications, ramifications, and consequences. If we look backward, we can picture Sade collecting

[1] This is a contradiction in terms, but the contradiction is inherent in the thought of the time. I shall reserve my criticisms of sadism until I have objectively analyzed it.

[2] "Sade was a serious thinker. . . . Sade is too much a part of the eighteenth century to be dismissed as a mad eccentric." (H. Vyverberg, op. cit., pp. 226-28.)

I am also obliged to point out that the object of this discussion is not to advance the simplistic proposition, "the philosophes were responsible for Sade's demented ravings and perversions." In the first place, we must differentiate between his perversions and his philosophy; although they are connected, we are dealing with his philosophy, and with that aspect of his sexual ideas which are pertinent to his philosophy. We are not concerned with his psychopathia sexualis, but with ideas, all of which were expressed before him in the eighteenth century. Furthermore, the word "responsible" is invidious and irrelevant, and betrays the historical process. It is rather a question of Sade and the philosophes being in the same movement of ideas, in the same historical intellectual movement, to the degree in which there is a coincidence of thought. (I am sorry if this incontrovertible fact distresses many lovers of the French Enlightenment.) If we take, for instance, Père Hudson in Diderot's Jacques le Fataliste, the question is simply this: Is Hudson a pre-Sadian character or is he not? What is his attitude toward other human beings?

In a word, in regard to the discussion of sadism and of prototstotalitarianism, in this study, as well as in regard to the influence of the eighteenth century on the French Revolution and on the twentieth century, it is essential to distinguish formative factors from causative factors.

the dispersed heritage of more than two thousand years of the revolt of instinct against culture, and igniting it with the spark that made it flame. If we look forward, we can picture his fame and his work glowing and smoldering under the cover of bourgeois smugness and cant, a beacon to misguided rebels of many kinds.[3] He has become a symbol, and properly so. He was the first to bring out, uncompromisingly and with striking power, the things about men and about their culture that they want most to hide, and which constitute a pervasive and enduring problem. That is why he is "unspeakable," why he has been permanently banished. He announces the symptoms of illness and weakness in culture; he reveals the ever-latent forces of evil in men, and their sources. Nihilism (not only as a philosophy, but as a psychology) is the worm at the core of our culture. It is the flaw we must constantly overcome. Sade was the first to bring the full truth of this danger into the general consciousness of the Western World. The reaction to him and to his work by those who prefer to keep the shadows out of sight is proof enough.

We should bear in mind that Sade's revolt is a total one: against a postulated God, whose wickedness (the second horn of Bayle's dilemma) is also Sade's justification, against nature itself (although nature is also his justification), and against all standards and limits which society makes as moral claims upon its members. Even in atheism, he goes beyond other atheists who apostrophized Nature almost as another divinity.[4] For Sade, nature is evil, and catastrophic to man, even as "God" is. His demand is for absolute freedom, in thought, imagination, and in act; freedom to follow the impulses of instinct without regard to human or divine laws.[5]

We may take as Sade's first major thesis that man is a completely "natural" being; and that, since all is indifferent in nature,

[3] "The reaction against Rousseau's ideas began even before 1800 in the works of a man whose thought, however subterranean and unavowed, was to set its mark on most literary productions in the next hundred years—the Marquis de Sade." (A. E. Carter, *The Idea of Decadence in French Literature*, p. 4.) The influence extended far beyond belles-lettres.

[4] D'Holbach, for instance: "Oh Nature! Sovereign of all beings! and you, her adorable daughters, virtue, reason, truth! be forever our only divinities." (*Système de la nature*, tome II, chap. 11.)

[5] "The idea of God," he declares, "is the only wrong for which I cannot forgive men." The reason for this, according to Simone de Beauvoir, is that "in order to deliver man from the idols to which he is alienated by society, it is necessary to begin by insuring his autonomy in the face of heaven . . . in choosing God, [man] renounced himself, and that is his unpardonable fault." ("Faut-il brûler Sade?" p. 1206.)

everything that nature suggests to us is also indifferent, therefore permissible. To prove his point, Sade, in one place, quotes a passage from Montesquieu's discussion of suicide to which we referred in the first volume of this study.[6]

Since we are purely natural beings, we are not responsible for what we do, but are determined by cause and effect, and by the mechanical laws of the nervous system. "Man . . . has no other laws than those imprinted on minerals, on plants, on animals." [7] As the materialists had declared, we are born good or vicious; Sade's characters defend themselves time and again by saying that they were born with certain tastes, as indeed he defended himself on the same grounds. We are also born with certain animal impulses and needs, and with a love of cruelty peculiar to the species, in degree at least. Says the infamous Duke de Blangis, in *Sodome et Gomorrhe;* "I have no need to constrain my inclinations in view of pleasing [God]: it is from nature that I have received those inclinations, and I would offend her by resisting them. . . . I am in her hands only a machine which she moves at her will, and there is not one of my crimes that does not serve her purposes." [8]

When we examine nature, we find, according to Sade, that she excludes and abhors all virtues, since they countermand her impulses.[9] Nature subsists on an equilibrium of what we call good and evil (as Robinet had argued), one of creation and destruction. Therefore our crimes and depredations are a valid and useful contribution to her processes.[10] Charity is against nature.[11] The parent's responsibility to his offspring and the child's gratitude toward his progenitors are declared time and again to be outside of nature.

---

[6] *Histoire de Juliette,* IV, p. 241. Sade fails to distinguish between "permissible" in the sense of "authorized" and in the sense of "not excluded by a rule or prohibition."

[7] *Ibid.,* V, pp. 176–77.

[8] Quoted by Lely, II, pp. 331–32. Also, *Histoire de Juliette,* II, p. 97. *La Philosophie dans le boudoir:* "Is a man the master of his tastes? . . . their wrongness is nature's; they were no more the masters of arriving in the world with different tastes than we are to be born bandy-legged or well-built." (P. 12.) Again, we are compared to a drum, which must necessarily emit a sound when struck by a stick; our "organization" and "outside forces" are the analogous elements. "Therefore it is madness, extravagance, not to do whatever we feel like doing. . . ." (*Histoire de Juliette,* I, p. 22.)

[9] *Histoire de Juliette,* I, pp. 10, 13.

[10] *Ibid.,* IV, p. 184; V, p. 177.

[11] *Les Infortunes de la vertu,* p. 161.

See if animals know [these ties]; no, of course, and yet it is always they we must refer to when we wish to know nature.[12]

It is false that one loves his father; it is false that one can love him; we fear him, but we do not love him; his existence irritates us, and does not please us; self-interest, the holiest of nature's laws, invincibly urges us to desire the death of a person whose fortune we are awaiting; and in this regard, it is doubtless true that it not only would be easy to hate him, but still more natural to kill him. . . .[13]

Nature tells us that theft belongs to her laws, since she has not made men equal, but either strong, to take from the weak, or weak, to avenge themselves with cunning.[14] Nature applauds murder. Exactly as the Catholic apologist, Bergier, had predicted, in his refutation of the *philosophes'* defense of suicide, their argument that man is an item of indifferent value in the natural order justifies murder for Sade, as well as suicide. Only our pride, he declares, makes murder "a crime." It is not merely the idea that everything nature suggests is proper and that a human life has no special value. When we destroy creatures, we allow nature the possibility of creating new ones. Nothing is really destroyed, in fact, but only recombined. There is no murder, only change of natural form.[15] Sade concludes that civil laws stand in contradiction to nature—an idea which again recalls Diderot (in his unpublished writings), Rousseau, and several others, with the difference that for Sade this legitimizes disobedience. "What respect can you expect a man to have for laws that restrain all that nature has imprinted in him?"[16] Obviously, then, no laws are valid, except those which conform to nature and therefore are not needed. Sade accepts this conclusion, and damns all lawmakers. All ends are valid, any means is legitimate.[17]

Sade's second postulate, one that is consequent to the first, is the unlimited right of the strong. In *Les Infortunes de la vertu,* he

[12] *La Philosophie dans le boudoir,* p. 223.

[13] *Histoire de Juliette,* II, p. 61. Parents' care of children is only a matter of custom and pride (*Boudoir,* p. 224). The daughter in this work derives intense enjoyment out of torturing her mother. Sade also declares that the inexistence of a "cry of the blood" proves there is no natural tie (*Boudoir,* p. 223).

[14] *Ibid.,* I, p. 154.

[15] *Infortunes,* pp. 56–57; *Boudoir,* p. 74; *Histoire de Juliette,* II, pp. 137–38; III, p. 15; IV, p. 231 ff.

[16] *Histoire de Juliette,* V, p. 129; III, p. 28.

[17] *Ibid.,* I, p. 117. This first point is summarized in the preamble of the "Statutes of the Society of the Friends of Crime." (III, p. 18.)

tells us, following good eighteenth-century theory, that "man is really born isolated, selfish, cruel and despotic; he wants everything and gives nothing in return. . . . The poor must suffer. It is one of nature's laws. Their existence is necessary to create prosperity." When Justine asks the bandits to justify their outrages, she is told, "Because right is with the strong and you are weak." Sade's statement about the poor brings to mind certain adherents of "social Darwinism" in the nineteenth century. He also supports that view by arguing, like Rousseau, that the law of the strong still obtains in civilized societies, power being exercised through wealth instead of by brute force.[18] A concept of the survival of the fittest permeates Sade. "My will to have power over others and to destroy them being the same in the feelings of all others towards me, war among all men is the law of the world." Juliette, contrary to her sister, understands these truths intuitively. While weak, she accepts as right the injustices done to her.

> Well! I said to myself, I have only to try to be rich in turn, and I shall soon be as impudent as this woman, I shall enjoy the same rights and the same pleasures. Let us beware of being virtuous, since vice triumphs always; let us dread poverty, since it is always despised. But, having nothing, how shall I avoid misfortune? By criminal acts, of course . . . crime serves nature's intentions as well as good conduct and virtue: Let us go forth into the perverse world . . . let nothing be an obstacle. . . . Since society is composed only of dupes and swindlers, let us by all means play the latter role.[19]

Juliette finds that her reasoning is invariably confirmed by experience. As the wicked Noirceuil explains, when she is taken aback by the injustice of her innocent victim's suffering, from which she has ignobly profited, "All this is in the order of things; . . . misfortune is the plaything of prosperity; . . . the weak must be the food of the strong. Look at the universe, at all the laws which rule it."[20] Consequently, injustice is the only justice. To punish a criminal is the only real injustice, since he was following the motive of "natural equity" in his atrocities, while the law perpetrates atrocities without any motive. Thus "natural equity" is set up against "human equity," or "artificial equity."[21] Follow-

---

[18] *Infortunes*, pp. 151–52, 162.
[19] *Histoire de Juliette*, I, p. 139.
[20] *Ibid.*, I, pp. 274–75.
[21] *Ibid.*, I, pp. 162–64.

ing Rousseau, apparently, Dorval shows that society is founded on the primary injustice of property, a theft imposed by force and authorized by nature. The strong consented to laws only because they preserved his usurpation, and because he knew he would not be bound by them in his further depradations. Thus theft, nature's institution, is continued under a coat of legality, and becomes the principle of economic competition, while the armed robber, who is the only doer of natural justice, is punished. And yet, such "natural justice" is made all the more necessary by the effects of legal economic exploitation. On the other hand, the exploitation is also just, since the strong have the natural right to victimize the weak; and the attempted reprisals of the weak are unjust, since nature has destined them to be victims. Consequently, the use of legal force by the strong, as an addition to their natural force in order to maintain and extend their exploitation, is also just.[22] After all, when the law punishes theft, it is only punishing it because it is an aggression upon another theft. All that we can say is that in nature's eyes there is no offense in any act which is successful.[23]

The result is the proclamation of a completely anarchic freedom. "O you, who dabble in governing men, beware of binding any creature! Let him make his own arrangement, let him find what is proper to him, and you will soon see that everything will be all the better for it."[24]

Still another result is the thrill of pleasurable sensations: for the weak, the masochistic pleasure of submission and suffering; the pleasure of sadism for the strong.[25] This leads us to the third principle of the Sadian philosophy. Egoistic pleasure is the sole value in a world in which acts are morally indifferent; the greater the pleasure, the greater the value of the act.

"Scorn everything that is contrary to the divine laws of pleasure," Sade urges.[26] Since chastity does not produce pleasure or happiness, the initiate, Eugénie, is urged to utmost debauchery and lasciviousness: ". . . your body is yours, yours alone." Underlying these words is belief in the absolute independence of the indi-

[22] This, basically, is La Mettrie's doctrine.
[23] *Ibid.,* I, pp. 154–61.
[24] *Ibid.,* I, p. 90.
[25] *Ibid.,* pp. 160–61. See the passage quoted in the first volume.
[26] *Boudoir,* p. 7.

vidual, and in the sacred "I." The only justice is to do what you desire at the expense of others.

> Eh! Why should I hesitate to satisfy myself, when the action which I conceive, whatever wrong it may do to my fellow-man, can give me the most exquisite pleasure? For, after all, supposing for a moment that in doing such an action I am committing an injustice towards my neighbor, it happens that in not doing it, I commit an injustice towards myself. . . . Now, between these two necessary injustices, should I be so much my own enemy as not to give preference to the one from which I can derive some pleasant titillation? [27]

This argument inevitably leads to the conclusion that no one's life is of value compared to our self-interest.[28] "When will you be convinced that everything that vegetates down here is only for our pleasure?" [29] Even if an action brings us only slight pleasure, at the cost of great hurt to many others, it is what we should do, "because there is no comparison between what others feel and what we feel. . . . What does the suffering of others matter to me?" "Have we ever felt a single impulse of nature which advises us to prefer others to ourselves and isn't it everybody for himself in this world?" [30] No individual is more precious than another, consequently, "the action which serves me by hurting another is perfectly indifferent to nature." [31] We may state Sade's proposition in generalized form: all men are identical in value, or in lack of it; but since each man is an egoist, he becomes most valuable, or rather uniquely valuable, in his own eyes.

If pleasurable sensation justifies any act, then that act which produces the greatest intensity of that sensation is most justifiable. It happens that human beings are so constituted that what Freud was to call their cruel, or aggressive impulses fulfills this requirement. Vice alone can make us experience "that moral and physical vibration, source of the most delicate voluptuousness." The suffering of others gives us pleasure; therefore we must prefer it.[32] The

[27] *Histoire de Juliette*, I, p. 254. Sade also occasionally makes use of the argument from relativism; e.g., *Les Infortunes*, p. 172.
[28] *Ibid.*, p. 111.
[29] *Ibid.*, IV, p. 153.
[30] *Boudoir*, pp. 93–99. This is a long defense of cruelty and crime.
[31] *Boudoir*, p. 136 ff., 48.
[32] *Sodome et Gomorrhe*, in Lely, II, p. 331; *Boudoir*, p. 138 ff. Cf. Bayle, La Mettrie, etc.

more barriers we break the greater the pleasure; it is a physical matter of shocks to the nervous system.[33] "But crime is so *délicieux,* Olympe said to me; I know nothing that excites me sexually like crime; love is so insipid by comparison." [34]

Pleasure follows a gradient corresponding to the crime. This is because "cruelty is itself one of the branches of sensitivity." [35] We can begin with "little pleasures: harshness towards the wretched, refusal to help them, the action of plunging them ourselves into misfortune." [36] Perversity is better. What delight in corrupting innocence, cries the chevalier in *La Philosophie dans le boudoir,* "to stifle in that young heart all the seeds of virtue and religion that her teachers planted in it." [37] Murder is the ultimate form of pleasure. To kill the object of voluptuousness is the absolute of possession and mastery. "As for the cruelty which leads to murder, let us dare to say boldly that it is one of the most natural feelings in man; it is one of his sweetest inclinations, one of the keenest he has received from nature. . . ." [38] But the greatest pleasure will come from torturing and killing small, helpless children.[39]

The next logical step is the systematic humiliation and degradation of the selected victims. Men, having no status outside the natural order, should not be treated any differently from the way we treat other objects, or animals, in that order.[40] The first rule of nature "is to enjoy myself, no matter at whose expense." [41] The philosophical conclusion is re-enforced by the psychological analysis. Eighteenth-century writers had expatiated on the pleasure we derive from humiliating and oppressing others, and they had also

[33] *Ibid.,* IV, pp. 246–47.

[34] *Ibid.,* IV, p. 141, also, I, pp. 230, 266. Sade does not respect timid, unreflective vices which passively follow nature's blackness, but only crimes of revolt which defy the universe and nature. "I shall imitate her but while detesting her," cries Almani on the brink of Mt. Aetna (de Beauvoir, p. 1219).

[35] *Ibid.,* I, p. 230; VI, pp. 88–89.

[36] *Ibid.,* II, p. 83.

[37] *Boudoir,* p. 15.

[38] *Ibid.,* IV, pp. 246–47.

[39] *Boudoir,* pp. 208–9.

[40] Spinoza considers animals as natural objects for our use, and also places man within the natural order, but does not draw Sade's conclusion.

[41] *Histoire de Juliette,* I, p. 135. Simone de Beauvoir writes that Sade wanted men treated as singular individuals, not as objects: "to enjoy humiliating the flesh, it was necessary to give it value." (*Op. cit.,* p. 1016.) Camus, on the other hand, affirms that to Sade men are only objects. Both statements are correct, and each expresses a partial truth. Sade does want men to be treated as things, because the pleasure comes from the fact that they are not things, but are being treated as such.

maintained that pleasure, or at least happiness, was the supreme goal of life. To say that such happiness depends on reciprocal consideration, or to say, even more absurdly, that it comes from denying and sacrificing the claims of ego is, according to Sade, to talk utter nonsense. He never tires of ridiculing the rationalists' theory that the wicked man is always secretly unhappy, the good man happy.

The filiation with the seventeenth- and eighteenth-century analysis of the lust for pride and power is evident throughout. "Ah, dear friend," says the infamous Lady Clairwil to Juliette, "if, like me . . . you had the courage to find pleasure in the contemplation of others' misfortunes, merely by the satisfying idea of not undergoing them oneself, an idea which necessarily produces a voluptuous sensation . . . you would certainly have gained a great deal for your happiness. . . ." [42] Dolmancé, in *La Philosophie dans le boudoir,* is even clearer. When a man enjoys, he says, he wants all others to serve only him, and to be their despot, for pleasure is less keen when another enjoys, too: "he would like to be the only one in the world able to feel what he is feeling; the idea of seeing another enjoy like himself brings him down to a kind of equality which dims the inexpressible attractions that despotism holds." By hurting, he becomes a tyrant; "and what a difference for *amour-propre! . . .*" [43] Noirceuil emphasizes the value of innocent victims: "innocence, virtue, candor make the object more beautiful; misfortune gives it to us, subjects it to us: all these qualities should serve then only to excite us more and we should regard them only as vehicles of our passions." [44] His theory is later illustrated by his mistreatment of his wife, by his subjecting her to foul and revolting practices, then to torture and death. In the countless examples Sade offers us, we see that the sadistic pleasure derives from a feeling of absolute power over another human being, from an affirmation of one's being, to the point of godhood, by the denial of another's.[45] Therefore the greater the abasement, the greater the joy. Extinction of the other is the logical end, followed even by his absorption in acts of cannibalism.

[42] *Ibid.,* II, p. 102.
[43] *Boudoir,* pp. 210–11.
[44] *Histoire de Juliette,* II, p. 83.
[45] Cf. Voltaire: "Tes destins sont d'un homme, et tes voeux sont d'un Dieu." (*Discours en vers sur l'homme,* II.) We have seen that the theme runs throughout the century, from Abbadie and Pope to Laclos and Rétif.

Murder, explains another character, is "the desire to exercise one's power." [46]

Nihilism is the denial (or, in satanism, the reversal) of Kant's ethical maxim, that every man must be treated as an end, never as a means. From Plato and Aristotle to Spencer and Hitler, writers have affirmed that certain men are born to serve as means for the ends of others. It is for them to act in accordance with the same principle if, in the struggle for existence, they reach the position of master. Noirceuil's mistreatment of his wife, like the fate of all of Sade's victims, is the denial of worth to human beings *qua* human beings, the denial of all rights and dignity, their reduction to the status of instruments. There is a good example of this in the early *Les Infortunes de la vertu* (1787), a volume in which Sade's thought is still disguised and attenuated, so that it is possible to quote from it in this regard. In a monastery, dissolute monks submit the girls they capture to enslavement and degradation, and finally to death. Justine is one of the captives.

> She was forced to put up with all his whims, cuffs, floggings and various enjoyments, and the slightest repugnance to any of the odious services to be performed was punished by severe tortures. She accompanied him everywhere, dressed and undressed him, waited on him hand and foot. She was always wrong, always beaten; and at the supper table her place was behind the master's chair, or at his feet, or under the table like a dog, or on her knees.[47]

The human being is denied, reduced to an object, with no more rights or status than a piece of furniture which is subject to the pleasure and power of whoever owns it.

As Sade's philosophy attains its greatest ethical amplitude, it aims directly at the destruction of the basic facts, or assumptions, of moral experience. It is not only, as Camus has put it, "a lawless universe in which the only master will be the boundless energy of desire"; it is a denial of all other-directed impulses and

[46] *Ibid.*, IV, p. 247. Simone de Beauvoir's approach to these data is through a personal analysis of Sade himself. She concludes that it is only through these acts that Sade can escape from the isolation of his self (as others do in a normal act of love), and to achieve a synthesis of body and spirit with the other. This analysis may be correct; but for Sade, as he expresses himself in his writings, it is a question of something much closer to eighteenth-century thought: the pleasure derived from satisfying the drive of affirming one's existence by denying the other's.

[47] The picture is remindful of a photograph in an exhibition concerning the Nazi concentration camps, which showed naked girls being made to run around in a circle, while the guards looked on and laughed.

of all altruistic moralities. There is no natural feeling which tells us to prefer others to ourselves. Let us take a few examples. To help the sick is unpardonable folly. "We must make every possible use of a living creature," but with the ill, let nature take its course, and certainly not risk exposing ourselves to "breathing the infected air of the sick room." [48] Ruining a friend by bearing false witness against him is upheld as a source of pleasure. So is ingratitude.[49] No promise or contract has validity beyond the time of its usefulness to us.[50] Pity, "far from being a virtue, is only a weakness, born of fear and misfortune," and the greatest enemy of his philosophy, to be crushed first and foremost.[51]

In a word, the only Natural Law is the law of nature. "Do you think this despotism which you exercise pleases the weak?" Juliette asks Saint-Fond.

It pleases everybody [he replies]; all men tend to despotism; it is the first desire nature inspires in us, quite far removed from that ridiculous law which is attributed to her, the sense of which is not to do to others what we should not like to be done to us—for fear of reprisals, they should have added, for it is quite certain that only the fear of being paid back could have attributed to nature a language so distant from its laws. I affirm then that the first and strongest inclination of man is incontestably to put his fellows in his power and to tyrannize them with all his might. The child who bites his nurse's nipple, who breaks his rattle again and again, lets us see that destruction, evil and oppression are the first inclinations that nature has engraved in our hearts . . . from which it results that the harshest, fiercest, most traitorous and wicked man will necessarily be the most happy.[52]

Nature, then, evokes no moral experiences; they are only chimerical, the result of social prejudices. "Nothing is more immoral than nature; it never imposed any limits on us, never dictated any laws. . . ." [53] Nature tells us only to do to others what we would

---

[48] *Histoire de Juliette,* III, p. 217.
[49] *Ibid.,* II, pp. 270–71; IV, pp. 141–42. "I love ingratitude . . . it awakens in the soul of the injured person little pangs of remorse that I love to arouse; we force him to be unhappy about having done something for us, and nothing is as delightful as that."
[50] *Ibid.,* I, p. 112.
[51] *Ibid.,* IV, p. 100, etc. This La Mettrie had said, too.
[52] *Ibid.,* II, pp. 149–51. The reversal of the virtue-happiness equivalence is obvious.
[53] *Ibid.,* I, pp. 71–72.

not like them to do to us.[54] There is no obligation; first, because no one does anything except for his own satisfaction; and second, because to receive a favor is a humiliation which itself is payment for the benefactor and sufficient reason for the beneficiary to hate him.[55] Justice is the supreme folly, for it bids us to attend to the interests of others, not our own. In actual practice, we find "just" whatever is in our interest, according as we are weak or strong; and this is precisely the law of nature, that is, the law of injustice. The mind recognizes no right or wrong outside of self-interest, which means that no moral values are possible. "All passions have two meanings, Juliette: one very unjust relative to the victim; the other singularly just relative to the person who expresses his passion." [56]

It is interesting to recall that Freud agrees with the contention that aggressiveness and not the Golden Rule is natural to us. The stranger not only has no claim to my love, he writes, but

> I must confess he has more claim to my hostility, even to my hatred. . . . If it will do him any good, he has no hesitation in injuring me, never even asking himself whether the amount of advantage he gains by it bears any proportion to the amount of wrong done to me. What is more, he does not even need to get an advantage from it; if he can merely get a little pleasure out of it, he thinks nothing of jeering at me, slandering me, showing his power over me; and the more secure he feels himself, or the more helpless I am, with so much more certainty can I expect this behavior from him towards me. . . . If the high-sounding ordinance had run, 'Love thy neighbor as thy neighbor loves thee,' I should not take objection to it. . . . I imagine now I hear a voice gravely adjuring me: 'Just because thy neighbor is not worthy of thy love, is probably full of enmity towards thee, thou shouldst love him as thyself!' I then perceive the case to be like that of *Credo quia absurdum.*[57]

Thus all the human work above that of nature is denied and torn away by Sade. "Since woman was formed for man's enjoyment, it is criminal for her to resist"—an idea we have noted in earlier writers. Sade's philosophical exposé is carried out into action by his

[54] *Ibid.*, I, pp. 249–50. The golden rule is the voice of the weak and is never uttered by the powerful.

[55] *Boudoir*, pp. 138–41.

[56] *Histoire de Juliette*, I, p. 186.

[57] *Civilization and its Discontents*, pp. 81–84. Cf. Sade: "Now I beg you to tell me whether I must love a being merely because he exists or resembles me and whether just because of these relations I should suddenly prefer him to myself?"

characters. Florent, in *Les Infortunes de la vertu,* whose life is saved by the wretched Justine, mocks the moral law of reciprocity by raping her in return. The punishment that follows is only for her, not for him.

In this perspective, any hierarchy of values becomes impossible. All acts are equivalent. Since the only rule of "justice" is egoism, vice, and virtue, so-called justice and injustice become purely relative, local prejudices or customs. If it were true, Montesquieu had written in the *Lettres persanes,* that justice is only a human convention, "it would be a terrible truth that we should hide from ourselves." And why, demands Sade, should we hide from ourselves such a basic truth? Is there any truth about ourselves that we should not face? It is better for men to know the truth about themselves and each other.[58]

The truth, for Sade, is that there is no such thing as Montesquieu had said, in his definition of justice: "a relationship of suitability which really exists between two things, regardless of who considers them." Justice has no real existence, because there is no such objectivity. No act has any intrinsic or objective value; the murderer trembles not because his act is evil in itself, but because it is forbidden, and he would feel the same, under like circumstances, about some minor misdeed, such as entering a forbidden room in a house.[59] The feeling of the absurd, writes Camus, "makes murder at least indifferent, and therefore permissible . . . if nothing has meaning, if we cannot affirm any value, everything is possible and nothing is important. . . . We can feed the fires of the crematories and we can devote ourselves to caring for lepers."[60] "Virtue and vice," cries Sade, "all is identical in the grave."

Sade agrees, then, though from a totally different viewpoint, with those eighteenth-century formalists of Natural Law theory who held that positive law does not create justice, right or wrong. For him, however, what matters is that the law tries to resolve the conflict between personal interest and general interest in favor of the latter. Since the sole value he admits is personal interest, the law is, *ipso facto,* unjust.[61] Consequently, no one has the

[58] *Histoire de Juliette,* IV, pp. 12–13.
[59] *Ibid.,* IV, pp. 248–49.
[60] *Op. cit.,* p. 15.
[61] *Histoire de Juliette,* pp. 178–79. Laws, he says, serve only to multiply crimes or to make them secret. In Nietzschean fashion, he blames laws and morals for holding down human greatness, will and imagination.

despotic right of submitting me to his ideas or edicts; no one has the right to blame me or to punish me for violating them. "And by what incredible injustice will you name *moral* what comes from you, *immoral* what comes from me? To whom shall we refer to know which of us is right?" [62] Sade's philosophy leads, as is obvious, to a dream of the *Uebermensch*. It leads also to the gratuitous act, to the absurd act which Lautréamont and the surrealists were to flaunt. Juliette, for instance, converted to the philosophy of nihilism, goes out into the street, to shoot the first person who happens to pass by.[63] There are innumerable other episodes, absurd in their motive and in the immolation, except that they produce perverse pleasure. "You are right," says Juliette, "the most exquisite crimes are those which have no motive: the victim must be absurdly innocent; if his faults make what we do to him legitimate, they no longer leave to our iniquity the pleasure of acting gratuitously." [64]

Conscience, for Sade, is purely a matter of conditioning. Since there are no objective moral judgments or universal values, it is possible to manipulate the nervous system so as to form a conscience that would torment us each time we did not commit what is known as a crime, if it were conducive to our satisfaction. It is possible to feel sorry that one has done too much evil, or not enough. Remorse is useless; it cannot undo what has been done, and only spoils our pleasure. Remorse comes from our illusion of free choice, and from fear.[65] Sade's ideas echo those of La Mettrie and resemble some of Diderot's writings. His theory of conditioning is basic to much of eighteenth-century moral and political thought.

The upshot of Sade's nihilism is the proclamation of anarchy. The present mixture of good and evil leads to confusion; but in a social order in which evil only is esteemed, there is a clear road. In a society of vice and evil, there will be no unhappiness due to fear, remorse, laws, and conventions.[66] Every man will do his own justice, and all, abandoned to nature, will be led better than by the stupidities of criminal law.

[62] *Ibid.*, VI, pp. 168–71.
[63] *Ibid.*, II, pp. 125–27.
[64] *Ibid.*, IV, p. 141.
[65] *Ibid.*, I, pp. 19–20, 121, 254–55; III, p. 234. Sade's characters do occasionally experience remorse for not having been sufficiently vicious. Cf. the article "Remords" in the *Encyclopédie*: "If man were naturally wicked, it seems that he would have remorse for virtue, and not for crime."
[66] *Les Infortunes de la vertu*, [62].

What need is there for man to live in society? Return him to the rustic forests in which he was born, and there let him do whatever he pleases. His crimes then, as isolated as himself, will have no disadvantage, and your restraints will be unneeded. Savage man has only two needs, fornication and food. . . . Nothing of what he does to satisfy one or the other of these needs can be wrong. Anything that gives him other passions is due only to civilization and society.[67]

This is the conclusion, implicit in Rousseau's criticisms, which he fought by seeking another way—and which Sade accepts.

One of Sade's most notorious pieces is a kind of pamphlet, introduced near the end of *La Philosophie dans le boudoir*, entitled "Frenchmen, one more effort, if you wish to be republicans." It is a plea for a "society" with complete license to commit murder or other crimes, a plea based on the execution of Louis XVI, who represented God and symbolized transcendent authority. The tenor of Sade's argument is that all men are criminals, and we should stop pretending that the good are punishing the wicked. Camus has summarized the import of this tract:

We cannot at the same time choose crime for ourselves and punishment for the others. We must open the prisons or prove our virtue, which is impossible. As soon as we accept murder, even a single murder, we must admit it universally, 'One more effort if you wish to be republicans' means: 'Accept the freedom of crime, which alone is reasonable, and enter forever into the state of insurrection as one enters into the state of grace!' [68]

Let men go to the root of their absurdity, and "a new universe" will be created. Freedom, then, expresses itself inevitably as crime, as the denial of others, and we see how sadism is in sharp opposition to the eighteenth-century current of primitivism. (Incidentally, this again shows that Rousseau was not a primitivist, for he understood exactly what Sade understood, but took the opposite path of social discipline.)

We come, finally, to Sade's treatment of sex. It is an error to consider his view of sex outside of its true place as a coherent element of his philosophy. His importance in this regard lies not only in his studies of the abnormal, although his description of six hundred kinds of perversions, in *Sodome et Gomorrhe,* was a notable feat. His attitude toward the sexual impulse and experience was an attitude toward men, society, and life. His rejec-

---

[67] *Ibid.*, VI, p. 170.
[68] *Op. cit.*, p. 59.

tion of the human being as end, rather than means, signifies his denial of man as a moral or spiritual being. This stand is crystallized in the sexual use and abuse of men and women. Sex thus becomes the focus of the Sadian revolt, doubtless because it is the primary energy and vitality of the life force and of the will to power and possession. An irrational, animal force, it has always been subjected to rational control, to social and moral discipline, in the name of social order, morality, the other world, the superiority of the spirit. It is the natural target for the rebel and for the nihilist.

Sade has no concept whatsoever of love, of the human function of Eros; and none of the mediating function of sexual experience in creating unity and exalting the human person. The three elements in his philosophy are absolute freedom of all sexual impulses, the culmination of these impulses in crime, and the justification of nihilism. This is not necessarily to be taken as a linear progression. On the contrary, it is clear, in the development of his heroes and heroines, that complete release from inhibitions may be obtained only as a result of their philosophical evolution and the destruction of inhibitory values. The function of the philosophical disquisitions in his novels is not only to justify, but to teach.

One of Sade's perceptions is that our pleasures and passions, especially those derived from crimes, are forms of sexual energy and satisfaction.

> —In that case, said Delcour, you think then that all passions can be intensified or nourished by that of lechery?
> —It [lechery] is to the passions [replies Saint-Fond] what the nervous fluid is to life: it supports them all, lends them all strength. . . .
> —Thus you imagine that we may be ambitious, cruel, avaricious, vengeful out of the same motive as lechery.
> —Yes, I am certain that all these passions [cause sexual excitement]. . . . There is not a single project of a crime, no matter what passion inspired it, which did not make the subtle fire of lechery run in my veins: lying, impiety, calumny, thievery, hardheartedness, even gluttony. . . .[69]

Theft is especially considered by Sade from the sexual viewpoint.[70] Murder, however, is the greatest stimulus, above all, as we have

[69] *Ibid.*, II, pp. 140–41.
[70] *Ibid.*, I, p. 166.

seen, when the victim is innocent and when it is preceded by torture and sexual abuse. Death, the ultimate truth and act of life, can be experienced subjectively only once. But if one can die only once, he can kill several times and thus enjoy the "ecstasy of death." One can feel like God. Some of Sade's characters can reach the acme of sexual enjoyment only at the moment of murder. They describe their experience in detail, and modern criminology and psychology have confirmed Sade's findings.[71]

In fact, the Sadian sexology has, both in its main lines and in many details, been amply substantiated by modern psychiatry. It is true that what culture has denominated perverted impulses are natural and universal.[72] The role of controls and of violation of controls is described by Freud in terms which summarize Sade's view. The control of instinctual demands, he says, reduces pain, but "brings with it an undeniable reduction in the degree of enjoyment attainable. The feeling of happiness produced in a wild, untamed craving is incomparably more intense than is the satisfying of a curbed desire. The irresistibility of perverted impulses, perhaps the charm of forbidden things generally, may in this way be explained economically."[73] Like Sade, Freud rebels against "a sexual life identical for all." He, too, condemns our society because it fails to take into account "the inborn and acquired sexual constitutions of individuals and cuts off a considerable number of them from sexual enjoyment, thus becoming a cause of grievous injustice." The only outlet not censured, says Freud, "is further circumscribed by the barriers of legitimacy and monogamy." Sexuality as a source of enjoyment for its own sake is intolerable to European civilization. However, he continues, "only the weaklings have submitted to such comprehensive interference with their sexual freedom."[74]

---

[71] *Ibid.*, II, p. 127; III, p. 15. The Middle Ages had recognized the fact that the sexual orgasm ("the little death") seems to release man from himself, and is connected psychically with annihilation.

[72] Sade defends his portrayal of aberrations. "We are still so ignorant of that science [of human nature] only because of the stupid modesty of those who have tried to write on these matters. Chained by their absurd fears, they speak only of those puerilities known to all fools, and do not dare, by placing a bold hand on the human heart, to offer to our eyes its gigantic *égarements.*" (*La Nouvelle Justine*, quoted by Lely, pp. 554–55.)

[73] *Civilization and its Discontents*, pp. 32–33.

[74] *Ibid.*, pp. 74–76. H. Marcuse writes that originally "the sex instinct had no limitations, but without the most severe restrictions, sex manifestations would counteract the sublimation on which culture depends." Perversions "express the

Sade precedes Freud in his understanding of eroticism in the child, and of the importance of the first sexual impressions in determining the nature of the libido.[75] He understood that sex enters into family relations. Freud says that the natural tendency in the child is toward incest and sadism. Sade had written, "Nature inspires in a young child the desire to sodomize his sister. . . . Horrible wickedness, conceived in the bosom of innocence and nature; he has enjoyed his sister, he wishes to hit her and to make her suffer." [76] He also anticipates the role of hormones and physiopathology.

> When anatomy is perfected, it will easily reveal the relation of a man's physical make-up to his tastes. Pedants, executioners, jailers, lawmakers, tonsured scum, what will you do when we reach that stage? What will become of your laws, your morality, your religion, your gallows, when it is shown that such and such a flow of body fluids, such a kind of fibres, such a degree of acidity of the blood or the animal spirits suffice to make a man the object of your punishments or of your rewards?[77]

Sade (as we noted in the first volume of this study) wanted to strip the idol of love of its hypocrisies, and restore it to what he thought was its true status as animal pleasure, not pure and lovely, not even merely bestial, but inherently and necessarily cruel. This was for him one way of uncovering the true man, man the animal, beneath the self-imposed halo of a being made in the image of God. He wanted to study man not only as he shows himself, but

---

rebellion against the subjugation of sexuality under the order of procreation, and against the institutions which guarantee this order. . . . The perversions seem to reject the entire enslavement of the pleasure ego by the reality ego. Claiming instinctual freedom in a world of repression, they are often characterized by a strong rejection of that feeling of guilt which accompanies sexual repression. . . . Phantasy . . . links the perversions with the image of integral freedom and gratification. In a repressive order, which enforces the equation between normal, socially useful, and good, the manifestations of pleasure for its own sake must appear as *fleurs du mal*. Against a society which employs sexuality as a means for a useful end, the perversions uphold sexuality as an end in itself." Thus they challenge the performance principle and threaten to reverse the process of civilization. "The fusion of Eros and the death instinct . . . here seems to be loosened. . . . And the loosening of this fusion makes manifest the erotic component in the death instinct and the fatal component in the sex instinct." (*Op. cit.*, pp. 49–51.)

[75] "It is in the mother's womb that the organs are made which are to incline us to such and such a whim; the first objects presented, the first words heard, finish determining the spring; tastes are formed, and nothing in the world can destroy them." (Quoted by Lely, *loc. cit.*)

[76] *Ibid.*

[77] *Ibid.*

in all the horrible forms his passions may lead him to take. If Sade is repulsive, it is because men can also be repulsive, as many in our own time know only too well.

We do not have to agree with Sade's philosophy to admire his lucidity and his courage, especially in comparison with the blind defense of sexual restrictions we find in most eighteenth-century moralizers, and their weak repetition of hollow moralities; weak not because they were necessarily wrong, but because of their ignorance of the genesis of these restrictions and of human nature. Unlike other radical moralists of the eighteenth century such as La Mettrie and Diderot, Sade did not make sexual freedom a *terminus ad quo*. He made the sex impulses basic to all human behavior, basic to its many disguised forms. He realized that the vitalities in human life are destructive—his error being to make them entirely so. He understood the intimate relation of sex to the aggressive instincts, to the power drive in all its forms. "There is no man who does not wish to be a tyrant when he is sexually excited," and this intoxication of tyranny leads to its expression as cruelty toward the *object* whom he is *using*. Simone de Beauvoir properly speaks of "inflicting sexual enjoyment" on a person, and notes that it may be "a tyrannical violence" imposed by "an executioner disguised as lover." [78] The sexual climax, Sade wrote, is "a kind of rage." Sex, then, is the blind impulse which demands the total possession of beings, even at the price of their destruction.[79] Control of the sexual instinct, Sade knew, implies control of the other, the destructive instinct. Freedom for the one means freedom also for the other. This view is again in contrast to the half-way approach of Diderot, who would free the sexual instincts, but not the aggressive. It was this total release of the aggressive instincts that Sade demanded, and that constitutes his nihilism. Thus the sexual activity of man becomes ultimately, in his mind, the nucleus of a philosophy of life.

Since the Renaissance, and especially throughout the eighteenth century some men had been knocking chinks and holes in the walls of hypocrisy and self-delusion. The Christian apologists had warned that certain ideas of the *philosophes* contained the possibility of a nihilistic outcome. Indeed, we have seen how many of the *phi-*

---

[78] "Faut-il brûler Sade?" p. 1010.
[79] The phrase is that of Albert Camus, *L'Homme révolté*, p. 56. For Sade, says Camus, nature is sex, a lawless universe of unlimited desire.

losophes themselves tried to call a halt, or were appalled by the blackness into which they had dared to peer.

The eighteenth century lay in the shadow of Pascal. His concept of original sin and of the evil in human nature, his hatred for life and for man were a constant challenge. Pascal saw man as aspiring restlessly to absolutes, to both infinities, the great and the small, and to God; but really, inasmuch as he longed to encompass both infinities, to godhood. While the eighteenth century absorbed and even developed Pascal's analysis, its moderate rationalists sought to stave off the consequences. Is it really necessary, as Pascal had asserted, to know the beginning and the end, the infinities and the absolutes? We must rather reconquer the human, as Voltaire had urged, and overcome man's alienation in the world by historical and rational action. Man's restlessness could be stilled, they thought, by the establishment of a humane morality and a just social state. But this implied the reality and possibility of justice and moral values, the traditional supports of which their own rational criticism and their analysis of human nature undermined. Knowing man's egoism and irrationality, they persuaded themselves too easily that they had found ways to channel his selfishness, and to induce or compel him to act "rationally," that is, in ways favorable to society's demands.

The seeds of eighteenth-century nihilism blossom in the incarnadine flowers of Sade's rebellion. Sade embraces the absurd, demands the absolutes, and returns to Pascal—but without God. He rejoins the Augustinian-Calvinist-Jansenist doctrine of man's total depravity, but accepts it joyously and exploits it. There is no election for salvation, but there is the election of the happy here on earth. The only grace is power. Sade, the culmination of eighteenth-century radical thought, demands that modern man say "Yes" or "No," choose between the sacred and the absurd. It was this either/or against which the *philosophes* had fought, seeking the compromise solutions of rationalism.

Sade disturbed profoundly the consciences of his contemporaries and of the later generations. They tried to bury him, like decent, respectable people, but they have had to deal with him. What he brought to light about human nature and the human condition could never be buried again. In Edmund Wilson's words, he gives expression to human malignance in a way "that makes it forever impossible not to recognize the part it plays in all fields of human activity." [80] In the Kafkaesque trial which modern man has had to undergo, he is a star witness.

It was Sade's desire to tell the whole truth about man. What he told was not the whole truth. But he did tell that part which others had suppressed or only hinted at. The hollow ambiguity of moral philosophies, even of that which urged men to "follow nature," or to combat vices as "against nature," is laid open by him. We have only to read *Le Misanthrope* to realize how much Molière, for instance—as Rousseau understood—feared the whole truth about man and justified (even as Pascal had done) the necessary vice of untruthfulness. Others before Sade—notably the Christian writers and Rousseau—had realized that "nature" is the greatest danger for social man; but none had dared to uncover the bottom-most depths.

Sade would have us plunge into the utmost sensations of living, the only value justifying action—as life is the only ultimate value. But life is absurd, and absolute freedom for the ego is the truth of the absurd. So, Sade tells us, we should live this absurd, plunge into it until the very bottom of our night, defy the sticky mass of undifferentiated beings with their refuge in myths and convention, rebel against the self-delusion of values and restraints, rebel against the meaninglessness and the nothingness of the world by treating the world on its own terms. He was the first to face the failure of rationalism—though Voltaire knew of it and suffered of it, and Diderot played with it—its failure to make of men human beings. Bayle had shown, even before, that religion, too, had not succeeded. Sade knew what modern psychiatry has rediscovered. "The repeated attempts that have been made to improve humanity," one psychiatrist has written, "in particular to make it more peaceable—have failed, because nobody has understood the full depth and vigor of the instincts of aggression in each individual. Such efforts do not seek to do more than encourage the positive, well-wishing impulses of the person while denying or suppressing his aggressive ones. And so they have been doomed to failure from the beginning." [81] Sade's contribution, in this regard, is clear: the study of the sex instinct in all its force, forms, and dimensions;

[80] "The Vogue of the Marquis de Sade," p. 175.
[81] Klein, in Lorand, *op. cit.*, p. 73.

the universality of these forms in normal people; the connection of the sexual instincts with the aggressive instincts, and their presence, as libidinal energy, in all forms of human behavior.

Sex and death are the two great preoccupations of our existence and of our unconscious mind, the stimuli to our acts and accomplishments. Before Freud, Sade already realized their hidden role in our lives and spoke of it without shame or reserve. The desire to possess and the desire to destroy are forms of the desire to affirm our being and to persist in being. And he recognized what import they may hold for our moral values. In doing this, he saw through the delusions of eighteenth-century self-interest ethics. Like Mandeville, he ironically demands a formalism of untainted virtue which Kant, writing from the same vantage point in time as Sade, was to call for in all seriousness. He derides the eighteenth-century concept of "social virtue," developed by the *philosophes*.[82] He realized that it was the Christian ethic of renunciation dressed in new garb, with the reward transplanted—even more nebulous, even more demonstrably false—to this life. The individual's interest and that of the generality (as Rousseau had explicitly stated) are always opposed; to prefer the general interest is to seek one's own unhappiness, and this is against nature, therefore wrong.[83] The theme of Sade's most important novels—the Justine-Juliette series—is, as we see, precisely the denial of the *philosophes'* greatest attempt to unite nature and reason, their rationalization that virtue inevitably produces happiness, and that the wicked man, despite his prosperity, is secretly uneasy and unhappy.[84] Sade himself took the alternative course and carried the self-interest psychology to an ultimate conclusion that destroyed the basis of ethics.

That Sade foretold the course of the crisis of Western civilization is obvious. How this work was continued by later rebels, such as Stirner and Nietzsche, has been traced by Camus in *L'Homme révolté*. Sade's impact on literature was continuous throughout the nineteenth century, as is visible in Stendhal, Baudelaire, and many others.[85] The problems raised by Sade are the core of the

[82] *Histoire de Juliette*, I, p. 190 ff.
[83] *Ibid.*
[84] *Ibid.*, I, pp. 188–89; II, p. 151, etc.
[85] Baudelaire, in his *Journaux intimes*, writes, "We must always go back to Sade, that is, to natural man, to explain evil." Stendhal paints the world as without a moral sphere, without love or friendship; he emphasizes the joy of cruelty, of mastery of others, brutal egoism, the law of the strong, who triumph ruthlessly until they are defeated by the stronger.

nineteenth century's most important novel, Dostoevski's *The Brothers Karamazov*. "Yes, yes!" cries Lise. "You have uttered my thought, they love crime, everyone loves crime, they love it always, not at some 'moments'! You know, it's as though people have made an agreement to lie about it and have lied about it ever since. They all declare they hate evil, but secretly they all love it. . . . Listen, your brother is being tried now for murdering his father, and everyone loves his having killed his father." [86]

But Sade speaks with loudest voice to our own time, and through our own time, for it is our age that has had to live the truths he revealed, to live through the night he uncovered. It is in the twentieth century that the failure of rationalism, revealed in history and in psychology, has plunged our arts and often our acts into the absurd of nihilism. The role of the artist has been perverted from that of overcoming chaos through form, to the admission of chaos by arid formalism, or even to the expression of chaos through complete subjectivity. And the role of political power has been similarly perverted. After World War I, the state of mind in Germany reflected the bitter rejection of rationalistic illusions about man and life.[87] It also accompanied the writers who, in France, were to embrace Nazism, such as Céline and Drieu La Rochelle.[88] The crimes of the Nazi torturers, like those of Sade's characters, start in an affirmation of vital force, which becomes a cold, logical affirmation of the indifference of beings and acts, and ends in violence for the sake of sensation. In both cases, we have the identical phenomena of delight in crime as the expression of a total negation, one which demands the destruction of all moral value in acts that deny the human personality and terminate in

[86] In concluding her article, S. de Beauvoir writes that Sade shouted what each of us admits to himself with shame: that others are indifferent to us. To indifference, he preferred cruelty. "If we can hope ever to overcome the separation between individuals, it is on the condition that we do not ignore it; or else the promises of happiness and justice envelope the worst menaces." (*Op. cit.*, p. 1230.)

[87] Cf. the lines from *The Threepenny Opera*: "humble virtue always wins;" "How does a man survive? He feeds on others. He likes to taste them first, and then eat them whole, if he can."

[88] The latter writes, "Man need never have left the forest. He is a degenerate, nostalgic animal. . . . The violence of men! They are born only for war, as women are made to have children. All the rest is a tardy detail of the imagination which has already shot its bolt. . . . It is necessary to have killed with one's hands in order to understand life. The only life of which men are capable, I tell you again, is the spilling of blood, murder, and coitus. All the rest is decadence." (*Le Jeune Européen*, quoted by Elliot Paul, *The Last Time I Saw Paris*.) As for Céline, his *Voyage au bout de la nuit* is a hymn to the unspeakableness of men and of life, a proclamation of utter nihilism.

the destruction of human life, the absolute destruction. The pleasure of seeing or of knowing that millions of other human beings are suffering and miserable because of what one has done, that one holds power of life and death over them, and that one can finally will their extinction, is pure sadism.[89] Similarity even in details is often striking.[90] In fact, Sade began, in his early *Les Infortunes de la vertu,* with a defense of vivisection. Man, he writes later, is "a completely material kind of plant"; and so, having no value in himself, is to be treated as an object, and particularly, "as an object of experiment." "The other is nothing to me," says the surgeon who is about to vivisect his daughter; "there isn't the slightest relation between him and me." His work abounds in descriptions of those walled-in places where the all-powerful captors, "showing to their assembled victims their absolute power-lessness and enslavement, repeat the Duke de Blangis' speech. . . . 'You are already dead to the world.' "[91] They are walled cities of power and hatred, in which an account book of crimes and massacres is kept meticulously. And the determination to extinguish whole races of people has its precise counterpart in Sade's mass murders and plans to wipe out whole cities and nations. We have, in both cases, the claim to absolute freedom of action, and "dehumanization carried out coldly by the intellect."[92]

If God is dead, the eighteenth-century Christian apologists had warned, human nature is so constituted that the cry will arise, "All is allowed." This is indeed what happened. Unable to tolerate his nothingness, rebelling against a universe without justice or moral realities, the nihilist wishes to affirm his existence by being like

[89] On the part of the victims, apathy reflects the masochistic will to surrender and slavery. Sadism omits, or rather would destroy, the feeling of guilt.

[90] Hundreds of examples in the Nazi record are available. Here, from a newspaper report, is a typical instance of a guard, "accused of confining Polish professors in cages and feeding them crumbs, like chickens. When this sport paled, the professors were dispatched with lethal injections." The same person was "accused of ordering lashings, delivered to the accompaniment of a gypsy band; of burying victims alive, and kicking them back into the coffin when they tried to sit up; of leaving prisoners hanging by their hands until they died; of forcing defiant priests to march past his cap for three days barefooted, so that they might learn to salute the Nazi authority; etc." Such acts of sadistic individuals are not the main fact, however. The essential point is, of course, the conscious adoption by the government of a philosophy of nihilism and its consistent application to masses of people.

[91] *Ibid.,* p. 67. This is precisely what new arrivals at the concentration camps were told.

[92] Camus, *op. cit.,* pp. 61–62. Cf. the statement by Adolf Eichmann: "I will leap into my grave laughing because the feeling that I have five million human beings on my conscience is for me a source of extraordinary satisfaction."

God; and a finite creature can express the *absolute* of godhood only by crime and destruction. To be like God is to say "all is allowed" and to refuse any law but one's own. Absolute power, or the release from limit, moral and physical, can fulfill itself only by control of others' lives and absolute destruction. By reducing all others to nothing, the Unique one not only, as Maurice Blanchot says, proves the equal nullity of all beings, but affirms his own godhood, since before God, all else is as nothing. God is independent, because he has no responsibility to others. And yet, this independence can never be achieved by men, because the strong always needs others to affirm his strength; he needs his victims, and so is dependent on them.

The characteristic of Sade's revolt was not—overtly—hatred of death and injustice, as was that of Ivan Karamazov. It was directed against culture, in the name of God's injustice and nature's; not against the Creation, but against man's creation. It was, perhaps even more, a revolt against men—against their self-delusions, their refusal to recognize the universe for what it is, their pretension of erecting a moral life justified by God and the world. It was the decision to accept injustice and death, and to live them. That is why the Sadian revolt is the greatest danger humanity must face. It involves the total destruction of culture, that is, of everything specifically human, and of life itself. The history of mankind may perhaps be understood as a long struggle against death: on the animal level, by procreation; on the individual level, by activity directed toward food, shelter, and health; on the cultural level, by the invention of religious myths; on the intellectual level, by experimental medicine and psychoanalysis. This is, in essence, a struggle against nature, to escape from nature.

The character of eighteenth-century ethical thought is that of the conflict between two norms, nature and reason, or nature and culture. To accept the sacred was to subordinate or deny nature. The *philosophes*, in the main, fought hard to reconcile the two, through theories of Natural Law and by rational constructions. The nihilist, on the other hand, and Sade in particular, rejected reason and culture in favor of nature. The counsel of unselfishness, or of enlightened self-interest, is not a first impulse of nature, Sade declares, but comes from reason and culture. Rational and cultural values are denied all validity: "The first impulse of nature is always right." How shocked Rousseau would have been, for he, too, had written exactly those words! There is only the individual, and the human work of constructing a transcendent social organism is an intolerable limit on what he considered "the activity of the incoercible human element." [93] Civilization, however, in the words of Justice Roscoe Pound, "involves the subjection of force to reason, and the agent of that subjection is law." Freud tells us that civilization requires the sacifice of sexuality and aggressiveness.[94] It requires and it signifies overcoming the death instinct. He defines the inner meaning of sadism as a mixture of that instinct and the sexual impulse. This he calls "the most powerful obstacle to culture." [95]

The philosophy of nihilism is a nonviable one, and it annuls itself. Although Sade showed courage in uncovering truths about human nature, the philosophical system he draws from those truths is false and untenable, as well as dangerous to human life. It is riddled by a fatal inner contradiction. To be consistent in the absurd, one should not try to justify his acts. True nihilism, if it were possible, would require no valuation of right and wrong; but even the nihilist (precisely as Diderot had said) must argue that nihilism is "right." Sade is constantly "justifying." He justifies a wife's deceiving her husband. He insists on the "right" of the strong to disobey laws and terms laws an "injustice." The latter statement is doubly contradictory: it not only contradicts its sup-

[93] M. Heine, quoted by Lely, II, p. 545. Sade fought for the sacredness of individual singularity; but society requires its limitations by an agreed common measure. Mme de Beauvoir points out the frustration of the eighteenth-century hope of "reconciling individuals within their immanence," a hope belied by the conformity inflicted by the Reign of Terror. On the other hand, she warns, if we recognize only the transcendence which unites each to his fellows, then individuals are sacrificed to new idols, today to tomorrow, individual freedom to collective accomplishments. "Prison, the guillotine will be the logical consequences of his renunciation. Hypocritical fraternity ends up in crimes in which virtue recognizes his abstract face." (*Op. cit.*, p. 1229.)

[94] *Op. cit.*, pp. 73, 91. "Since man has not an unlimited amount of mental energy at his disposal, he must accomplish his tasks by distributing his libido to the best advantage. What he employs for cultural purposes he withdraws to a great extent from women and his sexual life. . . ." Sade, in his demand for unlimited eroticism and instinctual expression, is the enemy of civilization.

[95] *Ibid.*, p. 98. The relation of the death instinct to culture is further analyzed in the following lines: "In sadism, where it bends the erotic aim to its own will and yet at the same time gratifies the sexual craving completely, we can obtain the clearest insight into its nature and its relation to Eros. But even where it shows itself without any sexual purpose, even in the blindest frenzy of destructiveness, one cannot ignore the fact that satisfaction of it is accompanied by an extraordinarily intense narcissistic enjoyment, due to the fulfilment it brings to the ego of its oldest omnipotence-wishes. The instinct of destruction, when tempered and harnessed (as it were, inhibited in its aim) and directed towards objects, is compelled to provide the ego with satisfaction of its needs and with power over nature."

posed nihilism, but is inconsistent in its failure to recognize (as La Mettrie had) the strength and tyranny of *society* as a "right" as valid as the strength and tyranny of the individual. What is natural and instinctual is characterized as "legitimate," "good," "sacred." Sade's nihilism is a principle, a belief in what is right. A consistent nihilist must say that it is indifferent whether one is a nihilist or not, since there is no way to judge his acts or another's. He cannot say nihilism is "true," or that if it is, its truth is a reason to adopt it. This fundamental contradiction is again obvious when Sade declares that the greatest pleasure (*jouissance*) comes from the greatest crimes. He also says that there are no crimes.[96] Now in this form the contradiction is particularly significant. It follows that if all acts, being indifferent, were allowed, if man lost his sense of crime, there would be no more *jouissance!* The fact that *jouissance* comes from crime is indeed the very proof that right exists, since crime is the violation of right. Furthermore, the consistent believer in the absurd performs tortures and murders, not primarily for pleasure, but only to express absurdity; although, in truth, even in the pure *acte gratuit* there is an implicit assertion of value against the nullity of the universe.

Nihilism, then, is untenable, since value judgments cannot be avoided. For Sade, in fact, value is egoistic pleasure, a solid, irrefutable value. But by setting up this value, he at once opens the door to going beyond the absurd. We see this in his frequent statements that only the types of pleasure he enjoys (sex and destruction) are real, or that they are *better* than other types of pleasure. He is thereby introducing a principle of valuation which implies the possibility of other values, and of other value systems. It is amusing that in his own life Sade frequently complained about his son, whom he called a scoundrel, an ingrate, "ce coquin qui se dit mon fils." [97] And we recall that the members of the Society of the Friends of Crime *pledge* not to murder each other.

A second inconsistency which occurs time and again in Sade's

[96] "Crimes are impossible to man . . . blind instruments of [nature's] inspiration, has she not told us to embrace the universe? The only crime would be to resist." (*Boudoir*, p. 232.)

[97] In a letter to his mistress's son, Sade affirms the opposite of his philosophy. Speaking of the boy's mother, he writes: "Nothing takes [a mother's] place. . . . We no longer find those disinterested attentions of a mother, that precious *sensibilité* which no self-interest touches; in a word, my dear friend, the hands of nature are no longer there." (Lely, II, p. 510.) This statement may be considered hypocritical. Sade's biographer, however, should not attempt to excuse him when he lies. In Sade's philosophy, this is not necessary, since there is no reason not to lie and be hypocritical.

books lies in the fact that on the one hand he deifies nature and justifies all impulses in her name, and on the other hand, he declares that man is not bound by nature, but may defy her as he wishes. Thus fornication is justified by nature, but we may and should freely defeat nature's intent of procreation. Here the inconsistency is superficial, since Sade would argue that pleasurable sensation is nature's basic law, and having children would interfere with it. Elsewhere the statement is broader.

> No being on earth has been formed on purpose by nature . . . in a world constructed like ours, there had to be creatures like the ones we see in it; just as there are doubtless very different ones on another globe, in that ant-hill of globes with which space is filled. But those creatures are neither good nor bad, nor beautiful, nor precious, nor created; they are the foam [the word is taken from La Mettrie], the result of the blind laws of nature. . . . [This creature] can be or not be, without the element from which it emanates suffering from it; it owes nothing to that element, and that element owes it nothing. . . . The relations of man to nature, or of nature to man, are then nil; nature cannot chain man by any law; man does not depend on nature in any way, they owe nothing to each other, and can neither offend each other nor serve each other. Once he is launched, man is free from nature. . . .[98]

When it comes to perversions, Sade must inevitably go further. "To recapture nature," he declares, "it is often necessary to outrage her." [99] Perversion, which was originally advocated as a revolt in the name of nature against cultural limitations, now becomes a revolt against nature itself. In fact, says Juliette, "once you are accustomed to defying nature's laws on one point, there is pleasure only in transgressing them all." [100] Thus he would have men completely within nature and determined by nature, yet free to violate and defy nature—though everything is natural! Sade eludes the inconsistency by arguing that the more we upset nature's orders, the better we are following them.[101] In other words, nature's law sanctions all our impulses, including those that tell us to violate her law, and even to destroy her. She directs man, by his passions, to destroy, and he turns this passion against nature herself.

[98] *Histoire de Juliette,* IV, pp. 230–31.
[99] *Ibid.,* II, p. 17.
[100] *Ibid.,* II, p. 143.
[101] *Ibid.,* III, p. 104.

While it may be argued that this is a logically defensible proposition, it is nonetheless again a self-defeating one. For how, then, shall we condemn positive laws, morality, custom, on the ground that *they* violate the law of nature?

Still a third inconsistency is Sade's view on lack of human communication. "All creatures are born isolated and without any need of each other." But if one can confirm his being and enjoy only by making victims of others, if—to follow Simone de Beauvoir's modern analysis—one can satisfy the need to overcome isolation only by possession of the other—then obviously men do need each other and do enjoy enterprises in common. In fact, virtue, too, becomes necessary to sadism, on the same grounds. "Your gentle virtue, Justine, is essential to us." This is, of course, a fundamental fact of human psychology.[102]

Sadism is self-defeating not only because of its logical weaknesses. It leads to an exhaustion of sensation and of pleasure.

> The habit of crossing all bounds makes them [*les scélérats*] soon find quite simple what had at first seemed revolting to them; and, from one extravagance to another, they reach monstrosities the execution of which still leaves them short, for they would need real crimes to have a real thrill, and unfortunately, there is no real crime. Thus, always falling short of their desires, it is no longer they who are lacking to horrors, it is horrors which are lacking to them.[103]

Sadism is the perfect example of what Hans Morgenthau has called "this limitless and ever unstilled desire which comes to rest only with the exhaustion of its possible objects." The *libido dominandi* "is of the same kind as the mystical desire for union with the universe, the love of Don Juan, Faust's thirst for knowledge. These four attempts at pushing the individual beyond his natural limit toward a transcendent goal, this resting point is reached only in the imagination but never in reality."[104]

The moment of ecstasy destroys the object that provides it. Thus we have what Camus calls "an impossible quest to escape

---

[102] The Sadian terminus is implicit in Rousseau's statement that as soon as man has artificial needs, he requires other men to satisfy them; "and when finally his desires embrace all of nature, the concourse of all mankind is scarcely enough to sate them." (Vaughan, *op. cit.*, I, p. 447.) Mme de Beauvoir considers that for Sade "no common interest [or enterprise] is possible, since there is only the reality of the self-enclosed subject" (1216), but expresses a contrary view ten pages later.

[103] *Ibid.*, I, p. 120.

[104] *Scientific Man and Power Politics*, p. 13.

despair, which ends in despair." We have an enslavement to en-slavement.

The holocaust and the apocalypse—these are the termini of nihilism. In his ever-mounting frustration and furious crises of excitement, the Sadian nihilist desires finally to exterminate the human race and to pulverize the universe itself. Murder, as Sade has made clear, allows nature to create new life. What we must murder is creation itself. "It is she [Nature] that I desire to out-rage, I should like to spoil her plans, to block her advance, to halt the course of the stars, to throw down the globes that float in space. . . ." [105] Since this is an impossible desire, since man cannot be God, the nihilist's revolt is doomed to frustration, as it sinks down into the bog of base and aimless savagery. It is obvious how far Sade has gone beyond eighteenth-century naturalism, his start-ing point.

To the extent in which Sade has revealed the truth about man, he is the answer to all those in the eighteenth century who praised "natural man" and said that society has corrupted him by creating an artificial man to war with him. Sade's man, as we now know, is indeed what men would be *naturally,* if "artificial" pressures were not exerted to restrain them, that is, if men could live out-side of a culture. The essential weakness in Sade's nihilism is, as Rousseau understood, that the so-called "artificial" is *natural* to men living in any possible social community. In carrying to its final limit the eighteenth-century reduction of man to the natural, Sade admitted only those aspects of human nature which were precisely the opposite of the ones admitted by optimists like Shaftesbury—those aspects which we have in common with ani-mals. His assumption is that what is most vile is most sincere and natural. He denies that pity, sympathy, justice, the surpassing of self, and the demand for limit are natural, whereas in fact they constitute a large part of the initial adjective in the phrase, "hu-

---

[105] *Justine,* IV, pp. 40–41; also *ibid.,* I, p. 112. Also, "To attack the sun, deprive the universe of it or use it to burn up the world, those would be crimes! . . . the impossibility of outraging nature is, in my opinion, man's greatest torture." (Quoted by de Beauvoir, pp. 1032, 1222.) If this dream is satisfying, comments Mme de Beauvoir, "it is because the criminal projects into it his own annihilation together with that of the universe; if he survived, he would be frustrated." Geoffrey Gorer has pointed out still another paradox. If nature's aim is destruction, and no act of destruction can irritate or insult her, the supreme insult (the one from which the sadist should gain the greatest pleasure of transgression) would be the justice of virtue.

man nature." The only *human* dimension he allows is the unique capacity for evil. Perhaps charity and helping the weak are indeed, as Sade says, a crime against nature; but they are not crimes against humanity! This again indicates the lack of identity, the discrepancy between the "natural" and the "human." There is ample reason to believe that men live not only for desire, but also for creation and for love, to do and to give. The dehumanization of sex by the denial of its psychic values cannot be substantiated.[106] Although sadism attempts to make man wholly natural, actually, in its inevitable cruelty and frustration, it separates man from animals and takes him out of the level of the strictly biological. "The truly natural man," writes Robert E. Fitch, "is one who strives for an unnatural end which is beyond, not below the natural." [107]

This is certainly as profound a truth about *homo duplex* as that which Sade discovered. Man, insofar as he is an organism, is superior to many things in nature, but does not transcend them. He is superior to *all* other known things, in his attainment of an intellectual level of abstraction, a psychological level of self-consciousness, a moral level of ethical judgment. And in these attainments he does truly transcend nature. Modern man, having passed the stage of myth, is deprived of external guidance and support, and must shift for himself. If he were to be left only to the nature he does not transcend, there would be no hope. Sadism, Nazism, or the surrender to inert despair (as in Samuel Beckett), would be his inevitable lot. But because of the other part, the human part of his nature, he can project an image of himself as he would like to be, and casting his net around the stars, pull himself up to them.

[106] See Freud, *op. cit.*, pp. 71–72.
[107] *The Decline and Fall of Sex.*

Seven

ETHICS AND POLITICS

AT THE OUTSET of this study, we emphasized the fact that the pivotal, ever-compelling concern of eighteenth-century thinkers was with the problem of man—his nature and destiny, his life, both individual and social. The problem of man is essentially ethical. It is also metaphysical, to be sure, and political. But metaphysics and politics may be considered as extensions or phases of ethics, bearing, in the one case, on its presuppositions, and in the other, on its implementation. Having begun, in the first volume of this study, with the metaphysical problems which were closely related to ethics, it behooves us to close our investigation with a view of the political implications. We shall not attempt to give a full account of political programs and systems; this, of course, would be quite another study. Our aim is more limited: to indicate, in rather summary fashion, the determining effect of ethical views upon political. If this can be done, we shall have fulfilled the major purpose of our entire inquiry: to show the interrelation and interdependency of the metaphysical, psychological, moral and political perspectives and problems of the eighteenth century. We may thus be enabled to perceive its organic wholeness, at least in its central and most enduringly significant aspects.

Such a relationship, which to some degree obtains among all political theorists, was particularly strong in the eighteenth century. The basic ethical problem was posed in terms of private interest and general interest, of natural impulse and cultural imposition, and of the necessity to reconcile the contraries.[1] Political the-

---

[1] It was the general view that most passions further particular ends rather than the general welfare.

430

orists never failed to speculate on the qualities of human nature and of human interrelations, often proceeding in the sequel to a search for natural laws of political forms and functions.[2] But while some envisaged harmony as ensuing from such natural factors, others equated the empirical with disorder and demanded the creation of an artificial and enforced harmony.[3] These tendencies correspond to the two parallel currents we have examined: the transformation of Natural Law into a theory of unalienable rights, and the drift to utilitarian social control, displacing the locus of right from individuals to the community. There were many who, in fact, held government to be the agent of morality—either to remove evil, as Hume thought, or to institute positive good, as French writers were inclined to insist. (The converse of this question we have already examined: whether moral values depend on or are independent of the laws and sanctions of government.) Unlike our own age, the eighteenth century had little awareness of the autonomous realities and dynamisms of power, or of the fundamental incompatibilities which, to some degree at least, set ethics and politics apart from each other, if not against each other. And yet its own proposed use of political power to *make* men moral itself betrays the ambiguity of any political "morality," which must, in Niebuhr's words, "deflect, beguile and use self-interest for the harmony of the whole." [4]

At the same time, as Basil Willey has pointed out, it is the French, not the English writers of the eighteenth century who were revolutionaries, dreaming of "Nature" as a slogan, or as a program that would overthrow altars and even tyrannies.[5] Morelly and Rousseau are two instances, among others, which we shall

[2] E.g., Chastellux: "andrology, or the science of man in general, would serve as the basis of physical and moral medicine, and from this science politics would be born." (*De la Félicité publique*, I, p. 135.) Le Trosne, a Physiocrat, declares that "there exists a natural, immutable and essential order, instituted by God, to govern civil societies in the most advantageous manner for sovereign and subjects," having a physical basis and the necessary cause-effect relation which obtains with laws of the physical order. "Only unhappiness can result from its violation." (*Op. cit.,* p. 302.) Linguet was typical in his separation of natural laws of legislation and government from laws which everywhere have sprung up arbitrarily, and in demanding the reform of the latter. (*Théorie des lois civiles*, Londres, 1767, pp. 34–50.)

[3] Shaftesbury, to cite a very early example of the kind of thinking which later developed into such theories, said consider the whole, and the individual will be cared for; to which Mandeville replied, consider the individual and the whole will look after itself. (See *Fable of the Bees*, ed. Kaye, p. lxxii.)

[4] *Children of Light*, p. 73.

[5] *Op. cit.*, pp. 155–56.

later consider—though the applicability of the word "Nature" is highly dubious. Theirs was an approach which made the ethical and the political well-nigh inseparable. An essential part of it, or consequence of it, was the abstract character of their thinking. They were willing to make short shrift of history (both its concrete legacies and its lessons), to write it off as an error or deviation from rational norms, and were inclined to remake society *de novo*—though this is not true of Rousseau's proposals for Poland. Montesquieu and Burke were the two great opponents of this view, and so the wrath of all its proponents fell upon their heads. For Montesquieu and Burke, some change is necessary—in part, at least, to return an aberrant system to its proper modes of functioning, even as Voltaire's God maintained an eternally established cosmic order by occasional correction of irregularities. But for them change is, in general, to be resisted, especially when proposed on abstract grounds, and is at all events to be held within the framework of the established system. In fact, however, new ideas were being generated in response to a changing world (itself changed because of new ideas about man and the world, some of which led to new technology and new economic establishments). The new ideas demanded new institutions. The structural complex was changing, but not fast enough or radically enough, as the inherited institutions fought for their survival, not realizing that they were fighting against historical process itself, a fight that must always fail.

If one part of political theory was derived from a concept of laws as regulating the life of institutions in their internal functioning and in their relations with nature (climate, soil, etc.), another part concerned their relations with human nature. It is this aspect which we propose to treat here. While anti-positivistic and anti-historical thinkers (who were opposed, for instance, to Montesquieu) rejected conclusions which impeded the remaking of society *de novo*, there was no gainsaying the connection between political theory and the theory of human nature. With the exception of Rousseau, who emancipated his political thinking from the belief that nature is the norm, it was claimed that we should not violate human nature, but only direct it. We have seen that the analysis of the laws of natural behavior eventuated, as a result of the sensationist pleasure-pain psychology, in a reduction to egoistic motivation—a conclusion which did not exclude varying degrees of sympathy, or of joy found in virtue, in service, or in patriotism. But the distinguishing feature of human beings and societies was the one which Hobbes had pointed out in a passage we quoted much earlier. Among bees and ants, "the common good differeth not from the private." [6] Hobbes assumed, doubtless incorrectly, that such animals were inclined to their private good, and that the common good ensued from it naturally, because of "natural consent" (contrasted with conventional). But, contrary to Hobbes, Mandeville and the Physiocrats took a similar position in regard to human affairs. It was roughly the view of others, too, whom we may describe as liberals, that a minimum of regulation of the pluralism of personal interests would best serve the general welfare. A more or less "natural" reconciliation was thus envisaged. A second group of political writers were far more impressed by the opposition of natural and cultural interest. Their program verged toward a collectivist or totalitarian way, toward a monism which contemplated transforming personal interest so that it coincided with a predetermined public interest.[7] A third, smaller

[6] *Leviathan*, II, chap. 17.

[7] "In fact, the problem of individual happiness and that of collective happiness never coincide; the first depends on a personal choice, the second is the result of a political order." (R. Mauzi, *op. cit.,* p. 14.) "Totalitarian democracy," writes J. L. Talmon, "far from being a phenomenon of recent growth, and outside the Western tradition, has its roots in the common stock of eighteenth-century ideas." It became an identifiable trend during the French Revolution. "The ethical ideal of the rights of man acquired the character of an egalitarian social ideal. . . . Nothing was left to stand between man and the State." (*The Rise of Totalitarian Democracy,* p. 249–50.)
I am pleased to acknowledge my debt to Prof. Talmon's epoch-making book, although my own investigation which proceeds along rather different lines was completed before I read his work. I believe that Talmon oversimplifies in some cases and also errs in a few interpretations. Nor does he attempt to treat the liberal side, and so to give a balanced picture—that is not his purpose. My analysis does not place the origin of totalitarian thinking in "a too perfectionist attitude" toward liberal individualism (p. 249) or in a desire to liberate man "from all dependence," but relates it to the basic ethical problems and attitudes of the age. I do not blame the *philosophes'* belief in a human nature (p. 29), but rather their simplification of human nature, the separating of it from the contingent and the historical, their inability to realize its stubbornness in its resistance to "molding," and consequently the degree of coercion and conditioning that would be necessary for their purposes. I do not believe—as it will become clear—that liberalism hopes that a state of ideal harmony will eventually be attained (p. 2). It seems to me that there are a number of inaccuracies in Talmon's sharp separation between totalitarianism of the Left and of the Right—in general, but especially as they pertain to the eighteenth century. (One point among others: "The Left proclaims the essential goodness and perfectibility of human nature." See pp. 5–8, 264.) Finally,

group rejected the dominion or transcendence of the collectivity and thought that society should sanction, more or less completely, the instinctual drives of personal interest.

Returning once more to our separation of the Montesquieu-Burke type of outlook from that of Morelly-Rousseau, we find in the latter a show of restoring the "natural" law or pattern of things, which, in reality, is a cover for an anti-natural position. The former view, on the other hand, protests against "warping by the force of positive institutions, the order of society, according to some preconceived idea of expediency, without trusting sufficiently to those principles of the human constitution, which, wherever they are allowed free scope, not only conduct mankind to happiness, but lay the foundation of a progressive improvement in their condition and in their character." [8] Both groups agreed that the accidental developments of a particular cultural history, its institutions and traditions, are not necessarily in conformity with the "natural laws." But the difference in the attitude toward the proper prerogatives of existing institutions, and in the methods for correcting both their deviations and the aberrant behavior of individuals is one of total opposition. For the "liberals," for instance, the very fact that institutions may deviate from conceived norms is a reason for not using them to mold individuals with monistic regimentation. The others, however, trust the intellect to discover natural political laws, to remake institutions in their image, and in some cases, to remake individuals by the mechanical force of institutions. The application of the term "liberal" to Montesquieu and Burke is rather unusual, and requires justification. The word is, of course, a matter of definition and perspective. From the viewpoint of resistance to change, they are properly labeled "conservatives," in opposition to "liberals." From a deeper perspective, however, that of the pluralistic, libertarian type of society they favored, they are properly called liberals, in opposition to monistic collectivists or totalitarians. It is this second point of view which has the greater significance, and which is of concern to the subject of this chapter. Burke, in our own time, has been

---

Talmon seems unaware of the *other* challenge to humanism and liberalism—the challenge of nihilism.

[8] Dugald Stewart, quoted by R. V. Sampson, *op. cit.*, p. 73. This attitude may also be attributed to those inclined toward anarchism.

claimed by the conservatives. But his historical role in the eighteenth century was most significantly (though not exclusively) that of a liberal, opposing inflexible absolutes, both in theory and in practice.[9]

One notion, however, was accepted without challenge on all sides: the political institutions of a society (even by their abstention from positive action) have a great power of determination over the moral life, as well as the physical life, of individuals, and so over their happiness. Endowed with this power, they have a concomitant responsibility. We may cite a few typical examples of the endless restatement of this belief.

One responsibility was for the welfare of the citizens. D'Alembert, in his divisions of ethics, lists first, what men owe to each other, and second, "the ethics of legislators," or what society owes to its members.[10] This idea, that government exists for the welfare of the governed, was a movement of protest against the Ancien Régime, one which had swelled continuously from the time of Fénelon and Boulainvilliers and was paralleled by developments in politics and political theory in seventeenth-century England.

A second responsibility was for the morals of the citizens, in order to ensure their proper contribution to the national welfare. "If it be true," says Vauvenargues, "that vice cannot be annihilated, the science of those who govern is to make it work toward the public good." [11] Charles Leroy belittles moralizing and moral theory and especially the foolish preaching of disinterestedness; it is only "by legislation that practical morality can be perfected . . . private interest reconciled with the general." If you do this, "you will make virtue commonplace, and you will ensure public happiness; reform the laws, and morals will reform themselves; men will become virtuous when it will be shameful not to be . . . the great art of legislation consists in placing men's self-interest in the observation of laws. . . . Morals are therefore tightly linked to the science of laws." [12] All the elements are here,

---

[9] It should also be noted that the doctrine of unalienable rights is no more inherently "liberal" (in the usual use of that word) than it is "conservative"; it has been used by men of both persuasions.

[10] *Elémens de philosophie*, p. 211.

[11] *Op. cit.*, III, p. 33 (Max. 157).

[12] *Examen critique du livre intitulé "De l'Esprit,"* Londres, 1760, pp. 48-50.

in Leroy's statement: self-interest motivation, reliance on feelings of "pride," the admixture (as in Montesquieu) of moral and political connotations in the word "virtue," unlimited faith in the powers of legislation. Just as the word "virtue" assumes a public character, so does the word "happiness." Philippe Fermin, a supporter of the *status quo* in all things, expressed his agreement in these words: "Only the establishment of laws, then, can oblige subjects to act according to their true interests, and to enter into the surest and best path to lead them to their destination, which is happiness." [13] Here the note of coercion is more marked.

It is clear that the two responsibilities often coalesce. Chastellux, one of the most optimistic writers of the time, and one particularly concerned with "public happiness," wrote to refute the pessimists who asked, "What will come out of it all? Won't men always be the same?" We can be quite sure, he affirms, "that legislation, morals and habits have such an empire over the passions that they can bring infinite differences to the social state; and as these differences can only be between two principal points, good and evil, it is sure that legislation and morals can make men more or less happy." [14] Chastellux gives credit to Montesquieu and Helvétius for having preceded him.

The jurist, Barbeu du Bourg, makes this confident generalization: "Morals are generally pure under a government which takes great care to inculcate scorn and horror for vice, and to inspire love of order and decency, and to give the first example." [15] In Samuel Formey, we again see the transfer of the goal of individual happiness to a public or social status. Just as "a man tends towards his happiness in proportion as he tries to contribute to that of others," so will a society increase its happiness (which is its aim) "in proportion to its contribution to the happiness of the human species." [16] And Marmontel, near the close of the century: "Good laws are those which make the greatest possible number happy, those which reconcile the common good of all and the good of each. The laws must be changed." [17]

In statements such as these, we can see how most men of the

---

[13] *Dissertation sur la question, S'il est permis d'avoir . . . des esclaves,* Maestricht, 1770, p. 82.
[14] *De la Félicité publique,* pp. 209–10.
[15] *Op. cit.,* p. 52.
[16] *Le Bonheur,* p. 140.
[17] *Oeuvres posthumes,* XI, pp. 113–14.

eighteenth century looked upon politics and ethics as inseparable. It is sometimes difficult to tell which is handmaiden to the other. For the one as for the other, happiness, virtue, and the reconciliation of private and public interest are the constant goals. For both, the great body of law is written in the large letters of human nature. As James Madison put it, "But what is government itself but the greatest of all reflections on human nature?" [18] Or, as Rousseau states it in the fourth book of *Emile,* "Those who want to treat politics and morals separately will never understand anything about either one." [19]

From these propositions, there were few total dissenters. Duclos argued that a man might observe all the laws and be a dishonest man; far more valuable is the free and voluntary observance of customary feelings and procedures "which make up the safety or the sweetness of civil society." [20] With this Romilly agreed. Indeed he went one step further and suggested that to make laws the guardian of moral virtue was to reverse the cart and the horse. "Far from laws sufficing without morals and virtue, it is from these, on the contrary, that they draw their force." A virtuous people could more easily exist without laws than a people without morals and with admirable laws. "When one is just only with laws, one is not just even with them." [21]

These protests were exceptional. But there were, as we have said, considerable differences of opinion in regard to the proper use, and the proper extent of the use of legislative and governmental power. In the general evolution of ideas, the political parallels the ethical. As individualistic hedonism gives way to

[18] *The Federalist,* No. 51.

[19] "The fact that eighteenth-century thinkers were ardent prophets of liberty and the rights of man is so much taken for granted that it scarcely needs to be mentioned. But what must be emphasized is the intense preoccupation of the eighteenth century with the idea of virtue, which was nothing if not conformity to the hoped-for pattern of social harmony. They refused to envisage the conflict between liberty and virtue as inevitable. . . . When the eighteenth-century secular religion came face to face with this conflict, the result was the great schism. Liberal democracy flinched from the spectre of force, and fell back upon the trial-and-error philosophy. Totalitarian Messianism hardened into an exclusive doctrine represented by a vanguard of the enlightened, who justified themselves in the use of coercion against those who refused to be free and virtuous." (Talmon, *op. cit.,* pp. 4–5.) In fact, it is not too much to say—at least in regard to this important group—that the Age of Enlightenment was one in which a few enlightened men contemplated forcing all others to be "enlightened."

[20] And even this is not enough, if pride, fear or self-interest, and not conscience, is the motive. (*Op. cit.,* pp. 62–70.)

[21] In Sabatier de Castres, *Dictionnaire,* II, pp. 504–5.

social utilitarianism, so, in politics, do partial, empirical, and pragmatic solutions give ground to absolutist rational doctrines of the supremacy of the social whole. To be sure, the theory (which we examined in the third chapter) that moral judgments are the creatures of instilled social experience, or of custom and will, does not lead inherently to a totalitarian political outlook any more than it does to a liberal one. But, as we are about to see, it is peculiarly congenial, and quite necessary, to such a society. Moreover, authoritarian training in moral theory and authoritarian training in political ideology are scarcely separable.[21a]

The group we have denominated "liberals" insisted as much as any other on the importance of government's role, and especially on the need for "good government." Nevertheless, they held that the role should be a restricted one. This was necessary in order to prevent it from hindering the natural rights of individuals in society beyond the need to protect those same rights.[21b] In this basic respect, there is a kinship between these French groups and the Anglo-Saxons, Locke, Burke, and Jefferson, however much they may have differed in other matters, or however much they differed among themselves. In the liberal view, the welfare of the State and of the individual are identical; but the emphasis in the meaning of the word lies in that of individuals with their inherent differences. Such an attitude has ethical implications. It assumes the dignity and the supreme worth of the individual. It may imply a confidence in the goodness of human nature. In the eighteenth century, however, this was only exceptionally the case—contrary to the traditional opinion. Neither in their analysis of human nature (as we saw earlier) nor in their politics, did these thinkers bank on the goodness of human nature. They counted rather on the admixture of rational prudence with self-interest, or on a harmony that would arise by virtue of natural law from the cancellation, checks, and balances, or counterpoise of conflicting

---

[21a] R. Mauzi writes, concerning eighteenth-century ethics: "The purpose of morals is to fashion the individual in such a way that while believing he is following his own nature only, he unfailingly directs himself toward the happiness which nature and philosophy have prepared for him. . . . Happiness therefore depends on a secret shaping of character, molded by philosophy. . . ." (*Op. cit.*, p. 258.)

[21b] It should be clear by now that transpositions of vocabulary, though entirely justifiable by the fundamental drift, are only approximate. Both partisans of "big government" and of "little government" united diverse elements. The former wished to control abuses of aggressive individuals or groups, but also to control character and thought. The latter supported pluralism, but also demanded almost unrestricted property rights.

interests; or yet on the ability of a government, which followed human nature and natural laws, to support and favor such a resolution.[22] In no instance is there a political theory among this group based on the belief that moral altruism or love of the general good is stronger than egoism and self-interest. But whereas our second group of writers thought that the great task of government was to make self-interest identical with a conceived general welfare, and to "remake" men if necessary, the liberals conceived of the general welfare as arising out of the very pursuit of self-interest, in a competitive society restricted by certain basic rules.

The role of government remains nevertheless great and crucial. "Nature," wrote Turgot, "has given all men the right to be happy." [23] But the cruelties of competition, he adds, make it necessary for a superior power, which embraces in its view the happiness of all, to conciliate and modify the conflict. Like an adroit pilot sailing against the wind, passions and even vices can be channeled in the direction of public welfare. But for Turgot this is really a matter of social, political, and economic arrangements, rather than of direct pressure on men. He calls this "the most difficult, and the most interesting of problems." This is also the sense of the Swiss jurist Beaumont's insistence that government enhance rather than pervert Natural Law. "Do legislators want to make people docile to their laws? Let them found them on the nature and original relations of men; let them avoid the arbitrary; let them be only the expression of the laws which each man finds in himself." [24] Morellet echoes the same view, but in a more extreme form: "It is a question of knowing what laws should have been made according to justice, and the unalienable and imprescriptable rights of property and liberty. . . . Seek only to determine what is just, and you can be sure that you will have found what is good for all of society. Justice above all, and if one may so say, even above public welfare, because it can never be contrary to public welfare." [25]

Thus the protective or guiding function of government, but also the limits imposed on it by justice and the rights of individuals are emphasized. In all these and other statements, happiness is the ultimate goal, and the function of government is viewed in relation

---

[22] The *Federalist* papers are an outstanding example.
[23] "Premier Discours aux Sorbonniques," *Oeuvres*, I, pp. 205–9.
[24] *Principes de philosophie morale*, 1754, p. 15.
[25] "Sur la liberté de la presse," *Mélanges*, 1818, III, pp. 41–42.

to it. As Maupertuis put the matter: "The problem which the legislator has therefore to solve is this: A multitude of men being assembled, to procure for them the greatest sum of happiness possible. It is upon this principle that all systems of legislation should be based." [26] The government is protector, and not tyrant. Despite all social changes, the laws which God originally gave men are those which are best for their happiness and remain the basis of all reasonable legislation, even though they are no longer by themselves sufficient, according to Maupertuis.

D'Alembert belongs to this group of liberals. Like the others, he believes in equality in the sense that all should receive the same protection from laws, but opposes equality in the metaphysical and social sense which, he holds, would lead to anarchy.[27] It is the responsibility of those who govern to see to it that "the economy and the balance" of a society is such that no one is forced, by natural needs, to crime.[28] Contrary to the collectivist radicals, d'Alembert clearly separates, to some degree at least, morals and politics. Morally, we must condemn adultery more than fornication; but the politician will be more concerned with the latter, since it results in dependent citizens. Governors and governed, he declares, stand in a relation of reciprocal respect and obligation; this is the foundation of "the true liberty of citizens."

Montesquieu's attention is divided between the two aspects of the problem of establishing optimum political conditions, that of encouraging desirable behavior, and that of maintaining a viable State. It is the latter aspect which dominates his inquiry into a healthy society and into the remedies for ill societies. But he does not neglect the other. We have seen that Natural Law is for him at once basic and remote. He is satisfied with the prescription that positive law should not flagrantly violate it. Slavery, for instance, is an institution to be condemned despite its usefulness. Contrary to Machiavelli, Hobbes, and to later theorists of power politics, Montesquieu, both implicitly and explicitly, in his *Traité des devoirs,* is opposed to considering politics as something absolutely independent of ethics. We are always dealing with human beings, with the best and the right. "When the principle of a government [i.e., honor, virtue, or terror] is once corrupted, the best laws be-

---

[26] "Eloge de Montesquieu," *Oeuvres,* III, pp. 407–8.

[27] *Elémens de métaphysique, Oeuvres,* I, p. 217 ff.

[28] D'Alembert believes in a limitation, or equitable distribution, but not in equality of fortunes (*ibid.,* pp. 214–15n.).

come bad, and turn against the State." [29] On the other hand, politics has its own laws and requirements, and different kinds of States have quite different moral outlooks. For the politician, there is no one absolute right or truth which he must follow and apply, as having universal, rigid validity. Neither morals nor politics is equated with "scientific" law. Montesquieu is in this regard a positivist. He does not want revolutionary new beginnings based on rationales for the ideal society. He does want reform, but always within the context of established institutions and their history, as corrections of their deviations. His abstract laws of the workings of the various forms of government never point to the overthrow of existing political or social institutions, but are only attempts to generalize (often too hastily) and to codify useful principles. In his examination of governments, the relation of ethics to politics appears, in each instance, as one of a particular form of government to a universal human nature. Government, for Montesquieu, is, from the most idealistic viewpoint, a regrettable necessity, one which shifts the responsibility for individual virtue from the shoulders of the individual, making it easier for him to be wicked.[30] But Montesquieu, who writes that "reason never produces much effect on the minds of men," [31] is as far as can be from utopianism, and his idealistic regret is of value only as an indication.

Never does Montesquieu approve of a government oppressing individuals for any purpose. As a would-be positivist he does, to be sure, look into the workings of tyranny (just as he does into those of slavery). He sees it as the self-interest of a few imposing itself by force and using—quite properly, within the objective statement—the spring of fear or terror to maintain itself. It is clear from Montesquieu's chapters on England, on liberty, and on morals, that he favors individual liberty and natural rights within bounds. The government should be a play of interest groups, a mechanism of checks and balances. The established mores, when not vicious, have precedence, and laws should be in their spirit; laws should strengthen and not violate or attempt to change them, and not attempt to perfect them. Laws can, however, influence mores; Montesquieu does not deny this, but only

---

[29] *De l'Esprit des lois,* VIII, chap. 11.
[30] *Lettres persanes,* XIV.
[31] *De l'Esprit des lois,* XIX, chap. 27.

urges that they be used in this way with restraint. It is true that liberty unchains struggles which are often violent and unjust, and presents the danger of popular passions, private ambitions and demagoguery. But liberty, in a representative republic, possesses its self-righting forces and mechanisms, and a devoted citizenry may be relied upon.[32] We are reminded that "law is not a pure act of power"; there should be no laws where none are needed and, again, rulers should not seek to remake people in an image of perfection.[33]

A moderate government of checks and balances, such as that of the English constitutional monarchy, one which encourages freedom and individual development, does not rely primarily on the virtue of the citizens—that is, on their sacrifice of self-interest for the general interest.[34] One might say that if a government is to favor the legitimate expression of individual natures, it will not at the same time expect of them something which is contrary to the norm of nature. It will rely rather on the natural impulse to prestige, pride, and power, and utilize these for the general welfare by a sound system of rewards and preferment.[35]

Montesquieu's democracy (a form of government which he admires in theory but does not favor in practice) in some interesting respects anticipates the popular, egalitarian State of Rousseau and other States of totalitarian complexion from the French Revolution on. Virtue—the sacrifice of self-interest for the common weal—is its "principle," that is, "the human passion which moves it." [36] Montesquieu has peered deeply into the nature of such a State. Equality, he understands, does not fit well with egoism, or a strongly competitive society. Only two recourses are possible. One is to have confidence in the goodness of human nature; but both the episode of the Troglodytes and the chapters in *De l'Esprit des lois* testify to the certain failure of such a course. The other is to create a repressive society by using the total power of government and education. Virtue, in Montesquieu's sense, is discipline—self-discipline, or enforced. There must be a repression

---

[32] *Ibid.*

[33] *Ibid.*, XIX, chaps. 6, 14, 21.

[34] Montesquieu tries to exclude moral ideas from his "political virtue," but this is quite illogical and was a way of fending off criticism for his exclusion of virtue from monarchy.

[35] *Ibid.*, III, chap. 7: "each goes to the common good, thinking to serve his private interests." The notion of virtue would reverse this formula: each goes to his private good, thinking to serve the common good. The goal is the same.

[36] *Ibid.*, III, chaps. 1, 3.

of "private passions" so that they may be sublimated into public ones.[37] Laws, then, must prevent luxury and excessive accumulations of wealth.[38] Laws must enforce "the continence of women," for Montesquieu understands that the sexual instinct is a focus of the revolt of egoism against social discipline.[39] The popular, egalitarian State also "needs all the power of education; . . . the honor of monarchies is favored by passions, and it favors them in turn; but (political) virtue is a self-renunciation, which is always a very painful thing. This virtue may be defined as the love of laws and country. This love, demanding a continual preference of the public interest to one's own, gives rise to all particular virtues. . . . Everything, then, depends on establishing this love in the republic; and it is to inspire it that education must dedicate itself." [40] But even laws and education are not enough. Example must back up law, and institutions and traditions not be allowed to change.[41] Denunciation is permissible.[42]

Now Montesquieu believes it possible, though very difficult, for laws to do these things. In his *Pensées,* he clearly states that in a small republic, people can be so educated that they will all be virtuous, and that "laws make good and bad citizens." Wicked men are generally so because circumstances make their crimes appear profitable in comparison to the risk or shame involved. "Good laws can make these circumstances rare; bad laws multiply them." [43] The point, then, is not that Montesquieu doubts the power of laws to control and mold human nature, but that he doubts the wisdom of so doing. He has clearly understood that a popular, egalitarian society tends toward collectivism and monistic control, and he prefers a free, open, pluralistic society. Twice he warns us that "the power [sovereignty] of the people has been confused with the liberty of the people," and that in certain States "the constitution is free, and the citizen is not." [44] He advises us that when mores are to be changed, they should be altered not by

[37] *Ibid.*, V, chap. 2.
[38] *Ibid.*, VII, chaps. 1, 2. "In proportion as luxury establishes itself in a republic, its spirit turns toward private interest. People who need only necessities, have nothing to desire but the glory of their country and their own." But luxury befits a monarchy. See V, chaps. 5, 6, for application to land holdings and inheritances.
[39] *Ibid.*, VII, chap. 8.
[40] *Ibid.*, IV, chap. 5. Later Montesquieu defines this love as the love of equality and of frugality. (V, chap. 3.)
[41] *Ibid.*, V, chaps. 4, 7.
[42] *Ibid.*, XII, chap. 20.
[43] *Pensées, Oeuvres,* II, pp. 428–29.
[44] *De l'Esprit des lois,* XI, chap. 2; XII, chap. 1.

laws, but by instilling new mores.[45] He knows the weakness of
human nature, and the constant regimentation such a society
would require.[46] He does not believe in the worth of a society
which denies "the rights of the personality and of human liberty,
that freedom in choice which alone can preserve the notions of
right and wrong in all their integrity." [47] He does believe that in
the kind of society he prefers, and with the right kind of education and good examples, man's natural sense of justice can be
preserved and selfish motives of conduct controlled, so that individual liberty and social order can be reconciled in a somewhat
precarious balance.[48]

Though the Physiocrats had a realistic view of human motivation, they were optimists in their belief that conflict of interests
(at least on the economic level) would best work out, for the
general interest and harmony, if allowed to pursue its natural
course. They did not want republics, for (following Montesquieu's
theory) republics were founded on virtue, which they termed "a
prejudice against nature, that makes a man devote himself to
maintaining the public security against the extension of his private
property." [49] A communistic society would be even worse. It would
destroy private interest, the *natural* foundation of society, and
together with the individual's property, absorb the individual himself.

The "logic" is clear: society is founded on self-interest; self-
interest can satisfy itself only when it is unhampered; the public
good can only result from the private good. The "anti-social" character of private interest is the result of a fallacious dichotomy of
private and public. Self-interest "contains" an inherent recognition
of the reciprocity of claims and of the harmfulness of harming
others. This Natural Law is, as we have observed, a rational law,
since it distinguishes and prefers "calculated self-interest" to
"blind, avid, and exclusive self-interest." [50] Free competition is

---

[45] *Ibid.*, XIX, chap. 14.

[46] See, for instance, *ibid.*, V, chap. 5, par. 2, 3. It must be noted, however, that not
all details of Montesquieu's democratic republic agree with Rousseau's or the "people's republics" of our time. In some respects, he envisions mechanisms, such as
political parties and pressure groups, which characterize our representative, liberal
democracies. It is simply that his rational divisions do not correspond neatly to the
decisions of later history.

[47] Barrière, *Un grand Provincial*, p. 328; Pensée 615, II, 1266.

[48] See A. S. Crissafulli, "Montesquieu's Story of the Troglodytes," *PMLA,* 52:389,
1943.

[49] Weulersse, *op. cit.*, p. 94.

[50] *Ibid.*

society's defense against the latter, and as Victor de Mirabeau said, in a well-ordered society "each works for everyone else while thinking he is working for himself." [51]

The Physiocrats thus turn their backs on the idea of using the full power of the State and see the social problem as primarily moral and economic, rather than political. As Mirabeau wrote, "when political speculations in a nation trouble it, they alter its substance. . . . If the products of property and the retribution due to work are restored, men will return by themselves to the moral order." [52] Nevertheless, the Physiocratic doctrine points in two rather different political directions. On the one hand, it reinforces the theory of the natural rights of man, which no government may infringe. Necessity, or the instinct of self-preservation, says Le Mercier de la Rivière, is a right which others have the duty to respect. Property, all agree, is a primitive "appetite." The right to pursue self-interest implies the liberty to do so. There is no fear of chaos, because the law of reciprocity imposes itself, since without it (as Quesnay writes in his *Droit naturel*) "nobody would be sure of keeping the use of his faculties or the enjoyment of his natural rights," but (in Mirabeau's words) would instead expose himself to reprisals: "no rights without duties, no duties without rights." Consequently, Le Trosne flatly condemns the notion, which the collectivists will exalt, that public interest must prevail over private; this "vague, indefinite principle" is only a cover for usurpation. An injustice which calls for suppression cannot be denominated a private interest, he urges. If it is, however, a legitimate right, then the accusation is false, because the exercise of rights "can never be contrary to public interest." Under this false principle, he charges, freedom and property have been invaded and restricted, submitted "to human legislation." [53]

On the other hand, Physiocracy leads to extreme political conservatism. It is not difficult to see how such a doctrine of natural rights, hoisted under the flag of Natural Law, can be used to

---

[51] This is similar to Montesquieu's theory concerning limited monarchy.

[52] *Philosophie rurale*, I, pp. 134–35. Destructive political influences, according to Mirabeau, reduce morals to "private interests." This combination of ideas is indicative of the Physiocrats' thinking. Abundance, he later says, "excites virtues." We care about the fate of others "as soon as we are not worried about our own" (*ibid.*, p. 218). "Man's fundamental genius, tending toward tyranny, subsists always; but he becomes humanized in proportion as his status draws him closer to the need for association and the community of enlightened self-interests." (II, pp. 100–1.)

[53] *Op. cit.*, p. 102. Talmon's classification of the Physiocrats among the proto-totalitarians is an egregious oversimplification.

prevent change, regulation, and govermental interference with abuses. As later history has confirmed, the freedom of the individual from governmental control, under the guise of natural rights, can become a pretext to prevent public authority from protecting the rights of all against the strength and aggressiveness of a few. This is already clear in Le Trosne. The only justice, he asserts, is respect for individual rights. Such rationalizations as a pragmatic morality (*"une morale de convenance"*), "the reason of State," clash of interests, the "public interest," he warns us, depart from Natural Law and become what each wants. Again, this fine doctrine, which surely contains a solid truth, may be used in two ways. We can see how Le Trosne would use it, when he declares that intervention to protect the people (*salus populi*) is most dangerous, and that the general welfare must be subordinated to absolute property rights.[54]

There have been many contradictory interpretations of the Physiocratic political doctrine. This is due in part to divergent opinions in the School and to apparently contradictory statements. In part, it is due to logomachies. Many have interpreted Physiocracy as absolute monarchy. A few have denied this, and Mario Einaudi, in particular, has proven that the royal powers are to be subject to judicial control, very much as the United States Supreme Court serves as protector of fundamental rights, which are above the reach of positive law.[55] While this is true, it is still possible to speak of despotism or absolutism (and the Physiocrats themselves termed it "legal despotism"), since the governmental functions, provided they do not trespass on the fundamental rights, are united within the hands of the monarch, without any division of powers, or popular voice other than that of public opinion.

Since positive law only formulates a pre-existing law, an absolute monarch, the Physiocrats judged, can best apply the natural order to the social situation. He will not violate the natural order which makes property the basis of society, because he is coproprietor. Le Mercier de la Rivière says this is a "natural government,"

---

[54] *Ibid.*, p. 92 ff. Natural Law, in general, could be used as a critical, revolutionary method—as Locke, Paine, and Jefferson did—or as a justification for established institutions and prejudices, to shatter the self-confidence of individual reason and to narrow the sphere of creativity—as Blackstone and Burke did. Blackstone built on Mandeville's theory, which was not unlike the Physiocrats', that selfishness leads to a natural harmony. See D. J. Boorstin, *op. cit.*, pp. 50–53.

[55] *The Physiocratic Doctrine of Judicial Control, passim.*

because the natural order is to keep all members of a society in mutual dependence, so that each, acting in his own interest only, "cannot help acting at the same time in the interest of others." This concept unites the ethical and the political theory of the Physiocrats—and incidentally, explains Diderot's initial enthusiasm for La Rivière.[56] Furthermore, while the Physiocrats wish to protect absolute natural rights against encroachment by government, those rights do not include political rights or individual civil rights other than those of individual security as determined by law, and (primarily) unrestricted property rights—or, to be exact, the right of economic warfare.[57]

An analogous logomachy is involved in the question of proto-totalitarian tendencies. Baudeau said that "The State molds men to its liking," and de Tocqueville interpreted this as "a true summary of the Physiocratic political doctrine, leading to the most fearful form of democratic despotism." [58] Einaudi objects to this view, pointing quite justly to the theory of absolute individual rights and their protection by a judicial guardian. He correctly notes its opposition to Rousseau's general will, which refuses to distinguish between a higher order of fundamental laws and a lower order of man-made laws. Nevertheless, the Physiocratic doctrine tends—unconsciously, perhaps, and despite itself—toward the proto-totalitarian view. According to Le Trosne, "Indeed, there is nothing which cannot be obtained from men, when we learn how to manipulate [*"manier"*] them, to catch them by their dearest interests. . . . We must especially apply ourselves to directing public opinion: that is what governs men more than reason." History, he continues, shows there is nothing of which men are not capable. "It is only a question, then, of knowing how to direct opinion in order to *master* and to *transform* men." [59] Thus

---

[56] It also explains the Physiocrats' criticism of Montesquieu, whom they accused of seeing only positive law, relativity, variations, conditions. Their search for a basic natural law, universal to all society, parallels their search for a universal natural moral law. They distinguished their "legal despotism," conserving and governing, from Montesquieu's "arbitrary despotism," commanding and destroying. The sovereign, wrote Mirabeau, can control men's social and antisocial drives (*L'Ami des hommes*, I, pp. 23–25). It is not seen that such despotism can violate the "laissez-faire" commitment.

[57] Freedom of the press, however, is called for.

[58] Einaudi, *op. cit.,* p. 3.

[59] Le Trosne, *op. cit.,* pp. 294–96 (italics added). Mirabeau writes, "Morals depend on laws; they must be the result and not the basis of legislation." (Quoted by Weulersse, *op. cit.,* II, p. 110.) According to La Rivière, "Good laws necessarily make good morals; the true teacher of moral man is the public system of government."

while the Physiocrats, on the one hand, place great reliance on public opinion to limit the monarchical power, on the other hand, they conceive of the necessity of the government (which it is supposed to limit) molding this opinion. It would seem that they did not really trust their own principle of the natural harmony of egoisms, unless those egoisms were properly "enlightened." [60]

A later generation of Physiocrats, however, including Chastellux, Morellet, and Dupont de Nemours, veered toward the espousal of political rights and liberal forms of government. In fact, according to Henri Sée, "these examples prove in the clearest way the progress accomplished by the liberal doctrine in the last third of the eighteenth century." [61]

One of the leading figures in the group of liberals was Voltaire. The Sage of Ferney, who among the *philosophes* was least given to systematic thought, never formulated a body of political theory. His unfavorable view of human nature made it impossible for him to conceive of any utopia or indeed to think that any form of government was necessarily the best. That very view also deterred him from the laissez-faire of the Physiocrats. At the same time, it kept him far from the collectivist group, who thought that men could be molded and remade so as to become harmoniously coordinated social units. Like Montesquieu, he placed great weight on government exercising its proper regulatory functions, as well as on civil rights. "A government which could take care of everything would do more in a year than the entire order of preaching friars has done since its inception." [62] Unlike Montesquieu, he distrusted the play of group interests and intermediate bodies, each with what Rousseau would have called "its private will," none concerned primarily with public interest. But, whereas Rousseau sought to overcome this with his "democratic" general will, Voltaire distrusted the people, and preferred an enlightened despot, who could stand above all private wills. (Rousseau, to be sure,

[60] Mirabeau in effect declares this; see Talmon, p. 276. Talmon emphasizes the synthesis of economic freedom and political absolutism which might lead to a totalitarian State [of the right]; economic interests lead to harmony, but political interests are an obstacle to it (pp. 44–45). "Eighteenth-century believers in a natural system failed to perceive that once a positive pattern is laid down, the liberties which are supposed to [inhere in] this pattern become restricted within its framework, and lose their validity and meaning outside it. The area outside the framework becomes mere chaos, to which the idea of liberty simply does not apply, and so it is possible to go on re-affirming liberty while denying it." See also p. 35.

[61] *L'Evolution de la pensée politique*, p. 215.

[62] Letter to Bastide, 1760 (*Oeuvres*, XLI, p. 53).

distrusted the people quite as much as Voltaire, and his popular sovereignty is a mask for control.) In this important sense, then, Voltaire was not a liberal. If we may divide eighteenth-century political theorists between those who had a greater fear of anarchy, and those who, like Montesquieu and Diderot, dreaded despotism more, we must, on this score, place Voltaire among the first group. It was the second group which supported the division and balance of powers, and the interplay of particular interests. On the other hand, Voltaire did believe in an open society, as his constant challenge of abuses, his demand for reforms and for individual rights, both natural and civil, testify.[63] That is why his political "philosophy" is elusive and even appears chaotic. He balanced a desire for individual freedom and the rule of law against a desire for progressive reforms in the general interest, which were being blocked by the lesser, group interests of the time. And yet, abhorring tyranny, he was obliged to set up a distinction between absolutism and despotism—which meant, in the final analysis, trust in an enlightened despot. Thus he was not willing, like other *philosophes* who took the side of the Parlements, to sacrifice reform for a principle of law which they hoped would lead to constitutional government, and thence, eventually, to reform.[64]

Voltaire was bound to ask himself this question: if men's wickedness is not all natural, but is furthered, or partly caused by social conditions, by government, and education, what can be done about it? If there is nothing radical that can be done (his opposition to the abbé de Saint-Pierre shows that he had scant faith in the legislative control of behavior), we are left with a fundamental pessimism, not so complete, however, that there is no room for a constructive program of limited melioristic action. This is Voltaire's outlook. His occasional defense of man is largely a matter of anti-Christian polemics; it is also partly theoretical and partly melioristic. The several occasions on which, in his later years, he conceded that the people are more educable than he had thought do not change his basic judgment. It is for this reason that he had

---

[63] For a list of these rights, see *Dictionnaire philosophique*, art. "Gouvernement," *Oeuvres*, XIX, p. 296.

[64] It is true that Voltaire also expresses great admiration for the British constitution, which is stable and yet protects liberty; and that late in life he developed an admiration for republics (notably Switzerland and Holland) as the best possible form of government. But he does not think of either of these as applicable to France.

little influence on the French Revolution with its optimism and sweeping revolutionary programs. He was a historicist and a pragmatist with little optimism. The job to be done was one of a limited correction of abuses, not an endeavor, based on abstract truths, to change the bases of society and direct it anew toward a "rational-natural" ideal.

Voltaire was disinterested in theoretical solutions, because he knew how the world works, how men seek power and immediate advantage. Like Burke, he realized that we live in an empirical world in which power and self-interest are ever-present realities. This practical, pragmatic approach has its limits, and is not impervious to criticism. It ignores the reality of ideals and their power. It tends to neglect the need of a viable, dynamic society to know in what direction it is moving, to have goals and a philosophy, and to head its practical actions, with a beyond-the-immediate vision, toward them. It must give its citizens an awareness of that purposiveness. All this Voltaire's political philosophy lacked, but Rousseau's—whether or not we relish it—offered.

Diderot's politics is as fragmentary as Voltaire's, and more incoherent in its multiple tendencies. His papers written for the "instruction" of Catherine the Great, unpublished until late in the nineteenth century, reveal a petty-bourgeois outlook in his opposition to luxury and his desire for a more equal distribution of national wealth and land-holdings.[65] Here, as in the *Encyclopédie* and his *Pages contre un tyran,* he is opposed to despotic rule and "divine right," and favors constitutional government with elective assemblies composed of property owners. Boldly he proclaims the right of open opposition and individual liberties, "without which men are reduced to the condition of animals," and so cannot achieve the happiness they desire. Especially he is against benevolent despotism. Under a benevolent despot, he urges in the *Réfutation d'Helvétius,* men are lulled into a false security, forget their liberties, lose the habit of self-government and the unalienable right of criticism. They fall into a "sleep of death," become "a herd whose pleas are despised, under the pretext of being led into fat pasture." For Diderot, humanist and liberal, human values are more important than mere well-being, freedom more valuable than security. So that a benevolent despotism is

[65] See M. Tourneux, *Diderot et Catherine II.*

the most dangerous of all despotisms.[66] He warns Catherine against witch hunts and thought control—a sure way to check the growth of minds. "Without realizing it, people begin avoiding a certain kind of dissenting ideas, as they avoid an object that would hurt them; and when they get used to that pusillanimous and cautious gait, it is hard to get back to a frank and outspoken way." Here and in the *Encyclopédie*, then, Diderot wants a moderate program. Freedom and property must be assured, commerce unrestricted, taxes levied according to the ability to pay, laws applied equally to all.

There is, however, another phase of Diderot's political ideology which puts him much closer to the opponents of the pluralistic attitude. "The system of the individual must not be preferred to that of the species" (art. "Particulier"). He has great faith in the power of laws to form a society in such fashion that a bad action "will punish itself." Under the sway of abstract rationalism and the belief in a universal human nature, he turns his back on the great work of Montesquieu. "Customs and manners are everywhere the result of legislation and government." This reverses Montesquieu. Good laws are good everywhere. Men and morals are therefore dependent on laws. "Arrange things so that private good is so tightly linked with the general, that a citizen can scarcely harm society without harming himself; assure virtue its reward, as you have assured wickedness its punishment." [67] And elsewhere: "men would have no need of being governed if they were not wicked; and the purpose of all authority is consequently to make them good." [68] In the article "Législateur," he urges legislators to use education to inspire "passions useful to the State." [69] Against Rousseau's subjective conscience he writes: "What is the voice of conscience without the authority and the menace of laws?" [70] And to Falconet: "The improvement of morals depends on good legis-

---

[66] *Oeuvres philosophiques*, ed. Vernière, pp. 619–20. For Diderot, Voltaire would be guilty of an inconsistent pessimism—one applied to the people and not to the ruler, a pessimism oblivious of the fact that power aggravates the natural inclination to injustice.

[67] *Entretien d'un philosophe, Oeuvres*, II, p. 517. Also, *Lettres à Sophie Volland*, I, p. 116.

[68] *Ibid.*, VII, p. 182.

[69] *Ibid.*, XV, p. 426. But in the same article he denies that the individual makes a total surrender to society, and insists that government must protect individual rights.

[70] Article "Grecs," quoted by P. Vernière, in Diderot, *Oeuvres philosophiques*, p. 504n.

lation. Any other device is only temporary." [71] In this trend of thought, Diderot unites morals and politics tightly. But he does not unify his priority of individual rights and happiness with the utilitarian outlook of general welfare.

Despite these steps which are neither entirely contradictory to, nor entirely consonant with, his liberalism, Diderot firmly refused to go along with the final consequences adduced by Helvétius or Morelly. Strangely for one who has such unlimited confidence in the conditioning power of laws, he does not have the same trust in the power of education. Perhaps he considers education to be an attempt to operate directly on the rational faculties, whereas laws function through the affective agencies of behavior. If this is true, then he did not grasp the totalitarian concept of "education." At all events, throughout the *Réfutation d'Helvétius,* he emphasizes the determinism of biological inheritance and rebels against the idea that men can be completely conditioned. In particular, he doubts the value of public education. [72] To Catherine he says, "We must teach to enlighten; but do not expect too much from it." Even in a well-ordered society, the wicked man "gains more as a wicked man than he loses as a member of society." Paul Vernière is the first to have realized that Diderot criticizes Helvétius' basic theory for political as well as for moral reasons. [73] One of the most important meanings of Diderot's thought in the *Réfutation* lies here. The eighteenth century, while advancing steadfastly toward liberalism and rights, also initiates moves toward the two extremes of anarchism and totalitarianism. Diderot sees the danger clearly. He rises up against it, as a humanist and a liberal.

Perhaps he was also impelled to react against Helvétius by the strain of anarchism which, speculative though it was, persisted in him, and which followed the important primitivistic current. As he wrote to Catherine, "I want society to be happy; but I want to be happy, too; and there are as many ways of being happy as

---

[71] *Ibid.* Also, in the *Supplément au Voyage de Bougainville,* "If laws are good, morals are good; if laws are bad, morals are bad." (*Ibid.*)

[72] *Réfutation,* III, pp. 450–51. In his *Plan d'une université,* he realizes the positive values of public education.

[73] "If Diderot criticizes Helvétius for moral and political reasons, if he feels intensely what danger threatens real man as soon as a strong power takes him for a mechanism, if he wants to safeguard the original richness of each conscience, it is because he wants his reader to understand 'the essence of order' and not only make him conform to that order." (*Op. cit.,* p. 559.)

there are individuals. Our own happiness is the basis of all our true duties." Here we recall his attacks on property and his vague long-ing for a state without laws, without vices and virtues.

The *Encyclopédie,* as a whole, bears the stamp of Diderot's moderate liberalism which was to be the most widespread attitude in the second part of the century. (We must not look to that great work for the most radical or most advanced thinking on con-troversial subjects.) It is quite clear, in numerous articles, that the scope of authority and the role of government are held to be limited by the rights of individuals, which are held, in the Lockean tradition, to be prior to government. It is not always clear what the rights are, but they do include life, property, and security under law.

We need not tarry long on outstanding late-in-the-century liberals whose theories do not, overtly at least, have a close rela-tion to a well-defined moral philosophy. Raynal, in many regards a liberal, holds up the British constitution as a model and demands political and economic liberties. Volney is more interesting in his insistence that there is no such thing as public happiness other than the sum of the happiness of individuals. This attitude is in sharp contrast with that of the group of thinkers we shall examine next. Laws, for Volney, exist both to fulfill egoism, and "to temper the conflict of egoism, to maintain the equilibrium of forces," thus inhibiting the natural impulse to domination at others' expense. By protecting rights and regulating relations, they will allow each man a large measure of freedom for individual self-realization —which is the purpose of society. Only a representative govern-ment can ensure the freedom and equality which, within the bounds of reciprocity, are unalienable.[74] A third liberal was Con-dorcet. Under the influence of Thomas Paine, he became the out-standing French exponent of the rights of man—of unalienable personal and civil rights which were not the gift of the State. The famous Declaration passed by the Assemblée Nationale in 1789 is in harmony with his extreme optimism and his Cartesian ra-tionalism in its search for universality and immutability. He was also a proponent of universal suffrage and representative govern-ment, of political parties and compromise of interests. However he tended toward some of Rousseau's theories, demanding, for instance, popular ratification of laws. Like Rousseau and many

[74] *Les Ruines,* chap. IX, XVI, XVII.

others in the final two pre-Revolutionary decades, equality seemed more important to him than civil liberties, and he did not realize that Rousseau's doctrine favored the first at the expense of the second. He also emphasized public education—not as a method of indoctrination and control, however, but as the only way to make equality and rights real.[75]

The eighteenth century witnessed a revival of political ideals, in reaction to the power-realism of Machiavelli and Hobbes. While this was partly a return to Natural Law, especially in the first half of the century, it was increasingly to become a conviction that a new society could be and had to be planned. Not many tried to do the actual planning (like Morelly or Rousseau). Most contented themselves with pious generalities, like d'Holbach or Robinet. The latter, for instance, tells us that natural liberty is that of doing what nature permits (what is in conformity with natural moral sentiments); civil liberty is that of doing what the law permits. Since laws are properly only the expression of moral sentiments, civil liberty is the same thing as natural liberty.[76]

The universal desire for happiness, the identity of needs and of motives seemed a sufficient basis for directing governments and laws toward the omnipresent goal of a concordance between personal and public interest. These facts seemed enough, too, to insure the logical conclusion that needs and *therefore* rights were mutual, reciprocal, and self-limiting. Thus two directions are indicated by these two propositions. The second led to the *philosophes'* important contribution to modern liberalism. More than the attack on abuses and the demand for reforms, more even than the theories of representative government (which were better taught and illustrated in England), the doctrine of rights and the defense of human liberty and dignity rise immortally out of the Enlightenment. We have seen how the Natural Law theory swerved toward one of natural rights. But no period of history is simple, linear, or univalent. The same factors which produced

[75] For a summary of Condorcet's political theories, see Sée, *op. cit.*, pp. 278–97; for a general study, J. Salwyn Schapiro's excellent biography. Talmon groups Condorcet among the proto-totalitarians, because he believed in a fixed order which, if realized would make politics an exact science (*op. cit.*, pp. 18–19, 26–27). This classification is, however, a simplification. Elements of both tendencies can be found in Condorcet.

Finally, we should not omit the name of Honoré de Mirabeau, son of the Physiocrat, whose moderate liberalism guided the first years of the French Revolution.

[76] *Op. cit.*, I, p. 245.

these demands also produced theories of indoctrination, of conditioning and control, which compromised them.

We must also ask what basis these men found in human nature —on which they always had an eye—for rights, liberties, democratic processes, and a liberal society. All of them distrusted and despised the common people, though in widely differing degrees they thought them subject to some enlightenment. We must refer back to the evaluation of human nature.[77] The few who really thought men to be naturally good could logically conclude that culture should not deprive them of their natural rights, and that it is not necessary to do so. (Rousseau did not really believe man to be good—quite the contrary; logically, he casts aside natural or unalienable rights.) Those who held man to be incorrigibly evil were concerned primarily with the preservation of order, and distrusted the idea of unalienable rights as the source of a war of all against all.[78] Those who considered man to be inherently neither good nor evil, or simultaneously both, endeavored (like Montesquieu, Voltaire, and Diderot) to strike a balance, but there was also a tendency to submit individual right to collective right.

"The excessively optimistic estimates of human nature and of human history," writes Reinhold Niebuhr, "with which the democratic credo has been historically associated are a source of peril to democratic society; for contemporary experience is refuting this optimism." [79] We must again note that with the exception of a small number of extremists (Chastellux, Condorcet, etc.), the "optimism" of the French Enlightenment was not about human nature, as Niebuhr and many others have said, but rather about what *could be done with men,* such as they were. This fact and the fact that various shades of open or implicit pessimism about human nature were the actually dominant tone in the eighteenth century are what really give point to Niebuhr's ensuing remark: "A free society requires some confidence in the ability of men to reach tentative and tolerable adjustments between their competing interests and to arrive at some common notions of justice which transcend all partial interests. A consistent pessimism in regard to man's rational capacity for justice invariably leads

[77] See *An Age of Crisis,* chap. 8, 12.
[78] Cf. F. Neumann, *op. cit.,* pp. 74–75.
[79] *Op. cit.,* p. x.

to absolutistic political theories; for they prompt the conviction that only preponderant power can coerce the various vitalities of a community into a working harmony." [80]

It was precisely in this intellectual framework, and because of the weakness of the enlightened self-interest and virtue-happiness solutions, that the emphasis on coercive tactics, which were in perfect accord with utilitarianism, grew stronger. The denial of the natural harmony of egoisms (as suggested by the Physiocrats but countered by the recognition that the passions and vitalities are not ordered and limited) and the inefficacy of the rational alternatives required, it seemed, a stronger defense of culture against nature. "It was then declared that in the interest of individuals, individual interest must be identified with the general interest, and that it is up to the legislator to carry out this identification." [81] In reality, this is to deny personal interest, insofar as it deviates from what has been decided is the *proper* "personal" interest, that is, the one which suits the collective whole. This is the real meaning of statements such as Raynal's: "The human race is whatever we want it to be; it is the way it is governed which determines it to good or evil." [82] The abbé Terrasson had reached a similar conclusion from "nature's view," which is to conserve the species and ignore the individual. "Thus moral politics tries to accomplish the good of the greatest number possible without worrying about a few individuals, and even at their cost, if necessary." [83] This tendency is in accord, too, with the general transference of the locus of value from the individual to society which we observed in the purely ethical sphere. It was on this ground, precisely, that slavery was generally defended. We remember that Turgot labeled slavery an injustice, but regrettably, a useful one. "There are enormous [injustices] which certainly have given great satisfactions to their perpetrators," and often without re-

[80] Not ungermane to our discussion is James Madison's ridicule of the optimism of Robert Owen's New Harmony Community: "Custom is properly called second nature; Mr. Owen makes it nature itself." (Quoted by R. L. Ketcham, "James Madison and the Nature of Man," p. 66.) Ketcham comments about Madison: "Life was usually guided by avarice, vanity, cruelty and depravity, but there was reasonable hope that free institutions would brighten the future in some cases. In fact, his views were close to what one would expect from a philosopher of the Enlightenment."

[81] Halévy, *op. cit.*, I, p. 23. He calls this the "principle of artificial identification of interests."

[82] Quoted by H. Wolpe, *op. cit.*, p. 88.

[83] *La Philosophie applicable à tous les objets*, 1754, pp. 37–38.

morse.[84] (This statement, incidentally, wrecks the virtue-happiness equivalence and reveals its possible discordance with the theory of general interest—as well as denying the natural identity of private and public interest.) Melon, the economist, had put it more crudely. The disadvantage of one is compensated by the gain of another. When the individual is hurt for the good of the nation, "then that hurt has so great a compensation, that it becomes as nothing for the Legislator." [85] Such a view is also in accord with the recognition that culture is not to be confused with nature; that society requires the limitation, regulation, and even the denial of subjective demands for ego-satisfaction.

In addition, both the new directions in Natural Law and the abandonment of that doctrine, we recall, weakened the tie which had held duties and rights in close relation (though favoring the former). Often rights were proclaimed as primary. But another outcome was also possible. Natural Law by making its commands the basis of political laws had assured those rights which were consistent with society. When political laws displaced such commands and became self-sufficient (whether conceived of as the expression of reason or of will), rights no longer had any status except as granted by laws, which were largely directed by the concept of "general welfare." On the other hand, Natural Law, if maintained at all, no longer counts except as a system of moral principles external to the political solution. The social problem really escapes from the moral problem into the realm of pure power—though this is not recognized. The identification of ethics with politics has the effect of absorbing the former into the latter. "Henceforth," comments Paul Léon, "the only question will be that of creating a political force to which the constituent atoms of society will be submitted; a unique force, the State will incarnate it either in a single individual or in an assembly conceived as an individual *en grand,* representing the physico-mathematical unity of social life." [86] Thus it was hoped to found a human harmony which is *not* the natural, though it was constantly proclaimed to be, inasmuch as it is based on natural laws—a fascinating confusion of mechanism and result. This, to be sure, is a perspective. It is possi-

---

[84] *Oeuvres,* III, p. 378.
[85] *Essai politique sur le commerce,* n. p., 1734, pp. 61–62. Helvétius and others were in agreement, as we have seen.
[86] *Op. cit.,* p. 210.

ble to change the optics, and to view the same phenomenon as the reduction of politics to ethics, the intention being to determine values and behavior by means of rational planning and manipulation. However such an ethics is one in which the "moral" tends to disappear.

In the hands of the writers we are about to examine, the appeal to the "natural" becomes a mere expedient rather than a teleological authority. What, after all, is a "natural order" which leaves nothing of natural autonomy? Their outlook, in the last analysis, was not far from La Mettrie's reduction: social welfare is the only standard of right and wrong in an "artificial morality." [87] Self-interest, so often defended as legitimate (because natural) tends, as the century grows old, to be considered as the chief evil. To *"régler l'amour-propre"* was seen as the goal. However, the conscience, a *tabula rasa*, could be trained to conformity to a society's purposes according to the simple laws of cause and effect, by which human nature, like all other natural phenomena, was controlled. (Thus Natural Law had to be excluded, and determinism embraced.) [88] Regardless of how one may feel about this attitude, it had a further weakness in many instances: its adherents often had no certain idea of a healthy society, or of the remedies that should be applied to the existing one. The discussion was therefore formal and abstract, rather than functional. Thus "general interest" was taken as an abstract entity, as a thing existing in itself, and group ("particular") interests were assumed to be opposed to it; whereas the former term, if meaningful, doubtless signifies a varying compromise or common denominator among particular interests. And liberalism, as in d'Holbach, slipped easily into a tendency favoring collectivist authoritarianism.[89]

There are few indications that the political use of coercive conditioning was considered in the first half of the eighteenth century. Montesquieu's chapters on democracy are the closest to it. Such a line of thought had to await Hartley's *Observations on Man* (1749) and Condillac's *Traité des sensations* (1754).[90] The British,

---

[87] *Discours préliminaire,* I, pp. 8, 46–47. "Natural morality" refers to the truth attached to pleasure.

[88] These attitudes are also related to the desire (as in Hume, Gay, and Hartley) to create a science of the mind, using the Newtonian method and the principle of attraction (association) to derive a moral science and a social science.

[89] The abbé de Saint-Pierre went so far as to demand interdiction of discussion of religious and metaphysical questions, thus turning his back to his own principle of freedom of opinions. (Barni, *op. cit.,* I, p. 71.)

[90] Hartley was translated in 1755.

having their liberties and a stable representative system, were not inclined to speculation of this kind. A possible exception is Soame Jenyns. In his *Free Inquiry into the Nature and Origin of Evil* (1757), Jenyns deduces from his acceptance of the unique self-interest motivation the conclusion that men must be manipulated by deceits, like religion and patriotism. Human nature cannot be changed; but it can be controlled.[91] In France, however, the climate was more congenial to the ideas of Hartley and Condillac. Condillac, we recall, affirmed that all higher faculties depend on associations, that habits are repeated association and that our whole temperament is acquired. He did not himself consider the training of the senses a matter for the educator, and limited it to early years; but he explained the personality solely as an aggregate of sensations and recognized in general the importance of conditioning the senses.

Morelly's theories were developed quite independently of Condillac's. He considered happiness to depend entirely on a social organization in which individual satisfaction would be deliberately subordinated to public good. In the *Code de la nature* (1755) he outlines a society which is actually a complete superseding of what the eighteenth century would have called "nature" by "culture," in the form of a communistic totalitarianism. Morelly carries out, on the economic side, the egalitarian, co-operative society which Rousseau, limiting it to the political, was to achieve only partly. Recognizing the competitive aspects of human nature, Morelly's program suppresses them ruthlessly, except where they can be channeled to public welfare and kept under public control. Self-interest ("that universal plague") is reduced, and submitted to the common interest as determined by an authoritarian welfare State. All this, to be sure, is advocated under the sacred standard of *nature*, which existing societies contradict.[92] And yet Morelly clearly recognizes the evil virtualities of human nature and sees the whole problem as one of control! "To find a situation," runs a chapter heading, "in which it will be almost impossible for man to be depraved or wicked, or at least, *minima de malis.*" [93]

Morelly's postulates are Newtonian and sensationist. Just as celestial bodies operate by an equilibrium of centrifugal and

---

[91] B. Willey, *op. cit.*, p. 54; A. O. Lovejoy, *The Great Chain of Being*, pp. 203–4. Machiavelli writes: "The individual judgment must be stunned and practically drowned; that is part of the armament. To govern is to make people believe."
[92] *Code de la nature*, pp. 150, 156.
[93] *Ibid.*, p. 160.

centripetal forces, so does society, by the forces of self-love and social affections (an idea set forth in Pope's *Essay on Man*).[94] The human heredity is physical only, and each individual is completely malleable; in other words, in accord with the logic of sensationism, man is neither good nor bad, but only what he is made to be. In the light of these data, we can smile at Morelly's pretention that he wishes only "to second Nature by Art." [95] He also pretends that we need only abolish property in order to cause men to think solely of the common good, which will be the source of their own. In the course of the development, however, it transpires that a "mechanical" education is also necessary to combat "unruly passions" and to forestall bad habits.[96] A man would then never need "to use his mental faculties, except to know and enjoy the advantages of a wisely constituted society." He would never think of disobeying laws, "accustomed from his earliest years to bending himself to its laws."

All this is, supposedly, to keep man in accord with nature.[97] This "nature" requires that the members of a society should have the same dependency "as the union and dependency of organs . . . in a living body." [98] Thus we have equality, for "the citizens of a Republic are individually and collectively in a mutual dependency." But for this, Morelly admits, nature is not enough, and must be supplemented by art. God has allowed human reason to erect its own laws and create "a moral world." [99] The "laws" which Morelly actually lays out, in the fourth part of his book, are a model of totalitarian control, of a society planned in detail, including a puritanical regulation of sexual relations and population control. He decrees the communal raising of children, with rigid regulation and conditioning; "the motives of exhortation will be private happiness, inseparably attached to the common good." [100] No laws may even be changed or interpreted other than literally. The millennian utopia is realized. History is abolished, and permanent stability attained.

It was Helvétius who, as a disciple of Condillac, provided the political application of his theories. According to Jules Barni, one

[94] *Ibid.*, pp. 141–42.
[95] *Ibid.*, p. 170.
[96] *Ibid.*, pp. 173, 175–76.
[97] *Ibid.*, pp. 184–85 note.
[98] *Ibid.*, p. 219. Rousseau will express the same idea.
[99] *Ibid.*, pp. 260–61.
[100] *Ibid.*, p. 317.

school of philosophers, from Plato to Mably, identified politics with morals—a "noble but fatal" error, one leading to oppression.[101] This is certainly the case with Helvétius, in whose writings one can observe how making ethics dependent on the interests and vagaries of legislation is destructive to the former, leading to (or departing from) his crucial statement, "We must consider actions as indifferent in themselves"; [102] leading also to this other pithy declaration, so like one we have quoted from Rousseau: "Ethics is then only a frivolous science, if it be not blended with politics and legislation." [103] This again connotes the absorption of morality by utility. "Wherever luxury is necessary, it is politically inconsistent to consider gallantry as a moral vice; and if we insist on calling it vice, we must admit that there are useful ones. . . ." [104] It is for the State to determine, according to its needs, which acts are to be praised or blamed, and for the legislator to set the bounds according to public interest.[105]

Culture cannot extirpate natural impulses, but it can channel them into the desired mold. There is, moreover, a close relation between the idea that law determines justice and the idea that morals and politics are identical, as well as with a third idea, that legislation can and must make self-interest and general interest identical (i.e., identical with the latter). We cannot think of accepting a laissez-faire doctrine, Helvétius would hold, because there is no *natural* genesis of a desire to further the good of all at one's own expense, but rather to hurt others for one's own benefit.[106] "The entire art of the legislator consists, then, in forcing men to be always just to each other out of a feeling of self-love." [107]

[101] *Op. cit.*, III, pp. 148–49.
[102] *De l'Esprit*, p. 168.
[103] *Ibid.*, p. 161. Also: "morals and legislation, which I regard as a single and identical science." (P. 239.)
[104] *Ibid.*, p. 158.
[105] *Ibid.*, p. 168. Helvétius favored an enlightened despotism.
[106] The development here brings Hobbes and Pascal to mind. He also says: "The homage given to virtue is passing; that given to force is eternal. . . . Force is everything on earth." (*De l'Homme*, IX, pp. 8–12.) Virtue is another way of seeking power.
[107] *Ibid.*, p. 238. On pp. 377–78, he calls the motive "love of pleasure." "But man is made to be virtuous; indeed, if force resides essentially in the greatest number, and if justice consists in the practice of actions useful to the greatest number, it is evident that justice is, by its nature, always armed with the necessary power to repress vice and to force men to virtue." (P. 228–29.) In his "Epître sur le plaisir," Helvétius speaks of "the love of pleasure, motive of all actions, necessary spring of societies, which makes their happiness a glory, shame or misery, according as it is directed by legislators. The perfection of legislation is to make individual happiness useful to the happiness of society."

This is possible because men are neither good nor evil (words which refer only to actions, not to intent) but subject to shaping by the law of self-interest. The precise weapons are honor and shame; but women, one of the principal motives of all activity, may also be used as rewards, instead of wasting the pleasure they give us in mere debauchery.

The vices of a people "are always hidden in its laws." [108] By studying human nature, the legislator can make of men what he wants, provided he makes it evident that their well-being is involved, that is, provided the idea of virtue is associated with the idea of happiness.[109] (Helvétius does not envisage the possibility of leading men by appeals to their enthusiasms, ideals, emotional forces, nor would he consider this reliable.) In other words, morality depends on legislation, rather than the contrary. Some individuals will suffer; that is unimportant. "When a vessel is overtaken by long calms, and famine has commanded in an imperious voice that the unfortunate victim who is to be eaten by his comrades be selected by lot, he is slaughtered without remorse; that vessel is the symbol of every nation; everything becomes legitimate and even virtuous for the public safety." [110] The justification of the Terror is already announced in these words.

Furthermore, no grouping or body can be tolerated whose self-interest does not coincide with the general interest.[111] Just as any individual who harms the public interest in following his instincts is a criminal and must be punished, for he has no rights in opposition to the general interest, so are minorities dangerous because they, too, often are in opposition and they must therefore be rigorously repressed.

To the legislative springs, Helvétius of course adds those of education. "The difference in one's education," he writes in *De l'Esprit*, "produces the difference in one's feelings." [112] Nature is only our first habit. The theme of education, as a force molding passive wax, is emphasized in *De l'Homme*. "Man is a machine

---

[108] *Ibid.*, p. 155. Consequently, "one cannot hope to make any changes in the ideas of a people until its laws have been changed; and it is by legal reform that moral reform must be begun." (P. 159.)

[109] (*De l'Homme*, Introduction.) "To direct the movements of the human puppet, it is necessary to know the strings that move it." "He who, in order to be virtuous, would always have to overcome his inclinations would necessarily be a bad man." (P. 373.)

[110] *De l'Esprit*, pp. 80–81.

[111] *Ibid.*, pp. 151–52.

[112] *Ibid.*, p. 231.

which, set in motion by physical sensitivity, must do everything it does." [113] Conscience is a faculty of judgment tending to direct choice toward what is considered advantageous, and it can be trained absolutely to choose one good over another.

Helvétius, like Rousseau, recognized social facts as having their own reality, alongside the facts of the individual, and strove to weld an indissoluble link between the two. As Charles Frankel has said, he "turned Condillac's emphasis upon the primacy of human needs as the origin and test of value into a principle of social planning. With knowledge the educator could manipulate the desire for pleasure and the aversion from pain in such a way as to maximize the general sum of happiness. Consequently, education could be the business of the lawmaker as well as of the schoolmaster." [114] Then "it is of little matter that men be vicious; it is enough that they be intelligent." [115] The important consequences are those which Frankel notes—the use of one part of Locke's philosophy "to destroy the other part of his philosophy which rested on self-evident natural rights. Yet it is probable that Helvétius did not realize how far reaching the implications of his substitution of utility for natural rights really were." [116]

The ideal of a perfect identification of personal and general interest means, in fact, for Helvétius and those who have followed along similar paths, the conditioning or indoctrination of the individual so that he will act in accord with a principle which is held to be universally true: whatever serves the general interest, best serves the private interest. In such a political philosophy two dangers inhere. One is totalitarianism and the extinction of individual rights; the other is the opposite, the denial that my interest is identical with the general, leading to a nihilistic attitude such as we have seen in several writers. The second is reinforced by the shift from moral responsibility to social responsibility, which may be conducive to a reaction against repression in the form of consciously evil acts. Jules Barni pointed out that Helvétius does not ever substantiate the supposed identity of personal interest (the unique and universal motive) and the supervening public interest. How do I serve my own welfare in sacrificing my security, liberty,

---

[113] *De l'Homme*, VIII, pp. 1–2.
[114] *Op. cit.*, p. 58.
[115] *De l'Homme*, quoted *ibid*.
[116] For the relation of Helvétius to Cartesianism and science see *ibid.*, pp. 59–61. He emphasized science "as the external manipulation of individual behavior in the light of indubitable fixed principles."

fortune, or life? Is public utility a sufficient rule? But Helvétius does show us where it leads: "Public humanity is sometimes pitiless." (Totalitarianism is always based on utility and asserts that justice comes after law.) Again, is it true that public utility is the only rule of virtue, or that public esteem is determined only by the usefulness of acts? Helvétius doubtless wished to attack despotism and fanaticism, but did not see that his own philosophy led to the same results, despite the fact that he claimed to be concerned with the happiness of individuals and considered it the fundamental duty of government to ensure their happiness.

Helvétius' great effort was to preserve the "natural" basis of morality (self-interest) and at the same time, to surmount its selfish implications, as society must do, by creating situations in which self-interest will require men to be just. Optimistically, believing that this can be done by legislation, he makes short shrift of the fact that such a self-interest will involve suppression by the individual of his primary impulses of pleasure and pain, that is (by definition) of his self-interest (except insofar as reason may conceive of an eventual satisfaction—a theory in which Helvétius had scant confidence). By saying, in effect, that the individual must be *forced* to *act* morally, Helvétius is renouncing the hope for a moral existence—as he also does by reducing virtue to pleasure and its criterion to public utility and approval.[117] By never saying what the public good is, or who determines it, he opens the door wide to totalitarian institutions. Helvétius, like Diderot and d'Holbach, sees man as ruled by inclinations, instincts, and appetites which are stronger than any so-called obligation. The extreme alternatives are to let nature rule (either because the individual alone counts or because it is thought that a natural harmony will ensue), or to impose a cultural coercion. Helvétius, like Rousseau, opts for the second alternative.

D'Holbach believed that "in going back to the nature of man, one can deduce from it a Political System, a harmony of intimately connected truths, a chain of principles as sure as any of the other branches of human knowledge." [118] But these were only general rules; it would take much experimenting to improve politics, and even then utopia could never be achieved. The chief weakness of

---

[117] The human and the inhuman person, according to his theory, act out of the same pleasure-pain motives.

[118] *La Politique naturelle*, I, chap v, quoted by Ch. Frankel, pp. 70–71.

current politics, according to d'Holbach, was its refusal "to concern itself with morals, which it attributes to the domain of religion." [119] Actually, government is more powerful than morality,
which can only urge. Government can compel and reward.[120]
When a country is overrun by vice and extravagances, it is only
the government that is to blame.[121] Contrariwise, the problem of
"making men happy through virtue" can be solved by "enlightened politics." [122]

The purpose of government is, then, to oblige the members of
a society to "practice the rules of morality." [123] It is also the purpose
of government to lead people to happiness. But, as we have seen,
happiness is incompatible, according to d'Holbach, with vice, disorder, or injustice.[124] It is obvious that he assigns to government
a wider and more "oppressive" role than we do in our concept
of liberal societies. The government, master of the objects in
which men place their happiness, "has a necessary influence on
their conduct, enkindles their passions, turns them in the direction it pleases, modifies and determines their mores. . . ." [125] It
can make the most abominable actions approved or applauded.
Clearly, then, it is not the people and the mores which should
determine the government, but the contrary. If education, example, institutions, and "the opinions suggested to us from childhood" show us virtue as useless and contrary to our happiness, we
shall be vicious, and vice versa.[126] D'Holbach, of course, thinks
only of putting such powers to noble uses. Men are wicked and
corrupt only because they are not governed according to their nature or *taught* its necessary laws.[127] In a well-organized society,
virtue would really be its own reward, and vice its own punish-

---

[119] *Système social*, III, p. 88.

[120] *Ibid.*, I, p. viii.

[121] *Ibid.*, I, p. 62.

[122] *Ibid.*, I, p. 164. His formula is summarized as follows: "Ethics is made to point
out the paths of virtue to men; education should serve its principles; habit should
make its practice familiar; public opinion and example should uphold it; legislation
should give it the sanction of authority; the government should make it more persuasive by means of rewards; punishments should make all whose perversity deafens
them to the voice of reason tremble." (*Ibid.*, III, p. 163.) Elsewhere, d'Holbach assigns to education the role he here gives to ethics. (*Le Christianisme dévoilé*, p. 25.)

[123] *Ibid.*, p. 125.

[124] *Ethocratie*, p. 1.

[125] *Système de la nature*, I, pp. 157–58. "One can make of men whatever one
wishes." (*Ibid.*, I, p. 13.)

[126] *Ibid.*, I, p. 162.

[127] *Ibid.*, I, pp. 315–16, and especially pp. 318–19.

ment.[128] Most wickedness comes from unenlightened self-interest; enlighten men, make them happier, and they will be better.[129] It is also significant that d'Holbach is the only one of his group to insist on conjugal fidelity and on chastity. In fact, he even attacks the penchant for pleasures as a disposition "contrary to *public* happiness." [130]

D'Holbach's confidence is based on his analysis of the motives of conduct (self-interest, happiness) and on determinism; two factors which make it possible, he believes, to anticipate results with something approaching scientific certainty. Even physical methods (food, drugs) can change human character.[131] Self-love and passions must not be stifled, but utilized, enlightened, redirected toward public welfare.[132] The so-called moral instinct, which gives us an immediate feeling of love for virtuous actions and horror for criminal actions, "is due only to habit, acquired by frequent exercise." [133] Governments, seconded by education, must therefore seduce, instill, chastise, provide motives.[134] "The legislator's task is to induce, interest, even force each one, for his own interest, to contribute to the general interest." [135] It all comes down to the fact that a man must love his own welfare, and so, the means to it, wherefore we have no right to expect him to be virtuous contrary to his happiness.[136]

And yet there are indications that d'Holbach sees limits to this process. Reason, nature, and moral principles are universal certainties which are always to be respected, and never arbitrarily thwarted by public will.[137] Any cult contrary to reason must be banished; this is contrary to the assumption of Rousseau's civic religion, that man is not sufficiently reasonable.[138] He supports individualism and does justice to the uniqueness and variety of

---

[128] See the important passage, *ibid.,* I, pp. 348–49.

[129] *Ibid.,* I, p. 387.

[130] See *Système social,* III, pp. 91–94.

[131] *Ibid.,* I, p. 135.

[132] *La Morale universelle,* I, pp. 30–33; *Système,* I, p. 386.

[133] *Ibid.,* I, pp. 52–53.

[134] *Système,* I, pp. 386–88. On education, see also *ibid.,* I, pp. 150–51.

[135] *Morale universelle,* I, p. 33. Cf. Rousseau's "we must force him to be free."

[136] *Système,* I, p. 163.

[137] In this respect, d'Holbach defends nature against culture (*Système,* I, p. 164); but his concept of "nature" is also teleological; it includes "the essence and purpose of society," as well as mutuality and reciprocity (*ibid.,* I, p. 152). This is in sharp contrast with the amoral, ateleological character of Montesquieu's "natural politics," which referred only to necessary laws of interaction, and not to a goal, nor to the satisfaction of individual natural desires.

[138] *Morale universelle,* II, p. 249.

life. He declares that men cannot be alike in thoughts, taste, feelings, or consequently in conduct. The inherited "organization" is all-important; and the same motives or pressures will produce different reactions in different individuals.[139] Freedom—the right to pursue happiness in any way not harmful to the same right of others—is sacred.[140]

Much like Marx, d'Holbach saw a harmony in the apparent paradox of determinism and the possibility of acting; the inevitable progress of mankind is to be achieved by men who choose the right side. He thought that attempts to improve the individual in an immoral, degenerate society will usually be fruitless. To escape from the vicious circle which this statement sets up, he seems to rely, as will Marx, on an élite who will be able to discover, follow, and finally impose the mystique of progress. An optimist, he did not even foresee the consequences which Morelly, Mably, and Rousseau were quite willing to accept. Here we may contrast him with Diderot who, intensely concerned with the problem of the superior person and the relation of greatness to morality, distrusted the uses to which leadership might put absolute power.[141]

So inseparable are morals and politics for Rousseau that we have already been led to observe their interrelation time and again. We need only emphasize some general conclusions. The essential signposts are those we have noted in *Emile:* that what is natural in the state of nature and in society are two different things; and that it is necessary to "denature" man, in order to make of him a social being. Perhaps the outstanding illustration is given to us in *La Nouvelle Héloïse,* where Julie and Saint-Preux discover that "the purest law of nature" (under the aegis of which they had proclaimed their independence of social conventions or controls) does not lead to happiness, and must itself be purified.[142] For Rousseau, too, human nature is the point of departure for political theory. The pertinent fact of human nature is that "nobody wants the public welfare when it does not agree with his own; therefore this agreement is the object of the true statesman who wants to make people happy and good." [143] For Rousseau, as for others,

[139] *Système,* I, pp. 129–33.

[140] *Ibid.,* I, p. 154.

[141] For Burke's realization of this, see *Reflections,* Everyman edition, pp. 144–45. But Burke also speaks of converting unsocial energies to social (p. 154), and d'Holbach, like him, claims to base "policy" on justice (p. 152).

[142] The expression is used in Lettre XXI, and is followed, in Lettre L, by Julie's conclusion that real love "is able to purify our natural inclinations."

[143] "Lettre à M. de Beaumont," III, p. 65.

the crux of the problem is the conflict between natural man and social man; his efforts, in *Emile, La Nouvelle Héloïse,* and the political writings, was to show how *homo duplex* can be transformed into a consistent social being. To accomplish this requires the formation of harmony of wills among men, which in turn requires a co-operative and unified society, having only one will. In *La Nouvelle Héloïse* we see how transparency and harmony are lost, in the basic social microcosm, as a result of independence, of following "pure nature," which (in society) is passionate and egoistic. So, too, in the social macrocosm. There must be a complete absorption of all divergent wills into one collective will.

> What makes human wretchedness is the contradiction between our state and our desires, between our duties and our inclinations, between nature and social institutions, between man and citizen. Make man one, and you will make him as happy as he can be. Give him completely to the State, or leave him completely to himself. . . . Make men consistent with themselves, being what they want to appear and appearing what they are; you will have put social law within their hearts: social men by their nature and citizens by their inclinations, they will be one, they will be good, they will be happy, and their happiness will be that of the Republic. For being nothing except by it, they will exist only for it; it will have all they have and will be all they are. To the force of constraint you have added that of will. . . . It [the Republic] will be all that it can be when it embraces all. . . . In another system there will always be something in the State which does not belong to the State, be it only the will of its members; and who does not know the influence of this will in affairs? When people want to be happy only for themselves, there is no happiness for the fatherland.[144]

Rousseau realized that in the purely naturalistic framework, each individual will decide for himself, according to his own interest and pleasure, what is right and wrong. He was acutely aware (following Helvétius) that each social group will do the same. There can be no harmony, but only the intestine war of a competitive society (as depicted in the second *Discours* [145]) unless these "particular wills" are absorbed and surpassed.[146]

---

[144] Vaughan, *op. cit.,* I, p. 326. We need not emphasize here how this is developed in the *Contrat social,* and in the projects for Corsica and Poland.

[145] See also *Narcisse,* Preface, V, pp. 105–6, and 106–7n.

[146] R. R. Palmer errs, in his generally excellent book, in opposing Rousseau and Helvétius. The former, he writes, "held that men were good by native spontaneous inclination." (*Op. cit.,* p. 200.) This is to confuse "goodness" (a first movement of

The role of the State is therefore essential. "I saw," he writes in the ninth book of the *Confessions,* "that everything depended basically on political science, and that, no matter how one views the problem, every people is just what its government makes it. The great question of the best possible form of government seemed to lead me back to the other question: 'What form of government is most suited to produce a nation which is virtuous, enlightened, wise—in short, in the highest sense of the word, as perfect as possible?' " What matters, however, is Rousseau's precise concept of the role of government. In the *Contrat social,* he outlines an ideal system of political institutions for pacifying and controlling egoistic aggressiveness by repressing and transforming particular wills into a monistic collective harmony.[147] With such institutions, proper laws can be made and executed.

But Rousseau is not attracted by the thesis that laws are by themselves sufficient to the great task. Time and again he indicates the limits to the operative effectiveness of laws.[148] He alone does not want merely to *use* self-love and self-interest, but to sublimate them. This is what is meant by "changing" men, by "denaturing" them (in his own words).[149] In the *Contrat social* it is clear that the self is surpassed by an *identification* with the general interest, by an emotional involvement which is empathetic and not sympathetic, by the absorption of each individual cell into the total organic life of the "corporate self." It is not a question of advancing the general interest *because of* self-interest, but rather of true "citizenship," of true and committed "patriotism." [150] The *philo-*

---

uncorrupted men) with "virtue," a discipline required to overcome the egoistic aggressions aroused by social living.

[147] "By new associations, let us correct, if possible, the fault of the general association. . . . Let us show him, in art perfected, the remedy for the evils which art only begun did to nature." We must change man from "a fierce brigand, which he wanted to be, into the firmest support of a well ordered society." (Vaughan, *op. cit.,* I, p. 454.)

[148] In *Narcisse* he declares that laws "may sometimes contain the wicked, but never make them good" (V, p. 108). In the *Discours sur l'inégalité,* he says that "except only in Sparta, *where the Law principally supervised the upbringing of children,* and where Lycurgus established morals which made it almost unnecessary to add laws, laws, generally weaker than passions, contain men *without changing them"* (Vaughan, *op. cit.,* I, pp. 190–91, italics added). See also *Lettre à d'Alembert,* ed. Fuchs, pp. 88–89, 90.

[149] Somewhat paradoxically, Rousseau at one point maintains that character itself cannot be changed, but only repressed; we can cultivate the best in it. (*La Nouvelle Héloïse,* ed. Mornet, IV, pp. 70–71.)

[150] "It is not enough to say to citizens: *Be good;* we must teach them to be so; and example itself, which is the first lesson, is not the only means we must employ.

sophes, Rousseau complained in *Emile,* ordered the whole in relation to the ego. Making the individual the center of the world, they urged him to do good because it was the best for himself. We have seen how Rousseau rejected these solutions. The society he projects is ordered in relation to the whole, and integrates the ego into the whole, so that the individual never thinks of a scission between his self-interest and the general interest and never confronts the need for a sacrifice in which Rousseau has little faith.[151] Individual happiness is still Rousseau's goal, but he conceives of it as realizable only through the collective good. This is as true for the microcosmic social group as for the macrocosmic. The harmony of the little society at Clarens, in *La Nouvelle Héloïse,* is built on no other principle. It surpasses and absorbs all its individual components and transforms their natural drives into social ones.

This is not accomplished by any one mechanism. It involves a *total* mobilization of the social resources. Laws and rules, rewards and punishments are indispensable, but not enough. Rousseau would rely heavily on indoctrination and thought control. In his projected *magnum opus, La Morale sensitive,* he intended to teach "that the human being lets himself be shaped by a thousand external causes which act on his body and soul. . . . Jean-Jacques continues to affirm that surrounding objects, that sensations have an all-powerful influence on him." [152] In other words, although Rousseau refuses to limit man to the sensationist explanation in the *Profession de foi,* he is quite ready to exploit its political potential.[153]

Indoctrination and thought control can utilize a variety of mechanisms. A very important one is the education of children. From the very beginning Rousseau conceives of education as a training for citizenship.[154] In "Economie politique," he calls it

---

Love of country is more efficacious; for, as I have already said, every man is virtuous when his private will is in complete conformity with the general will; and we willingly will what people we love will." ("Economie politique," Vaughan, *op. cit.,* I, p. 250; also p. 251.)

[151] We can apply to Rousseau the statement of Duclos: "The happiest State would be that in which virtue would not be a merit. When it begins to be noticed, morals are already altered." (*Considérations,* pp. 12–13.) For Rousseau, virtue is the essential thing, and virtue (sacrifice of self-interest) is not natural. Consequently, man must be refashioned.

[152] Robert Osmont, in Rousseau, *Oeuvres,* Pléiade, I, LXVII.

[153] There is also a clear statement in this regard in *La Nouvelle Héloïse,* IV, chap. 12 (ed. Pomeau, p. 475).

[154] "Lettre à M. Grimm," *Oeuvres,* I, p. 25.

"the most important business of the State." [155] Through education, a watchful *("attentif")* government, "constantly alert to maintaining or recalling love of country and good morals in the common people, forestalls from afar the ills which sooner or later result from the indifference of citizens for the fate of the Republic, and contains within tight limits that personal interest *which so isolates individuals* that the State is weakened by their power and has nought to hope for from their good will." [156] It is in his *Considérations sur le gouvernement de Pologne* (1772) that Rousseau reveals the full implications of his program of education. It may well serve as a model for the totalitarian State. This is the most important article, he says.

> It is education which must give the national form to souls, and so direct their opinions and tastes that they are patriotic by inclination, by passion, by necessity. A child, when he opens his eyes, must see his country, and until he dies see nothing but it. Every true republican sucked the love of his country with his mother's milk: that is, of laws and of liberty.[157] This love comprises his whole existence; as soon as he is alone, he is nothing. . . .[158]

A somewhat detailed outline follows. The law must regulate the matter, order, and form of studies. All children are to be "brought up together, and in the same manner" by the State, those who cannot pay to be called "children of the State." Education is to be nonintellectual and is to emphasize physical culture. Games are to be public always, arranged in such a manner "that there is always a common end to which all aspire, and which excites competition and emulation." The aim is to accustom children early "to rules, to equality, to fraternity, to competition, to living under the eyes of their fellow-citizens and to desiring public approval." It is to inspire in them vigor of soul and patriotic zeal, to reverse the way we have seen "undisciplined members" of society behave. Without this, laws will be vain.[159] In most respects, this program could be taken as a model for the education practiced

---

[155] Vaughan, *op. cit.*, I, pp. 257–58. The admiring reference to Sparta makes his reason clear.

[156] *Ibid.*, italics added.

[157] By "liberty" is meant national independence, not individual liberties.

[158] Vaughan, *op. cit.*, II, p. 437.

[159] But Rousseau admires as great lawgivers Moses, Lycurgus, and Numa Pompilius, for imposing "an iron yoke" upon their peoples, a stamp, a discipline, an exclusive unity and patriotism from which they could never escape. *(Ibid.*, pp. 427–30—all revealing pages.)

today in Soviet Russia and other Communist societies.[160] Rousseau's own model is beyond doubt the two remarkable chapters in
Montesquieu's *De l'Esprit des lois* on education in republican
governments.[161] The similarity in theory and in the ends of the
conditioning process is striking—the notable exception being the
collectivization of property, a step Rousseau was never willing to
take.

In *La Nouvelle Héloïse,* planned deceit is utilized as another
weapon of control. "In a republic, citizens are controlled by morals, principles, virtue. But how can we control servants and mer-
cenaries except by constraint and compulsion? The whole art
of the master is to conceal this coercion under the veil of pleasure
of self-interest, so that they think they want what they are being
obliged to do." [162] As one examines the details of this perfect
society which are described in the same letter, one wonders
whether this co-operative harmony may not also be called exploitation. The complex plans for "containing the servants" and for
depriving them of all sex life reduce them to the status of things;
they are not considered as existing in themselves, but only as a
function of the group interest, or even of the self-interest of their
masters. They are, explicitly, to be kept and treated as children.
The very competitions, the reward of which is admiration, ap-
plause, and "the looks of the spectators," are the same acts and
motives which Rousseau had condemned in the second *Discours*
as destructive of natural transparency and creators of vice through
amour-propre. Now they are mechanisms for manipulation. What
was fatal to natural goodness may be productive of social virtue.[163]
In truth, there are two societies at Clarens; the egalitarian, transparent group of the masters, and the benevolently exploited and
manipulated society of servants and workers. Each has been
socialized, but in a different way: the first by openness, the second

[160] It should be noted that competition and emulation (condemned by Rousseau in
its present anarchic form) is basic both to his plan and to the Russian; however it
is manipulated and directed toward sacrifice of egoism for the group, and takes
place in public.

[161] Livre IV, chap. 5, 6. The reader is urged to consult these chapters. Montesquieu
describes his ideal totalitarian democracy with an obvious nuance of sympathy. The
influence of Plato is also obvious.

[162] Ed. Mornet, III, chap. 202. There are other examples in this letter (Part IV,
chap. 10).

[163] In a letter to Ustéri (15 July 1763), Rousseau writes that human passions are
necessary to the maintenance of the State: "no more emulation, no more glory, no
more ardor to be preferred."

by contrived integration into a "corporate self" (the "house they regard as theirs") in which their self-interest has been fused with the supposed "general interest." As in totalitarian societies, everything is planned and arranged for the selected purpose, and there is an irreduceable minimum of personal freedom. It is a striking fact that Rousseau should have written all these pages on the methods and techniques of "forming" good servants. One feels that there is some analogy with the larger society. His own explicit comparison ("in domestic economy as well as in the civil") and his use of the word *police* ("polity") reinforce this impression. Rousseau does say there is a difference between servants and citizens; but his attitude toward human beings is the essential. Moreover, the difference is said to be that citizens are moral, while servants are motivated by gain. In order to make such nonselfish citizens, however, exactly the same processes will be applied as to the servants! [164] In fact, we already find such a generalization in *La Nouvelle Héloïse*, when Julie explains that we should leave undeveloped the faculties and talents of those who are destined to an inferior lot in society, "like the gold mines of Valais whose exploitation the public welfare does not allow." [165] Two classes of citizens with inequality of opportunity are thus established, and the individual is pitilessly sacrificed to "the general welfare."

We have, then, a little society in which there is constant and complex indoctrination and manipulation, the adroit use of emulation and self-interest, but always with the end (as in contemporary totalitarian societies) of surpassing the level of self-interest and instilling reflexive devotion to what Rousseau here calls "the masters" or "the chiefs" (leaders)—for which words we may again substitute the "republic" and its "leaders." ("I have never seen a polity in which self-interest was so wisely directed, and in which nevertheless it had less influence than here. Everything is done out of devotion.")

Several other points require brief notation. Rousseau specifically rejects the doctrine of counterpoise, in favor of re-formation and an absolute of dedication which permits of no dissent, expressed

---

[164] Cf. *Considérations sur le gouvernement de Pologne, Du Contrat social*. The *Considérations* is pervaded by a totalitarian spirit and the same scorn for the people, which we see in *La Nouvelle Héloïse*; they must be managed, deluded, and remade into selfless citizens devoted fanatically to the fatherland.

Rousseau's egalitarianism never goes beyond the political, never becomes economic or social.

[165] V⁰ partie, chap. 3.

or reserved, from authority. Harmony and concord are imposed ("they are *united,* so to speak, despite themselves," and "forced" to do good to each other), in order that those who are controlled may serve better. A principal mechanism of control is denunciation, and an inculcation of its moral rightness (cf. Montesquieu), as a form of action in which love of duty is preferred to personal feelings. In these ways, declares Rousseau, the normal state of war is ended; masters are no longer usurpers, but benevolent guides who insure the common good.[166] Nature, finally, is transformed into culture. "Servitude is so unnatural to men, that it cannot exist without some dissatisfaction." But in this artificial society, "no one can stand having his zeal compared with his comrades'." The process of the socialization of "natural man" is achieved.[167]

There are, as we have said, two distinct though interwoven societies at Clarens. Within the larger group, the four élite souls ("the beautiful souls") enjoy a privileged existence which testifies to the artistocratic dualism of Rousseau's society. Julie and Saint-Preux, before his marriage, had wanted to live in a state of nature, even within society. Rousseau shows the impossibility of such egoistic self-fulfillment, the necessity of a rational, ordered existence, and of sacrifice to virtue (communal values and welfare). In this intimate world, all discord and strife are eliminated, but by the frankness and transparency of noble and congenial souls, by self-discipline rather than by imposed discipline. In this extremely artificial world, in which nature is sacrificed to the rational rule of culture, some of the natural values of primitive human relationships can be recaptured, preserved from the corruption of unguided (i.e. natural) societies. Unfortunately for Rousseau's consistency (or more deeply the reverse: the true sign of his consistency), the fact is that even this ideal paradise is tainted by artifices and deceit, which are the real weapons used by Wolmar to overcome the love he knows still exists between his wife and Saint-Preux. It is the same lesson as in *Emile,* the same as in Rousseau's more abstract political theory. Here, too, the goal is a static society, exempt from time and history. Here, too, the security of

---

[166] Cf. *Contrat social,* especially chap. 1: we must justify the loss of natural independence.

[167] Here, as in the *Contrat social,* Rousseau is aware of the crucial problem of finding the proper "guides" or legislators. "To have [honest people] it is not enough to seek them, they must be made; and only a good man can know the art of making others."

this fragile harmony is "guaranteed by the watchful presence of M. de Wolmar"—who is the analogue of the "guide" in the *Contrat social*.[168] Julie's garden, like that of Candide, is the great symbol of its writer's outlook:

> How much work do you think it took me [Julie asks Saint-Preux] to put it in this state? . . .
>
> My word, I said to her, you just let it alone. This place is charming, it is true, but rustic and abandoned. I don't see any sign of human work. You closed the gate; the water came I don't know how; nature alone has done all the rest; and even you could not have done as well as she.
>
> It is true, she said, that nature has done it all, but under direction, and there is nothing there which I have not planned.[169]

What is most striking in *La Nouvelle Héloïse* is the constant impression of a completely and perfectly rational way of life, in which every detail is foreseen, planned, and calculated, even the nonrational (or suprarational) "communication of souls." Wolmar or Julie, in turn, is always explaining his or her "method." It is quite clear that the purpose is to disfigure nature, in order to make it more natural, according to a preconceived rational idea of what nature should be!

[168] The quotation is from Ronald Grimsley's brilliant analysis, "The Human Problem in *La Nouvelle Héloïse*," p. 181. Grimsley also notes: "The elimination of love, on the other hand, makes it possible for the self to remain satisfied with a world that is in some sense timeless because it does not need to evolve or be modified." This is as true of Karl Marx as of the *Contrat social*. Grimsley indicates the human flaws in this utopia. But they were already beautifully laid bare in the El Dorado episode of *Candide*: the restlessness and dissatisfaction characteristic of the human animal, his striving for absolute self-expression and self-affirmation. "Happiness," says Julie finally, "bores me."

[169] *La Nouvelle Héloïse*, IVᵉ partie, Lettre XI. In the detailed explanation which follows, we see that all the effects of nature are "tricked." We have throughout *La Nouvelle Héloïse* the dichotomy of appearance and reality which Rousseau had condemned so severely and which he pretends to abolish. This also applies to Julie's method of raising the children (in which the general ideas of *Emile* are already announced). The children are brought up under "an inflexible yoke," but apparent or direct discipline is avoided. Apparent freedom masks constant guidance and constraint, often based on rather intricate artifice. We can see here the duplicity of Rousseau's vocabulary which is frequent throughout his writings. Management and constraint are called "freedom," artifice is called "nature," though it is, in Rousseau's mind, nature "made to work" by artifice. The symbol of the garden is brought in again: "I weed the garden," says Julie (V, p. 3). There is little intellectual education before adolescence, but an effort to "imprint early in ineffaceable letters" certain modes of feeling and behavior.

A close analysis of the *Contrat social* may well substantiate the view that Rousseau's aim is to make the people believe they are free, exactly as he does with the servants and the children in *La Nouvelle Héloïse*. See my forthcoming article, "Rousseau et la voie du totalitarisme" (Annales de philosophie politique, tone v, 1963).

As one reads the strategy for the large republic, it becomes fairly clear that there, too, the goal is to make the people think they want what some have decided they ought to want. We shall not go into the program of the *Contrat social*. Let us only summarize the various mechanisms suggested in several works to achieve the socialization of man in the co-operative society: obscurantism, an élite of leaders, inculcation of "virtue," of citizenship and patriotism, the processes of "education," a nominal egalitarianism, prohibition of luxury and individualistic competition, "censorship" (by which Rousseau describes control of opinions and mores), the mobilization of such resources as the theater, the press, and public games or festivals, an obligatory State religion, absolute submission to the general will with no political parties, no individual or group rights of dissent or opposition, and finally, reliance on "guides" to formulate and indoctrinate the "general will" with which the "generality" cannot be trusted. Clearly, this is nothing less than mobilization of the total resources of the State to weld the society into a monistic unit.[170]

Just how far Rousseau would go is clearly and specifically set forth in his *Projet de constitution pour la Corse,* in which the details of individual and family life are regulated and regimented in the way which Morelly (and Plato) had done and which bears an appalling analogy to some aspects of the Chinese Communist program. And Rousseau asserts that all this is done in the name of *nature* and of *liberty*.

How will all these mechanisms operate? They will all focus on the repression of the conversion of "natural inclinations." It has not been sufficiently emphasized that this objective is present in Rousseau's mind from the very outset.[171] It is consistently present through each and every pertinent writing (the second *Discours* not being contradictory to it); consistently, it emphasizes control of the sexual drives and keeping women "in their place." [172] The

---

[170] The great difficulty which Rousseau admits not having overcome is that the lawgiver, or guide, must be exempt from the vices and temptations which he is trying to eliminate. See L. Gossman, "Rousseau's Idealism."

[171] See *Réponse au Roi de Pologne, Réponse à M. Bordes, Oeuvres,* I, pp. 34–35, 49, 50n.

[172] E. g., *Réponse a M. Bordes," Oeuvres,* I, pp. 49, 50n; *Discours sur les arts,* ed. Havens, note 285, p. 244; *Lettre à d'Alembert,* ed. Fuchs, p. 111; *La Nouvelle Héloïse,* VI, chap. 6 ("the strength of soul which produces all the virtues depends on the purity which nourishes them all"), and Pomeau edition, pp. 102–3, 338–39, 341, *Emile, passim.*

theme of *La Nouvelle Héloïse,* in part, *is* the problem of sexual relations in society. This socio-political conception is not merely rational. On the contrary, it counts almost exclusively on the manipulation of emotions; and, in *La Nouvelle Héloïse,* attributes great importance to the establishment of harmonious, "transparent" and nonaggressive interpersonal relations within the small social nucleus.

Rousseau is almost alone among his fellow theorists in not holding up the goal of finding the "natural laws" of government.[173] Society itself is not natural. We must, then, pledge ourselves wholly to the work of culture in its transformation of nature. Our examination of Rousseau's moral theories has shown, to quote Charles Frankel's excellent formulation, that he believed that "reason could never argue anyone into having a feeling of obligation." [174] However, we must also remember that he never counted —like some others—on that "natural goodness" (which he defended as an attribute of our original nature) having any operative effect in the social state. The rest follows from this. His system of conditioning and repression exists in virtue of his persuasion that men, in society, are wicked *because* of their natural impulses toward each other—a point which he made clear in his replies after the first *Discours,* in *Narcisse,* and in the second *Discours.*[175] His totalitarian absorption and transformation of the individual social atoms into the monistic unity of an organism rests on his perception of a state of war, a state of moral nihilism, existing *naturally* among men in society. He turns away from a synthesis of nature and culture, and as Sade was to select nature, so he selects culture.

Rousseau's opposition to the *philosophes* thus presents a curious duality. On the one hand, he stands for worship of the natural (the simple and sincere) in opposition to scientific progress, luxury, the arts. On the other hand, the *philosophes* worshiped

---

[173] Cf. his opposition to Diderot's "Droit naturel" and his theories on the origin of society.

[174] *Op. cit.,* p. 78.

[175] As Starobinski has shown, immediacy and transparency are lost in society. Men would be "good" if they followed their first impulses (like Rousseau!), if they acted without prudence, calculation, reflection. But all that is lost to the corruption of *amour-propre.* Goodness is no longer sufficient. Now *virtue* is needed. To have virtue we need repression of natural impulses, indoctrination, guides, etc. "But unfortunately, personal interest is always in inverse relation to duty." (Vaughan, *op. cit.,* I, p. 243).

nature in the sense that it provides laws and motives which bring
about harmony, happiness, and progress, while he espouses the
opposite thesis, that the rational (unnatural) society and man
(conditioned) alone could realize his ideal. Moreover, his preference for a simple, rustic society fits perfectly with his political
theories, since the avoidance of sophistication and complexity
would make it easier to achieve his ends. Sparta is therefore the
model, Athens the foil.[176]

The abbé de Mably was one of the most important theorists,
one whose ideas influenced the thinking of the Revolutionary
leaders, including Robespierre and especially Babeuf. He opposed
the doctrine of enlightened despotism, but his practical attitude
toward social questions was a conservative one.[177] In the realm
of pure speculation he theorized about a collectivist, communistic
State, in which, like Rousseau, he makes no pretense at discovering
natural laws, but relies on reason and will. In his *De la Législation* (1776), he starts from the common premise that legislation
must be based on a knowledge of human nature and happiness.
The lawmaker's task is to promote the social qualities on which
society depends. The law of nature is equality; it obtains in
society, too, as a necessary condition for prosperity. Equality
depends on common ownership of all goods. (Mably is thus led
to exclude Rousseau's thesis of property as basic to the origin
of society.) Mably takes care to warn us that equality, once destroyed, cannot be re-established. The legislator must therefore
work with might and main against luxury, avarice and ambition,
and so bring the State closer to the views of nature. Mably also
gives to laws vast scope and power. "Can you be unaware of the
fact that virtues and vices, which ruin States or make them

[176] Benjamin Constant's analytical criticism of the *Contrat social*, in his *Principes
de politique*, seems more pertinent and valid with the passing of time.
A minor protototalitarian and disciple of Rousseau was S. N. H. Linguet. See his
Théorie des loix civiles (1767) I, pp. 348–53.
[177] See his *Considérations sur le gouvernement et les lois des Etats-Unis d'Améri-
que*. This antiliberal attitude, dominated by distrust of the people and the need to
repress them, is fundamentally the same as in his theoretical State. When Mably
rails against despotism and demands that the government express the will of the
nation, he is not necessarily favoring a *liberal* society. Elsewhere, he favors a limited
monarchy and subordination of the executive to the legislative; but here again he
gives the legislative unlimited authority, unconditioned by "fundamental laws" or
a constitution. On the other hand, he stoutly maintains the right to resist oppression
by insurrection (*Des Droits et devoirs du citoyen*, Lettre IV). While there are some
liberal elements occurring in Mably's voluminous writings, we shall see that the
main drift of his thinking is anti-liberal.

flourish, are rare or common only as far as the legislator takes particular care to cultivate good *mores?"* [178]

It is because he relies on the indoctrinating power of education and laws that Mably demands the popular suffrage of a *democratic* State. Le Mercier de la Rivière had argued that men must act according to the natural order (pleasure-pain), and that conflicting particular interests could not therefore be taken as the arbiters of public interest; passions and *mauvaise volonté* dominate the majority. To this Mably replies that the allegations are true, but only because we have corrupted wills by private property, and because we have not wisely directed them: "the whole art of politics consists in directing our affections in such a manner that we take pleasure in sacrificing ourselves for society." [179]

We must begin by regulating morals. The passions are an instrument for those who govern to play on. "Why couldn't you bring out how useful they would be in the hands of a skillful politician? . . . If I play a certain key on a clavecin, I am sure of producing a certain sound. I believe, in truth, that it is the same with man. . . . Man would be happy if politics learned the springs of the heart well enough to move the passions at will, and to give them the extent, the activity and the enthusiasm necessary to the success of its enterprises; and it is this marvelous art which I claimed to teach." [180] Hope, pity, anger, fear, shame, and esteem —these are the springs to be moved, or the keys to be struck. "Prudence" must above all be cultivated; for men, seeking happiness, will be just "only insofar as the chiefs or magistrates of nations work ceaselessly to oppose the progress of imprudence in citizens." Men are not reasonable enough to be prudent, true enough; "but they are capable of being disciplined, they adopt the ideas, customs and morals that we may decide to give them." [181] The force of example and habit can make them act in a desired fashion before they reflect about it, or consent to it.[182] Men, by and large, are little better than animals, devoid of reason, led by what flatters them, incapable of rational foresight. "It is these imbeciles who, by their number, by the stupidity of their brutal

---

[178] *De la Législation*, pp. 344–45. Mably also emphasizes the necessity of social education to inculcate good habits.
[179] *Doutes . . . , Oeuvres,* 1789, XI, pp. 244–49.
[180] *Principes de morale,* X, pp. 216–19.
[181] *De la Superstition,* XIV, pp. 175–76.
[182] *Ibid.,* pp. 288–89.

instinct and their physical force make reason tremble and exercise the most blind and violent tyranny in the world. We must spare their prejudices and fear to irritate them." [183] We must, in other words, consider the people as children and the government as their parents or guardians who must "shape them to the practice of their duties." We must direct their self-love in such a way that they neglect their private advantage and are (by a proper system of laws) rewarded for the sacrifice. The third part of the *Principes de morale* is largely a study of the psychology of children and adolescents, with the avowed purpose of forming them in a desired mold. "Let us study man as he is, in order to teach him to become what he should be." [184] We must make the imbecilic multitude "the worthy instrument of great men who make it act." [185]

It is obvious that Mably's "democracy" is not that of Jefferson and the Anglo-Saxon tradition, but, distrusting and despising the people, belongs to the French tradition of directed, egalitarian "popular democracy," which, developed by Montesquieu (in his chapters on democracies), Morelly and Rousseau, leads to the "people's democracies" of Robespierre and the modern Communist States. The multiple analogies with Rousseau's thinking are obvious. The same union of morals and laws is a metaphor for repressive indoctrination by a monistic State.[186] Nor is it surprising that Mably, like the others, is puritanical in regard to sexual license and to luxury—such repression being a crucial form of the socialization of the egoistic antisocial drives.[187]

Kingsley Martin has pointed out that theorists like Mably and Morelly emphasized virtue rather than happiness. Happiness was only the incidental result of virtue, and it was virtue which laws

[183] *Ibid.*, pp. 391–92. This theme, we recall, has a continuous history from Bayle and Fontenelle on. See especially my article on the controversy over truth and falsehood.

[184] *Principes de morale*, X, p. 354.

[185] *Ibid.*, p. 397.

[186] See *Entretiens de Phocion*, p. 73. Mably goes so far as to claim that happiness is identical for all men, wherefore the government must discover its nature and apply it (*ibid.*, p. 41).

[187] See *ibid.*, X, pp. 90–96 for a detailed statement of this position; also p. 291 ff. and especially pp. 58–76: "in the eyes of politics, there is no minor virtue . . . the most essential laws for the happiness and safety of States are those which concern the details of morals" (p. 64). This repressive doctrine is further developed in the *Considérations sur . . . les Etats-Unis*, p. 338 ff.; legislators and governments "must neglect no measures" to inculcate virtues.

should foster.[188] "Is it not certain," wrote Mably in the *Entretiens de Phocion*, "that the polity ought to make us love virtue and that virtue is the only object which legislators, laws and magistrates ought to have in view?" And, we may add, is it not certain that this is equally true of Rousseau's political thought? And is it not also the same virtue of which Montesquieu speaks—the repression of self-interest and egoism in favor of the general welfare of the collective whole?

Let us glance briefly at Sabatier de Castres, a typical example of the *philosophe* turned anti-*philosophe* with the advent of the Revolution. The key to his whole system—absolute monarchy, nobility, intolerance, foisting of superstition—is his view of human nature. The Golden Rule is contrary to human nature, he assures us, and must be imposed by force, threats, or deceit. Man is so selfish that he would always be unjust and aggressive, "if the laws of society did not repress his natural tendencies very early. . . . In a word, he is so inclined to evil that there is no man who by the age of twenty would not have been a homicide, perhaps a fratricide and even a parricide, if his power had equalled his will." [189] Sabatier's plan is, then, to have the government artfully utilize men's vices: ambition, cupidity, jealousy, hatred, fear, superstition, hypocrisy, love of lies, and the marvelous. Hypocrisy, for instance, obliges scoundrels to the exterior practice of virtue; better a pretty mask than an ugly face. "Vices are opposed to vices and can serve as a counterweight." [190] Borrowing perhaps an image from Mably, Sabatier writes: "The art of governing man and peoples is really only that of directing passions and making them tend to the proposed end. They are the different keys of the political keyboard." [191] In a later work, Sabatier boasts of a plan which would make it as ridiculous not to be a royalist as it would be to dress in the Chinese style. "Man is the first instrument of

---

[188] *French Liberal Thought in the Eighteenth Century*, Boston, 1929, p. 243. This statement must, however, be supplemented by another fact: happiness being the only natural motive and value, they claimed to be inspired by the desire to make men happy. In successful republics of ancient times, remarks Mably, "each citizen could become happy only as he seemed somehow to forget himself and care only about public happiness." (*Principes de morale*, X, p. 279.) This is again, of course, the persistent desire to reconcile, unify and identify private and public interest.

[189] *Pensées*, 1794, pp. 36–37.

[190] *Ibid.*, pp. 60–70. We are reminded of Nicole, and of the theory of counterpoise.

[191] *Ibid.*, pp. 50–51.

man, and the talent for using him is the most necessary science for those who govern." [192]

We may close this phase of our investigation with a quotation from Robespierre which brings together and summarizes many of the preceding ideas:

> What is the fundamental principle of democratic or popular government, that is to say, the essential spring which maintains it and makes it move? It is virtue. I am speaking of public virtue . . . of that virtue which is nothing but love of country and its laws. But as the essence of the Republic or democracy is equality, it follows that love of country necessarily includes love of equality. It is also true, that this sublime feeling involves preference of the public interest above all one's private interest, whence it follows that love of country also presumes or produces all virtues; for are they anything else but strength of soul which makes men capable of these sacrifices? . . . Thus everything which tends to animate love of country, to purify morals, to elevate souls, to direct the passions of the human heart towards the public interest, must be adopted or established by you; everything which tends to concentrate them in the abjection of the personal ego, to awaken the infatuation for petty things and scorn for great ones, must be rejected or repressed by you.[193]

Finally, we must, however briefly, refer to the third current of political thought in the eighteenth century—anarchism, or the rejection of any political and social authority. Anarchism, two students of the subject have noted, arose with the domination of the State.[194] These scholars see anarchism as the rejection of authority over men, or of power as the source of obedience, a movement which began in the eighteenth century "because then the entire social body was the object of a vast process of desacralization." [195] With the struggle against religion, human relations were naturalized, leading to the alienation of the individual from the social body. Thus the *philosophes,* though they defended the State and even sought its extension, laid the groundwork for anarchism. Starting with Hobbes, who made of the State an artificial creation, laws were held to be the creation of arbitrary will,

---

[192] *Lettres critiques,* Erfurt, 1802, p. 71 ff.
[193] "Discours du 7 février 1794, sur les principes de morale politique qui doivent guider la Convention."
[194] A. Sargent et C. Hamel, *Histoire de l'anarchie.* We must not forget the important role played by travellers' tales since 1640.
[195] *Ibid.,* p. 12.

rather than in the nature of things.[196] "Men, as if starting from a dream, found themselves alone on a refractory earth. The gods no longer walked among them . . . their presence no longer made life divine."

While the first two groups saw men as good and evil, or as evil, anarchism appealed principally to a few extreme optimists who thought that society had corrupted a good human nature. Among the first was Gueudeville, in Lahontan's *Dialogues curieux* (1703).[197] Later, Meslier's famous clandestine writings, popularized by Voltaire and by d'Holbach, were infused with hatred of all authority and of the social order. Calling for revolution, for the murder of the king and nobles, Meslier's appeal has been described by Lanson as a *"Carmagnole anticipée."* [198] A complete anarchist, he is animated by hatred for the State and for whatever enslaves (i.e., limits) man. With Meslier, however, we are really no longer in the realm of utopian primitivism, but rather in the camp of nihilistic revolt. "This priest who, after all, had ruined his life and was really taking it out on the whole world for his own disappointments, brought nothing but his blind passion, his fierce negations, his festering grudge against authorities and Authority, his nihilism, his despair." [199]

Utopian anarchism is found in the fourth part of *Gulliver's Travels,* but it is only, for Swift, a reflection on the viciousness of men. Burke, in his youthful *Vindication of Natural Society* (1756), foresees and satirizes anarchism as an outcome of deistic rationalism. Such reasoning, according to Burke, tells us that the law of the State, because of its nature, is war, and that all political society rests on tyranny, injustice, and violence—the violation of nature. The fruits of society are inequality, poverty, slavery, and vices.[200] Government is therefore an antisocial institution. Such reasoning

---

[196] *Ibid.,* p. 14. See our discussion of Natural Law.

[197] Ed. G. Chinard, Baltimore 1931, pp. 42–43, 96, 183–88, 258.

[198] Cf. Jean Marchal, "Requiem pour un curé," p. 54 ff. Voltaire disguised this and made of Meslier "the anodine preacher of a bourgeois deism." Lanson attributes his inspiration to Spinoza, but Marchal doubts that he was cultivated enough to have read him.

[199] *Ibid.,* p. 59. This hatred probably went back to the fact that his father forced him to become a priest against his will. Meslier made an overt connection between death and nihilism: "Soon I shall be nothing. . . . The dead worry about nothing, concern themselves with nothing and care about nothing. I shall thus finish this by nothingness: therefore I am scarcely anything more than nothing, and soon I shall be nothing." (P. 62.)

[200] Burke may well have read Rousseau's *Discours sur l'origine de l'inégalité* (1755), or Lahontan.

is also associated, Burke goes on, with the belief in an absolute truth and law, discoverable to reason, and from which positive law must not stray lest it become injurious. There is no doubt that Burke, even at this date, grasped some of the innermost characteristics of radical philosophic thought.

In France, Dom Deschamps, in the following decade, carried forward the current of primitivist anarchism. The State, he argues, exists only on the basis of moral inequality; there can be no moral state until society is dissolved and natural equality restored.[201] Diderot sympathized with Deschamps, in his secret longings, and there are anarchistic implications in his wish to end the scission between the moral order and the physical.[202] But he never for an instant considered these dreams as a serious possibility in the domain of reality. On the contrary, Diderot's nihilistic writings envisage rather a tyrannical imposition of social control. This is also true for La Mettrie.[203]

To some extent, it is true for Sade, too. More often, his characters demand a nihilistic anarchism.[204] In the *Histoire de Juliette,* Sade demands tyranny for the *canaille* and freedom for the rich and strong. This combination doubtless best represents his thinking: a repressive society but one of exploitation, as in modern Fascist movements.[205]

[201] *Le Vrai système,* p. 85. Deschamps thus follows the simplistic logical line from which Rousseau departed. See also p. 140 and especially p. 146 and note (f). He did not see, as Rousseau did, that creativity ("perfectibility") distinguishes man from other animals, so that as a species, he is never "satisfied," but creates new needs for himself, wherefore we must look in another direction.

[202] See also Raynal, *Histoire,* I, pp. 41–42.

[203] See also d'Argens' *Thérèse philosophe* (p. 96). Punishment is imposed for the general welfare, "which in all cases is preferable to private good." Relatives should also be punished, as this reinforces motivation. Our natural disposition is hostile to public good. "Men must therefore be constantly incited and forced to experience those sensations which are useful to the general happiness."

[204] *La Philosophie dans le boudoir,* p. 141. See also Simone de Beauvoir, *op. cit.,* pp. 1214–15.

[205] *Histoire de Juliette,* V, pp. 243–46; VI, pp. 173–75; III, p. 102 ff. The people must be kept in ignorance, corrupted by lies and other devices. The most ruthless exploitation is developed in II, pp. 156–59, which also urges the imposition of strict morality on the people, the absolute dehumanization of a slave labor class, and the distinction between a master race (not national) and inferior races. Also of interest in this regard is the advice, which we later find appealing both to Fascist and to collectivist totalitarian States, that the primacy of loyalty to the family must be replaced by loyalty to the State. "Do not imagine that you can make good republicans as long as you isolate in families children who should belong only to the republic; in giving to only a few individuals the affection they should spread over all their brothers, they inevitably adopt the frequently dangerous prejudices of these individuals; their ideas and opinions became isolated and particularized and all the

In relation to collectivist societies and utopian anarchism, brief mention must be made of Babeuf and his followers who, during the Revolution, sought implementation of some of the theories we have mentioned. They desired an end to property and social inequalities of all kinds. "A people without property and without the vices and crimes it engenders . . . would not need the great number of laws under which the civilized societies of Europe groaned," Buonarroti, one of the commissioners of the execution committee of the Babouvistes, wrote about their theory.[206] It was based on the same naïve optimism we find in Morelly, Deschamps, Rétif de la Bretonne, and other anarchists or communists of the eighteenth century.[207] The same optimistic theory of the withering of the State will occur again in the writings of Marx and Engels. True sons of the Enlightenment (or one important aspect of it), they were pessimistic about man and free societies, and counted on institutions to reform morals.[208]

Nihilism and totalitarianism are not, as the preceding discussion has indicated, necessarily unrelated. The denial of moral value and of human value may lead either to individualistic revolt or to ruthless repression and dehumanizing of individuals. The former, in fact, implies the latter; but the agent and also the ends are different. The first denies the general interest, the second the private interest. Both wish to put an end to the war within, between natural man and social man.

Early in the century, the tenor of "secular morality" and also of apologetic writings had stressed self-interest (even when indicating its proper limits). These writers, though not unaware that society has its requirements, did not speak often of the general interest;

---

virtues of a citizen ["a state-man"] become absolutely impossible to them. . . . If it is most disadvantageous to let children suck in from their families quite different interests from those of the nation, there is, then, the greatest advantage in separating them from them." (*La Philosophie dans le boudoir*, p. 183.) Marriage should therefore be abolished.

[206] D. Guérin, *La Lutte de classes sous la première république*, II, p. 348. On Babeuf, see also Talmon, *op. cit.*, p. 20, and all of Part III.

[207] For Rétif, see A. Lichtenberger, *Le Socialisme au XVIIIᵉ siècle*, pp. 206–20.

[208] What Reinhold Niebuhr writes about the nineteenth century can be applied to the eighteenth. Bourgeois liberalism, he says, saw the competitive economic life as tame and capable of being tamed. Marxism sees the demonic fury of the struggle [cf. Morelly, Rousseau, Mably] but expects men "to be as tame and social on the other side of the revolution as Adam Smith and Jeremy Bentham thought them to be tame and prudential on this side of the revolution." He concludes that "the social harmony of which Marxism dreams would eliminate the destructive power of human freedom; but it would also destroy the creative possibilities of human life." (*Op. cit.*, p. 60.)

they concentrated on an acute analysis of individual psychology rather than of the social collectivity. We have observed the gradual emergence of the notion of general interest as a way out of self-centeredness into a moral society, the consequent shift of the locus of value and the replacement of motive or intent, as criteria, by consequences. As Diderot wrote, "Services rendered to the fatherland will always be virtuous acts, whether they are inspired by the desire to preserve one's well-being or by the love of glory." [209] Montesquieu emphasized a prestige concept of honor. He was also the first important writer to indicate the possibility of molding public opinion and directing men, as well as exploiting their faults and foibles.[210] Helvétius, d'Holbach, and the others do not tell us precisely what they mean by "general interest." [211] By integrating the two "interests," they indicate only a way of enabling the State to exploit the vices or weakness of individuals for what is conceived to be their ultimate good, and to control their behavior by conditioning and indoctrination. They have in mind an abstract, permanent self-interest of individuals, thinking thus to create a scientific objectivity, but forgetting completely the existential reality of the sentient being from which they originally derived their principles.[212] "Make men happy through virtue' (induced or imposed) is a good slogan, but when these theorists think of society in general, they have little regard for the aspirations of the individual.[213] They love humanity and lose the concrete person. "Patriotism" as an all-absorbing collective force takes shape.[214] It will receive concrete form and realization during the dictatorship of Robespierre and his associates.

[209] *Encyclopédie,* "Intérêt," in *Oeuvres,* XV, p. 230.

[210] ". . . each goes to the common good, thinking he is going to his own interest . . . This false honor is also useful to the public." (*De l'Esprit des lois,* chap. VII.)

[211] Although "the greatest happiness of the greatest number" is generally implied the definition of general interest as that of the majority is usually avoided, since it would create the problem of justifying the sacrifice of the minority, or of any individual. Sometimes it is considered to be the sum of individual interests; but plusses and minuses do not make a sum or form a homogeneous whole. The only way to this end is the elimination of aberrent private wills.

[212] Whence the weakness of such abstractions as d'Holbach's "help others so that they will help you." Thus morality, we have seen, degenerates into a code of rules and the rebellious individual is led to ask, like Sade, "Why should I prefer your happiness to mine?"

[213] Talmon speaks of "the subordination of the actual, concrete man to the image of what he should be" (p. 263).

[214] D'Holbach, for instance, already uses threats of public condemnation; he deems the bad citizen "guilty of ingratitude . . . the enemy of the fatherland." (*Système social,* chap. XII.)

In one way or another, it was necessary to annihilate the basic dichotomy their own thinking presented: virtue is what is useful to the public or the State; but we can love in others only what is useful to ourselves. The very assumption that virtue is the preference of the general good (or the good of others) to that of the individual freed of subservience to divine will became the great focal point, often unavowed, of the ethical problem. In this cloud lurked the face of nihilism; and the extreme counter to it was a protototalitarianism which liquidated the issue by absorbing the individual into the total organism. It seemed necessary to turn self-love from a disruptive, antisocial force into a harmonious, co-operative force, to subject an empirical natural datum to rational control. This involved re-educating the masses "till men were able to will freely and willingly their true will." [215] Helvétius, Rousseau, and the others realized that this meant freeing man from history; it implied, in other words, the belief that man by his reason can unmake what history has made, and create "the good society," the millennian utopia.

La Mettrie had indicated another path. The individual is the center of his study. He does not conceive of conditioning as a program, but avoids the anarchism whose moral basis he uncovers by giving to society an equal "right" of power, that of purging itself of elements it considers criminal. Once this concept is accepted, we know only too well, in repeated episodes since 1793, how far purges can go. No moral justification is offered by La Mettrie (or others)—only political expediency, often called "necessity."

We must not forget that "liberal" and "totalitarian" were concepts that did not exist in the eighteenth century. This is why the lines are often muddled, why a Diderot or a Condorcet could write in ways which to us seem to head in opposing directions, but did not seem so to them. Consequently we can really speak only of protototalitarians or protoliberals, that is, of theories which do head in one direction or the other—but which often do so in terms that to us are clear and unmistakable. Eighteenth-century writers, however, were too close to their own ideas to be aware of potentialities which only application to real situations could uncover. The abbé Gauchat did foresee some implications of Morelly's *Code de la nature*. He accuses Morelly of treating men

[215] Talmon, *op. cit.*, p. 251.

as animals and laws as "mechanisms of education." He blames
Morelly for advocating a society which is to be maintained without moral law, by the destruction of passions, self-love, and
property. The result, he charges, will be to destroy the essential
difference between an animal and a human society.[216] Gerdil saw
in the *Contrat social* a system for the coercion of the individual
and commented ironically on Rousseau's reconciliation of freedom and constraint.[217] Diderot, in his criticism of Helvétius, had
the clairvoyance to see that a logical *idée fixe* could lead to
catastrophe. He refused to be carried away by the rationalistic
idealists—who were, as Gauchat's criticism points up, really pessimists; despairing of human nature and despising human beings,
they saw no way of governing people except by treating them as
children or animals, spanking and rewarding, and regimenting.[218]

Hobbes, we again recall, had distinguished human societies from
natural societies, such as those of ants, in which private and
public interest have no separate existence.[219] An attempt to create
this condition among human beings cannot succeed without
dehumanizing them into a parody of social insects. This is one of
the paradoxes of our condition; we must have rebellious, even
unsocial impulses, to be human. The eighteenth-century theory
of bringing about a state in which self-interest and general interest
coalesce into equivalence thus has totalitarian implications, of
which many of those who were attracted by it as a simple, rational
theory did not dream. And totalitarianism, though an antithesis
to anarchistic nihilism, is itself fundamentally nihilistic, since it is
ultimately based on arbitrary will and force. It is, to be sure, a
revolt against nature in defense of culture. But it assumes for
culture the absolute power over men that nature has over insects.
It is a revolt, in highly rationalistic forms, against the failure of the
rational in history. It assumes that truth is dangerous, moral values
without objective basis, and the dignity of man inexistent.

[216] *Op. cit.*, pp. 141–42.

[217] See Kingsley Martin, *op. cit.*, pp. 204–5n.

[218] Jefferson wrote to Dupont: "We both consider the people as our children, and
love them with parental affection. But you love them as infants whom you are
afraid to trust without nurses, and I as adults, whom I freely leave to self-government." (Weulersse, *op. cit.*, p. 84.)

[219] Although some antiliberals may have spoken of a "natural society" as their end,
that phrase has meanings quite different from what it appears to have, referring to
mechanisms rather than results. In manipulating natural laws of behavior, they
never confused the norms of nature with social norms.

The political theories of the *philosophes* rest ultimately on several principles to which they accorded the status of scientific truths. The pleasure-pain *reductio* led to the wish for natural satisfactions and free expression of the self; when combined with the belief that nature is good, the result was utopian anarchism. The same principle, however, when combined with the *tabula rasa*, associationist psychology and determinism, produced a theory of conditioning of behavior; and in conjunction with an estimate of man as selfish and aggressive, the results were concepts of a repressive society having a totalitarian color. The moral anarchism of nature bred its opposite, dominance of the State. Some of the greatest thinkers of the century—Diderot, Burke, Condorcet— were aware of both extremes and refused them both. They spoke for individual rights within a context of social discipline or self-discipline. They sought, not a fusion of self-interest and general interest, but the maintaining of a compromise—or a tension— between the two. This was the only way, they thought, that both could be preserved and maximized, and neither sacrificed to the other in the search for their "fusion" or "harmony." This was also the outlook embodied in the American system of government, as we see it expounded in *The Federalist*.

So that, omitting the fringe group of anarchists and nihilists, whose systems were not taken seriously at the time, two types of society were envisaged: the competitive, representative, capitalistic society, and the egalitarian, organic-co-operative (sometimes communistic) society. These were upheld by two groups of writers. The thinking of the liberal group was largely empirical (despite an admixture of rationalism); [220] for one reason or another, they doubted the unlimited efficacy or desirability of conditioning and indoctrination and recognized the sway of historical or natural factors beyond the power of rational control. The second group, the antiliberals, were rationalistic idealists, inasmuch as they thought that the discovery of the scientific laws of behavior furnished the rulers of society with unlimited power of manipulation and control. There are really two assumptions here: first, that there are a few virtuous leaders, who infallibly know what is best and right, in view of the general welfare; second, that it is possible for such men to wield the power necessary to shape the behavior of other men. "Remaking mankind" invariably means that a few

[220] See Vyverberg, *op. cit.*, pp. 158–59.

"superior" men remake other men into what they think they ought to be.[221]

Political thought in the eighteenth century falls, consequently, into two major patterns. One held that government has the power and the duty to change the modes of behavior, feeling, and thinking of the individual.[222] The other limited the function of government to the administrative regulation of the mechanisms of the State, the equitable adjustment of conflicts of interest, and the protection of individual rights. This group divides in turn into two sub-groups: those who opposed enlightened despotism and favored intermediary powers (or the division of powers); and those who, like the Physiocrats and Voltaire, distrusted the intermediary power groups as inimical to general welfare and preferred the benevolent despot. However, the benevolent despot is never conceived as acting upon the inner sanctuary of the individual conscience, judgment, and emotions, but only as regulating their effects, as through their expression they affect others. On the one hand, the desire is to reform government, so that a sufficient but limited regulation of discordant forces in society may be achieved. On the other hand, the intention is rather to penetrate within men themselves, to mold them in view of obtaining a harmony of wills, a collective organism of unified or unanimous parts—that is, to eliminate discordant forces at their very root, rather than to balance and moderate their free expression.

Two other factors contributed to an outlook favorable to a totalitarian type of thinking. For some, an order of the world was uncertain or false; in the absence of God, the social community

---

[221] Lest there should be a misunderstanding, it must be emphasized that the ethical doctrine of utilitarianism does not, by itself, lead logically or necessarily to any particular kind of State. Both sides, in the eighteenth century, were utilitarians. However, it is necessary to consider the peculiar context in which eighteenth-century French utilitarian thinking developed, especially the psychology we have examined, and the belief that the State had both the responsibility and the means to solve the "great problem," that is, to unify private and general interest, to harmonize wills in a true organic unit. Other parts of this context were the fusion of ethics and politics and the postulation of a single truth and of a definitely right order of things.

[222] "If it is good to know how to use men as they are, it is much better yet to make them such as we need them to be; the most absolute authority is that which penetrates inside of man (*"jusqu'à l'intérieur de l'homme"*), and is exercised no less upon will than upon actions. It is certain that people are in the long run what government makes them." ("Economie Politique," Vaughan, *op. cit.*, I, p. 248.) See *Contrat social*, II, chap. 7, where Rousseau speaks of the necessity of "changing human nature" and "altering man's constitution," substituting dependence for independence.

became the largest existing whole, the only one capable of surpassing the particular will of individual or family. A second factor,
the fusion of morals and politics, led easily to social repression, as
a result of the analysis of human nature whose selfish and aggressive components (including the sexual) were refractory to socialization or discipline in the name of the common good. "The
morals of a people," wrote Duclos, "are the active principle of its
conduct, laws are only the brake." The identification of ethics and
politics destroys ethics by making it dependent on momentary
situations, on tides of power, on legislation and its vagaries. "Everything," wrote Helvétius, "becomes legitimate and even virtuous
for the public welfare." It also destroys the proper function of
politics, which is not the establishment of moral values, but the use
of power to implement and protect them.[223]

The great humanists of the period demanded the right of
participation in government, the widest possible scope for individual freedom, and the protection of what we now call civil rights.
This moderate group (Condorcet excepted) was impressed by the
complexity of human events and their irreducibility to rational
simplicity. They believed that nature required some enlightenment and some direction, but that no government which was
either perfect or stable is possible. Their outlook was prolonged in
nineteenth-century liberalism; but England and America had
deeper roots in their own traditions and philosophers. Nevertheless, nineteenth-century liberals were more inclined to the optimism of a Chastellux or a Condorcet than to the cautious skepticism of a Montesquieu or a Voltaire. They resembled the liberals
in the belief in freedoms; but resembled the rationalistic idealists
and the most optimistic liberals in the belief that time would produce all the knowledge necessary to solve all social problems, in
view of the identity of human reason and the certainty of scientific
law.

The rationalistic idealists did not believe in the sufficiency of
enlightenment and of rules which might be established. While they

---

[223] See also the opinion of Hans Morgenthau: "Politics must be understood through
reason, yet it is not in reason that it finds its model. The principles of scientific
reason are always simple, consistent and abstract; the social world is always complicated, incongruous and concrete." This is in contrast to what a Physiocrat said
in 1768: "It will suffice to have that amount of capacity and patience which a child
who is good at arithmetic employs, to become a good politician or a truly good citizen." (*Scientific Man Versus Power Politics*, Chicago, 1946, pp. 14, 17.)

proclaimed that the existing feudal order was an irrational system of force preventing the establishment of the order of nature and reason, they also distrusted nature (which had produced the situation of force); consequently, they wished to place total force in the State, which would use it to order, to mold, to repress. An order of anarchic force was thus to be replaced by an order of rational force operating in the service of the organic whole. It is, incidentally, a somewhat amusing paradox that these men constantly attacked Christianity for repressing nature, while their own program was aimed at the same results, including even (with the exception of Helvétius) the discipline of sexual activity.

In these anti-liberals, we have, then, a convergence of pseudo-science, ethics, and politics, all devoted to a single purpose—the reshaping of nature and of accumulated habit. By controlling thought and emotion, desired behavior is to be produced. Men are to be remade into truly social beings, who have no thought of personal interest outside of an established general interest. History is to be ignored and abolished. In its place, definite and final truths, absolute laws are to be installed. The possibility of an antinomy between individual and so-called "public" happiness is always ignored or denied. The *absolutist* character of this kind of thinking is notable; it assumed that in human nature and institutions there are certainties, certain predictability and certain utopias. The terminus of such a theory of progress is a static society in which progress is no longer necessary, since that transposition of the certainty of physical laws into moral (and political) affairs, which Rousseau proclaimed as the ultimate *desideratum,* is to be achieved.[224] We have seen what these "laws" were. We must emphasize the fact that they displaced and replaced Natural Law—and unalienable (civil) rights—as outside the framework of physical nature and law, and so devoid of operational predictability. Natural Law was not a political solution, but at least it was, supposedly, knowable to all men. On the other hand, the people could not be trusted to know or to follow the laws of a rational, organic society—for nature (according to one of these laws) does not dictate the sacrifice of self-interest. The desired modes of thought, feeling, and behavior must, it is obvious, be determined and instilled by some person or persons. The idealization of the legislator, or Rousseau's "guide," as the voice or incarnation of

[224] Contrast with this Voltaire's attitude toward El Dorado.

the true general interest, is thus another terminus of this type of theory.[225] Equality is often substituted for liberty, which is necessarily sacrificed to it, inasmuch as the two are not compatible.[226] Liberty is transmuted into a concept of what one ought to wish to do. Thus, in Rousseau's words, we force people to be free, induce them to "discover" a general will which actually pre-exists their vote, and to which they are "guided" by the élite leaders who already know the general will (which, Rousseau says, is only what best serves the general welfare). The possibility that human nature may corrupt *any* institutions man can devise is conveniently overlooked.

In truth, liberty is not an objective, but an enemy. The objective is the termination of an unjust society and the establishment of a just society, the replacement of wrong by right. When private interest and general interest are made to coincide, the war between men will come to an end.[227] We will have a true society, an organism rather than a conglomeration. While we can speak only of analogies with twentieth-century totalitarianism, rather than of a derivation, the pattern of thought was first set down in the eighteenth century. Moreover, the influence on Marx and Engels is indubitable.

Although the anti-liberals may occasionally speak of natural right, that term is in effect reduced to egalitarianism (which is not necessarily liberal) and the pursuit of happiness, which is conceived as that of the generality. As Sabine has shown, the two principles, utility and natural right, really led to opposite practical conclusions. "The conclusion that Helvétius drew from the principle of utility was that a wise legislator would use pains and penalities to make men's interests harmonize, which need not imply any great degree of liberty. Natural Law, on the contrary, implied that men's interests were naturally harmonious if they were left free. . . ." [228]

There are two contrasting ways of approaching the problem of human nature and social harmony. One is to overcome the beast in man through fear and violence. If this could be done, says Boris

---

[225] Rousseau differs from the others in that he does not pretend to be following scientific law, but only rational will; he could not very well look for the natural laws of an institution which he described as artificial and unnatural. Nevertheless, as we have noted, he seeks the same certainty of physical events.

[226] See Sampson, *op. cit.*, pp. 228–29.

[227] The anarchists, we recall, thought of ending the war in a different way.

[228] *A History of Political Theory*, p. 567.

Pasternak's Dr. Zhivago, our ideal would be a circus tamer with a whip, not Jesus Christ. The other way is through love and good will. In the eighteenth century, the Christian tradition was rejected as a fallacy and a failure, and as a rigid institution of power and oppression. Scientific thought led some men to the alternate solution. But men cannot be made over by legislation, and there is doubtless a limit to the artificial patterns which can be imposed by indoctrination and prison camps. Abstract philosophies are bound to discover that there is another world of lived experience, of existence. "Collectivism," writes Martin Buber, "is based on the organized atrophy of personal existence." It gives us "massed, mingling, marching collectives, individuals packed together, and armed and equipped in common, with only as much life from man to man as will inflame the marching step." In contrast to collectivity, Buber holds up the ideal of community, "the being no longer side by side, but with one another." This is not dissimilar to the opinion of the psychiatrist, Erich Fromm. Analyzing Herbert Spencer's affirmation that "remoulding of human nature into fitness for the requirement of social life must eventually make all needful activities pleasurable, while it makes displeasurable all activities at variance with these requirements," since any kind of activity consistent with life can be made pleasurable, Fromm comments as follows:

> Spencer touches here upon one of the most significant mechanisms of society: that any given society tends to form the character-structure of its members in such a way as *to make them desire to do what they have to do in order to fulfill their social function*. But he fails to see that, in a society detrimental to the *real* human interest of its members, activities which are harmful to man but useful to the functioning of that particular society can also become sources of satisfaction. Even slaves have learned to be satisfied with their lot; oppressors, to enjoy cruelty. The cohesion of every society rests upon the very fact that there is almost no activity which can not be made pleasureful, a fact which suggests that the phenomenon that Spencer describes can be a source of blocking as well as of furthering social progress. What matters is the understanding of the meaning and function of any particular activity and of the satisfaction derived from it in terms of the nature of man and of the proper conditions for his life. . . . Only by analyzing the nature of man and by uncovering the very contradictions between his *real* interests and those *imposed* upon him by a given

society, can one arrive at the objectively valid norms which Spencer strove to discover.[229]

History and psychology both indicate that the two extremes of utopian anarchism and utopian collectivism are nonviable, cannot achieve their announced ends. The war within man and the war between men is the price we must pay for being human beings. The great liberal figures of the eighteenth century realized this. They point to a third way, one of humane reason, a way which seeks to maximize both community (as in *Candide*) and individual self-realization. They knew that a social organization must be judged not merely in terms of its functional efficiency, but also in terms of the free existence and human development it supports. But there would be no utopia, and no absolutes.

[229] *Op. cit.*, pp. 196–97.

EPILOGUE

THE METHOD pursued in this work has comprised an analytic study of texts and a synthesis of their relationships, leading to interpretations of eighteenth-century thought and outlook, and of their historical significance. It has been my hope that the analysis of the texts and their relations is sufficiently objective so that those who may not agree with the interpretations will be able to construct alternate hypotheses and conclusions. In regard to the significance of ideas in our cultural history, I have thought it proper to look both backward and forward. On the one hand, the historian must live both in a given age and beyond it, in order to appreciate its complexities and its half-veiled insights. On the other hand, it is surely of equal importance to understand the reverberations of ideas among the generations which follow, even until our own time. Without this dual perspective, history risks that diminution which we call "antiquarianism."

In each chapter, we have explored the questions which concerned the men of the eighteenth century and have noted those which they ignored. We have observed what basic assumptions they brought to the solution of problems and the methods they used. We have asked what they were looking for, why, and what results they obtained. One general result of our study was to show the complexity of tensions in eighteenth-century thought. Just as for the twentieth century, or for other periods, simplistic views of the eighteenth century, though popular and appealing, are fallacious and misleading.

The subject we are dealing with is part of a total intellectual and social movement which constitutes our cultural history. Because of the scientific, technological, philosophic and social evolution, the inherited cosmology, ethics, and politics were also changed. In the "crisis of the European conscience," as Paul Hazard called it (and which we have interpreted as a more or less continuous phenomenon from the Renaissance on, with its first great ethical climax in the eighteenth century), the metaphysical re-examination of man's place and destiny in the world had been the prime mover. Partly contingent on it, but more closely dependent on the new science, was the intensive exploration of human nature and psychology. This, in turn, became the basis for new approaches to ethical problems which, severed from theological dicta and often from a priori principles (such as Natural Law), gave rise to naturalistic theories.

The great problem, in ethical terms, became the validation of ethical value and obligation. Following the methodology in vogue, this was attempted through an analysis of the genesis and development of moral judgment. The genesis of moral experience indicated the status of the moral life: whether it was natural or artificial, primary or secondary, instinctual or rational—a decision which, in the eighteenth century, was bound to have deep effects on constructive theorizing in regard to the principles of ethics.

"The object of ethical enquiry," writes Schweitzer, "is the discovery of the universal basic principle of the moral."[1] This was assumed to be justice and virtue conceived as altruism (though occasionally other principles, such as self-realization, were proposed). However, because of the reduction of human motivation to egoism (or with some more optimistic analysts, to a coexistence of egoism and altruism), the problem, in terms of morals, became that of the socialization of egoism in favor of virtue. Thus egoistic utilitarianism, a first and persistent result of secular morality, was gradually transformed into the predominant current of social utilitarianism, and to some extent into an emotional altruism and altruistic patriotism. At the same time, as a result of four major factors—the character of upper-class society, certain genetic theories, the unconvincing validation of values, and an exacerbated revolt of egoism and instinct against the social superego—both anarchistic, utopian primitivism and nihilism continued, throughout the century, their attempt to invalidate the rule of culture.

Most men, in the eighteenth century, felt that the supreme task

[1] *Op. cit.*, p. 217.

of ethics was to put an end to this battle. We shall not attempt to
summarize all that has been covered in this volume. One fact
stands out. There was almost unanimous agreement that human
nature must not and could not be violated in its basic demand for
happiness. Virtue and happiness, even altruism and happiness,
were fused and confused. Thus began a search for means to
reconcile happiness with the demands of culture (morals being
one principal instrument of culture, whether or not it be considered to possess an independent status in human nature, or
even in the world at large). "To make men happy by virtue: that
is the great problem which ethics must undertake to solve." [2]
Paradoxically, this involved the denial of nature, and the rationalistic assumption that a universal human nature existed which was
susceptible of finding happiness in approved ways—a theory which
much of the materialist doctrine contraverted and which nihilists
rejected. By their avowed intention to reconcile nature and culture, the moralists actually established their opposition, and made
the problem of "reconciliation," in reality, one of choice. They
sought to integrate man into nature as a uniform part of physical
nature.[3] But they had to cope with the fact that he is exceptional
in several of his faculties and potentialities, as is indicated by his
dissatisfaction with the natural course of events and by his effort
to control it and supersede it—this being the very essence of moral
experience. Endless conflict and dissension with the "natural"
follow.[4] Nor could the eighteenth-century moralists escape the
fact that human societies differ from others because they rest on
convention and law which, not being imbedded in a total order
of nature, can be violated. The sexual impulses were one major
illustration and focus of dispute.

It was possible, of course, to reduce the moral order to a social
manifestation of the physical order (self-love). This idea was congenial to more than one outlook: to the laissez-faire Physiocrats,
to the rebellious nihilists, and to some who sought to resolve the
scission on the side of culture, through conditioning and repres-

---

[2] D'Holbach, *Système social*, III, p. 164.

[3] See R. Hubert, *op. cit.*, pp. 270–71, A. Vartanian, *Diderot and Descartes*, p. 28,
and Diderot, *Oeuvres*, II, p. 521.

[4] Modern biologists, like George Gaylord Simpson, are convinced that "the proposals of naturalistic ethics have generally failed through either misunderstanding
of the evidence or not recognizing that man is a product of evolution and yet is
unique, that he is much more than merely a new species of animal."

sion. Others persisted in attributing to man an irreducible moral nature, sometimes considered as a sense, more often as a rational intuition of Natural Law. But in one case or the other, it was necessary to control or suppress "passions," to enlighten or manipulate the reason, so as to determine will. By and large, it was found well-nigh impossible to overcome the analysis of human nature which, stemming from La Rochefoucauld, Pascal, Nicole, and Abbadie, had been "scientifically" confirmed by Condillac. This analysis led to the uniqueness (or dominance) of self-interest motivation, and either to the possibility of unlimited conditioning envisaged by the pure sensationists or to the "fortunately born–unfortunately born" dualism of the man-machine school. In either view, virtuous behavior is a coincidence of the pursuit of pleasure with the demands of the social group, and the practical moral-political problem is to cause the latter to be experienced as the former. Virtue is something "outside of us," in a way, a classification of an inherently indifferent act—or else, "inside of us," as an impulse to pleasure, in the form of a pleasurable altruism. There was nothing to do but to use this motive, and no longer expect men to do the right on the ground that it is their responsibility as men.

It seemed, then, that there was no moral way to make men moral. They would not, knowingly, do the right out of respect or love of right. We may say that many eighteenth-century moralists were not interested in making men moral, not believing it possible. With intention replaced by consequence, and consequence judged in the light of social standards of the desirable, morals really became a matter of *managing* men. As long as the act was "virtuous," it could be done from the most nonmoral or perhaps even from an ignoble motive, and still be deemed worthy. That is why, ultimately, humanitarianism becomes substituted for ethics. Viewed in this light, Kant's revulsion is quite understandable. To state the matter differently, many eighteenth-century moralists did not distinguish the good from the right, or the bad from the wrong.[5] This confusion was less frequent among those who adhered to tradition, or to Natural Law, because they believed that obligations inhere in certain relationships, so that a good might not be a right. They recognized "right" as a judgment

---

[5] Helvétius' reasoning is an excellent example: self-interest is the unique principle of judgments and acts; this fact became a right and the ethical rule; therefore the right and the useful are identical.

sui generis. But the *philosophes* were treading on new ground. Their aim was to construct a secular and social system of ethics that would effectively steer between the equally odious poles of supernatural authoritarianism and anarchy, between a priori rationalism and indiscriminate acceptance of the natural.

They had therefore to avoid the hidden reef that underlay their making happiness (pleasure, or self-interest) the sole motive and the highest value: the conclusion of Rameau's nephew, that right is whatever produces happiness. We have observed their self-defeating efforts to accomplish this, by making virtue the surest or the sole way to happiness—arguments, it may be claimed, which were themselves quite nonmoral, and merely another kind of egoistic calculation which lacked, moreover, both empirical confirmation and the universality and certainty of law. In answering the question, Is there a right and wrong outside of the subjective act of choice? The most common species of reply—utility to self, to the greatest number, or to the "whole"—has weaknesses which were felt or understood at the time, and which later philosophers have amply criticized. The question is essential, since it involves the objective status or validity of obligation. But another question which seemed equally essential methodologically was that of the nature of moral determinants and their *modus operandi* in the choice of conduct. The prescriptive moralist is enjoined to show how his prescriptions are relevant to and potentially efficacious in the phenomena of behavioral choice. The eighteenth-century naturalists, however, were very far from a logic which might enable them to do this.

Although the establishment of ethical value is not necessarily dependent on any particular metaphysical position, the metaphysical revolution stemming from the late Renaissance led, in the eighteenth century, to results which were not always favorable to ethics. The end of theocentricity and the consequent contingency of the human deprived acts and existence of cosmic meaning or value, posing the problem of finding another substratum, that is, of legitimizing what man creates for himself and adds to the nonhuman natural world. The result, as Hegel later saw it, was the alienation of modern man from a dead nature, from an impersonal world governed by inexorable laws indifferent to him. But the unconscious tendency was to refuse this alienation, and to seek to establish oneness with the world by a philosophy of naturalism. While naturalism is a wholly defensible philosophy, and may be in complete harmony with morality and humanism, the peculiar shape of eighteenth-century naturalism tended to be constricted and defective from these viewpoints. In order to avoid alienation, it tried to absorb man into nature narrowly conceived as physical and often as mechanical, diminished the importance of human differentia and distinctiveness (but inconsistently—e.g., the defense of suicide), tried to explain the complex in terms of the elementary (cf. Diderot's criticism of Helvétius), denied the transcendence of the individual over his body or his culture, and at times, that of culture over nature. But the very effort to establish a social ethics of enlightened self-interest and utilitarianism, or of altruism, in part contraverted such a view, despite simultaneous efforts (necessitated by the general position) to seek so-called "natural" laws of ethics and politics, that is, laws which would coincide with the quest for happiness. On the one hand, it was claimed that men are entirely submitted to nature, and that nature is normatively valid (an important source of nihilism); on the other hand, plans were simultaneously entertained to induce or to make men repress or rise above nature.

While the avowed purpose was to free man in order to follow natural laws (which primitivists and nihilists sought to do more consistently), the actual purpose was to free man in order to create a human world and to realize what *separates* man from nature and makes him transcend it. But the temper of the time did now allow a clear espousal of such a supranatural thesis. The vision of Democritus and the vision of Plato were both accepted, in part. Those eighteenth-century writers who represented the original, distinctive thinking of the age affirmed the accidental character of life and man, his insignificance in the whole, his submission to a universal law indifferent to him. The ethics of this outlook might well have been—as it was for a few—an acceptance of natural facts similar to the cosmic indifference. Yet there is much in their thought which also affirms the unique worth and dignity of life and man. He is the center and the criterion. The world of facts is submitted to his unique values, so that good and evil become real. A. Monod declares correctly that when the *philosophes* "call nature good, they mean that they accept it such as it is, without making any value judgments about it." [6] And yet they constantly

[6] *De Pascal à Chateaubriand*, 1916, p. 506.

found themselves wanting to, and obliged to make such judgments. As C. C. Gillispie astutely puts it, the conflict was not only between science and religion, but between "science and any naturalistic moral or social philosophy. For your moralist knows what kind of nature he wants science to give him, and if it gives him only a descriptive account, irrelevant to the good, he will . . . repudiate . . . or . . . he will change it." [7]

And so it was, precisely, not only with their view of man's place, but with their central ethical fact, that of happiness (pleasure, self-interest) as the unique natural motive and value, which might lead to the conclusion that acts are equivalent except as to their consequences for subjective pleasure. The subjection of man to uniform natural law left the conclusion, "whatever is, is right." But these conclusions the moralistic *philosophes* never accepted; this is precisely what they devoted themselves to overcoming. "It was necessary to separate society from nature once more." [8]

The time of alienation had come, but the Enlightenment was not prepared to accept it fully. There were many manifestations of this refusal. It is visible in the attempt to make reason coextensive with nature, rather than transcendent. It is dramatically present in the desperate quest for happiness in the face of deep feelings of inner emptiness, boredom, meaninglessness, insecurity—all signs of the confrontation with naked existence in an absurd universe. The eighteenth century was not willing to accept the fact which it had (after Pascal) discovered: that spiritual frustration is the human condition; that the absolutes and certainties we most want are not available; that we are free and alone, except for other men who are like ourselves. In a word, that we long to be gods but must remain men.[9]

It was Voltaire who came closest to it, and that is why, despite other lapses, such pieces as the *Poème sur le désastre de Lisbonne, Candide,* and the *Histoire d'un bon bramin* make of him one of the greatest humanists of the age. For whether one was an atheist or a deist was not necessarily crucial. Voltaire and Diderot both said that if God were a do-nothing God, if his justice was not ours,

[7] Review in *Victorian Studies,* p. 169.

[8] Carl Becker, "The Dilemma of Diderot," p. 70.

[9] A few nihilists embraced the alienation, but were carried away by the destructive implications—a sure sign of despair and defeat. The nineteenth century will struggle with it on the fringes of "respectable" literature, while waiting for the twentieth to face it fully and live with it.

then it was the same as if there were no God. When God withdraws to the status of universal soul, said Rétif de la Bretonne, or the source of intelligence and matter, then individual organisms become indifferent to him, or at least we must act as if they were.[9a]

But alienation was not accepted either by naturalists or by those who still sought refuge in a universe suffused with the moral will of God or in a semipantheism, which did not give to man his full burden of responsibility and anguish. Here, as in the practical ethical conflict (as it was formulated) of natural man versus artificial man, it was desired to avoid or terminate conflict, to seek reconciliation and harmony. However this cannot be done except by settling for life at the lower level (animals have no "conflicts" of this kind, but no moral life), or alternatively, by a complete denial of nature in the interest of culture.[10] If we were to settle for love at the level of physical intercourse, or for force without right, there would indeed be no conflict, but then man is no longer human. The *philosophes* argued that might is not right and hoped to put an end to the conflict between them. They dreamed of a society of nature where there were no inner (and for some, no outer) conflicts. But such creatures would not really be men at all. It is through conflict, through the tragic splitting of right, through alienation from pure nature, that man progresses into morality and humanity. To put it differently, the Enlightenment oversimplified the complexities of human nature, of human interrelations, and of our place in the world.

Man, despite dreamers, despite extremists on one side or the other, is condemned to be man, an animal physical and moral, selfish and generous, egoistic and social; in the tragedy of his conflicts, of his victories and his defeats—and not merely in his reason and power—lies the glory of being what Buffon called "the king of nature." Consequently, the distinction between nature and culture, viewed from a certain perspective, and between nature and moral value cannot be overcome or abolished; nor, on the other hand, can the two be severed and dissociated, in such a manner

---

[9a] "Salvation lies then in acting as if the fruits of knowledge were no longer forbidden; to take upon oneself . . . the risks and responsibilities of the human condition. . . . There we have, prefigured in the Enlightenment, all the dilemmas which are ours. . . ." J. A. Bédé, review of M. Chadourne, *Rétif de la Bretonne, ou le siècle prophétique.*

[10] Thus Rousseau's solution (in his socio-political thought) was the substitution of the State for God, the absorption of the individual into the collective Whole.

that we can consistently oppose them to each other, and choose one or the other. They are neither absolute contraries, nor can they be completely reconciled. There is, in fact, no pure or logically satisfactory category which we may term, in absolute or exclusive fashion, "nature" or "culture." There are conflicts between radical egotism and social demands, between man's psychological endowments and the requirements of social life; but only in a loose sense may these be spoken of as a conflict between nature and culture, since nature is involved in all we do, and culture is man's nature. We may, more properly, speak of *some* natural impulses being in conflict with society, or with some societies. As in a classical tragic dilemma, man must live simultaneously in the realms of facts and demands, which produce two different types of valuation. "The world of culture is the world constructed by man in view of values"—both natural and moral, objective and subjective, empirical and rational—a world of meaning.[11] A few liberal *philosophes,* notably Voltaire and Montesquieu, accepted the conflicts and the unhappiness as part of the human condition, which allows of no utopian solution, no stable El Dorado, but in which men would forever have to struggle to attain a tenuous harmony of contraries—a definition of the human, a struggle unending, but not without hope.[12]

The intellectual dilemma is reflected acutely in the tensions and ambiguities contained in the words "nature" and "reason," on which we made some observations at the very outset of our inquiry. "Modern man ends by seeking to understand himself in terms of his relation to nature, but he remains even more confused about the relation of reason in nature and man than the Stoics were. The thought of the French Enlightenment is a perfect exposition of this confusion." [13] Nature and Reason "had absolute normative functions in eighteenth century ethical, political and social theory." [14] But we have seen how equivocal both words were, having so many contrary meanings that they lose meaning. So it

[11] P. D. de Gusmão, "El derecho como cultura," pp. 127–28.

[12] As Hans Morgenthau has well expressed it, there is a tragic antinomy in human experience between lust for power (a ubiquitous empirical fact) and its denial (a universal ethical norm). The dichotomy is irreducible. There can be no renunciation of the ethical denial without renouncing the human nature of man. There can be no denying the lust for power without denying the conditions of existence. (*Scientific Man vs. Power Politics,* p. 16.)

[13] R. Niebuhr, *The Nature and Destiny of Man,* I, pp. 19–21.

[14] H. Haydn, *The Counter-Renaissance,* p. xvi.

is that some exalted reason over nature, others the contrary, and still others wished to reconcile them, often while talking about entirely different concepts.

For the Physiocrats, reason was that meaning or aspect of nature which includes and satisfies reason. There was reason as intuition, or again, as an anti-natural human faculty working against amoral and unmoral nature. Still others considered this last reason to be "natural." More basically, the function of reason in the moral life was generally misunderstood. Unlike Hume, the French writers asked, Why be moral? and when they could not find convincing logical reasons for being moral (an impossible question), went off in other directions which removed them from the moral realm. The function of reason, however, is not to convince men that they should be moral, but to help them discriminate between possible acts. In this sense, reason does enlighten men and is not without effect on the making of wiser choices. Reason may not act as a motivating force; but, assuming that we do not know the right choice, it may show the way to more responsible choices. However the French thinkers usually confused the two functions; mistaking the way reason and enlightenment apply to human affairs, they were looking to these to ground that which they already assumed to be right.

By "natural" was meant empirical facts, or else that aspect of of nature which was in accord with moral and social commands, including conscience. "The licentious," Pascal had written, "tell men of orderly lives that they stray from nature's path, while they themselves follow it; as people in a ship think those move who are on the shore." [15] Nature was praised as good and the source of all good, with contrary ideas in mind; and the indifference of an unmoral nature was made (by La Mettrie, Diderot, and Sade) the sanction for human immorality or (by many others) a justification for repression of nature. "The entire disorder of human moral life comes from nature," wrote Bayle, "as from a putrid stream." Whatever good there is "comes from the trouble we have taken to pluck out the natural weeds and to plant others." [16] How different from Shaftesbury, Rousseau, and Bernardin! And how similar to Rousseau's actual program! Leibniz explains, "Now by moral I

[15] Pensée 383.
[16] *Oeuvres diverses*, III, pp. 220–21. Compare the image of the garden in *La Nouvelle Héloïse*. See also the satire in *Rasselas*, Everyman ed., p. 44. Sade's view of nature, at one end of the century, rejoins Bayle's, at the other.

mean that which is equivalent to 'natural' in a good man. . . . Further, a good man is one who loves all men, so far as reason allows." [17] This reduces itself to: moral is what is natural in a man who follows reason. The definition thus absorbs the natural into the rational. And yet the eighteenth century constantly purports to use reason to discover the natural and to make the natural the criterion of the good!

Clearly, from one viewpoint, nature includes reason and reason includes nature. From another, they are evidently in opposition. For La Mettrie, nature and reason are in eternal war; for Shaftesbury (and for Raynal) both come from God and can be reconciled. For Shaftesbury, again, to follow nature was to subject our individual will; for La Mettrie, it was to fulfill it. Sabatier pointed out that Natural Law and natural religion were opposed to nature; the *philosophes* "confuse nature with reason, instinct with duty." [18] We have seen Diderot, in one work, the *Supplément au Voyage de Bougainville,* use the word "nature" in the two contrary senses: to take fact as norm, and to assert rational or moral demands of culture. Nature, according to different writers, is both what is prior to reason and social habit, and what is approved by reason as conducive to culture. It leads to societies, and so to the imposition of controls upon itself—and yet such controls are sometimes called invalid if they contradict nature (i.e., impulse). Both nihilists and defenders of morality appeal to it. When Rousseau says, everything is good when it leaves the hands of God, he does not intend it as a sanction for the natural in society; when d'Argens has his Thérèse *philosophe* say, "Everything is good, everything is the work of God," he does intend just that. And Sade could say, everything is evil when it leaves the hands of God, therefore let us be evil. Virginie's fatal gesture of modesty, in *Paul et Virginie,* contradicts the natural instincts Bernardin praises and preaches, but for him it is a victory of uncorrupted nature. He does not see that if vices are "artificial," so are modesty and morality; that if the latter are natural, so are the former.

The fundament of every ethical code is self-denial; an imperative "thou shalt," or "thou shalt not" opposes our primitive will. Ethics, observes Schweitzer, cannot be conceived as a natural

---

[17] "On the Notions of Right and Justice," ed. Latta, pp. 282–83.
[18] *Lettres critiques,* p. 89.

happening which merely continues itself in man, in the same way in which insects sacrifice themselves.[19] One cannot both say that nature is norm and have a moral code. It is scarcely tenable to affirm that nature is good and the source of law, and to demand that culture confine and contradict nature. If nature is good and culture is responsible for vice and crime, then shall we ask culture to repress nature? If man is evil by nature, shall we look for natural remedies?

The "nature-reason" antithesis was a Procrustean bed which could not yield the key to a solution of the moral-social problem. The contraries could not be reconciled; they could not even be defined to produce a harmony of discourse. They remained abstractions and arbitrary simplifications. Both reason and nature could be opposed to contemporary culture, or nature could be opposed to reason and culture as allies. Man's relation to nature and to reason could never be satisfactorily settled. And the "scientific" approach could never yield values, for moral philosophy is normative, not descriptive; justice is not necessarily the rules of justice, as Thrasymachus claimed it was.

Thus it was that naturalists, placed in the position of finding self-love dominant in nature, were compelled to derive moral experience and to fashion moral values out of egoism. (This, however, was not as compelling for believers in Natural Law.) They attempted the feat of pretending to remain within nature while arbitrarily interpreting the word as it pleased them. Carneades had said justice is either nonexistent or madness. Natural Law theorists replied that nature gives us an antidote; d'Holbach, that justice was only intelligent selfishness, given man's need to live with others. "O NATURE," he exclaims, "Sovereign of all beings! and you her adorable daughters, virtue, reason, truth!" [20] If, as is generally said, the work of the eighteenth century was to put man back into nature, then truly, it may also be said that its work was to separate him from nature. Some writers did this by transferring valuation from the individual conscience (the realm of moral experience) to the so-called general interest and the organs of its determination, which thereby tended to become coercive and monistic. We have, in fact, encountered four different attitudes.

[19] *Op. cit.*, pp. 221–22.
[20] *Système de la nature*, II, p. 453. On d'Holbach's contradictions, see B. Willey, *op. cit.*, pp. 156–57, and our previous analyses.

Nature is good, and so we should follow it; it is good, but it (or a part of it) must be disciplined and denied; it is evil, so we must contravene it; it is evil, and we must follow it, since we are nature.

In consequence of this general confusion, we can understand the difficulty experienced by eighteenth-century naturalists in explaining how their ethics was a part of their view of nature and of man in nature. They wished to establish a unity or congruence of man and nature. On the one hand, this required a reduction of man into nature; on the other, it involved an interpretation of nature that made man's transcendence of nature *seem* unnecessary. As C. C. Gillispie has suggested, "the Enlightenment saw a moral revolt against physics, expressed in moving, sad and angry attempts to defend a qualitative science, in which nature can be congruent with man, against a quantitative, numbering science which alienates him by total objectification of nature." [21] And yet, the nature d'Holbach was appealing to above was really *human* nature, which he both distinguishes from nature as a whole (necessary and unmoral) and confounds with it.

The principle method of evasion from the trap involved in the concepts of nature was to redefine the "moral" to mean "socially useful and approved." This definition eliminates the requirement of finding virtue in nature or natural motivation. The proponents of this view usually did not note, nor would they admit, that their definition implicitly places culture above nature. Nor did it bother them to proclaim, at the same time, a natural (innate?) love of virtue! For virtue was only self-interest! It was held that we naturally conceive of and embrace this valuation, either immediately, or as a result of (enlightened) egoistic calculation. It is understandable that Kant, reacting against this philosophy, will take the idea of "natural man" not in an empirical sense, but teleologically, looking for constancy not in what man is, but in what he should be.[22] Eighteenth-century naturalists aimed to establish the objectivity and validity of moral laws; but by making nature its criterion and justification, they exposed values to the ambiguity of "nature," to a levelling process which could (and did)

[21] Review-article in *The American Scientist*, 1958, p. 70. "Alienates" in the sense that man is not explicable by such a science, and the rest of nature becomes something different, not possessing some of the things that explain man. It should be noted, however, that there were also other reasons for the materialists' concept of science.

[22] Cassirer, *Rousseau, Kant, and Goethe*, Princeton, 1945, p. 20. This reverses the eighteenth-century genetic approach; but the seed is in Rousseau.

culminate in the lack of valid criteria to distinguish among the various claims of the "natural." As Adam Ferguson was to put it: "employed to specify a conduct which proceeds from the nature of man, [the natural] can serve to distinguish nothing; for all the actions of men are equally the result of their nature." [23] Therefore, if there is to be moral value, if culture is to be possible, something over and above the natural must be recognized as valid and binding on the individual and his *natural* egoistic propensities. This the eighteenth century found in the social—which is perforce often at odds with the natural, and which, moreover, is partly responsible for corrupting the natural by its fomenting of disorderly desires.[24] If there is only the natural, there is, furthermore, no need for obligation; but the *philosophes'* moral writings are full of obligation. When it became evident that it is insufficient to assume that the value is given in nature, many moralists simply excluded some manifestations of nature as contingent, pathological, abnormal, i.e., as unnatural! This is to assume that the moral in man is *most* natural in him. Nihilistic revolts in philosophy, the arts, and in history have been precisely against this assumption, and against the denial of the essential, *naturally* valid quality of his other demands.[25]

There were, of course, many other cross-currents, contradictions, and antithesis in the philosophy of the Enlightenment, though we cannot attempt to mention them all. Karl Jaspers, for instance, notes the conflict between faith in reason and distrust of it. He sees the Enlightenment as a child of Descartes: "with what I validly think and can empirically investigate, I can achieve the right organization of the world." But he recognizes the strength of the countermovement led by men "who, although in complete possession of rationality themselves, at the same time saw its limits"—men like Pascal, Vico, and Bayle. "The philosophy of the seventeenth and eighteenth century seems to work itself out in these great antitheses." [26]

An important confusion which follows from the body of naturalistic reasoning was the frequently—but far from universally—expressed belief that men would make significant and ever-increasing moral progress. As we read numerous statements of this

[23] *An Essay in the History of Civil Society*, 1793, p. 15.
[24] R. Hubert, *op. cit.*, pp. 282–83.
[25] For a similar view, well argued, see R. V. Sampson, *op. cit.*, p. 71 ff.
[26] *Reason and Existenz*, pp. 21–22.

kind, it is evident that there is no real hope that man will change, that he will *be* better, but only that external conditions can be set up, or indoctrination so perfected, that he will *perform* better, that is, in accord with desired standards of social utility. Others put it in this fashion: man will become *enlightened,* so that he realizes virtue is the best way to happiness. As Volney states it in *Les Ruines,* "man will become wise and good because it is his interest to do so." The "good" is prudential, and does not regard the will to accept moral obligation. Mably, d'Holbach, Helvétius, Morelly, Bonnet, Mirabeau, Saint-Lambert, Duclos, among many others, entertain hopes of the kind. The argument is expounded to perfection, in exactly these terms, by Hume.[27] We have, then, a hope for the *social* redemption of the species. Condorcet alone, perhaps, believed in an actual change in character, in improvement of the moral and physical constitution. "Who knows, for instance, whether the time will not come when our self-interest and our passions will have no more influence on the judgments which govern our will than we see them have today on our scientific opinions, a time when any action contrary to the right of another will be as physically impossible to most men as a barbaric action committed in cold blood is today." [28] Condorcet was to find out, soon thereafter, how "impossible" barbaric actions were to men! Other writers did not believe in moral progress, among them Montesquieu, Voltaire, and Diderot. Robinet held to an eternal equilibrium; [29] Voltaire and Diderot were tempted by Manicheanism.[30]

Passing now to another issue, we find in a philosophy which often proclaims the empirical and the relative, a real preference for the absolute.[31] The Physiocrats, for example, affirm a natural,

[27] *Treatise,* in Aiken, pp. 86–87, 90.

[28] *Esquisse,* 2e Partie, pp. 557–58.

[29] C. Rosso, "Il Paradosso di Robinet," *Filosofia,* 1954, p. 68.

[30] Voltaire's opinions changed from time to time. When he thinks of the injustices in the world, he writes: "This picture of the world, of almost all times and all places, you would like to change! That is the folly of you moralists. Climb into the pulpit with Bourdaloue, or take the pen like La Bruyère—a waste of time: the world will always go as it is going." (*Oeuvres,* 41:52–53, 1760.) Sometimes his pessimism is attenuated: "The world is getting a little better; yes, the thinking world, but the coarse world will always be composed of bears and monkey, and the *canaille* will always be a hundred to one." (30:549, 1777.) But he did believe that "preaching men reason" might do some good (6:503). For Diderot, see L. G. Crocker, "Diderot and the Idea of Progress," and R. Hubert, pp. 282–83.

[31] R. V. Sampson (*op. cit.,* p. 240) notes the ignoring of the relativity of values in time and place.

physical order containing an invariable moral law as its consequence. They hoped that by transposing utility to Natural Law, it would impose itself as an absolute. The same may be said of Voltaire. Sampson notes that the attack on metaphysics did not generally preclude a belief in Natural Law; that even Helvétius has an unshakable conviction in a universal Law of Nature, discernable by right reason in men of every time and place—at a time when Natural Law was being pitilessly assaulted, by Helvétius, among others.[32] In other words, as our discussion of nature and reason has already made clear, the supposed empiricism of the *philosophes* was vitiated by rationalism—not, however (as Talmon proposes) by the premise of universals in human nature, but by a simplified and abstract conception of human nature, and by the other factors we have brought out which induced a way of looking at facts, of selecting some and ignoring others.

We need not comment further on the uncertainty of making self-interest and general interest coincide, or on the actual sacrifice of the former. We have examined the difficulty of reconciling happiness, a subjective, capricious, chaotic criterion with the objectivity of announced social desiderata and moral law, and the error of taking psychological fact for ethical criterion. Do not men like Helvétius and d'Holbach really prefer virtue to happiness, culture to nature? To be sure, they refuse to choose between happiness and duty and pretend to offer both. In reality, they are demanding the same old sacrifices, and trying to make them valid and attractive with the sugar-coating of a naturalistic philosophy of egoism. We may say the same of Rousseau, in a somewhat different setting. Analogously, Voltaire and others fought against Original Sin, only to admit innate depravity in naturalistic terms. Or, when they would not admit the innateness of positive evil, their argument amounted, at best, to a declaration that man is capable of good deeds because they give him egoistic satisfactions, impulsive or rationally calculated. There is no attempt to distinguish the felt pleasure of an act from the pleasure of considering oneself as the subject of an act. Man is allowed moral knowledge, conscience, and remorse, but is denied the possibility of acting like a moral being.

The terms in which eighteenth-century French social philosophers were obliged to pose the moral problem—the reconciliation

[32] *Ibid.*, p. 229.

of happiness and virtue, of self-interest and general interest, of nature and culture—created an unbridgeable dichotomy which the attempted solutions (enlightened self-interest, virtue-happiness, etc.) were unable to dissolve, thus opening the way to the contrary but related extremes of nihilism and social tyranny. These were terms, we must realize, which they were compelled to use, and answers they were compelled to seek, because the psychology under which they were working seconded the narrowly conceived naturalism we have described. They had to fashion an ethical philosophy, imposing moral obligation, from suppositions and conditions which denied its very existence: compelled by nature to act in certain ways (to satisfy an instinctual pleasure-pain reaction), an individual has no freedom or moral responsibility. Since pleasure was obviously not synonymous with right action (except for primitivists and nihilists), it became necessary to inquire how we could establish a moral system conforming to man's egocentric tendencies, how he could be coerced, coaxed, or "enlightened" into believing that he should follow virtue for the sake of his happiness. When the *philosophes* said, "Do good," they said, do it because it is good for you, even though the individual really became lost as an existential entity in the halo of "general welfare" and other abstractions.

It was, to be sure, an attempt to fashion a realistic ethics. But such positivism is sufficient neither as a description of men nor as a prescription for moral values. Since it does not clearly discriminate between egoism and obligation, it cannot successfully assert the superior claims of the latter. It encouraged rather than weakened the argument: this is *not* good for me, it does not make me happy; I have only this life and my nature tells me to make it as happy as I can; nature is sacred and right, and from nature I learn to follow pleasure-pain motives, rather than the weaker impulses of sacrifice, sympathy or altruism. It enjoined men to prefer the interest of others, or of the whole, to their own by pretending it was in their own interest to do so, while acknowledging, often enough, that men are not pre-eminently rational or determined by ideas, and that individuals (as life often shows us) have more to gain by frustrating the enjoinder, leaving it to the fools to obey it.

Surely there should be scant wonder if in the passage between the Scylla of supernaturalism and the Charybdis of nihilism, the humanists often felt the appeal of the one and the temptation of the other. Nor is it hard to understand the eventuation of a strictly political morality, which enabled the shifting both of responsibility and of moral valuation from the individual's shoulders to society's. Such a tendency grows constantly in the second half of the century, but its terminus is already announced in Rousseau's article "Economie politique" (1755), in which he asserts that the body politic is a moral being with its own will which is the rule of right and wrong. His use of the general welfare concept opens a path to totalitarian conclusions. It was following Rousseau's views (and those we have grouped with him would have mainly agreed) that Dostoevski was to condemn, in *The Brothers Karamazov,* the interpretations of freedom as "the multiplication and satisfaction of desires," an interpretation which causes men to "distort their own nature." To be free is to desire what one *should* desire, and the decision for this is removed from the hands of the individual.[33] The Achilles' heel of all such views is the assumption that those who determine the general interest and direct the conditioning process will themselves be above the same natural temptations and drives of power and self-interest. What is also forgotten is that the word "freedom" is quite meaningless unless it includes the possibility of dissent. At all events, virtue, when it is assumed to be action favoring what is best for the generality, must take on a different garb according to who determines the criteria of the general good. How, then, can we be certain that the "best interests" will also be moral (satisfactory to ethical judgment)? It seemed convenient, therefore, to dispose of the problem by redefining "morality." The "managing" of people becomes the supreme moral and political task, as the two adjectives are fused in consequence of this progression of reasoning; a progression that began with the proposal to re-establish ethics (which involves a surpassing of egoistic instinct) on the basis of the natural egoistic instinct termed self-interest, pleasure, or happiness. Yet to those who opposed the ethical outlook on either extreme this had seemed the only route. They relished neither the pure Christian morality of love and sympathy, which had partly evaporated under the heat generated by the scientific revolution and

[33] In a recent interview, the Rector of the Communist University of Rostock stated that "Democracy is not the freedom to do what you want, but to do what is good for you." When asked, "Who decides what is good for you?" his reply was evasive and unintelligible. We are brought back to Rousseau's *Contrat social.*

the analysis of human nature; nor the extreme naturalism which legitimized the law of the strong, or proclaimed that our happiness depends on asserting our superiority over others, even by hurting them. Against these, a measured egoism seemed the best ground to take. But how limit the egoism? By natural process and prudence? By enlightenment? Or was it rather necessary to direct, condition, and indoctrinate it? We have seen how all three courses were proposed.

In the political sphere, the extremes of utopian anarchism and nihilism had little direct importance. The ethical thought of the Enlightenment worked out into two great rival directions, both of which have had continuous influence ever since. One was the liberal-utilitarian. This current of thought did not try to abolish the tension between self-interest and general interest by absorbing the former completely into the latter. It hoped rather that they could be placed in a situation of peaceful coexistence by the organization of a society tending toward freedom and justice, a society in which the rights of individuals, limited only by reciprocity and equal status before the law, would be respected and enhanced. Science would contribute its share to abundance and a better life. Self-interest would become enlightened self-interest, among nations as among individuals. Reason, tolerance, liberty, unalienable rights, legal equality, humanitarianism, progress through enlightenment—these are imperishable ideals which still underlie our civilization. We cannot forget that the Declaration of Independence, the Bill of Rights, and the Déclaration des Droits de l'Homme stand as immortal monuments symbolizing the legacy of the Enlightenment. In this same tradition we must add the theory of representative government and the separation of powers.[33a]

On the other hand, the need to protect culture by overcoming the ever-present motives and tendencies of the egoistic instincts, to put an end to the war of self-interest and general interest, to socialize man, led to the collectivist and protototalitarian moral-political philosophies and programs we have examined. Beneath

[33a] In addition to the writers of liberal tendency whom we discussed in the last chapter, we cannot ignore the fact that certain of Rousseau's theories exerted a powerful influence in the direction of democratic government. This is particularly true of his insistence on popular sovereignty, universal suffrage and (apparent) self government. A few writers, like Benjamin Constant, early pointed out the innermost tendencies, and his ideas influenced totalitarian theorists, as well.

all these factors, the rise of totalitarian or collectivist thinking rests on a still more basic cause. This was the loss of confidence in the will or the ability of individuals to order their inner selves in what we call a moral way—to orient their inner lives, and so their behavior, along the reciprocal or co-operative lines which are requisite to healthy societies. Western culture had indeed come to this pass. In the absence of an inner order, then, it seemed more and more urgent that order be imposed from the outside, that men's lives and inner selves be ordered for them, that they be relieved of this responsibility which was too much for them. Rivarol calls for "a conspiracy for order." This was not an invention of the *philosophes;* it was a fact of life. The naturalistic reduction of human nature and behavior from which this type of remedy sprang was the theoretical formulation of what seemed to be a realistic observation of phenomena. After all, if men are biological organisms and nothing else, subject to mechanical laws of cause and effect, they must be so treated. There is no use in pretending to universal respect, fraternity, equality, or to a "right" to be treated only as ends—a right which belongs only to creatures capable of giving themselves laws of moral obligation and of adhering to them. In this way the problem of the tension between morality and power was "solved" by placing all power in the hands of society, or rather, in those of its "guides" and rulers.[34]

This philosophy, as I have tried to show, is basically related to nihilism, accepts some of its premises, and is essentially an extreme form of reaction against it. Consequently it is furthered, in our own time, by the fact to which Sampson alludes, that we live in an age of disillusion with the agencies of progress on which the liberal-progressivist school had counted; disillusion, also, we may add, with moral ideals and the possibility of values which can be both substantiated and made efficacious. The result is one we have witnessed, and sometimes contemplate with equanimity: a rever-

---

[34] For the descendance of Marxism from the *philosophes,* see R. W. Sampson, *op. cit.,* pp. 6–7. According to Niebuhr, both discount the rational pretenses of man, but expect men to build societies governed by a remarkable "rational coherence of life with life and interest with interest." (*Nature and Destiny,* I, p. 21.) Cf. the statement of a Soviet Scholar: "Are the morals of a nation bad? The cause is bad laws, a deplorable form of government. To improve manners and morals it is therefore necessary to change the structure of the State. This is the aspect of the social doctrine of French materialism which Karl Marx had in mind when he wrote that eighteenth century French materialism leads directly to socialism and communism." (I. K. Luppol, *Diderot,* p. 302.)

sion to barbarism. The triumphs of scientific technology—because of the way they have been used in contemporary social orders, though they might also be a potent instrument for the advancement of liberal-progressive ideals—have given proportionately greater strength to the aggressive and destructive forces in man than to the rational and moral, thus precisely reversing the direction of history which the liberal-progressives had foreseen. It is perhaps an element of human tragedy that the discovery of the conditions which might make happiness and equality as nearly attainable as possible involves coming into possession of sources of power which men use to nullify those very potentialities.

These are matters in which the verdict of history has weakened or countered the hopes of the humanistic thinkers of the Enlightenment, without—we emphasize this—having yet proven them finally wrong. On the plane of ethical thought, however, we must conclude that the weaknesses of the eighteenth-century French utilitarian ethics strengthened the alternatives of nihilism and totalitarian control—the first of which had already risen out of metaphysical and ethical rebellion, the second of which was a direct product of an important phase of eighteenth-century moral and social thought. We have examined in detail the development of both alternatives, as well as the attempt to forestall or counter them. Particularly significant and prophetic as a warning is the passage from the *Réfutation d'Helvétius* which we underscored, in which Diderot expresses his heartfelt desire to refute amoralism, and his inability to make the attempt for fear that a failure would only justify and strengthen the enemy. This passage epitomizes the crisis of ethical thought in our culture, which came to a head at that time.

We may go further. It was not only the weakness of the rationalistic ethics which was at fault. It was also the accompanying inability to envisage other possibilities. A prime example of considering problems in terms of alternatives which are not exhaustive is to be seen in the all-embracing Natural Law–utilitarian antithesis. The belief of many utilitarians that positive law has no prior moral sanction, making it dependent on convention or force, in turn gives the nihilist and the protototalitarian an opening wedge —that is, produces another alternative in which relativism appears conducive either to extreme subjectivism or to total social control.

There are, however, still other alternatives. We may maintain the empirical relativism of instrumental values without having to abandon the universality of terminal values. Such relativism, moreover, does not annihilate the validity of a given cultural experience and thereby sanction a subjective revolt of egoism; nor does it deprive the individual of his dignity as a moral person, thus allowing the collectivity to assume total moral responsibility and control. In regard to the major antithesis of Natural Law and utility, we have seen how at times (in Voltaire, for instance) these two contraries tend to coalesce. But here, too, there are other alternatives. It may be argued, for instance, that moral principles have an objective certainty without being natural laws in the sense of traditional Natural Law. Even for the strictest utilitarianism, the maximization of welfare (or happiness) is an objectively certain principle prior to all positive laws. It is not, however, a self-evident principle, like Natural Law, but derives from the analysis of good or right. It does not set up this principle as a natural or rational absolute, but only states that when we make value judgments, we are making assumptions about maximum welfare. This immediately excludes the statement that all positive laws are moral. For Hume, similarly, a value judgment is simply what a benevolent impartial spectator would assert. He does not claim to offer a rule for value judgments of particular acts, only an account of what we mean when we make a value judgment. He offers an empirical theory which does not sanction the two eighteenth-century alternatives of nihilism or social tyranny, but neither does it provide an absolute justification. This helps to explain why there was so little communication between Hume and the French on matters of ethical speculation.

Another alternative would be to transcend the empirical, without, however, losing it and falling into the a prioris (frequently supernatural) of Natural Law. The Ancients had mostly linked obligation to egoism and self-interest. In the Middle Ages, these two motives were, in theory, surpassed on the earthly level, by postponing their satisfaction to a future existence. The eighteenth century returned to the Ancients. But Locke had already indicated and Kant was to renew the idea of obligation as a defining character of man, transcending self-interest. We may perhaps say that a conceptual morality is demanded by the reason, objectifying and projecting its own existence, giving a terminal value to every human being. An existential morality in human relations comes from the capacity to direct action in accordance with this universal and the configuration of particular situations.

We may suggest further that apodictic attempts to justify moral value and obligation of the kinds practiced in the eighteenth century are both self-defeating and supererogatory. Moral obligation is no more provable than the simplest axioms and numerical identities. But obligations do not have the rigid abstract forms of mathematical propositions; they have an empirical or concrete existence inextricable from the complex fabric of life, with its diverse patterns. To be sure, what matters to men is happiness and welfare (their own and that of others); but in their pursuit of these ends, they have come to live on a moral plane, to know right and wrong, and the obligation to do the right; and these have come to exist in virtue of their own demands, justice for justice, truth for truth. Whether God has made us moral beings or whether we have become such in the process of evolutionary emergence is irrelevant. We do not need an external substantiation of moral obligation: *we* are its substantiation. An essential component of our distinctiveness and definition is that we have added moral valuation to a nonmoral universe. This is, perhaps, the redemption of our bestial and sub-bestial iniquities. The existence of ethics depends, then, not on what is physical and common with other beings, but on such specifically human characteristics as conscious and self-conscious knowledge, the power to objectify, choice, purpose, and plan. It is not that the moral world is reducible to or completely explicable by these potentialities. The situation is rather that, as soon as they exist, the responsibility for *right* judgment, planning, and choice, for the determination of what *is* right, comes into being. The necessity to judge, choose, and plan involves the selection of criteria for judgment, choice, and planning. Nor is there a need to "prove" our obligation to carry out our obligations. If obligation exists, that is the prime obligation of all obligations, since no other can exist without it, and the word would be self-contradictory. Unless we knew that we ought to do the right, there would be no such category as right. Right and wrong, justice and injustice have no meaning in nature, as Diderot and many others claimed, but their meaning for man is an inescapable part of his nature. Who says "man" says a moral being.

Our very humanity is the origin, the ground, the sole and compelling justification of our moral obligations.[35]

If the verdict of history has not been entirely favorable to the ethical enterprise of the French Enlightenment, no discredit falls on its humanistic writers. They could not foresee the uses to which two centuries of upheaval were to put their ideas, nor could they easily escape working within the confines of their cultural moment. Many of their great hopes and ideas remain the living part of a liberal society; if we have not sufficiently realized them, the failure is ours more than theirs. It is nonetheless true that the thinkers of the Enlightenment, after starting with the empirical realism of Bayle, gradually lost their grip on the existential claims, experiences, and realities of both individual and social life. Starting with a bold individualism, they ended with the accent on collectivism. Their rationalistic ethics weakened the moral defenses of Western civilization—which they desired to protect—against the challenges of nihilism and totalitarianism. From the eighteenth century we have inherited a fundamental weakness of the social philosophy of democracies, confidence in an easy resolution of the tension and conflict between self-interest and the general interest. Later, when the defenses of culture were faced with the choices of reality, they proved inadequate, and under the mask of humanitarianism was uncovered the face of violence and cruelty. It is true that no one else has provided a satisfactory defense that could operate in a society both modern and liberal.

Consequently, while lauding the Enlightenment, in traditional fashion, for its legacy of liberalism, we must recognize that nihilism and totalitarianism (like liberalism, as theories not as facts) were also parts of its legacy; the small size of the group who furthered these outlooks is quite disproportionate to the historical importance of the problems they raised. History has not been made primarily by thinkers; and the economic, technological, and political events of the following two centuries determined the plight of humanistic culture and the power of its foes. Yet we are not entitled to forget that the eighteenth century contributed to the fashioning of authoritarianism and nihilism in morals and politics, both of which were inimical to the aims of many amongst its

[35] Bonnet, we noted in our first chapter, held that men have a different way of *being* in nature, one which inevitably puts all our relationships in a unique light of right and ought—the moral plane of existence. It should be noted that this argument is, in essence, the one advanced by Diderot in "Droit naturel."

intellectual leaders. Again we must remember that their ideas were not so much causative factors as formative factors.

We have tried, then, to see the eighteenth century in the full complexity of its problems and tensions. We have abjured simplistic formulas. We have not read history backwards, but have tried to present all important eighteenth-century viewpoints in their proper relationship—not just those which later history has selected to retain. We have taken sides neither with the eulogists nor with the damners. The Enlightenment gave ample grounds for both, but neither group sees it in its organic wholeness; neither realizes its historical necessity and its historical function. Robespierre said of the *philosophes:* "To them we owe in large part that kind of practical philosophy which, making a system of egoism, considers human society as a war of ruse, success as the rule of right and wrong, honesty as a matter of taste and convention, the world as the patrimony of clever swindlers." [36] That he spoke the truth is confirmed not only by the philosophies we have examined, but also by the parallel evidence of the theater, from *Turcaret* to the *Mariage de Figaro,* and of the novel. But the same sources would testify to the fact that it is far from the whole truth, and that we may draw opposite conclusions from other aspects of their philosophy.

It is sometimes said that the seventeenth century was a period of originality, discovery, genius; that the eighteenth merely broadened and popularized the work of its predecessor. The proposition, as stated, is true. But the historical significance of the eighteenth century lies in another discovery—that of the meaning for man and his culture of what had been discovered, and was still being discovered about nature, human nature, and man's place. True, a few individuals had at various or all times acquired a similar realization, but they were not heard. The eighteenth century brought into the open the untenability, in life and society, of the whole inherited religious-rationalistic value structure. After this point, the decisions of societies would no longer be bound by it, not even in theory. If it contained valid truths, they would have to be substantiated. The individual was faced with internal chaos, emptiness, anguish. Societies confronted the problem of reorganizing their approach to the relation of the individual and the whole. As power increased, the need to control it would become

[36] Speech to the Convention, 18 Floréal, An II.

ever more urgent and difficult, because of the inability to organize the structure of a compelling moral force which, working through social institutions, could control power for constructive and co-operative ends rather than for the destructively competitive ends which nature, as the eighteenth century had made clear, opposed to culture.

The function and significance of the Enlightenment in our cultural history lie far less in the ideals and panaceas it propounded—though these have rolled on to us with mounting reverberations—than to have brought the hidden flaws, the festering problems, the alternative courses into the light of day. It uncovered the crisis of our culture—the instinctual resistances, the inner war, the contingency, and the lack of certainty. Perhaps the greatest lesson of their enterprise is that the basic problems cannot be solved in terms of political reforms or enlightenment. The trouble is in us, in the human condition. But this is precisely the lesson of which many among them, who comforted themselves with rationalistic schemes for reordering reality, were unaware— a statement from which we should, however, exempt men like Bayle, Montesquieu, Voltaire, and Diderot who looked hard and true at the human condition.

Kant and Hegel, Kierkegaard, Marx, Darwin, Freud and Einstein, nationalism and imperialism, capitalism and its antagonists —these are essential factors among many others, in the structural complex of the twentieth century. The Enlightenment still has its place; but in the unending process of cultural evolution, its role in the formation of successive structural complexes becomes more diluted. It recedes to a background even as, at a further remove, the Greek world has. Much of its work, though useful in its time, now has only an antiquarian interest, is no longer a living part of our structural complex. With its explorations and theories in the domain of ethics and politics, however, it is a quite different matter. Here was not only a moment of transition, as outworn elements were brushed away. Here was the posing of enduring problems in a new light, often in a true light. Here was an attempt at answers, which still have their vigor amongst us, the uncovering of truths eternally applicable, of problems perhaps forever unsolvable. All the hopes for the best and all the fears for the worst are brought out into the open. That is why the *philosophes,* despite the fact that there have been better "philosophers" both before and after them, have an undying appeal. The generations beyond were to follow the paths they traced—the rational and the irrational, the exaltation of culture or nature, the primacy of the whole or the revolt of the part. Thus we may properly view the Enlightenment as a cultural moment in the timeless evolution of the structural complexes of culture. Some of it was ejected in the historical process, some remains and can be ejected only by a total revolution. What remains is its humanism, and paradoxically, as a result of its effort toward humanism, the antihumanism which grew out of its questioning of all values, out of its inability to accomplish what it wanted most to accomplish—to establish a humanistic ethics that could withstand the assaults of right or left, and a social structure which, together with the moral, would unite nature and culture for the happiness, the progress, and the brotherhood of man.

SUPPLEMENTARY BIBLIOGRAPHY

A. Sources

BATTEUX. *Les Beaux-Arts réduits à un seul principe.* 1746.   .

BEAUMONT, E. *Principes de philosophie morale.* Genève, 1754.

BERKELEY. *Essays, Principles, Dialogues, With Selections from Other Writings,* ed. M. W. CALKINS. New York, 1929.

BERNARD, J.-FR. *Réflexions morales.* Amsterdam, 1716.

BUTLER, JOSEPH. *The Analogy of Religion, Natural and Revealed, to the Constitution and Course of Nature.* New York, 1839.

CHÂTELET, MME DU. *Réflexions sur le bonheur.* 1806.

CLARKE, SAMUEL. *A Demonstration of the Being and Attributes of God* (6th ed.). London, 1725.

CONSTANT, B. *Oeuvres.* Pléïade, 1957.

CROUSAZ. *Traité du beau.* Amsterdam, 1715.

DARWIN, C. *The Descent of Man.* New York, 1896.

DIDEROT. *Oeuvres philosophiques.* Textes établis, avec introductions, bibliographies et notes, par Paul Vernière. Classiques Garnier [1956].

FOUGERET DE MONBRON. *Le Cosmopolite, ou le citoyen du monde.* Londres, 1753.

GUYON, CLAUDE-MARIE. *L'Oracle des nouveaux philosophes.* Pour servir de suite aux oeuvres de M. de Voltaire. Berne, 1759.

JOHNSON, SAMUEL. *The History of Rasselas.* London, 1956.

LAMBERT, MME DE. *Oeuvres.* 2 vols. 1761.

LINGUET, S. N. H. *Théorie des loix civiles, ou Principes fondamentaux de la société.* 2 vols. Londres, 1767.

MABLY. *Doutes proposés aux philosophes économistes, sur l'ordre naturel et essentiel des sociétés politiques.* La Haye, 1768.

—— *De la Législation.* Amsterdam, 1776.

MADISON, JAMES, et al. *The Federalist.* New York, 1945.

MIRABEAU, MARQUIS V. DE. *Théorie de l'impôt.* 1761.

QUESNAY. *Essai physique sur l'oeconomie animale.* 3 vols. 1747.

RÉTIF DE LA BRETONNE. *L'École des pères.* 3 vols. 1776.

ROUSSEAU, J. J. *Oeuvres,* ed. M. RAYMOND, etc., Editions de la Pléïade, Vol. 1. 1959.

—— *Rêveries du promeneur solitaire,* ed. MARCEL RAYMOND. Lille, 1948.

SADE. *Justine, or the Misfortunes of Virtue,* New York, 1935.

SMITH, A. *An Inquiry into the Nature and the Causes of the Wealth of Nations,* 2 vols. London, 1910.

STRUBE DE PIERMONT. *Ebauche des loix naturelles et du droit primitif.* Nouvelle édition, Amsterdam, 1744.

VATTEL, E. DE. *Le Droit des gens, ou Principes de la loi naturelle appliqués à la conduite et aux affaires des nations et des souverains,* 2 vols. Londres, 1758; also, Aillaud, 1835.

———— *Questions de droit naturel et Observations sur le Traité du Droit de la Nature de M. le Baron de Wolf.* Berne, 1762.

VOLTAIRE. *Dialogues et anecdotes philosophiques,* ed. R. NAVES. Classiques Garnier, 1955.

B. Critical Works

BARNI, JULES. *Les Moralistes français au dix-huitième siècle.* 1873.

BARNWELL, H. T. *Les Idées morales et critiques de Saint-Evremond.* 1957.

BARRIÈRE, PIERRE. *Un Grand Provincial: Charles-Louis de Secondat, Baron de La Brède et de Montesquieu* [Bordeaux, c. 1946].

BECKER, CARL. "The Dilemma of Diderot," *Philosophical Review,* 24:54–71, 1915.

BÉDÉ, J. A. "Review of M. Chadourne: Retif de la Bretonne, ou le siècle prophétique," *Romanic Review,* 51:58, 1960.

BINGHAM, A. J. "The Abbé Bergier: An Eighteenth-Century Catholic Apologist," *Modern Language Review,* 54:337–50, 1959.

BOISSIER, DR. RAYMOND. *La Mettrie, médecin, pamphlétaire et philosophe.* 1931.

BOORSTIN, D. J. *The Mysterious Science of the Law.* Boston, 1958.

BOTTIGLIA, WM. F. *Voltaire's* Candide: *Analysis of a Classic.* Genève, 1959.

BREASTED, J. H. *The Dawn of Conscience.* New York, 1933.

BREDVOLD, L. I. "The Meaning of the Concept of Right Reason in the Natural Law Tradition," *Univ. of Detroit Law Journal,* 36:120–29, 1958.

BRÉHIER, E. *Histoire de la philosophie.* 1947.

BRIFFAULT, ROBERT. *The Making of Humanity.* London, 1919.

CARRITT, E. F. *Morals and Politics.* Oxford, 1935.

CARTER, A. E. *The Idea of Decadence in French Literature, 1830–1900.* Toronto, 1958.

COCHRANE, C. N. *Christianity and Classical Culture.* Oxford, 1940.

COTTA, SERGIO. *Montesquieu e la scienza della società.* Torino, 1953.

CRESSON, A. *Le Problème moral et les philosophes.* 1954.

CROCKER, L. G. *An Age of Crisis. Man and World in Eighteenth Century French Thought.* Baltimore, 1959.

———— "Diderot and the Idea of Progress," *Romanic Review,* pp. 151–59, 1938.

———— "Hamlet, Don Quijote and La vida es sueño: the Quest for Values," *PMLA,* 69:278–313, 1954.

———— "Jacques le Fataliste, an 'expérience morale,'" in *Diderot Studies III,* ed. O. FELLOWS and G. MAY, Genève, 1961, pp. 73–99.

———— "Le Neveu de Rameau, une expérience morale," *Cahiers de l'Association internationale des études françaises,* XII:133–55, 1961.

———— "The Relation of Rousseau's Second *Discours* and the *Contrat social,*" *Romanic Review,* 51:33–44, 1960.

———— *Two Diderot Studies.* Baltimore, 1952.

DARDEL, ERIC. "Signification du mythique," *Diogène,* 7:50–71, 1954.

DARWIN, CHARLES. *The Descent of Man.* New York, 1896.

DERATHÉ, ROBERT. *Rousseau et la science politique de son temps.* 1950.

DEWEY, JOHN. *Human Nature and Conduct.* New York, 1930.

DIECKMANN, HERBERT. "An Interpretation of the Eighteenth Century," *Modern Language Quarterly,* 15:295–311, 1954.

DUNNING, W. A. *A History of Political Theories from Luther to Montesquieu,* 2 vols. New York, 1928.

EHRARD, JEAN. "Pascal au siècle des lumières," in *Pascal présent,* Clermont-Ferrand, 1962, pp. 233–55.

EINAUDI, MARIO. *The Physiocratic Doctrine of Judicial Control.* Cambridge (Mass.), 1938.

D'ENTRÈVES, A. P. *Natural Law. An Introduction to Legal Philosophy.* London, 1951.

EWING, A. C. "Utilitarianism," *Ethics,* 58:100–11, 1947.

FABRE, JEAN. *Chénier, l'homme et l'oeuvre,* 1955.

FERM, VERGILIUS. "Varieties of Naturalism," in Ferm: *A History of Philosophical Systems*. New York, 1950.

FRANKENA, WM. "Hutcheson's Moral Sense Theory," *Journal of the History of Ideas*, 16:356–76, 1955.

FREUD, S. *An Outline of Psychoanalysis*. New York, 1949.

FRIEDRICH, C. J. "Deux interprétations philosophiques du droit naturel," *Diogène*, 10:118–35, 1955.

VON FRITZ, KURT. "Relative and Absolute Values," in ANSHEN, R. N., *Moral Principles of Action*. New York, 1952, pp. 94–121.

GARNETT, A. C. *The Moral Nature of Man*. New York, 1952.

GIBSON, JAMES. *Locke's Theory of Knowledge*. Cambridge, 1917.

GILLISPIE, C. C. "The Natural History of Industry," *Isis*, 48:398–407, 1957.

———— Review (of books by N. Barlow and D. Lack), *Victorian Studies*, pp. 166–69, 1958.

———— Review-article of S. Sambursky, "The Physical World of the Greeks," *The American Scientist*, 46:62–74, 1956.

GOLDMANN, LUCIEN. *Le Dieu caché*. 1955.

GOSSMAN, LIONEL. "Rousseau's Idealism," *Romanic Review*, 52:173–82, 1961.

GRIMSLEY, RONALD. "The Human Problem in *La Nouvelle Héloïse*," *French Studies*, 53:171–84, 1958.

GUÉRIN, DANIEL. *La Lutte de classes sous la première république*, 2 vols. 1946.

GURVITCH, GEORGES. "Natural Law," in *Encyclopedia of the Social Sciences*, XI, 284–90. New York, 1933.

GUSMÃO, P. D. DE. "El derecho como cultura," *Humanitas*, III. 1956.

GUYÉNOT, E. *Les Sciences de la vie aux XVIIe et XVIIIe siècles*. 1957.

HAINES, C. G. *The Revival of Natural Law Concepts*. Cambridge (Mass.), 1930.

HALÉVY, ELIE. *La Formation du radicalisme philosophique*. Vol. I. 1901.

HALLOWELL, JOHN H. *The Decline of Liberalism as an Ideology*. Berkeley, 1943.

HAYDN, HIRAM. *The Counter-Renaissance*. New York, 1950.

HINTERHÄUSER, H. "Utopie und Wirklichkeit bei Diderot: Studienzum" *Supplément au Voyage de Bougainville*. Heidelberg, 1956.

HUBERT, RENÉ. "La Morale de Diderot," *Revue du dix-huitième siècle*, 2:329–40, 1914; 3:29–42, 1916.

HUXLEY, JULIAN. *Touchstone for Ethics*. New York, 1947.

JASPERS, KARL. *Reason and Existenz*. New York, 1955.

KETCHAM, R. L. "James Madison and the Nature of Man," *Journal of the History of Ideas*, 19:62–76, 1958.

KLINE, MORRIS. *Mathematics in Western Culture*. New York, 1953.

KLUCKHOHN, CLYDE. "Values and Value Orientations in the Theory of Action," PARSONS, T. and SHILS, E. A., *Towards a General Theory of Action*, Cambridge (Mass.), 1951, pp. 388–433.

KOYRÉ, ALEXANDRE. "Condorcet," *Journal of the History of Ideas*, 9:131–52, 1948.

LAW, R. G. "Rivarol's 'Morale indépendante' and Pascal," *Criticism*, I, 249–57.

LECKY, W. E. H. *History of European Morals*, 3rd ed., revised, Vol. 1. New York, 1889.

LEGROS, R. "Diderot and Shaftesbury," *Modern Language Review*, 19:188–94, 1924.

LÉON, PAUL. "Etudes critiques. Rousseau et les fondements de l'Etat moderne. I. Rousseau et l'idée du Droit Naturel," *Archives de philosophie du droit et de sociologie juridique*, 4:197–238, 1934.

LICHTENBERGER, ANDRÉ. *Le Socialisme au XVIIIe siècle*. 1895.

LINTON, RALPH. "The Problem of Universal Values," in SPENCER, R. F. *Method and Perspective in Anthropology*. Minneapolis, 1954.

———— "Universal Ethical Principles, An Anthropological View," in ANSHEN, R. N., *Moral Principles of Action*. New York, 1952, pp. 645–60.

LION, HENRI. "Essai sur d'Holbach," *Annales historiques de la Révolution française*, 1:42–63, 356–70, 1924.

LORAND, S. *Psychoanalysis Today*. London, 1948.

LOVEJOY, A. O. "Terminal and Adjectival Values," *Journal of Philosophy*, 46:593–608, 1950.

LUPPOL, I. K. *Diderot, ses idées philosophiques.* 1936.

MCKEE, D. R. *Simon Tyssot de Patot and the Seventeenth Century Background of Critical Deism.* Baltimore, 1941.

MAHER, L. D. "Pascal's Suicide," *Romanic Review*, 53:52–57, 1962.

MARCHAL, JEAN. "Requiem pour un curé: Jean Meslier et ses utilisateurs," *Ecrits de Paris*, juillet-août, 1958, pp. 48–62.

MARCUSE, HERBERT. *Eros and Civilization. A Philosophical Inquiry into Freud.* Boston, 1955.

MARITAIN, J. "Natural Law and Moral Law," in ANSHEN, R. N., *Moral Principles of Action.* New York, 1952, pp. 62–76.

MARKUS, R. I. "Hume: Reason and Moral Sense," *Philosophy and Phenomenological Research*, 13:139–57, 1952.

MAUZY, ROBERT. *L'idée du bonheur au XVIIIᵉ siècle.* 1960.

MELDEN, A. I. *Ethical Theories.* New York, 1955.

MORGENTHAU, HANS J. "The Evil of Politics and the Ethics of Evil," *Ethics*, 46:1–18, 1945.

MORLEY, LORD JOHN. *Critical Miscellanies*, Vol. III. London.

MORNET, DANIEL. *Diderot, l'homme et l'oeuvre.* 1941.

NEGLEY, GLENN. "Recent Schools of Ethics," in FERM, V. *A History of Philosophical Systems.* New York, 1950, pp. 563–73.

NEIL, T. P. "Quesnay and Physiocracy," *Journal of the History of Ideas*, 9:153–73, 1948.

NEUMANN, FRANZ. *The Democratic and the Authoritarian State.* Glencoe, Ill., 1957.

OGDEN, H. V. S. "The Antithesis of Nature and Art, and Rousseau's Rejection of the Theory of Natural Rights," *American Political Science Review*, 32:643–54, 1938.

PARKIN, CHARLES. *The Moral Basis of Burke's Political Thought.* Cambridge, 1956.

PAYNE, ROBERT. *Hubris.* New York, 1961.

PERKINS, M. L. "Unpublished Maxims of the Abbé de Saint-Pierre," *French Review*, 1958, pp. 498–502.

POLIN, RAYMOND. *La Politique morale de John Locke.* 1960.

POMEAU, RENÉ. *La Religion de Voltaire.* 1956.

PRAZ, MARIO. *The Romantic Agony.* London, 1933.

RAUSCHNING, HERMANN. *The Revolution of Nihilism.* New York, 1939.

ROSENTHAL, JEROME. "Voltaire's Philosophy of History," *Journal of the History of Ideas*, 16:151–78, 1955.

SAINTE-BEUVE. *Causeries du lundi.* Vol. 4. Garnier, n.d.

SAMPSON, R. V. *Progress in the Age of Reason.* London, 1956.

SCHAPIRO, J. S. *Condorcet and the Rise of Liberalism.* New York, c. 1934.

SÉE, HENRI. *L'Evolution de la pensée politique en France au XVIIIᵉ siècle.* 1925.

SERGENT, ALAIN ET HARMEL, CLAUDE. *Histoire de l'anarchie.* 1949.

SHACKLETON, ROBERT. *Montesquieu. A Critical Biography.* Oxford, 1961.

SIMPSON, G. G. *The Meaning of Evolution.* New Haven, 1950.

SMITH, ADAM. *An Inquiry into the Nature and Causes of the Wealth of Nations.* London, 1910.

SMITH, J. W. "The British Moralists and the Fallacy of Psychologism," *Journal of the History of Ideas*, 11:159–78, 1950.

SPINK, J. S. *French Free Thought from Gassendi to Voltaire.* London, 1960.

STANLIS, P. J. *Edmund Burke and the Natural Law.* Ann Arbor, 1958.

STAPLETON, LAURENCE. *Justice and World Society.* Chapel Hill, 1944.

STAROBINSKI, JEAN. *Jean-Jacques Rousseau, la transparence et l'obstacle.* 1957.

STRAUSS, LEO. *Natural Right and History.* Chicago, 1953.

SWABEY, MARIE C. *The Judgment of History.* New York, 1954.

TALMON, J. L. *The Rise of Totalitarian Democracy.* Boston, 1952.

THOMAS, JEAN. *L'Humanisme de Diderot.* 1932.

TORREY, N. L. "Boulainvilliers: the Man and the Mask," *Travaux sur Voltaire et le dix-huitième siècle*, 1:159–73. 1955.

TOURNEUX, MAURICE. *Diderot et Catherine II.* 1899.

TUFTS, J. A. "Ethics," in *Twentieth Century Philosophy*, ed. D. D. RUNES, New York, 1947, pp. 11–37.

UNAMUNO, MIGUEL DE. "La Foi pascalienne," in *Etudes sur Pascal*, par M. BLONDEL, etc., n.d., pp. 217–21.

VALLAT, HENRI. "Vie du Marquis de Sade," by G. LELY [Review]. *Studi Francesi*, 6:452, 1958.

VARTANIAN, ARAM. *From Diderot to Descartes. A Study of Scientific Naturalism in the Enlightenment.* Princeton, 1953.

———— "La Mettrie's *L'Homme Machine.*" *A Study in the Origins of an Idea.* Critical edition with an introductory monograph. Princeton, 1960.

VERNIÈRE, PAUL. "L'Idée d'humanité au XVIIIᵉ siècle," *Studium Generale*, 15:171–79 (1962).

VIVAS, E. "Animadversions on Naturalistic Ethics," *Ethics*, 46:157–77, 1946.

VYVERBERG, HENRY. *Historical Pessimism in the French Enlightenment.* Cambridge (Mass.), 1958.

WASHBURN, S. L. and DE VORE, I. "The Social Life of Baboons," *Scientific American*, June 1961, pp. 62–71.

WEISS, PAUL. "The Universal Ethical Standard," *Ethics*, 46:39–48, 1946.

WERNER, ALFRED. "Germany's New Flagellants," *The American Scholar*, 27:169–79 (1957).

WESTON, J. C., JR. "The Ironic Purpose of Burke's *Vindication* Vindicated," *Journal of the History of Ideas*, 19:435–41, 1958.

WEULERSSE, G. *Les Physiocrates.* Doin, 1931.

WILLIAMS, D. "The Influence of Rousseau on Political Opinion, 1760–95," *English Historical Review*, 17:414–30, 1933.

WILSON, EDMUND. "The Vogue of the Marquis de Sade," in *Eight Essays*, New York, 1954, pp. 167–80.

INDEX

INDEX